CW01583774

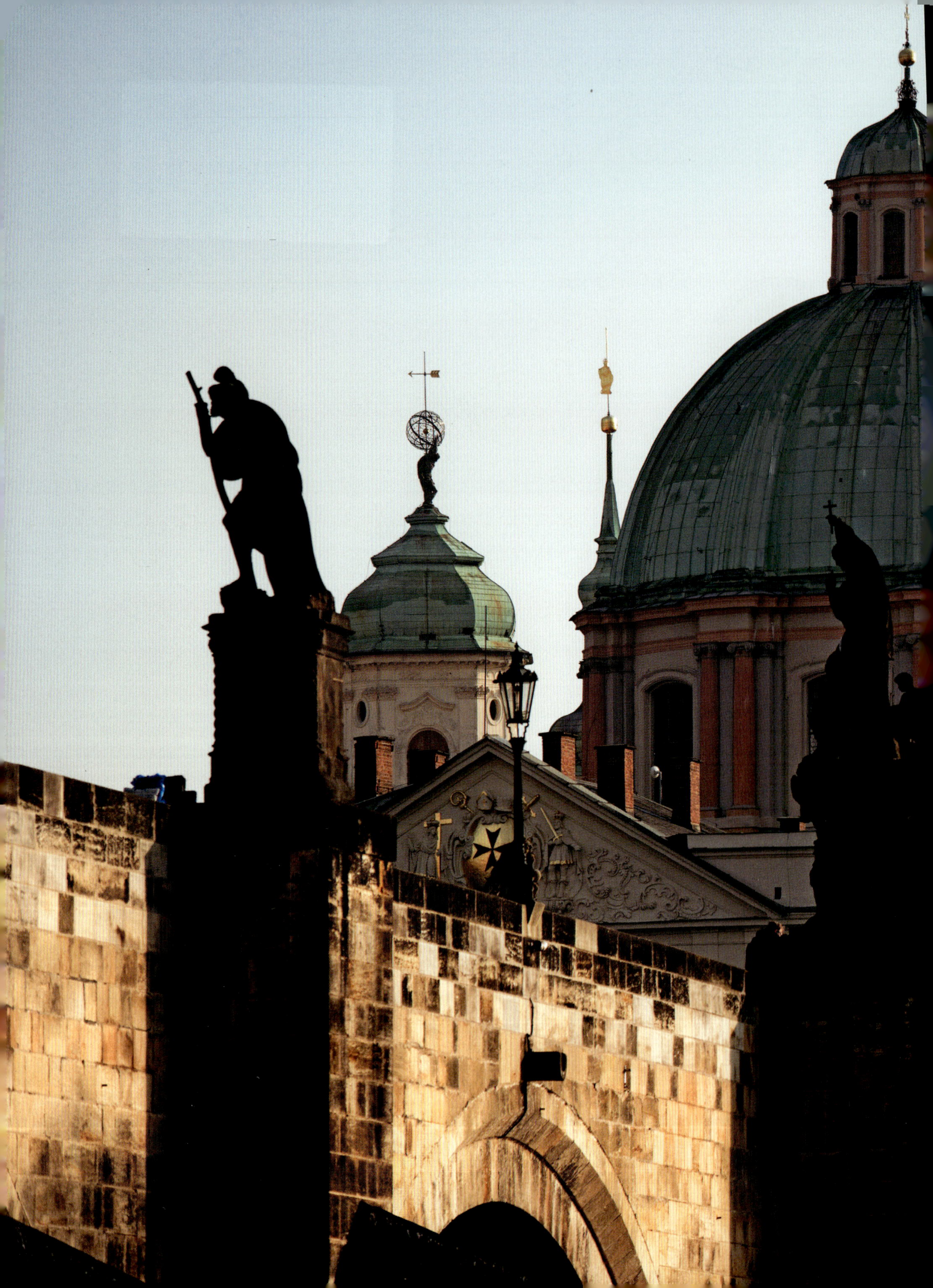

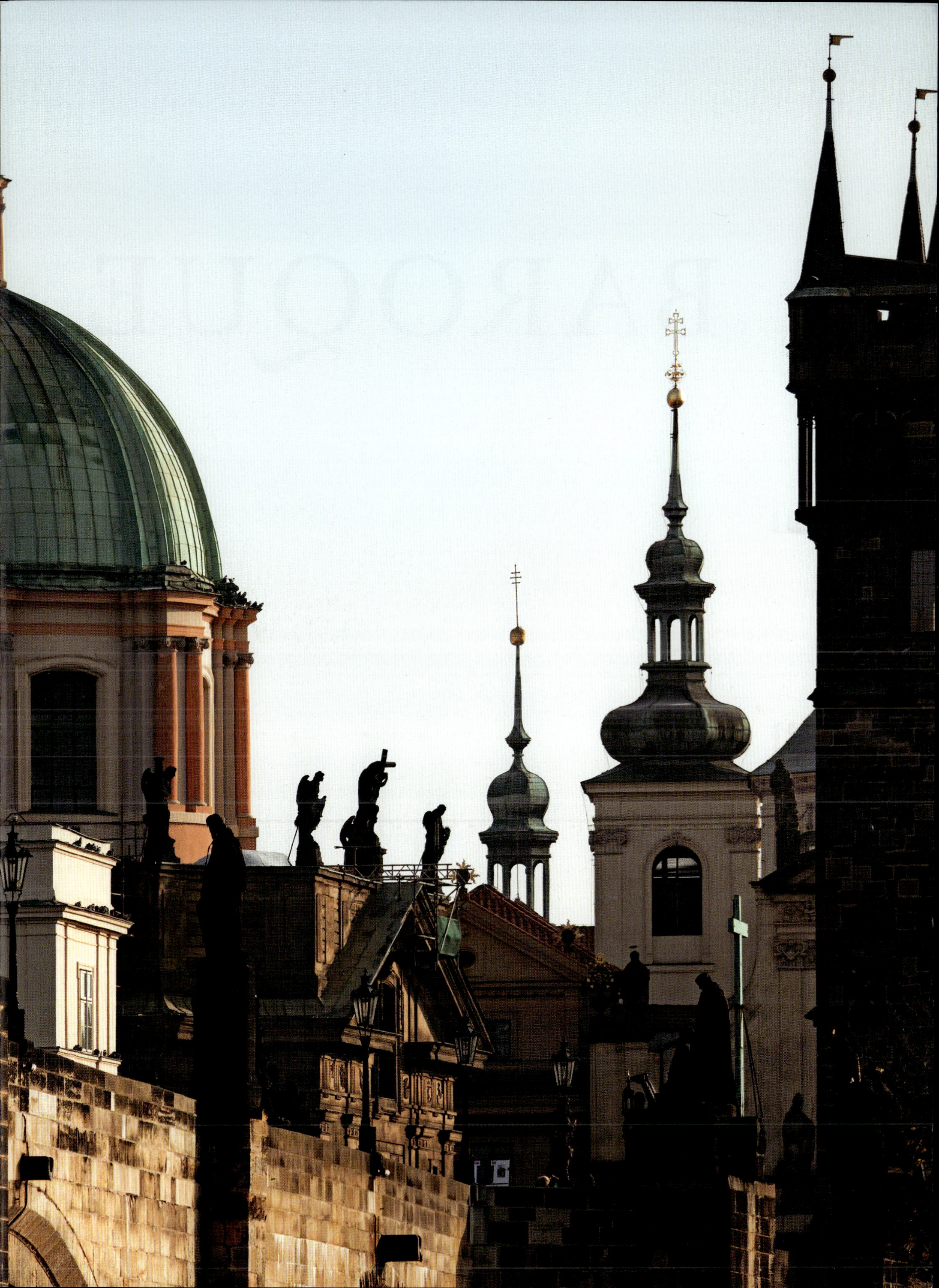

BAROQUE

PRAGUE

Vít Vlnas

Photographs by Oto Palán
Translated by Derek and Marzia Paton

Charles University
Karolinum Press

Originally published in Czech as *Praha barokní*, Prague: Karolinum, 2017
KAROLINUM PRESS is a publishing department of Charles University
Ovocný trh 560/5, 116 36, Praha 1, Czech Republic
www.karolinum.cz

© Karolinum Press, 2024
Text © Vít Vlnas, 2024
Translation © Derek & Marzia Paton, 2024
Photography © 2024
Oto Palán pp. 2–3, 8, 10–11, 1–5, 12, 34, 43, 45 (on the right), 50; plates 1–5, 6D, 8–12E, 13A–B, 14–21B, 22–23B, 24–31C, 32–40C, 40E, 41A, 41D–44A, 44D, 45–52, 54–73; Author's archive: pp. 4, 17; Archiv hl. města Prahy: pp. 23, 38, 44, 45, 62–63; Helena Kodíková: plate 41B; Muzeum hl. města Prahy: pp. 19, 21, 27, 30, 31, 33, 35, 39, 42, 51, 53, 55, 57, 59; plate 40G; Muzeum umění Olomouc: p. 28; Nakladatelství Karolinum: plates 53A–C; Národní archiv: p. 54 (top), p. 54 (bottom); Národní galerie v Praze: pp. 26, 46, 48; plates 21C, 23C–D, 31D, 40D, 41C; Národní muzeum: p. 56; plate 40F; Provincie kapucínů v České republice: plate 12F; Národní knihovna ČR: p. 22; plates 44B–C; Národní památkový ústav – státní hrad a zámek Frýdlant: p. 25; státní zámek Březnice: p. 15; Památník národního písemnictví: p. 60; Státní oblastní archiv v Třeboni: p. 47; plate 13D; Správa Pražského hradu – photo Jan Gloc: p. 40; plates 6A–C, 6E–F, 7A–B; Věroslav Škrabánek: plate 13C; Ústav dějin Univerzity Karlovy and Archiv Univerzity Karlovy: p. 37; Zámek Častolovice – Diana Sternberg-Phipps: p. 16; Židovské muzeum v Praze: p. 49

Edited by Milada Motlová (Czech) and Martin Janeček (English)
Cover and graphic design by Zdeněk Ziegler, typeset by DTP Karolinum
Maps by Jaroslav Synek
Printed in the Czech Republic by Těšínské papírny
First English edition

ISBN 978-80-246-4376-2

The manuscript was reviewed by Richard Biegel (Institute of Art History, Faculty of Arts, Charles University, Prague), and Lubomír Slavíček (Department of Art History, Faculty of Arts, Masaryk University, Brno).
The Prague series editor is Milada Motlová

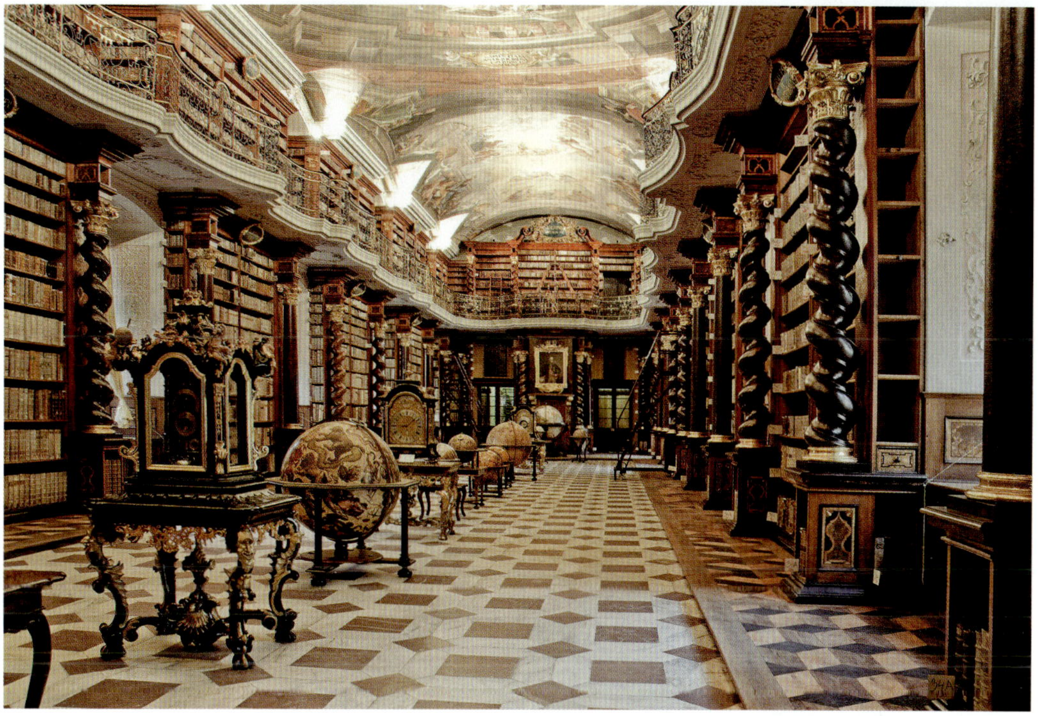

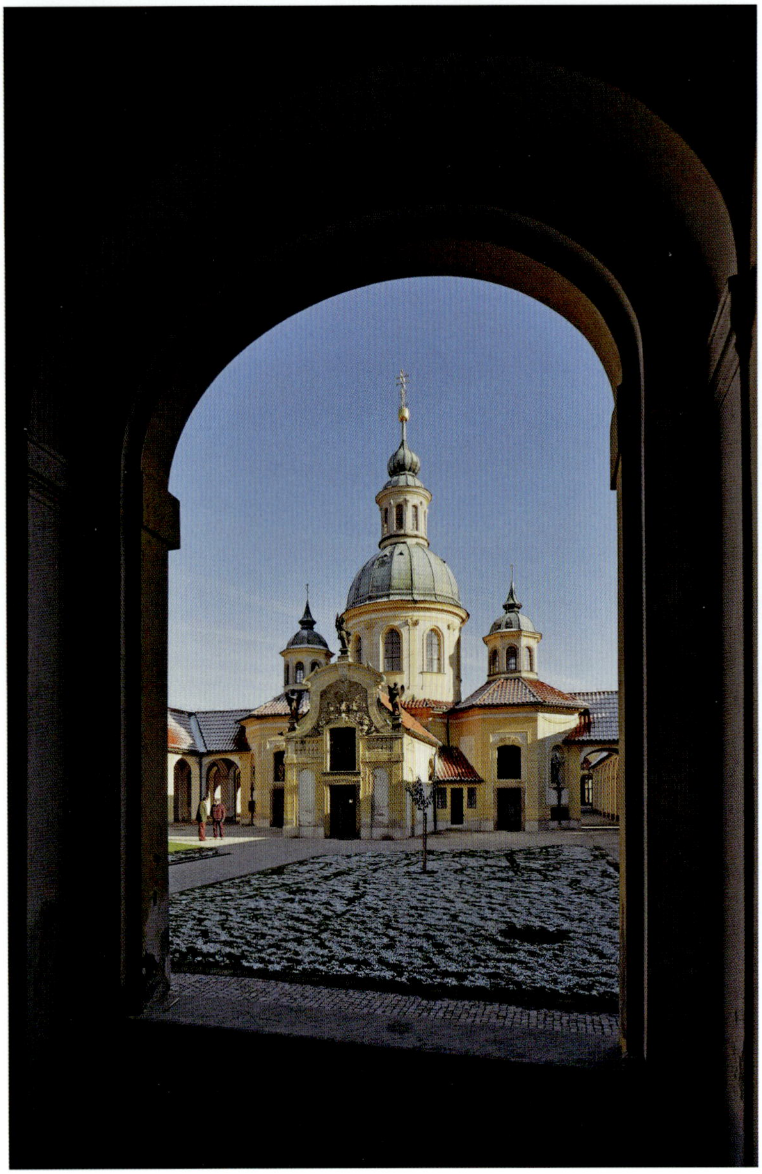

CONTENTS

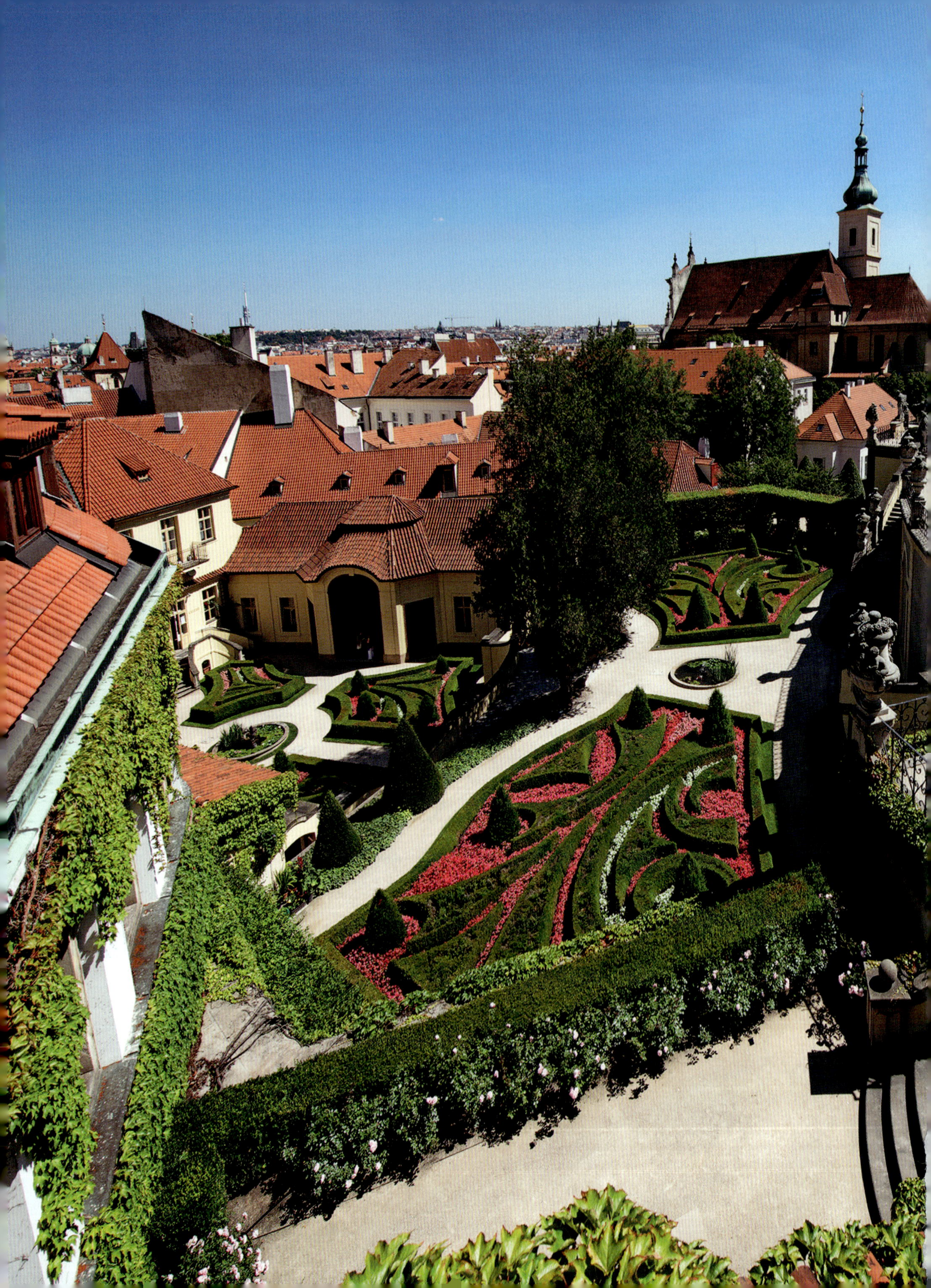

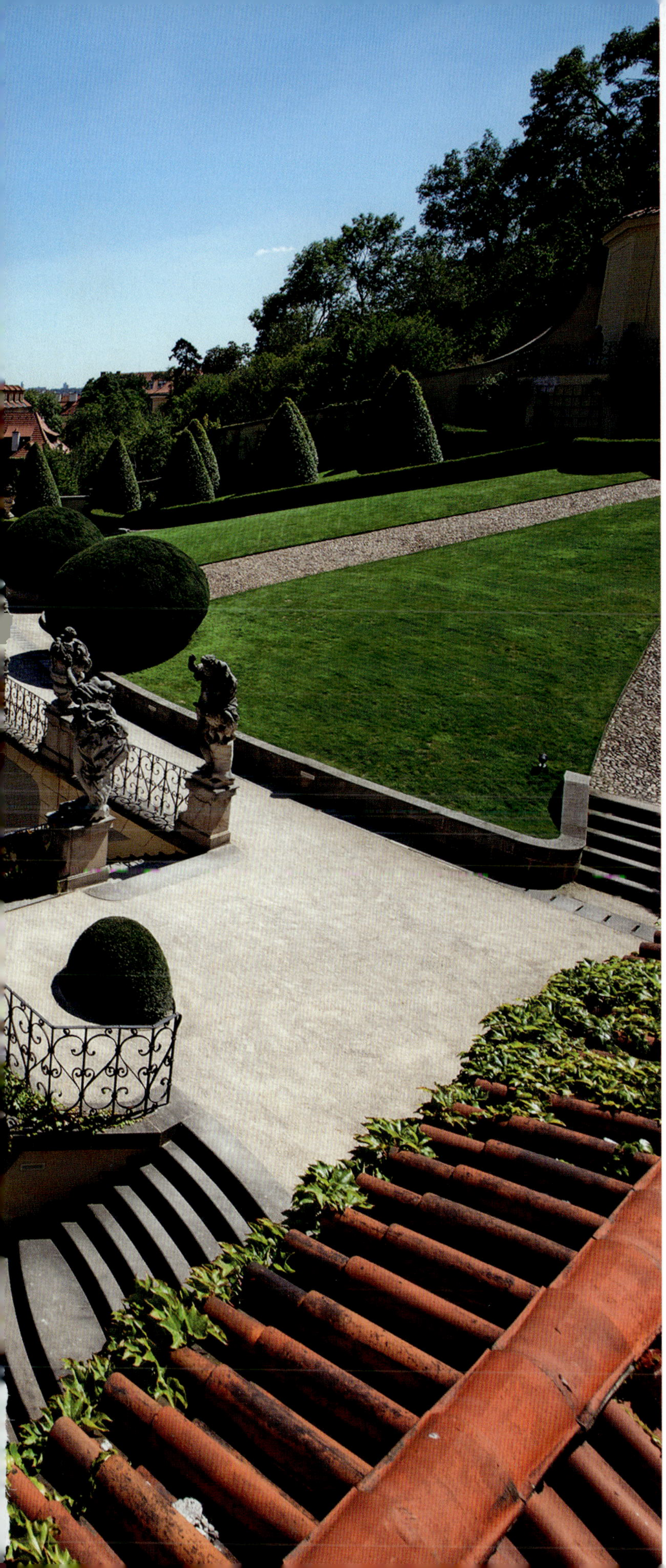

A CONCISE HISTORY OF BAROQUE PRAGUE

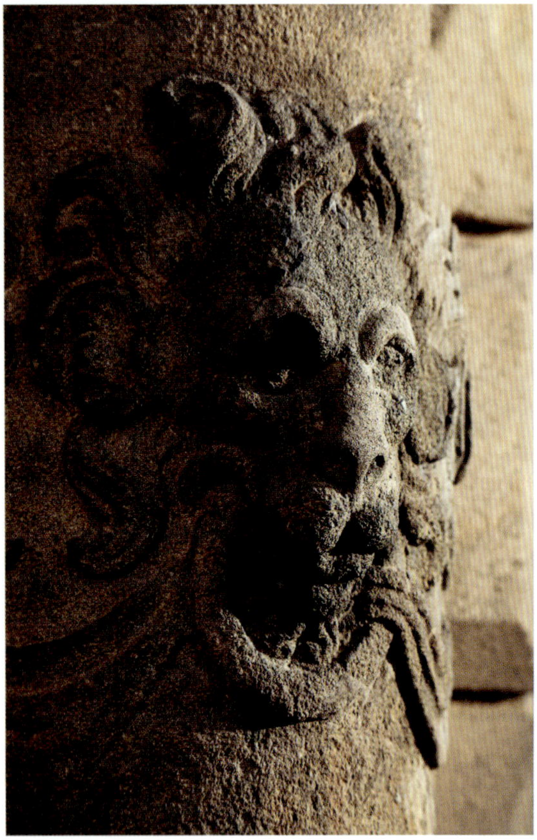

In his *Poselkyně starých příběhů českých* (A recorder of bygone events in Bohemia, 1700), the patriotic Baroque chronicler Jan František Beckovský, a member of the Order of the Knights of the Cross with the Red Star, writes that in 1613 a remarkable painting appeared on the façade of a house in Štěpánská ulice in the New Town of Prague. It depicted eight maidens attending to the double-tailed Bohemian lion – combing his mane, stroking his paws, decorating him with insignia of royal majesty, and holding a mirror up to his vanity. The beast was so taken with himself that he failed to notice that one of the maidens had, behind his back, slipped a harness and halter over his head. The inscription attached to it reads: 'Perhaps because the Bohemian lion now has a bridle and reins he is no longer free, but is now also well saddled, and therefore must go when and where he is led, having lost his freedom, power, and might.' Possibly, this was but an afterthought, originating only with the discovery of what had happened. Undoubtedly, however, the process of subjugating and taming the Bohemian lion had been taking place with the benign indifference of those who should have above all ensured his freedom.

The rebellion of the Bohemian Estates against the Habsburgs in 1618–20 was the spark that ignited the powder keg and divided Europe along political and confessional lines. Sometimes fortune favoured the troops of the emperor and his Roman Catholic allies, sometimes the Estates camp, reinforced by Protestants from the Holy Roman Empire. In the second half of 1620, war began inexorably to approach Prague. At the end of the summer, imperial forces, under the command of Charles-Bonaventure de Longueval, Count of Bucquoy, together with the army of Maximilian I, Duke of Bavaria, crossed the south-west border of Bohemia, and quickly advanced to the centre of the kingdom. Prague had been preparing, or at least trying to prepare, to defend itself since the summer, chaotically, uncoordinatedly. In early November, divisions of the Estates clashed with the enemy at Rakovník, about 60 km west of Prague, and then retreated to areas around Prague. The rebel commanders, Christian I, Prince of Anhalt-Bernburg (also known as Christian of Anhalt), and Georg Friedrich von Hohenlohe, took up a strategically advantageous position on the White Mountain, the misleadingly named hillock about 7 km west of Hradčany. Apparently, they assumed that the enemy would not attack. Despite the views of his general staff, Duke Maximilian, roused by the charismatic Carmelite friar Dominic a Jesu Maria, decided to engage in battle. Thus, on 8 November 1620, after the first failed attempt, when the vanguard of the joint Bavarian-Imperial forces launched a continuous attack, it began to be clear that it was to be not so much a battle as a skirmish. Many of the Estates' mercenaries, who for months had not been paid, fired once, as required by military honour, and then abandoned the battlefield. Others, however, were brave and had no intention of giving up without a fight. In less than two hours, however, the victory was decided in the Catholics' favour. The general view at the time was that the outcome was largely thanks to the contribution of Dominic a Jesu Maria, who had convinced the hesitant commanders that they should lead their men into battle. He had roused the

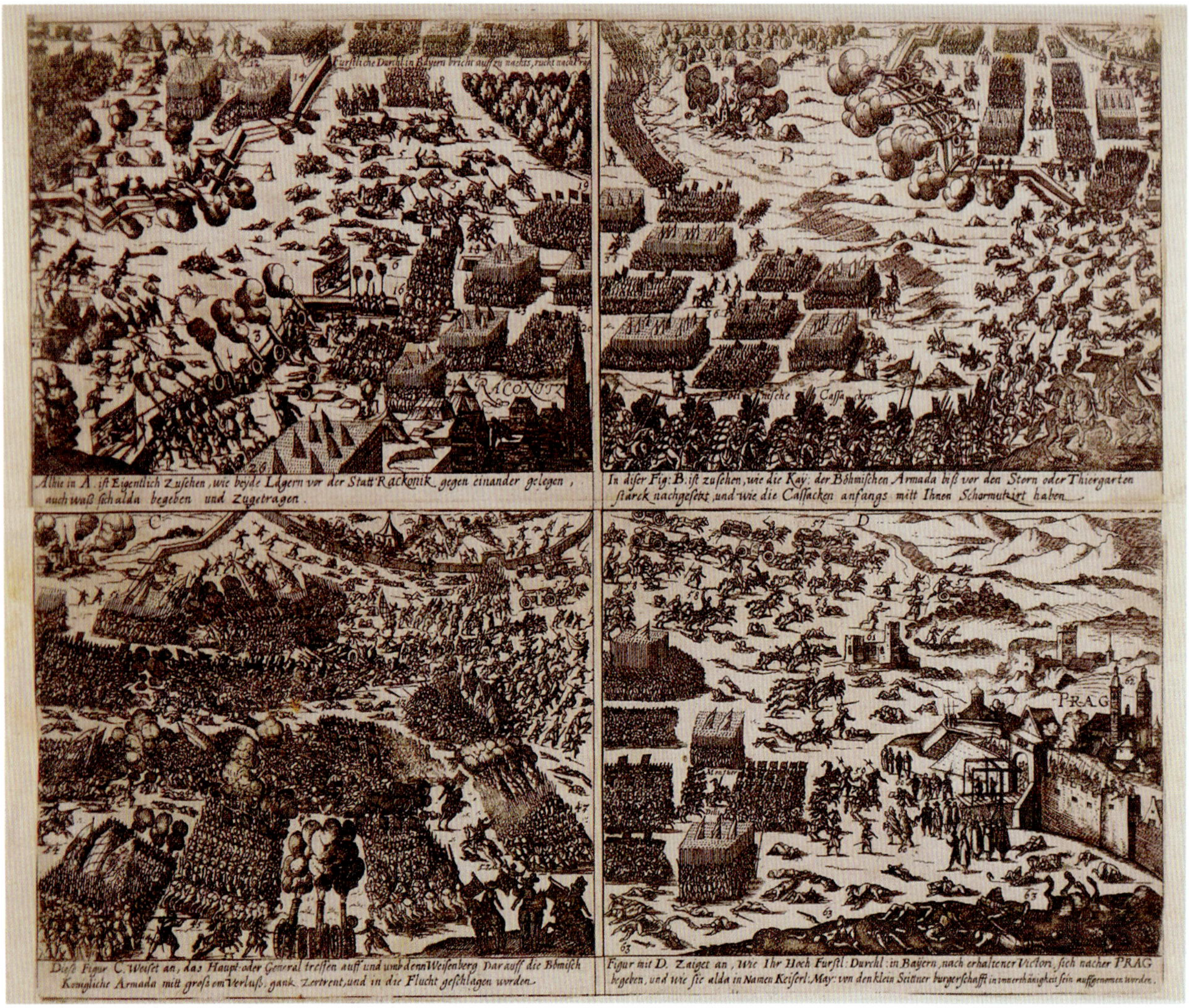

The Battle of the White Mountain, 8 November 1620

This engraving, though considerably schematic, graphically illustrates key moments in the crushing of the Bohemian Estates rebellion. On the upper left, we see the Imperial League army and the Bohemian Estates army in the fortified positions at Rakovník (60 km west of Prague). It was from here that the Estates forces retreated to Prague and took up suitable positions on the plain at the White Mountain. The scene on the upper right shows the first attack by the Catholic forces against those positions. The third scene is dominated by the general pandemonium of battle. In the centre, the isolated regiment of Count Heinrich Schlik is bravely fighting the numerically superior Imperial forces and their Bavarian allies, while the remainder of the defeated Estates army fled towards Prague. There, they were pursued by the victors, whose arrival at the city walls near Strahov and Pohořelec is depicted in the last scene.

soldiers not only with fiery words, but also with a small panel painting of the Blessed Virgin Mary adoring the Christ Child, which had been dishonoured by the Protestant iconoclasts. He had found it only recently in a ravaged manor chapel in Štěnovice (Stienowitz or Stenowitz) near Pilsen.*

*In period descriptions of the event, the better-known town of Strakonice – between Pilsen and Budweis – was mistaken for Štěnovice – just south of Pilsen. Hence the now traditional name for the painting of Saint Mary of Victory, *The Strakonice Adoration*.

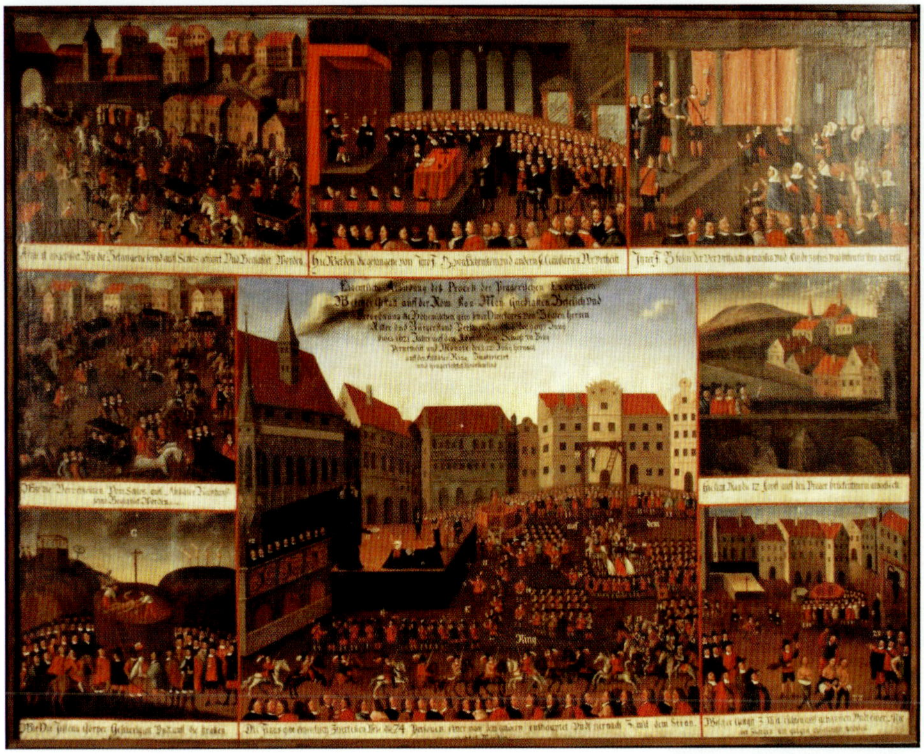

The Execution of the Leaders of the Estates Rebellion, Old Town Square, 21 June 1621, with accompanying scenes

The painting, made after one of many prints depicting the Prague executions, was commissioned by the procurator royal Přibík Jeníšek z Újezda, who participated directly in the trial of the rebel leaders of the Estates. The central image depicts Old Town Square on the day of the execution of the twenty-seven condemned leaders. On the upper left begins the series of accompanying scenes of events that chronologically preceded the executions or sometimes came after them. In the first picture, at the top, we see the transfer of the prisoners up Ostruhová ulice (today, Nerudova ulice) to Prague Castle, where, in the second picture, they are tried, presided over by Karl Liechtenstein, the governor (*Statthalter*). Their wives and children, in the third scene, beg, unsuccessfully, with Liechtenstein to show mercy. In the middle row, the first scene on the left shows the transfer of the condemned men to jail in the town hall of the Old Town, from where they will go straight to their deaths. As a warning, the heads of twelve of the executed were exhibited on the bridge tower on the Old Town side of the River Vltava, depicted in the scene on the far right of the second row. The body of Jan Jessenius was quartered and the executioner's henchmen impaled his body parts on spikes by the road below Šibeniční vrch (Gallows Hill, in today's Žižkov) beyond the city gates. The executions continued for a second day: for two hours the Old Town scribe Mikuláš Diviš was nailed by his tongue to the gallows; another three burghers, guilty of having ceremoniously welcomed Frederick V of the Palatinate, were ignominiously whipped out of the city.

Roused to action by Dominic, the mercenaries went on the attack, with the battle cry 'Santa Maria!', as Christian sailors had once done at the Battle of Lepanto in 1571. This is where the legend of Saint Mary of Victory was born, whose icon was taken, in 1622, in a ceremonial procession to the church of the Discalced Carmelites in the Quirinal District of Rome, known today as Santa Maria della Vittoria.

The Catholic victory was so clear-cut that it seems it could have been won without divine intervention. Poorly paid and ill-motivated to fight, the army of the Bohemian rebels, chased through half of Europe, fell apart more or less from

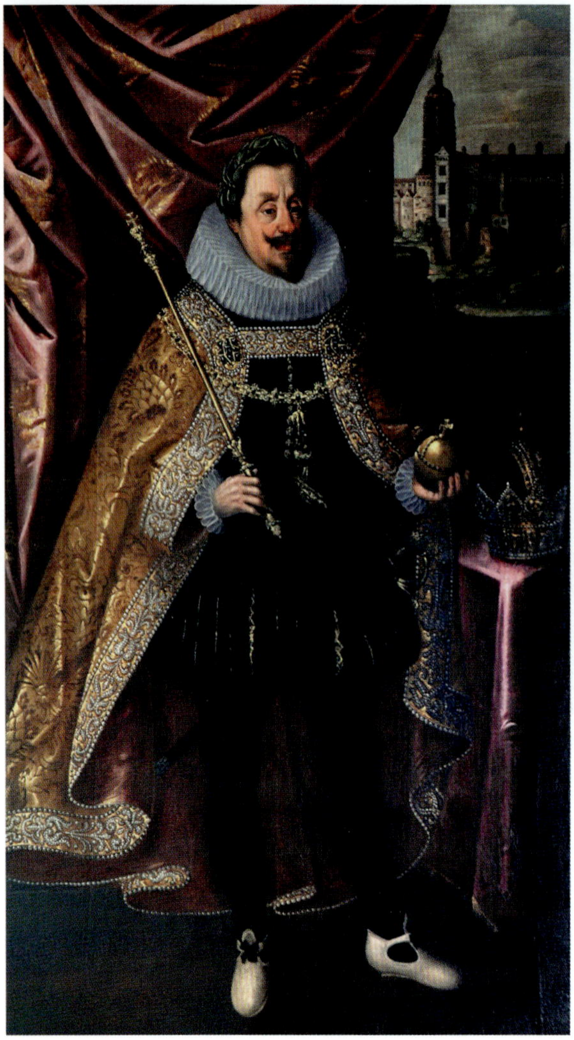

Portrait of Emperor Ferdinand II with a View of Prague Castle

Ferdinand II, the grandson of Ferdinand I, became heir to the Habsburg throne during the life of the childless Emperor Matthias. In 1617 the Bohemian Estates accepted this implacable Catholic as their new king, thanks in part to the disunity of the Protestants opposition. In the difficult years of the Estates Rebellion, Ferdinand, having been Emperor since 1619, displayed energy and decisiveness, but also icy calm, which stemmed from his unwavering faith. During the Thirty Years War, he was able, despite all the reversals of fortune in his war efforts, to push through his conception of absolute rule and to prepare the integration of central Europe in the Habsburg Monarchy. He was said to be a garrulous, witty, and kind ruler, a magnanimous friend, and a charming companion who adored music and enjoyed hunting. In matters of faith, however, this bigoted Catholic knew no compromise and most certainly never made light of his mission as a God-chosen ruler. His intransigence was eventually felt both by the defeated Bohemian Estates and by his general Albrecht von Waldstein, called Wallenstein.

within. The supreme political representatives showed no will to resist; indeed, not even Frederick of the Palatinate (Frederick V of Bohemia, the Winter King, r. 1619–20) really considered defending the kingdom. He and those loyal to him abandoned Prague the day after the battle. Unable to defend even its fortifications, the city passively surrendered to the victorious army. Emperor Ferdinand II, a Habsburg, who had been duly approved and crowned King of Bohemia three years earlier, this time did not intend to leave anything to chance. Karl Liechtenstein, the Moravian noblemen whom Ferdinand had appointed Statthalter in the Bohemian Lands, ensured that men loyal to him from the times before the rebellion were appointed to the town councils, and eventually he gave the order for the arrest of the begetters of the 'odious rebellion'. The exemplary mass execution of the twenty-seven leaders of the Estates Rebellion, on the Old Town Square on 21 June 1621 was the bloody epilogue to the Bohemian Estates Rebellion. Contemporary commentary by the anti-Habsburg camp said that the 'flower of Bohemia's nobility and gentry' had given their lives here. Among the condemned were indeed some of the most distinguished men of the age of Rudolph II. For example, Václav Budovec z Budova, an implacable tribune of the Bohemian Brethren, and Kryštof Harant z Polžic a Bezdružic, a humanist writer and composer, who overcame his initial fear, bravely went to their deaths here. The judges passed the most dreadful sentence on Jan Jessenius, a Breslau-born professor of medicine, a former imperial physician, later a rector of Prague University, and eventually an adept diplomat in the service of the Estates. While he was still alive, the executioner cut out his tongue on the scaffolding and, after beheading him, quartered his body. Thus ended the life of a man who had once excelled as an anatomist at Wittenberg University, carried out the first public autopsy in Prague, and repeatedly dedicated his scientific works to Habsburg monarchs.

For ten years after the executions, the heads of selected rebels remained exhibited on the gallery of the tower on the Old Town side of Charles Bridge as a warning to anyone who dared to oppose the new rules. The worst that was inflicted on the common folk of Prague, however, was fines and confiscations, which followed the executions of the leaders in the Old Town. During the rebellion, Prague had proudly claimed itself to be the foremost town in the kingdom – and for that pride it was now paying a high price. Hand in hand with severe sanctions came the victors' re-Catholicization of the population. The Battle of the White Mountain prepared the way for settling accounts with non-Catholics, which to the 'papists', from the standpoint of their triumph, seemed to be decisive and definitive. Here, not only political factors but also confessional ones were applied.

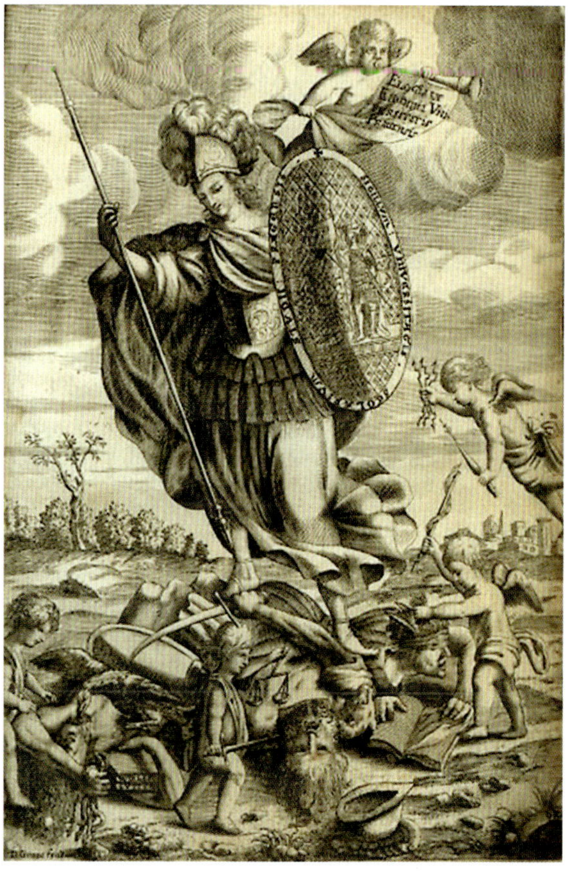

Academia triumphans:
An Allegory of the Caroline-Ferdinand University

From 1419 to 1622, Prague University was run by the Utraquists. Afterwards, it was transferred to the Jesuits. The longstanding dispute between the Jesuits and the Archbishop of Prague over its administration was not resolved until the decree of union issued by Emperor Ferdinand III in 1654, which merged the 'Jesuit' Clementinum faculties (of arts and theology) with the schools of the Carolinum (medicine and law). In memory of this act, the university was, until Czechoslovak independence in late 1918, officially called the Caroline-Ferdinand University.
This engraving from 1672 celebrates higher education in Prague in the form of an armed woman, recalling Pallas Athena of classical antiquity. The shield in her hand bears the image known from the medieval university seal. The glory of triumphant Academia is proclaimed by a cherub with a trumpet, while the other little celestial beings aid learning in its fight against ignorance and Protestant heresy.

It would be too simple to see Ferdinand II's measures as merely acts of revenge. For this deeply pious Catholic, however, returning the Bohemian Lands to Roman Catholicism was a serious mission, which stemmed from his sense of moral responsibility to God, by whose mercy, he believed, he had been called to the throne. After many discussions, an uncompromising though 'mild' path to re-Catholicization was chosen for the Kingdom of Bohemia, based on persuasion and personal example. But the use of force, including corporal punishment and military assistance, did not usually lead to the anticipated success. In any case, the consequences were fateful: after the prohibition of Protestant church services came the banishment of non-Catholic clergy and a ban on importing or printing 'heretical' books. The University of Prague, previously Utraquist, now became Jesuit. Protestant noblemen and burghers were eventually given a stark choice: conversion or emigration. According to very rough estimates, about a twentieth of the Prague population went into exile during the 1620s; this figure does not, however, fully illustrate the phenomenon of emigration after the Battle of the White Mountain. Many people converted and many others returned home after years of exile. Part of the usual strategy adopted by noble and burgher families was that though they were forced to leave they nevertheless left behind one or more reliable Catholic relations who then looked after the family property.

The gap between those who left the country was quickly filled by the 'new' Catholic educated class. They shared with their Protestant counterparts from the period before the Battle of the White Mountain an ardent love for their country, nation, and language. A 'Baroque' historical-patriotic conception was formed, built on the idea that Roman Catholicism was the original confession of the country. For two centuries, intruders had brought the poisons of Hussite, Bohemian Brethren, and Lutheran reform into Bohemia, sowing the seeds of destruction from which sprouted the rebellion of 1618–20. Armed with these ideals, the Catholic clergy of the seventeenth and early eighteenth centuries performed missionary work, a result of which was that the inhabitants of the Bohemian Lands, with rare exceptions, became Roman Catholics. Until Emperor Joseph II issued the Patent of Toleration in 1781, the profession of any faith other than the Roman Catholic remained, at least *de jure*, illegal.

The Catholic armies triumphed on the battlefields of the Thirty Years War for ten long years. The hundreds of exiles who had been forced to leave their home after the Battle of the White Mountain were given new hope by Gustavus Adolphus of Sweden: in mid-November 1631, Saxon divisions, allied at the time with the Swedes, drew closer to Prague. The city, deprived of its military defences, opened its gates to them. The new master of the Bohemian Lands was Hans-Georg von Arnim-Boitzenburg, a Saxon field marshal who was put up in Liechtenstein House in the Lesser Town. His troops conducted themselves as occupying forces usually do, yet the application of Saxon regulations somewhat restricted mass pillaging. With varying success, they maintained a delicate balance of forces among the Catholic town councils. The non-Catholc (partullary the Bohemian Brethern) exiles, now under the protection of Arnim's

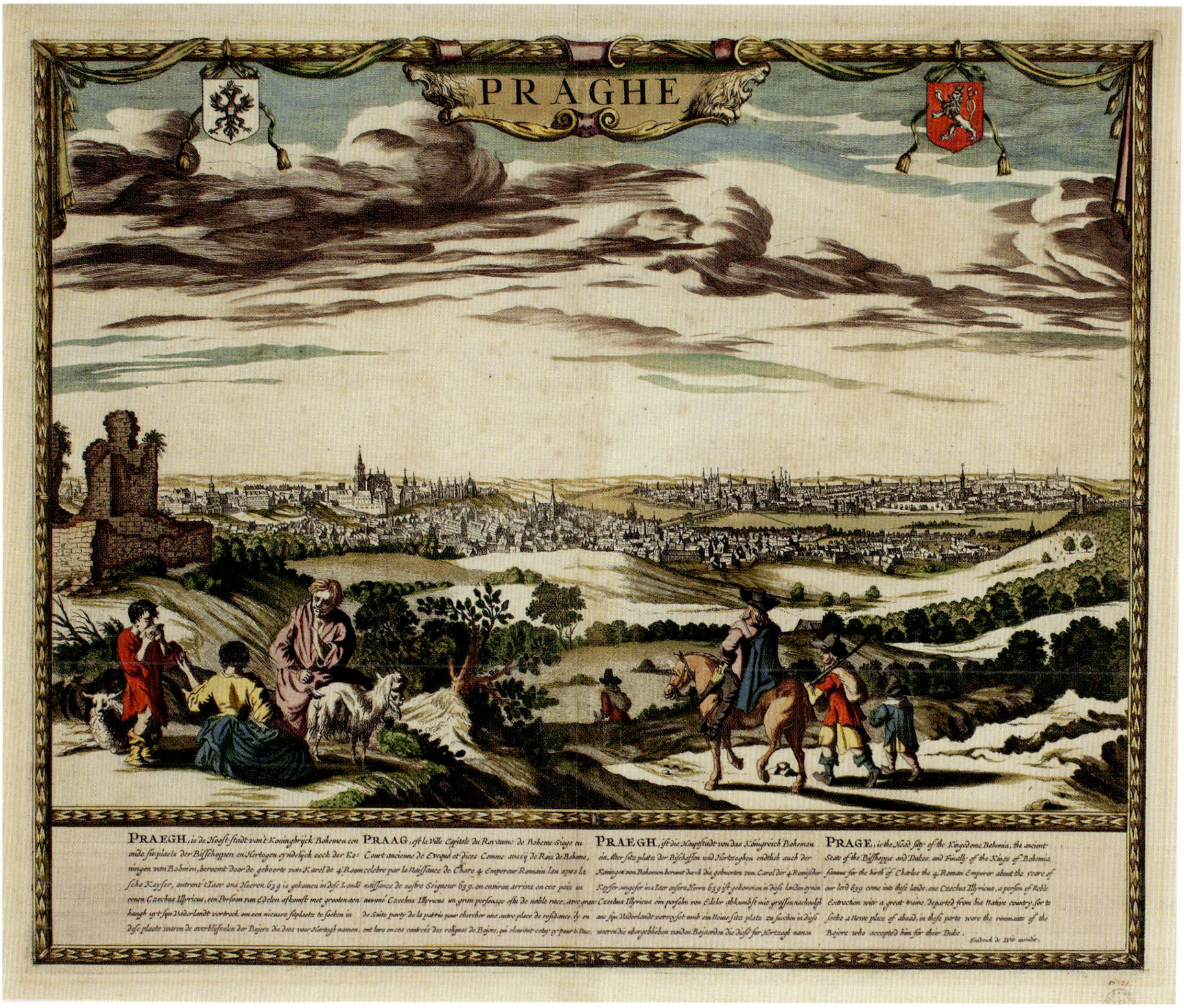

A View of Prague from the South-west, 1660

This hand-coloured engraving of Netherlandish origin shows the city from the top of Petřín Hill (Laurenziberg, in German). It is a variation on a well-known *veduta* by Wenceslaus Hollar, which was made in 1649 after the artist's own drawing from 1636. Its viewpoint makes it possible to present the city panorama from a sufficient distance and in dramatically modelled relief.

Although closer inspection of Baroque Prague elicited more than one critical comment from foreign visitors, the majestic silhouette of the town spread out over the two banks of the River Vltava caused unanimous rapture. 'The metropolis of Prague, the seat of the flourishing Kingdom of Bohemia, is one of the most beautiful towns in all of Europe', wrote, for example, Francisco da Fonseca, a well-travelled Portuguese Jesuit, who, in 1708, accompanied a diplomatic mission of his king to Emperor Joseph I in Vienna.

mercenaries, returned to their old homes and vociferously demanded the return of their confiscated property and some churches. The Protestants reverentially took down the heads of the executed rebel leaders from the bridge tower and buried them with dignity; unfortunately, we still do not know where. The Jesuits had to leave the city but the other Catholic religious orders remained, and in late 1631 and early 1632 Prague again became a place of religious toleration, albeit an imposed toleration maintained by the armed force of the Saxons. The occupying forces, like it or not, had to feed all the people of Prague regardless of confession. In the spring months of 1632, food shortages began to appear in the city and undernourishment gave rise to epidemics.

At that time, Ferdinand II reappointed Wallenstein to lead his armies, after having relieved him of his command the previous year and causing him great offence. With fresh units and quick manoeuvres, Wallenstein, a seasoned warrior, drove the Saxon garrisons out of Bohemia. Towards the end of May 1632, Prague fell. Besides Arnim's mercenaries, the remaining clusters of Bohemian exiles also moved north, their hopes of a lasting return home having been definitively dashed that spring. The six-month occupation had become, among other things, a test of the reliability of the Catholic administration of the three towns of Prague. In these difficult circumstances they had indeed proved themselves. In 1635, peace was signed in the capital of the Bohemian Kingdom between the Emperor and the Elector of Saxony, whose relations with his Swedish ally had somewhat cooled after the crushing defeat of the Protestant forces at Nördlingen the year before. Prague was not, however, relieved of wartime worries. New fortifications were hastily being built, the inhabitants were trained in the use of arms, and the monarch eventually agreed to Prague having a permanent garrison for its protection. The effectiveness of these measures was demonstrated as early as 1634 and again in 1639, when Prague was directly threatened by Swedish troops.

A direct Swedish attack came in July 1648, when Europe, plundered and exhausted, was already looking with hope towards the anticipated conclusion of the apparently endless conflict. With a rapid and well-concealed march, General Hans Christoph von Königsmarck reached the centre of Bohemia and his troops, without a fight, made their way into Prague in the area of Pohořelec and Strahov, traditionally the Achilles heel of the town fortifications. The political consequences of the Thirty Years War could not be fundamentally affected by this operation, but in the event of success it would certainly strengthen the bargaining position of the Swedes and their allies at the peace conference in Münster and Osnabrück, Westphalia. It has been plausibly argued that the main reason for Königsmarck's attack may have been his desire to seize Rudolph II's widely known art collections at Prague Castle, which, in the end, he fully succeeded in doing. On 25 July 1648, Hradčany and the Lesser Town woke up to the first day of Swedish occupation. Many prominent inhabitants of the two residential quarters (including Archbishop Ernst Adalbert von Harrach) became prisoners of the Swedes before they even knew what had happened, for the previous evening Prague had celebrated the marriage of Emperor Ferdinand III and Maria Leopoldina of Austria-Tyrol in grand style, with the celebrations having continued long into the night.

The city on the right bank of the Vltava meanwhile quickly organized an effective defence. The Swedish army, essentially comprising soldiers recruited from various German lands and Finland, met with surprisingly strong resistance. On Charles Bridge, along the river and the whole length of the city walls from Poříčí to Vyšehrad, resistance was put up not only by troops of the profes-

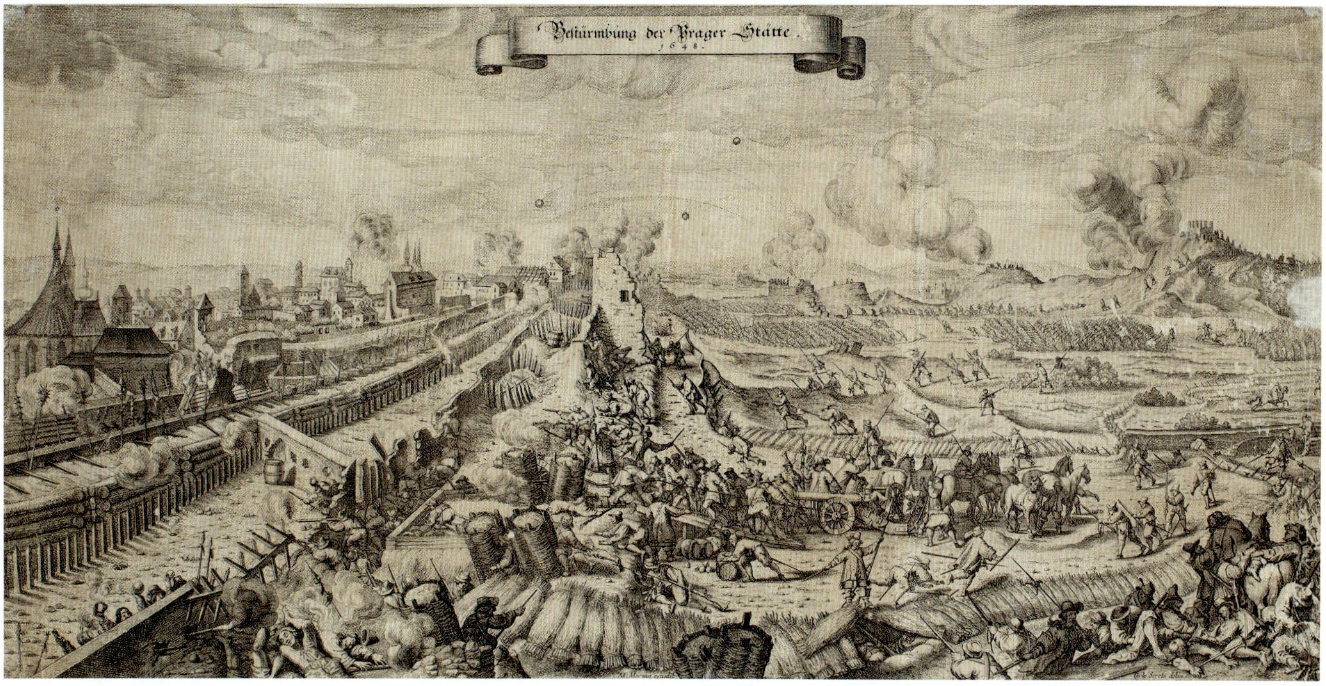

MATTHÄUS MERIAN THE YOUNGER, AFTER KAREL ŠKRÉTA: **The Swedes Attacking the New Town of Prague in 1648**

This vividly realistic scene most likely relates to the heavy attack of 13 October 1648, when the enemy succeeded in breaching the fortifications in several places. The New Town walls in the section between the Horse Gate and the Kutná Hora Gate are depicted here from a viewpoint where the National Museum now stands, looking towards what is now the Main Railway Station: on the far left is St Henry's Church; the hillocks in the background on the right are Vinohrady and Šibeniční vrch (Gallows Hill in today's Žižkov). Swedish troops are pulling a large cannon through a breach in the outer wall while defenders lob hand grenades at them and prepare to repel the attack with typically improvised pikes and swords.

sional Imperial Army, but also by self-confident companies of citizens who had been trained in the use of arms. Gradually, other 'civilians' became engaged in battles. They included students of Prague University – the Academic Legion led by the charismatic Jesuit priest Jiří Plachý (aka Georgius Ferus) –, divisions of noblemen and their servants, secular clergy, clergy of the religious orders, and also inhabitants of the Jewish ghetto. With some pauses, the fighting continued till November 1648. The Swedes besieged the right bank of Prague and repeatedly tried to make their way into the Old Town by crossing Charles Bridge. In the autumn, the fiercest attacks were carried out by marauders against the New Town fortifications in the area of the Horse Gate (Koňská brána, at the south-east end of today's Wenceslas Square) and particularly the Kutná Hora Gate (Horská brána) – neither of which exist anymore. The attacking troops penetrated breaches, though with colossal effort the defenders repeatedly repelled them. To the great joy of the people of Prague, the Peace of Westphalia put an end to the fighting. The pride of the city quarters, stemming from their successful defence, was immeasurable. 'This tower was the outer limit of Gothic fury, but not of Bohemian loyalty,' reads a commemorative plaque installed on the western façade of the Old Town Bridge Tower just after the war.

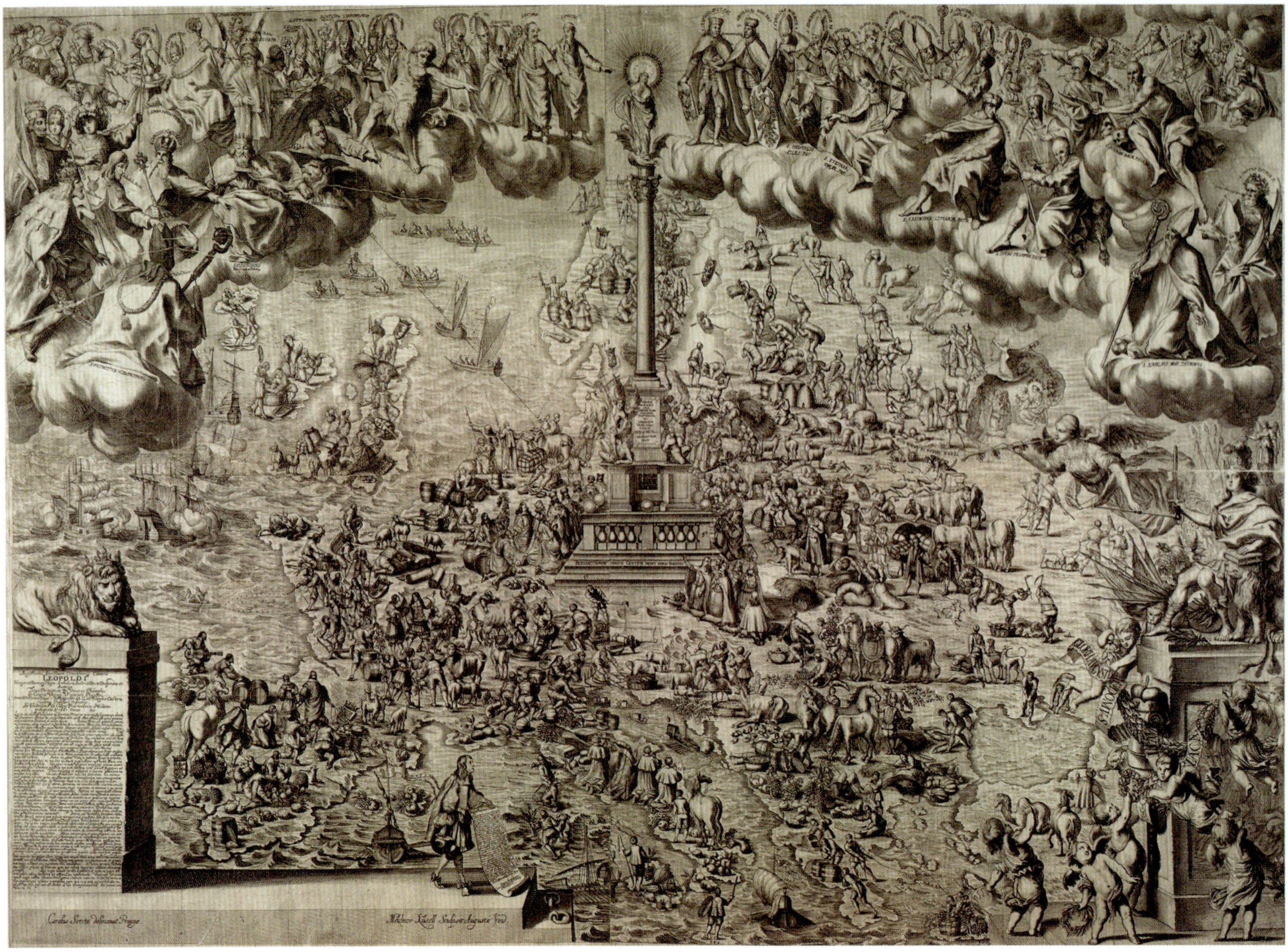

MELCHIOR KÜSEL AFTER KAREL ŠKRÉTA: **Prague as the Spiritual Centre of Europe**

This epic allegorical scene is part of a thesis of peripatetic and general philosophy defended at Prague University in 1661 by Count Johann Friedrich von Waldstein (Jan Bedřich z Valdštejna), a future archbishop of Prague. It shows Johann Georg Bendl's Marian column on the Old Town Square as the focal point of the continent, indeed, as the absolute centre of all Christendom to which all the nations of Europe look. In the celestial sphere to the right of Mary the Immaculate is a group of the patron saints of Bohemia led by St Wenceslas. This is a graphic example of the Catholic patriotic mentality in the Baroque period.

Almost immediately, the heroic story of the defence of the Prague towns on the right bank of the Vltava acquired a strikingly pro-Catholic and anti-Reformation nature. This time, the people of Prague were, it was said, assisted in their struggle against the heretical 'Goths' by St Mary herself; after all, even the Swedish prisoners had blasphemously attested that 'a witch in a blue cloak caught our flying grenades with her hand and threw them back at us'. In these circumstances, the cult of St Wenceslas as the heavenly protector of the Bohemian Lands was also brought up to date. A one-time member of the Academic Legion, Jan Norbert Zatočil z Löwenbrucku, later expressed the conviction, widespread at the time, that 'the Most Holy Trinity, at the pleadings and intercessions of the Most Holy Mother of God, the Blessed Virgin Mary, was pleased to liberate the towns of Prague from the difficult and dangerous Swedish siege'. By contrast, the Bohemian exiles in Protestant countries believed, often up until the last moment, that the conquest of Prague would help them to return home. Few people understood why the people of Prague themselves did not open the gates of their city to the Swedes, who were, after all, defenders of the 'true faith', and why they did not voluntarily surrender to Prince Carl Gustav of Sweden (the future King Charles X Gustav), who, as a relation of the Winter King, Friedrich of the Palatinate, could make apparently legitimate claims to the Bohemian crown. Jan Amos Komenský, better known outside the country as Comenius, famous throughout Europe as an educator, and last bishop of the Bohemian Brethren, fervently pleaded with Axel Oxenstierna, Lord High Chancellor of Sweden, to intervene politically in favour of his co-religionists:

'Consider the nation upon which Christ was pleased to look first before all European nations, seizing them from the darkness of the Antichrist, and who alone for a whole century withstood the fury of the Antichrist so that other nations could in the meantime receive enlightenment.' Such chiliastic proclamations were utterly useless for politics in practice and eventually Comenius would bitterly describe the circumstances of the non-Catholic Bohemian and Moravian exiles after the Peace of Westphalia with the complaint: 'not only have I or some of our people, adherents of our church, been forsaken; rather, the whole nation has been forsaken'. It was a tragic mistake of this great thinker. The future of the Bohemian nation no longer depended on those who had gone abroad, no matter how much their spiritual legacy had a truly profound influence on modern Czech culture. The 'founders' of the nation in the modern sense were those who had not left and had been able to maintain its continu-

The Coat of Arms of the Old Town of Prague

On 20 April 1649, for their contribution to the defence of Prague against the Swedes, Ferdinand III granted the Old Town privileges by which, among other things, he augmented its coat of arms. On the armorial miniature of this document, the emperor is portrayed in the company of allegorical figures of Piety and Justice (on the left) and personifications of Glory and Peace (on the right). The figures stand on pedestals decorated with captured war trophies, over which putti tread with the Hungarian and the Bohemian coats of arms. The putto on the left holds a palm of victory; his counterpart has lowered his torch to indicate that fighting has ended. The scene at the bottom in the middle recalls the defence of the Kutná Hora Gate in October 1648.

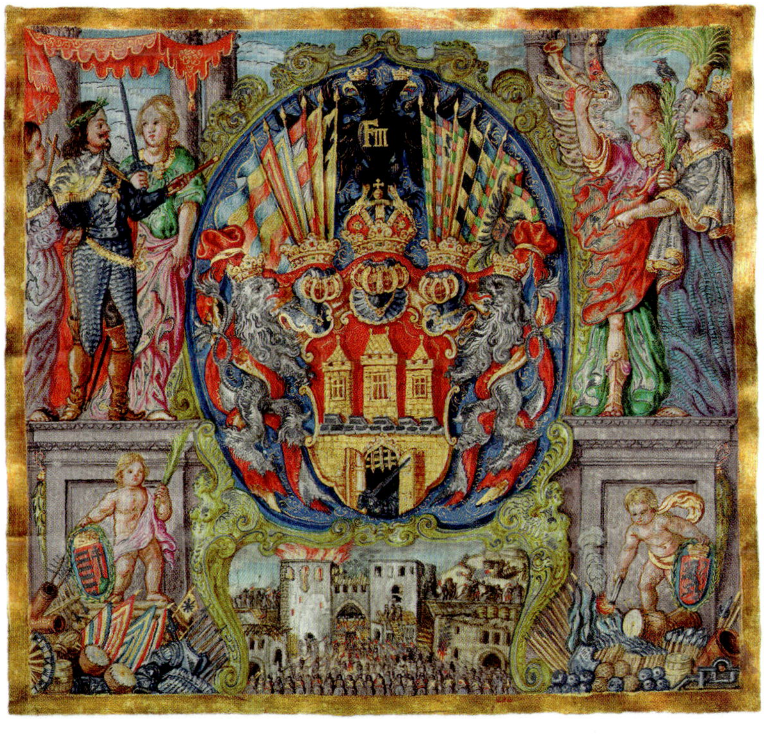

ity at home. Among them were descendants of the brave defenders of Prague against the Swedes. There was in fact less religious exultation here than there seemed to have been at that time.

* * *

The continuity of artistic life in Prague was not interrupted by the imperial court having moved once and for all to Vienna, nor was it fundamentally affected by subsequent wartime events. The nobles' and Catholic clergy's investment in the arts stemmed from the fashion for ostentation and also reflected changes in the political and religious situation in the capital of the kingdom. From the 1620s onwards, the interiors of Prague churches began to be slowly filled with magnificent carved altars dominated by monumental paintings of Christ, the Blessed Virgin Mary, and Catholic saints, and often inspired by current events. In the monastery church of St Thomas, the Hermits of St Augustine of the Lesser Town, who had already begun to beautify their friary, installed two monumental canvases in 1637 – St Augustine and the Martyrdom of St Thomas – commissioned in Antwerp from Peter Paul Rubens. The prestigious commission was the culmination of a small series of direct consignments from the workshop of the most famous Flemish painter to the churches of Catholic central Europe. The altar, also decorated with paintings by Rubens, can reasonably be compared only with those in the similar surroundings of Freising, in Bavaria, Neuburg an der Donau, Cologne, and, after that, Valtice (Feldsberg), in south Moravia, where Liechtenstein had moved some of his property. In 1640, a large series of paintings began to be made in the workshops of Prague artists for the monastery of the Discalced Augustinians at the Church of St Wenceslas in Zderaz (sv. Václava na Zderaze) on the corner of today's Resslova and Dittrichova streets, in the New Town of Prague. It comprised 32 lunettes with scenes from the life of the most important patron saint of the country. Of this series, eight paintings have survived to the present day, seven of which come from the workshop of the most influential Czech painter of the seventeenth century, Karel Škréta. The series followed on from two previous Prague series – the Renaissance wall paintings in the Wenceslas Chapel of St Vitus' Cathedral and the frescos by Baccio di Bianco in the chapel in Wallenstein House.

During the Thirty Years War, Wallenstein, at one point the Emperor's generalissimo, became the greatest Bohemian builder and investor in art since Rudolph II. His palatial house in the Lesser Town continues to attest both to his high demands on comfort and showiness and to his mentality in general. The scale of the building is Baroque but its range of forms is not entirely so. The interior division of the building perfectly reflects the period ideal of the princely residence with hierarchically arranged rooms. This military leader and politician, who in his day was second only to the emperor in importance in the country, built his seat symbolically close to Prague Castle. Only the residences of sovereigns in Vienna, Munich, and Salzburg could compare with it. To this day, the whole premises, including the garden with the grotto and riding school, stands apart from the neighbouring buildings by its high walls, giving

Wallenstein/Albrecht von Waldstein

Albrecht von Waldstein, known as Wallenstein, gained his first combat experience on the Hungarian battlefield in the wars against the Turks. During the Estates Rebellion, he went over to the side of the emperor and until the mid-1620s created an integrated territory in north-east Bohemia under his own sovereignty – the Duchy of Friedland. Financially independent, Wallenstein was able to recruit an army for Ferdinand II at his own expense. In 1625, he entered imperial territory as the general of these troops, successfully fighting against the Danes and their allies. When he occupied the whole German Baltic coast, he was at the height of his power and entered the world of European sovereigns as one of their equals. The persistent efforts of the Catholic League and the Bavarian Elector Maximilian I led, in 1630, to Wallenstein's dismissal as commander of the army. In no time, however, he was reappointed supreme commander, for the Habsburg domains were directly threatened by the Swedish-Saxon offensive. This was the beginning of the long period of his restrained warfare, circumspect manoeuvring, and secret negotiations with representatives of the anti-Habsburg alliance. Though no hard evidence of Wallenstein's treason was ever found, Ferdinand II, after some hesitation, eventually gave the order to have him killed. On 25 February 1634, in Eger (Cheb), near the westernmost tip of the country, the assassins dealt the 'wicked old perjured rebel beast' the death blow.

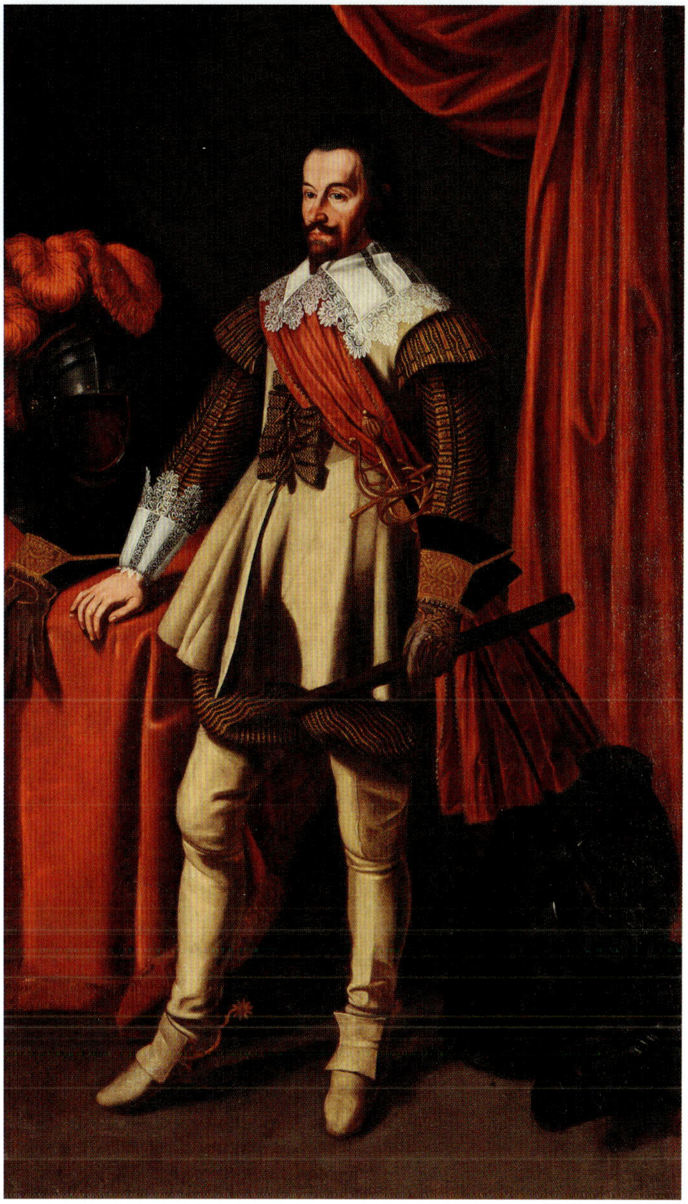

the impression that it is a self-enclosed organic whole. It was not only a ducal residence with everything that that entails, but was also the refuge and headquarters of a warrior. Stylistically, it is a synthesis of the latest achievements of the leading early seventeenth-century Italian schools of architecture.

To fund his project, the generalissimo had at his disposal not only superb urban planners and architects, but also outstanding specialists in the various building trades. Together with the Italian contingents, skilful stucco artists arrived at Wallenstein's residence, and their work gradually lent its characteristic features to all seventeenth-century central European architecture to such an extent that art historians, particularly in German, sometimes talk about *Stuckbarock* (stucco Baroque). Remarkable paintings were added to the stucco decoration of Wallenstein's Prague residence by artists like the Florence-born

Baccio di Bianco. Monumental bronze figures for Wallenstein and other prominent patrons, including Karl I Liechtenstein, were still being made in the mid-1620s by the Lesser Town workshop of Adriaen de Vries, a sculptor at Rudolph II's court. The strikingly shaped surfaces of these late works, fully open to the effects of light, correspond to the Baroque sensibility. But in Prague the great Mannerist artist de Vries found no one who would directly carry on his work, and with his death the only foundry capable of casting large bronze statues ceased to exist. Bohemian Baroque sculpture remained limited to wood, stucco, and stone; monumental metal sculptures here were henceforth all imported.

* * *

The nascent Baroque style was not really employed in the architecture of the towns of Prague until after the Thirty Years War. One must bear in mind, however, that even before the Estates Rebellion a 'proto-Baroque' had developed in Prague in the works of the imperial architect Giovanni Maria Filippi, particularly in the Lutheran Church of the Holy Trinity in the Lesser Town and the Matthias Gate at Prague Castle. These works attest not only to the refined architectural style, but also to contemporary links to Roman and indeed Spanish sources of inspiration. During the war, moreover, Catholics invested in beautifying the interiors of churches, remodelling them to reflect the current doctrine, and occasionally founded and built new religious houses or restored existing ones. Shortly after the Battle of the White Mountain, the interior of St Vitus' Cathedral, which had been badly damaged by Calvinist iconoclasts in 1619, was refurbished under the personal patronage of Ferdinand II. This restoration of the most important church in the country was meant to accompany its completion. According to the ambitious plans, attributed to the architect Giovanni Domenico Orsi, a massive nave with two aisles in the Roman style, probably with a cupola above the tomb of St Adalbert (Vojtěch), was meant to be built onto the medieval choir. The foundation stone for this work was laid by Emperor Leopold I in 1673, but ultimately only the foundations, buttresses, and part of the vaulting were built. The completion of this ambitious, costly project was halted mainly because of lack of funds.

Being so close to the seat of the monarch, the district of Hradčany was an important residential quarter of Prague. It remained so even after the monarch's court moved away from Prague, returning here only on special occasions. A favourite architect of the Bohemian upper nobility, Francesco Caratti, born near Lugano, designed a stately home for Count Humprecht Johann Czernin von Chudenitz. He began construction in 1668 on a plot near Pohořelec, carefully taking into account its physical position in relation to Prague Castle. Even when seen from a distance, the house provided a striking accent to the city skyline. Here, Czernin followed the examples of large Roman *palazzi*, which, according to contemporary admirers, his seat could not only be compared with, but even surpassed. It is the residence of a property tycoon who could afford to subsidize the state coffers of the Habsburg Monarchy by means of private

KAREL ŠKRÉTA: **Humprecht Johann, Count Czernin von Chudenitz**

Humprecht Czernin, a friend of Emperor Leopold I, reached the height of his diplomatic career in Venice between 1660 and 1663. Later, he increasingly spent time on his Bohemian estates and devoted most of his energy to collecting works of art and carrying out grand building projects. He was a cultivated patron of Baroque art.
In this painting by Karel Škréta, Czernin has just turned thirty. The artist has underscored the distance between his sitter and the viewer, giving Czernin an air of aloofness and a certain reticence, which are communicated with the suggestively fixed gaze of his cold blue eyes. We sense that under the mask of a perfect courtier is a tired, vulnerable man who is perhaps even prematurely disenchanted with the disfavour of his surroundings. The painter and his sitter probably understood each other; while on his embassy, Czernin collected a number of Škréta's Venetian paintings, which he then brought to Prague.

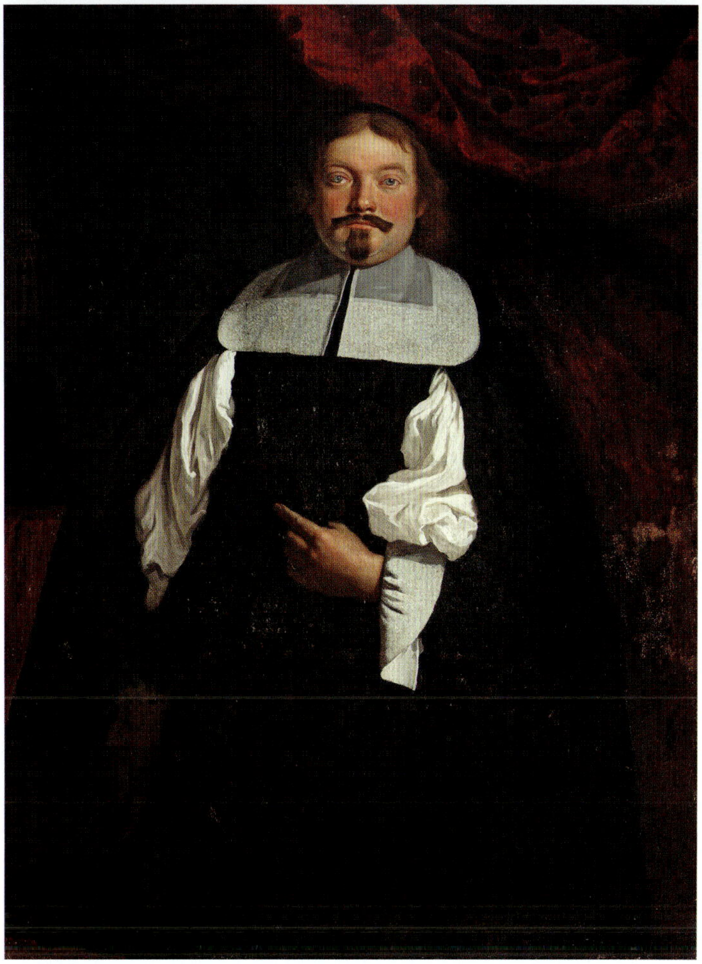

loans. Preserved correspondence and planning documentation attest to the lively negotiations between the builder and the architect; from these sources it is clear that Count Czernin was actively involved in designing the appearance of his house, though the building was not completed till the next generation of his family. Even from a distance, the viewer is astonished by the building, particularly its main façade, whose composition comprises twenty-nine vertical axes in the form of giant order engaged columns on strikingly distinctive bases of rusticated masonry. Caratti was inspired here by the works of Andrea Palladio, but emphasizes the balanced relationship between the horizontal and the vertical lines. A different impression is made by the more intricately composed façade on the garden side. Between the lateral 'towers', two ground-floor loggias (each a sala terrena) separated by a staircase, open out onto the garden.

The Early Baroque stage of building in the three towns of Prague closes with the works of Jean-Baptiste Mathey, an architect of Burgundian origin and Roman training, and was a citizen of Prague by choice. Born in Dijon, he was trained as a painter and spent almost two decades in Rome. It was there that he met the future archbishop of Prague, Johann Friedrich von Waldstein, a polymath prelate and demanding patron of the arts. Mathey came to Prague at

Waldstein's invitation in the first half of the 1670s, commissioned not to make paintings but to design prestigious architectural projects for him.

The first of these commissions was for the large-scale rebuilding of the Archbishop's Palace at Hradčany Square, from 1675 to 1679. In this edifice, today largely covered over by later remodelling, Mathey employed forward-looking elements of contemporary Roman architecture, giving the building its characteristic silhouette, and emphasizing the central part that comes to a peak with the roof-top pavilion. An interesting feature is the roof in the form of a ship's hull, the architect's tribute to an earlier Prague architectural tradition represented particularly by Queen Anne's Summer House in the Royal Garden.

Mathey's palatial house for Count Michael Oswald Thun-Hohenstein (today called Toskánský palác, the Palace of the Grand Duke of Tuscany), enclosing Hradčany Square from the west, is also Roman in expression. From its corner on Loretánská ulice, Ottavio Mosto's noble statue of the builder's patron saint, the archangel Michael, threatens all devils. Nearby, stands the new Martinitz House, designed by the Roman architect Carlo Fontana in the style of pure Baroque of Rome, the city where he had spent a good part of his life.

A dynamic trend in High Baroque architecture in Bohemia was applied, for example, in St Vitus' Cathedral and in the Royal Garden. The renowned Johann Blasius Santini-Aichl designed not only the lovely marble balustrade separating the cathedral choir from the nave, but also an impressive Italian-influenced façade for the earlier building of the dean and chapter next to the cathedral. Apart from these works, however, one encounters this architectural style in Hradčany more often outside the Castle precinct. Trained in Vienna, Giovanni Battista Alliprandi was probably the architect of the unfinished house of Wenceslas Adalbert Sternberg above the Deer Park Moat. Count Sternberg, a well-travelled gentleman and an exacting builder, had commissioned plans in 1692 from the renowned Domenico Martinelli for his Prague residence. The shape those plans would take, however, was fundamentally changed by increasing the number of plots on which the house was to be built.

The resulting building is remarkable particularly because of its strikingly shaped vestibule and its garden façade, into which the architect has incorporated an oval hall projecting upwards and outwards from the building. Count von Sternberg also built the Troja (Troy) manor house near the Royal Hunting Grounds (today's Stromovka Park), directly linked visually to Prague Castle. On plans by Jean-Baptiste Mathey, it is a luxurious country house on what was then the edge of the city, similar to the villas the count had seen near Rome, particularly in Frascati. In Prague and its environs, Troja is the first example of a comprehensive artistic project subordinated to a unified artistic point of view and ideological programme, ranging from its urban plan to the sculptural and painted ornamentation of its interior.

Several buildings in Hradčany were designed by Christoph Dientzenhofer and his son Kilian Ignaz, the latter of whom developed into one of the most distinctive figures of Bohemian architecture before the mid-eighteenth century. Together, father and son were involved in the planning of a new church for the

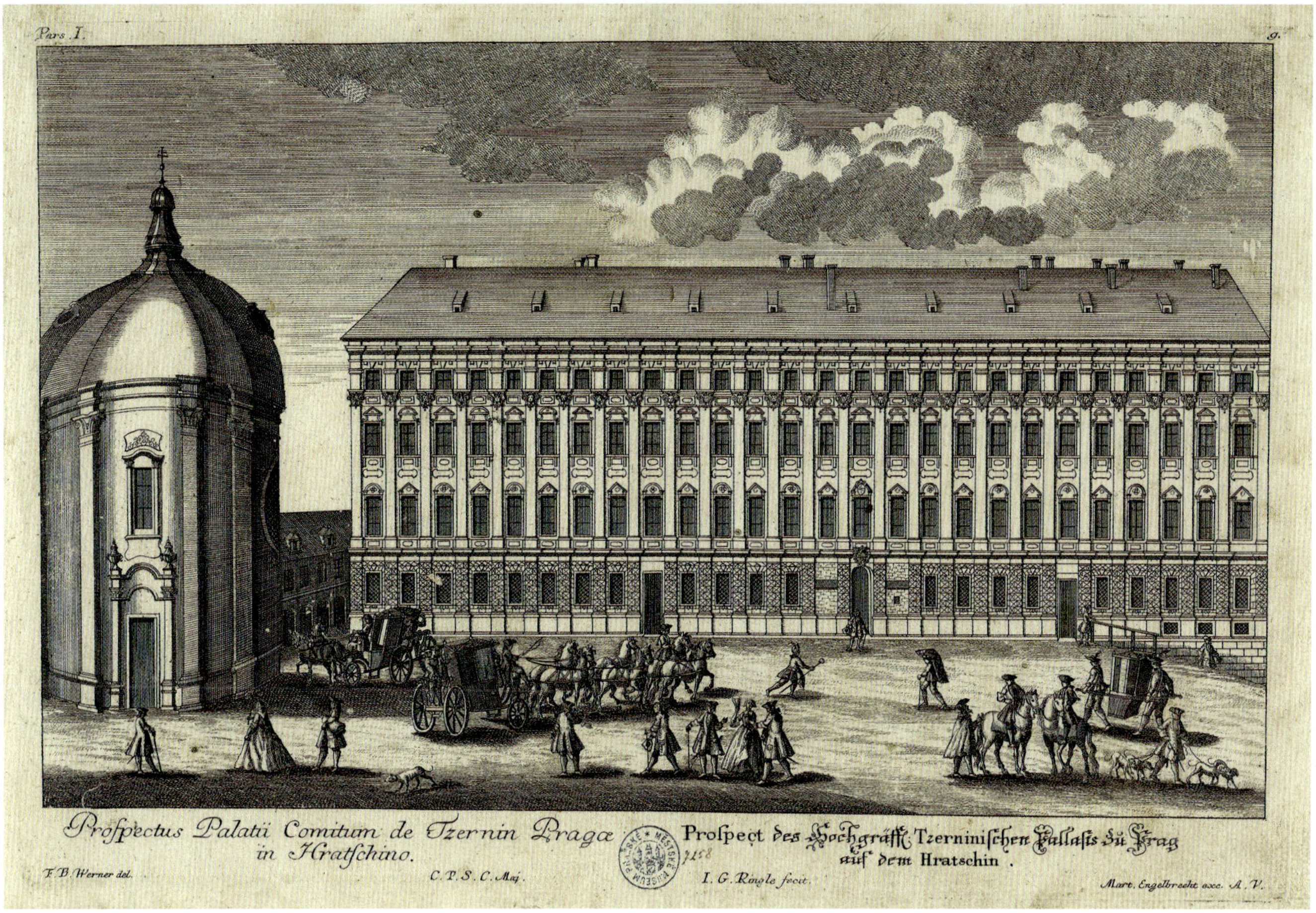

JOHANN GEORG RINGLE AFTER FRIEDRICH BERNHARD WERNER:
Czernin House in Hradčany

Count Humprecht Czernin began building his palatial Prague house in 1668 on plans by Francesco Caratti. Six years later, part of the Czernin picture gallery was installed here, the core of which Czernin had brought to Prague from Venice. This engraving depicts not only the monumental façade of the house but also the Chapel of St Matthew, built on the initiative of Count Franz Josef Czernin allegedly on the site of a church that had been dedicated to the same saint, and in which the body of St Ludmila was said to have temporarily been laid after being translated from the village of Tetín (about 40 km south-west of Prague). The central chapel, built between 1726 and 1732, was designed by František Maxmilián Kaňka and was decorated by Matthias Bernhard Braun and Wenzel Lorenz Reiner. It was demolished in the late eighteenth century.

Ursuline nuns. It was dedicated to St John Nepomucene, who is said to have performed the miracle here of healing the atrophied arm of the young Theresa Krebs. The Dientzenhofers were also involved in building the pilgrimage area around the copy of the Santa Casa (Holy House) of Loreto, Italy. The copy was built after 1626 on the initiative of Benigna Catherina von Lobkowicz, who was probably inspired by the imitation Santa Casa in the town of Mikulov (Nikolsburg), south Moravia. The Prague shrine, which became famous among pilgrims, was gradually expanded, transformed, and made richer up until the mid-eighteenth century. The best-known work of the younger Dientzenhofer at Hradčany is the Imperial Hospice in Kanovnická ulice. It was built from

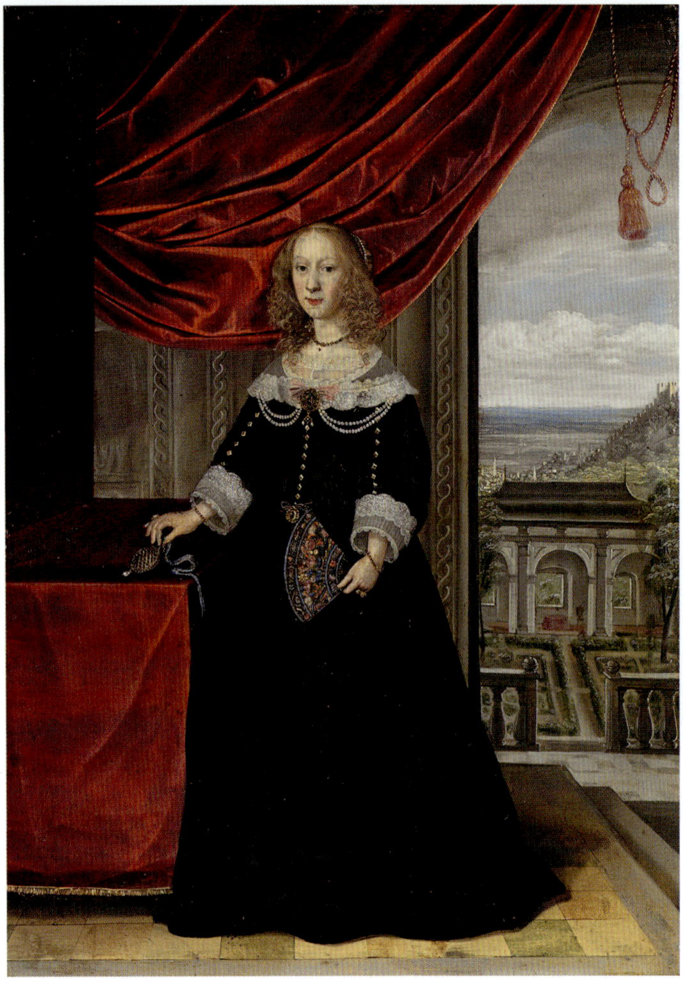

WOLFGANG HEIMBACH: **Portrait of a Young Lady with a View of Prague**, 1651

Behind the lady in this delightful little painting is a view of the no longer extant sala terrena opening onto the garden of Trauttmansdorff House in Loretánská ulice at Hradčany. The scenery is completed by the silhouette of Petřín Hill and the Hunger Wall and a section of the Prague skyline. The portrayed woman could well be Countess Eva Johanna von Trauttmansdorff (née von Sternberg), the wife of the then owner of the house.

1733 to 1737 on the site of an almshouse possibly established by Archbishop Jan Očko z Vlašimi in the reign of Charles IV (r. 1346–78). Here, the architect employed his favourite motive of an octagonal centre and gave the building a three-dimensional façade. The Baroque chapter in the architectural history of Hradčany closed with the grand redesign of Prague Castle in the reign of Empress Maria Theresa (r. 1740–80) on plans by the Vienna architect Nicolò Pacassi. The motley conglomerate of buildings of various style periods, as we know from old *vedute*, was replaced by a uniform, Neoclassically austere, and outwardly not particularly expressive architecture, which, however, cannot be denied monumentality and impressiveness, especially on the Prague skyline. Pacassi was a master of sophisticated planimetric composition based on the overlapping of planes and layers. This ingeniously conceived complex of buildings appealed to noble connoisseurs of architecture. We find it also behind the scenes in the First Courtyard of Prague Castle, which to this day functions as the honorary 'reception area' of the head of state. It was surely on purpose that the impressive backdrop of the Matthias Gate, finished in 1614, generally considered to be one of the first works of Baroque architecture in Prague, was incorporated into the Late Baroque façade. In his façade for the Archbishop's

Palace on Hradčany Square, obliquely facing the Castle, the architect Johann Joseph Wirch created a delicately shaped and flamboyant Prague counterpart to the work of the cooler Pacassi and his Viennese sophistication. The range of styles has come full circle.

* * *

In *An Account* of *Several Travels through* a *Great Part* of *Germany* (1677), the English physician, traveller, and man of letters Edward Browne writes that the Lesser Town of Prague is far merrier than the towns on the right bank of the Vltava, for it has nicer houses and the town houses of the nobility are grander. The French physician and numismatist Charles Patin considered the Lesser Town to have the most imposing architecture of Prague: 'It has nothing but town houses, more than three hundred, and they are the refuges of everything that gives Bohemia and the hereditary lands of His Imperial Majesty their riches.' This well-educated traveller greatly exaggerated the number of Lesser Town residences, however, for in 1653 the whole Lesser Town, together with Hradčany, had only 544 houses, of which those registered as belonging to the nobility number only 124. Baroque gentlemen on their journeys were understandably most interested in the huge Wallenstein House, together with the story of the man who built it. The fame of the Lesser Town as a place where the nobility lived in the Early Baroque period was increased by the house of another post-White Mountain upstart, Pavel Michna z Vacínova, which is stylistically more advanced than Wallenstein House. In the 1660s, the house of the supreme chancellor of the kingdom, Johann Hartwig von Nostitz, was built on Maltézské náměstí. Though a remarkable building, its architect is not mentioned in the records. Yet, considering its similarities with Czernin House, we may reasonably assume that the architect was Francesco Caratti.

By the mid-eighteenth century, the Lesser Town had acquired its characteristic appearance as a much-admired town of Baroque churches and palatial houses. The credit for that transformation goes first and foremost to two Lesser Town burghers, the Dientzenhofers, father and son. Their joint achievement was the Jesuit Church of St Nicholas (1702–11) on Lesser Town Square (Malostranské náměstí), the upper part of which the church opens onto with its monumental, expressively shaped, two-storeyed façade, one of the most impressive of its kind in all Bohemian Baroque architecture. The massive cupola, next to which stands the slender bell tower of the same height (finished by 1752), constitutes the decisive feature of the skyline of left-bank Prague, into whose intricately structured organism the architect has placed his church with surprising boldness and admirable sensitivity. The greenish dome of St Nicholas is to Prague what Brunelleschi's dome is to Florence and Michelangelo's cupola of St Peter's is to Rome. In Miloš Marten's philosophical dialogue *Nad městem* (Above the city, 1917) one of the character-discussants claims that the 'whole drama of the Latin spirit has been turned into the beauty that rises up from the joyful flowerbed of three churches in front of Charles Bridge, through the avenue of its statues, to the gigantic green rose of Saint Nicholas, and, with its

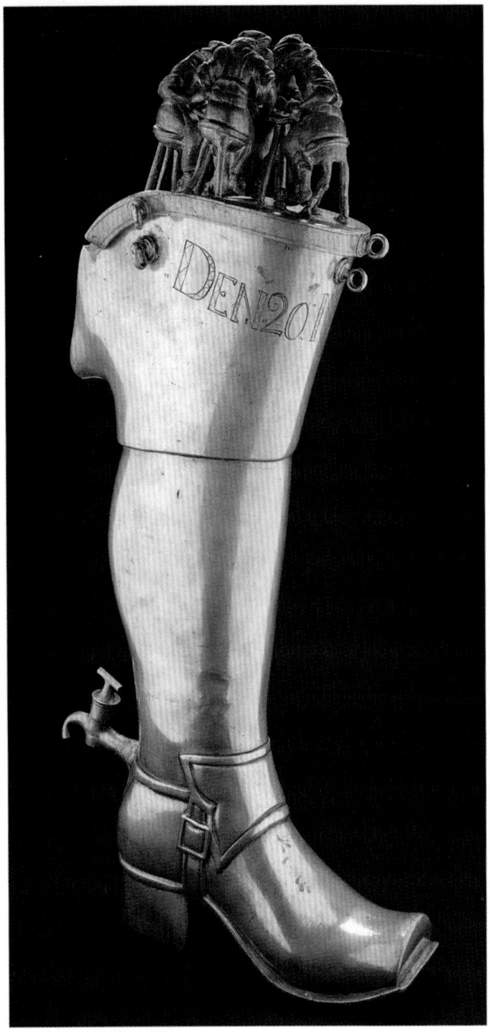

Wine Flagon of the Shoemakers' Guild, 1715

Wine jugs, whose shape and decoration were often related to the trades, were an important part of the common mid-morning repasts of guild masters. The pewterer Philipp Jacob Strolz probably made this charming vessel, in the form of a high riding boot, as his masterpiece.
Its lid is decorated with a group of four shoemakers at work.

proud brow, it creates, from the vortex of palaces, the harmony of the great line of the Castle and the Cathedral upon which charming wilfulness has placed the upside-down emerald chalice of the copper cupola like a beacon of triumphant light.' Another side of Kilian Ignaz Dientzenhofer's art is the admirable Augustinian Church of St Thomas, which was given a dynamic, almost sculptural façade after 1727. Smaller buildings erected on plans by this great architect can be seen on walks through the streets of the Lesser Town.

Another citizen of the Lesser Town was Johann Blasius Santini-Aichel, renowned as the designer of original churches in the style called 'Baroque Gothic', which to this day adorn the Bohemian and Moravian landscape. A few steps from his home in Ostruhová ulice (Sporrengasse, today's Nerudova ulice) is Santini's first work (perhaps from 1703): modifications to the Marian church at the house of the Theatine order. The initial plans were by the brilliant Guarino Guarini, but the church was later built probably on plans by Jean-Baptiste Mathey. Santini took the idea of his great predecessor and, presumably, teacher, and made it strikingly more dynamic, particularly by modifying the ground plan. Also in Nerudova ulice, which rises steeply up from Lesser Town Square

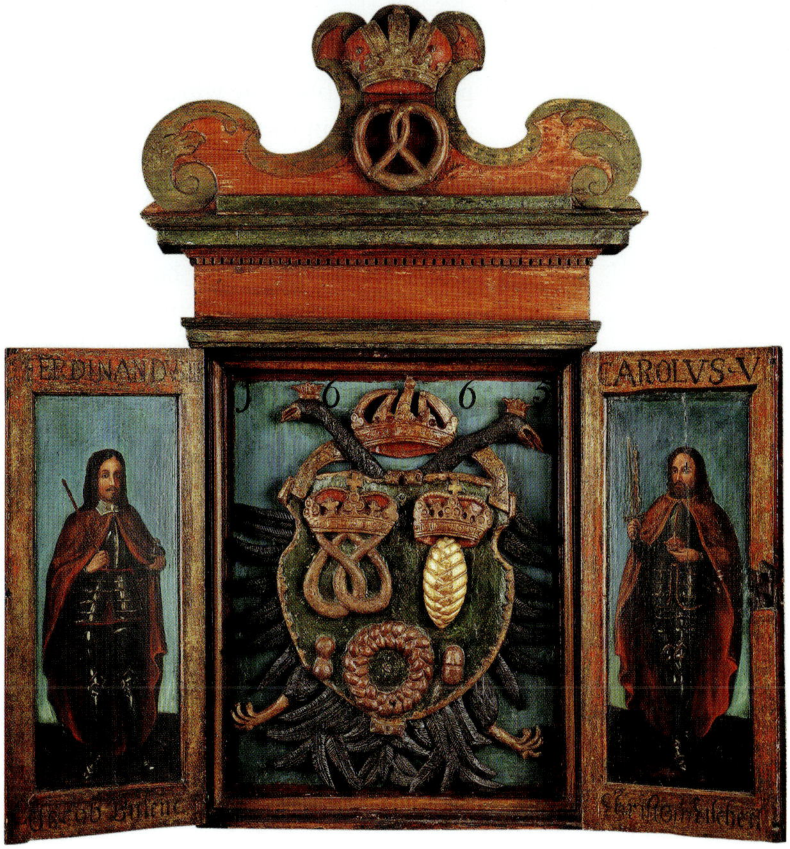

Shop Sign linked with the Bakers' Guild of the Lesser Town and Hradčany, 1665

Beginning in the late seventeenth or early eighteenth century, attempts were made to reform the outmoded guild system, for it was impeding the development of mercantilist methods and the establishment of factories. Important changes 'from above' were brought about particularly by the 1731 guild ordinance of Charles VI, on the basis of which general guild regulations were issued eight years later. The preserved items from the Prague guilds reflect the pride that the craftsmen had in their work and reveal their efforts to have the worshipful companies duly represented.

to the Castle and Strahov, stand, almost opposite each other, two palatial houses designed by Santini: Morzin House and Kolowrat House. The former was built, in about 1713/14, from several older houses which the architect unified with a wide façade that has three vertical sections, completed with striking sculptures by Ferdinand Maximilian Brokoff. Similarly, in the Kolowrat House (today, Thun House –Thunovský palác), built from about 1706 to 1721, the important role of the sculptor was assigned to the renowned Matthias Bernhard Braun, who created a pair of gigantic heraldic eagles bearing the pediment above the portal. Santini resourcefully coped with the sloping terrain, setting the building on a rusticated base upon which he then set the masterly composed façade, dramatically and playfully combining bas relief with exaggeratedly shaped elements. Recently, this ingenious architect has also been attributed with modifications to Fürstenberg House (also known as Berka House) in Valdštejnská ulice. The architectural history of the building is somewhat complicated and the changes that are assumed to have been by Santini (before 1714) are today particularly apparent in the innovative design of the ground-floor interiors.

In Santini's day, a number of other remarkable Baroque houses were built in the Lesser Town. After Caratti and Lurago, Giovanni Battista Alliprandi also found work there. It was he who introduced into the architecture of the nobility's Prague town houses characteristic features of the High Baroque such as articulated attics surmounted by statues and convexly and concavely curving pediments above the windows. They first appeared in Kaiserstein House, built about 1700, in the lower part of Lesser Town Square. In the palatial house of Count Přehořovský z Kvasejovic (today, Lobkowicz House), built from 1702 to 1707 at the foot of Petřín Hill, Alliprandi, probably under the influence of Johann Bernhard Fischer von Erlach (but perhaps also influenced by the *maisons de plaisance*, country houses, in France), incorporated the oval of the main hall into the central structure of the building, which is flanked by wings curving inwards towards the garden. Noblemen and burghers who built their houses at the foot of Petřín and Hradčany took advantage of the terrain to create terraced gardens rising high up the slopes. In about 1712, Mauritius Vogt, a polymath of the Cistercian monastery in Plasy, describes Petřín as a hill with 'splendid orchards, summer residences, and marvellous underground caves', remarking that the Lesser Town is where 'most of the gentry live, the nicest German is spoken, and the best wheat beer is brewed'.

* * *

The Lesser Town is linked to the Old Town by Charles Bridge, which until the nineteenth century was the only bridge over the River Vltava. During the High Baroque, the bridge was gradually changed into a unique open-air sculpture gallery, which is to this day not only the foremost tourist attraction in Prague but also, indeed mainly, compelling evidence of the artistic quality, variety of expression, and depth of content of Prague sculpture from the late seventeenth century to the first quarter of the eighteenth. Probably from the time it was built, Charles Bridge traditionally had a Crucifixion with figures of the Virgin Mary and St John the Evangelist. Though damaged or destroyed in various wars, it was always erected again, most recently after the Swedes attacked in 1648. The pier opposite it was decorated with a stone wayside shrine. For a while, a statue of King George of Poděbrady (r. 1458–71) also stood here until it was torn down during the occupation of the Lesser Town and Hradčany by troops led by Rudolph II's cousin, Leopold, Bishop of Passau, in 1611. Since the beginning of the sixteenth century, one of the piers has been guarded by a knight of popular literature, in full armour – Roland or, as he is known in Czech, Bruncvík – probably as a reminder of the rights of the Old Town local authority to control bridge traffic.

It was the Old Town that had single-mindedly led the decoration of the stone bridge with statues of the saints. The bronze St John Nepomucene by Johann Brokoff, erected in 1683, allegedly on the place where the saint was martyred, did not remain alone for long. The idea of celebrating the popular martyr, who had been thrown off the bridge into the Vltava, was linked with ambitious plans for a unique set of sculptures, probably inspired by the Ponte Sant'Angelo in Rome. The Prague bridge soon surpassed its model when the city authorities, university faculties, religious orders, ambitious nobles, and self-assured patricians competed with one another in presenting proposals to fund more and more sculptural groups. This growth, however, was not random or unchecked; the authorities of the Old Town, for example, saw to it that figures of the key

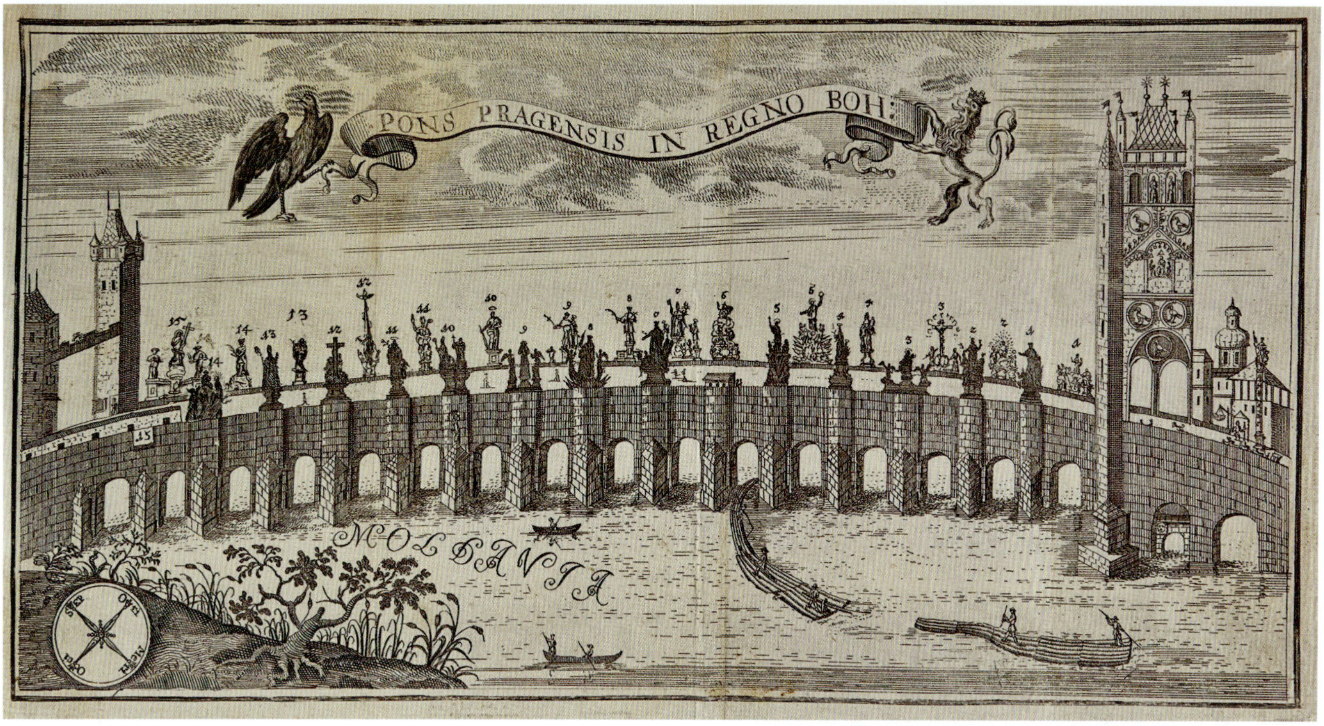

View of Charles Bridge from Střelecký ostov 1729

The sculptural decoration of Charles Bridge became a tourist attraction shortly after it was completed. This print, originating in Augsburg, even describes it as 'world renowned'. The *veduta* disregards the true scale of the sculptures and the architecture. Here, the bridge changes into an emblematically conceived path lined with the figures of the Roman Catholics' heavenly intercessors. John Moore, a globetrotting Scottish physician visiting Prague towards the end of the Baroque period, writes: 'The corners of the streets, bridges, and public buildings, are all ornamented with crucifixes, images of the Virgin of all sizes and complexions, and statues of saints of every country, condition, age, and sex. People are to be seen on their knees before these statues in every part of this city, but particularly on the large bridge over the Moldaw [Moldau/Vltava] where there is the greatest concourse of passengers. This bridge is so profusely adorned with the statues of saints, that, crossing over it, you have a row of them on each side, like two ranks of musketeers.'

patron saints of the country would gradually appear on the bridge. The town hall was also able to block proposals that deviated from the purely sacral programme of decoration and too obviously drew attention to the patron. That was the case in 1720, when the local authorities rejected the proposal of the Count Franz Anton von Sporck to erect a sculptural group from Braun's workshop in honour of the reigning emperor, Charles VI. Thanks also to this supervision, an impressive set of Baroque sculptures was made in the course of several decades, resting on the base of the Gothic bridge and watched over by the medieval tower gates. The French sculptor Émile-Antoine Bourdelle (1861–1929) rightfully compared Charles Bridge to a centaur with a Gothic body and a Baroque head, though he probably did not intend this as a compliment.

* * *

The Old Town, Edward Browne wrote, 'is very populous, full of Buildings, private and publick' but the '*Kleine Seitten,* or *lesser Prague,* far exceeds the

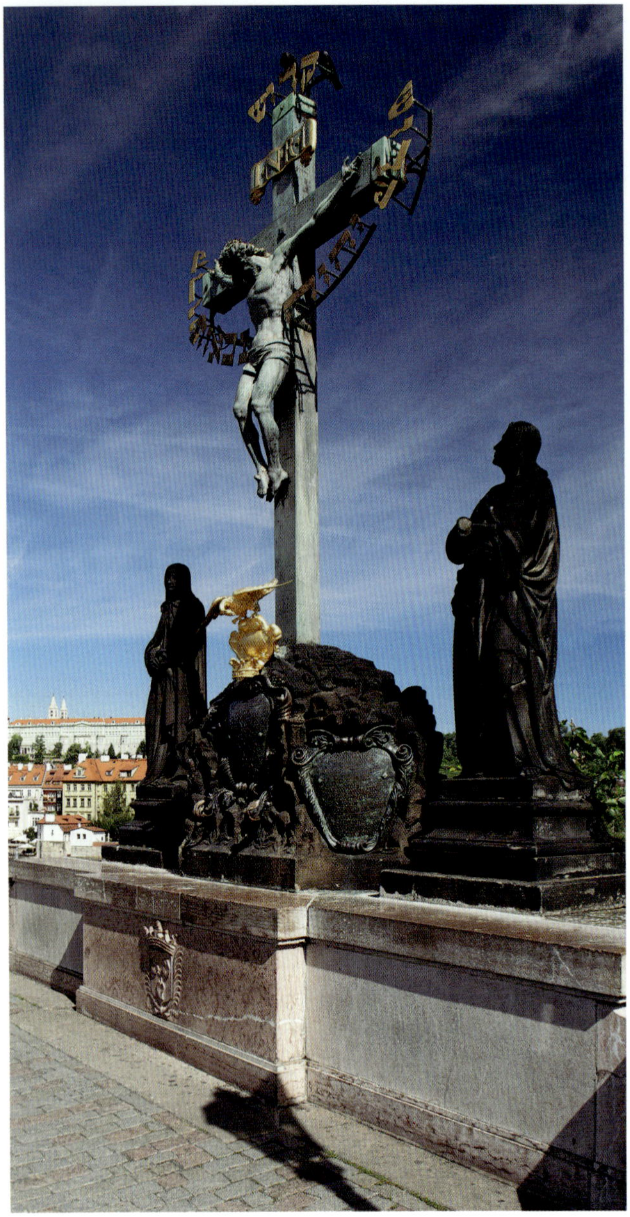

Calvary, sculptural group on Charles Bridge

The earliest part of this sculptural group as it is now constituted is the bronze *corpus* of Christ, which was made in Dresden probably in 1628. The gilt Hebrew inscription was added later. From an Old Testament canticle, the quotation 'Holy, holy, holy is the Lord of Hosts' (Isaiah 6: 3) is absolutely unique in this context, and for Jews it is considered disgraceful. The inscription was made with money from a fine of 1,000 guilder, paid in 1694 by Elias Backoffen, a leading member of the Landesjudenschaft (the organization of Jewish self-government in Bohemia). Backoffen was fined for allegedly having blasphemed God and the Cross in a coded letter to his friend, Berl Tabor. He was denounced by his colleague, Abraham Aaron Lichtenstadt, the head of the Landesjudenschaft. The court decision was based on circumstantial and inconclusive evidence. Moreover, Lichtenstadt's denunciation was intended to draw attention away from his own financial machinations. In Jewish self-government in Prague, it was unprecedented that an eminent member of the community would take advantage of Christian antagonism towards the Jews in order to humiliate a long-standing rival.

[Old Town] for pleasantness and beauty of Buildings and fair Palaces.' Another eye-witness describes this part of Prague as an overcrowded quarter of narrow streets and tall buildings. A list from 1653 states that the Old Town had 1,052 houses (of which 109 were registered as owned by nobles), which was slightly less than in the New Town with its 1,172 houses. One factor that contributed to the impression foreigners sometimes had of Prague as chaotic was the bilingualism of the right bank, where – unlike in the noble quarters on the other side of the Vltava – Czech was increasingly being used in addition to German. Nevertheless, the Old Town remained the foremost Prague town, for it had the university, the Jesuit academy, numerous convents and monasteries, and the largest church in the city after the cathedral. This church – Our Lady before the Thein (Týn) – soon, after the 'return' of its Catholic congregation, also became a monument to the Old Town burghers' pride in having successfully defended the city against the Swedes. And it also became a place where members of leading bourgeois families and guilds, as well as illustrious patricians, developed their individual and corporate identities. In front of the Thein Church, in the middle of the Old Town Square, loaded with symbolic meanings and historical contexts, the first Marian column in the Lands of the Bohemian Crown was erected at the command of Ferdinand III in 1650, and dedicated two years later. The obvious reason for erecting the column was the signing of the Peace of Westphalia in late October 1648 and the breaking of the Swedish siege of Prague from late July to early November 1648. In the microhistory of the city, however, the column mainly represented the definitive 're-Catholicization' of the Old Town Square, the triumph of Mary the Immaculate, not only over the enemies of the true faith, but also, symbolically, over the whole world. The most important sculptural commission of Early Baroque Prague, the column was executed by the master sculptor Johann Georg Bendl with a few assistants. The work stands out for the maturity and inventiveness of its design. Whereas the Blessed Virgin Mary's head is made after models

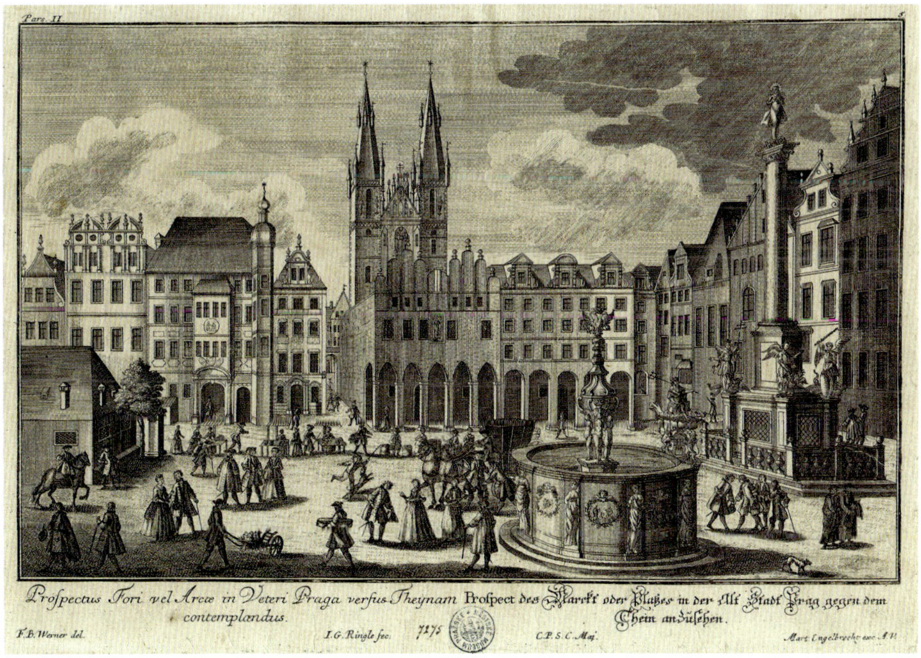

JOHANN GEORG RINGLE AFTER FRIEDRICH BERNHARD WERNER:
Old Town Square with the Krocín Fountain and Marian Column

In the late 1730s or early 1740s, a series of engravings with Prague subject matter was made after drawings by the Silesian painter of cityscapes, Friedrich Bernhard Werner. Despite their numerous imprecisions and obvious errors, the engravings provide unique evidence of the appearance of the town in the High Baroque and about life in the streets of Prague. The view of the east side of the Old Town Square (Staroměstské náměstí) shows the hustle and bustle, particularly round the Renaissance Krocín Fountain and Bendl's Marian column from 1650. Note the three historic houses to the left of the façade of Thein Church, which are today joined into a whole under the Rococo façade of Goltz-Kinský House.

from classical antiquity, the group of angels battling with demons or devils is characterized by dramatic movement and the realistic combination of robust bodies. Wrongly assuming it to be a monument to the victory of the imperial forces at the Battle of the White Mountain, hysterical participants of a public gathering demolished the Marian column on 3 November 1918, seeking by this Herostratus-like gesture to express their hatred for the Habsburg Monarchy, which had already come to an end four days earlier.

Long before the Baroque arrived, Jesuit fathers had settled in Prague. The 'court' builder of their Bohemian province was the versatile Carlo Lurago. He was not only an architect, but also a practising builder who stood at the head of a prospering construction company that also included much sought-after Italian stucco artists. For the Jesuit college in the Old Town, called the Clementinum, Lurago designed the sculpture-like west façade with vertical bands of windows inserted between pilasters of the giant order. Another component of this side of the Clementinum is the façade of St Saviour's Church, ingeniously composed as a counterpart, physically and symbolically, to the Gothic bridge tower on the Old Town bank of the Vltava, practically on the axis of one of the main Prague roads, demarcating the east and the west sides of the city. By its composition, the church portico is meant to suggest a triumphal arch. The symbolic apotheosis of the Church Militant and Church Triumphant, which the Jesuits employed right in the medieval core of the town, could not have been more telling. Bendl's statues of patron saints of the country and the patron saints of the Jesuits on the façade are grouped around the central figure of the Blessed Virgin Mary (the embodiment of the Church) and Jesus Christ as the Saviour of the world (Salvator Mundi). The literary historian Arne Novák, in his essay *Praha barokní* (Baroque Prague, 1915; published in French and English in 1938 and 1947) writes: 'This why the Baroque sculptors adorned their churches with whole throngs of saints and philosophers, such as the stone conclave that looks down from the balustrades of the Church of San Salvator – the Church Victorious, willing to intercede'.

The unique character of Křižovnické náměstí (Knights of the Cross Square), where, so typically of Prague, the Gothic is wed in remarkable harmony to the Baroque, is formed by the main façade of the Church of St Francis of Assisi. The church is administered by members of the Order of Knights of the Cross with the Red Star. Its General Superior, from 1668 to 1694, was the Archbishop of Prague, Johann Friedrich von Waldstein, and he entrusted the rebuilding of the Gothic hospital church to his favourite architect, Jean-Baptiste Mathey. Its gracefully proportioned façade, clad in sandstone blocks and articulated with giant order pilasters with additional pilaster frames and layered relief-like bossage, is turned towards the intimate space of the square. Above the tympanum, the façade visually comes to a peak with a cupola on a high drum. The pedigree of this astonishing building goes back not only to Rome and the rest of Italy, but also to the architect's native France. All in all, however, St Francis's Church is an entirely original work in which various impulses have been synthesized into the harmonious whole of its spatial concept and forms.

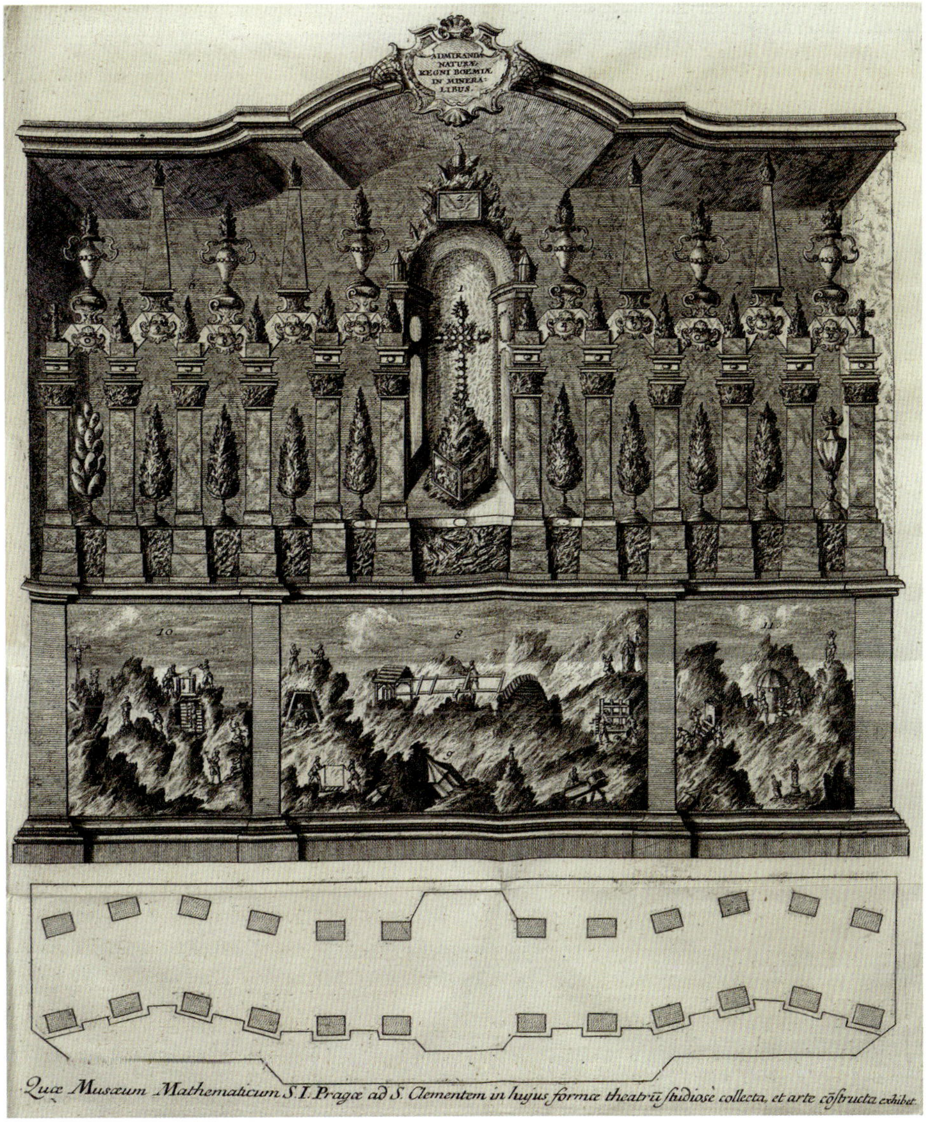

The Mathematics Museum in the Clementinum, a cabinet with an exhibition of minerals

The Museum of Mathematics, opened in five rooms of the Clementinum in 1722, was the first institution of its kind in the Bohemian Lands. The Jesuits assembled here not only books and scientific instruments but also a wide variety of exotic objects which Jesuit brothers had brought home or sent back from missions. These included herbaria, coins, prints, and ingenious automata run by clock movements. The pride of the museum was a systematically built-up collection of minerals, whose impressive Baroque installation is captured in this engraving from 1743.

The Old Town, including the Jewish ghetto, was severely damaged by a conflagration in the summer of 1689, which is remembered in Prague history as the French Fire. It was blamed on French-paid saboteurs, who allegedly carried out the dirty deed on the orders of the French Minister of War, the Marquis de Louvois, whose armies were at that time plundering the Rhenish Palatinate. On the first day of summer, 21 June, after a very dry spring, fire broke out in several places at once on the right bank of Prague. A total of 766 residential buildings (of which 318 belonged to Jews) were reduced to ashes, together with

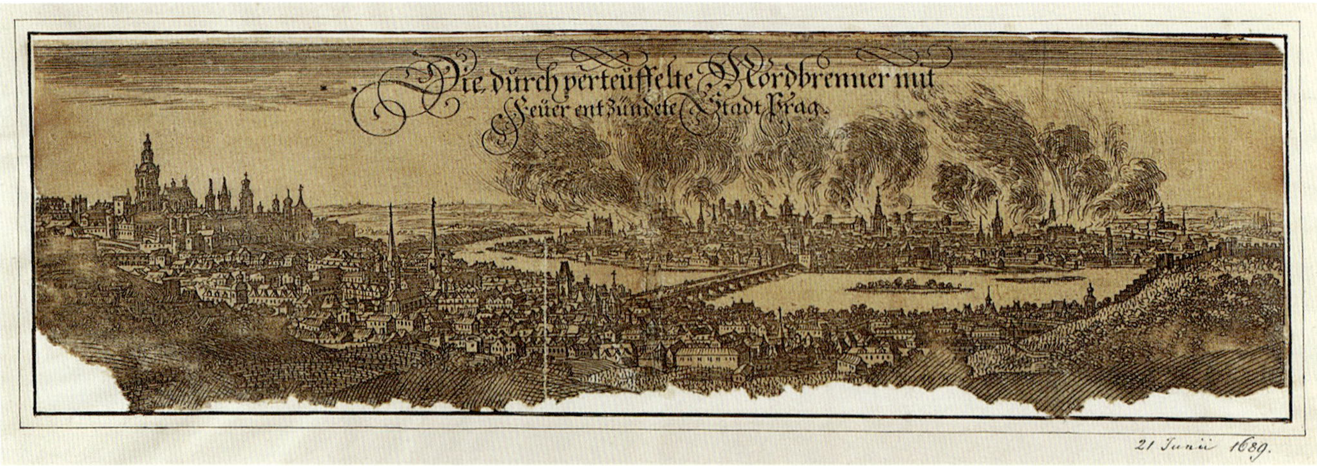

The French Fire of Prague, 1689

Fires were the scourge of early modern towns and in this respect Prague was no exception. In 1653, a blaze destroyed part of the New Town around the churches of St Peter and St Henry. In 1708, there was a fire on the boundary of the Old Town and the New Town of Prague and, in 1754, a large part of the ghetto was reduced to ashes. The greatest damage to life and property was done by the great fire in the towns on the right bank of the Vltava on 21 and 22 June 1689, which was said to have been started by French agents. Though the authorities continuously took fire-prevention measures and issued regulations, the danger did not go away. The source of disaster was most often open fire used for heating, cooking, and light, possibly glowing ashes, badly swept chimneys, and, more rarely, lightning. The roofs of most Prague houses were shingle and frequently had walls adjoining wooden extensions in which straw and other combustible materials were stored. Considering that water was often inaccessible, it becomes clear why the fires spread so swiftly.

six churches and convents, eleven synagogues, and the municipal flour mills of the New Town together with the sawmill and the water tower. The disaster also took its toll in human lives.

Like the even more destructive conflagration of the Lesser Town and Hradčany in 1541, the French Fire led to the restoration of the damaged buildings in an even grander and more modern spirit. The Third Estate were becoming rich and felt a need to show it. In the decades after the fire, houses of the middle classes, flaunting remarkable High Baroque façades, appeared on the right bank of the Vltava. They manifest the influences of Alliprandi, Dientzenhofer father and son, and Santini, though it is practically impossible to attribute these houses to any of one of those architects. In no time, the artistically knowledgeable noble builders entered the traditionally middle-class and ecclesiastical microcosm of right-bank Prague. After 1702, probably on plans by Alliprandi, the house of Zikmund Valentin, Count of Hrzán z Harasova, was built in Celetná ulice. It differs from the houses of its more conservative bourgeois neighbours not only by being markedly taller, but also by its 'Viennese' portal with a balcony borne by a pair of atlantes and by its dynamic lines. The most important secular Old Town building of the High Baroque was the house of Count Johann Wenzel Gallas. Gallas crowned his illustrious political and diplomatic career as Viceroy of Naples (where he died in 1719), and was therefore, after the emperor, the highest placed man in the Habsburg Monarchy. This grand residence, built on the site of several medieval houses, was erected after

1714 and completed in 1718 on plans by the Vienna-based imperial architect Johann Bernhard Fischer von Erlach. In the labyrinth of the Old Town streets which prevent one from stepping back sufficiently from this spectacular façade with its eleven vertical divisions, this edifice, exuding an air of 'Baroque great power' under the sceptre of Emperor Charles VI, seems like a messenger from another world. Inside the building is the most gorgeous monumental Baroque staircase in Prague, crowned with a ceiling fresco by Carlo Innocenzo Carloni. The impression the house leaves is increased by the outstanding sculptural decoration from the Prague workshop of Matthias Bernhard Braun.

Another architect who struggled with the problem of the densely built-up areas that stood in the way of elaborating grand urban plans was Kilian Ignaz Dientzenhofer in his project for the Church of St Nicholas, from 1732 to 1737, at the Benedictine abbey on Old Town Square. The cramped medieval plot of land led the architect to come up with an untraditional solution – namely, moving the main façade from the west to the south lateral wall of the church. The dramatically graduated portal leads into the brightly illuminated interior, in which the architect has masterly launched the intricate play of straight lines

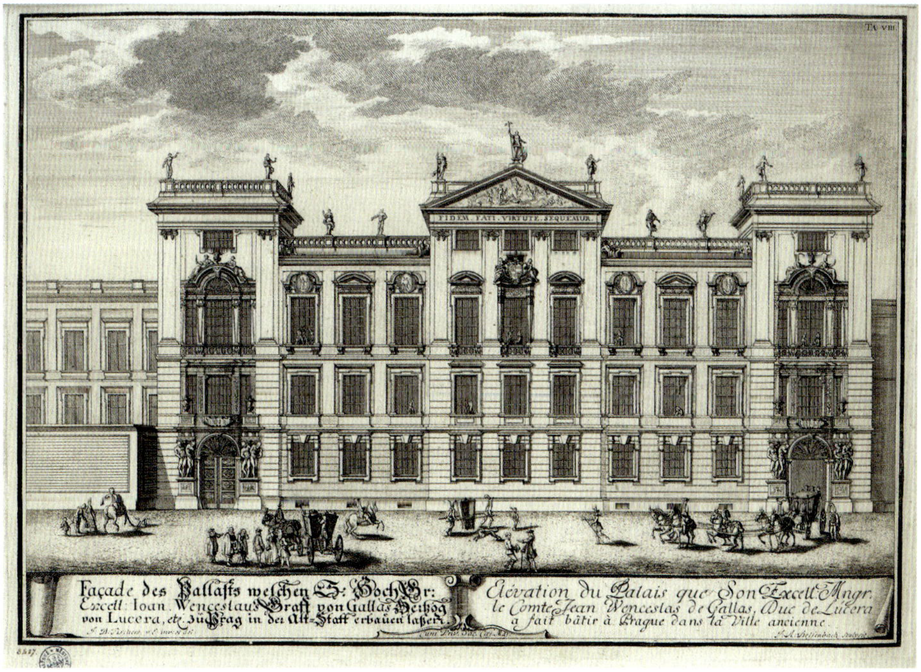

JOHANN ADAM DELSENBACH AFTER JOHANN BERNHARD FISCHER VON ERLACH:
Gallas House (Clam-Gallas House) in the Old Town

This grand panorama of the elevation was made in 1721 when the building was not quite finished. Four years later, the proud architect included it in a selection of his plans published in the last part of the album called *Entwurff Einer Historischen Architectur.* The monumental façade of the house is captured here as it never could have been seen in reality, for the surrounding buildings prevent anyone from standing back this far from the façade. Count Gallas was thinking about buying the houses across the street in order to demolish them, but this idea turned out to be too expensive.

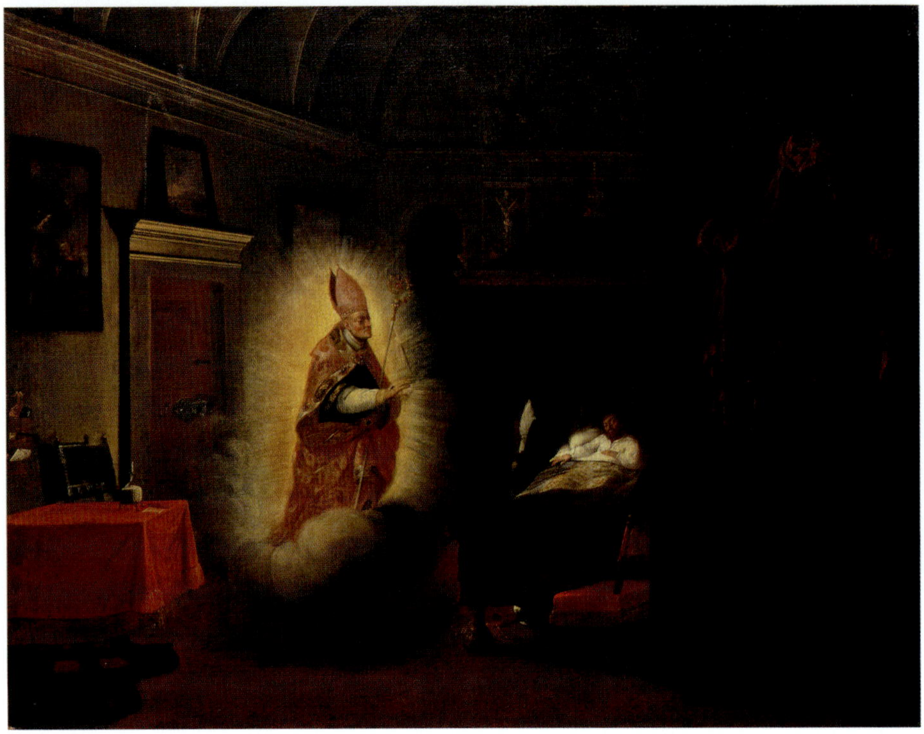

CHRISTIAN DITTMANN: **St Procopius Commands the Dreaming Burgher Soběslav to Change His House into a Church**, 1668/69

This painting from the series of scenes from the life of St Procopius, in the Church of All Saints at Prague Castle, provides unique iconographic evidence of the appearance of a rich burgher's home in the seventeenth century. Note the table with the lamp and the large pocket from which letters and small pictures protrude (a quodlibet, that is, a kind of *trompe-l'œil*). The room is also decorated with paintings, the larger of which portrays a female saint with a supplicant, and a smaller picture, a landscape, which rests on the cornice above the door. The righthand side of the scene is taken up by a wall with a home altar. The burgher Soběslav is sleeping on a large bed with a luxurious canopy, which often also served as a place to keep books.

and dynamic curves on the plan of a Greek cross. At the very end of the Baroque period, the massive monolith of Goltz-Kinský House, built from 1750 to 1765 on plans by Anselmo Lurago, energetically entered the space of Old Town Square, typical of which was the cluster of houses of the middle class. The austere character of the building, emulating Classicism, is weakened and visually broken up by the numerous decorative elements, particularly the sculpture on the attic and the richly developed stucco of the façade.

Other buildings of the Old Town also underwent High Baroque transformations. The versatile František Maxmilián Kaňka was a reliable architect in the service of the Czernins and other Bohemian noblemen. He drew up the plans for remodelling the university complex called the Carolinum, which was then built by 1718, in the very heart of the Old Town. He gave his buildings Baroque façades, but at the same time, with the erudition of a historical preservationist, he structurally secured the Gothic core of this labyrinthine complex of buildings, thus preserving it for future generations. Medieval churches were decorated with new façades and their interiors were remodelled. During the decades before Maria Theresa came to power, the Baroque permeated all parts of the city and imprinted it with its distinctive character. Construction work was not interrupted even by the subsequent battles for Prague. The graceful Pachta House (Pachtovský palác) built near Charles Bridge after 1770, a diminutive secular counterpart to the Archbishop's Palace at Hradčany, may justly be considered a capricious architectural epitaph to the Baroque in the Old Town.

* * *

The Baroque style also made its way into the streets of the still somewhat plebeian New Town, which had retained the character of a kind of an inner-city suburb, though here too important secular and, especially, church buildings were erected. The vast Baroque complexes of religious houses were wedged, initially without restraint and certainly inconsiderately, into the otherwise systematically laid-out medieval town. The first of them, built during the Thirty Years War, was the Capuchin friary on what is today náměstí Republiky (Republic Square), immediately followed by the adjacent building of the Irish Franciscans (Hibernians). Beginning in 1658, the vast complex of the Jesuit college was built at the Cattle Market, today's Charles Square (Karlovo náměstí). The building, begun with the participation of Martin Reiner and perhaps also Carlo Lurago, was finished 120 years later by Paul Ignaz Bayer and probably also the Late Baroque architect (and crypto-Protestant) Johann Joseph Wirch. Lastly, the convent of the Ursulines, with its exceptionally interesting church which projects with its side façade into what is today the avenue called Národní (National), was built after 1699 on plans by Marcantonio Canevalle.

Noble builders in the High Baroque acquired plots for their palatial houses mainly in the lower part of the New Town, roughly between what is today Václavské náměstí (Wenceslas Square) and Hybernská ulice (Hibernia Street). Later changes to the buildings and the town plan were more brutal than elsewhere in inner Prague, yet Baroque houses remain to this day in the streets Panská, Na Příkopě, Jindřišská, and Hybernská. The group of these buildings near the former monastery of the Irish Franciscans is a remnant of the noble residential area, which was built here after the mid-seventeenth century. The main entrances of the impressive noble houses faced the street forming the first section of the Royal Road, whereas their gardens stretched towards the boundaries of the quarter around St Peter's Church in the New Town. Swéerts-Sporck House, whose monumental façade was designed by Anton Haffenecker after 1783, is somehow a nostalgic epilogue to the construction of grand Baroque houses in Prague and also evidence of the relentlessly changing taste of demanding builders.

The line where the Old Town meets the New was lined with the residences of noblemen in the area of the original city walls. The former residence of the Piccolomini (Silva-Tarouca) family on the street Na Příkopě was built from 1743 to 1752 on the unique 'palatial' plans of Kilian Ignaz Dientzenhofer, but was completed by Anselmo Lurago. In the New Town, Dientzenhofer was predominantly designing religious architecture. The most important of these works is the dynamically conceived Church of St John Nepomucene on the Rock, built

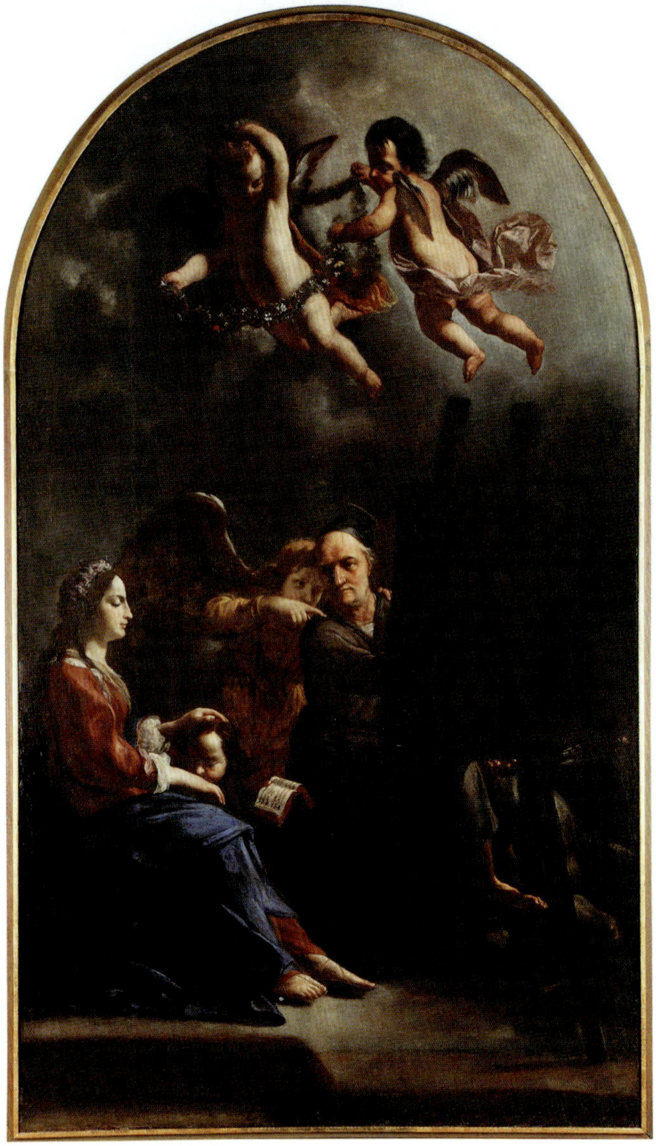

KAREL ŠKRÉTA: **St Luke Painting the Virgin**

Painters, sculptors, goldsmiths, embroiderers, illuminators, glaziers, and other artisans proudly sought to join the Prague Confraternity of St Luke, which was founded in 1348. Emperor Rudolph II augmented its coat of arms in 1595 and ordained that henceforth no one could 'consider them craftsmen or call them craftsmen, but, instead, would call them practitioners of the art of painting [...]'. Prague artists held their ceremonies and other meetings at the altar of their patron saint, Luke, in the Thein Church. For ten years, beginning in 1651, the altar underwent restoration and this canvas by Karel Škréta was placed on it in 1661. The tranquil scene, with Luke the Evangelist hard at work on a picture of the Blessed Virgin Mary, introduces the viewer to the setting of the master painter and his guild in the seventeenth century.

from 1730 to 1738. It was once the lively centre of the cult of the great saint of the Bohemian Baroque. The emblem of John's relic, his incorrupt tongue, ideologically dominates the dramatically dynamic façade with two obliquely placed towers. The plan of St Catherine's Church (1737–41) in the New Town was determined by an earlier, medieval church that stood here. Dientzenhofer conceived St Catherine's as a deep, aisleless (single-nave) church, whose striking vertical pilasters provide it with rhythm. Here, the role of creating space has also been assigned to the ceiling frescos by Wenzel Lorenz Reiner, the great master of this technique in High Baroque Prague, who was also a friend and frequent collaborator of the architect. Kilian Ignaz Dientzenhofer is also credited with designing the graceful, stylistically harmonious suburban house of Michna z Vacínova, which has the sobriquet Amerika (1717). Today largely concealed by the modern buildings around it, the house remains one of the last survivals of the world of formal gardens and summer houses which were spread

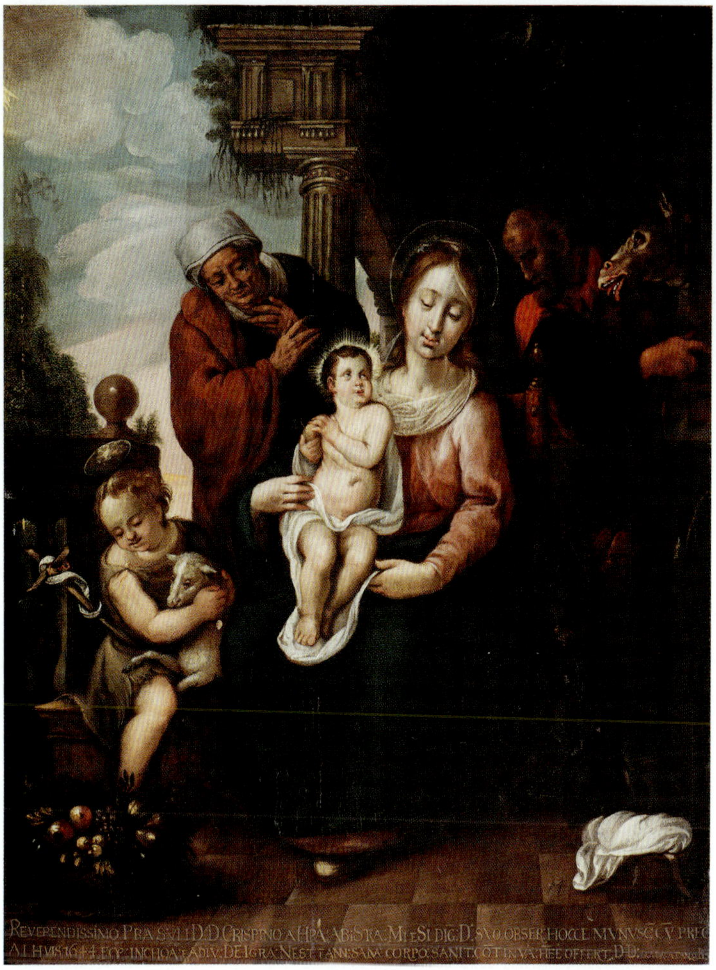

DAVID NORBERT ALTMAN:
The Holy Family with St Elizabeth and St John the Baptist

Every painter in the seventeenth and eighteenth centuries who sought membership of the Confraternity of St Luke had to demonstrate his skill by presenting a masterpiece, specifically, a 'painting of the Virgin Mary in a red gown and wrapped in a blue mantle, such that she is seated, holding her Child in her arms or on her lap, by some building and behind them a landscape or land with hills, woods, mountains, and a distant building, which is called a *landšoft*, and all of that [...] must be properly painted and made'. Though the guild records mention dozens of these masterpieces, only one has been preserved to this day. On 10 January 1644, it was presented to the elders of the Old Town guild by the painter David Norbert Altman, who was immediately accepted as a master. That same year the proud artist added to his work a long dedication to the abbot of Strahov, Crispin Fuck. Altman's painting is stylistically an interesting example of the transition from the sophistication and aesthetic polish of Rudolphine Mannerism to the emotional involvement and realistic detail typical of the advent of the Baroque.

throughout the upper New Town during the Baroque period. The whole area was described by Mauritius Vogt as a calming, undulating landscape whose houses seemed to vanish in the midst of gardens and vineyards. The rugged terrain, with a great number of areas not yet built up within the town walls, also caught the attention of Edward Browne, causing him to compare the capital of Bohemia to Lyon, France.

* * *

In his encyclopaedic survey, Vogt drily summarizes it thus: 'The city of Prague is therefore a school for the administration of commerce, the arts, languages; it is the dormitory town of the upper nobility and an assemblage of convents and monasteries, which number about forty, not to mention presbyteries.' This statement may reasonably be seen as an answer to a question that continues to rack the brains of scholars of the modern age: how can one satisfactorily explain that in the late seventeenth and the early eighteenth century Prague became one of the most important cities of art in central Europe, even though, unlike other capitals, it had not been the continuous seat of a monarch's court? In the High Baroque, the capital of the Kingdom of Bohemia became a focal point, no longer passively accepting artistic impetuses impulses from elsewhere, but

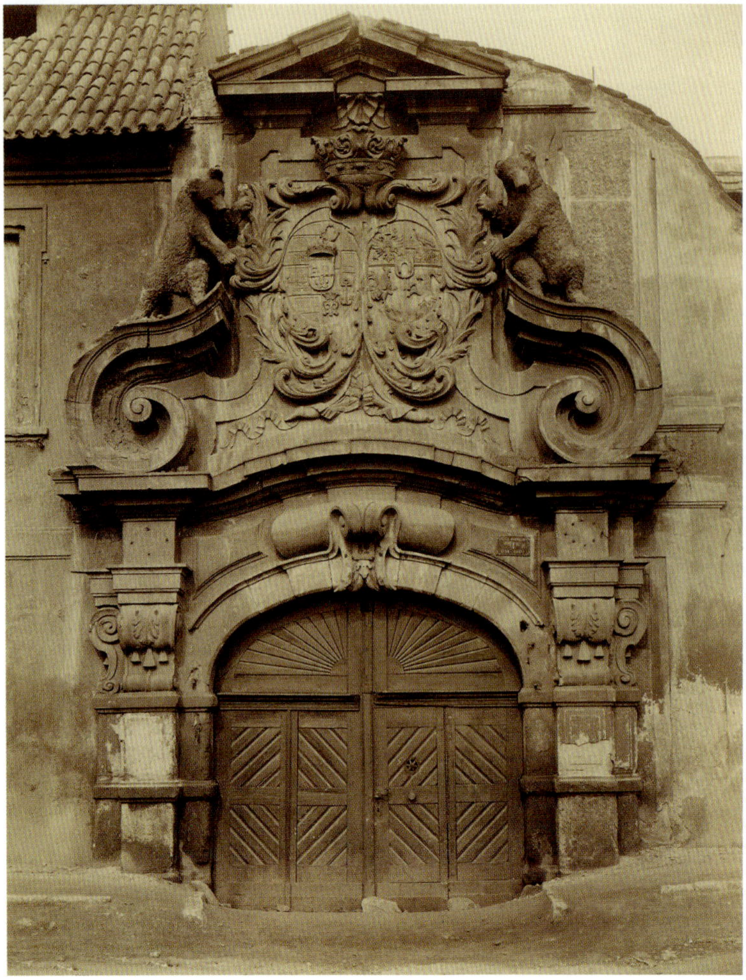

Garden gate of the former Slavata Summer House in Smíchov

This photograph, taken in 1880 by Jindřich (Heinrich) Eckert, a leading Bohemian photographer of the period, shows how the wall of the former garden on the outskirts was gradually disappearing into the ground as the land was rising with the regulation of the banks of the Vltava. This also adds to the impression made by the overlarge pediment above the Early Baroque portal, whose sides curl up into striking voluted wings. The central field bears the coats of arms of Count Johann Georg Joachim Slavata and his wife Maria Margaretha née von Trautson. The winsomely gawky figures of two little bears, supporters of the coats of arms, from the workshop of the sculptor Hieronymus Kohl, give this work the name the Bear Gate. Unlike the summer house, the portal has been preserved to this day; since 1906, it has been part of the collection of stone statuary and architectural ornament in the Lapidarium of the National Museum, Prague.

itself creating incentives for future stylistic development in Bohemia and the neighbouring countries. Though the people of Prague could still only rarely welcome the king of Bohemia in their city, the only archbishopric and only university – not to mention the many supreme provincial offices – in the country were here. Twenty-six Roman Catholic orders had their houses here and the city remained an important commercial and manufacturing centre as well as a transport hub. Only one other 'big city' in the Lands of the Bohemian Crown could rival Prague – and that was Breslau (Wrocław) in Silesia. Yet simply because most of its inhabitants were not Catholic, Breslau could not hope to attain the standing of a Baroque metropolis. The driving forces of the cultural development of Prague were the commissions made by the land-owning nobility, richer in Bohemia than elsewhere in the Empire, and the Roman Catholic clergy, mainly the religious orders. But the self-confident members of the bourgeoisie, professional associations, and lay confraternities also contributed greatly. Bohemia and Silesia were the only lands of the Habsburg Monarchy which could show continuously positive economic results. Even as war with the Turks dragged on in the south-east and war with the Bourbons dragged on in the west, the Lands of the Bohemian Crown were an oasis of peace and

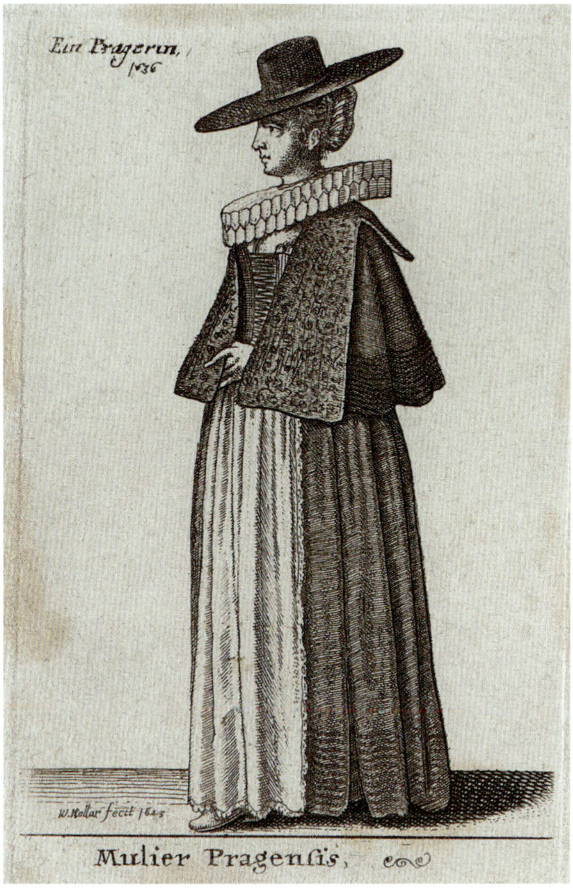

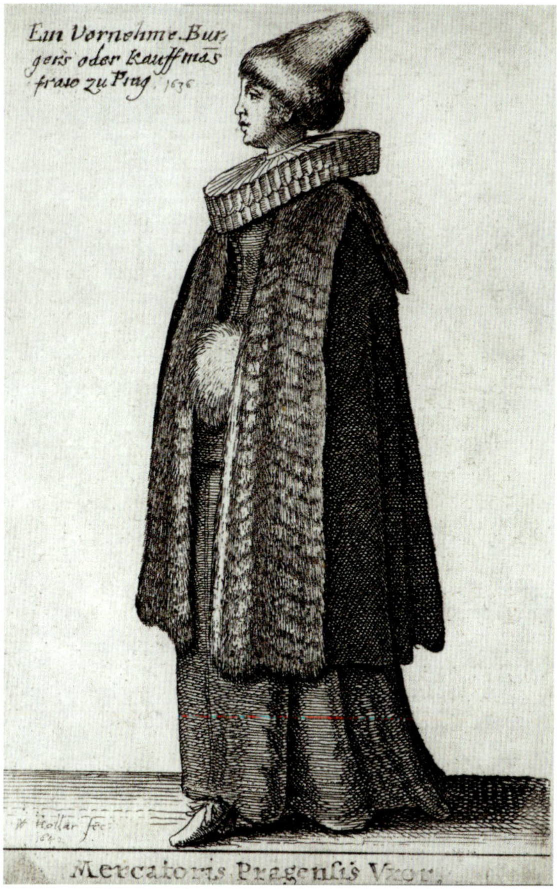

VÁCLAV HOLLAR: **A Woman of Prague**
VÁCLAV HOLLAR: **A Prague Merchant's Wife**

These illustrations of the wives and daughters of Prague burghers were included by the famous engraver in a series of costume studies called *Theatrum Mulierum*, published in London in 1643. Authors of Baroque travel writing mostly referred to Prague women with appreciation. In 1710, for example, Carl Adolph Redel claimed: 'concerning the women, many are very lovely, especially those with white skin and black eyes and hair'. Lady Mary Wortley Montagu, a writer and the wife of the British Ambassador to the Ottoman Empire, was more critical when, in 1716, she snidely noted in a letter that the ladies of Prague imitated Vienna fashion rather eccentrically: 'The person is so much lost between head-dress and petticoat, that they have as much occasion to write upon their backs, "This is a Woman," for the information of travellers, as ever sign-post painter had to write, "This is a Bear".'

quiet, free of enemy soldiers. The absence of a permanent seat of the monarch here made the capital of Bohemia a 'nobleman's paradise', as was stated by contemporary observers: a little world of splendid houses, of lavish festivals and sophisticated musical and theatrical life. Various elites joined forces in an effort to create and increase intangible cultural and social assets. Noble and bourgeois families, like institutions and religious orders, could profit from such assets, even if they were financially unquantifiable. Investment in the arts, particularly in painting and sculpture, constituted an important part of the creation of this virtual wealth – all the more so since they were as a rule closely linked not only by individual or group strategies of representation, but also by efforts to save one's soul and preserve the memory of individuals and families.

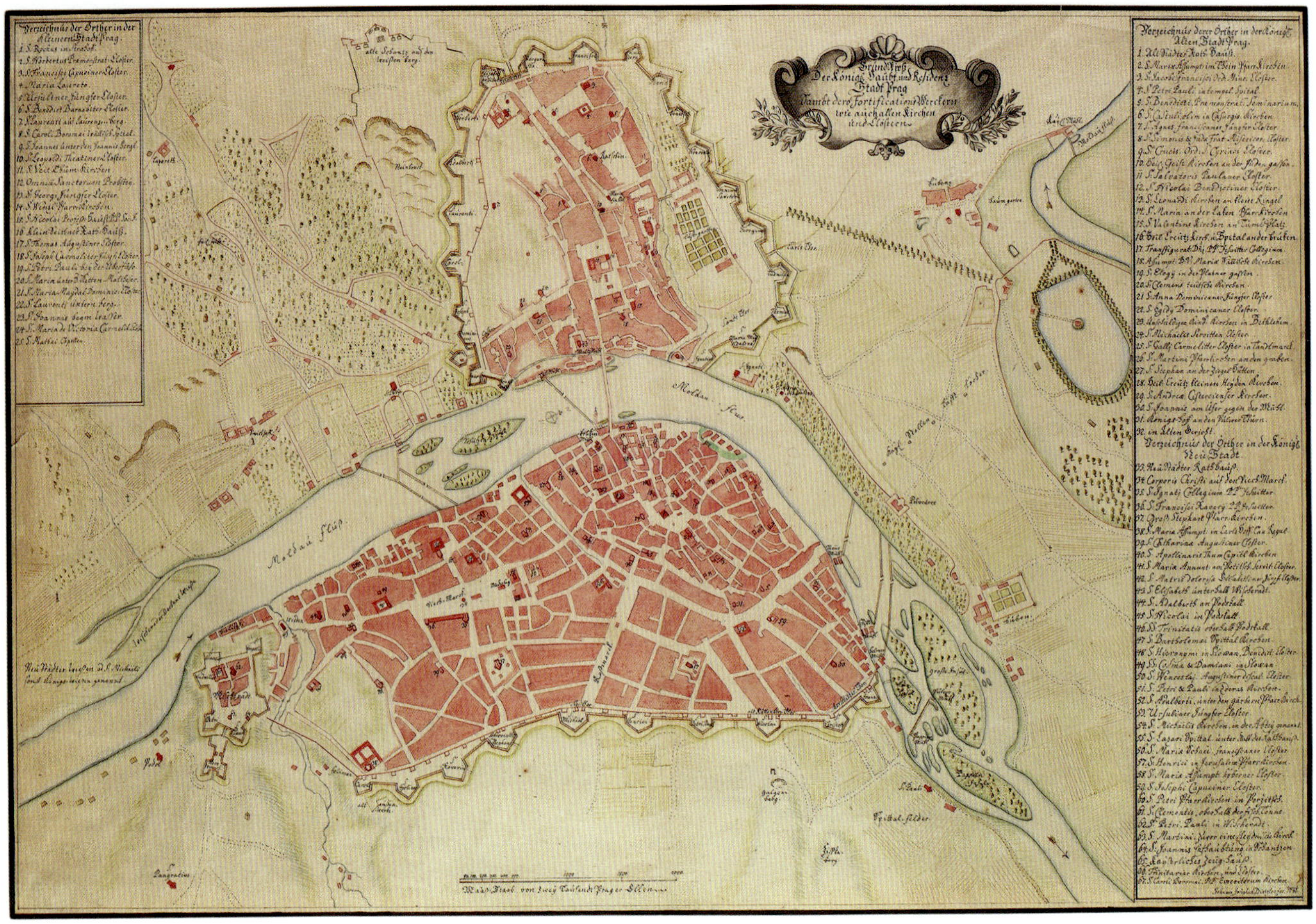

JOHANN JOSEPH DIETZLER: **Map of Prague from 1741**

This meticulously drawn map shows the city with its bastion fortifications completed. The draughtsman has paid great attention to the immediate environs of Prague as well, which were abundant in vineyards and gardens with the summer houses of nobles and rich burghers. The avenue (shown just below the cartouche) that linked Hradčany with the Royal Game Preserve (today's Stromovka) is particularly noteworthy.

The demanding requirements of the clients were willingly met by the artists. Prague in the first half of the eighteenth century was firmly linked to the European-wide network among client-builders and architects, sculptors, painters, and other master craftsman and builders. Traditionally, it was Italians and Dutch, people who often had experience of working in Vienna, the imperial capital, who applied their skills in Prague. But increasingly often artists from all corners of the Monarchy received commissions here, as did local masters. The Dientzenhofers, father and son, members of a widespread dynasty of builders from the foothills of the Alps, and Johann Blasius Santini-Aichel, the grandson of an Italian stonemason who had settled in Prague, became the chief proponents of the radically dynamic trend in Bohemian Baroque architecture, whose roots were in Rome and Turin. Baroque Prague remained open to various languages and cultures, though no longer to the extent that it had been in the reign of Rudolph II.

There was, however, another side to the story. The slow but sure waning of the political importance of Prague in the Habsburg Monarchy left its mark on demographics. In about 1600, during the reign of Rudolph II, Prague had a population of roughly 60,000 and was the most populated city in the Holy Roman Empire of the German Nation; it even surpassed the traditionally large cities of the empire and the Hanseatic League. Two other metropolises of the Habsburg Monarchy, Vienna and Breslau, each had populations of about 30,000 people. The fourth largest city in the western half of the Monarchy was Graz, with a population of about 10,000. In the reign of Rudolph II, the towns

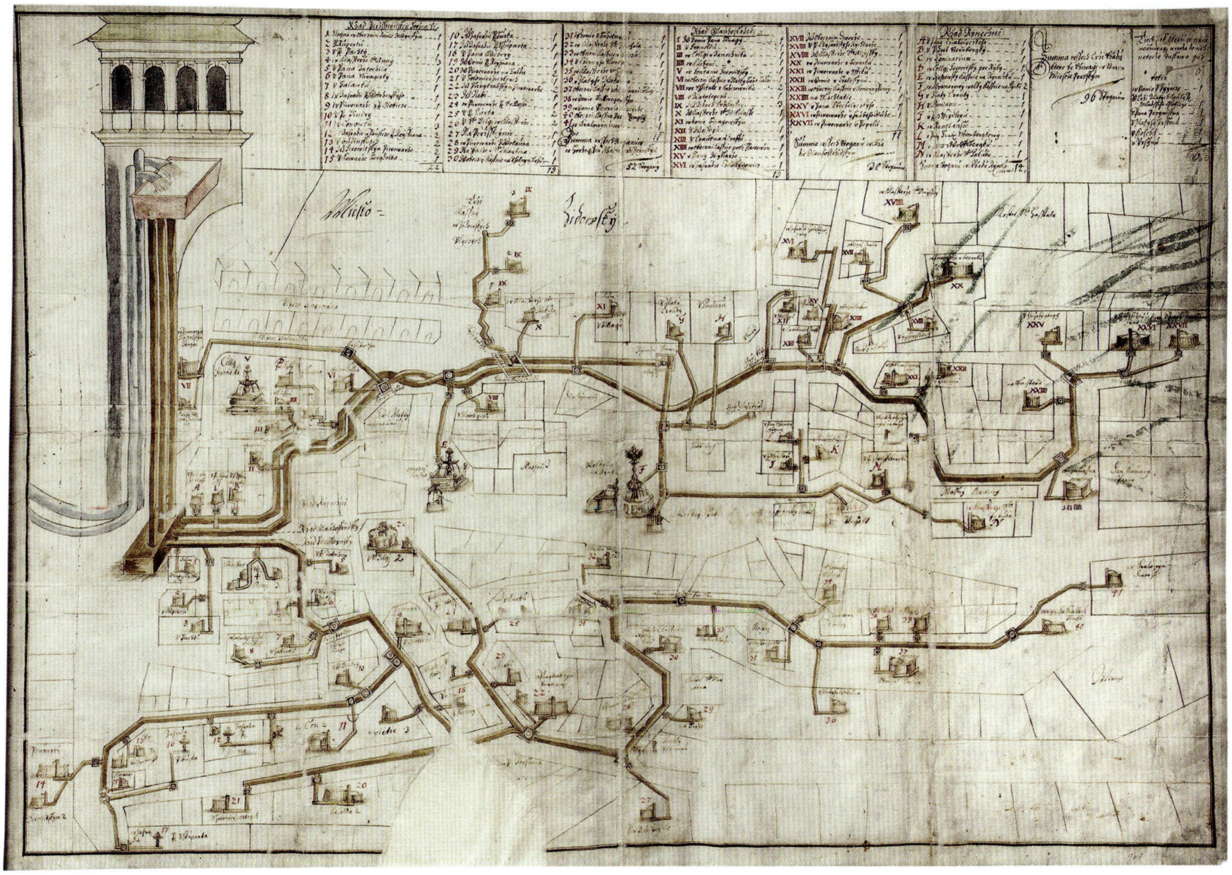

The Earliest Plan of the Water Mains of the Old Town of Prague, from 1684

The Old Town already had its own water tower in the early fifteenth century. The plan shows that water was distributed from here by three water mains, consisting of pipes made of pine logs. The shortest was called the Town Square Main (Rynečný) and also supplied the now no longer extant Krocín Fountain on Old Town Square. Another, called the Long Avenue Main (Dlouhá třída) went all the way to the Powder Tower and a branch of it near the Church of the Holy Spirit supplied the fountains in the Jewish Town. The Perštýn main took water into the south part of the Old Town, flowing into the area called V Kotcích. The detailed list in the upper part of the plan mentions 96 active supply points plus six other disused ones. This number attests to the increasing demand for sources of water in private homes. In particular, breweries, hospitals, butchers' shops, and also convents and monasteries, which raised fish in hatcheries for fasting days, used a considerable amount of water. Though anyone could draw water from public fountains free of charge, private consumers paid quite high prices for it.

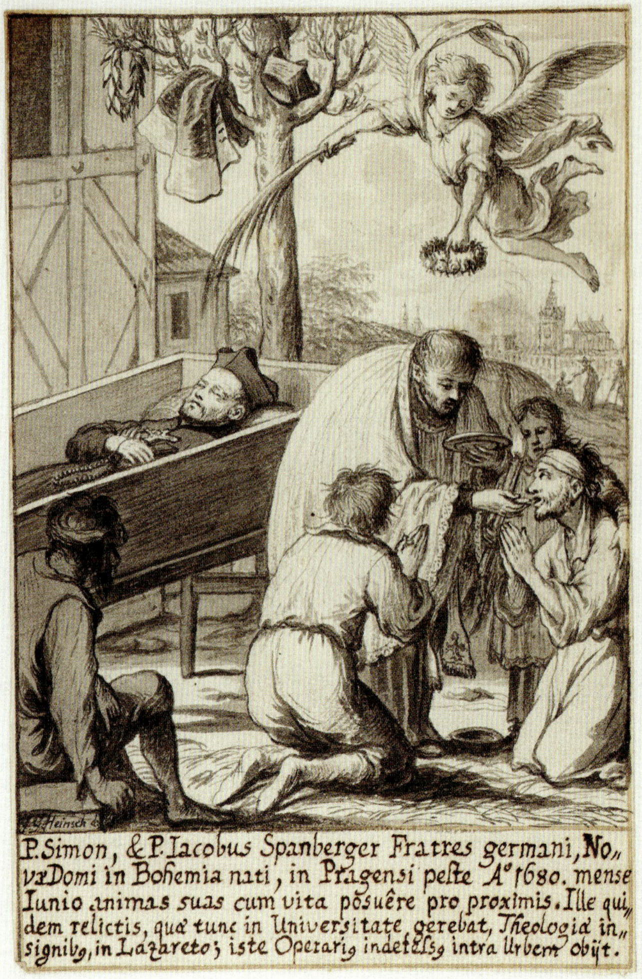

JOHANN GEORG HEINSCH: **The Jesuit Brothers Spanberger during the Plague in Prague, 1680**

During plague epidemics, the Jesuit fathers selflessly cared for the sick, providing them with spiritual comfort, and, consequently, themselves often dying of the disease. The Great Plague of 1679–81 claimed the lives of almost half of the Jesuits of the Clementinum college. Among them were the brothers Simon and Jacob Spanberger, natives of Jindřichův Hradec (Neuhaus), a town in south Bohemia. Together they took care of plague sufferers in the Bethlehem Chapel in Prague. The elder brother, Simon, a professor of moral theology, died in an infirmary on 6 June 1680. Twenty days later, Jacob, too, died of the Black Death at the age of 43. Heinsch's drawing portrays Jacob administering the Host to two sick people near the open coffin in which lies the body of Simon Spanberger. An angel is bringing the two brothers a palm branch and a wreath as signs of their self-sacrificing martyrdom.

of Olomouc (Olmütz) and Jihlava (Iglau) had about 7,000 inhabitants each, Brno (Brünn) and Košice (Kaschau in German and Kassa in Hungarian – in Upper Hungary, today's Slovakia) had about 5,000 each. By comparison, Elizabethan London, the first modern megalopolis, had a population at that time of about 250,000, whereas Naples and Paris each had 200,000 and Istanbul may have had as many as 400,000 inhabitants!

In 1612, the new Habsburg emperor, Matthias, moved his seat from Prague (associated with Rudolph II, his elder brother, whom he detested) to Vienna, which he knew intimately. Ferdinand II acted similarly seven years later, moving the court from Graz to Vienna, the capital of Lower Austria. Nevertheless, for decades afterwards, the Bohemian Estates sought to compel the Habsburg emperor to return to Prague Castle. Discussions of this possibility were held also among the people close to the emperor. Thus, for example, during a short stay in Prague in 1673, Leopold I wrote about the Spanish ambassador, 'Balbases [Pablo Spínola Doria, the 3rd Marquis of Balbases] has fallen completely in love with this town; he says that he cannot understand why we have our seat in Vienna and not here'. For the Habsburgs, Prague continued to be the place of Bohemian coronations, an occasional refuge from plague and also the scene

Torah shield (1708)

This is the earliest preserved Torah shield in the Bohemian Lands. It was made by the Lesser Town goldsmith Johann Georg Kogler the Younger, and was donated to a synagogue by Zalman Munk and his wife Haneli of Vienna. This extraordinary relic is a silent witness to the turbulent history of the Jewish Community of Prague. During the Estates Rebellion, the Jews remained loyal to the Habsburgs, and, moreover, were protected by the influential financier Jacob Bassevi, an adviser to Karl von Liechtenstein and Albrecht von Wallenstein. In 1648, the residents of the ghetto courageously helped to defend Prague against the Swedes. The government rewarded their loyalty with important privileges, which included a ban on expelling Jews from the country. Numerous Jewish immigrants from eastern Europe headed to the Bohemian Lands and particularly to Prague in the second half of the seventeenth century. Though the authorities limited the number of inhabitants of the ghetto and regulated their business activities, they were unable to get by without the financial skills of the Jews and especially without their money, which flowed into the state coffers. That was also a reason why whenever it seemed that Prague was on the verge of a pogrom, usually provoked by fires, epidemics, or events like the killing of Shimon Abeles, the armed forces of the state protected the Jews against the Christian mob.
Not until after Maria Theresa came to the throne, when the inhabitants of the ghetto were accused of acting treasonously during the Prussian occupation in 1744, did the Jews of Prague face harsh measures.

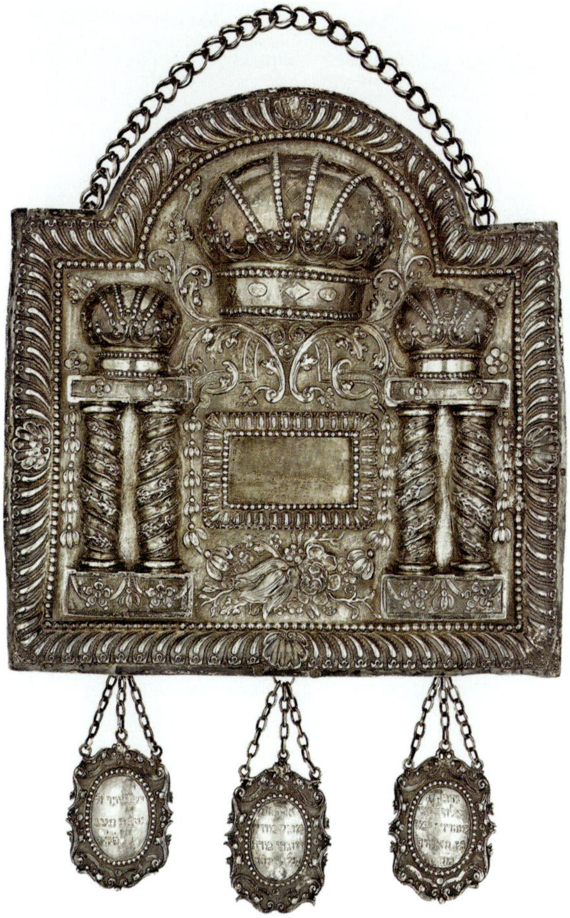

of diplomatic talks with princes of Northern Germany. Later, its advantageous geographic position was appreciated by Charles VI, who met Frederick William I of Prussia for intimate conversations here in 1732.

Imperial Vienna in the meantime became larger and more powerful. In the mid-seventeenth century it surpassed Prague in number of inhabitants, since Prague had been devastated by emigration after the Battle of the White Mountain and the ravages of the Thirty Years War. In 1664, almost half of the houses in the centre of Vienna belonged to noblemen and in subsequent decades whole blocks were systematically built here for members of the court. After 1683, when the main theatres of the Ottoman wars moved farther to the south-east once and for all, Vienna overflowed the perimeter of its medieval town walls and new suburbs began to sprout up along the main transportation routes. In about 1700, the population of the imperial metropolis reached 100,000. In the same period, Prague had about 40,000 inhabitants; it again reached a population comparable with what it had during Rudolph II's reign only after another 150 years of war, plague, and emigration, but also of economic and cultural growth.

Information about the meagre population growth seems to be confirmed by lists of Prague houses. Whereas 3,011 of them were registered in 1653, their number had fallen to 2,926 by about 1757. But these figures attest rather to the growth in wealth and thus also to the growth in the demands of the town's

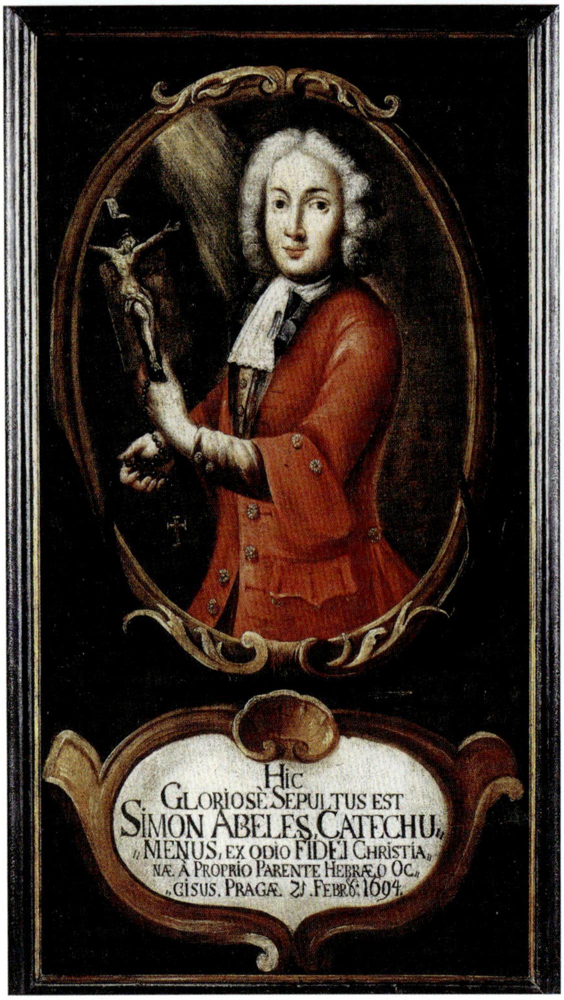

Shimon Abeles

This idealized portrait of the young Christian martyr does not quite correspond to the dark tragic nature of the true story, which has no hero. Encouraging Jewish children to run away from their parents with the prospects of their future conversion to Roman Catholicism was a common missionary practice of the religious orders, particularly the Jesuits. Thus, in 1693, the twelve-year-old Shimon Abeles, the grandson of the head of the Prague Jewish Community, ran away from his parents. At first he was preparing himself for baptism in the Clementinum, but later neglected his religious education, and eventually, probably with the implicit consent of the Society of Jesus, returned home to the Jewish quarter. According to some of the preserved sources, Shimon had been a wilful, disobedient child who often came into conflict with his father, Lazar Abeles, and he was repeatedly given harsh beatings. When, on 21 February 1694, Lazar and his relation Löbl Kurtzhandel again punished Shimon, the drunken Löbl struck the boy so hard that he fell against the edge of a chest and broke his neck. The two men tried to conceal the misfortune but were soon discovered and arrested. The court found them guilty, not 'merely' of having beaten the boy, but of premeditated murder committed *ex odio fidei*, out of hatred of the faith, though no evidence exists to support such an interpretation. Lazar Abeles hanged himself in jail. Kurtzhandel was executed in October 1694 in a particularly painful way, and his torture only ended with his conversion to Christianity.
Shimon Abeles's funeral was held in the Thein Church in the presence of seemingly all Catholic Prague. The Jesuits sought to construct a martyr legend about him. The story became widespread throughout central Europe and contributed to anti-Jewish sentiment among Christians.

population. The Baroque period was distinguished by the building of houses for members of the nobility, often erected on the sites of several earlier city houses. Happy to expand their houses, rich burghers did the same.

* * *

The Baroque splendour of Prague churches and noblemen's houses, multiplied by the stunning impression left by secular and church festivals with all the pomp of the opulent painting, sculpture, and music accompanying them, stood in stark contrast to the less pleasant aspects of life in the early modern city. Prague of the seventeenth and eighteenth centuries remained dirty, neglected, dreary, and dangerous. The paving of its streets left much to be desired and public lighting was only first installed for the coronation of Charles VI in 1723. The burghers of what is today Letenská ulice in the Lesser Town lodged a complaint with the authorities against their fellow citizens for having dumped so much rubbish and manure in the steep street called Ostruhová (today's Nerudova ulice) that only a narrow path remained for pedestrians. Furthermore, it was said that the servants of the noble houses of Sternberg and Thun had dumped muck from their stables in front of the gate and occasionally buried carrion in it. All it had to do was to rain a bit and, in the absence of a sewage system, all this filth suddenly ended up in the lower streets round the River Vltava. In 1714, the Prague public health committee presented Emperor Charles VI with a report on the subject of lavatories. The inhabitants of the left bank of Prague, according to the report, intentionally let their cesspits overflow into open tanks (something like primitive septic tanks), which when it rained then flowed out in reeking torrents into the whole Lesser Town from Hradčany downwards. Carl Adolph Redel, a man of letters, whose descriptions of central European towns were published in 1710, writes that wide open sewers ran between the side walls of Prague houses, carrying away everything possible. It is no surprise that in such circumstances epidemics repeatedly took their cruel toll. Plague used to visit the towns of Prague with relentless regularity. In 1680, it claimed the lives of about 12,000 people and, from 1712 to 1714, perhaps even one or

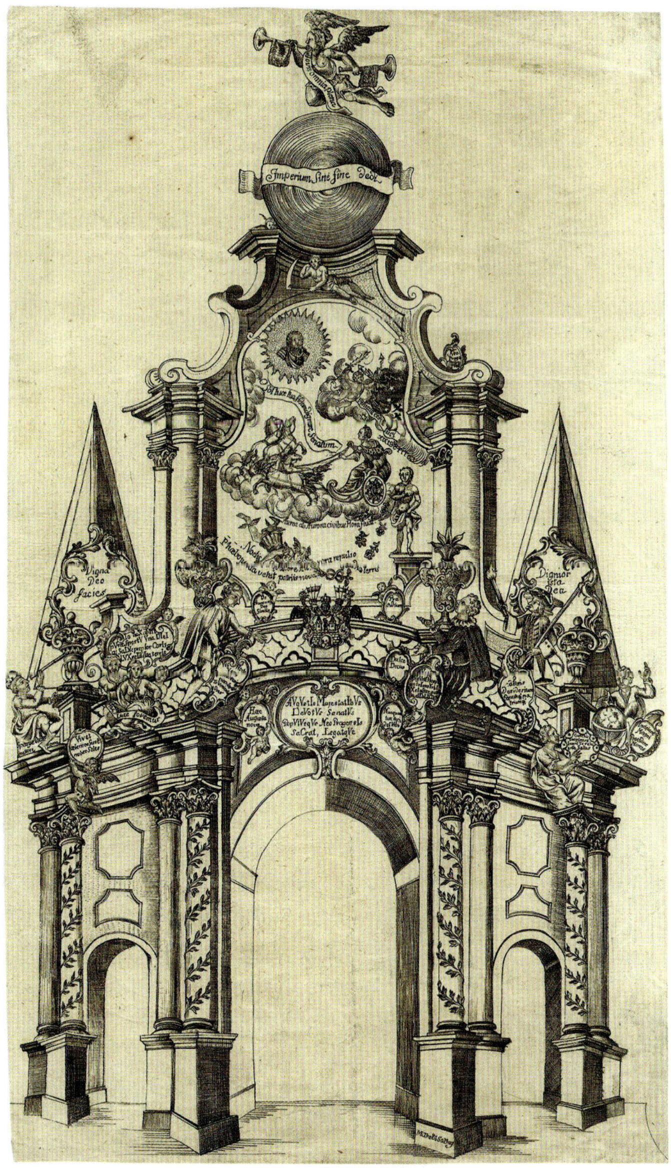

Triumphal Arch Erected by the New Town of Prague for the Entry of Archduke Charles of Austria into Prague in 1703

In September 1703, the younger son of Emperor Leopold I, the future Emperor Charles VI, set out across Northern Germany, the Netherlands, and England to Portugal, in order there to win the Spanish crown from his rival, the Dauphin, Philip of France. In Prague, he was welcomed with all the pomp due to a monarch, except that the military presence had to be performed by the town militia, because the soldiers of the Prague garrison were fighting for the Habsburgs on the Rhine and in Italy. The triumphal arch, erected in honour of Charles by the town hall of the New Town, was decorated with Apollo's quadriga together with a portrait of the young archduke and an allegorical figure of Fama. The inscription wrapped around the globe reads: *Imperium sine fine dedi* (I have given them empire/ power without end). Under the sceptre of Charles VI the rule of the central European Habsburgs would truly achieve its largest territorial scope.

two thousand more. There was, allegedly, not a house in Prague at that time where someone was not taken ill with the plague.

Despite repeated calls for measures to prevent fires, Baroque Prague was continuously threatened with fire. Redel was allegedly surprised to see that even the houses of the rich and noble had wood-shingle roofs. He was told that a wooden roof was light, so it could be easily thrown off if a fire seemed imminent and thus the house could be saved. That may have been true, but during the great fires of Prague the burning shingles, carried off by the heat and the wind, naturally helped to spread the fire. It was usually the Jewish ghetto that was the worst hit. It was there that the greatest number of plague victims were reported and also where the cramped buildings provided the least resistance to the raging flames. It was a sad fact of life in the early modern town that the Jews regularly became the target of accusations of having intentionally spread disease and started fires. After the French Fire in 1689, which hit the Jewish Town particularly hard, the town hall of the Old Town even proposed relocating the ghetto. The new home of the Prague Jews was envisaged in some peripheral area of the New Town or possibly on the island of Štvanice on the Vltava or the area around what was then the village of Libeň (now a Prague district). The plan was ultimately abandoned and the ghetto was restored in its original place. For lack of time and money, wood was again the main building material, which did not exactly increase the buildings' resistance to fire. During his sojourn in Prague in 1733, the Swedish theologian, philosopher, scientist, and mystic Emanuel Swedenborg drily remarked: 'I also walked through the Jewish square and their town. Everything there is filthy.'

* * *

Baroque festivals in this town of contrasts, however, were grand affairs, productions that were unusually opulent and diverse. Hemingway's description of Paris in the 1920s as a 'moveable feast' can be fittingly applied to Prague of the seventeenth century and especially of the first half of the eighteenth. The rhythm of life in the town was directly determined by the cycle of a wide variety of festivities, particularly Church holidays, such as the feast days of the Blessed Virgin Mary and of the patron saints. Students, guilds, religious orders, and numerous lay confraternities had their particular holidays too. Apart from that, the birthdays and weddings of the ruling house were celebrated, as were the imperial victories on the battlefield and the arrivals of new archbishops.

In processions of thousands of people, banners fluttered and statues of saints and the Mother of God were held high. The façades of houses and churches, glowing with translucent allegorical pictures and ingeniously composed inscriptions, remained illuminated long into the night. Neither before nor afterwards had Prague experienced so many celebrations, produced so lavishly and with almost profligate splendour. At that time, one looked at the world around oneself as an enthralling theatre in which illusion was raised to the level of reality, often even above it. The production of the festivities indulged that

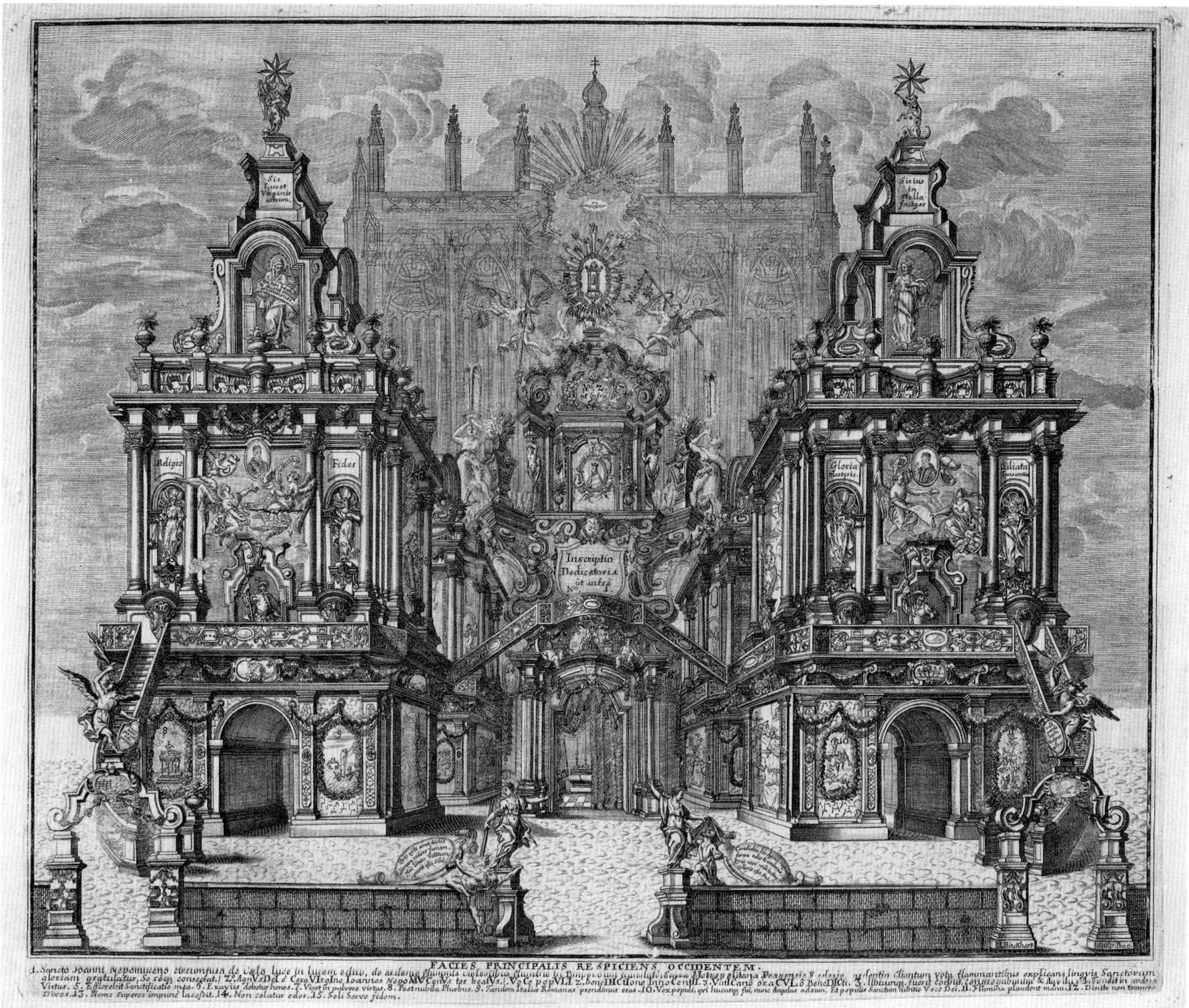

ANTON BIRCKHARDT AFTER JOHANN EZECHIEL WODNIANSKY:
The decoration of the area in front of the west façade of St Vitus' Cathedral for the celebrations of the canonization of St John Nepomucene in October 1729

In its production and pomp, the eight-day celebration in honour of the canonization of the most venerated saint in Baroque Bohemia surpassed everything that people had been accustomed to. In front of the makeshift façade of the cathedral an intricate triumphal arch was erected on the land of the chapter cemetery. Four columns of an unbuilt Baroque house were changed into towers decorated with scenes related to the life, miracles, and posthumous glorification of St John Nepomucene. The imposing amphitheatre had three gates. Similarly, the chapel above the tomb of St Adalbert was brimming over with Nepomucene symbols and the façade of the cathedral was covered with a system of cascades decorated with figures of dolphins and river gods, together with a whole range of allegories.

outlook. All of Prague, on terraces along both banks of the river, changed into one glorious stage. The Baroque festival was not only expensive to produce, but it also followed precise rules and was closely managed. In these festivals, all forms of artistic expression, from architecture to painting and sculpture to music and the verbal arts practised by preachers, intermingled. A festival thus

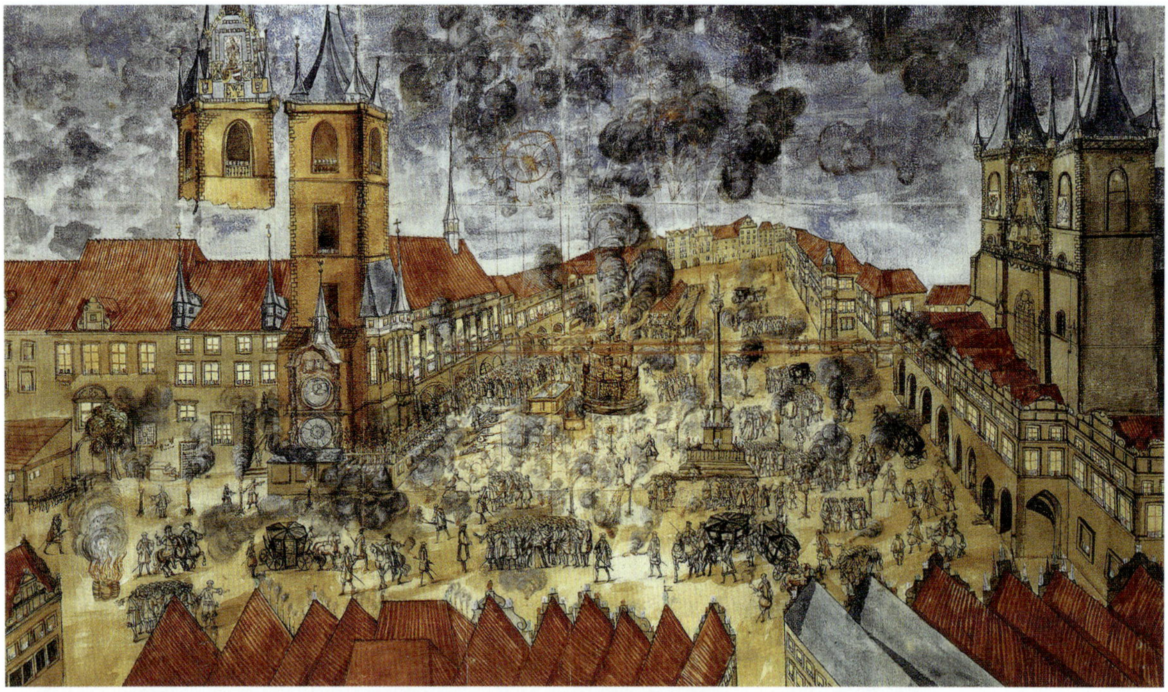

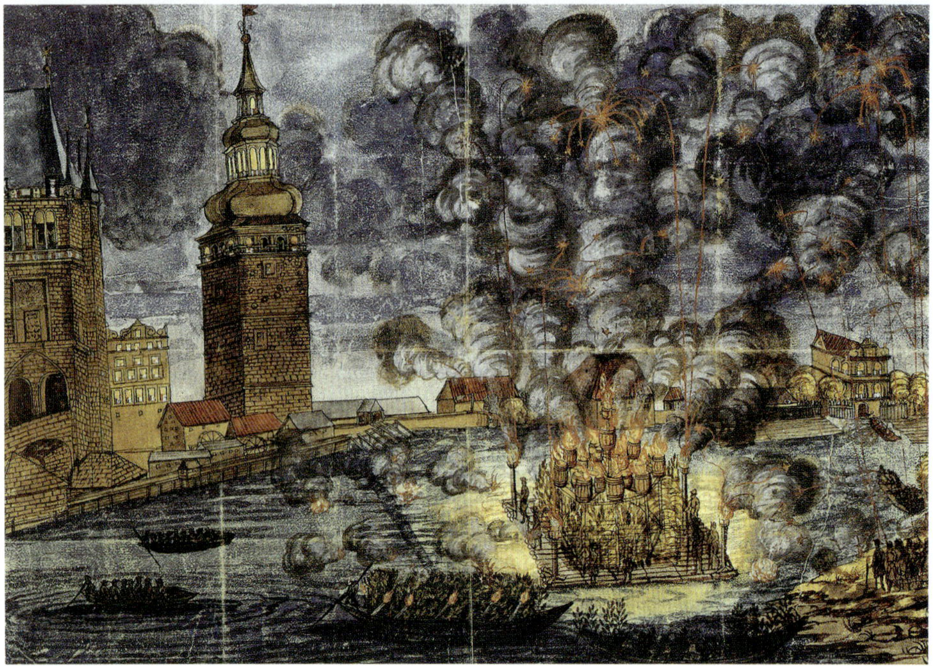

The Decoration of Old Town Square and a Fireworks Display during Celebrations on 9 October 1667 to Mark the Birth of the Son of Emperor Leopold I
A Regatta on the Vltava at Old Town Bridge Tower during the Celebrations on 9 October 1667 to Mark the Birth of the Son of Emperor Leopold I

In late September 1667, a long-awaited heir – the Archduke Ferdinand Wenceslaus – was born to Leopold I and his wife Margaret Theresa of Spain. The towns of Prague celebrated the joyous event on 9 October of that year. The centre of the festivities was Old Town Square, above which, after dusk, fireworks burst and flared, accompanied by visual and sound effects. On the towers fluttered illuminated banners with heraldic emblems, allegorical scenes, and monograms of members of the ruling house. On the River Vltava at Charles Bridge, a flotilla of illuminated boats with musicians and fireworks sailed forth. The lower of these two documentary drawings has also captured the dimensions of the raft carrying an ingenious pyramid of lights, from which hundreds of rockets are being launched into the evening sky. The celebrations were joined in by the religious houses of Prague and also by many burghers, who decorated the façades of their homes fittingly. The wishes for a long and happy life for the Habsburg prince, expressed in flowery inscriptions and festive sermons, were unfortunately unfulfilled: Ferdinand Wenceslaus died three months later.

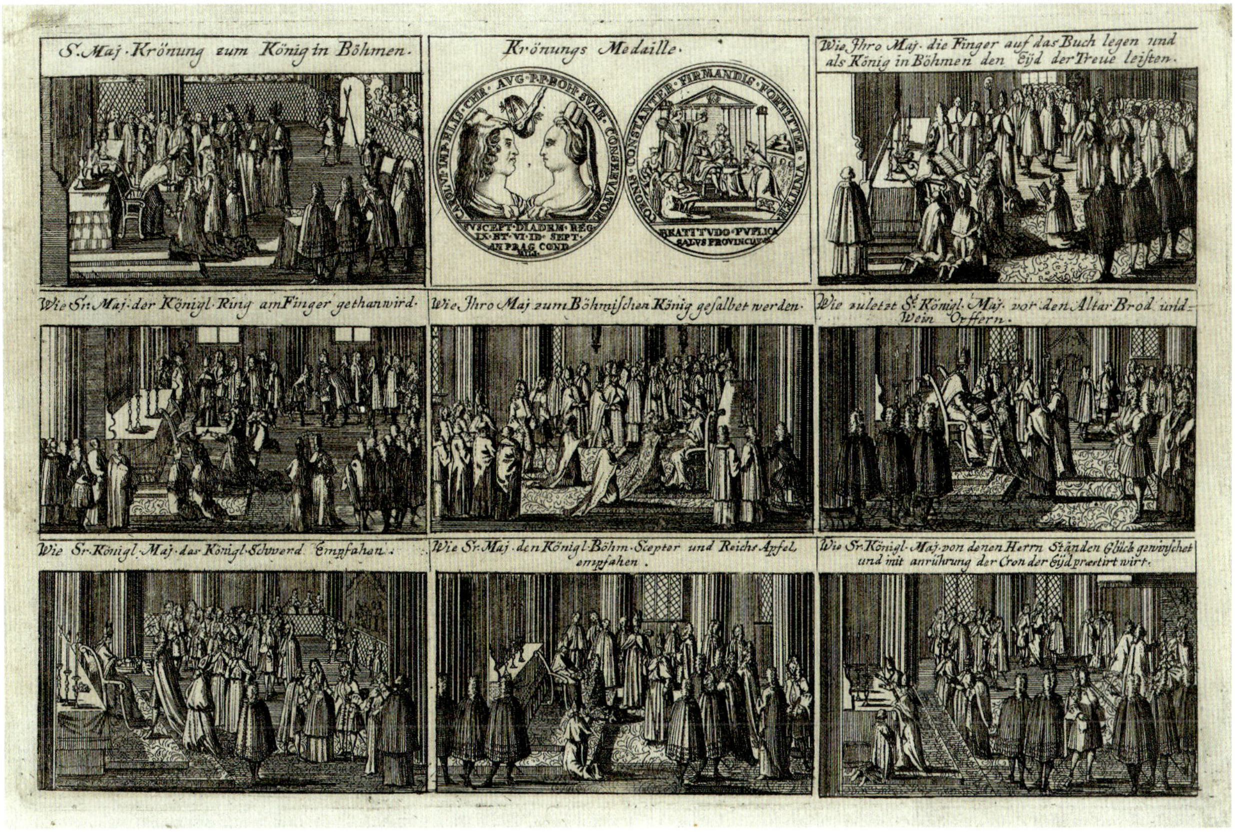

The Coronation of Charles VI as King of Bohemia

Though this anonymous engraving appears to be a contemporary record of the coronation of Charles VI in 1723, the artist of the work which this has been made after was definitely not an eyewitness to the event in St Vitus' Cathedral and instead turned to abundant earlier models. In eight of the nine frames, it presents important moments in the coronation ceremony. They are, from left to right: in the upper band, the coronation of the king of Bohemia (followed by the obverse and reverse of the coronation medal) and the monarch taking the oath; in the middle band, the ring being placed on his finger, the anointing of the monarch, and the king offering bread and wine at the altar; the lower band shows the presentation of the sword, then the imperial sceptre and orb, and, finally, the Bohemian Estates paying tribute.

represented a true *Gesamtskunstwerk* (total work of art), but, unlike Gothic cathedrals, it existed only for an historic moment. The glory of the Baroque was built from transient materials. Everything was made of wood, wax, cloth, stucco, and papier-mâché, intended to leave a fleeting impression in the course of just a few splendid days. What remains of it now is only fragments of painted or sculptured decoration, synopses of plays for the stage, texts of sermons, sheet music, descriptions, and illustrations – and stacks of bills in the archives.

Prague experienced its first truly Baroque festival in 1627 during the translation of the remains of St Norbert from the Protestant city of Magdeburg to the abbey church of the Premonstratensian canonry at Strahov. The most stunning festival of this type, however, was held a century later – the celebration of the canonization of John Nepomucene in October 1729. In front of the makeshift west façade of St Vitus' Cathedral a piece of intricate ephemeral architecture was built: four massive buttresses, the remains of an attempt to complete a Baroque

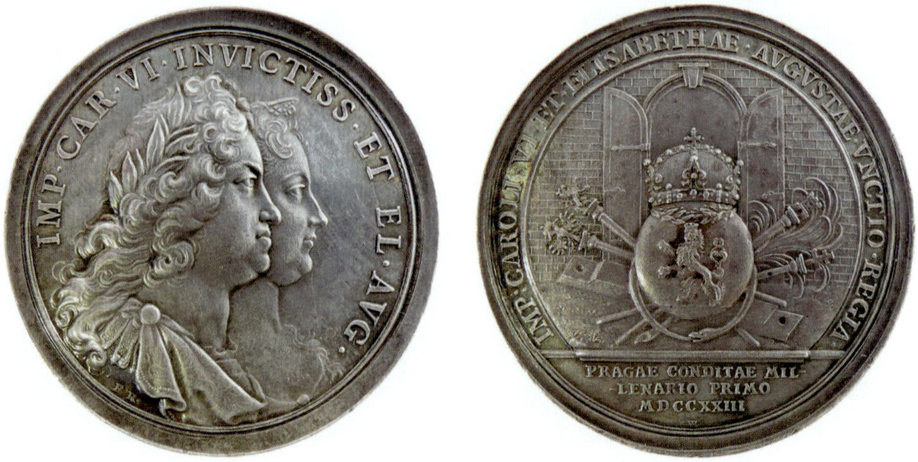

Medal commemorating the coronation of Charles VI as King of Bohemia and the thousandth anniversary of the founding of Prague, 1723

The obverse of this silver commemorative medal, designed by the court emblematist Carl Gustav Heraeus, bears a double portrait of the 'invincible' emperor and empress. The subject matter of the reverse is the millennial anniversary of the founding of Prague by the prophetess princess Libuše. (The fictitious date of 723 comes from the chronicle of Václav Hájek z Libočan, published in 1541.) The basis of the composition is a wall with an open gate, recalling the gate of the Roman god Janus and symbolizing the promise of good fortune. Depicted in front of the gate is the Royal Orb of Bohemia crowned with the royal diadem and a laurel wreath. Wound round the globe is a snake swallowing its own tail, the uroboros, a symbol of time as a closed circle and also of the beginning of a new age. Behind the orb, a palm branch lies across the legendary threshold (*práh*, in Czech), which, according to Libuše's prophecy, gives the city its name (*Praha*) and reminds us that people will respectfully bow their heads as they enter it. The four sceptres represent the lands ruled by Charles VI.

building, were changed into a tower abundantly decorated with scenes relating to the saint's life and cult. The interior of the church was also a magnificent sight to behold. From the triforium gallery, a flood of artificial flowers and palm branches cascaded down to the chancel. Above the high altar hung a huge dark red baldachin embroidered in silver, in the middle of which was raised a standard painted on both sides with motifs of the martyrdom and glorification of the new saint. From both sides of the standard there extended a band of fourteen monumental paintings with scenes of St John Nepomucene. For those eight days of celebration (the octave) the towns of Prague were festively decorated to give a dignified welcome to pilgrims from all over the country and abroad. Their first steps often led not to the cathedral but to the statue of John Nepomucene on Charles Bridge, splendidly decorated and illuminated for the occasion. Every year in May, a special chapel was built around this bronze statue, exquisitely decorated with countless wax candles. In Prague, on St John's Day, 16 May, no statue of this saint would have been without flowers and at least one light.

On the eve of St John Nepomucene's feast day a large fleet of decorated and illuminated flatboats, crewed mainly by musicians, sailed out from Holy

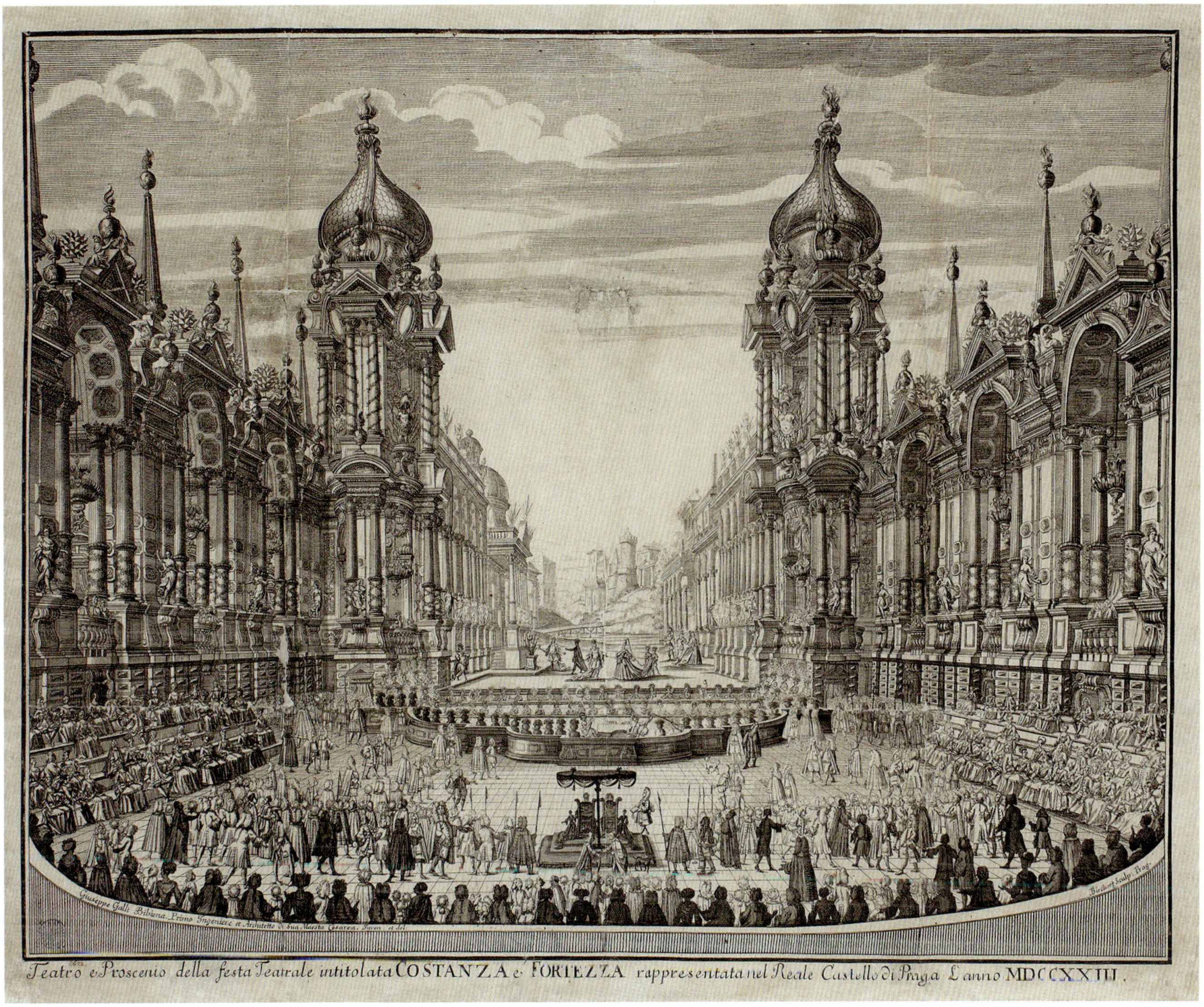

ANTON BIRCKHARDT AFTER GIUSEPPE GALLI DA BIBIENA: **Summer Theatre at Prague Castle: The Opera *Costanza e Fortezza*, Produced to Mark the Coronation of Charles VI in 1723**

The festivities accompanying the coronation of the imperial couple in Prague in 1723 included a magnificent production of Johann Joseph Fux's opera *Costanza e Fortezza* (Constancy and Fortitude), whose libretto is by Pietro Pariati. The architect of the theatre and also the scenographer of the production was Giuseppe Galli da Bibiena, who, in addition, designed seven large prints documenting the event. These prints were made in advance of the performance and were presented to important visitors together with copies of the printed libretto. This print shows the interior of the theatre as it would have been seen by a member of the audience in the middle box at the back, that is, the point in the theatre farthest from the stage, on which the first act of the opera, set on the banks of the Tiber near Rome, is being performed. The stalls are dominated by the raised dais on which, from the thrones below the baldachin, the imperial couple is watching the performance, surrounded by the little archduchesses and their bodyguards. The other members of the audience are sitting on the tiers of benches and in the boxes on the sides. To the left and the right of the proscenium rises a striking two-storey tower in which there are musicians playing brass instruments and timpani. The other musicians have taken their places in three rows in the orchestra pit and on the steps at the base of each tower. The opera was performed by about a hundred instrumentalists and an important role was played by the choir and dancers as well. The theatre, according to some reports, could hold an audience of about 4,000. The performance lasted from half past eight in the evening till one o'clock in the morning. After the first night, Jacob Heinrich von Flemming, a Saxon field marshal and man of the world, remarked that although the arias had been lovely, the voices 'passable', and the dance numbers mediocre, the performance had maintained a suitable standard, and, apparently, enough space had been found for everyone in the amphitheatre.

Cross Church (sv. Kříže) in the Old Town. With the rejoicings of the many spectators and to the ringing of bells, a swarm of lights on the darkened surface approached the arches of Charles Bridge and the tones of oboes and strings sounded from the boats. In his novel *Temno* (The dark age, 1915), Alois Jirásek successfully evokes the atmosphere of these water pageants: 'Ahead resounded trumpets and drums. A gentle breeze carried their voices to the banks and above the priests' boat billowed a canopy from whose golden fringes and precious embroidery flashed gleams as it did from the brass crosses of the gently fluttering banners. The boats sailed quietly on. They solemnly passed tall, old poplars and willows and blossoming apple trees in the gardens on the left bank. In the background, above the Lesser Town, Hradčany soared in majestic, hushed beauty. The pealing of bells was carried above the River Vltava, in part now darkened by shadows, in part still shining in the streaming, misty, wet gleam and glint of the waves.'

Beginning in 1715, when the water music for St John Nepomucene Day was first performed, numerous composers, including František Xaver Brixi, Jirí Ignác Linek, and Jan Antonín Koželuh, wrote motets and litanies for the occasion.

The counterpart of the religious festivities were celebrations linked with the dynasty and political events. With great pomp, the births of members of the ruling house were celebrated, and with no less pomp their deaths were mourned. In churches, *castra doloris* (castles of grief) were erected, decorated with emblems and inscriptions extolling in ingenious allegories the lives and deeds of the late aristocrat. Fireworks, military parades, the *Te Deum* under the vaulted ceilings of a church, the tolling of bells, and the firing of salvos created the background to grand celebrations of the victory of imperial arms over the perfidious French and, mainly, the Turk, the cursed 'hereditary enemy of the Christian name'. The road the Habsburg Monarchy took to become one of the great European powers was lined with a chain of Baroque festivals.

It was the royal coronations, however, which were celebrated with the greatest pomp and ceremony. Though historic circumstances limited their political importance, the act of the consecration of the monarch by God Himself remained the symbolic expression of the sovereignty of the Lands of the Bohemian Crown. The turbulent political events of the seventeenth century meant that the first 'Baroque' Bohemian coronations, which were held during the Thirty Years War, were somewhat rushed affairs. The essence of the hallowed ritual continued to consist in its being timeless, invariable, and repeatable. The scenario for the coronation, which was at the same time a Solemn Mass, continued in the Baroque period to refer to the order of service used in the coronation of Charles IV in the fourteenth century. In fact, however, over the years changes had been made to almost every aspect of this politico-religious theatre, including the props and scenery.

The most spectacular and also most expensive coronation was that of Charles VI in September 1723. It became part of contemporary Habsburg policy that was shaped by fears of a coming dynastic crisis. In Prague, two mentali-

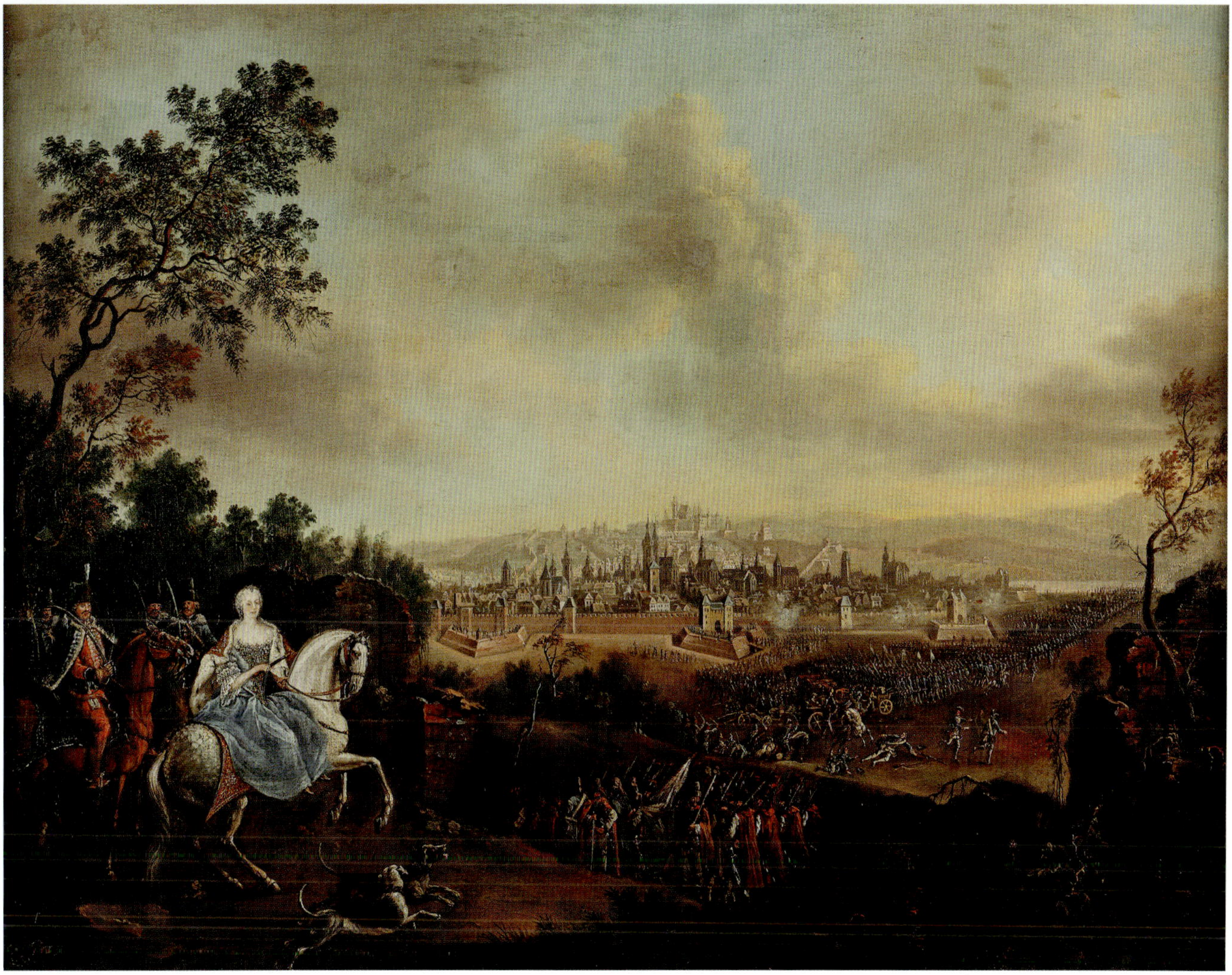

JOHANN TOBIAS SONNTAG: **Maria Theresa at the Head of the Hungarian Troops as the Saviour of Prague**

Emphasizing the participation of Hungarian troops in the victorious campaign, this painting, made after a period engraving, is a symbolic tribute to the heir to the Habsburg throne for her liberation of Prague. Obviously Maria Theresa did not lead her troops from the saddle and did not physically take part in the battles for the Bohemian Lands. By portraying her at the head of the army, the painter has consciously made a mistake, yet he has accurately conveyed the decisive role of the young monarch in these historic events.

ties met and briefly united. The state-dynastic idea of Charles VI, based on the Roman imperial tradition and unwavering faith in the historic mission of the House of Habsburg on the one hand and the historical-mythical past of Bohemia on the other. Memories of the prophetess-princess Libuše – who, according to the chronicle of Václav Hájek z Libočan (published in 1541), had founded Prague in 723, exactly a thousand years before Charles's coronation – acquired contemporary meaning in connection with the expectation that a woman was about to come to the throne: Charles VI had not sired a male heir who would live long enough to succeed him and so his eldest daughter, Maria Theresa, born in 1717, seemed destined to inherit the Empire.

Charles VI's coronation, in 1723, and the eight days of celebrating St John Nepomucene in October six years later were both the culmination and the close of the era of great Baroque festivities in Prague. It was not simply that the monumentality and pathos of the dynamic Baroque festivities were at that time beginning to yield to the Rococo sensibility and intimate scale of things. The external effect of the opulent stage scenery drowned out its spiritual message, the means that Baroque festivities used attained such perfection that they ended up being merely empty form. The pressure to limit the festivities came from elsewhere. Mercantilists were arguing that an overabundance of church holidays was ruining the economic life of the country, while the town councils were complaining about unproductive expenditures connected with the preparations of these spectacles. The end was not long in coming. In the Enlightenment model of the world there was no more room for the impractical luxury of Baroque festivals, spending money on the fleeting beauty of triumphal arches, and thousands of the emperor's subjects uselessly spending their precious working hours on processions instead of toiling in fields and factories. The new age created its own festivities and though they still contained some Baroque features, their content was completely new.

* * *

After the sudden death of Emperor Charles VI at the age of 55, in autumn 1740, the Austrian succession became even more uncertain. Three neighbouring states of the Habsburg Monarchy came forth with territorial claims against Charles's daughter and heir, Maria Theresa. Prussia intended to acquire the economically and strategically important Silesia and County of Glatz. The whole of Bohemia together with Upper Austria, the Tyrol, and smaller Habsburg domains on the western edge of the Empire were claimed by Charles Albert, the Prince-Elector of Bavaria, who was also determined to become King of Bohemia. Moravia, which would be given the status of a kingdom, was then to fall to Saxony, together with part of Lower Austria and Upper Silesia. In the event of their victory, Maria Theresa's enemies intended to leave her with only the Hungarian lands. With surprising speed, Silesia, a rich and populous province of the Bohemian Crown, fell into the hands of the Prussians. In many places, its German-speaking population, mostly Protestant, welcomed Frederick the Great's soldiers as liberators. The heir to the Habsburg throne remained more or less alone against the coalition of predators; of the major European states only Great Britain was at first willing to provide limited diplomatic and financial assistance. With the death of the last male Habsburg, a real danger thus arose for the lands of the Bohemian Crown that they would be torn apart, leading to nothing less than the destruction of the historic Bohemian state and the division of its population, including people ethnically Czech, under the sovereignty of several 'successor' states.

In the autumn of 1741, these enemies invaded Bohemia from three sides. This was the first real test of the modern bastion fortifications of Prague, which had been built from the withdrawal of the Swedes in 1648 to the 1720s at a total

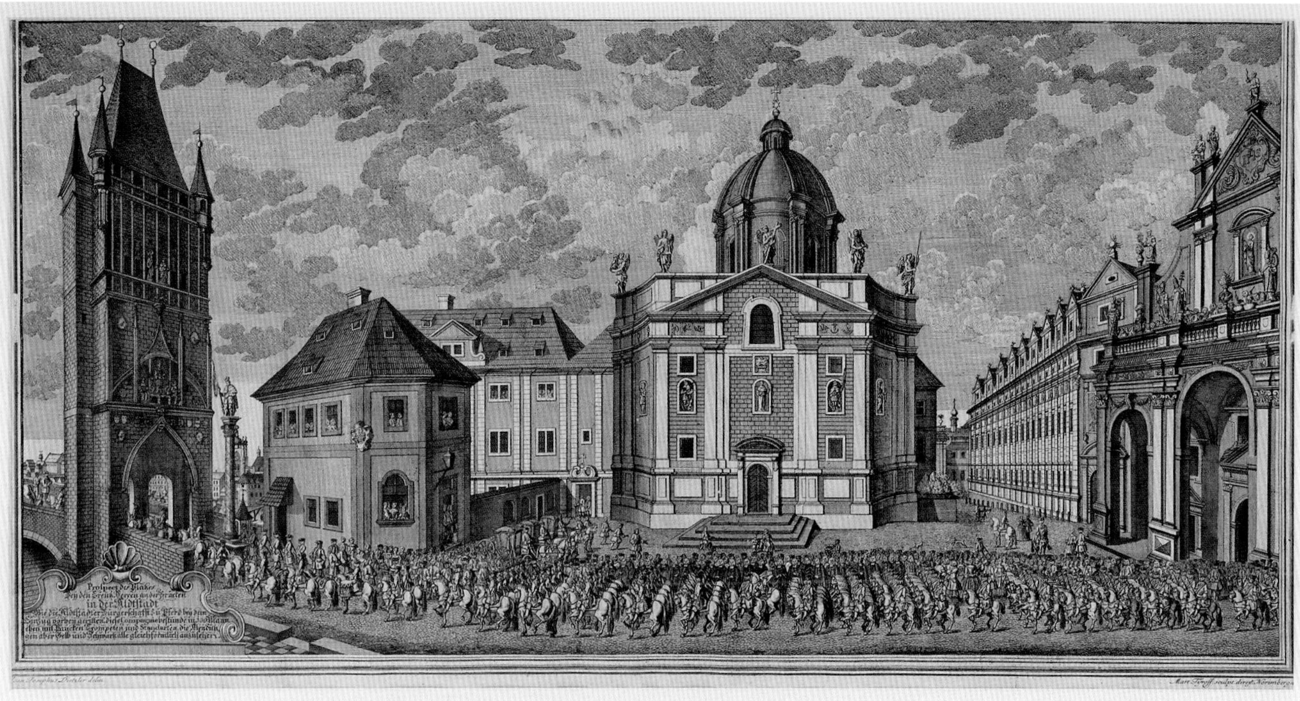

MARTIN TYROFF AFTER JOHANN JOSEPH DIETZLER: **Maria Theresa's Triumphant Entry into Prague on 29 April 1743 (A Procession on Křižovnické náměstí)**

The preserved illustrations of the coronations of the monarchs of Bohemia in the early modern period are for the most part just outlines, often entirely fictional. In memory of Maria Theresa's coronation in Prague, however, the Bohemian Estates commissioned a series of detailed documentarily accurate prints after drawings by Johann Joseph Dietzler. The individual scenes not only portray the course of the ceremonies, but also faithfully capture the appearance of Prague in the Late Baroque.

cost of more than two million guilders. This investment now turned out to have been insufficient. In a rapid pre-dawn attack on 26 November, French soldiers captured the city. Charles Albert, Prince-Elector of Bavaria, who a month later was elected Emperor Charles VII by the electoral college (without a Bohemian vote), entered the country not as its conqueror and occupier, but as its legitimate new monarch. In this spirit he delivered his manifestos to the population and the Estates; initially at least, this intention was respected by the French army as well, which was pretending to be an army of liberators.

After Silesia, Bohemia also seemed to be lost and Maria Theresia's situation seemed to contemporary observers to be just as hopeless as the possibility of preserving the integrity of the Habsburg lands. The political representatives of the Bohemian Kingdom, who at first unanimously supported the new Habsburg monarch, were in fact mainly pursuing the interests of their own estate. The conduct of the Bohemians once Prague had fallen into French hands stood in ever sharper contrast to the attitude of the Hungarian Estates society. In June 1741, Maria Theresa accepted the Crown of St Stephen in Pressburg (today's

Bratislava) and the Hungarian Estates immediately afterwards provided effective military assistance to their queen. The French army would thus, in the course of 1742, become acquainted with the dreaded hussars, whose incursions disrupted army provisioning in Bohemia. The forces of Maria Theresa succeeded in occupying a considerable part of Bavaria, including Munich. The French and the Bavarians were abandoned by their Saxon allies. Frederick the Great also took advantage of his victory in the Battle of Chotusitz (near to Čáslav, eastern Bohemia)), on 17 May 1742, to sign a separate peace with the new Habsburg monarch. The French continued to fight alone but they no longer had Fortune on their side.

Whereas during their Bohemian campaign, the French army under Marshal Belle-Isle pursued broader political interests, the Prince-Elector of Bavaria took seriously his mission as the new king of Bohemia and was determined to rule responsibly. The Bohemia Estates hesitated. Though the political representatives of the country did not question Maria Theresa's claim to the Crown of St Wenceslas, in these circumstances her representatives in late 1741 and early 1742 paid tribute mostly to Charles Albert as King of Bohemia. Not forgetting their opportunism, Maria Theresa nevertheless conducted herself as a great political figure. By the summer of 1742, her army had liberated a considerable part of Bohemia from the occupying forces. The French garrison decided to withdraw from besieged Prague and, on 12 May 1743, Maria Theresa's hastily prepared coronation as Queen of Bohemia was held. Though the ceremony took place following exactly the same arrangements as that of Charles VI twenty years before, this time it was not primarily a matter of confirming the sovereignty of the Kingdom of Bohemia and the inviolability of its rights. By this ceremonial act, the young monarch declared her right of succession to the Bohemian throne and her firm intention to retain this Habsburg hereditary land as a single entity.

Though in private she ironically compared the Bohemian crown to a fool's cap, Maria Theresa was not belittling the meaning of the historical kingdom for whose maintenance she was making such an effort. With this metaphor, she was, instead, bitterly remarking on the willingness of the highest representatives of the country to proclaim king anyone who came along. That was why during the coronation in Prague the guilty Bohemian Estates, who had been at fault, had to tolerate the presence of representatives of the political elite of Moravia and Silesia and also of Hungarian magnates, to whom the monarch ostentatiously demonstrated her favour. Joy at the newly crowned queen was mixed with fear of punishment for betrayal, particularly among those noblemen and prelates who had paid tribute to the not quite 'King of Bavaria', Charles Albert, and were now outdoing each other in expressing their loyalty to the heir to the Habsburg throne. Unlike with the defeated rebels who had led the Bohemians against the 'Arch-House' of Austria in the sixteenth and seventeenth centuries, this time no one was executed. Maria Theresa's magnanimity towards the disloyal estates paid off politically. When, in 1744, Frederick the Great again invaded Bohemia, nominally as champion of Charles Albert's claim to the Bohemian throne, he met not only with cool rejection but also with open resistance.

Though the wars in central Europe were still far from over, a substantial part of the Austrian inheritance ultimately remained preserved under the rule of the 'new' House of Habsburg-Lorraine. The steps towards modernization and enlightened reforms, which were partly the result of the wars over the lands of the Bohemian Crown, changed the social climate to the detriment of Baroque culture, which was essentially coming to an end. But the Baroque – admired, cursed, and full of contradictions – indelibly left its mark on the essence of the Bohemian Lands, primarily in the appearance of the capital city.

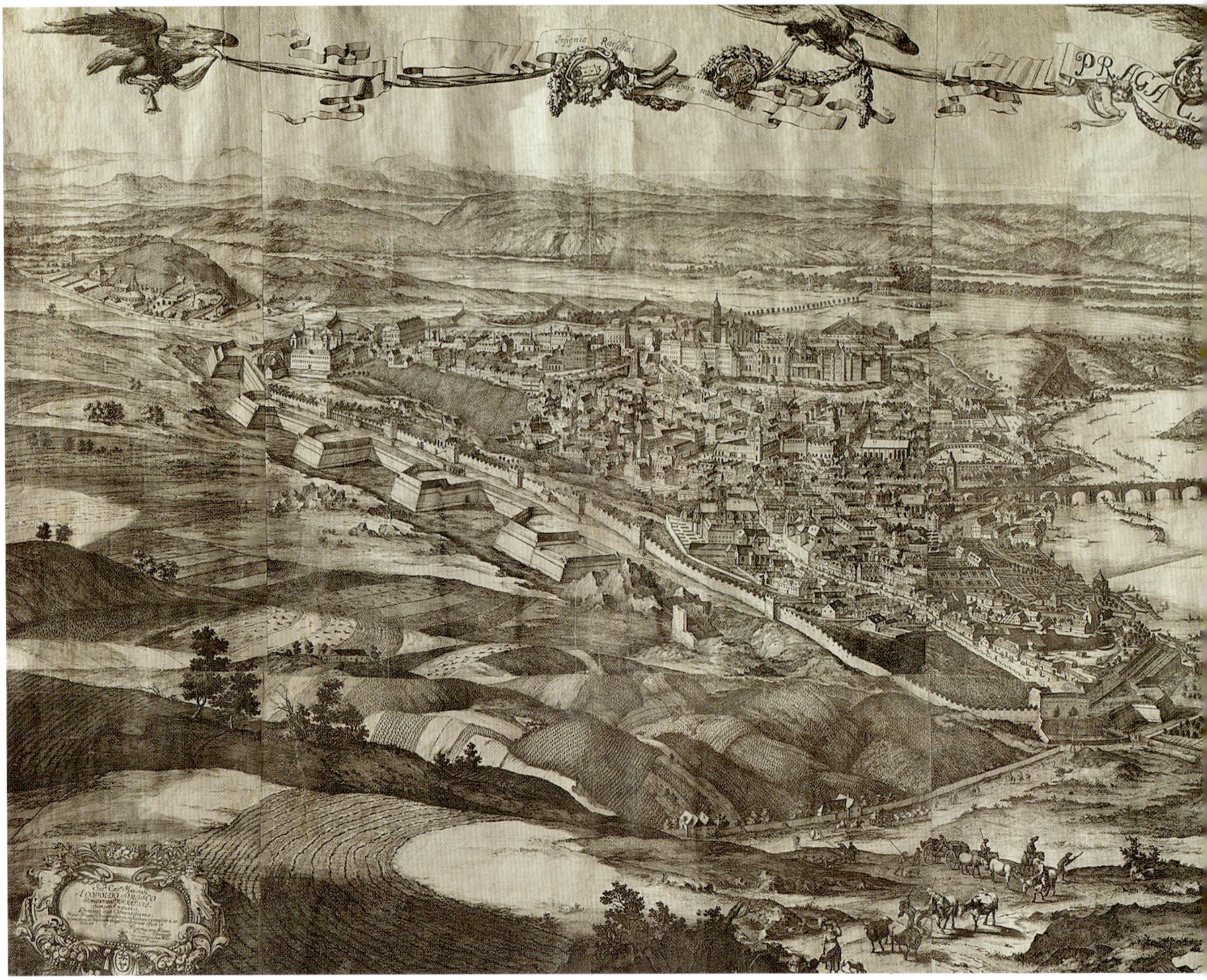

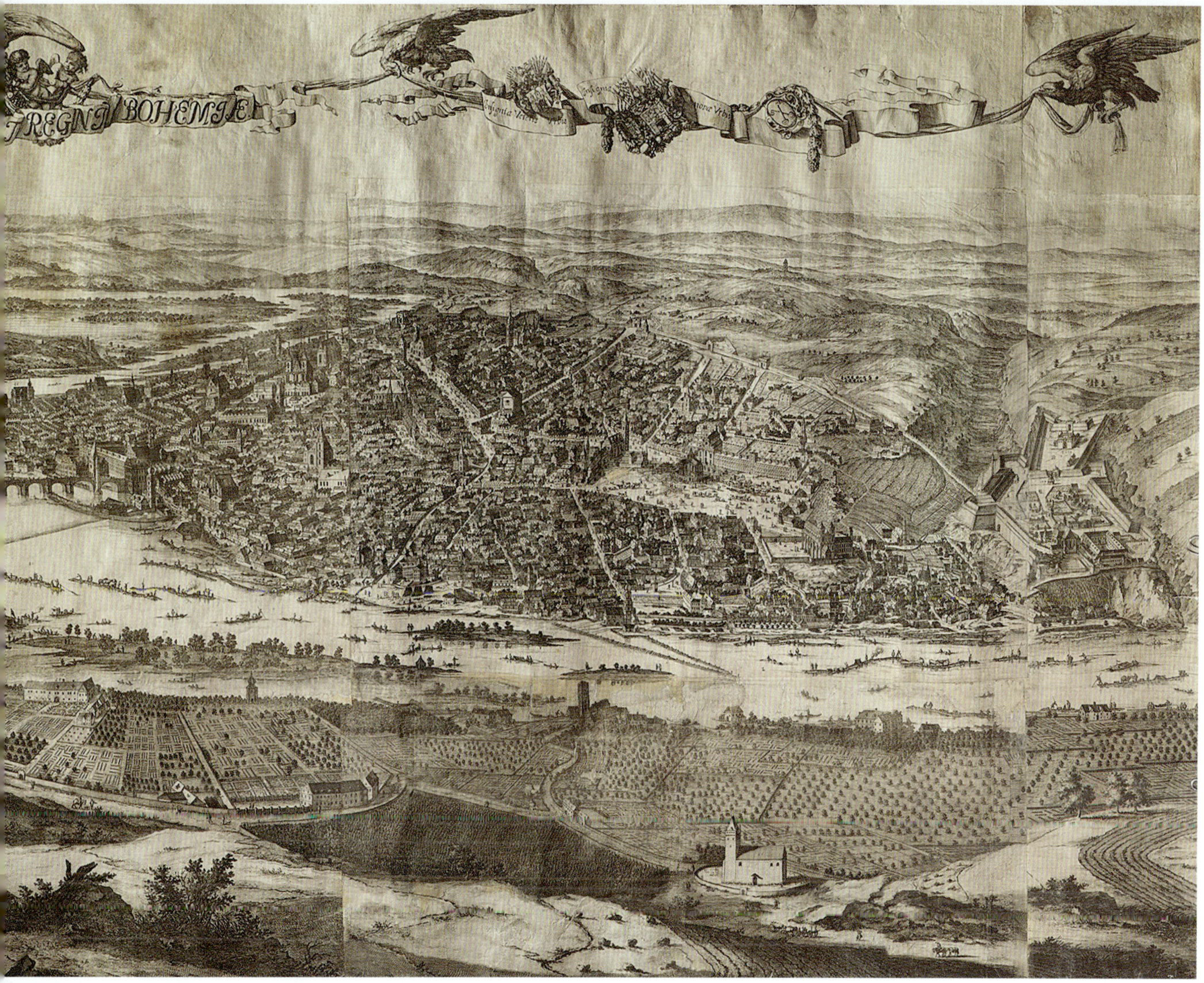

COENRAET DECKER AFTER FOLPERT VAN OUDEN ALLEN: **View of Prague from 1685**

This panorama, comprising fifteen prints from copper plates, was made for Emperor Leopold I by Coenraet Decker, an Amsterdam engraver, after drawings by Folpert van Ouden Allen, a Utrecht-born artist. A grand *veduta*, with a dedication to the monarch, it was published by Johann van Ghelen in Vienna. The work shows Prague from an imaginary viewpoint above what is today the Prague district of Smíchov. Ranging from Strahov monastery on the left to the site of Vyšehrad castle on the cliff on the right, it is an impressive work thanks both to the monumental scope of the cityscape and to its meticulously drawn details. Despite all its imprecisions and intentional distortion of perspective, this is an irreplaceable source of information about the architecture of Prague in the Early Baroque. The overall skyline remains the legacy of the Gothic and Renaissance periods, but is enriched with new landmarks like the palatial Czernin and Wallenstein houses and the churches in Karmelitská ulice and the Jesuit professed house on Malostranské náměstí (Lesser Town Square). On the right bank of the Vltava, we can clearly make out the two massive Jesuit colleges with their churches. The New Town Jesuit College at the Church of St Ignatius is depicted as completely built, though at the time the panorama was made it was far from finished.

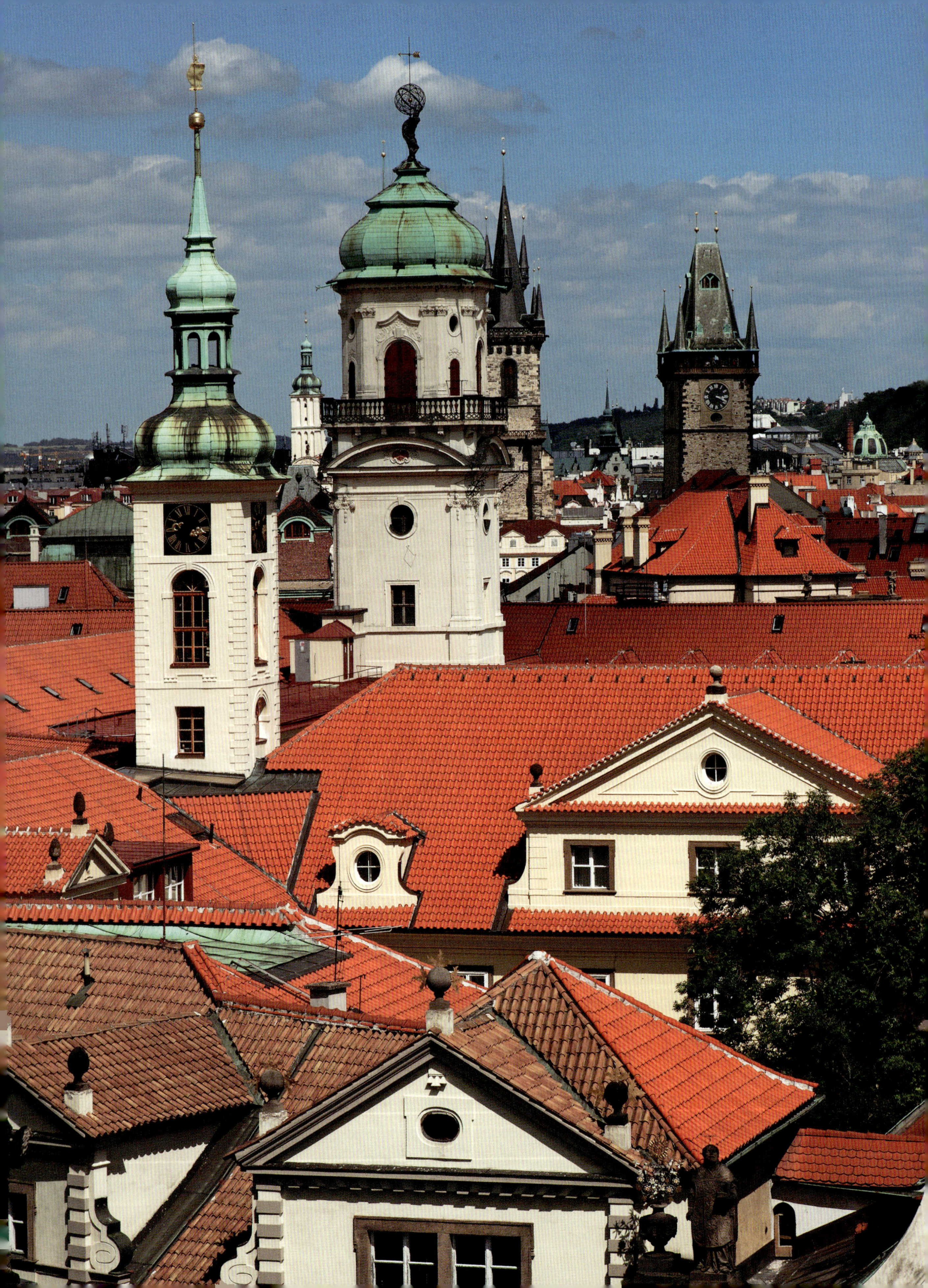

A GUIDE TO BAROQUE PRAGUE

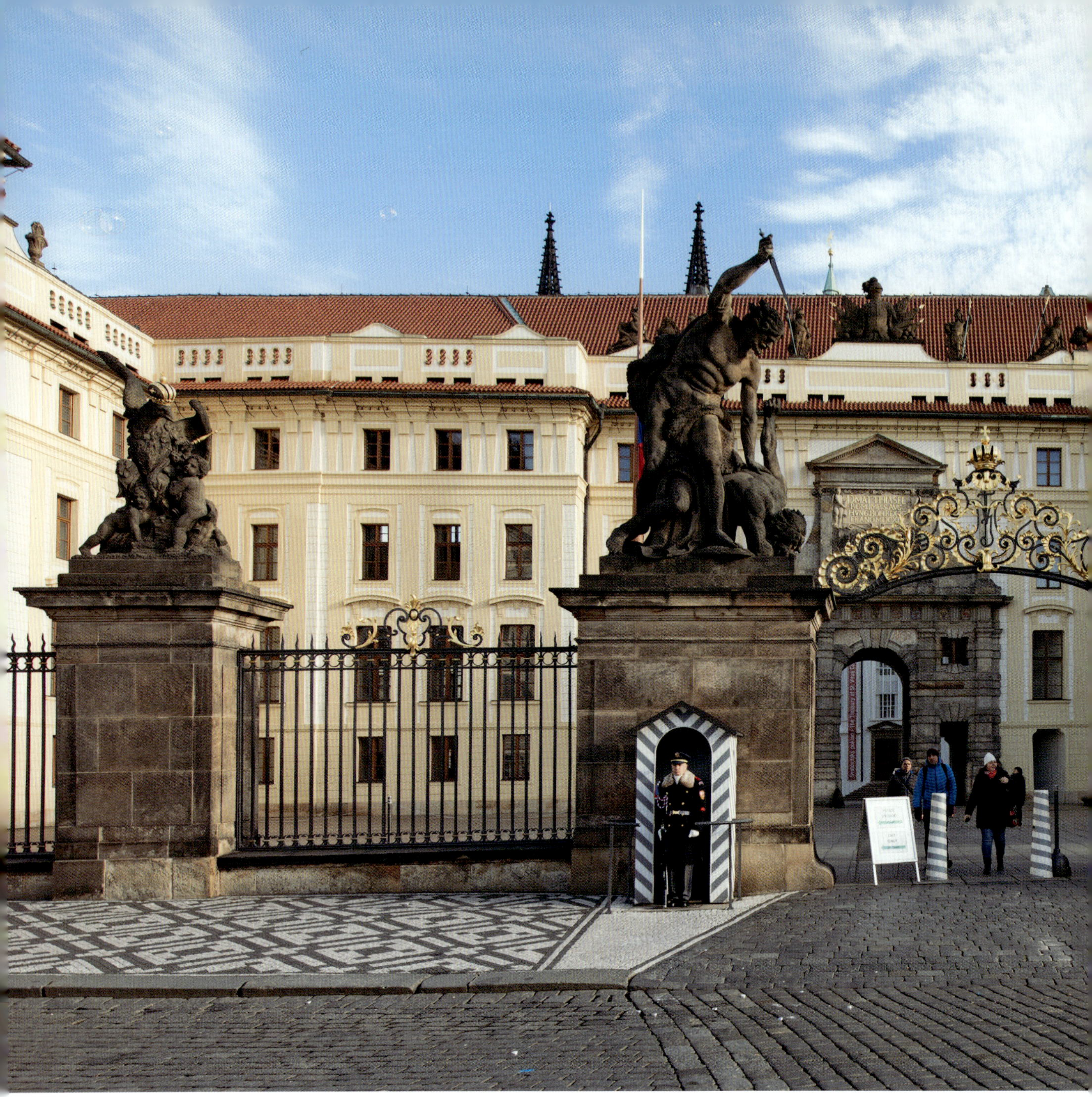

1/ ENTRANCE FAÇADE OF PRAGUE CASTLE WITH THE COUR D'HONNEUR
In 1755, Empress Maria Theresa expressed the wish to have the historic royal palace at Prague Castle 'changed, furnished for comfortable living, and extended'. The rebuilding, on plans by Nicolò Pacassi, was not finished till 1775. Among the new features is the *cour d'honneur* (First Courtyard) instead of the former Castle moat.

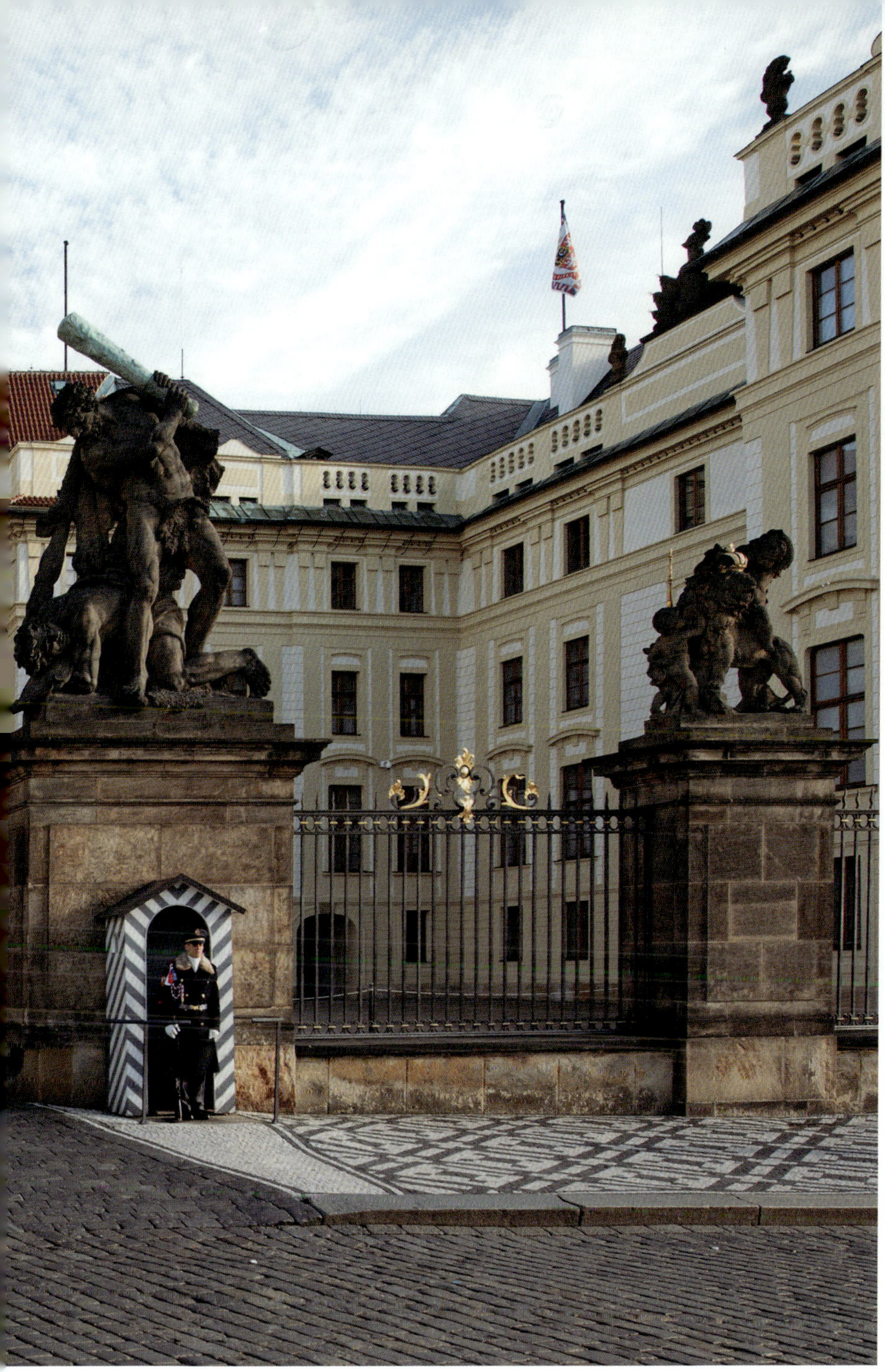

The Theresian entrance wing incorporates the earlier Matthias Gate, which, according to the inscription on it, dates from 1614, and is often considered the earliest example of non-church Baroque architecture in Prague. The masonry columns of the fence around the *cour d'honneur* were originally surmounted by sculptural groups made from 1767 to 1770 by Ignaz Franz Platzer. In 1902, they were replaced with freely executed copies by Čeněk Vosmík and Antonín Procházka.

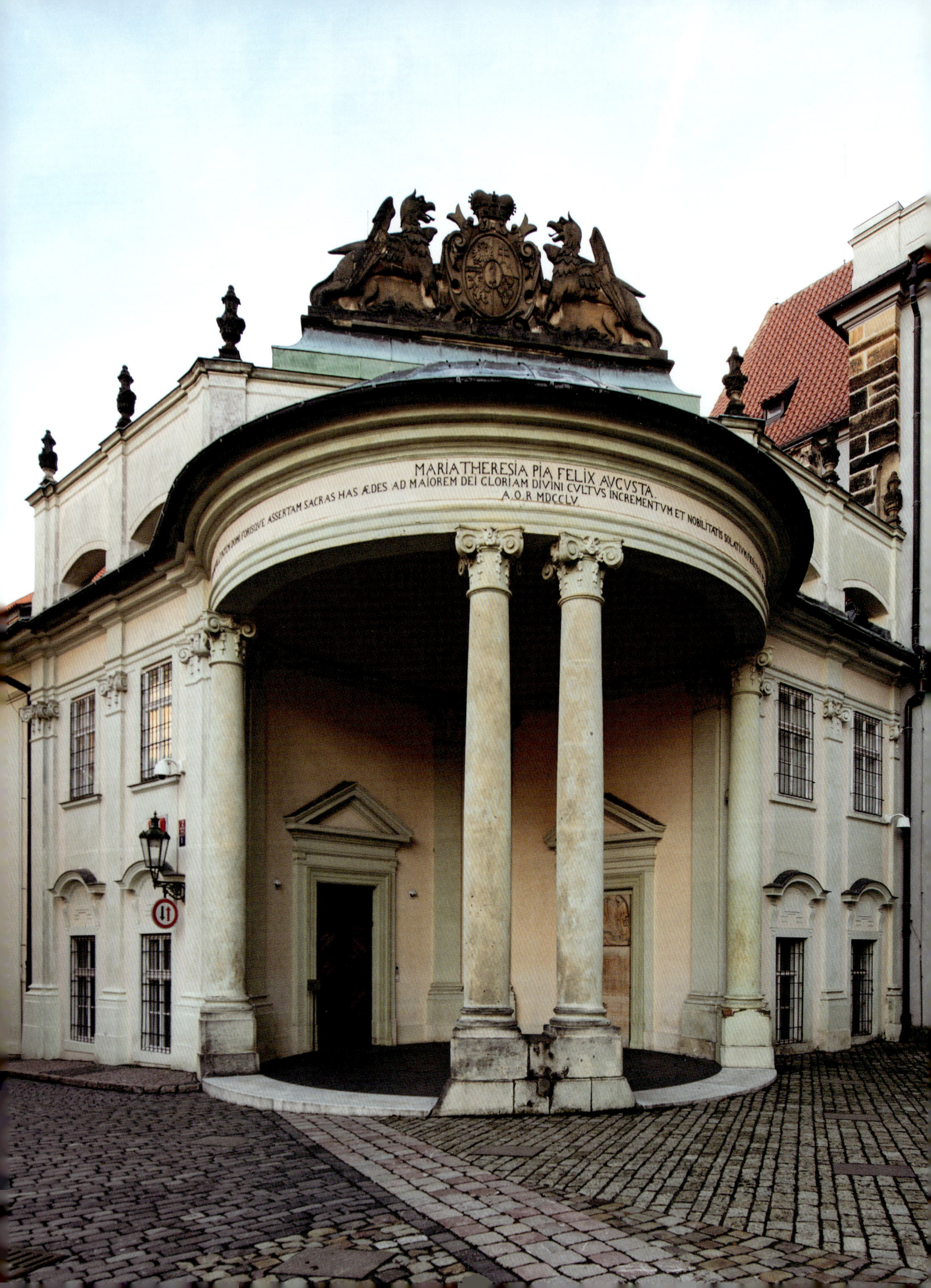
MARIATHERESIA PIA FELIX AVGVSTA.
DOMI FORISQVE ASSERTAM SACRAS HAS ÆDES AD MAIOREM DEI GLORIAM DIVINI CVLTVS INCREMENTVM ET NOBILITATIS SOLATIVM
A.O.R MDCCLV

2/ INSTITUTE FOR DISTRESSED NOBLEWOMEN
Maria Theresa founded this institution in 1753 for the care of unmarried daughters of noble families. In the Late Baroque style, the building was erected from 1753 to 1755 by Anselmo Lurago on plans by Nicolò Pacassi. The entrance section is distinguished by its circularly incised corner in the form of a pavilion. The building and grounds stand on a site with a rich architectural history dating from the tenth century. The institute was intended for thirty noblewomen older than 24 years of age; but orphans, if they had reached the age of eighteen, could also live here. The institute was always run by one unmarried female member of the ruling house; its first abbess was the 'learned archduchess' Maria Anna, one of the eleven daughters of Maria Theresa. After the Benedictine convent was dissolved by a decree of Joseph II in 1782, the right to crown the queen of Bohemia was transferred the abbess of the Institute for Distressed Noblewomen (das adelige Damenstift/Ústav šlechtičen).

3/ CHURCH OF ST GEORGE

The basilica of St George was founded in the tenth century. In about 1670 it was given an Early Baroque façade, perhaps designed by Francesco Caratti. The façade acquires its rhythm from the giant order of pilasters decorated with statues of the convent founders – the Venerable Mlada Přemyslovna and Duke Vratislav I of Bohemia. From the right, it is attached to the façade of the Church of St John Nepomucene, built from 1717 to 1722 on plans by Philipp Spannbrucker. The statues above its entrance are from the workshop of Ferdinand Maximilian Brokoff.

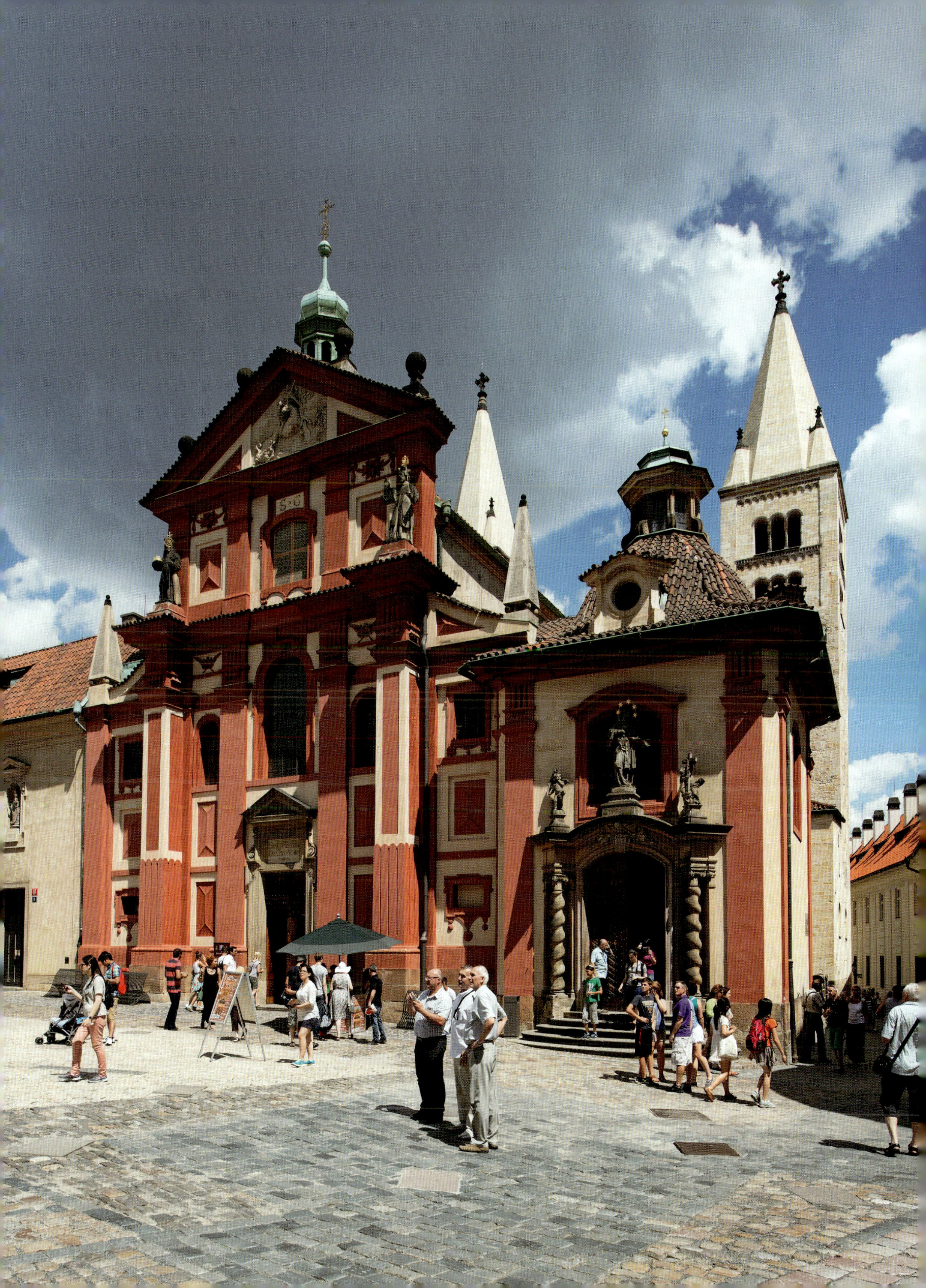

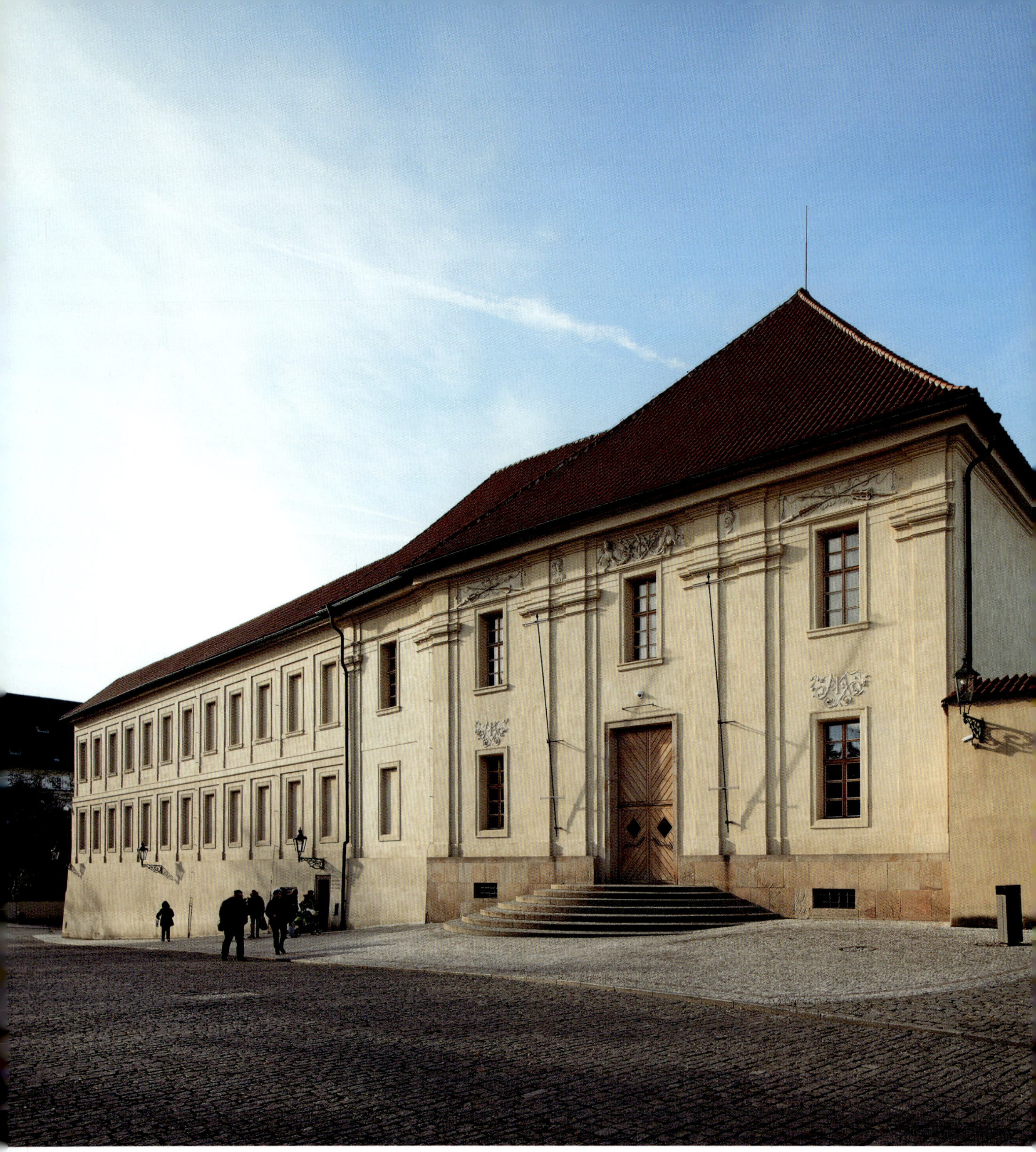

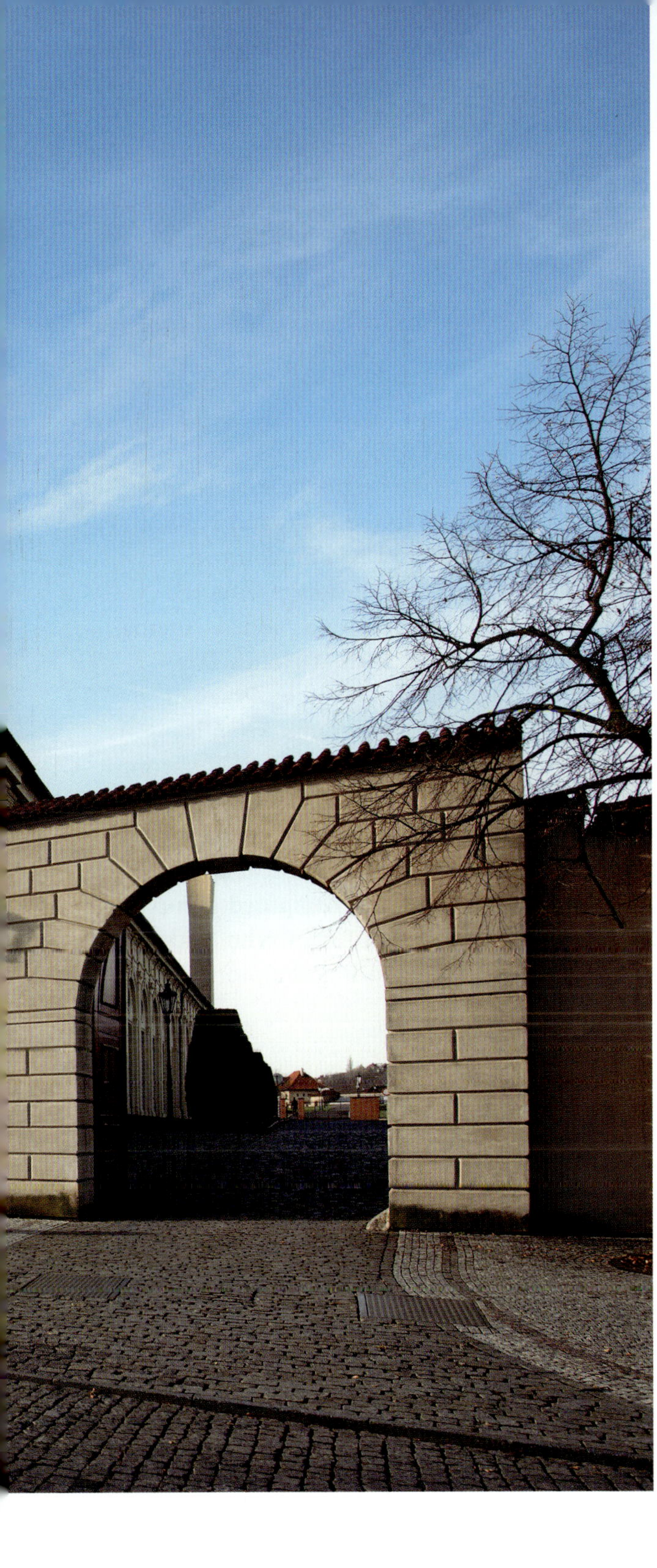

4/ THE RIDING SCHOOL
OF PRAGUE CASTLE, 1694–98

Because the earlier Renaissance buildings did not meet the needs of Baroque court entertainment, a large new Castle riding school was erected following a decision of the Bohemian Chancellery. It was built on plans by Jean-Baptiste Mathey, who also designed the monumental main façade, which is given rhythm by the Roman Doric pilasters. The arcaded courtyard of the building is also remarkable.

5/ THE ROYAL GARDEN –
ANTON BRAUN: NIGHT, 1733

The Baroque changes made to the originally Renaissance Royal Garden are linked chiefly to the 1720s and 1730s, the years when Emperor Charles VI had his court in Prague. That was also when the set of statues from the workshop of Matthias Bernhard Braun was added. Among them were the large allegorical sculptural groups *Day* and *Night*, the first of which was destroyed by Prussian bombardment in 1757. The surviving group, *Night*, is carved out of hard sandstone from the village of Toužetín, about 75 km northwest of Prague (45 km as the crow flies). The seated figure of a dreaming woman represents the Starry Sky, above whom rises the allegorical figure of the Moon. The artist of this effectively composed group was Matthias Braun's nephew, Anton Braun, who made his mark in the early 1730s as the leading sculptor of his uncle's workshop.

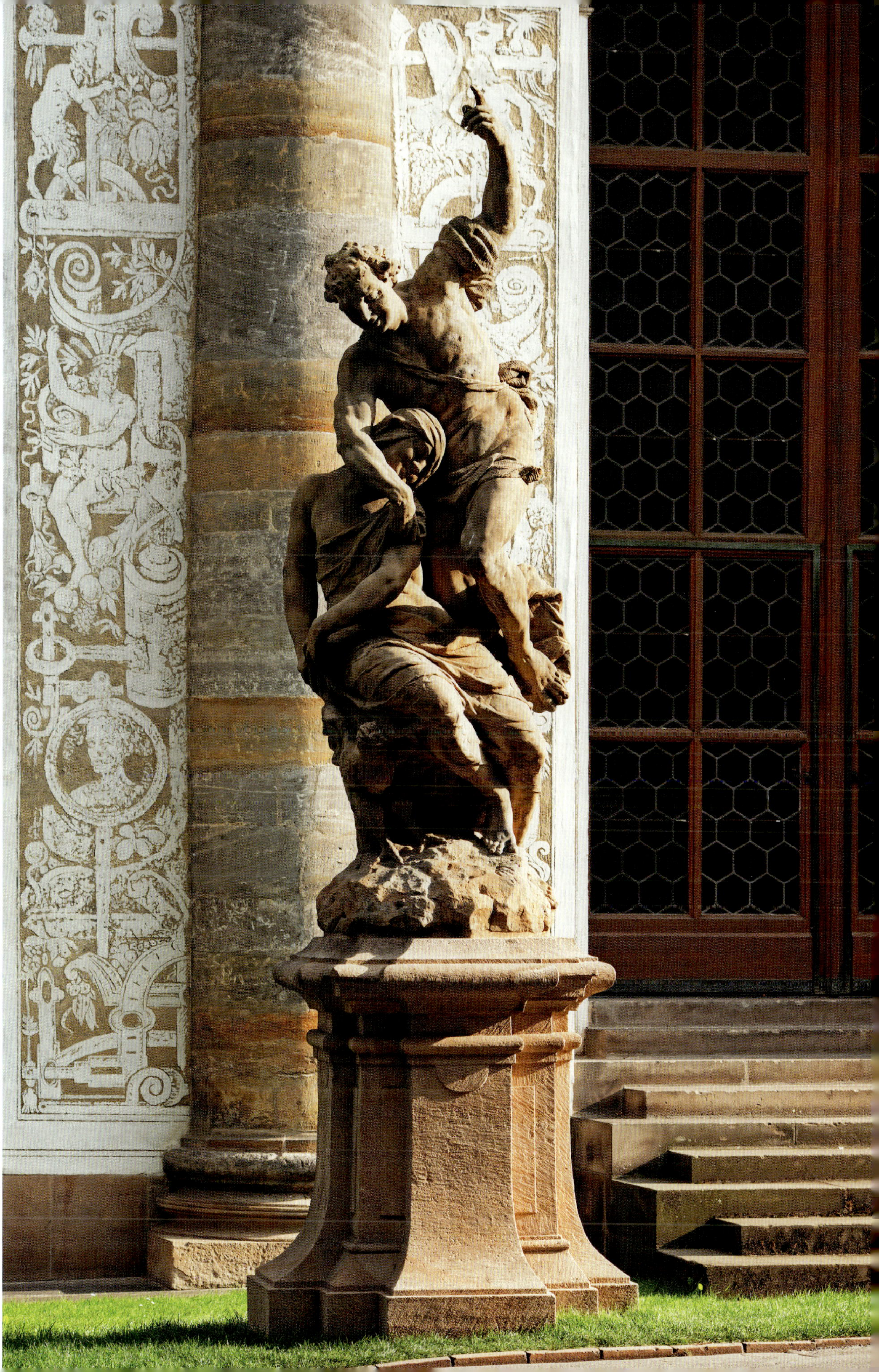

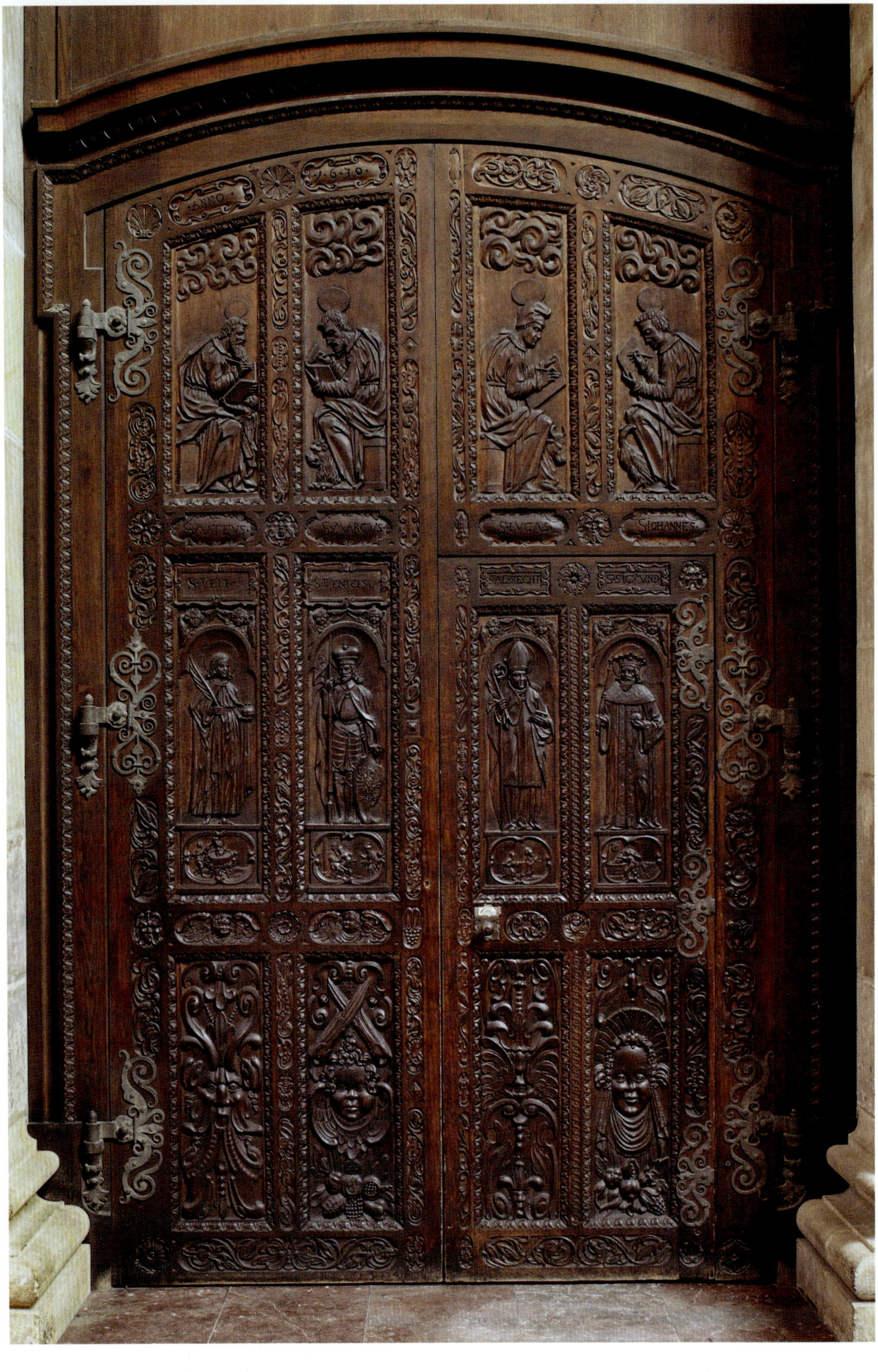
ANNO
1630
S·MARCVS
S·LVCAS
S·IOHANNES
S·VEIT
S·ALBRECHT
S·SIGMVND

(80)

6A–B/ THE CARVED WEST DOOR

In the Baroque period, one entered the unfinished Prague Cathedral from the west through a pair of doors whose intricately carved leaves were made in about 1630 by the carver and court cabinetmaker Caspar Bechteler. In the upper part of the leaves of the left door is a depiction of the Four Evangelists. Below them are Bohemian patron saints – Vitus, Wenceslas, Adalbert, and Sigismund of Burgundy. The decoration of the similarly carved leaves of the door on the right include the four Fathers of the Western Church and figures of the saints Procopius, Ludmila, John the Confessor (that is, Nepomucene), and Ivan. Today, these leaves are installed below the choir loft in the apse of the north transept.

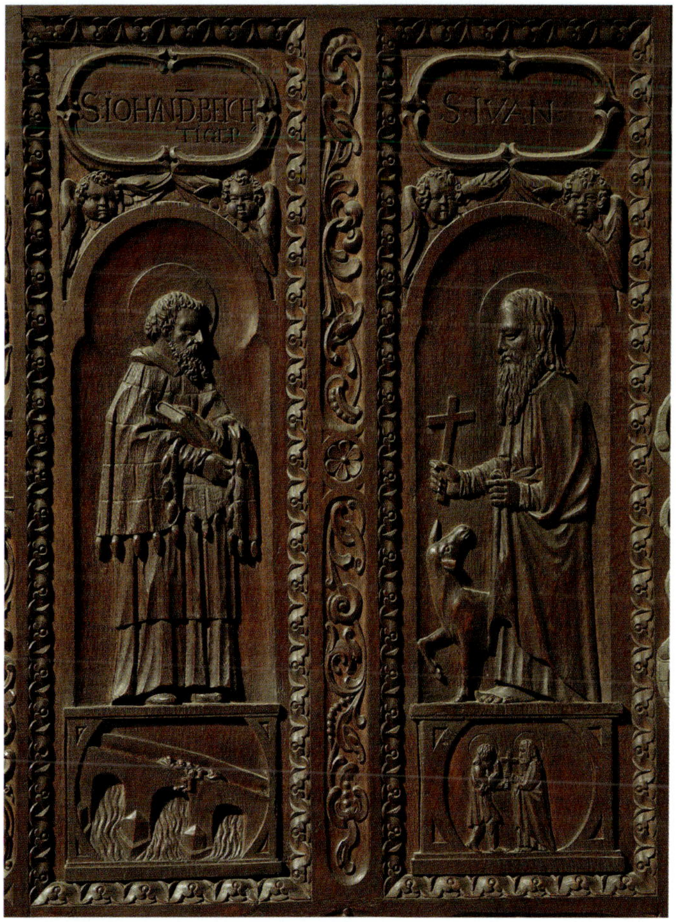

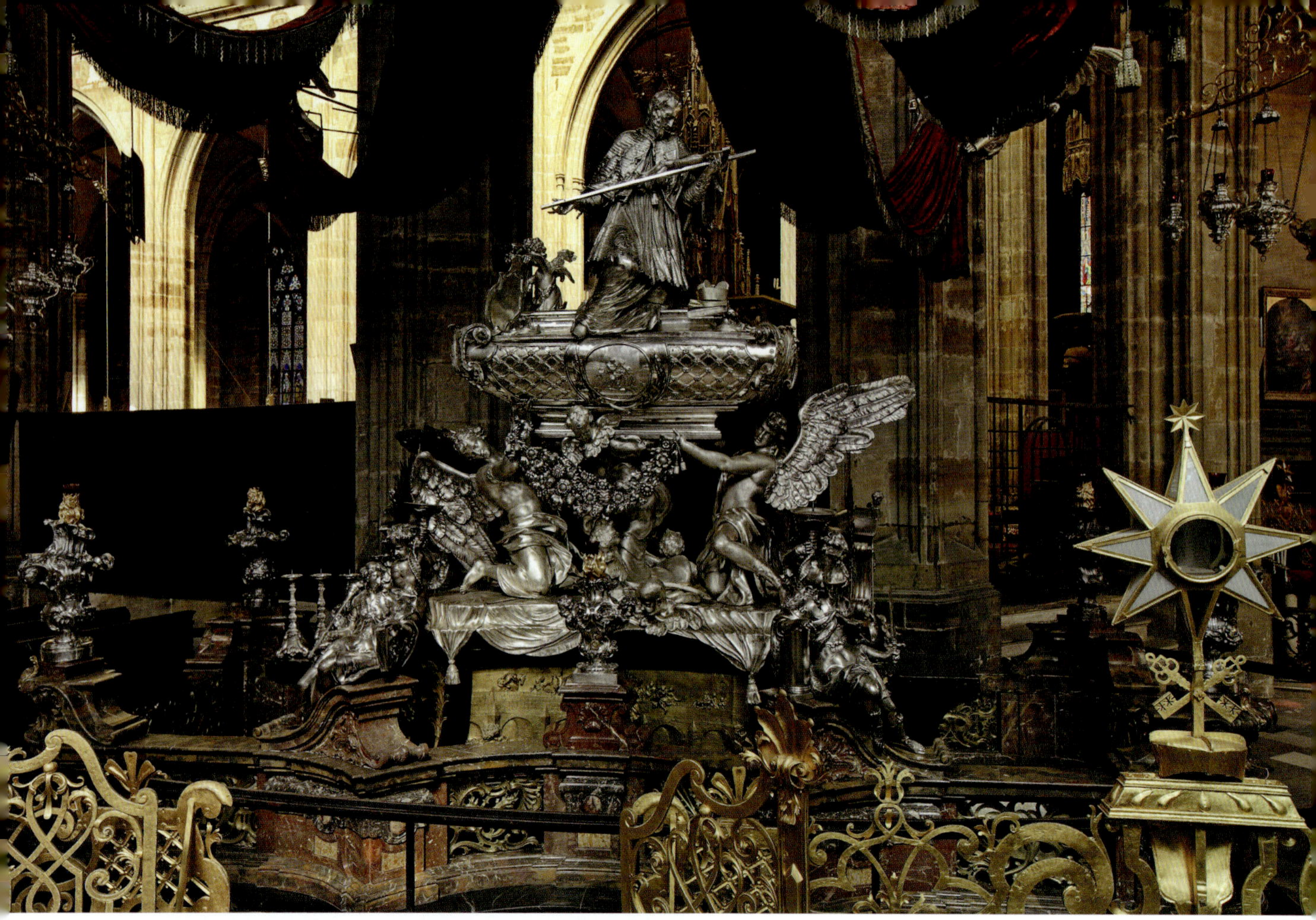

6C/ TOMB OF ST JOHN NEPOMUCENE, 1733–36

The history of the cult of St John Nepomucene is also the history of the increasingly opulent changes made to his tomb in the cathedral chancel. The existing monument was designed by the architect Joseph Emanuel Fischer von Erlach. The sculptural decoration was made by the Viennese silversmith Johann Joseph Würth after a model by Antonio Corradini. The mausoleum required a tonne and a half of silver from the mines in Kremnica (Kremnitz in German, Körmöcbánya in Hungarian), Upper Hungary (today's Slovakia). Its main part comprises a coffin borne by two angels. This coffin contains a second coffin, of crystal and lined with red samite, which holds the saint's remains. In 1746, the suffragan bishop, Zdeněk Jiří Chřepický z Modlíškovic, ordered from Josef Lauermann a marble balustrade with allegorical figures of the Virtues to surround the tomb, made by Joseph Seitz. In 1771, the capitular provost, František Kazimír Strachovský, commissioned the silversmith Ignác Novák to make the four silver angels who soar about the tomb and hold the corners of the huge baldachin. Alexander Kleist, who participated in the Prague coronation of Leopold I in 1791, remarked: 'Every archbishop sought to be immortalized in that Nepomucene monument; that is also why it is overloaded with silver angels, and consequently, due to a lack of space, four more angels, each of which cost 24,000 Rhenish guilders, circle around the tomb'.

6D/ AUGUSTIN PETER NEUREUTER: TOMB MONUMENT TO ST JOHN NEPOMUCENE, 1717

This engraving depicts the tomb in the form it had from 1692 to 1694. It was decorated with six allegorical statues of the saint's virtues and a spreading bower of repoussé metal, symbolizing the Garden of Eden. A figure of the martyr soared in heavenly glory at the top. In the years from 1721 to 1725 this tomb was replaced by a considerably more opulent one. Ten years later, the silver mausoleum we see today was installed.

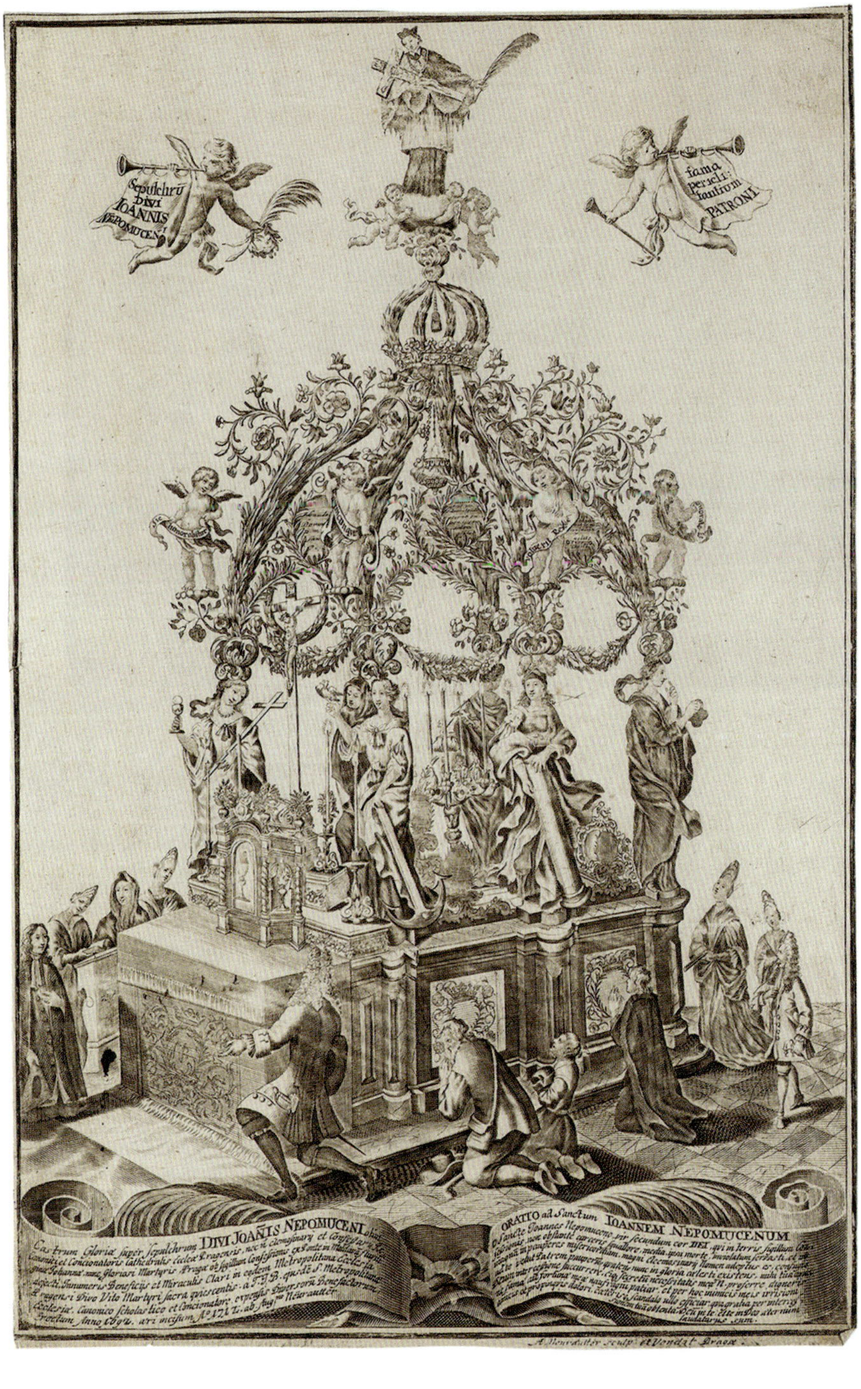

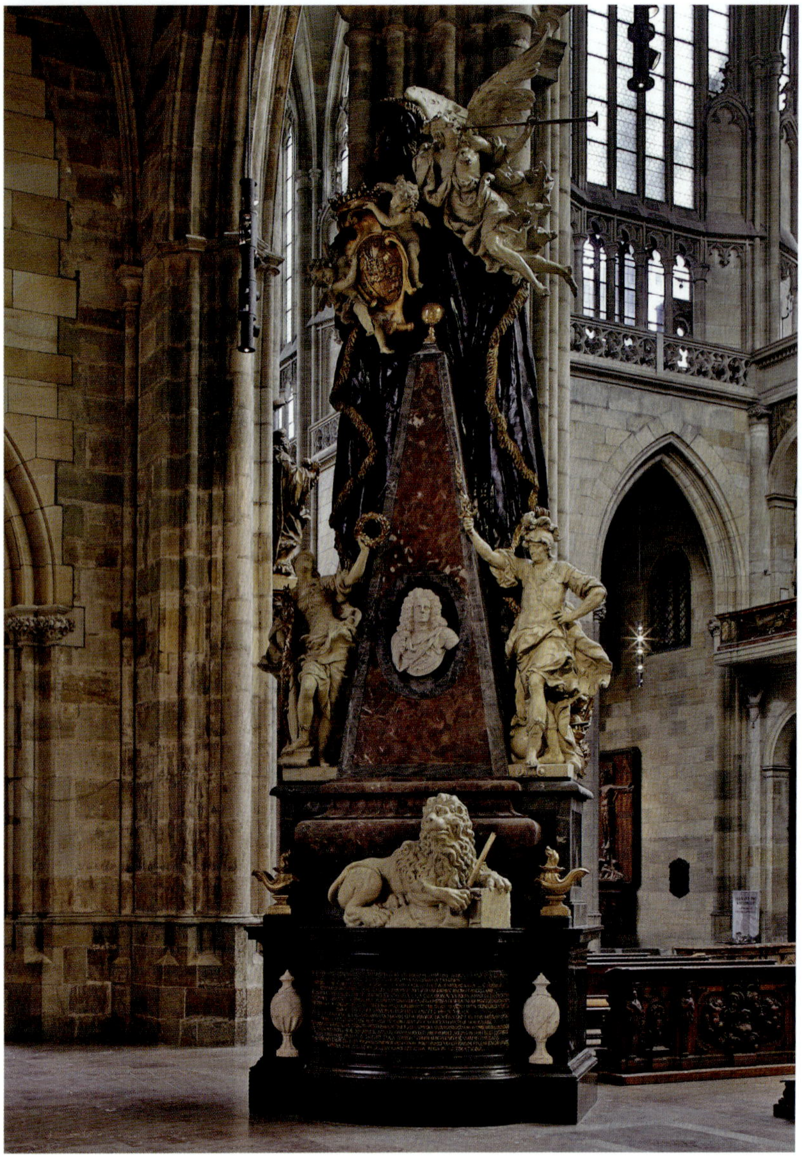

6E/ TOMB MONUMENT TO COUNT JOSEPH LEOPOLD, LORD HIGH CHANCELLOR OF THE KINGDOM OF BOHEMIA, 1723–25
The building of this monument to the distinguished general and politician was initiated by Schlik's brother-in-law, Gundacker, Count Althann, Imperial Director of Works. The decoration was designed by the court emblematist Conrad Adolph von Albrecht and the architectural design is by František Maxmilian Kaňka. The sculptural decoration is by Matthias Bernhard Braun, who applied his mastery as a portraitist in the marble bust of the deceased. The technically perfect execution of the obelisk-like monument, with marble of different colours, stucco and gilt, is the work of the sculptors Johann Wilhelm Hennevogel and Domenico Antonio Rappa, the builder and stonemason Giacomo Antonio Canevalle, the cabinetmaker Jacob Strasser, and the stucco artist Tommaso Soldati. The statues represent Minerva and Mars, above whom soar Fama and two putti holding aloft a cartouche with the Schlik coat of arms.

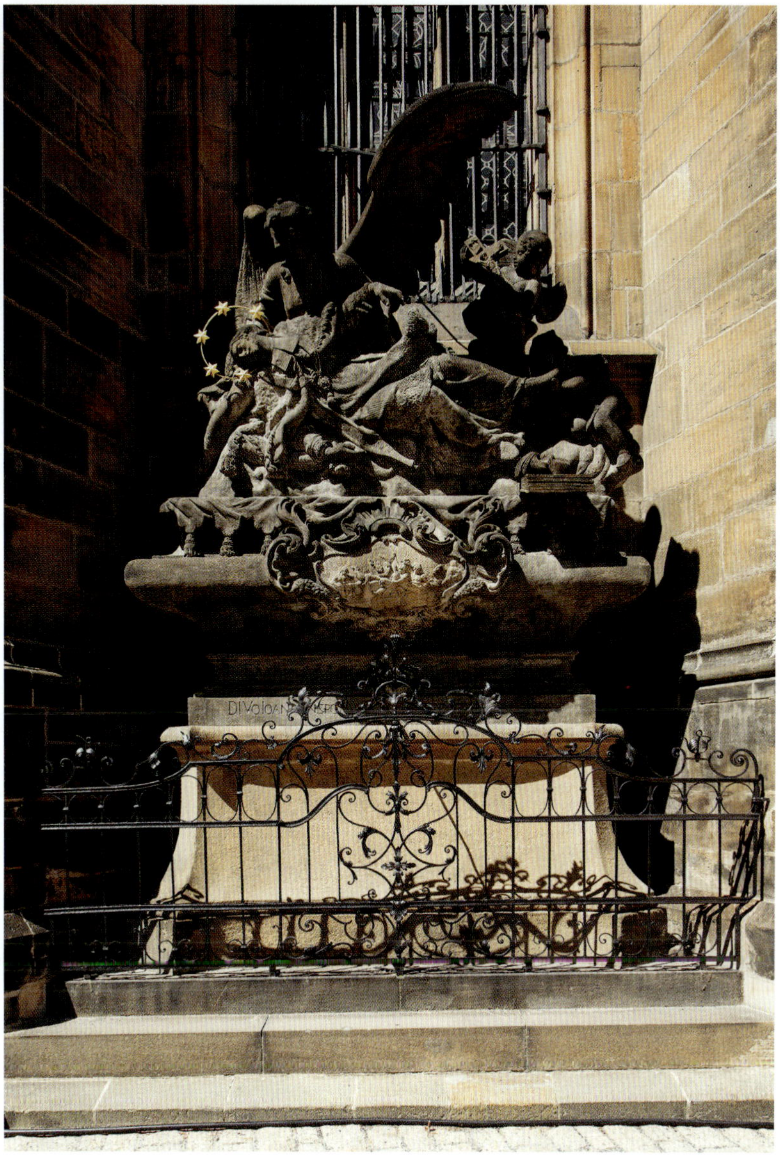

6F/ IGNAZ FRANZ PLATZER: CENOTAPH OF ST JOHN NEPOMUCENE, 1763

The most significant sculptor of the Late Baroque in Prague was commissioned by the verger Václav Křečinský to make this scene of the discovery of St John Nepomucene's body for the cathedral exterior. As is clear from the preserved drawings and wooden model, Platzer originally intended the work to be much more spectacular, but abandoned the idea because, among other things, the vertically conceived sculptural group would overshadow the Gothic window of the church.

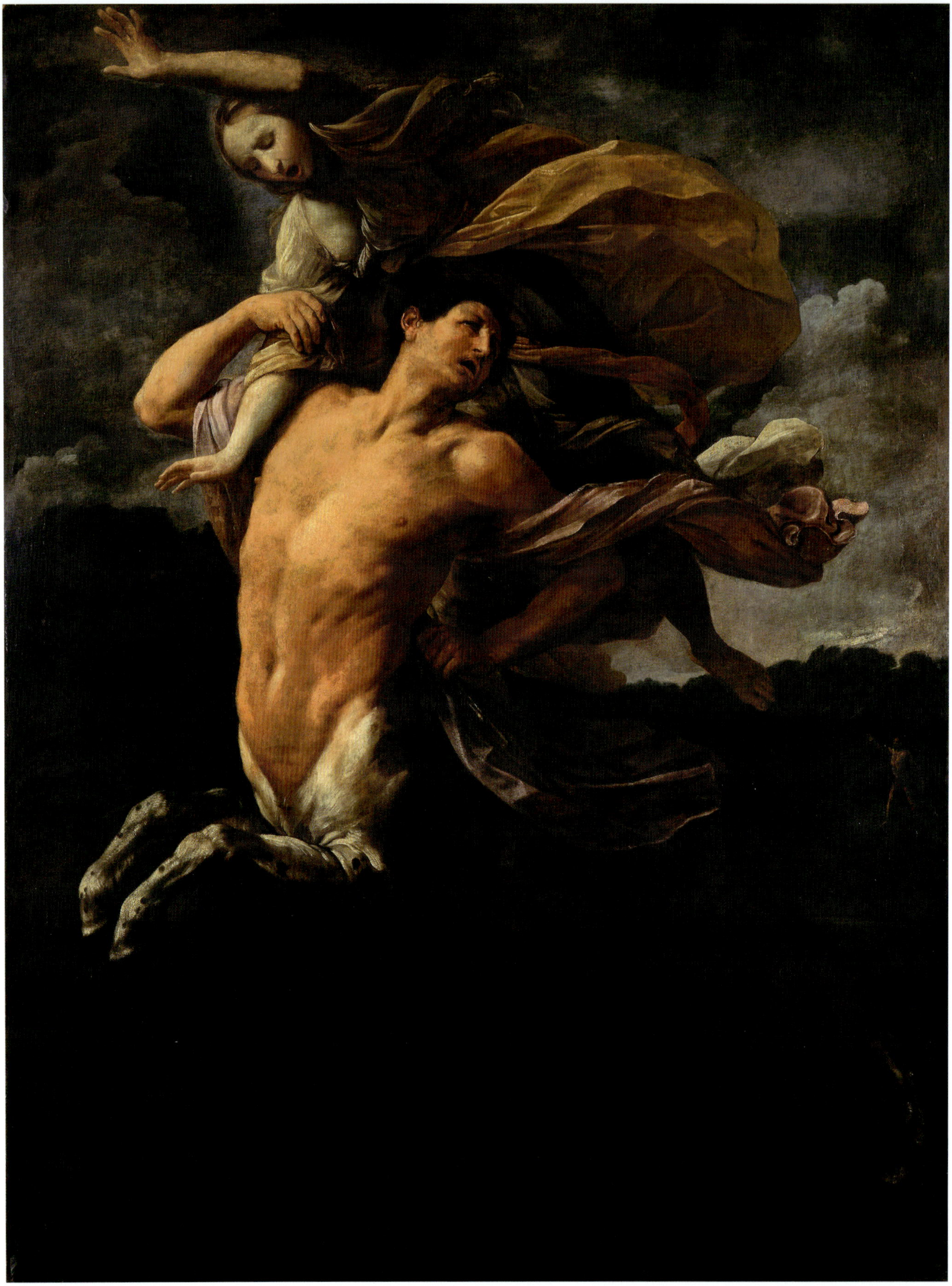

7A/ GUIDO RENI: THE CENTAUR NESSUS ABDUCTING DEIANEIRA, AFTER 1630

The renowned Prague Kunstkammer (art gallery) of Emperor Rudolph II came to a definitive end with its plundering by Swedish troops in 1648. But in 1655, Ferdinand III decreed that a new collection should be assembled at Prague Castle. It was based on the distinguished collection of the emperor's brother, Archduke Leopold Wilhelm, which already had the character of a Baroque picture gallery. Accessible both to artists and to people simply interested in art, it became a model for Prague noblemen building their galleries, a trend that came to a peak in the late seventeenth and the early eighteenth century. Though from the eighteenth century onwards, this imperial gallery was gradually depleted by selling off works of art or moving them to Vienna, many valuable paintings can still be seen today at Prague Castle. Among them is this canvas by the Bologna-based Baroque master Guido Reni, whose subject matter comes from the myth of Hercules. We have written evidence that it was in Prague as early as 1685. The Swedish architect Nicodemus Tessin the Younger compared this painting, in 1688, with Reni's work on the same subject, in the property of the King of France (today, in the Louvre, Paris). The Prague picture, remarked Tessin, was 'truly exquisite', better than the one in Paris. He also wrote that when he visited it, the imperial picture gallery in Prague consisted of 'a study, three galleries, and a main hall'. All these rooms, he wrote, were 'hung from top to bottom with excellent paintings'.

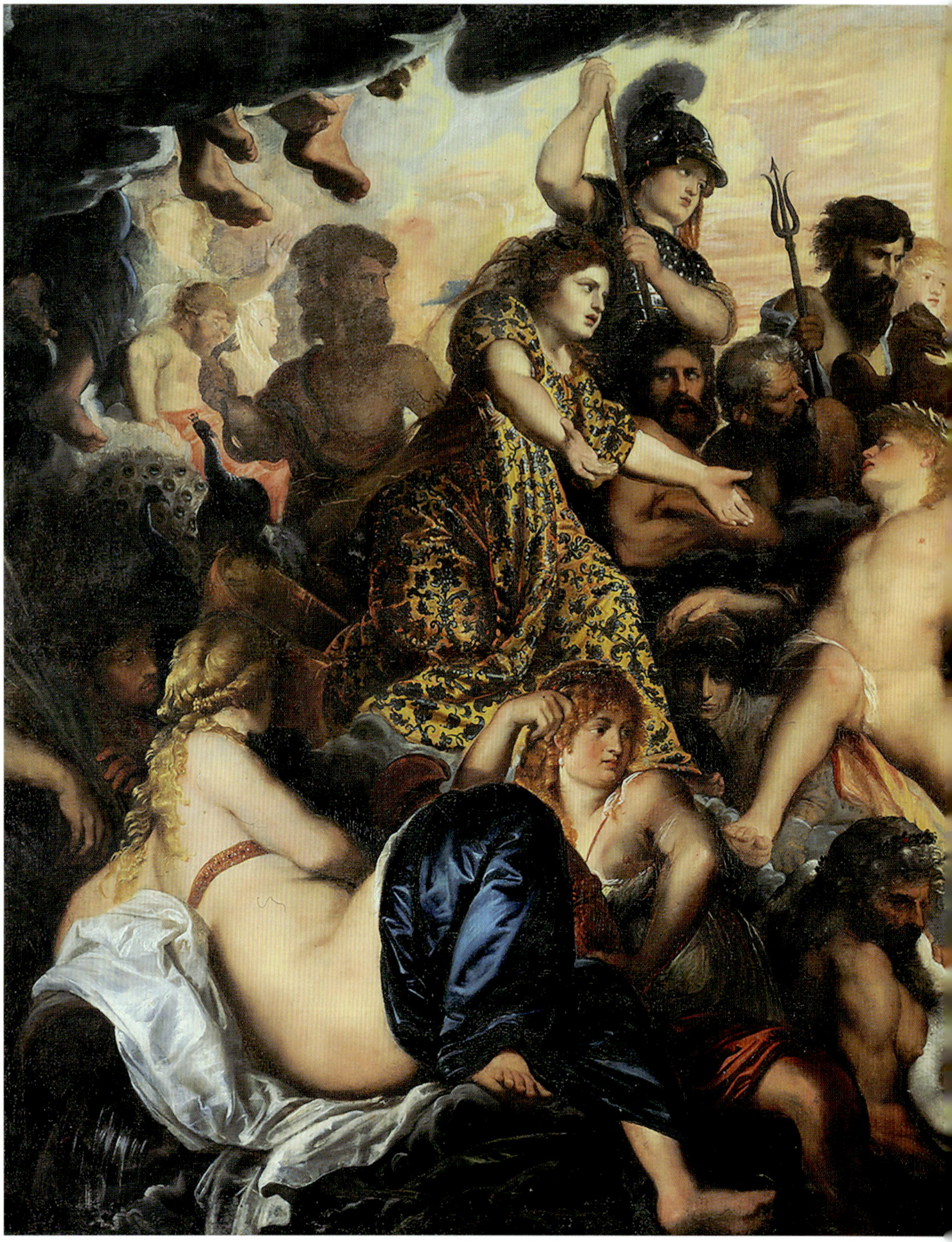

7B/ PETER PAUL RUBENS: THE COUNCIL OF THE GODS, 1602

The inventories of the Prague Castle collection first mention this early work by Rubens in 1685. It was made during the artist's sojourn at the palace of Vincenzo Gonzaga, the Duke of Mantua. The subject matter of this spectacular composition is the confrontation between, on the one hand,

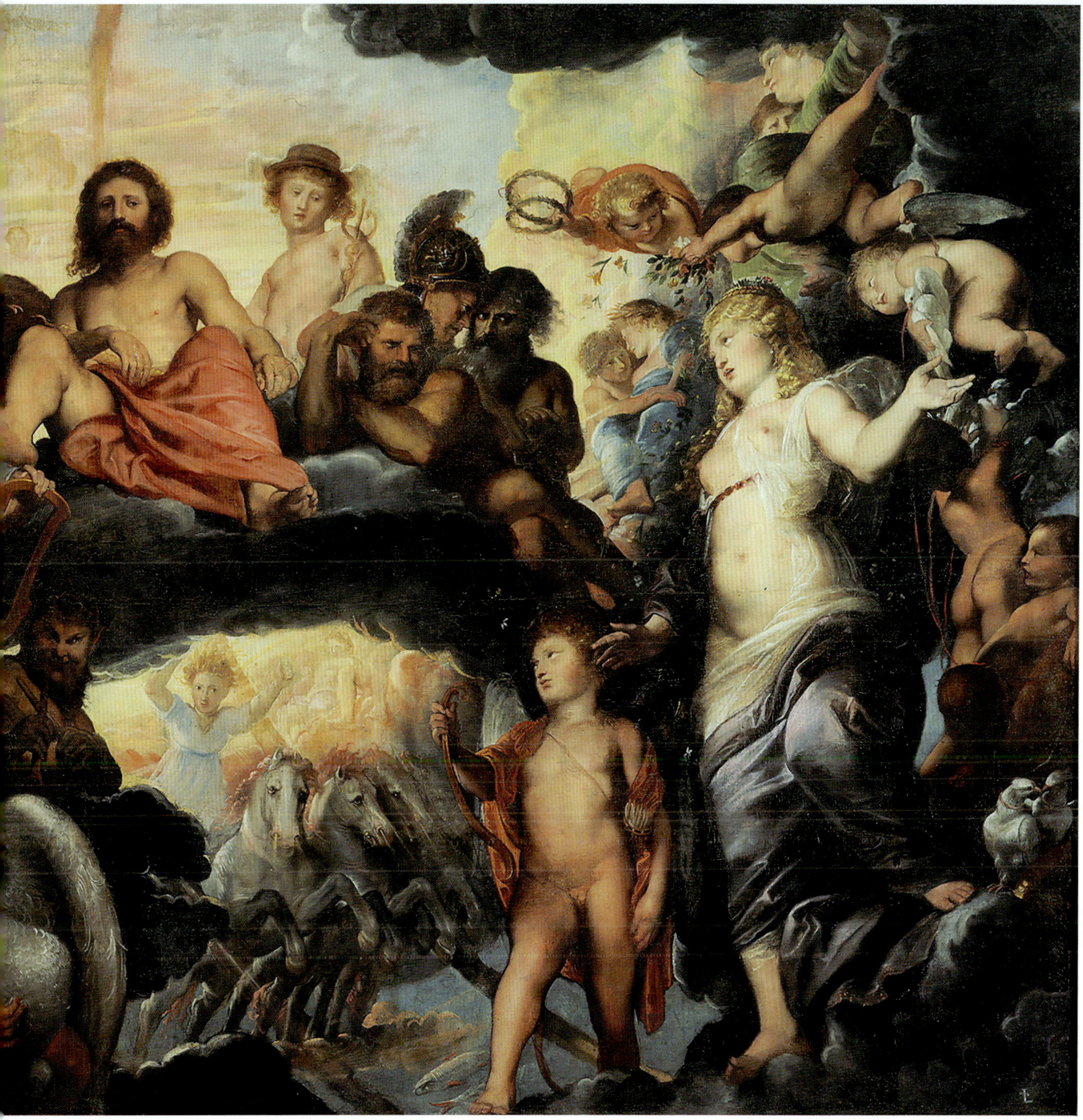

the goddesses Juno and Minerva, the personifications of wisdom, order, and the strength of marital bonds and, on the other, Venus and Cupid, here representing the unforeseen yet triumphant power of love (the group on the right). The picture contains various references to both Mantua and the period of its creation. The impetus for the painting may have been a particular social event at the Gonzaga court.

(90)

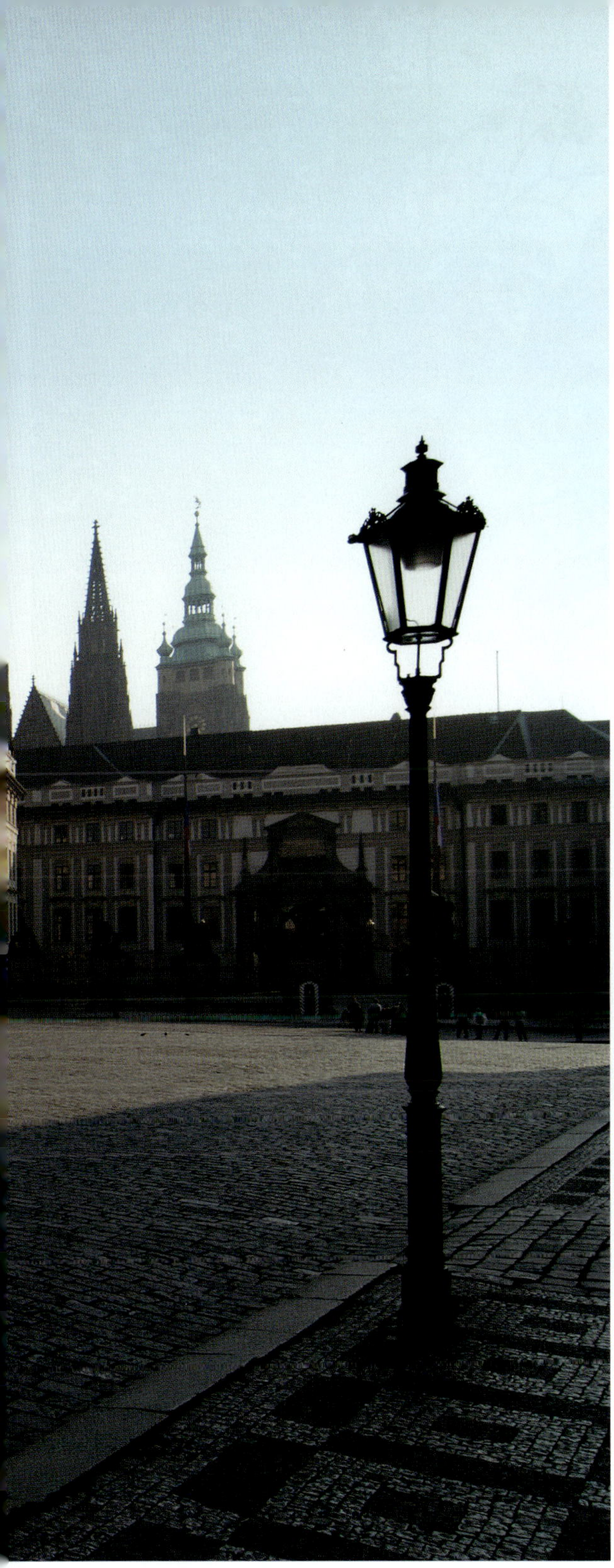

8/ ARCHBISHOP'S PALACE

Since 1562, this has been the official residence of the archbishops of Prague after it was given to them by Emperor Ferdinand I. The house, which had previously belonged to the Gryspek family, was remodelled several times. The Late Baroque façade it has today was designed by the architect Johann Joseph Wirch after 1764. Its sculptural decoration is from the workshop of Ignaz Franz Platzer. The arms of Archbishop Antonín Petr Příchovský are set on the central axis between the two sections of the cornice. The triple-axis main entrance, from 1676, is a remnant of extensive Early Baroque remodelling by Jean-Baptiste Mathey from 1675 to 1679, initiated by Archbishop Johann Friedrich von Waldstein. To this day, Mathey's architectural design has determined the shape of the building, which comes to a peak with the central pavilion; the Early Baroque articulation of the façades is particularly clear on the west side of the palace.

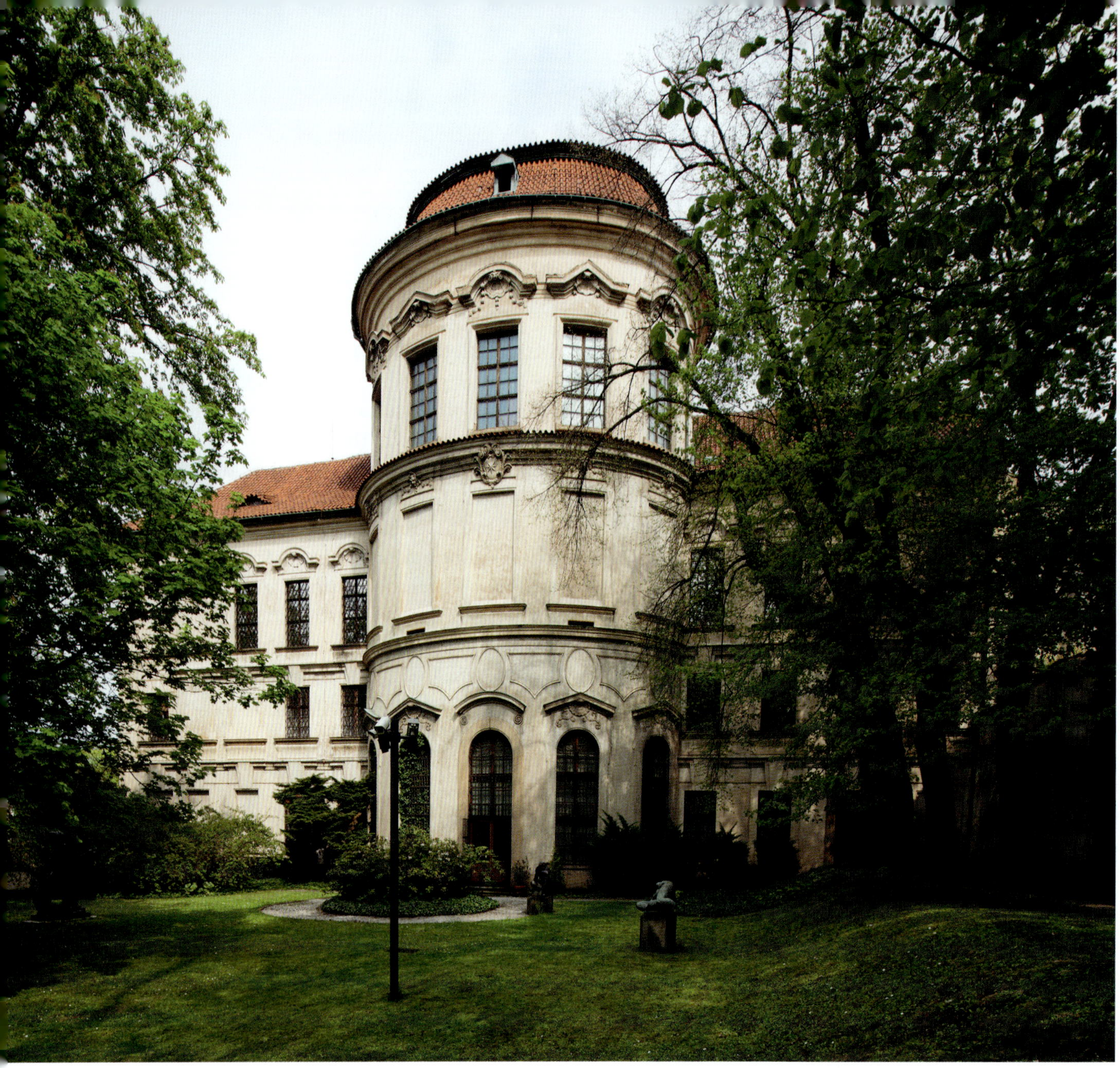

9A/ STERNBERG HOUSE

Sternberg House at Hradčany is located by an old road that connected the hill of the Castle with the valley of the Brusnice stream. Today's building is a mere shadow of the originally grand plan for the house, which was supposed to have three courtyards and whose main façade was meant to be right on Hradčanské náměstí. The building, erected from 1698 to 1708 by Count Wenzel Adalbert von Sternberg, is generally believed to have been designed by Giovanni Battista Alliprandi. The garden façade is enlivened by the oval avant-corps, which runs the whole height of the building, coming to a peak above the wings, and is decorated with the Sternberg coat of arms. The building, which has served as a museum since the nineteenth century, is today managed by the National Gallery.

9B/ THE CHINESE ROOM

The interior of the house is to this day still decorated with the impressive stucco work (1706) of Donato Giuseppe Frisoni and paintings by Michael Wenzel Halbax and Johann Rudolf Byss. The Chinese Room (Činský kabinet) has been fully preserved. It is decorated with wooden panelling and lacquered painting with chinoiserie, which are by Jan Václav Kratochvíl, to whom the emperor, in 1712, granted a monopoly on the painting of 'Indian' scenes. The walls of the small room originally had carved brackets for its porcelain from the Far East.

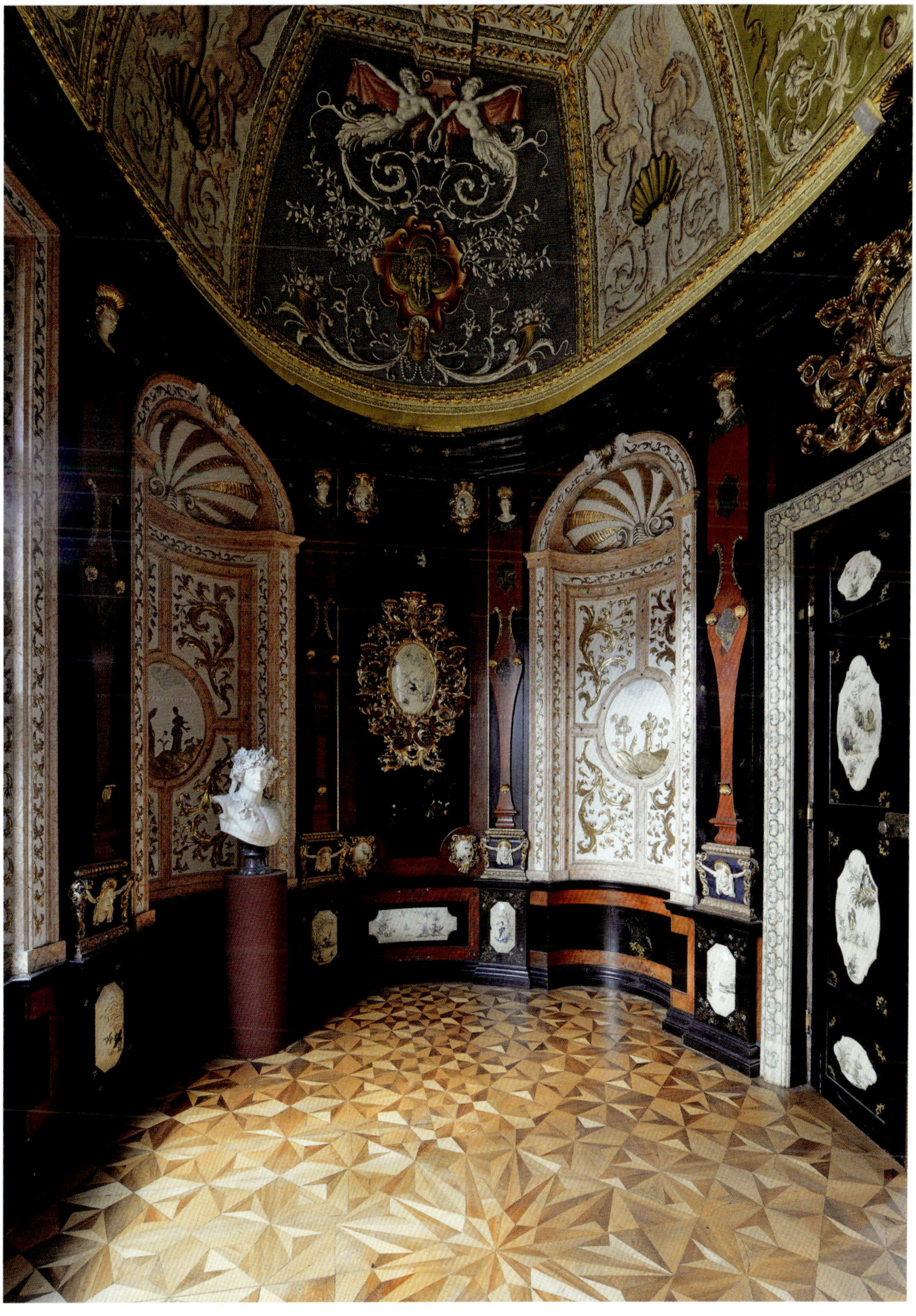

10/ THE MARIAN COLUMN ON HRADČANSKÉ NÁMĚSTÍ, 1724–36

The spectacular Marian column was erected to mark the last plague epidemic, in 1713–14, when a temporary altar stood on this site, at which services were held involving prayers for deliverance. The sculptural decoration of the column, paid for by the borough of Hradčany, is from the workshop of Ferdinand Maximilian Brokoff. Some of the sculpture has now been replaced by copies. It was initially meant to comprise only the patron saints of the country, but eventually came to include Charles Borromeo and Elizabeth of Hungary, the patron saints of Emperor Charles VI and his wife Elizabeth Christina.

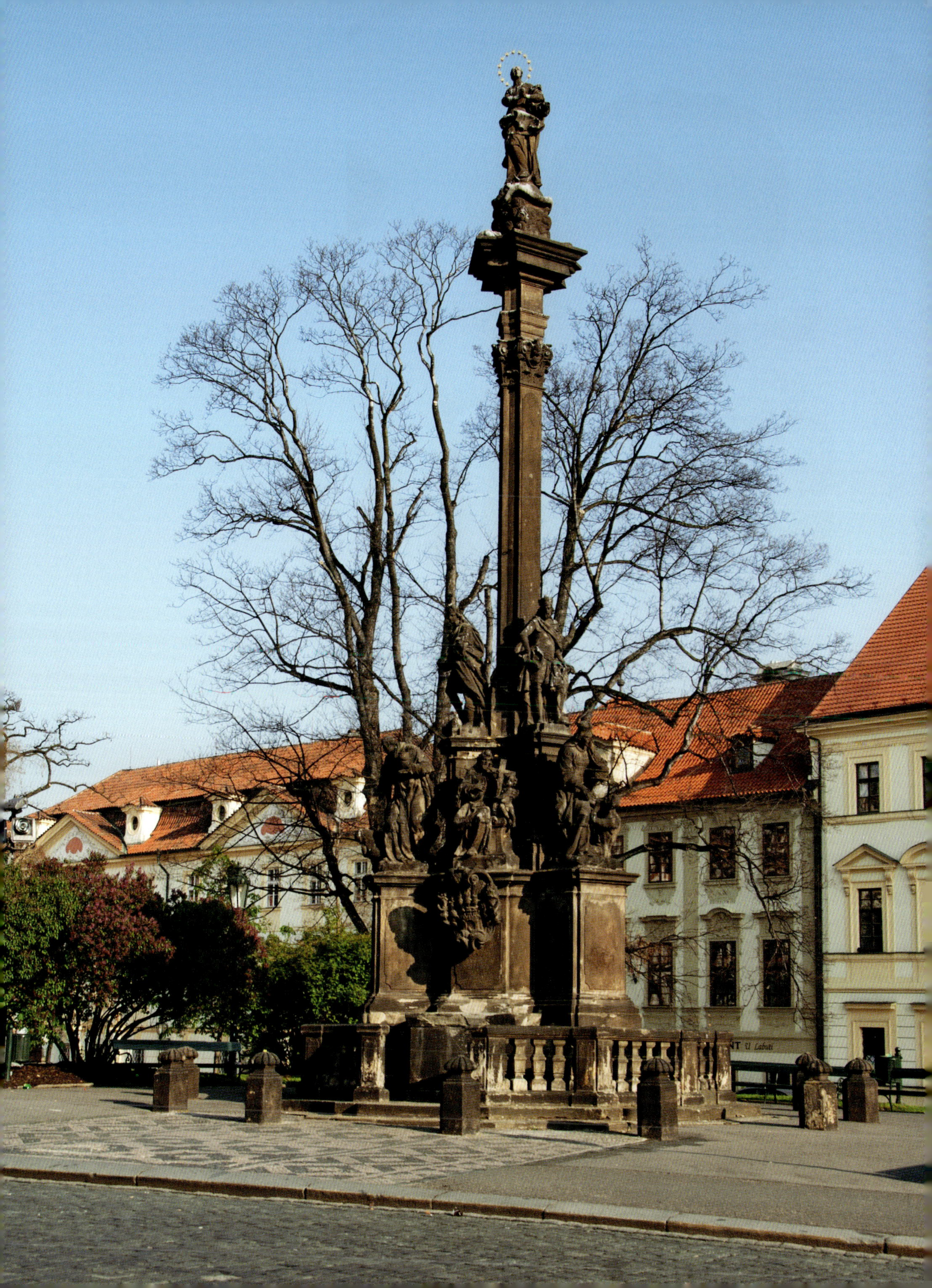

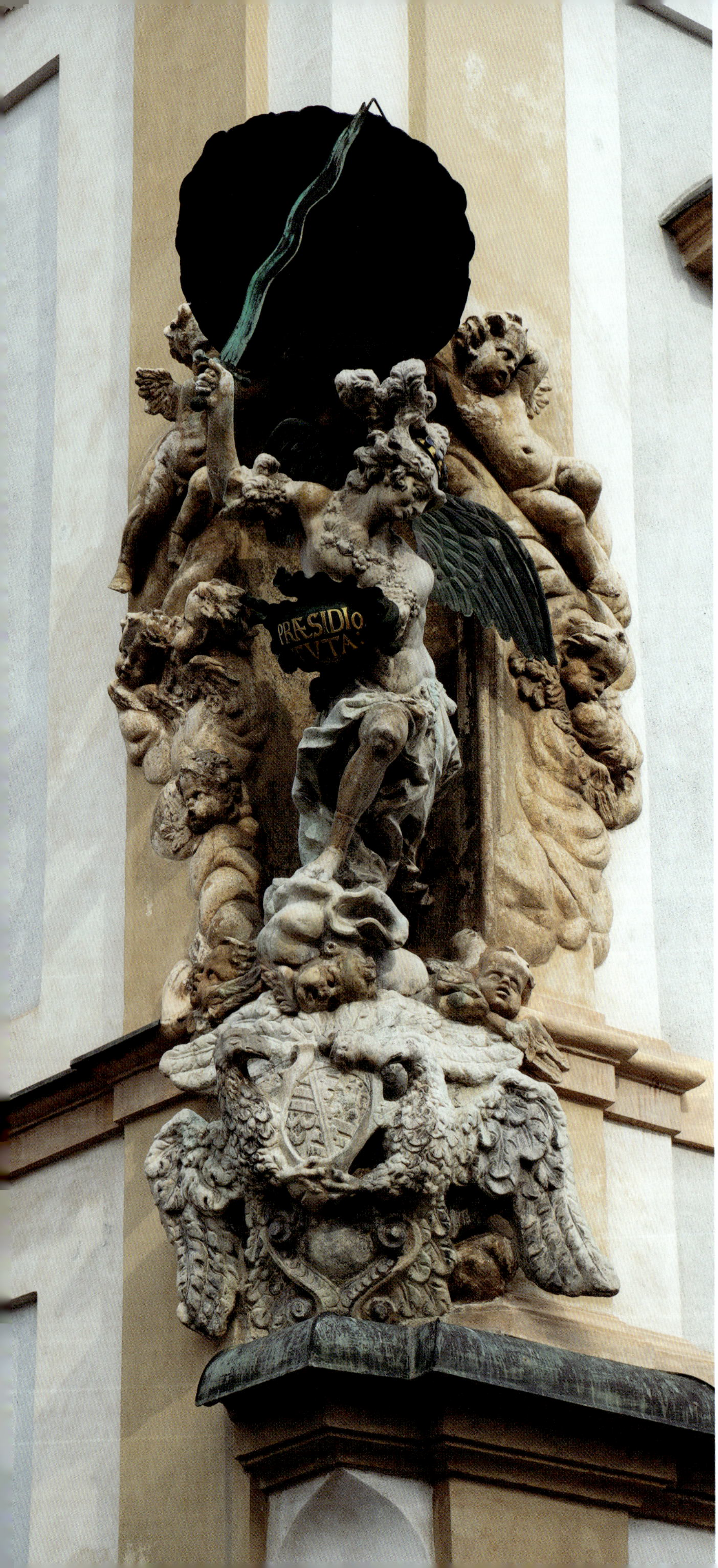
PRÆSIDIO
TVTA!

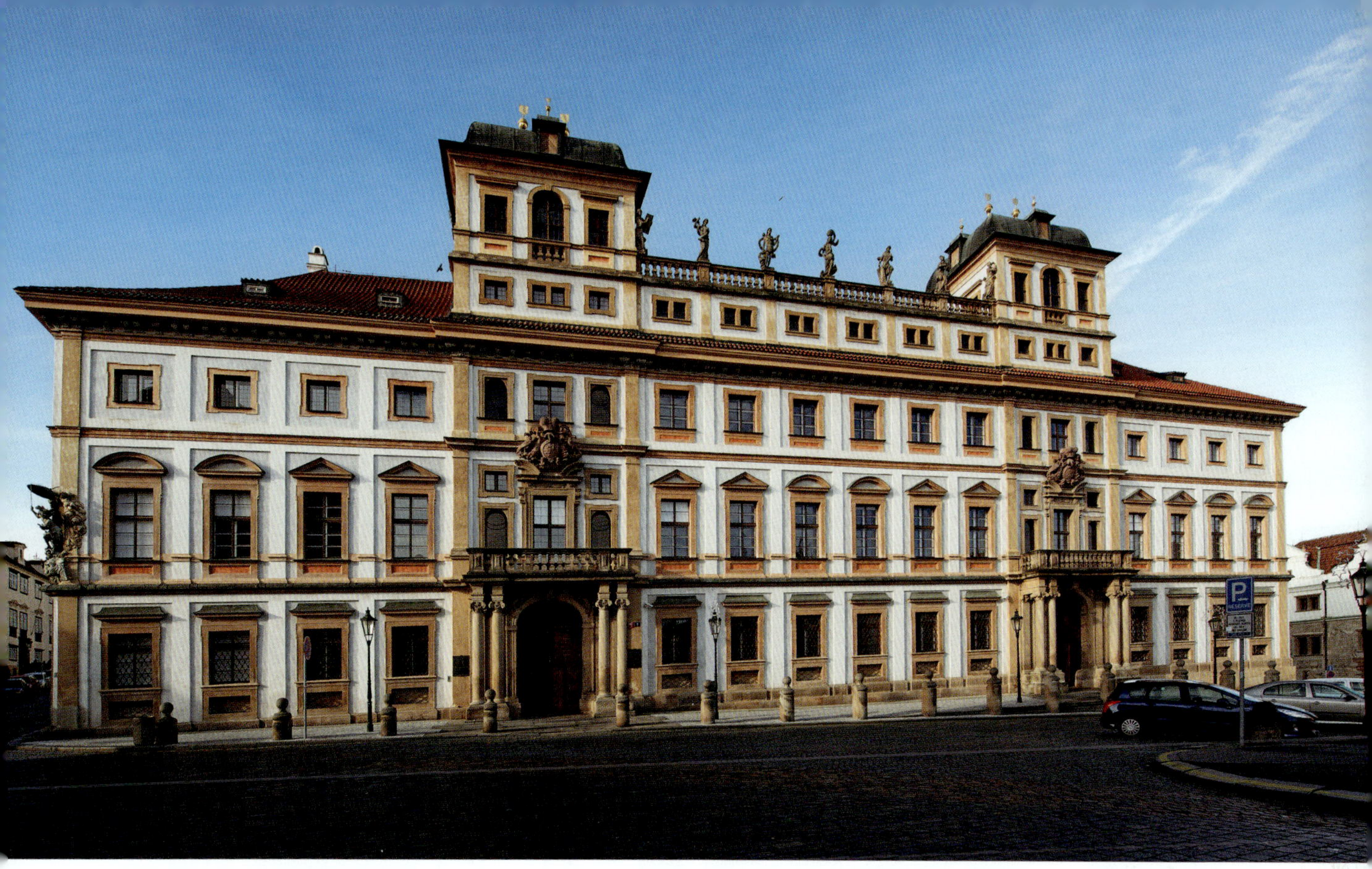

11A/ THE GRAND DUKE OF TUSCANY'S HOUSE (TOSKÁNSKÝ PALÁC), 1689–91

This clearly Early Baroque building, which visually closes off Hradčanské náměstí on the west side, was designed by Jean-Baptiste Mathey for Count Michael Oswald von Thun und Hohenstein. It remarkably combines elements of sixteenth and seventeenth century Roman *palazzi*. The current name of the house reminds us that it belonged to Anna Maria Franziska of Saxe-Lauenburg, the wife of Gian Gaston, the last Medici grand duke of Tuscany.

11B/ OTTAVIO MOSTO: ARCHANGEL MICHAEL

In the late seventeenth or early eighteenth century a statue of the Archangel Michael, a hallmark of Baroque Prague, was placed on the southeast corner of the house (the left side of the façade). The dynamic figure, with its many three-dimensional details, was created by the Padua-born sculptor Ottavio Mosto. The apocalyptic scene of the battle between the archangel and the Devil was inserted into the softly shaped *trompe-l'oeil* relief, which, with its heraldic motifs, commemorates the builder of the house, Count Thun-Hohenstein. Michael was his patron saint.

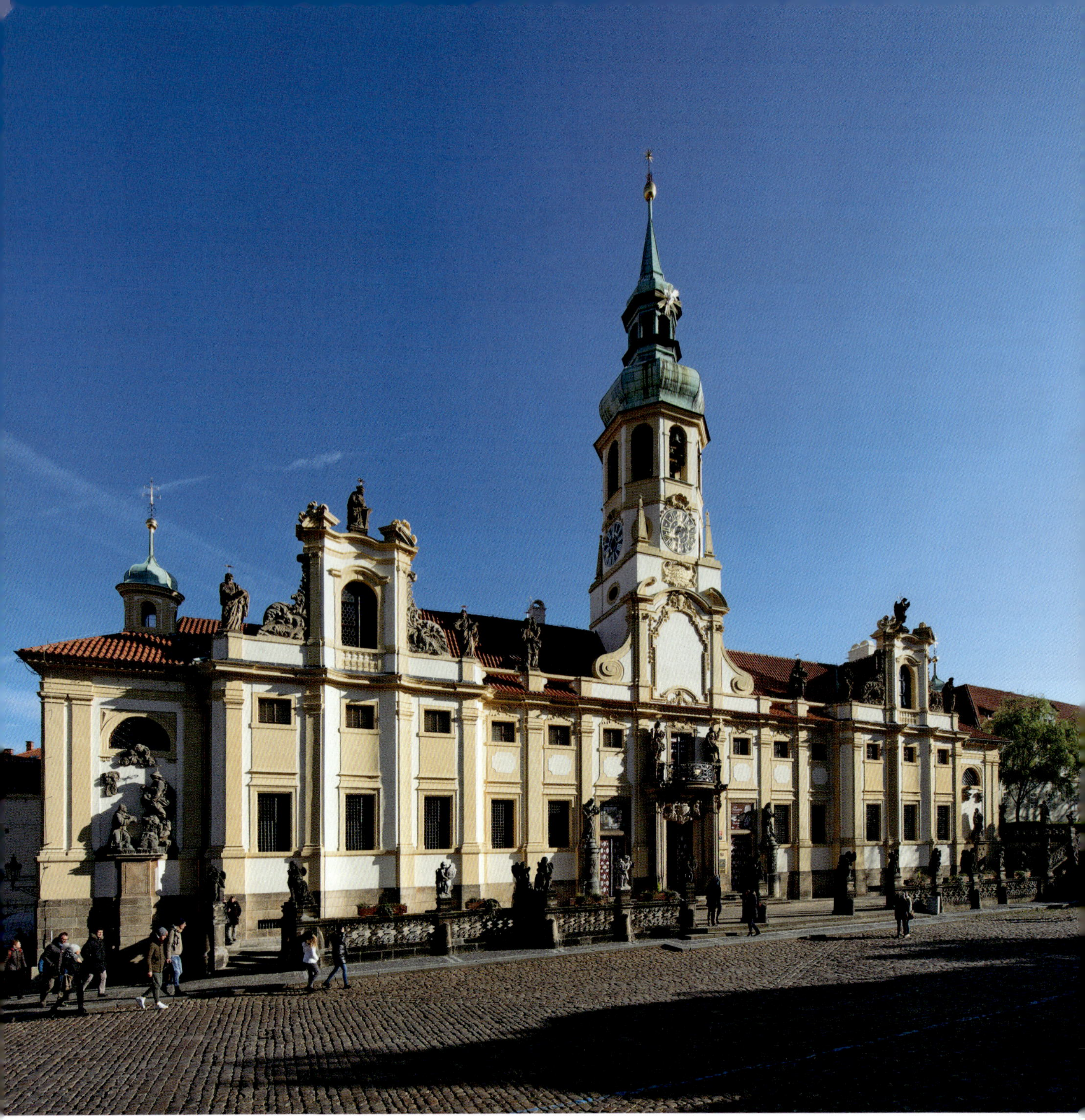

12A/ MAIN FAÇADE

The Santa Casa, the house in which, according to church tradition, the Blessed Virgin Mary lived, has been an important pilgrimage shrine in the Italian town of Loreto since at least the fourteenth century. The cult developed among Bohemian Catholics from the late sixteenth century onwards and about fifty Loreto chapels were gradually built in Bohemia and Moravia. The Hradčany copy of the Santa Casa was the work of Giovanni Battista Orsi and was paid for by Benigna Catherina von Lobkowicz. It was built in 1626–27. By the mid-eighteenth century a large pilgrimage area with cloister arcades on the first storey, chapels, and an entrance wing had been built around this core. The main façade now connects the Early Baroque chapels at the sides and the High Baroque central part from 1721–24, which comes to a peak with the tower above the main entrance. Its belfry, designed by Kilian Ignaz Dientzenhofer, contains the famous carillon (1683–91) by Claude Fremy of Amsterdam. The raised terrace in front of the building is richly decorated in sculptures, some of which are copies.

12B/ THE SANTA CASA

The exterior of the Santa Casa of Prague was originally decorated only in black-and-white painting on plaster. The series of relief sculptures that we see here today was completed by the stucco artist Giovanni Bartolomeo Cometa from 1671 to 1673. The sculptures are precise copies of scenes in the Italian Loreto, which were designed by Donato Bramante. These, however, are executed in less expensive, easier to shape stucco, rather than marble.

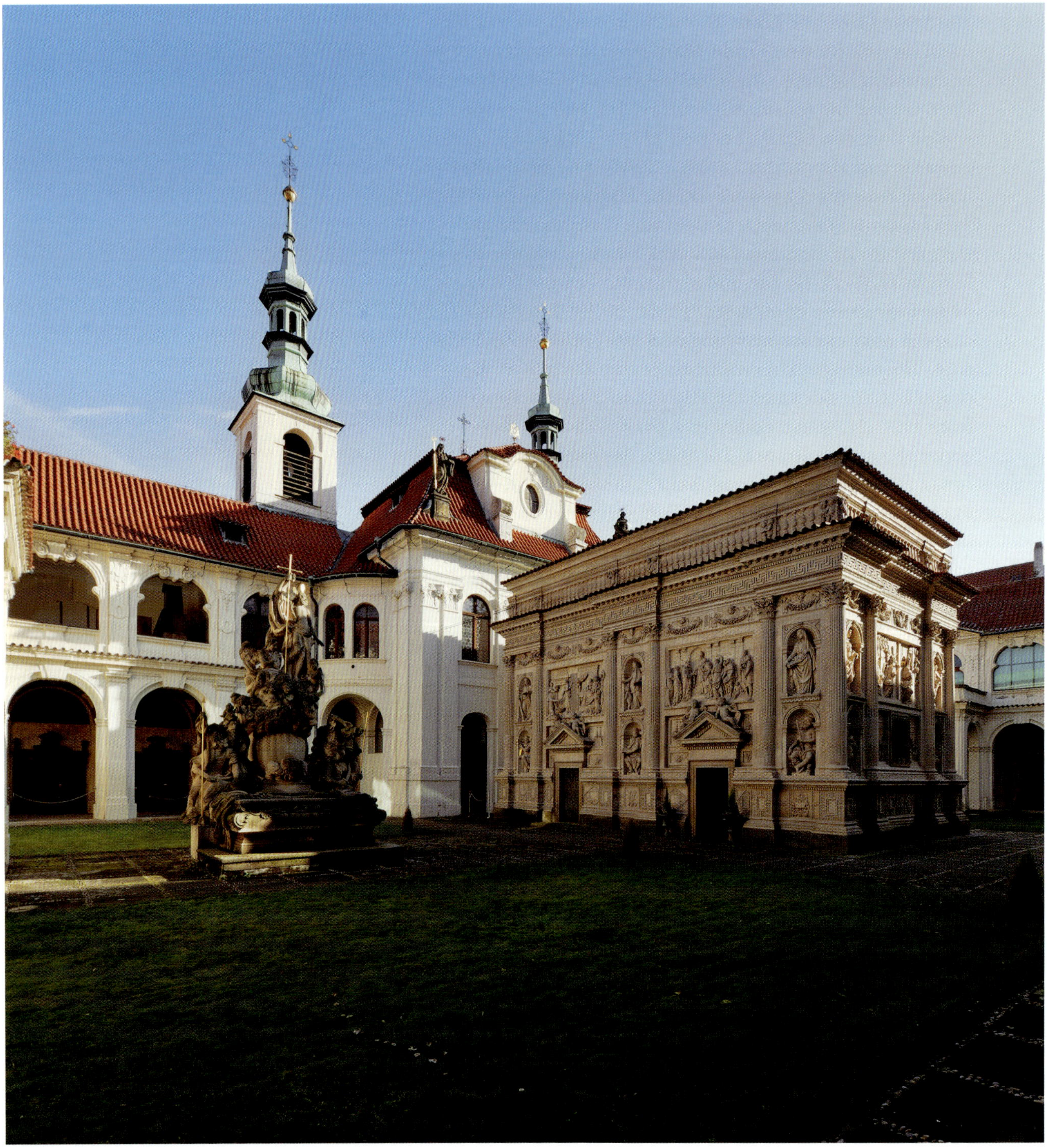

12C–E/ CHURCH OF THE NATIVITY

From 1717 onwards, the originally modest recessed chapel of the Nativity in the middle of the east wing of the Loreto cloister was expanded three times. The church as it exists today was built in 1734–35 by Johann Georg Aichbauer the Younger. Its interior was gradually completed in later years. The stylistically uniform interior of the church is rightly considered by art historians to be the most impressive Early Rococo interior in Prague. It is dominated by statues, made by Matthias Schönherr, and paintings of St Agatha of Sicily and St Apollonia on the side altars, the work of Anton Kern (1737–38). The frescos above the choir loft, depicting the Presentation in the Temple, are early works by Wenzel Lorenz Reiner, and consciously follow on from Kern's masterly use of colour, which in turn follows models of Venetian *trompe-l'oeil* Rococo. The remaining fields of the vaulted ceiling were later filled with Johann Adam Schöpf's *Adoration of the Magi* and *The Nativity* (before 1742).

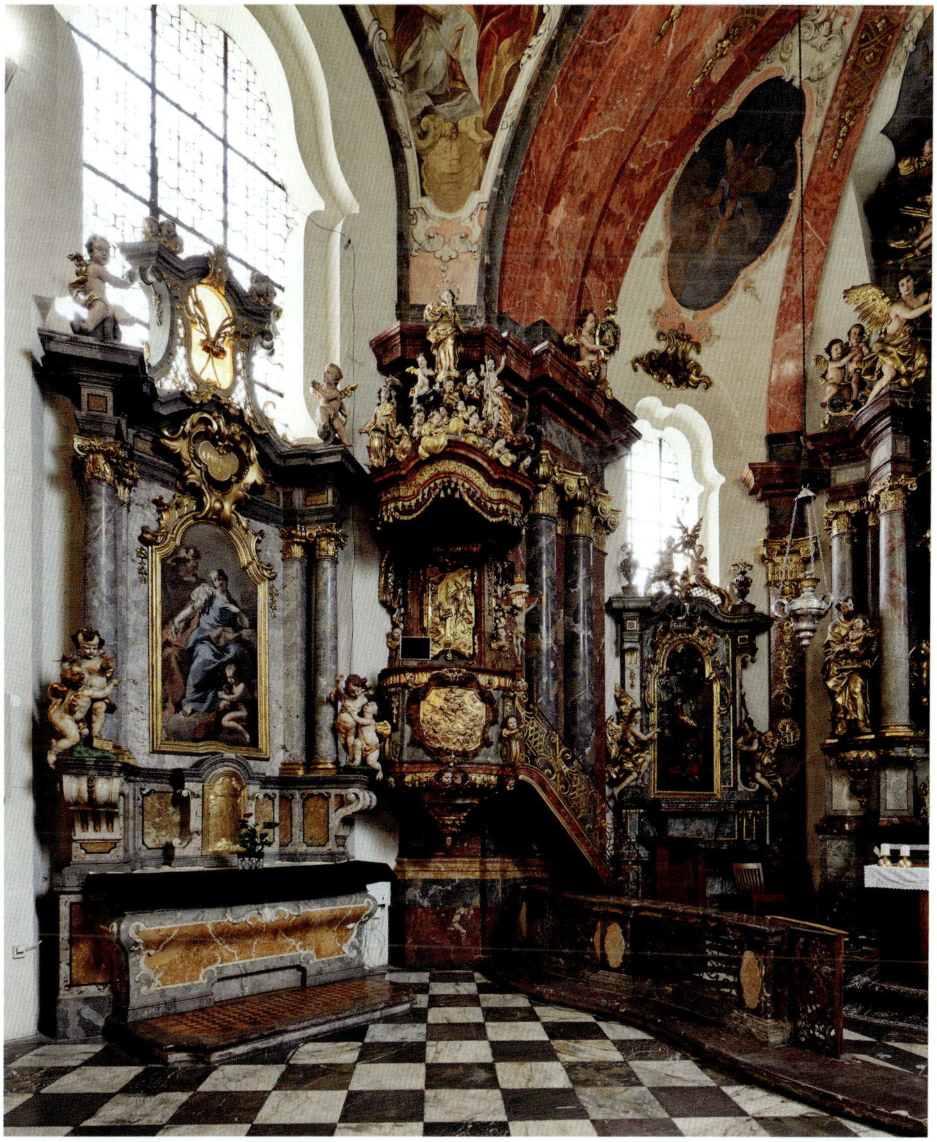

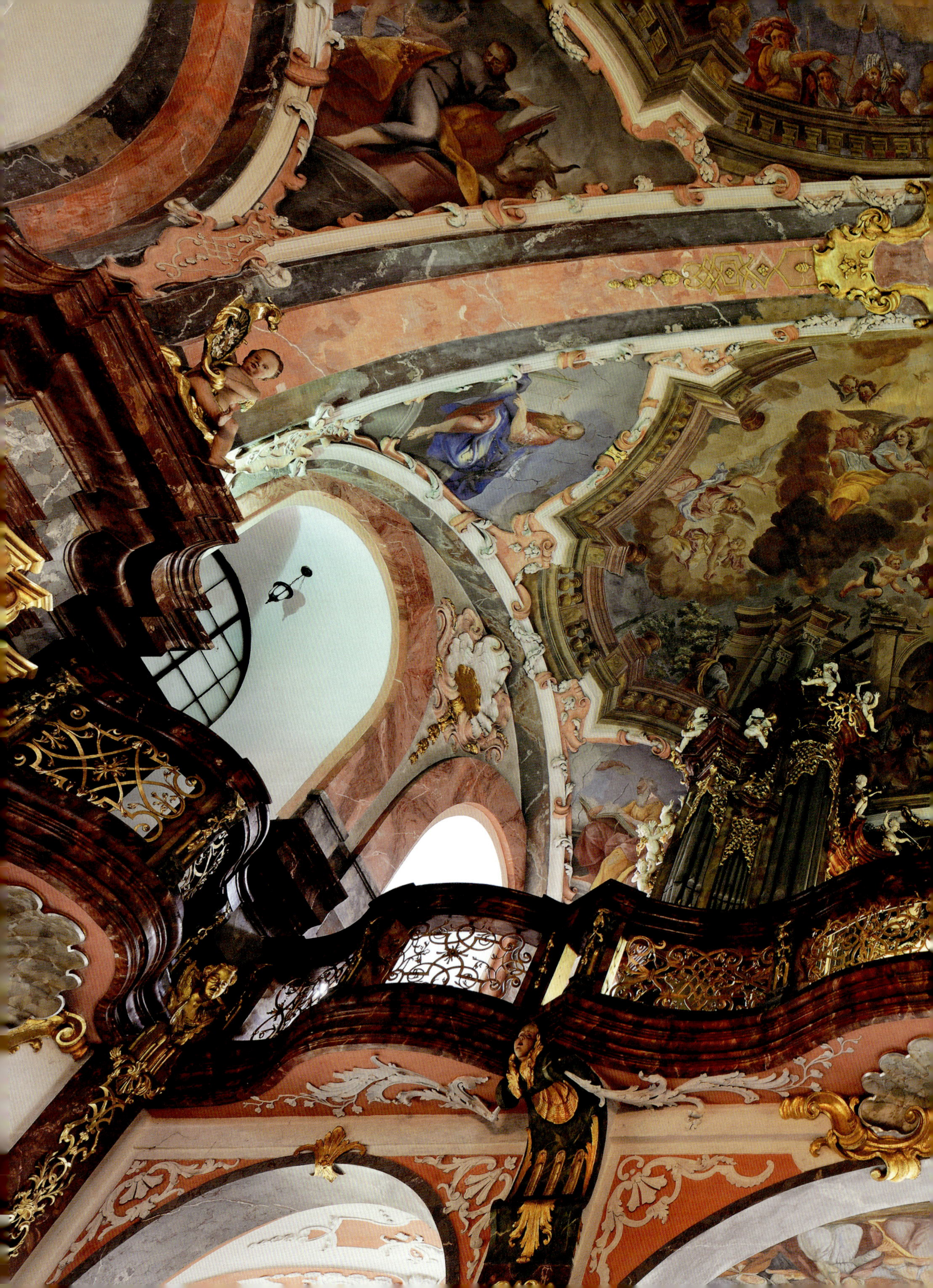

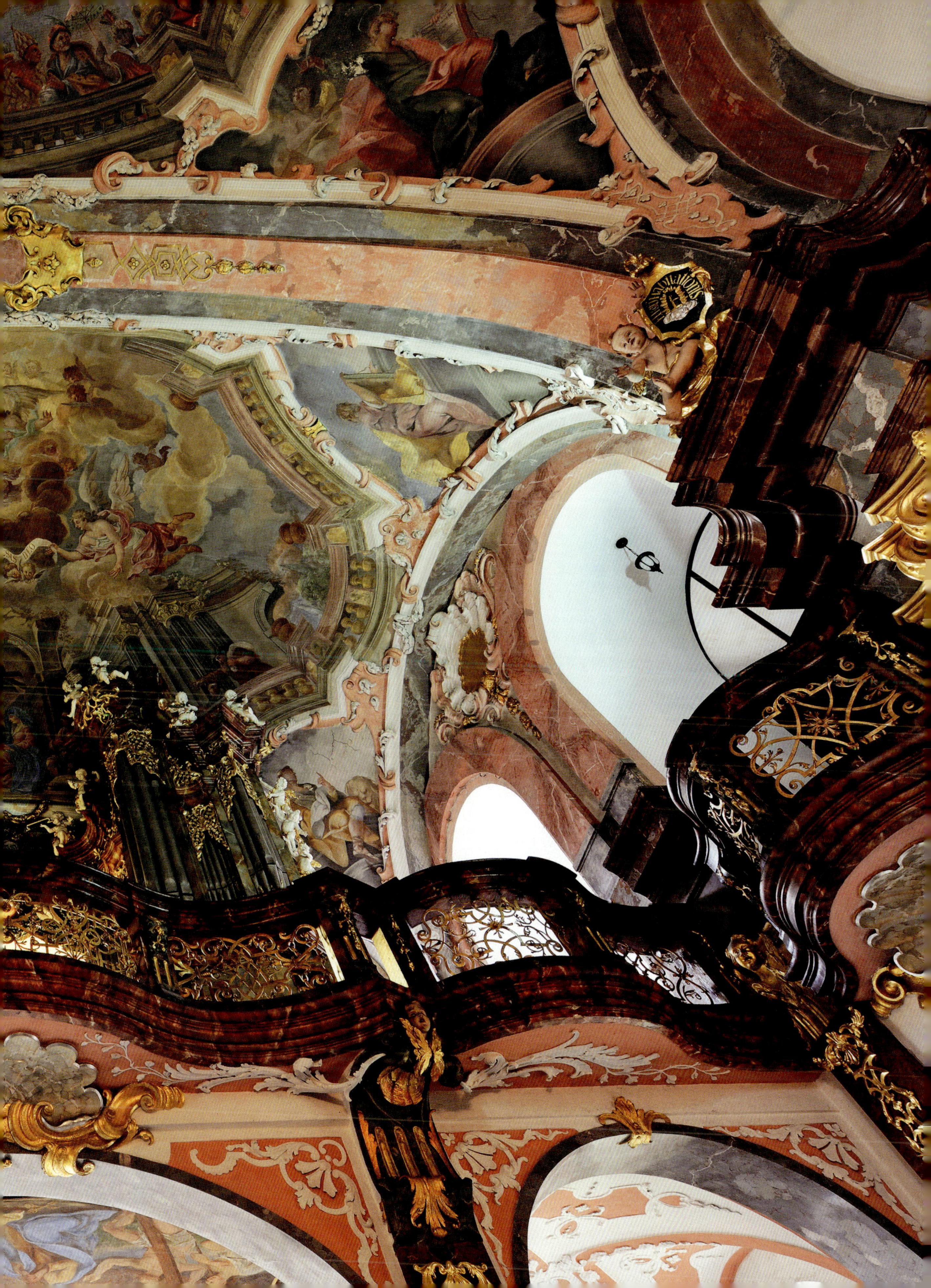

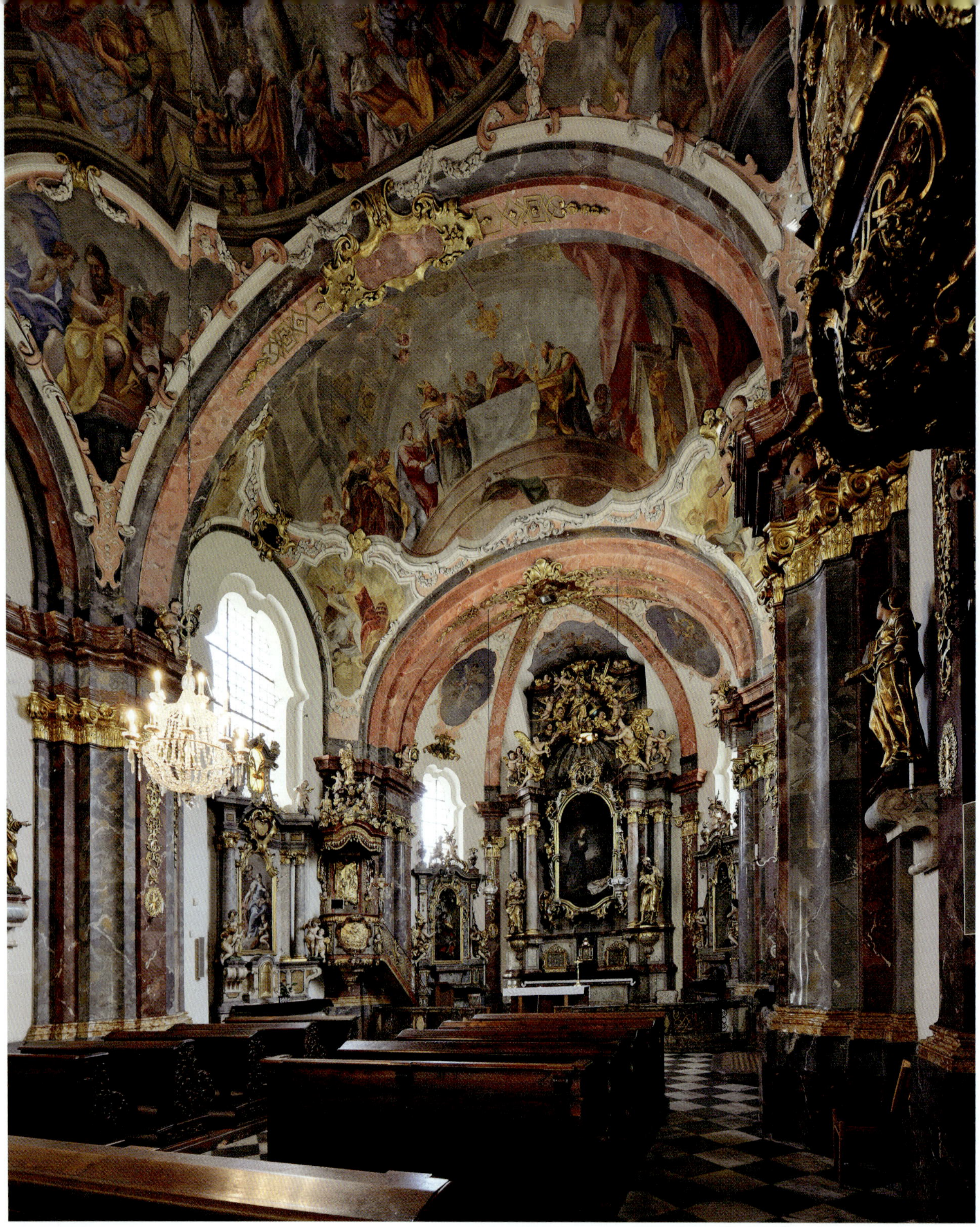

'A hidden place of Baroque eroticism and a very tryst of love is that Loretta. […] St Agatha offers the rosy fulness of her virgin breasts to the rays of the sun and the eyes of the beholders, and opposite, St Apollonia coquettes with the charm of her girlish lips.'
Arne Novák, 1915

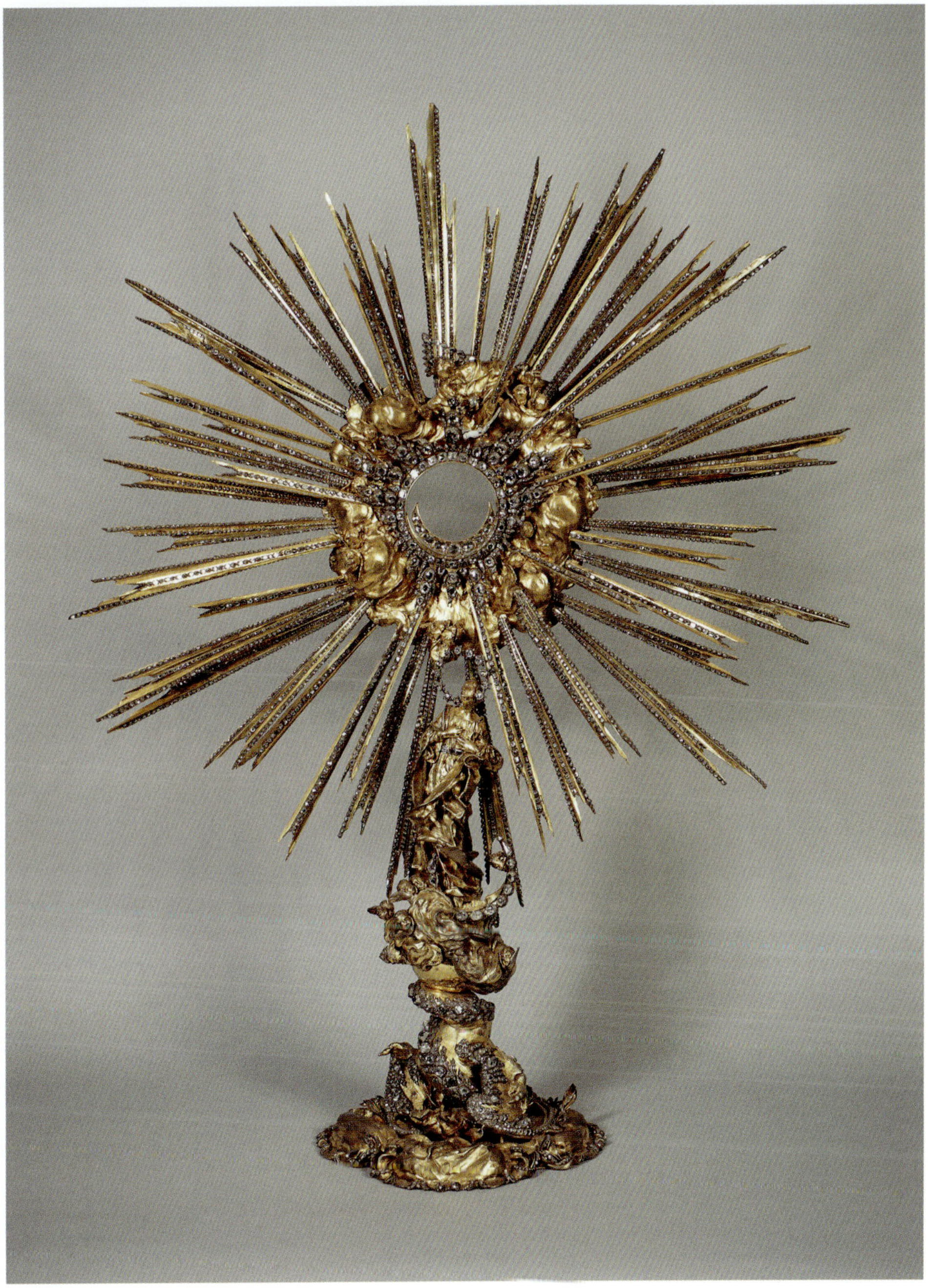

12F/ MONSTRANCE KNOWN
AS THE PRAGUE SUN, 1696–99

The treasury of the Prague Loreto includes a rich set of Baroque decorative arts items. The most famous is a monstrance designed by Johann Bernhard Fischer von Erlach and made by the goldsmith Johann Baptist Känischbauer together with the jeweller Matthias Stegner. It is decorated with 6,222 diamonds which were left to the Loreto in 1695 by Countess Ludmila Eva Františka z Kolowrat.

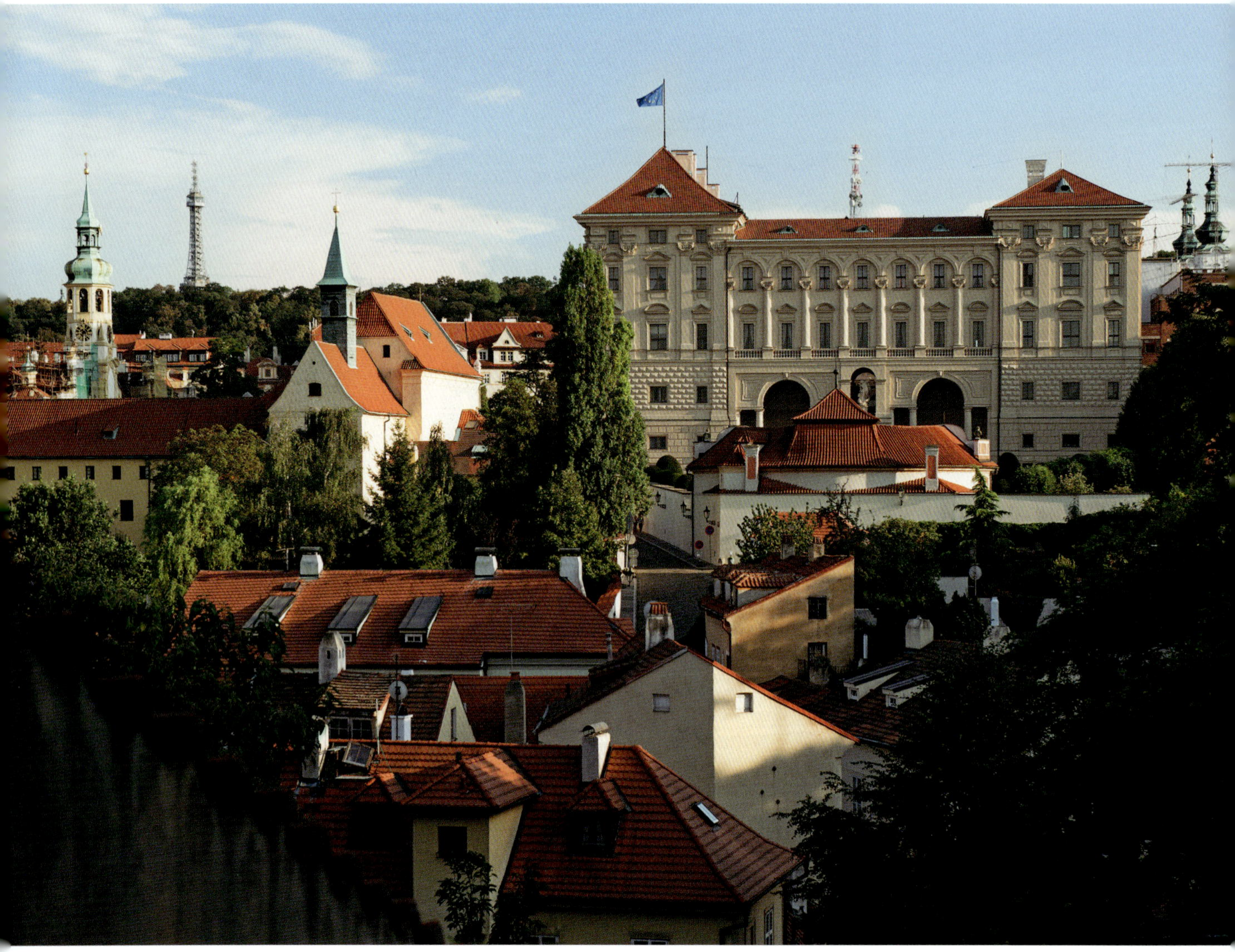

13A/ CZERNIN HOUSE
AS SEEN FROM NOVÝ SVĚT STREET

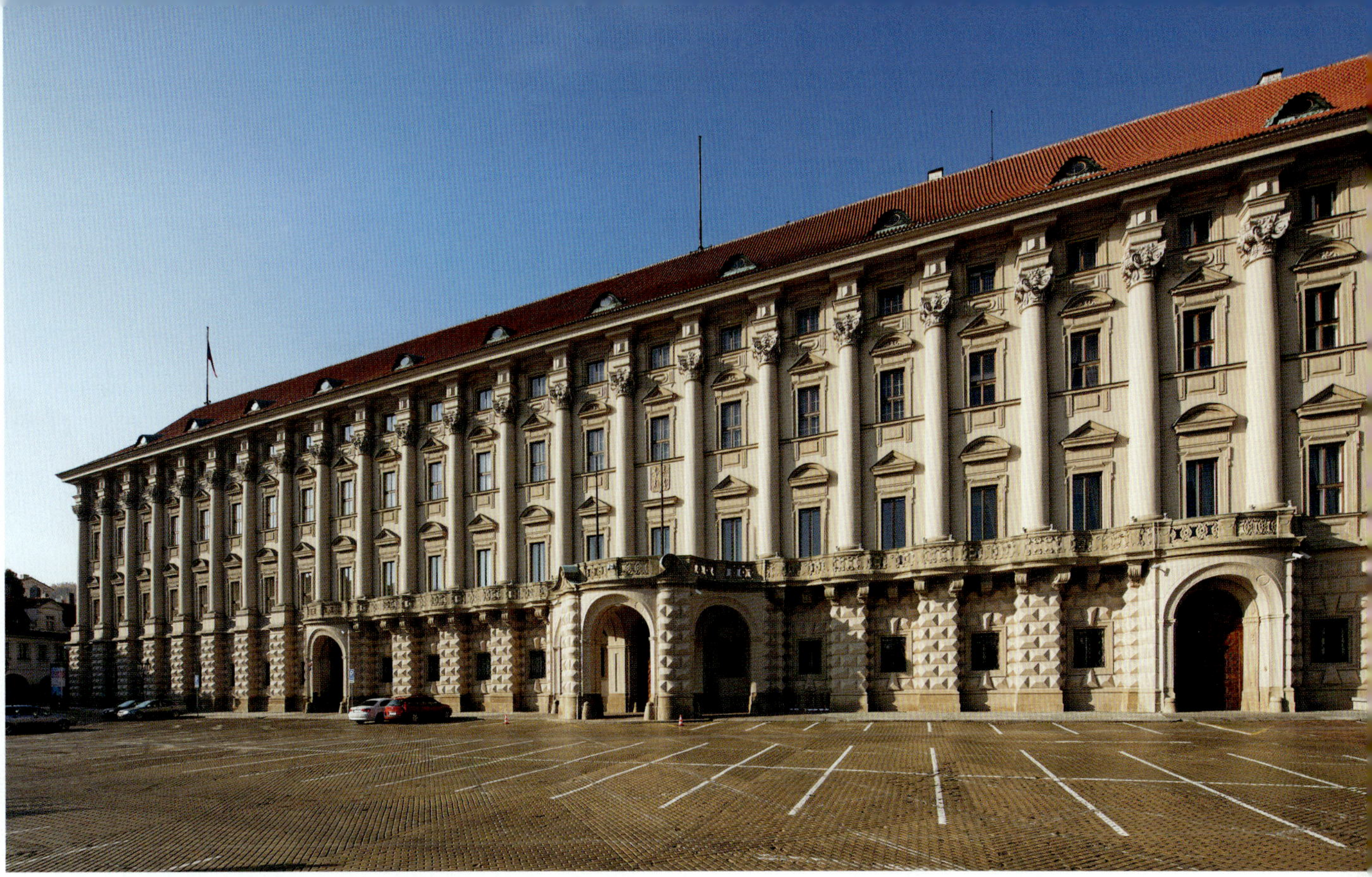

13B/ MAIN FAÇADE

Count Humprecht Johann Czernin von Chudenitz spent a long time searching for a suitable architect for his stately home; among those he approached was, apparently, Gian Lorenzo Bernini. The house was finally built on plans by Francesco Caratti, who entered the service of the count in 1668. By the time of his death in 1677, Caratti was able to get the house at least roughly built, but the decoration of the interiors required additional time, and ultimately Humprecht was unable to enjoy his home very long.
The house included a separate gallery, intended from the start for the installation of the paintings of the outstanding Czernin collection. Other members of the family at first continued to make the house grander, but eventually only invested in its repair. In 1851, the Austrian state bought the building from the Czernins, and turned it into barracks.
The monumental main façade, divided up by striking half-columns on high rusticated bases, adds to the impression made by the whole edifice. Its current appearance is the result of a sensitive remodelling from 1929 to 1934 by Pavel Janák, who adapted the building to the needs of the Czechoslovak Ministry of Foreign Affairs.

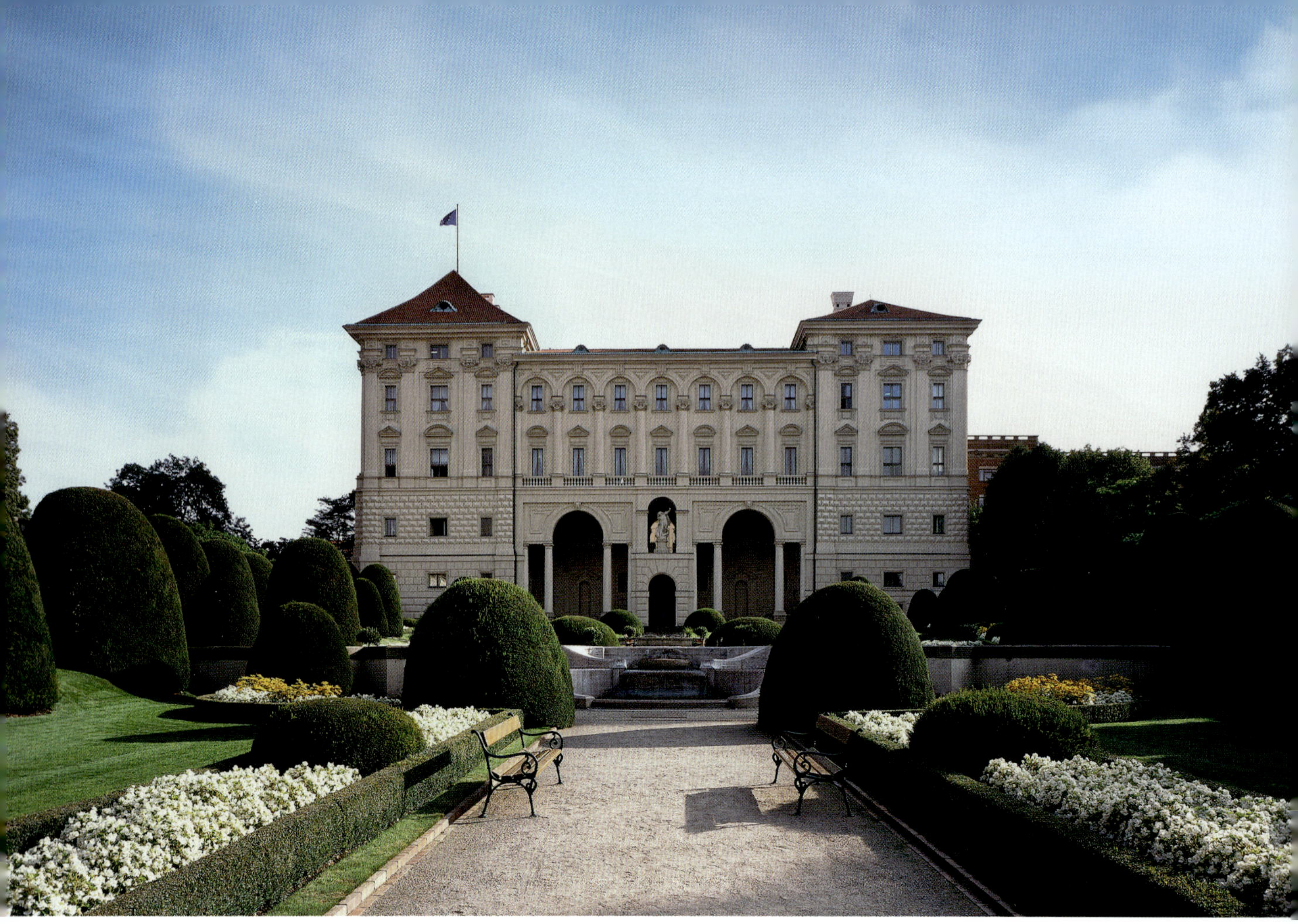

13C/ GARDEN FAÇADE

The façade on the garden side of Czernin House was also designed by Caratti as an imposing *trompe-l'oeil* backdrop, but its conception differs from the austere order of the 'Palladian' main façade. Reminiscent of the architecture of Roman villas, it opens widely into the adjoining garden through two vast sale terrene.

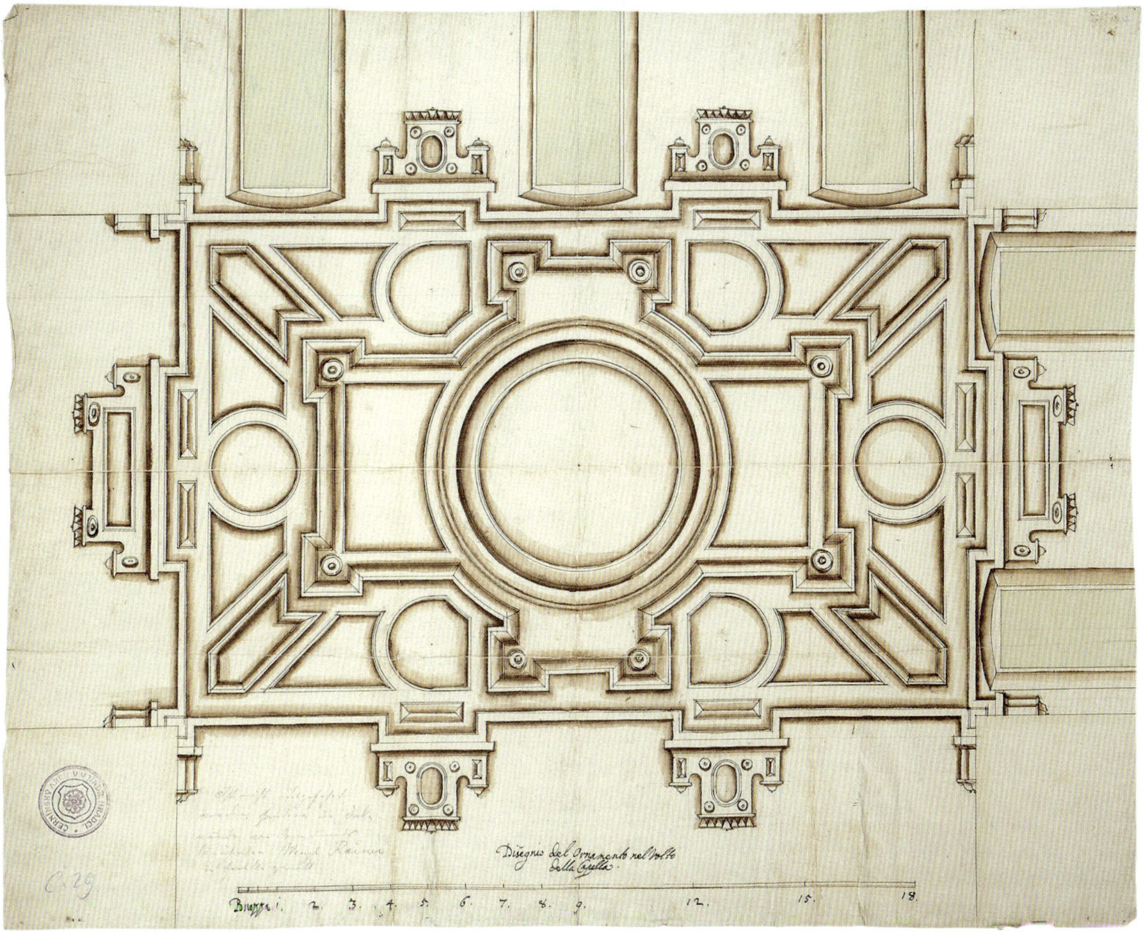

13D/ FRANCESCO CARATTI: DESIGN FOR THE VAULTED CEILING OF THE CHAPEL IN CZERNIN HOUSE, 1675

A large set of original plans has been preserved which make it possible to reconstruct in detail the development of Czernin House. The now no longer extant stucco decoration of the chapel ceiling is shown in this drawing by Caratti. In about 1720 it was removed and a fresco by Wenzel Lorenz Reiner took its place. The fresco in turn ceased to exist when the house was made into barracks in the nineteenth century.

14A/ CHURCH OF ST JOHN NEPOMUCENE AT HRADČANY

In 1701, the Ursuline convent at Hradčany was the scene of the purported miracle involving Theresa Krebs, a girl who fervently prayed to John Nepomucene to heal her atrophied arm. The cure later contributed to the canonization of the venerated martyr. In 1720, however, even before his canonization, the foundation stone was laid for the church that Abbess Maria Theresa, the Countess Berka, ordered to be erected in commemoration of the miracle. The church that was built from 1725 to 1727 owes its appearance to Kilian Ignaz Dientzenhofer. In an interesting way, the façade with three vertical divisions copes with the church being situated on the slope of Hradčany. The sculptural decoration comes from the workshop of Mathias Wenzel Jäckel.

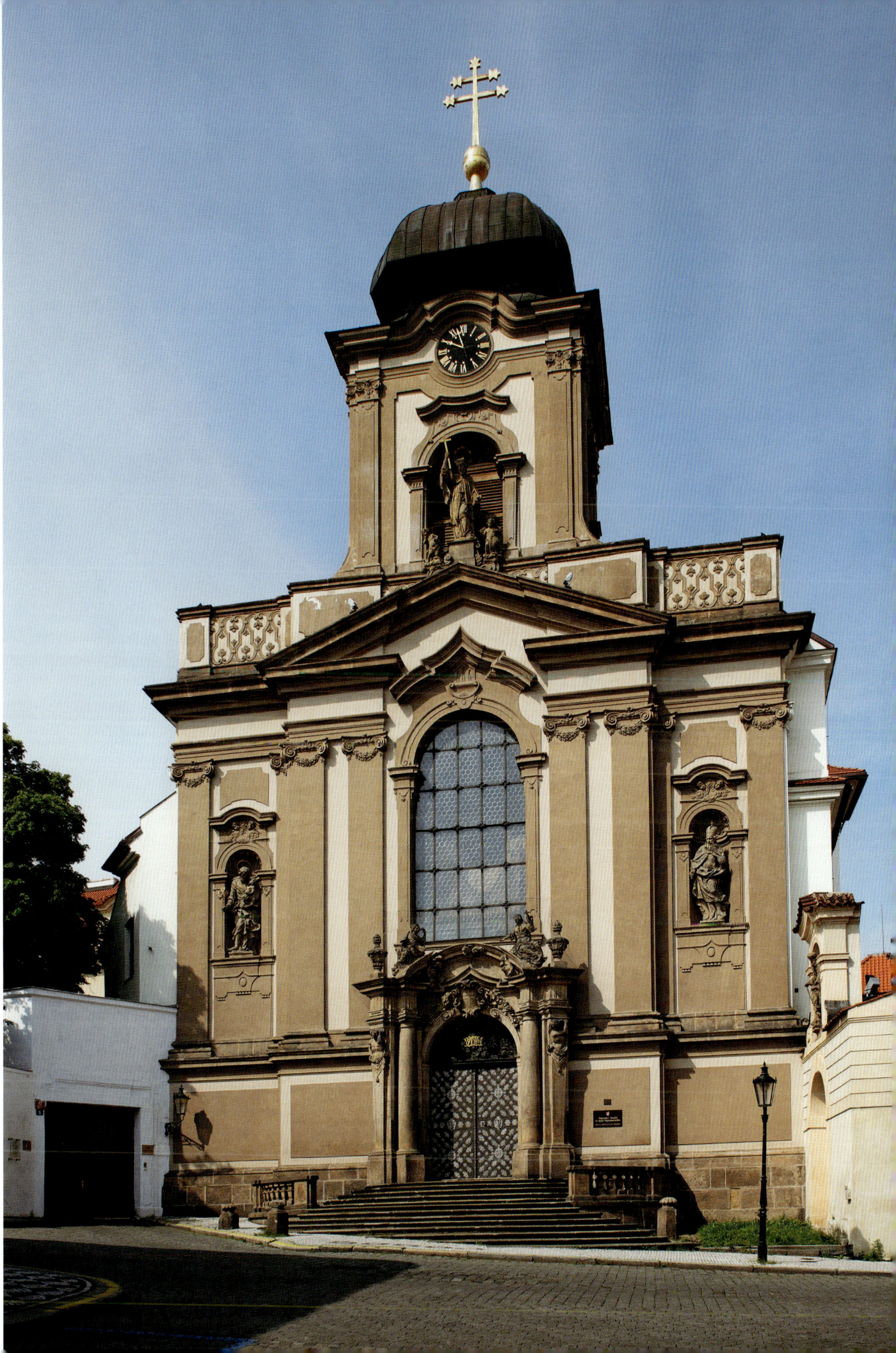

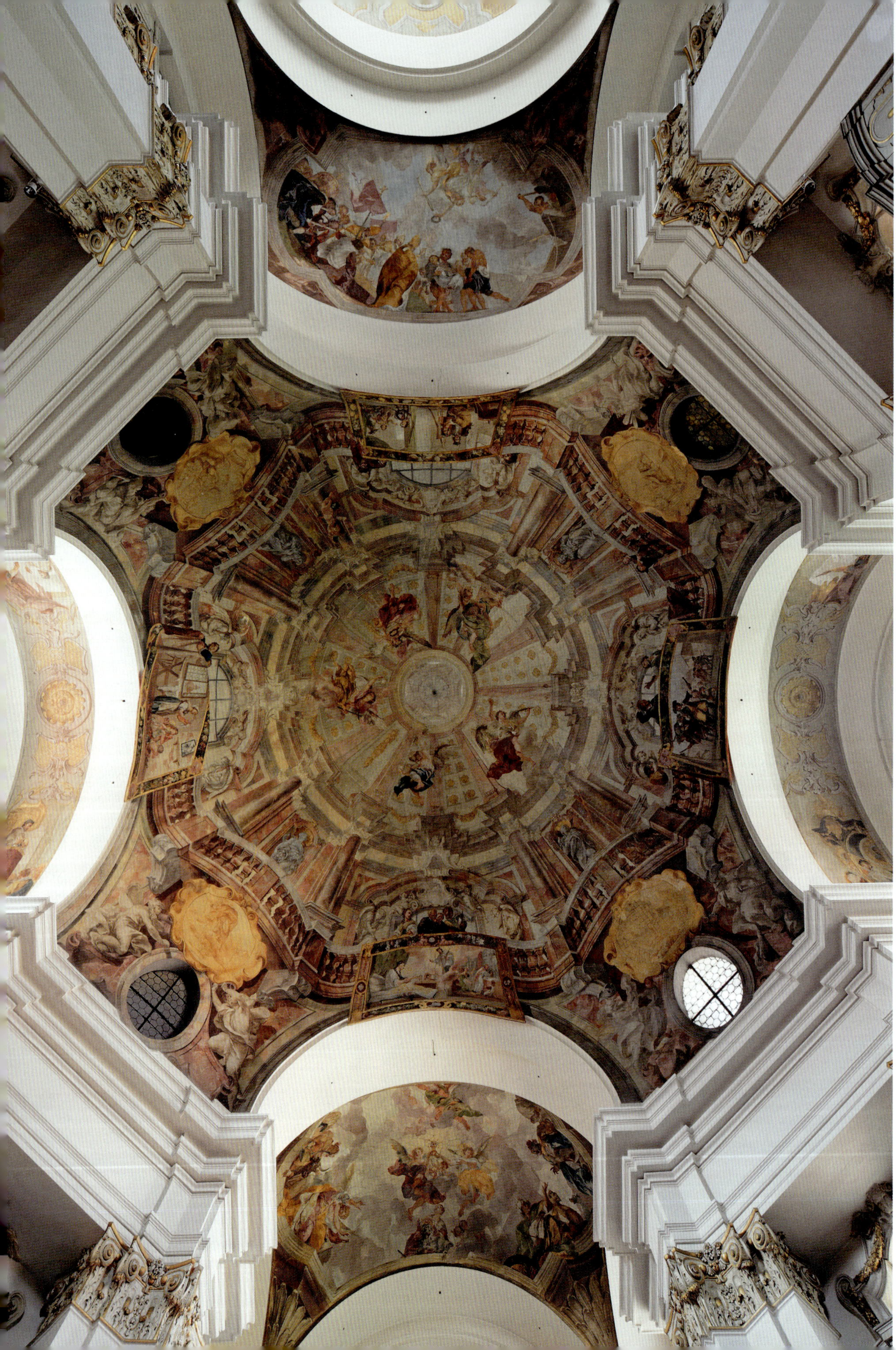

14B–C/ WENZEL LORENZ REINER:
FRESCOS DEPICTING SCENES FROM
THE LIFE, WORKS, AND GLORIFICATION
OF ST JOHN NEPOMUCENE, 1727

The magnificent fresco decoration of the church interior has no parallel in central Europe. The glorification of the revered saint martyred for preserving the secrecy of the confessional is developed here in several layers of meaning. The complex structure of the iconographic programme is based on *trompe-l'oeil* architecture, which is enlivened by allegories and various genre figures. In addition to the 'real' scenes, some parts of the legend of St John Nepomucene are also recalled in the monochrome decoration and in the painted tapestries and statues.

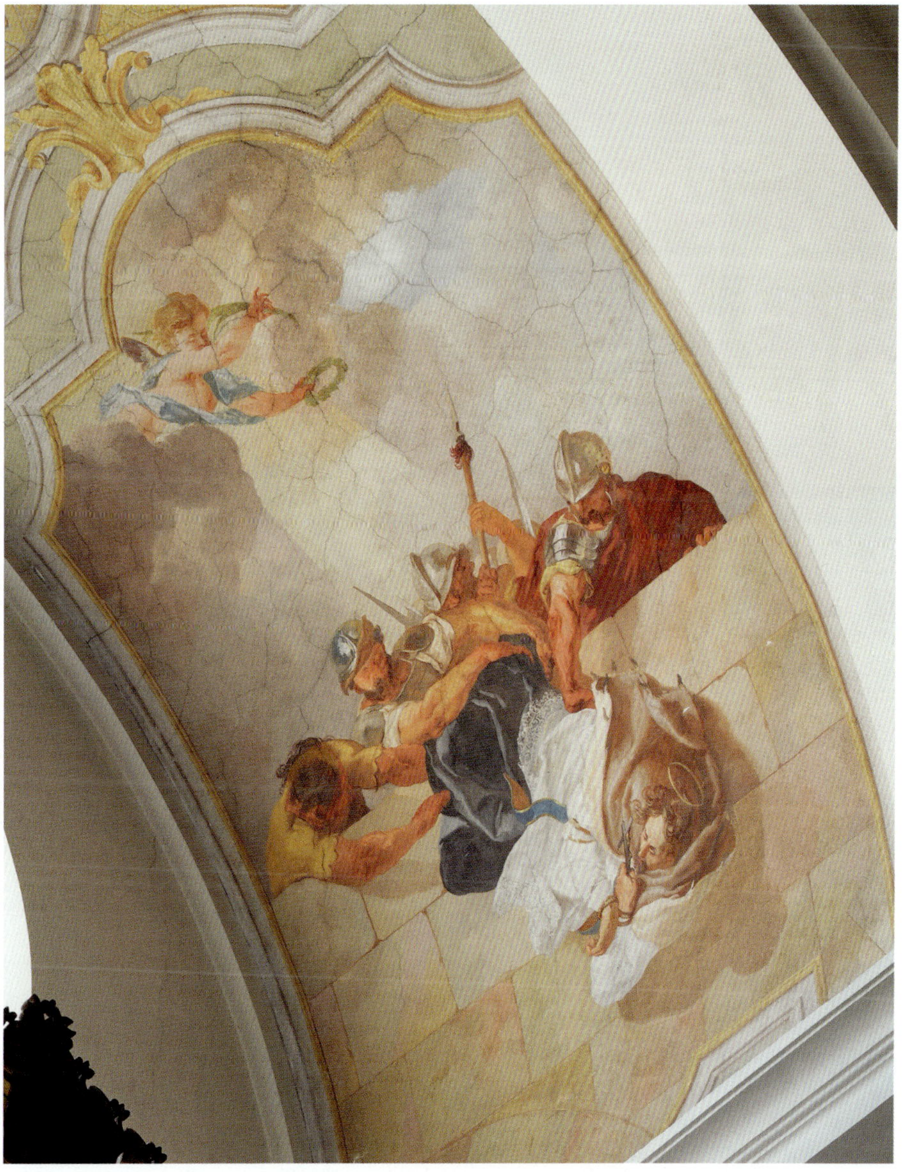

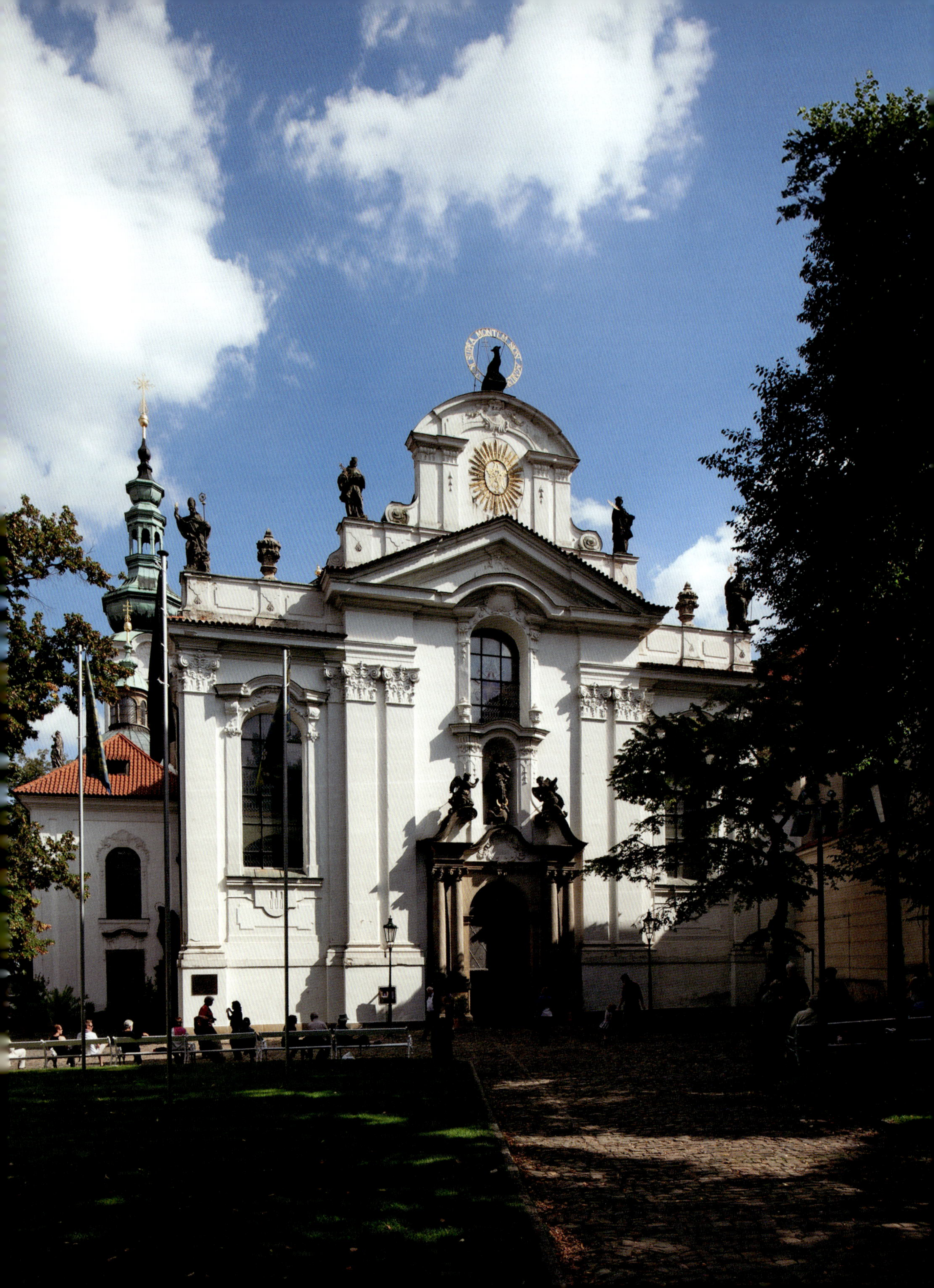

15A–B/ CHURCH OF THE ASSUMPTION

The ancient conventual church of the Strahov Premonstratensians was rebuilt at the beginning of the seventeenth century and given a complete Baroque makeover from 1742 to 1751. After the damages caused by the Prussian siege of Prague, the decoration of the interior continued until the 1770s. The result is the remarkable unified space in which, apart from the altars made with marble of many colours, a sober and solemn Rococo harmony of gold and white is used. The altar architecture was executed by the sculptor in marble Josef Lauermann and the sculptural decoration was supplied by the workshops of Johann Anton Quitainer and Ignaz Franz Platzer (the high altar). The ceiling paintings (1743/44) are by Georg Wilhelm Neunhertz.

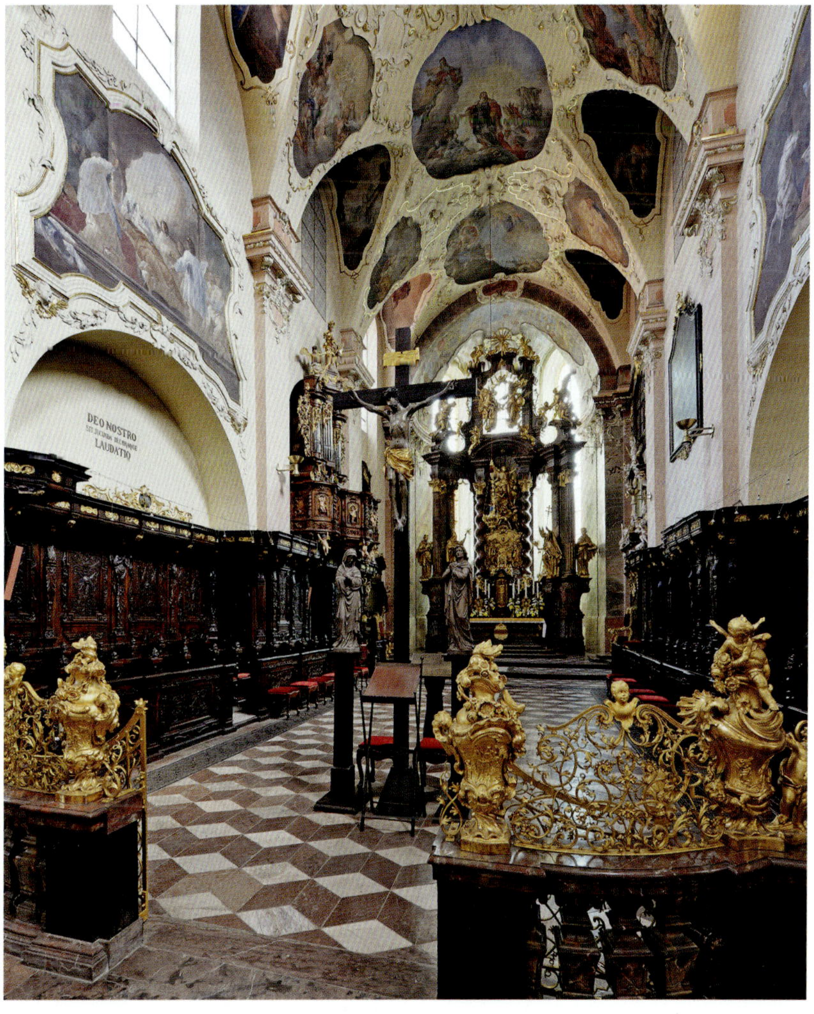

15C/ ALTAR OF ST AUGUSTINE – FRANZ XAVER KARL PALKO: ST AUGUSTINE (BEFORE 1760)
At the seaside, Saint Augustine meets a boy who is pouring seawater into a pit dug in the sand. In this way, he is suggesting to Augustine that his efforts to fathom the mystery of the Holy Trinity are even madder than this. The artist has set the scene in the early evening, employing a range of sophisticatedly muted colours and the harmony of figures and landscape.

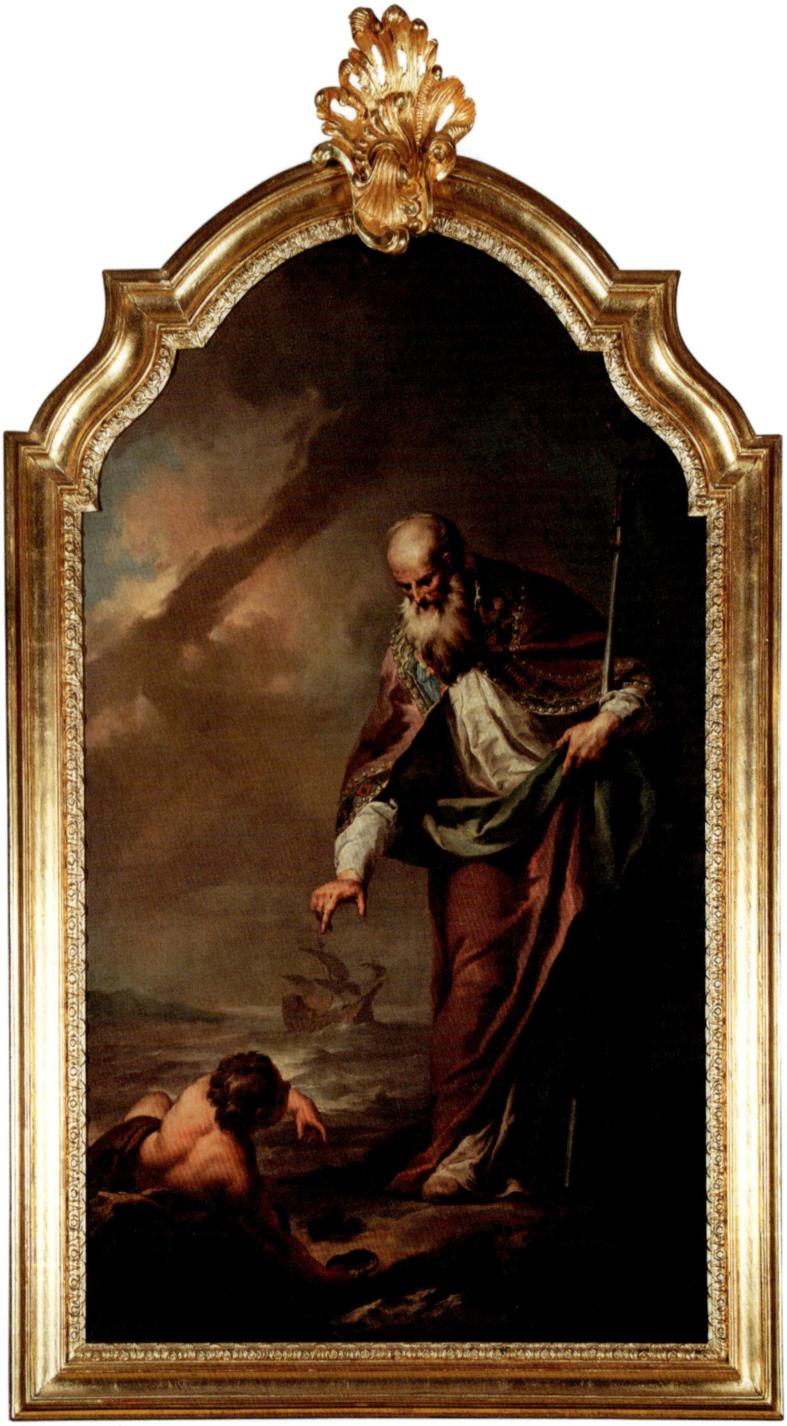

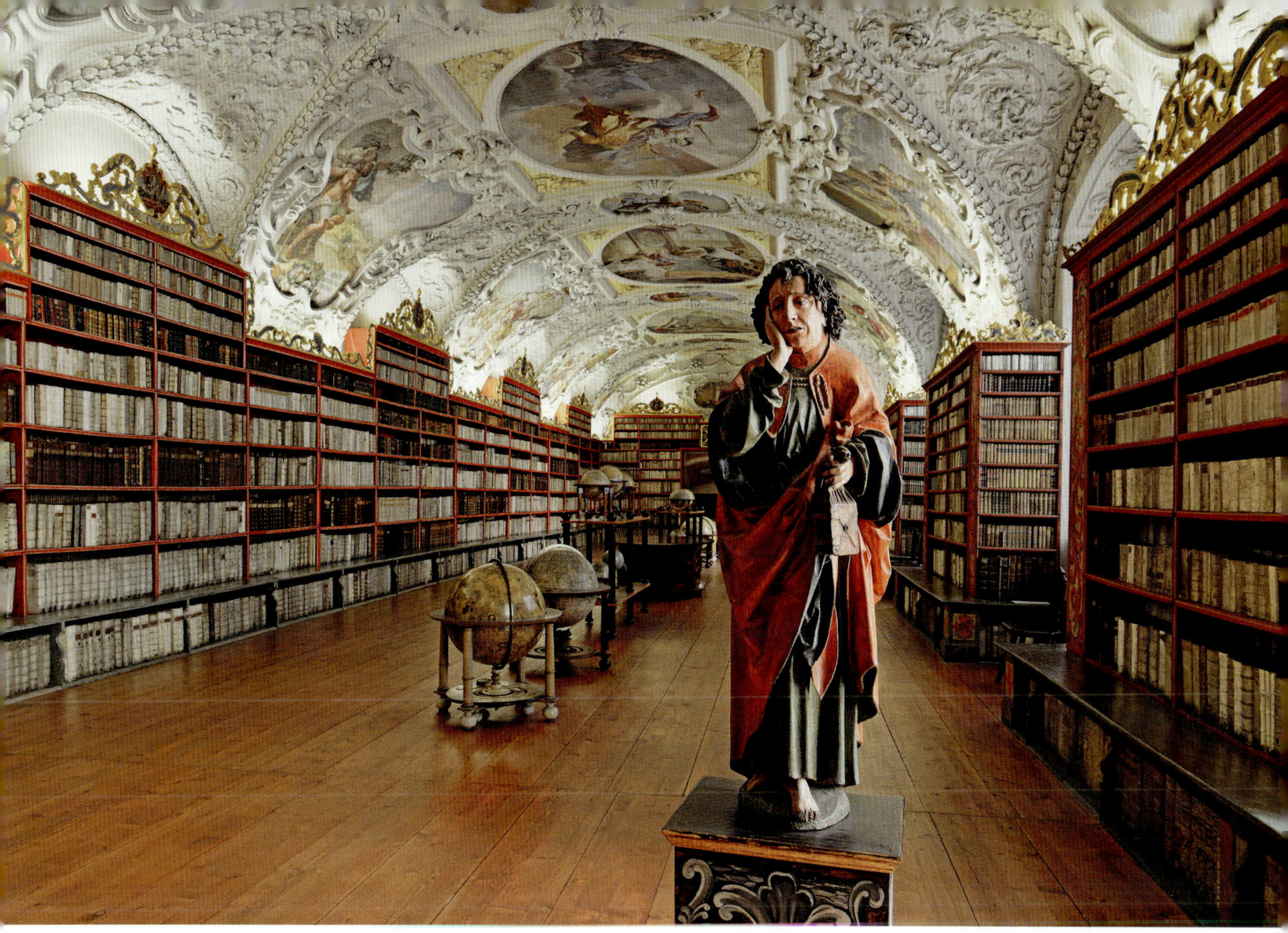

15D/ STRAHOV LIBRARY– THE THEOLOGY ROOM
The library of the Royal Canonry of the Premonstratensians comprises about 200,000 volumes, including illuminated manuscripts and incunabula. As part of the Early Baroque changes made under Abbot Hieronymus Hirnhaim, executed by Giovanni Domenico Orsi, this large library hall was built, from 1671 to 1674, into the upper storey of the west wing of the abbey. Changes were made to it between 1721 and 1727, when the painter Siard Nosecký, a Premonstratensian friar, painted the original richly stuccoed vaulting. The message of the thematically complex series of paintings is the manifestation of true wisdom, which the faithful acquire by fearing God. The furnishings of the Theology Room include a collection of historic globes and a Late Gothic wooden statue of St John the Evangelist.

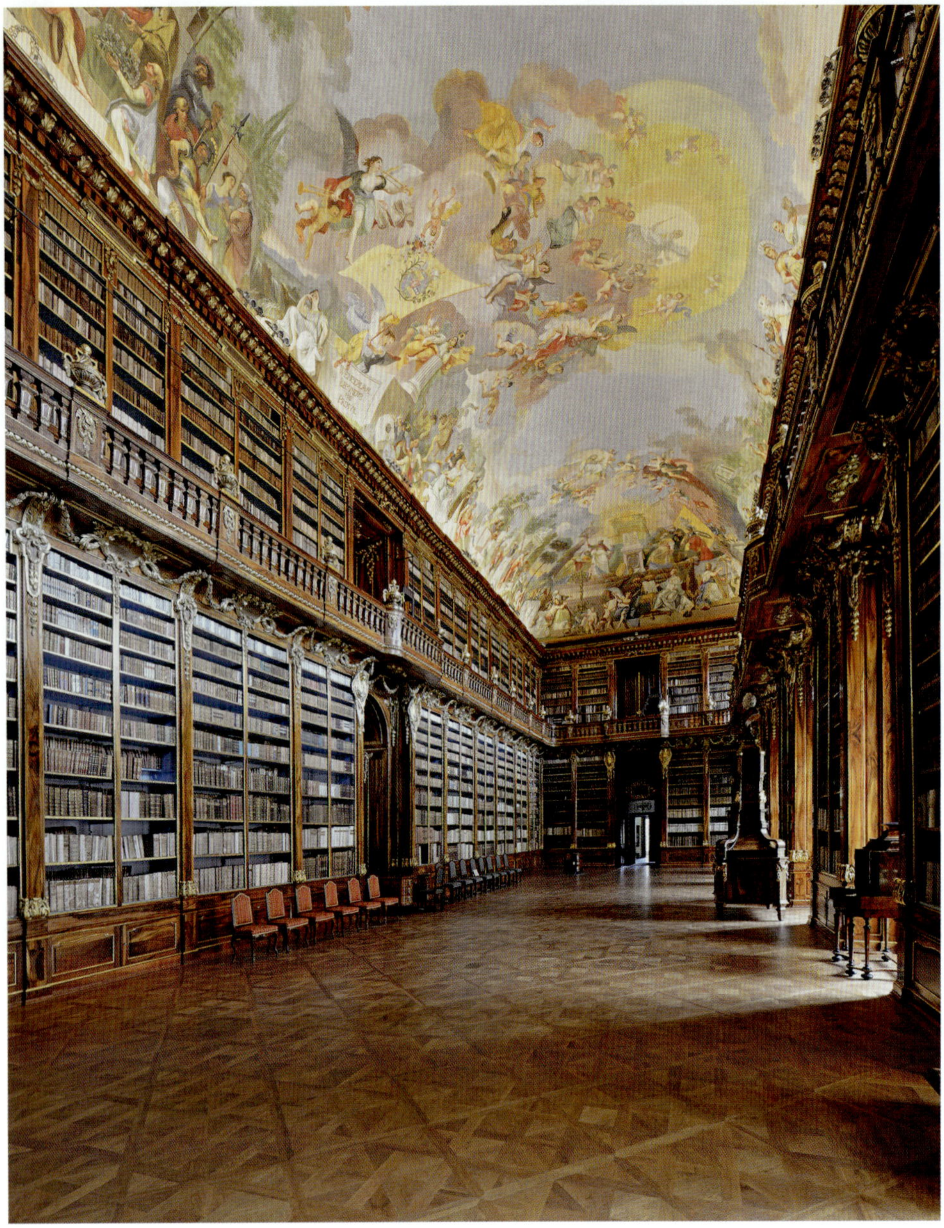

15E/ STRAHOV LIBRARY – THE PHILOSOPHY ROOM

In 1783, the growing collection of books of the Strahov canonry necessitated the conversion of a once Baroque granary into a new library hall. In 1792, the ceiling of this room was made higher to provide space for cabinets of walnut made in 1778 by Johann Lahofer for the Premonstratensian canonry in Louka near Znojmo, south Moravia, which had in the meantime been suppressed. The parquet flooring and wainscotting of the windows were moved to Strahov from the canonry in Louka. The ceiling of the hall is decorated with a fresco, *Man's Spiritual Evolution* (1794), by the renowned Austrian painter Franz Anton Maulbertsch. With this work, following on from a painting on the same theme in Louka, Baroque fresco painting in Prague symbolically came to an end.

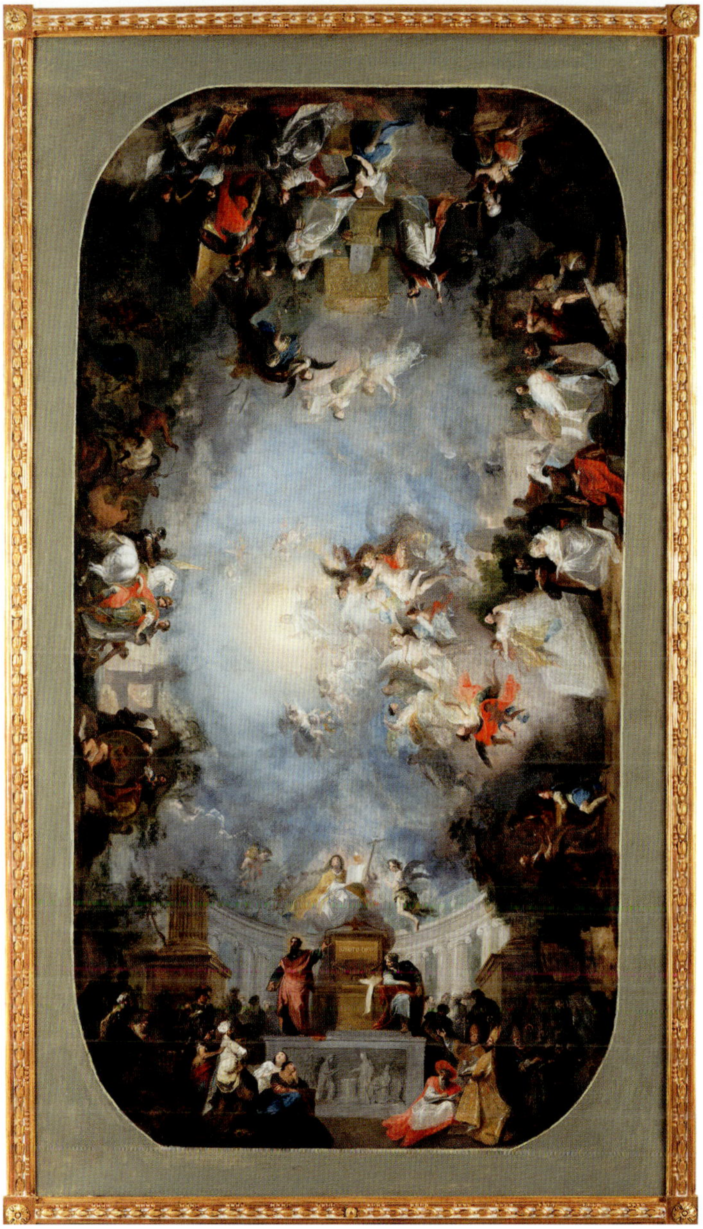

15F/ FRANZ ANTON MAULBERTSCH: MAN'S SPIRITUAL EVOLUTION, A MODELLO FOR THE PHILOSOPHY ROOM FRESCO, 1793–94
In many places, the fresco in the Philosophy Room reveals that the seventy-year-old painter's physical strength was diminishing, which is why part of the work was executed by his assistant Martin Michl. None the less, the modello in Maulbertsch's own hand is a masterpiece, and met with the admiration of his contemporaries. The subject matter of the highly developed composition takes place between two poles, represented on the two narrow sides by evocations of the Old and the New Testament. Man's spiritual evolution in the conception is represented here by the key scenes and selected biblical and classical figures, but the work also includes Bohemian patron saints and critical contemporary allusions to the Encyclopédistes (though not present in the sketch, they do appear in the actual fresco).

16/ THE STONE COLUMN
(U KAMENNÉHO SLOUPU), HOUSE SIGN

The house called U Kamenného sloupu (the Stone Column) in Úvoz street was bought in 1697 by the painter and woodcarver Christian Luna, who that same year made the little wooden sculpture of Mary the Immaculate, imitating Bendl's original on the Marian column on Old Town Square. In 1706, he placed it on a stone Corinthian column which he had attached to the façade of his house, and added a chronogram (LAPIDEA COLVMNA = L+I+D+ C+L+V+M = 1706). On each corner of the façade is an allegorical bust, Luna and Sol (Moon and Sun), an allusion to the name of the owner.

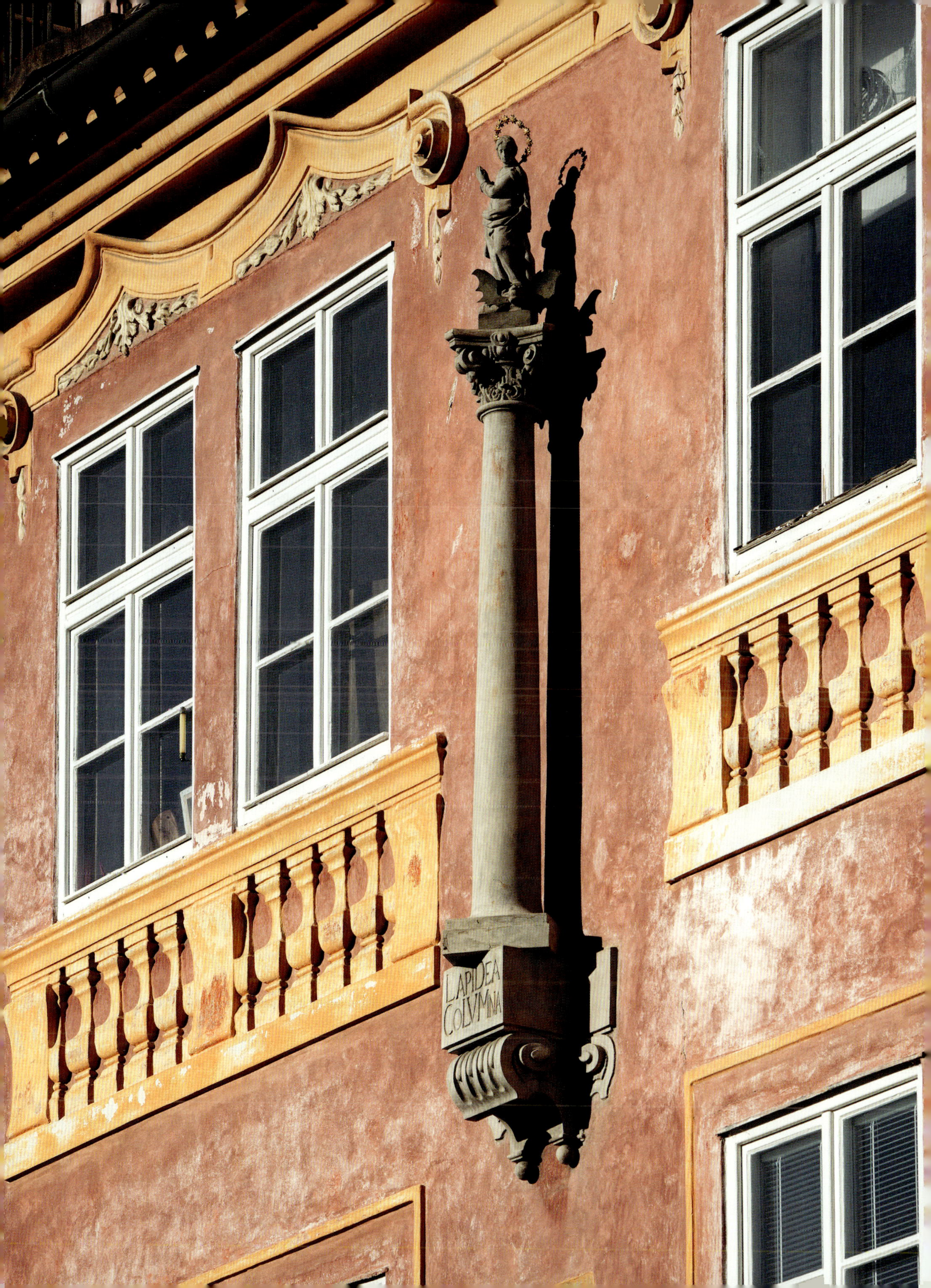
LAPIDEA
COLVMNA

17/ OUR LADY OF PERPETUAL HELP AND ST CAJETAN (OUR LADY OF PROVIDENCE / PANNY MARIE POD OCHRANOU BOŽSKÉ PROZŘETELNOSTI, 1691–1717)

The Theatine college in the Lesser Town was built on the initiative of Count Bernhard Ignaz von Martinitz in the late 1660s and early 1670s. The original plans for its conventual church were drawn up in 1679 by a member of the Theatine order, Guarino Guarini, one of the most distinguished architects of the dynamic Italian Baroque style. Construction work on the church on the steep slope of Ostruhová ulice (today's Nerudova ulice) did not begin, however, until 1691, perhaps on plans by Jean-Baptiste Mathey. In a later phase, the appearance of the building was changed by Johann Blasius Santini-Aichl, who is widely assumed to have been Mathey's pupil.

With five vertical divisions, the façade is probably Mathey's work; Santini is credited not only with modifications to the windows, but also, in particular, with the design of the main portal, which has a striking voussoir-shaped decoration at the top.

The interior of the church is more clearly the work of the younger of the two architects, Santini. He added dynamism to the originally static ground plan on a Greek cross by adding the spatial field and chancel apse and by inserting bevelled lateral fields into the front wall of the transepts. The passageways between the individual spaces acquired 'gothicizing' Santini-esque jambs. Of the art works in the church, Franz Xaver Karl Palko's painting of St Tecla (after 1760) and Michael Wenzel Halbax's marble altar of the Holy Family with the altarpiece (1707) merit particular attention.

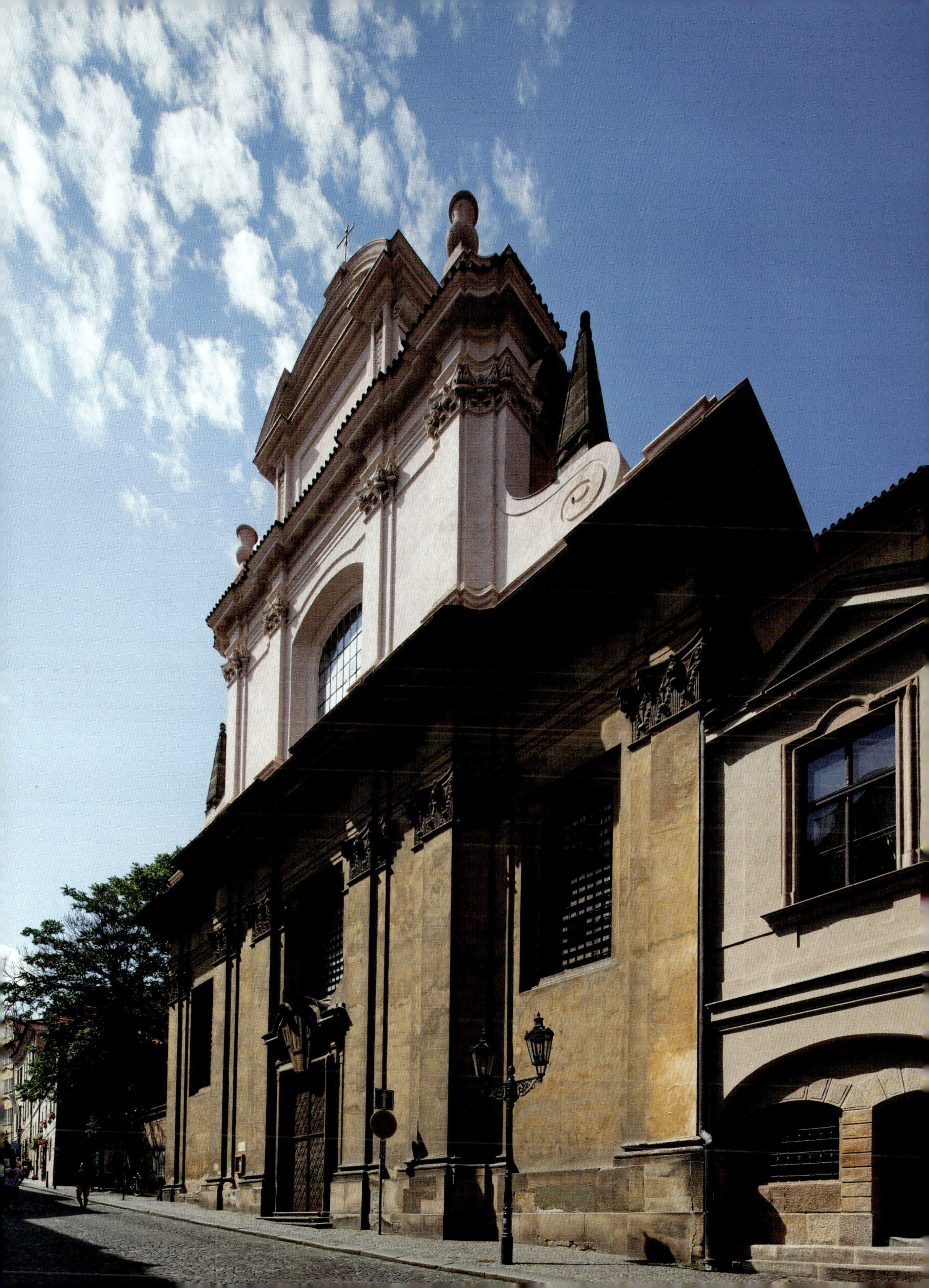

18/ KOLOWRAT HOUSE (AKA THUN HOUSE) (KOLOWRATSKÝ PALÁC, AKA THUNOVSKÝ PALÁC)

Count Kolowrat acquired this plot for his new Prague residence together with the neighbouring Slavata House after the Slavata line died out in 1693. The massive new Baroque building was designed by Johann Blasius Santini-Aichl, who was first mentioned in this connection in the archive records in 1706. The construction work was carried out from 1716 to 1721. The main entrance to the house is guarded by two huge eagles with their wings spread – heraldic emblems of the Kolowrat coat of arms. They were made by the workshop of Matthias Bernhard Braun, which also supplied the statues of the classical gods Jupiter and Juno on the cornice above the portal. Today, the building houses the Italian Embassy.

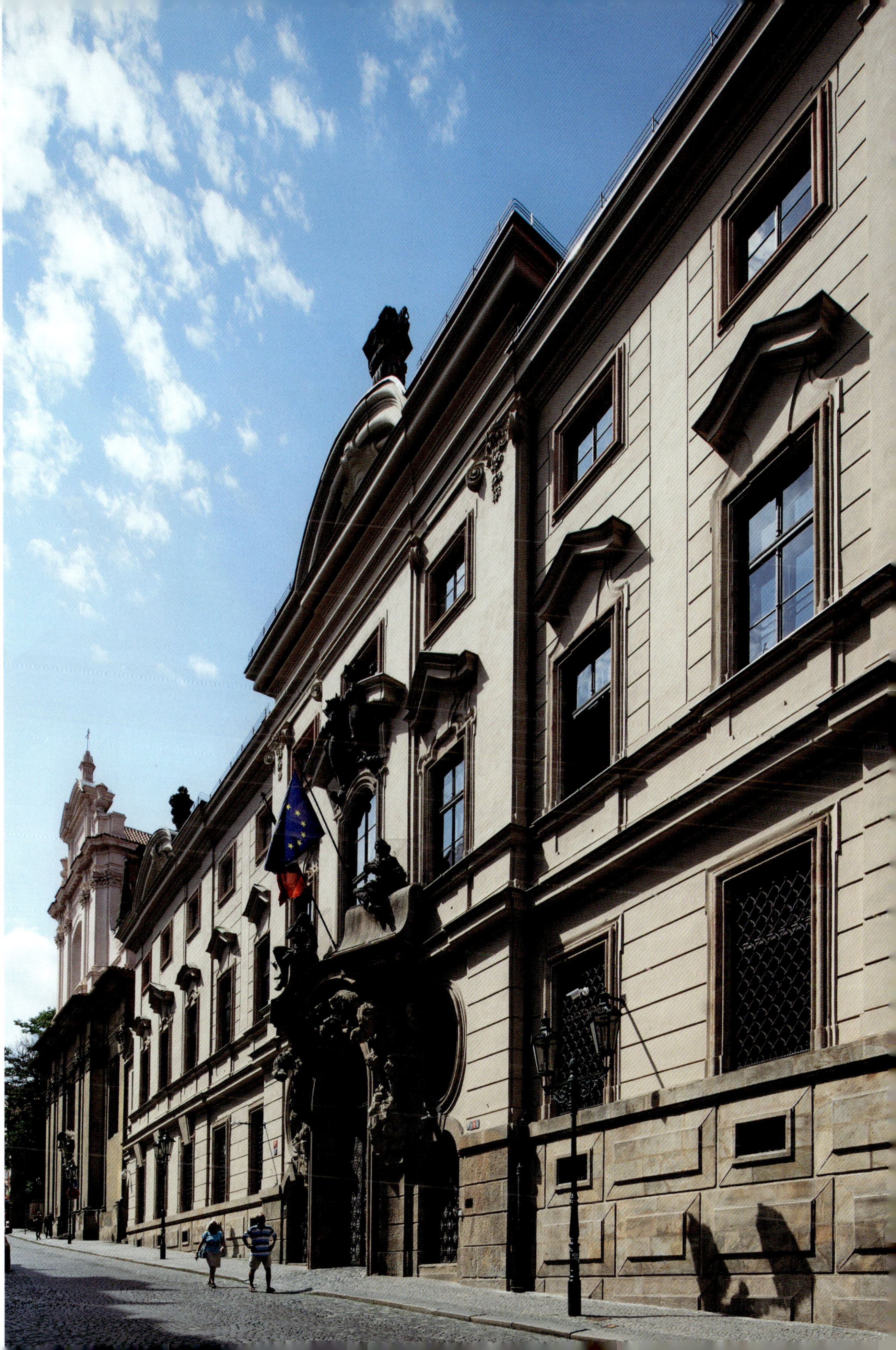

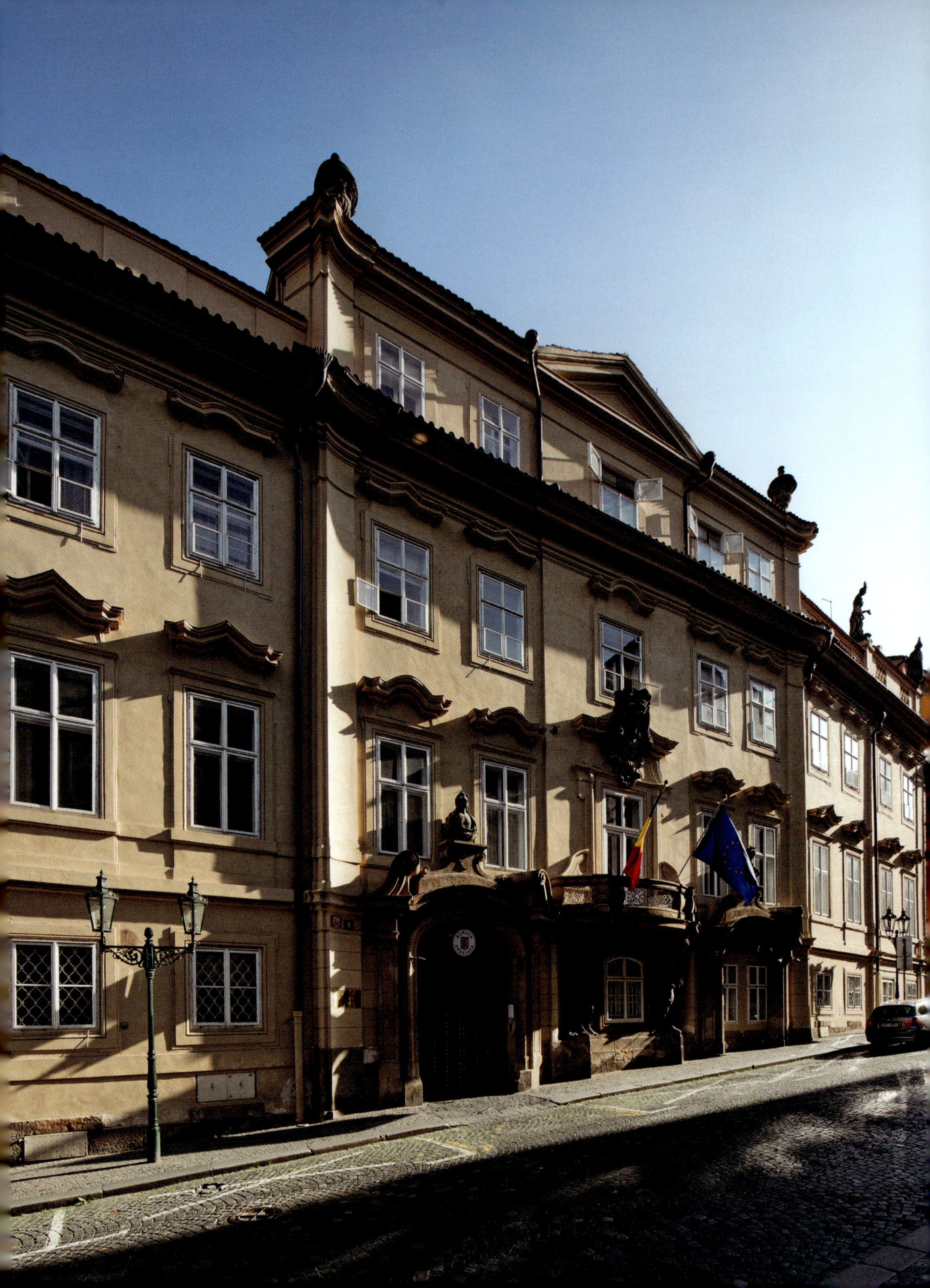

19/ MORZIN HOUSE (MORZINSKÝ PALÁC)
In 1713–14, Count Wenzel Morzin joined together four earlier houses in what is today Nerudova ulice to create this great edifice. His architect, most likely Johann Blasius Santini-Aichel, visually lightened the main façade by piercing it with two carriage entrances, of which only the one on the left is functional (the other has been made into windows). Between them, he placed a central balcony borne by figures of two muscular African men, which were made in 1714 by Ferdinand Brokoff. In addition to these atlantes, recalling the heraldic figures on the Morzin coat of arms, the Brokoff workshop supplied the allegories of the Continents on the attic and the lyrical busts of women representing Day and Night. The house is currently the Romanian Embassy.

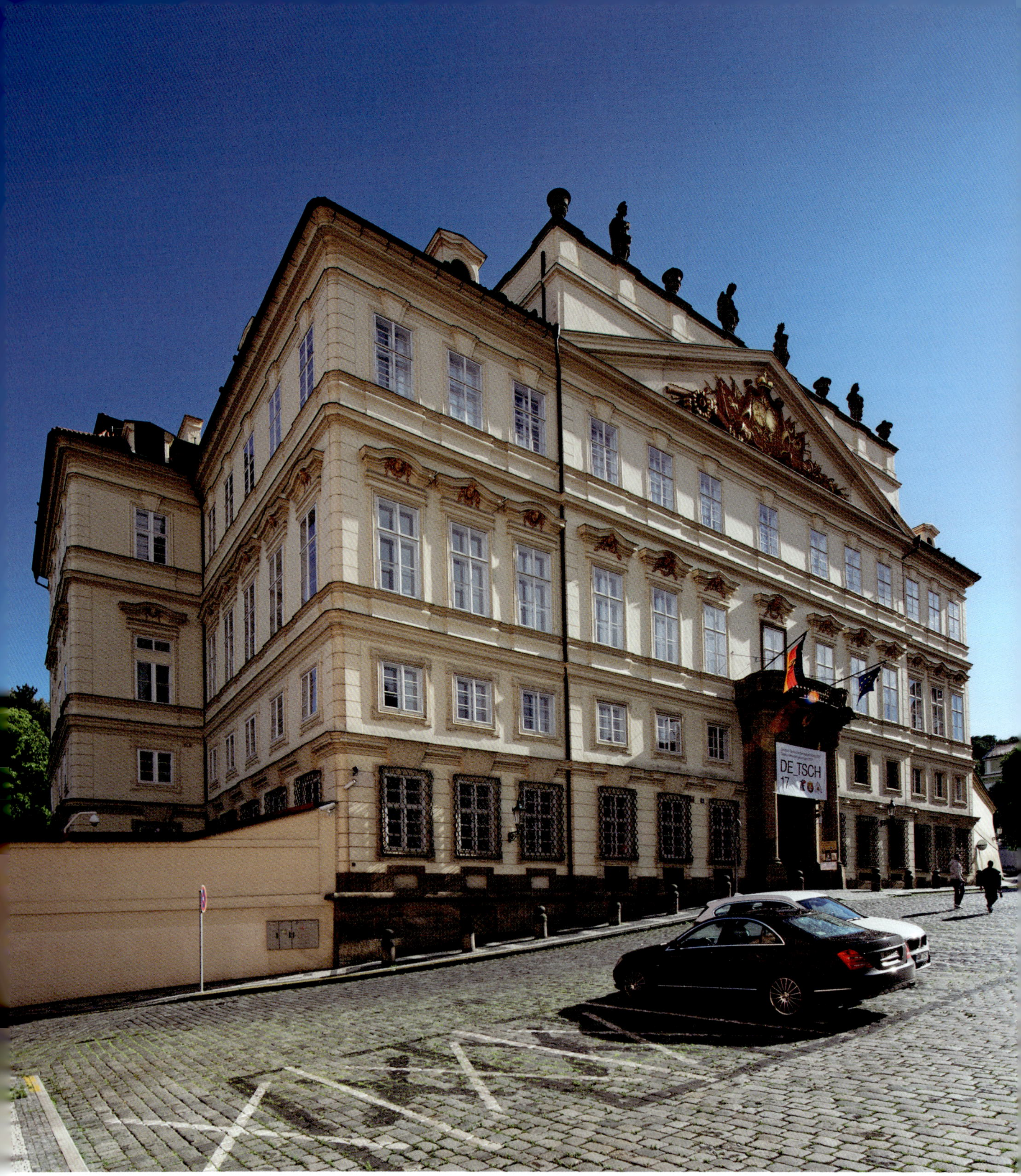
DE_TSCH
17

20/ LOBKOWICZ HOUSE (PŘEHOŘOVSKÝ HOUSE)

At the foot of Petřín hill, on the former vineyards of the Premonstratensians of Strahov, Count František Karel Přehořovský z Kvasejovic, Master of the Mint of the Bohemian Kingdom, built his High Baroque residence from 1702 to 1707. The plans were most likely by the Vienna-influenced architect Giovanni Battista Alliprandi, and the exceptional stucco decoration was made by Tommaso Soldati. Count Přehořovský was forced to sell the house at auction in 1717. In 1753, it became the property of the Lobkowicz family, who owned it until 1927. Today, it is the German Embassy.

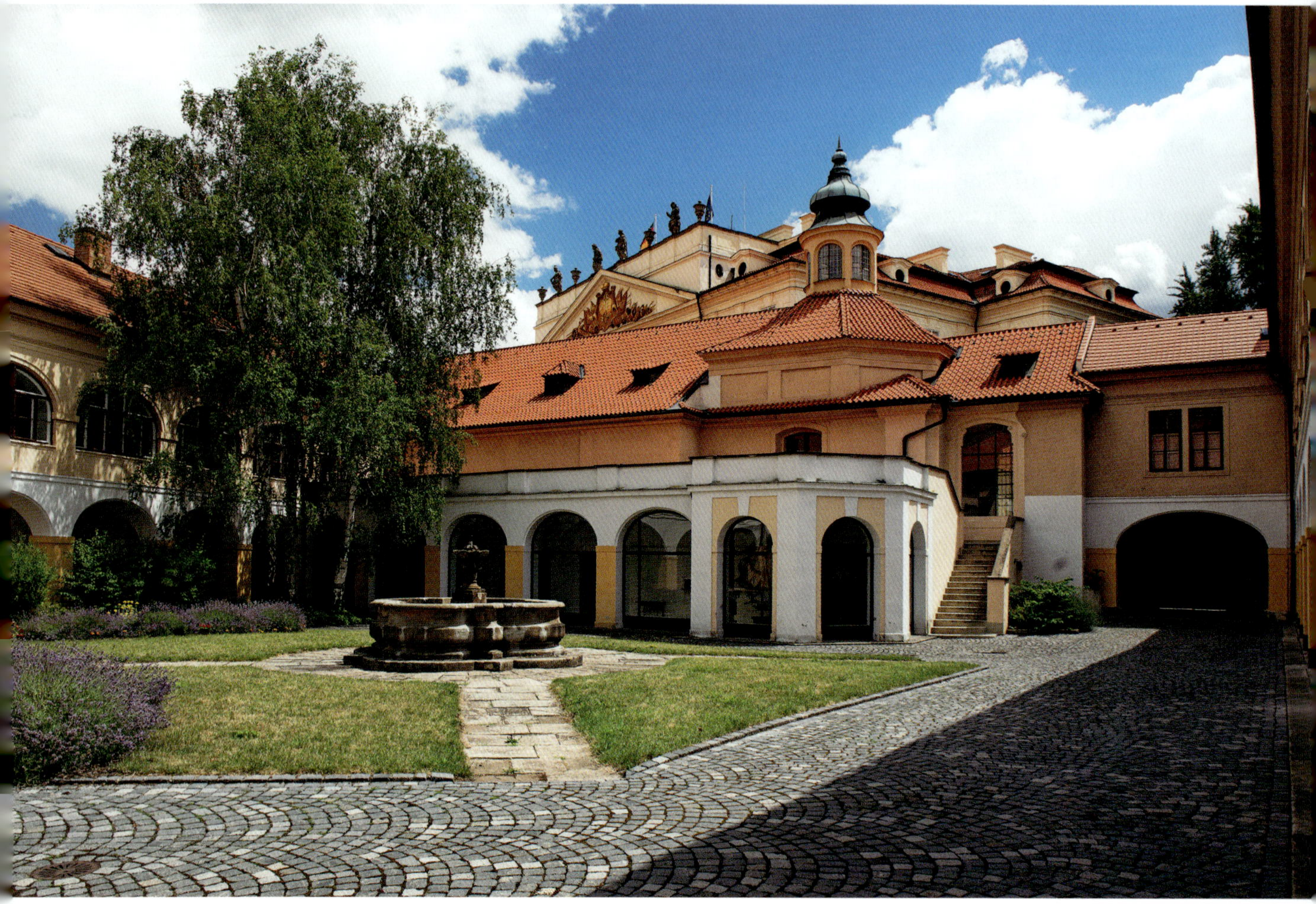

21A–B/ ITALIAN HOSPICE AND CHAPEL OF ST MARY AND ST CHARLES BORROMEO (P. MARIE A SV. KARLA BOROMEJSKÉHO)

The Italian community in early modern Prague was a colourful mixture of merchants, craftsmen, clergy, artists, and others employed by the monarch's court and the upper classes. Faithful to the Roman Catholic Church, they met in the Marian congregation of the Jesuit College in the Old Town. It was there that the idea first emerged to build an *ospedale,* a charitable institution for orphaned and sick members of the community. During the first half of the seventeenth century, a large area was built below Petřín Hill, which included a hospital, an orphanage, a church, a school, a garden, a cemetery, a brewery, and a tailor's shop. The church was dedicated to the Blessed Virgin Mary and to the Archbishop of Milan St Charles Borromeo, venerated as a protector against the plague. The church includes the greater part of the south wing along Vlašská ulice.

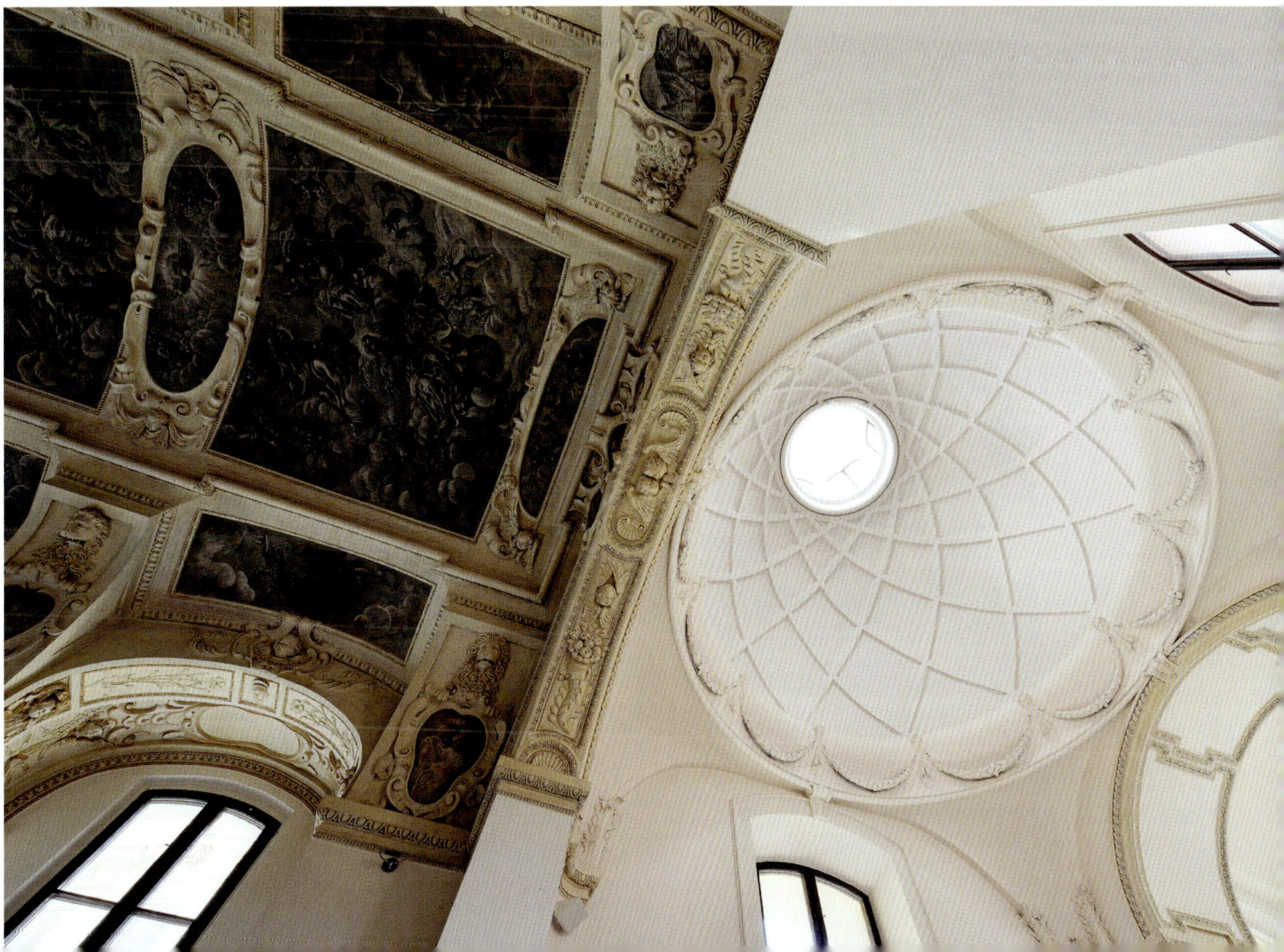

21c/ KAREL ŠKRÉTA: ST CHARLES BORROMEO VISITING PLAGUE SUFFERERS IN MILAN, 1647, Národní galerie v Praze

This canvas for the high altar of the church in the Italian Hospice (Vlašský špitál) was commissioned by Antonio Cassini, a member of the Italian congregation, from Karel Škréta, the most famous Prague painter at that time. In this scene of the plague infirmary, Škréta displays his mastery of composition and applies his knowledge of contemporary Neapolitan, Roman, and Bolognese painting. It is a kind of 'altar in an altar': the central idea of the composition is the depiction of an icon of the Blessed Virgin Mary adored by three virgin martyrs – Lucy, Agatha, and Barbara. The artist has depicted himself as the male figure to the right of St Charles.

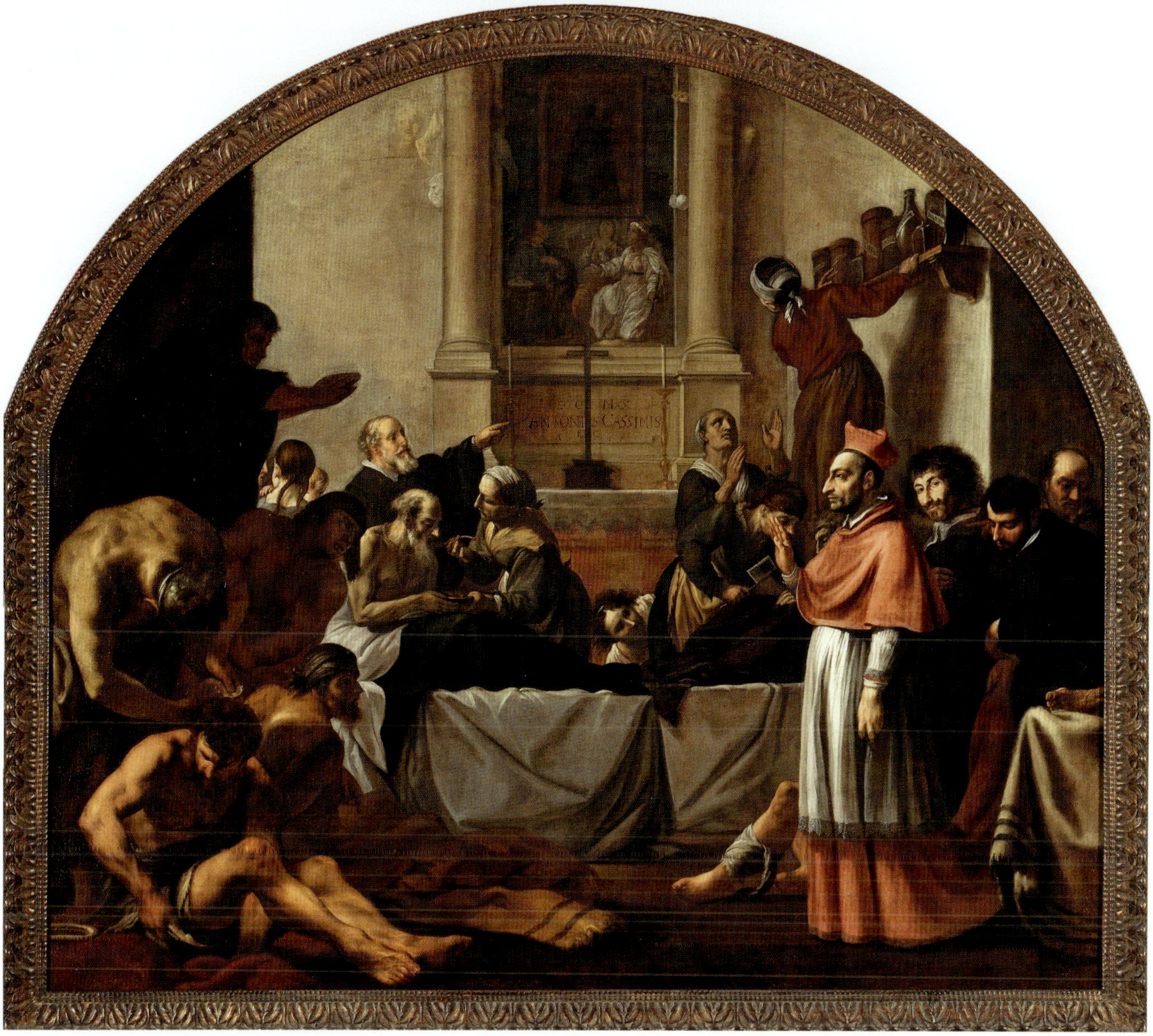
ANTONIVS CASSINIS

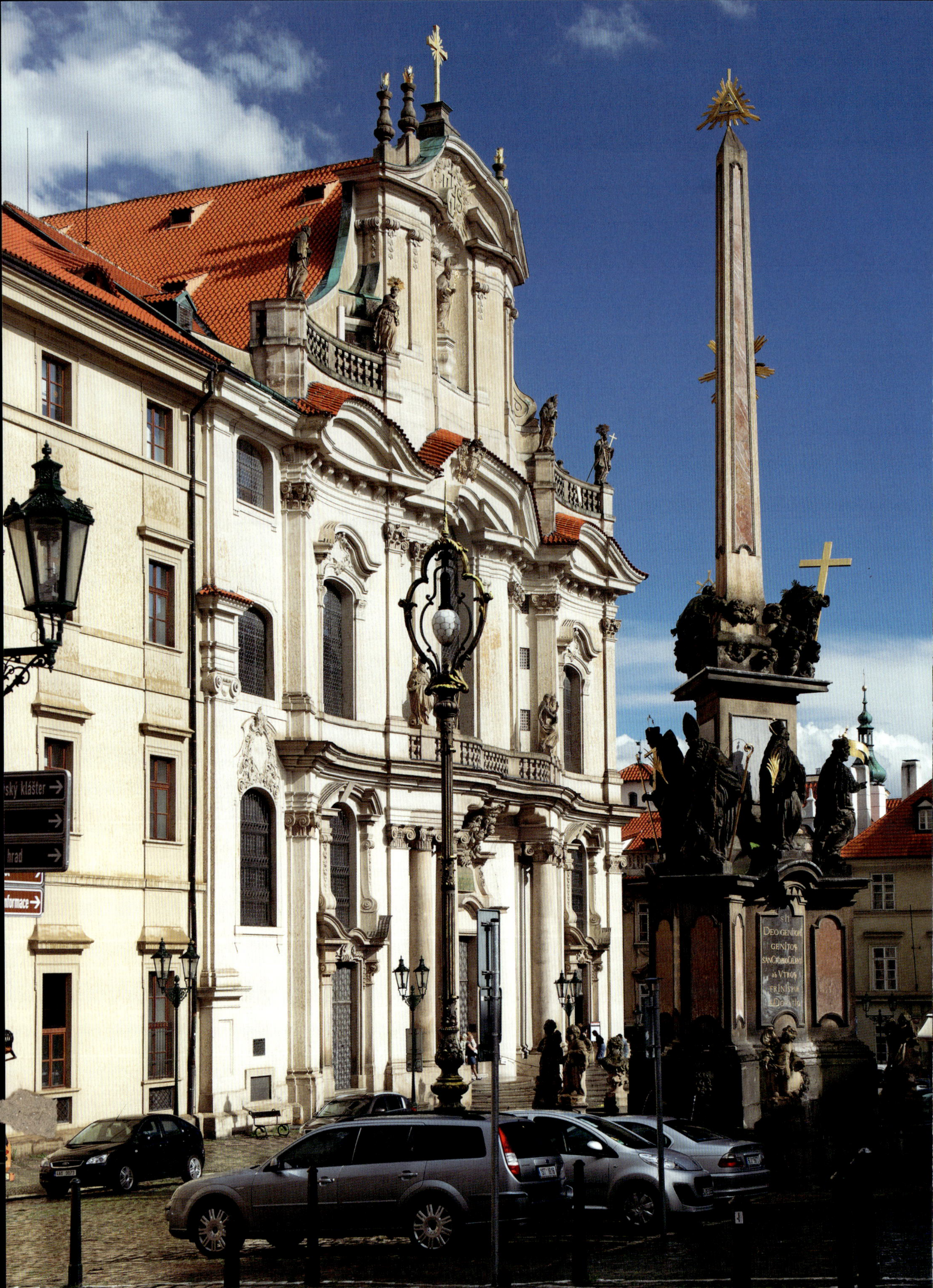

hrad

22/ CHURCH OF ST NICHOLAS (SV. MIKULÁŠE) IN THE LESSER TOWN

22A/ MAIN FAÇADE

This High Baroque church is, in its current form, the work of Christoph Dientzenhofer and his son Kilian Ignaz. Commissioned by the Jesuits who ran the adjacent professed house, it was built, with pauses, from 1702 to 1752. Churches dedicated to St Nicholas and St Wenceslas had stood on this site since the Middle Ages. The monumental west façade of the current church dates from 1702 to 1711. Here, Christoph Dientzenhofer has used the motif of convex-concave undulating walls, characteristic of the so-called radical group of Bohemian Baroque buildings. The inscription and coat of arms above the portal commemorate Count Franz Karel Kolowrat-Libsteinsky's funding of the building.

22B–C/ INTERIOR

The vaulted ceiling of the nave, altered after the Prussian bombardment of 1757, is decorated with a *trompe-l'oeil* fresco (1760/61) by Johann Lucas Kracker, depicting scenes from the life of St Nicholas and his glorification. In the crossing of the church there are four gigantic classicizing statues of the Fathers of the Eastern Church: St Cyril of Alexandria (here replacing St Athanasius), St John Chrysostom, St Gregory of Nazianzus, and St Basil of Caesarea (Basil the Great). These statues, made in 1769, come from the workshop of Ignaz Franz Platzer. Though they seem to be made of marble, they are in fact wood that has been painted white and gilded. Above them opens the view into the cupola, which is decorated with a fresco by Franz Xaver Karl Palko, made after 1752. Here, as he enters heaven, St Nicholas is welcomed by Christ, and is glorified by hosts of saints and angels.

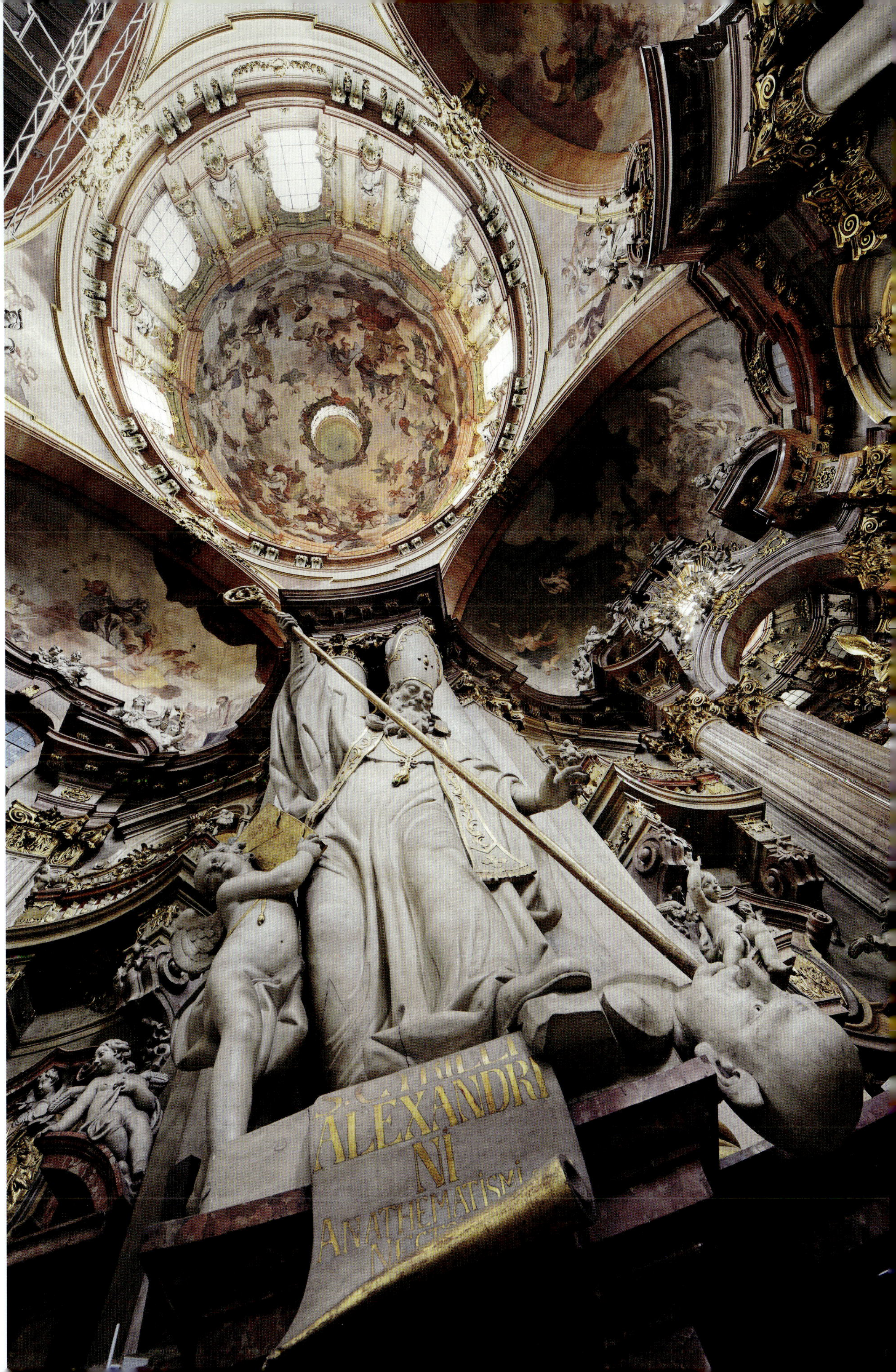
ALEXANDRI
NI
ANATHEMATISMI

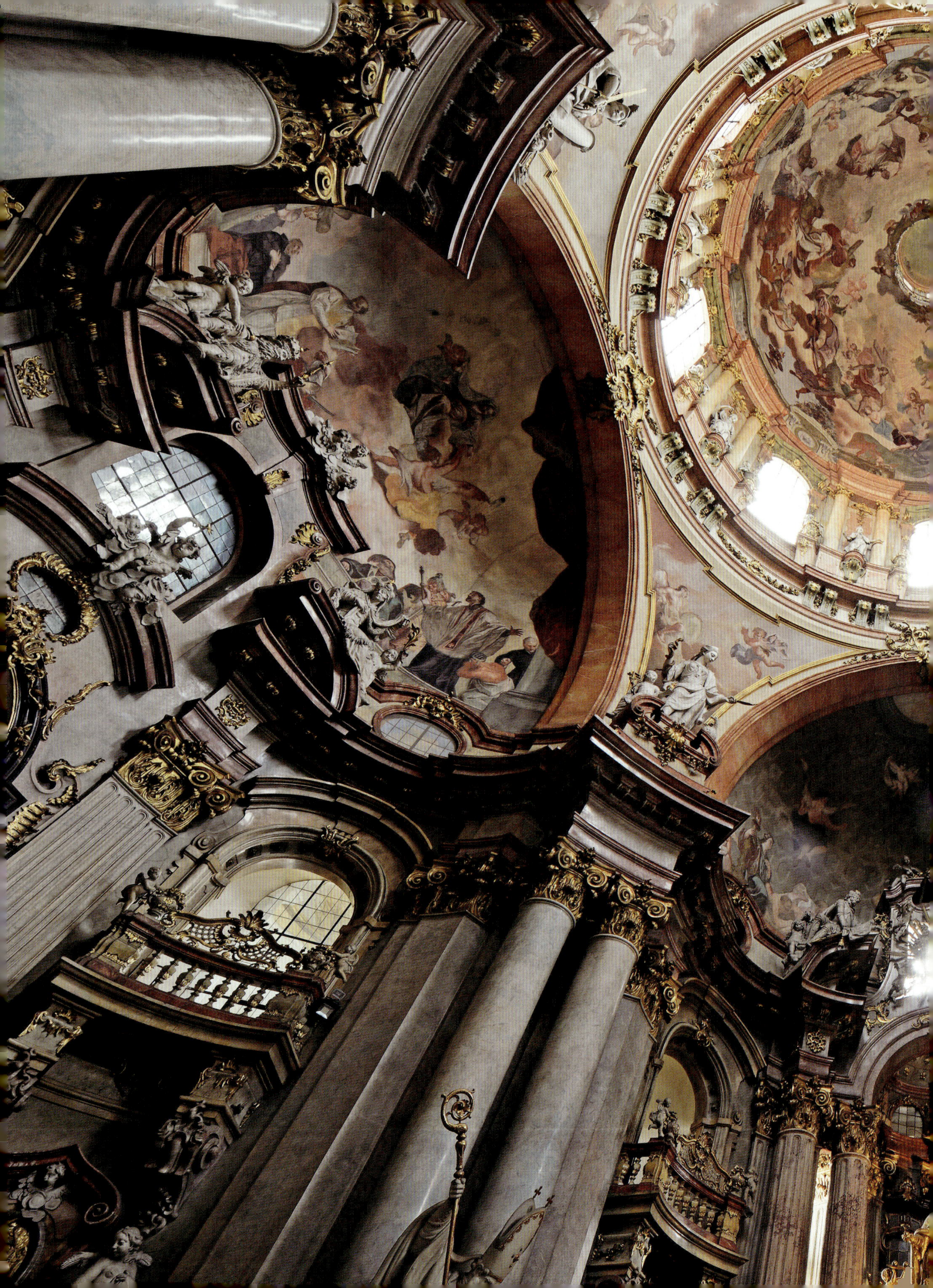

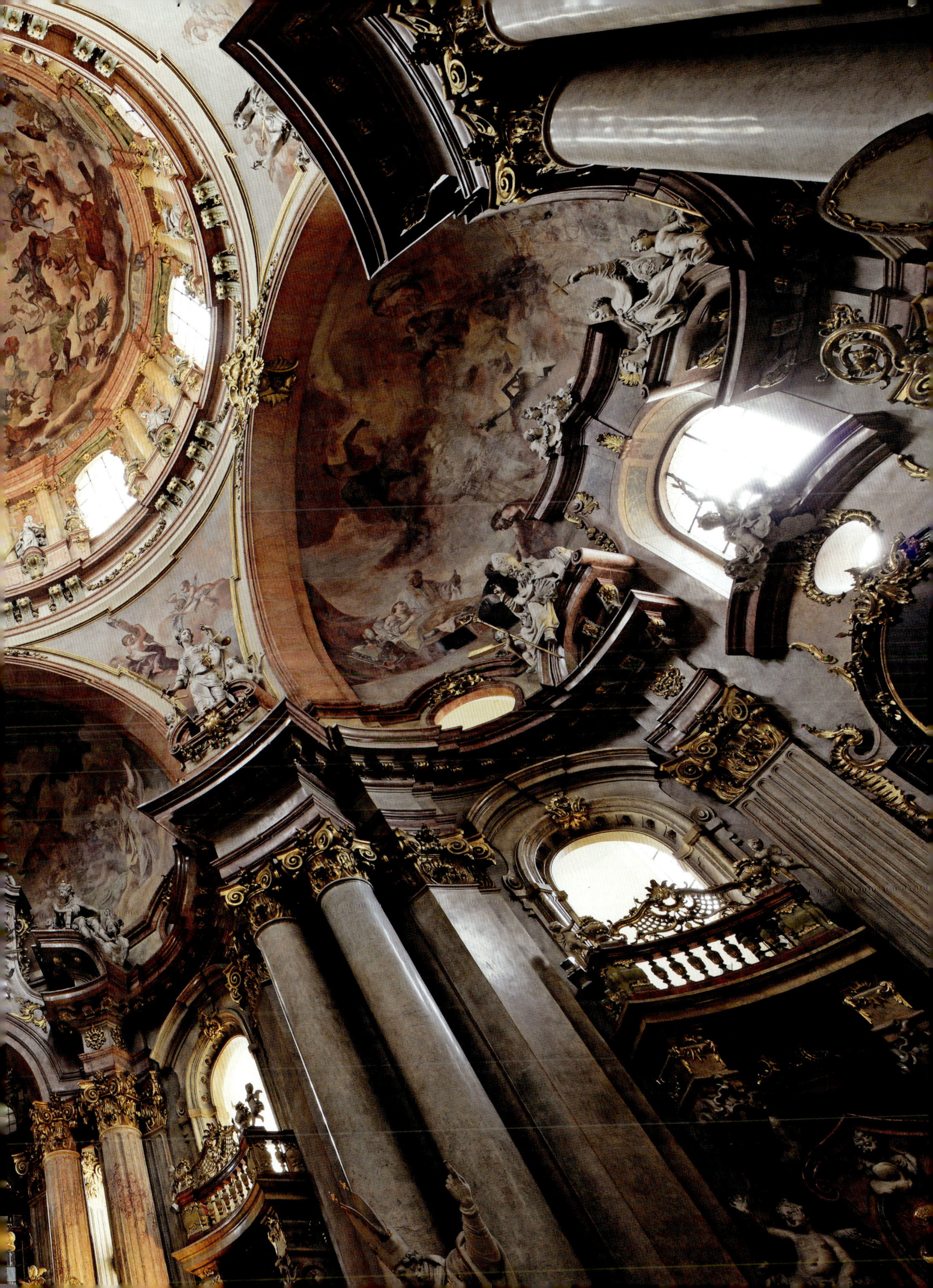

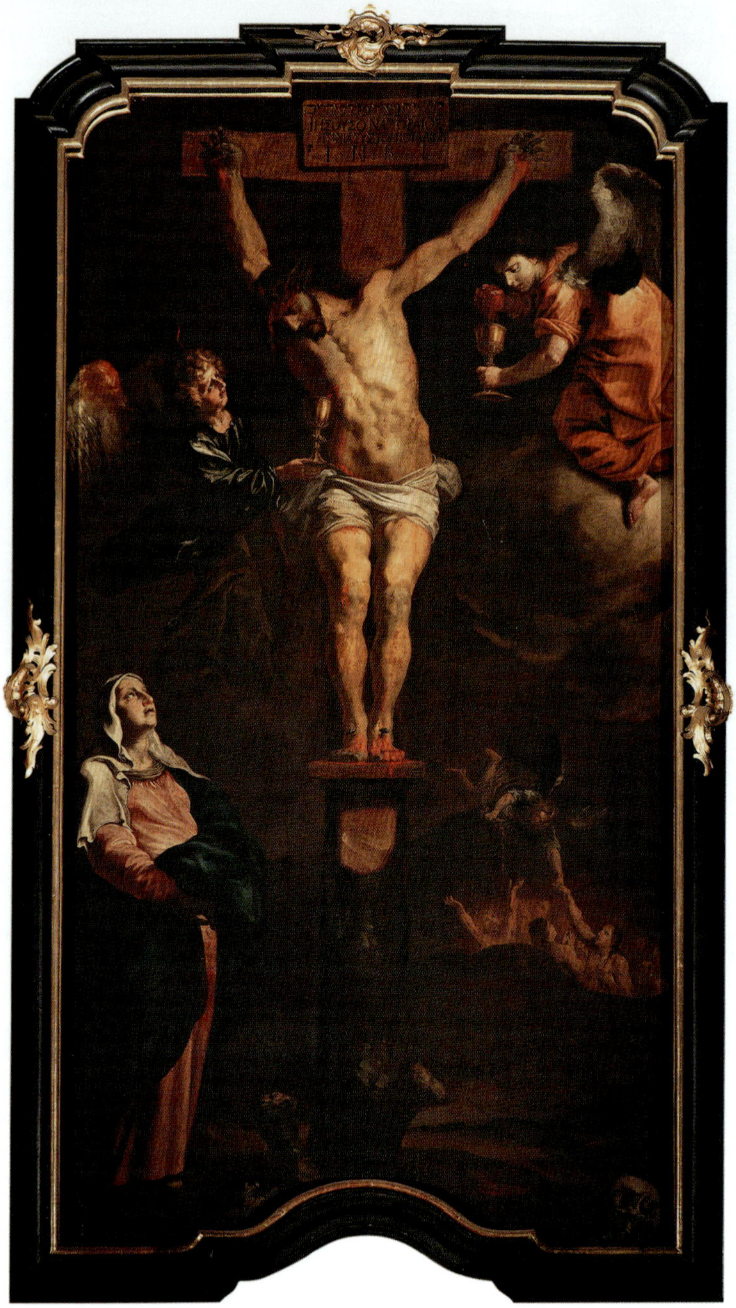

22D/ KAREL ŠKRÉTA: THE CRUCIFIXION WITH OUR LADY OF SORROWS AND SOULS IN PERGATORY, 1644
This canvas, well known and frequently imitated in its day, was made for the Chapel of St Barbara at St Nicholas' Church, where a burial society was active. The blood of Christ, together with the intercession of the Blessed Virgin Mary, frees the souls of the dead from Purgatory, as is graphically portrayed in the background.

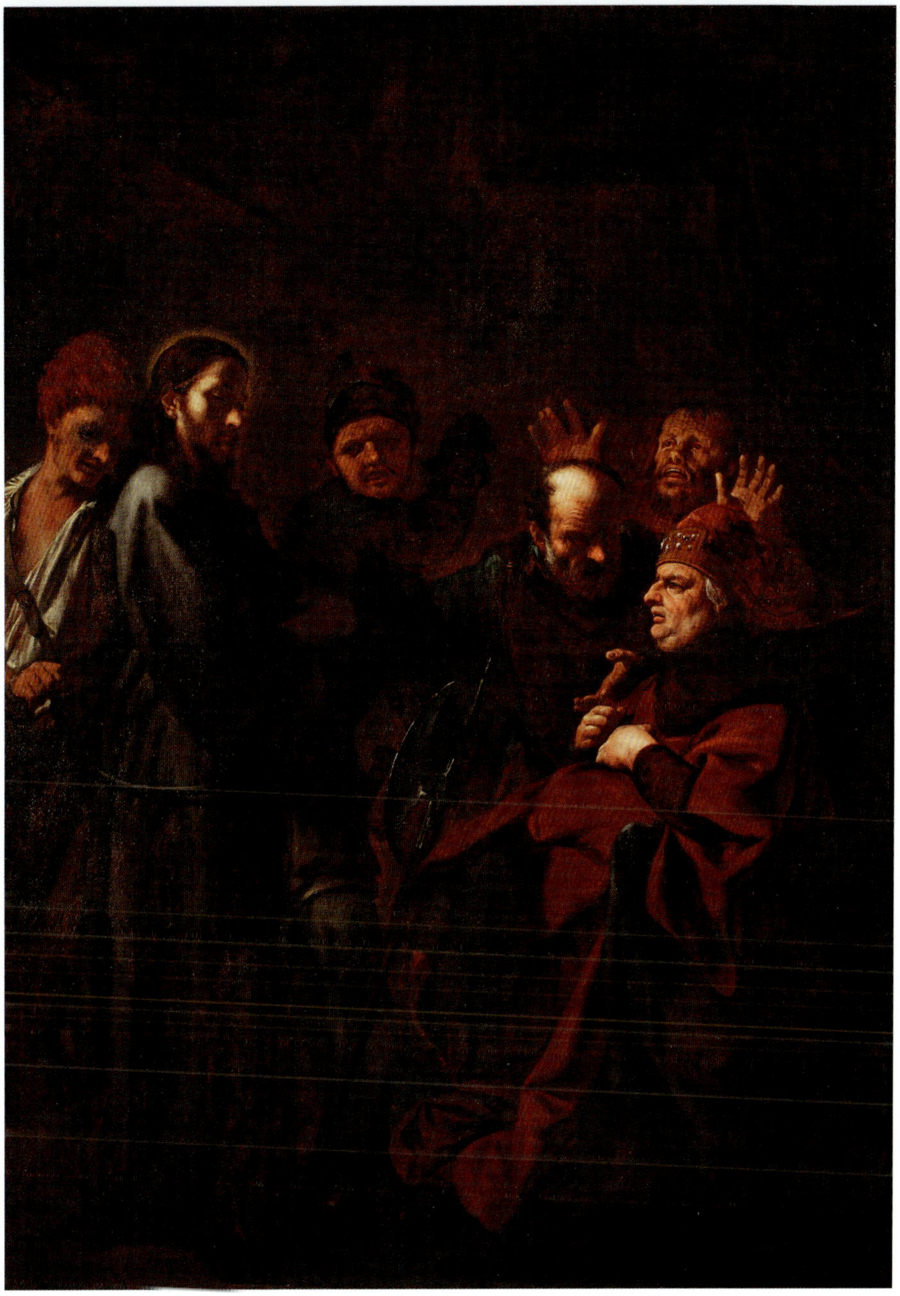

22E/ KAREL ŠKRÉTA: CHRIST BEFORE CAIAPHAS, 1673
St Nicholas' Church today contains a series of scenes of the Passion which Karel Škréta made for what was then still the original Gothic church of St Nicholas. These are scenes of extraordinarily expressive power and persuasiveness, closely linked with Jesuit spirituality. Their compositions draw mainly on the prints of Albrecht Dürer, but are linked in a number of ways to contemporary Italian painting. In *Christ before Caiaphas*, the Jewish High Priest is condemning Jesus as a blasphemer and, as a sign of his decision, rends his robe.

22F/ THE CHURCH SEEN FROM THE EAST

Looking at St Nicholas' from the east side clearly reveals the ingeniousness of Dientzenhofer's design in relation to the urban fabric. The cupola with the adjacent bell tower not only became the spatial focus of the skyline of left-bank Prague, but also neutralized what must have been the negative impression of the gigantic, almost monolithic, block of the Jesuit professed house (1674–91), which was callously wedged into the earlier small built-up area. The distinctive Grömling House in the middle of Malostranské náměstí was built in place of four earlier houses and was given its Late Baroque character by the architect Josef Jäger after 1772.

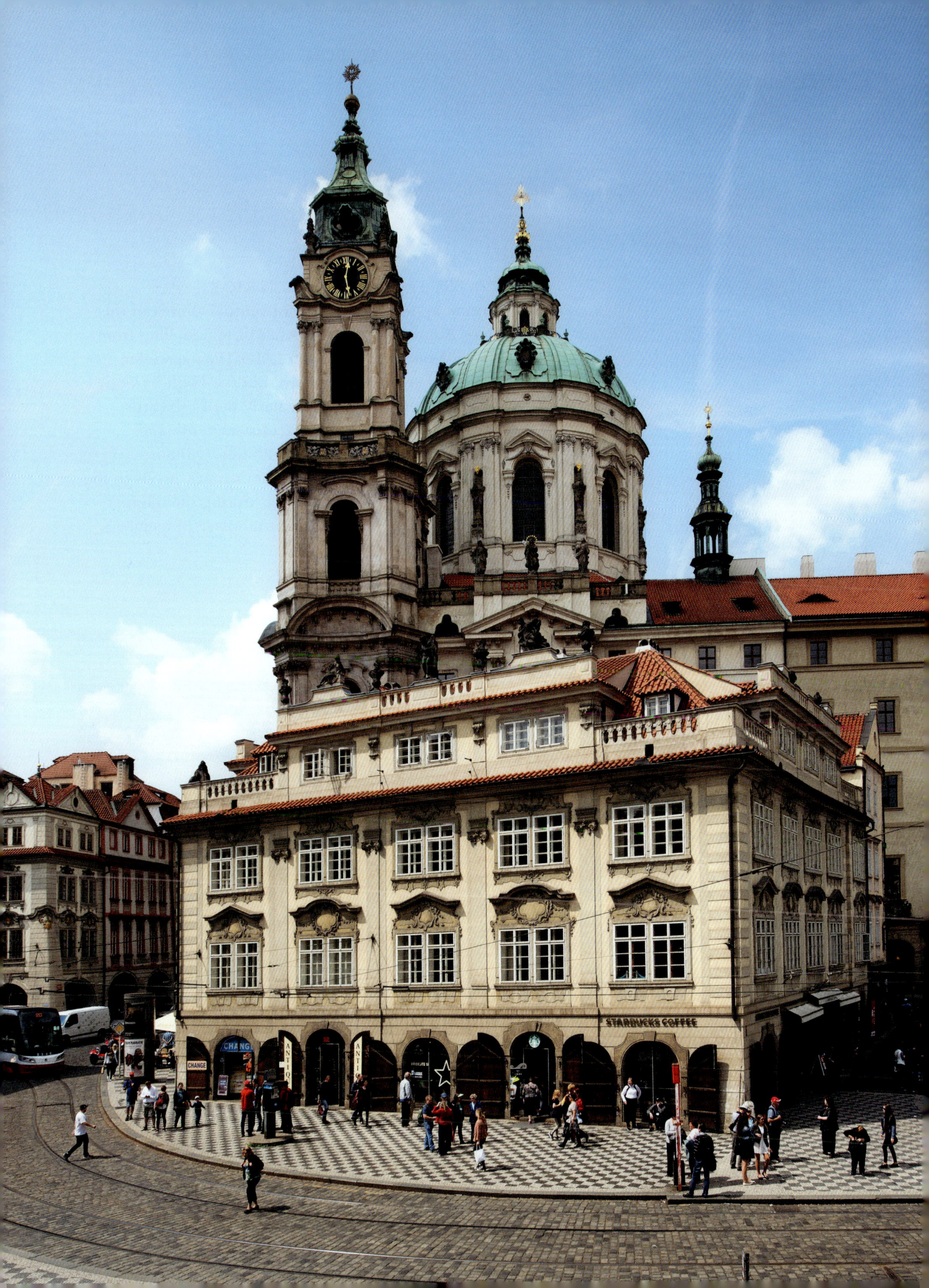
STARBUCKS COFFEE
CHANGE

23A–B/ WEST FAÇADE AND INTERIOR
The current appearance of the conventual church of the Discalced Augustinians is the result of remodelling from 1727 to 1731 on plans by Kilian Ignaz Dientzenhofer. Distinguished artists were involved in the High Baroque decoration of the church, particularly the fresco artist Wenzel Lorenz Reiner and the sculptors Ferdinand Maximilian Brokoff and Andreas Philipp Quitainer. The great number of remarkable tombstones attests to the fact that the church was, as early as during the reign of Rudolph II (r. 1576–1612), the burial place of members of the Prague élite.

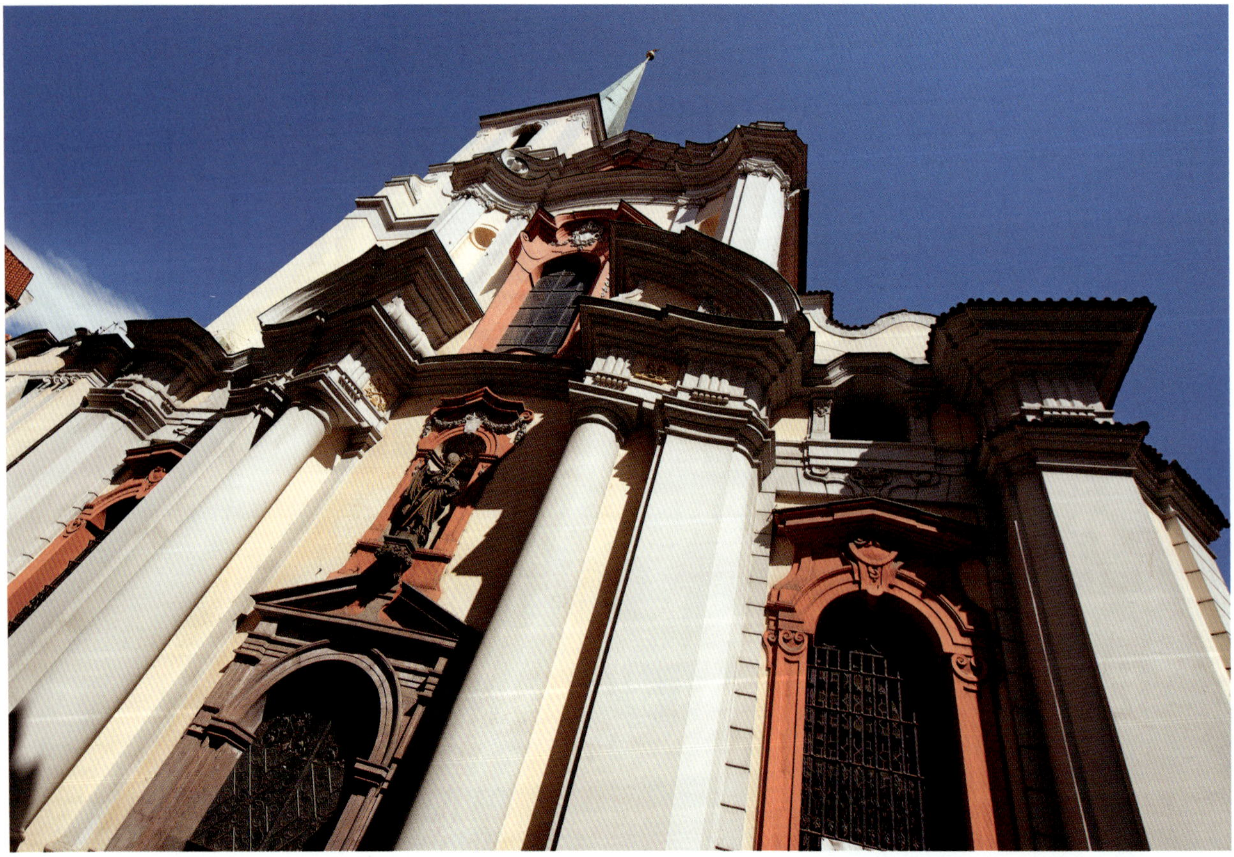

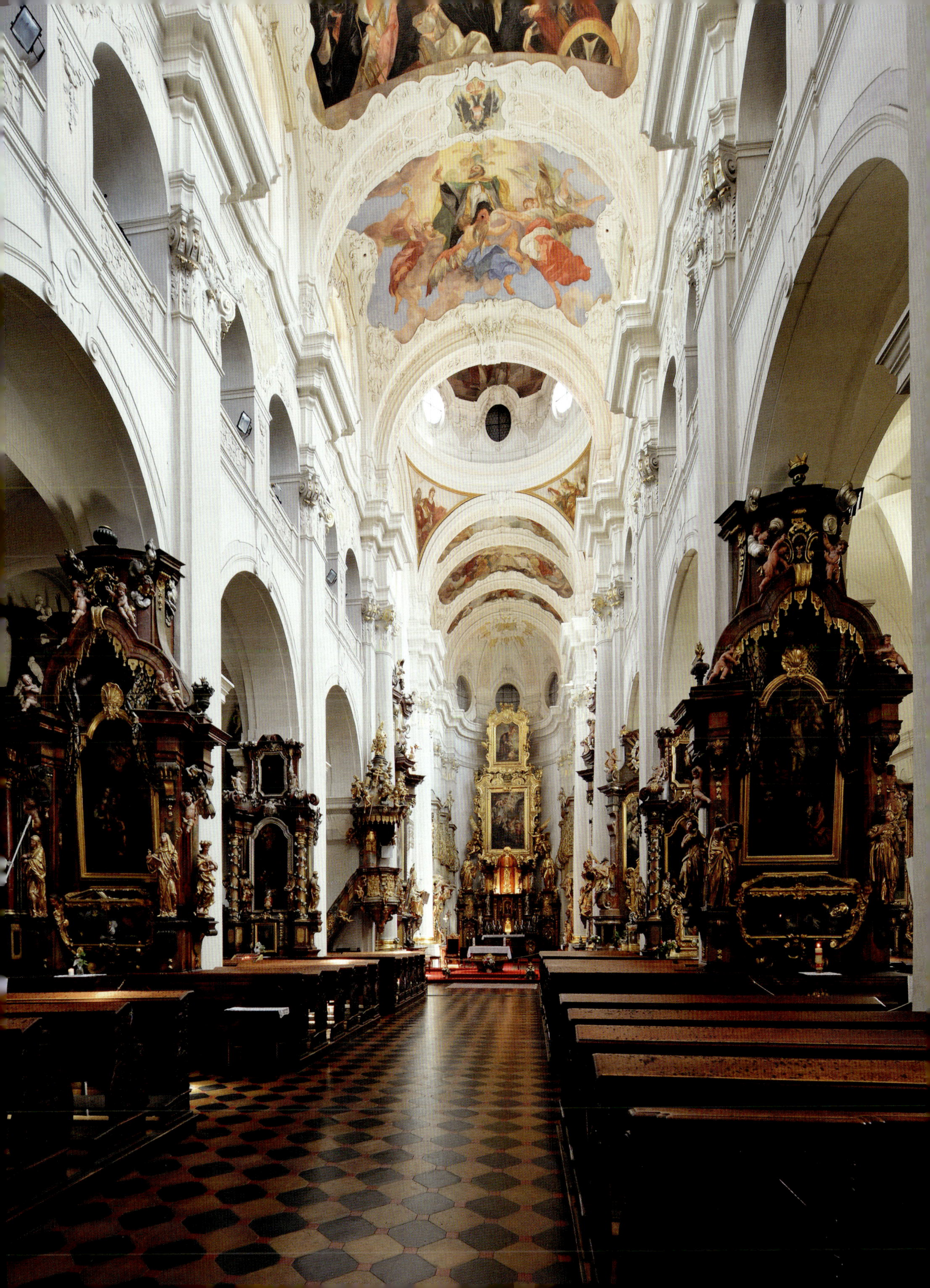

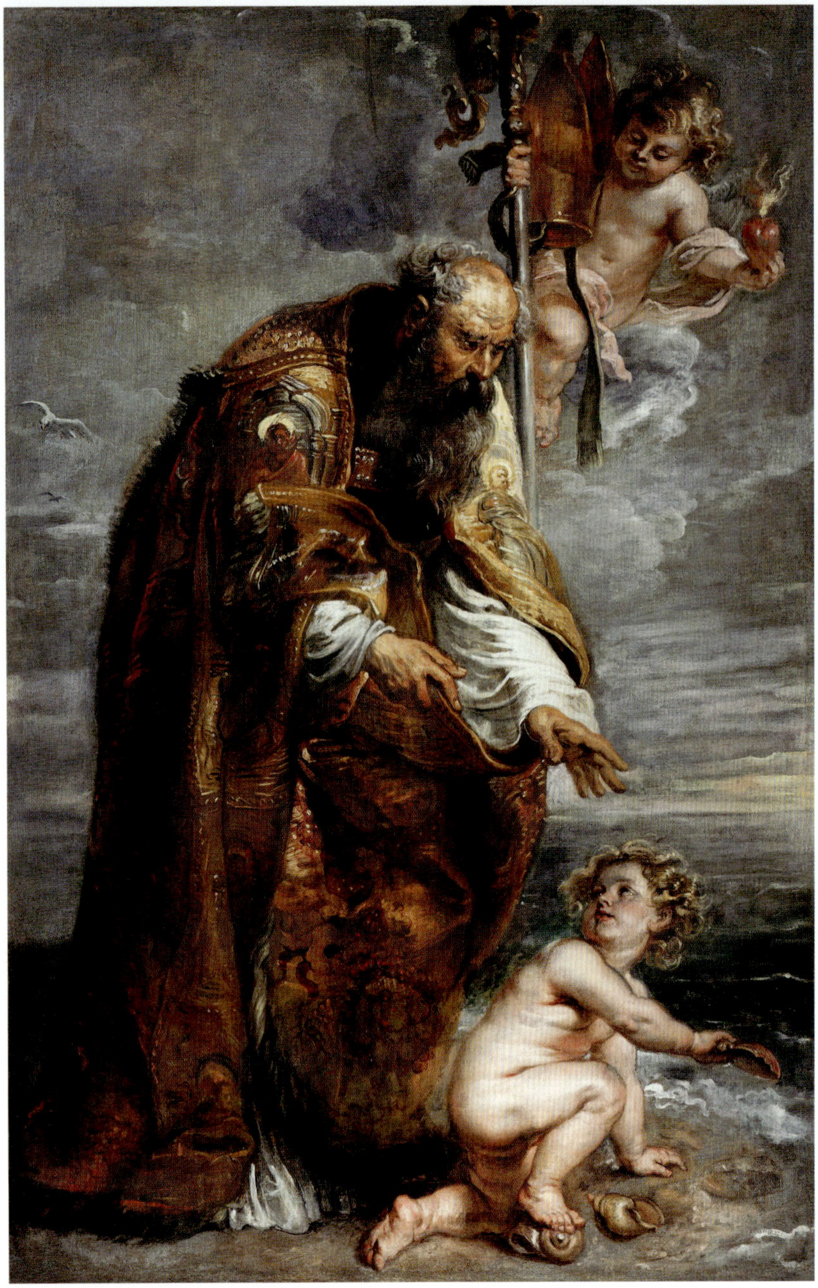

23C/ PETER PAUL RUBENS: ST AUGUSTINE, *c.*1636–37
These two paintings, commissioned by the prior of the Augustinians at St Thomas', Jan Baptista (Crystellius) Svitavský z Bochova, directly from Rubens's workshop in Antwerp, are the most important art works imported to Prague during the Thirty Years War. Whereas the larger canvas portrays the dramatically depicted martyrdom of Thomas the Apostle in India, with many references to Classical models, the second canvas is distinguished by a mood of calm introspective meditation. Both works were already on loan to the public picture gallery in the nineteenth century, and copies were hung in the church.

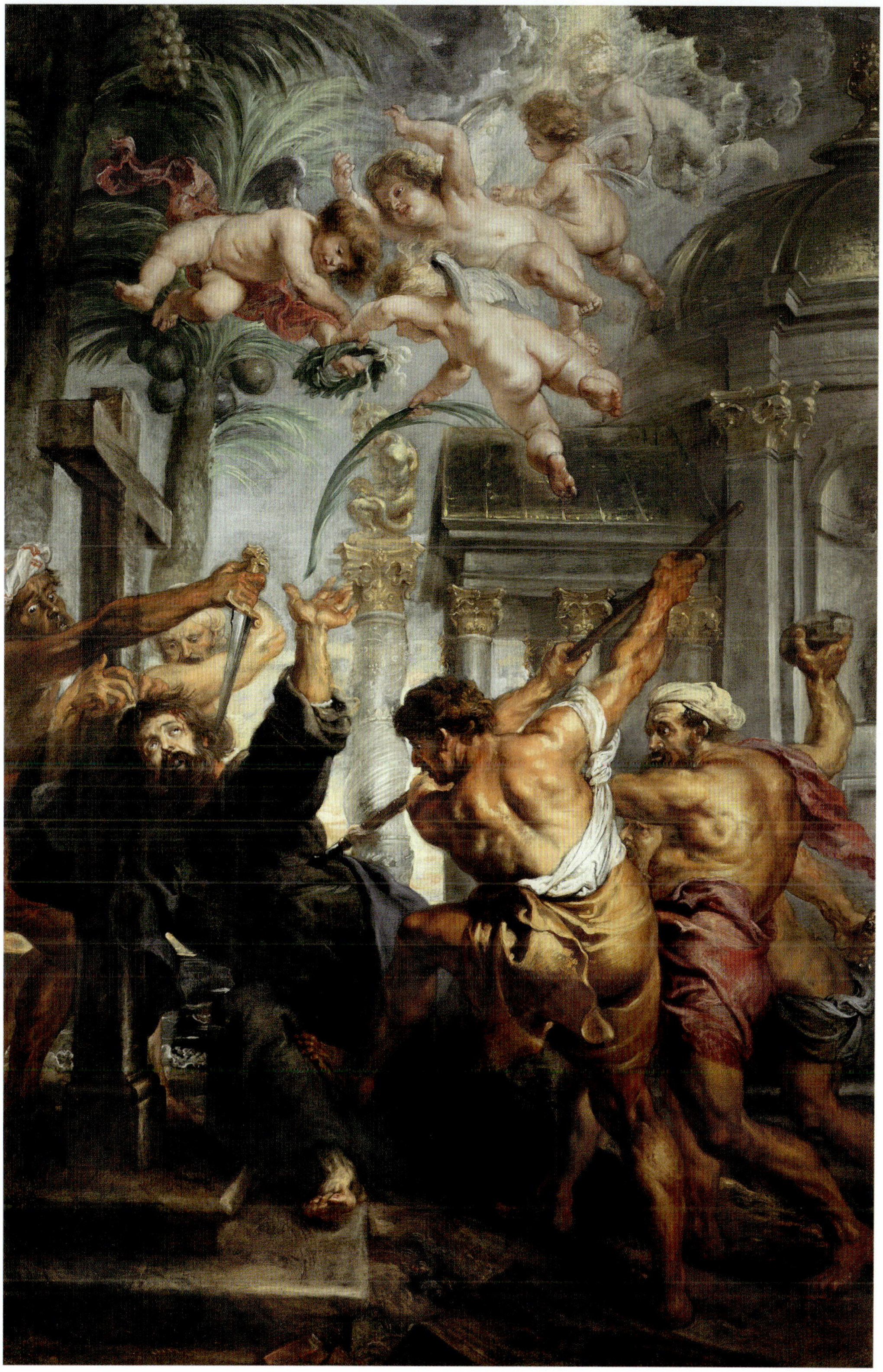

24D/ PETER PAUL RUBENS: THE MARTYRDOM OF ST THOMAS, *c.*1636–37

24/ THE GOLDEN STAG (U ZLATÉHO JELENA), HOUSE SIGN, *C.*1726

Johann Caspar Friedrich von Freinberg, a rich burgher of the Lesser Town, had his house next to the Augustinian friary thoroughly remodelled after 1723. Part of its High Baroque architectural design, attributed to Kilian Ignaz Dientzenhofer, is the unusually imposing conception of the house sign. Ferdinand Maximilian Brokoff has depicted here the surprised Roman soldier St Hubert kneeling in amazement in front of the stag, between whose horns the Cross has appeared.

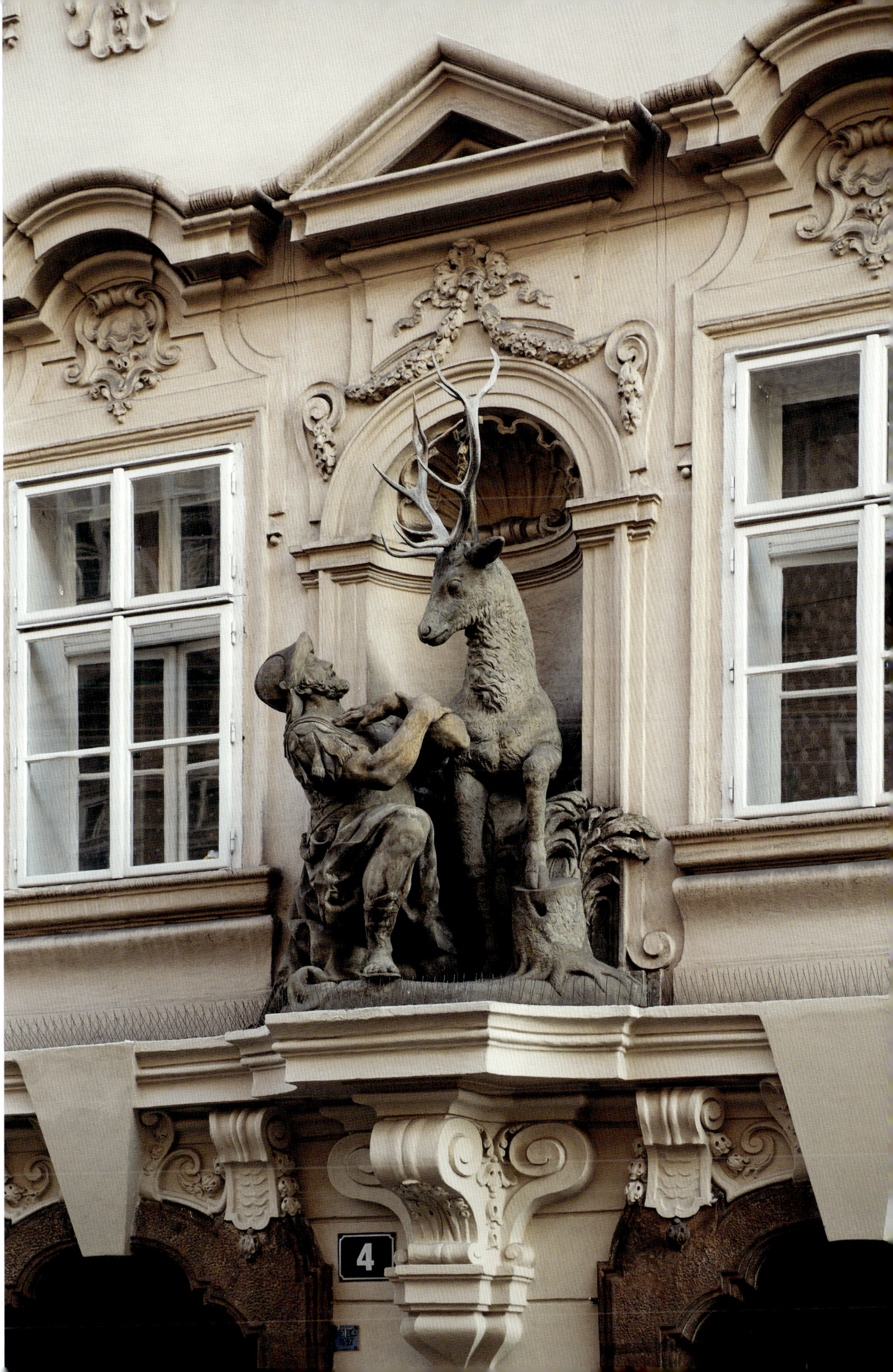
4

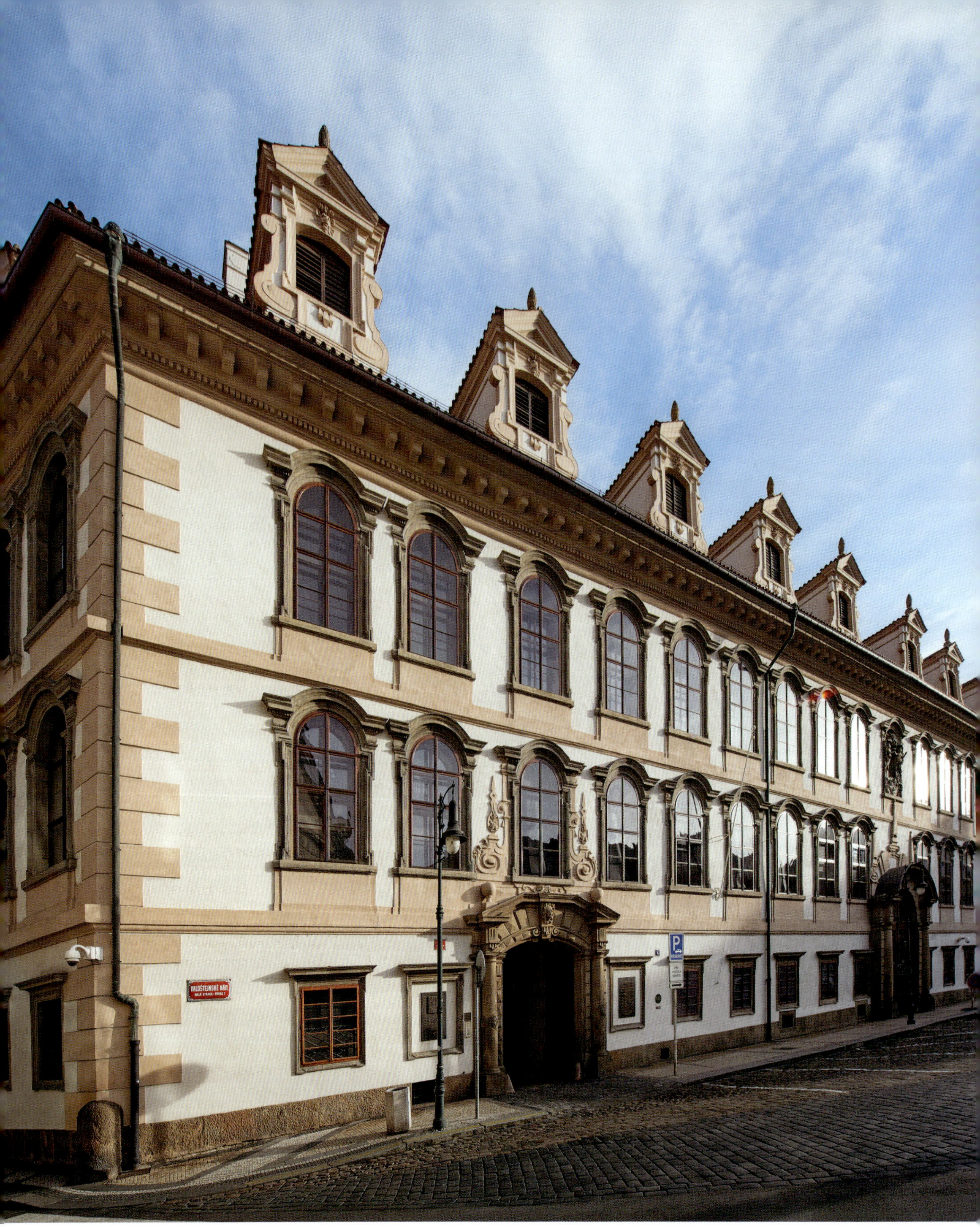

25A/ MAIN FAÇADE

The vast house and grounds, built from 1623 to 1629 for the emperor's generalissimo, Wallenstein, was erected on the plots of thirty houses and gardens of burghers. This is the first palatial Prague house of a new Baroque type, including its own riding school and sala terrena. The main architects are generally considered to have been Andrea Spezza and Giovanni Pieroni, whose relationship to each other and whose individual contributions remain unclear. The articulation of the main façade of the house, facing Valdštejnské náměstí, does not even suggest that behind it, apart from two staircases, is the main hall, which occupies the two upper storeys. Above the central portal, which is in fact blind, there is a cult image of the Madonna of Valle Vigezzo.

'But I was most pleased with the Palace of Count Wallenstein, Duke of Friedland, General unto the Emperor Ferdinand the Second, who being suspected to Usurp that Kingdom, was afterwards killed at Egra [Eger]. This Palace was built upon the Ruins of an hundred Houses, purposely plucked down to make room for it [...].'

Edward Browne, *A brief account of some travels* [...], 1685

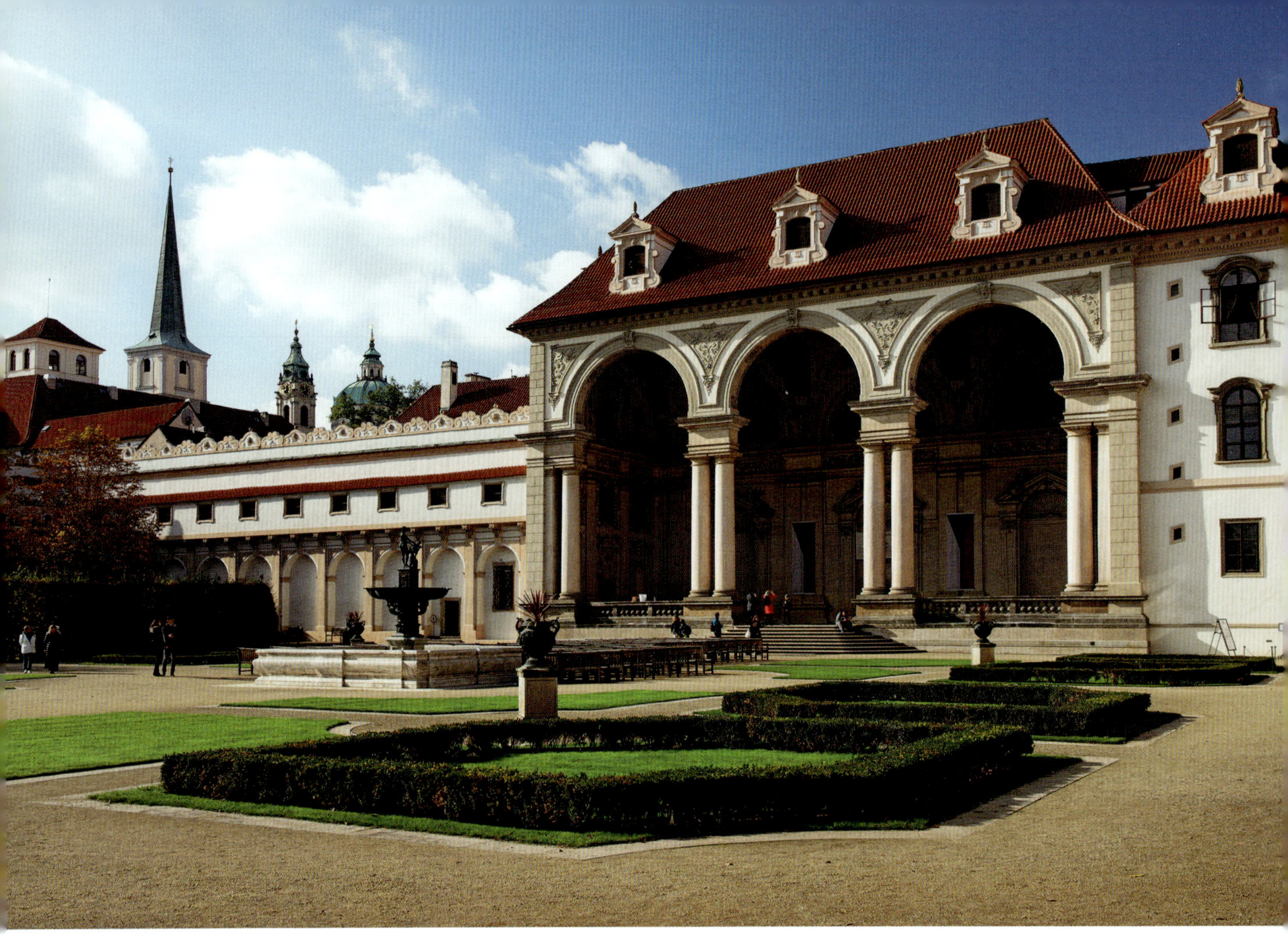

25B/ SALA TERRENA

The house opens onto the garden through the three tall arches of the sala terrena, the interior of which is decorated in stucco work and paintings by Luigi Baccio del Bianco with subject matter from the Trojan War. The painted decoration of the whole house and its grounds has several thematic levels, uniting astrological, mythological, and military-imperial motifs. Bronze casts of statues by Adriaen de Vries are placed throughout the garden (the originals were taken as booty by Swedish forces in 1648). A grotto (artificial cave) with an aviary runs along part of the inside of the perimeter wall. On the east side, the grounds are enclosed by the free-standing riding school, which today serves as the National Gallery.

25C/ LEATHERN DRAWING ROOM

Named after the material used for the wall covering, what is today known as the Leathern Drawing Room was originally one of three reception rooms. It was called the Knight's Hall, for it contains the equestrian portrait of Wallenstein, painted in 1631, and attributed to Christian Kaulfersch the Elder.

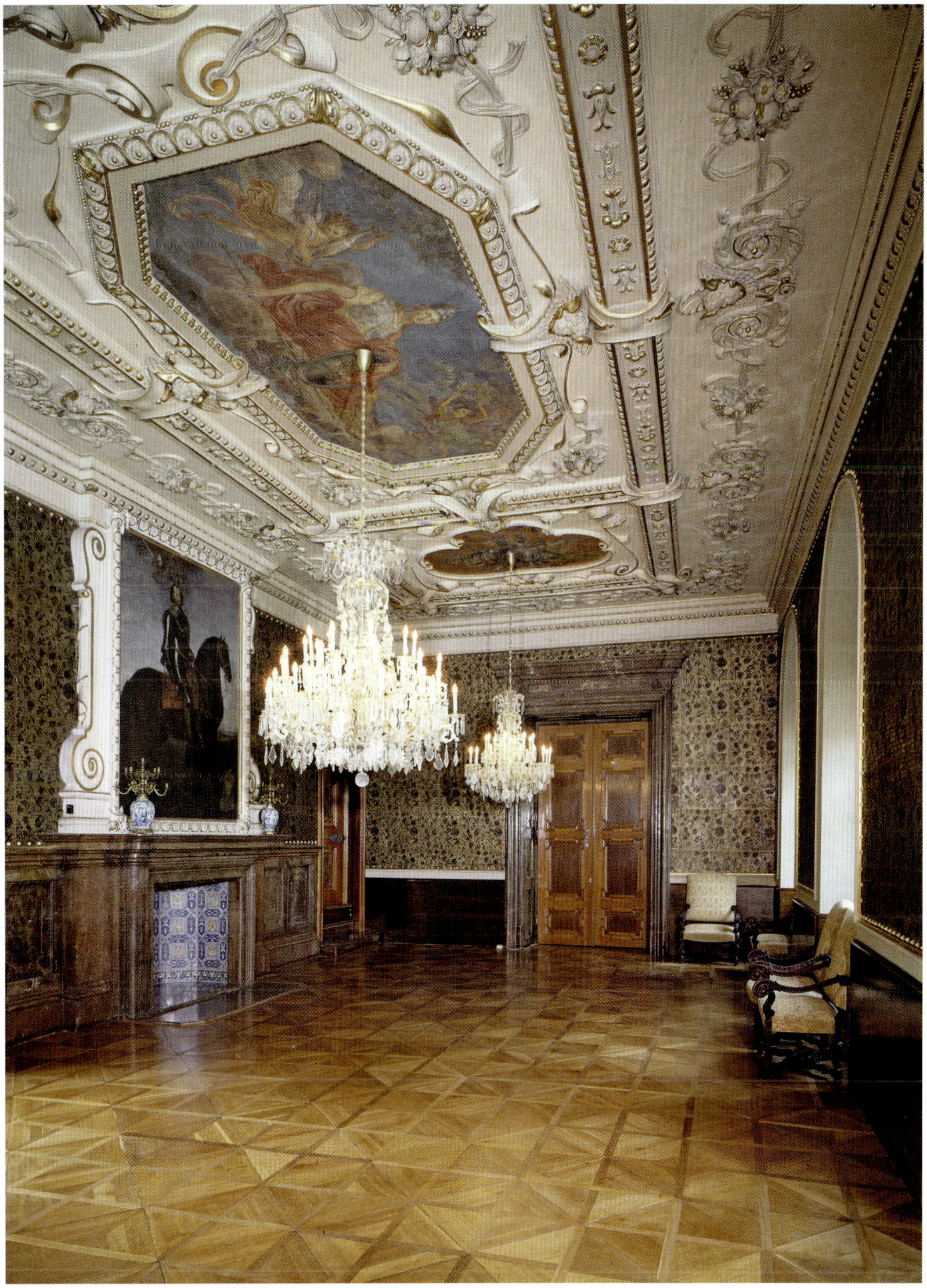

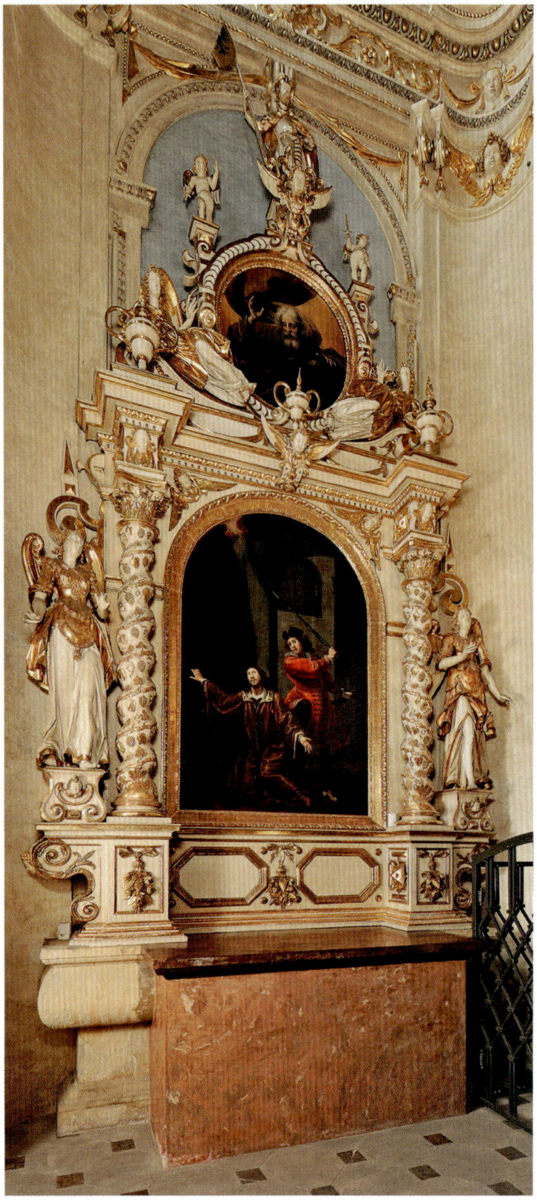

25D/ THE WENCESLAS CHAPEL

Preserved to this day in the north-west corner of the house is a private chapel, dedicated to St Wenceslas (Václav). The life and works of this Bohemian patron saint, who was also one of the patron saints of Wallenstein, are depicted here in paintings by the Florence-born Luigi Baccio del Bianco. The sculptural decoration of the intricate Mannerist altar is by the court sculptor Ernst Johann Heidelberger.

25E/ THE GREAT HALL

The unusually large main hall of the house, originally called the Lifeguards' Hall, is richly decorated with stucco works by Santino Galli and Giovanni Domenico Canevalle. The warrior iconography culminates in Luigi Baccio del Bianco's ceiling painting of the god Mars in a chariot. Since the nineteenth century, the central figure of the scene has usually been interpreted, probably incorrectly, as a crypto-portrait of Wallenstein. Considering Wallenstein's interest in astrology, the iconography of the scene may instead be emphasizing Mars as one of the seven planetary deities and the builder's 'lucky star'.

25F/ WALLENSTEIN GARDEN (VALDŠTEJNSKÁ ZAHRADA) →

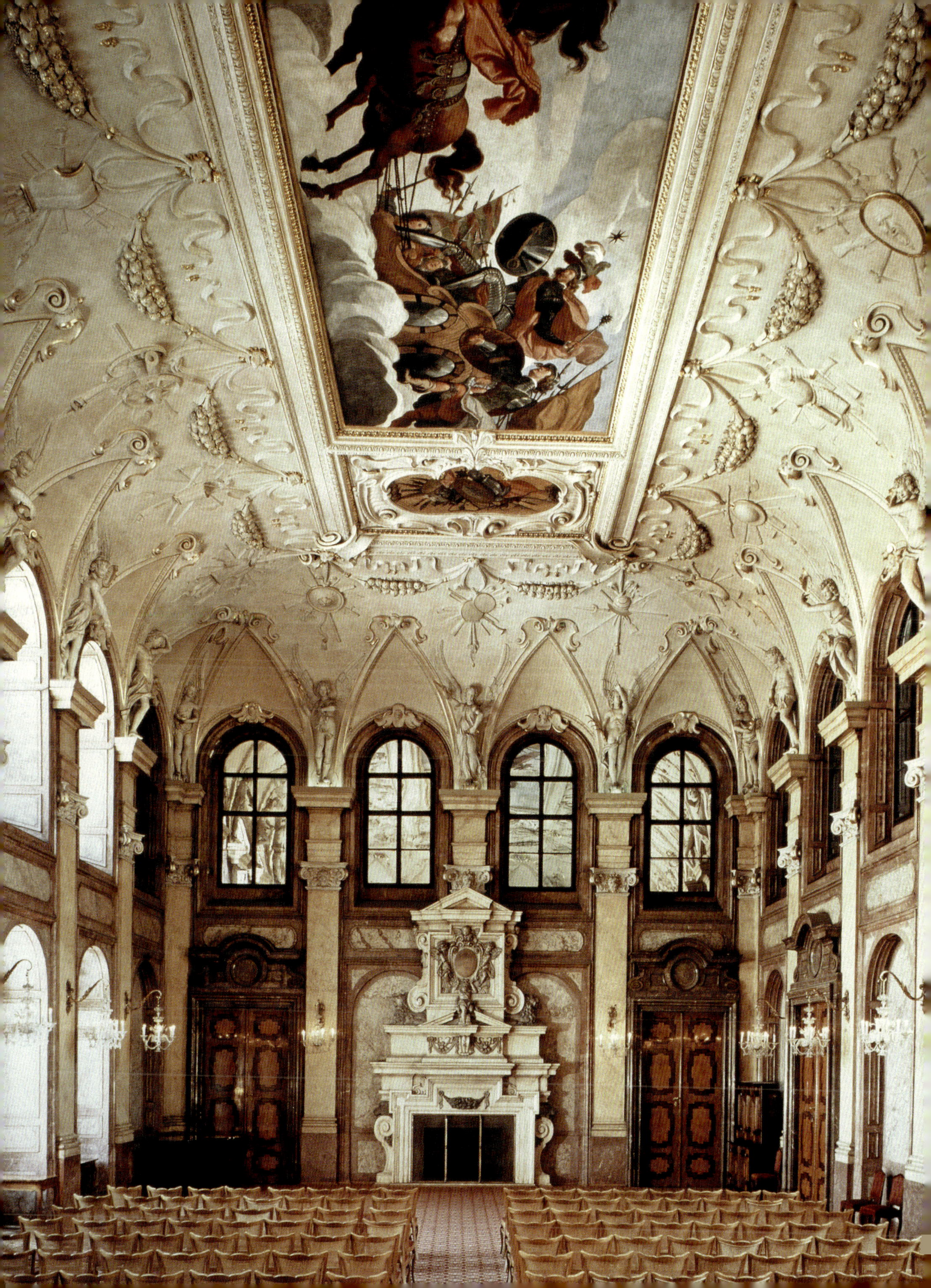

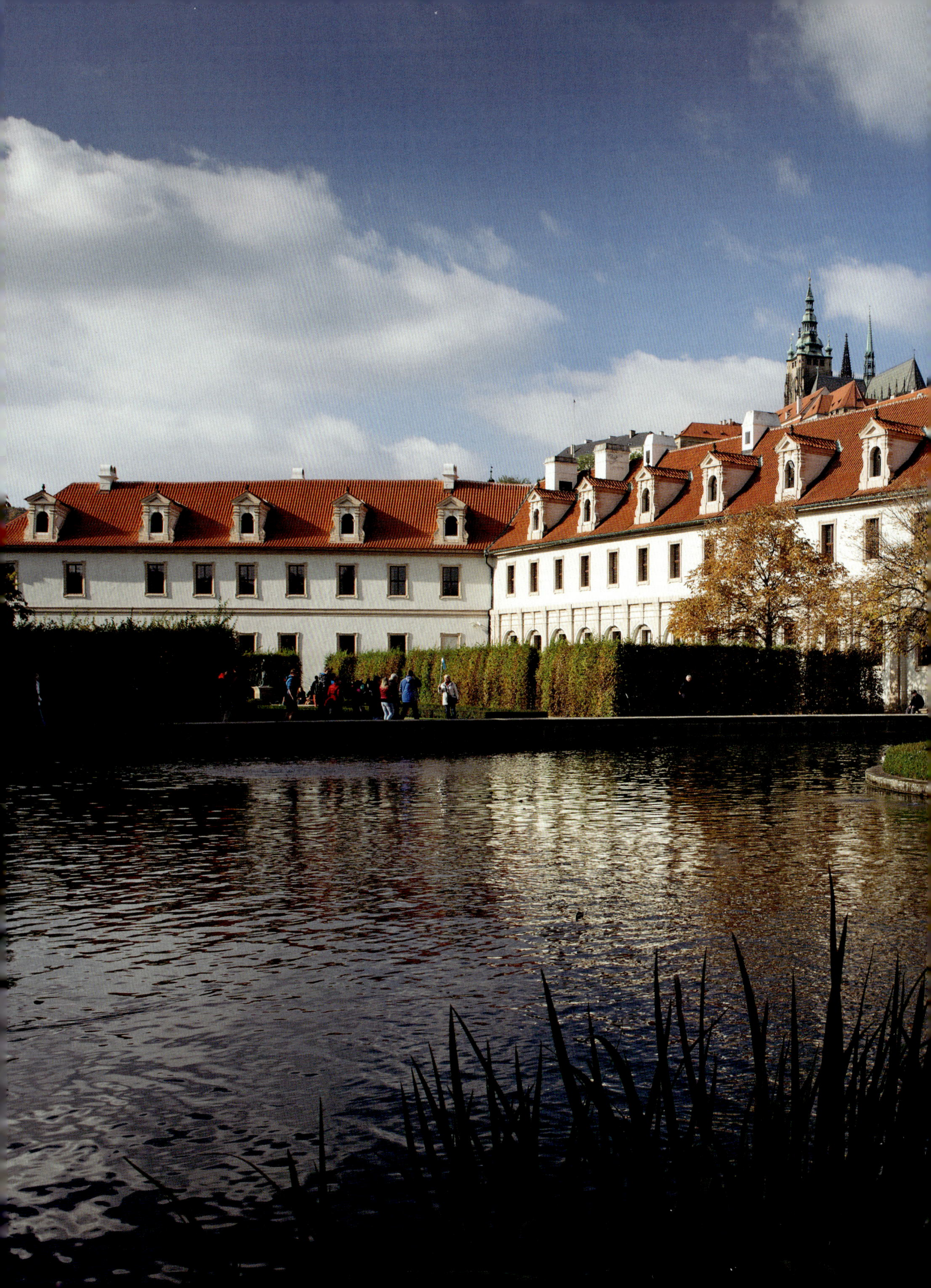

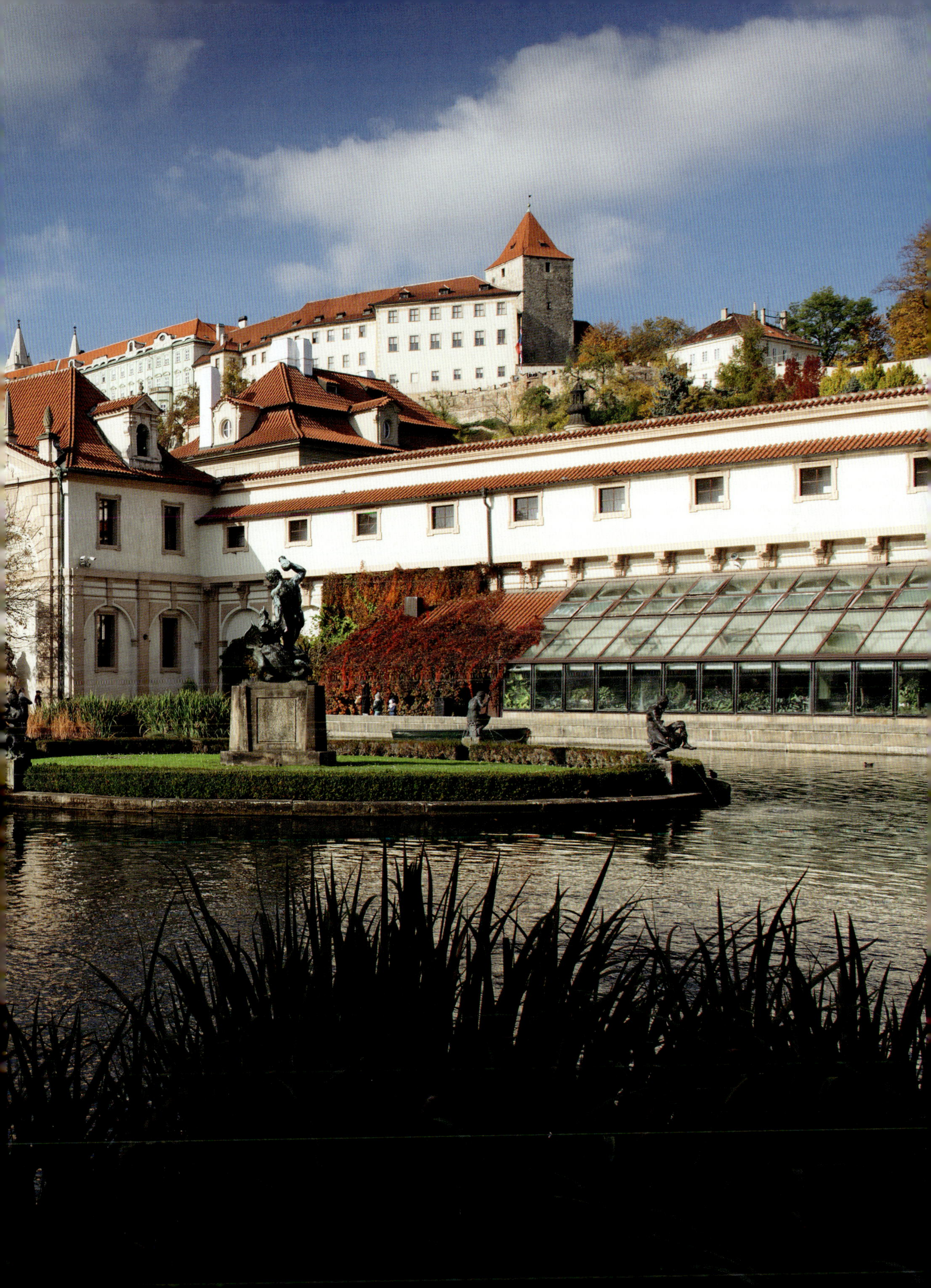

26A–C/ LEDEBUR GARDEN (LEDEBURSKÁ ZAHRADA)

Baroque terraced gardens, rising up from the valley of the Lesser Town along the side of the Castle hill, are among the most romantic places of old Prague. They are perhaps at their most beautiful in spring and early autumn. The garden adjacent to Ledebur House (Ledeburský palác) was probably made after 1697, when the grounds belonged to the Trauttmansdorff family. The garden is generally considered to have been laid out either by František Maxmilián Kaňka or Giovanni Battista Alliprandi. Ledebur Garden is spread out over five terraces.

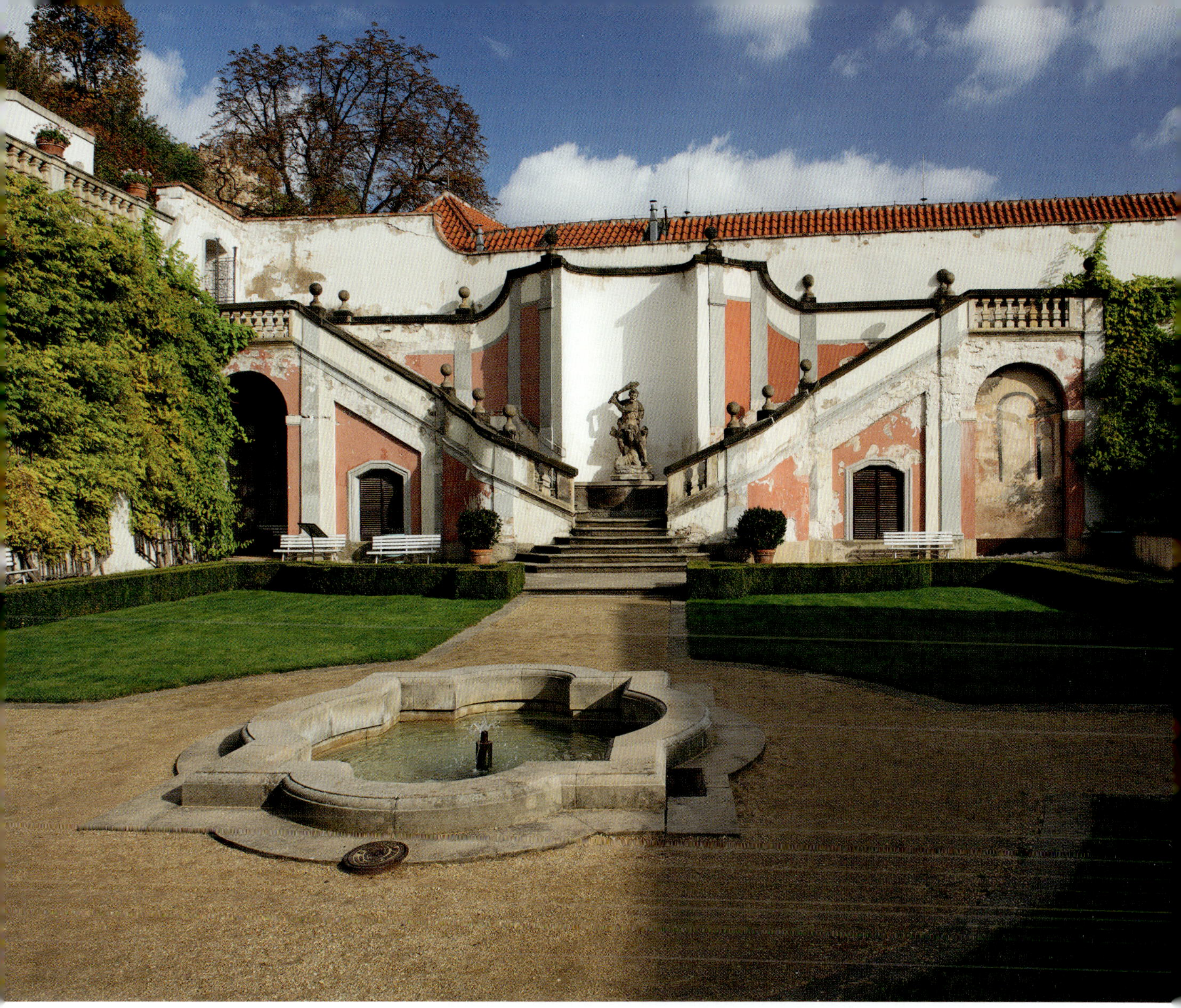

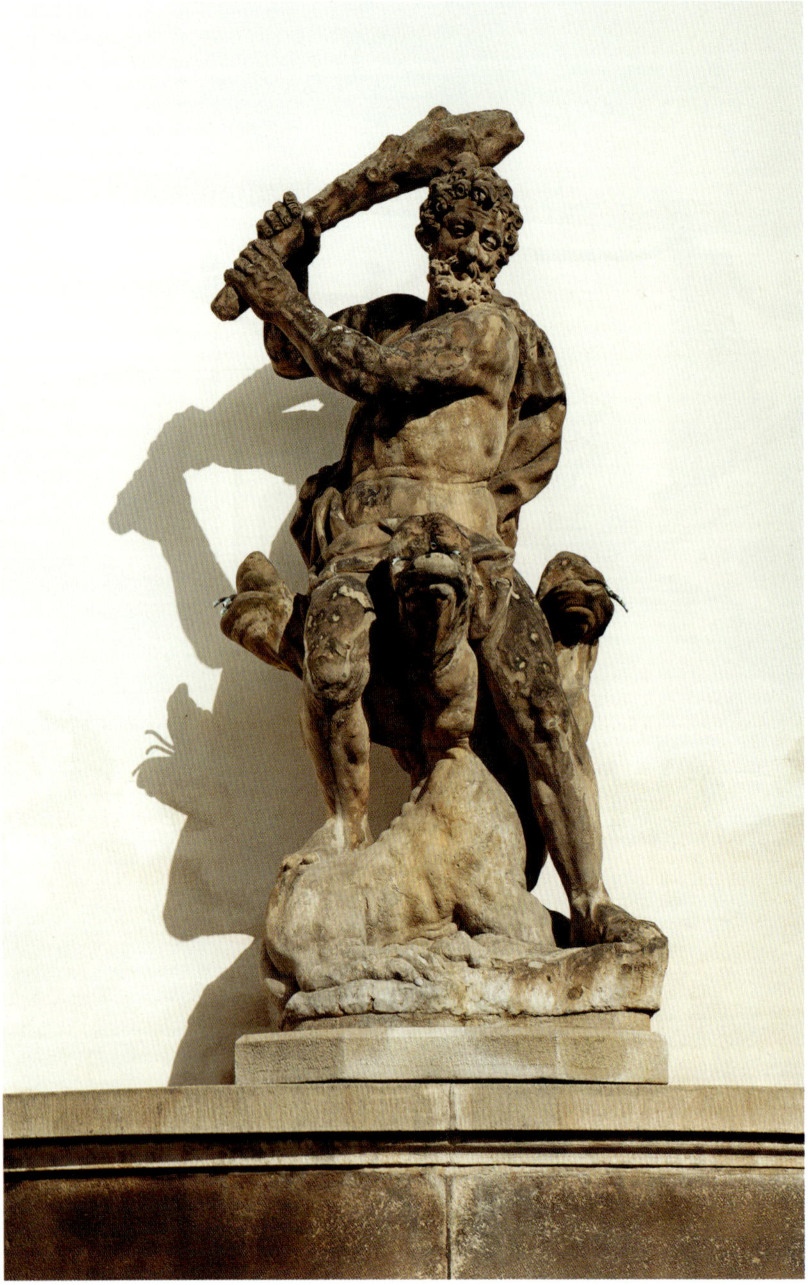

The house opens onto the lowest of the terraces through a tripartite sala terrena decorated with *trompe-l'oeil* paintings of architectural views. From the other side, the parterre is enclosed by convex-concave retaining wall with a staircase and a statue of Hercules wrestling with Cerberus, the three-headed hound who guards the gates of the Underworld. The wall was once decorated with a battlefield painting by Wenzel Lorenz Reiner.

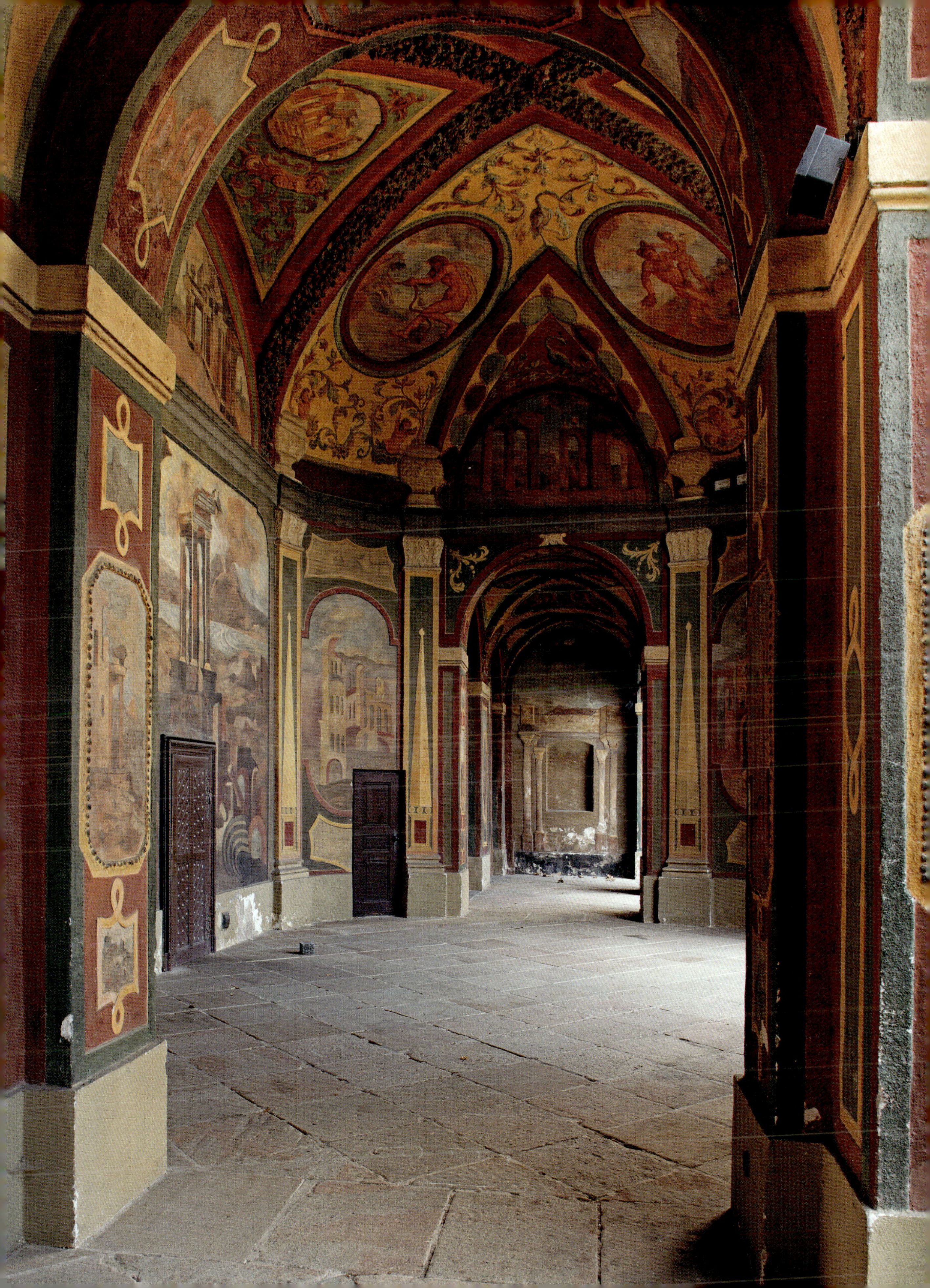

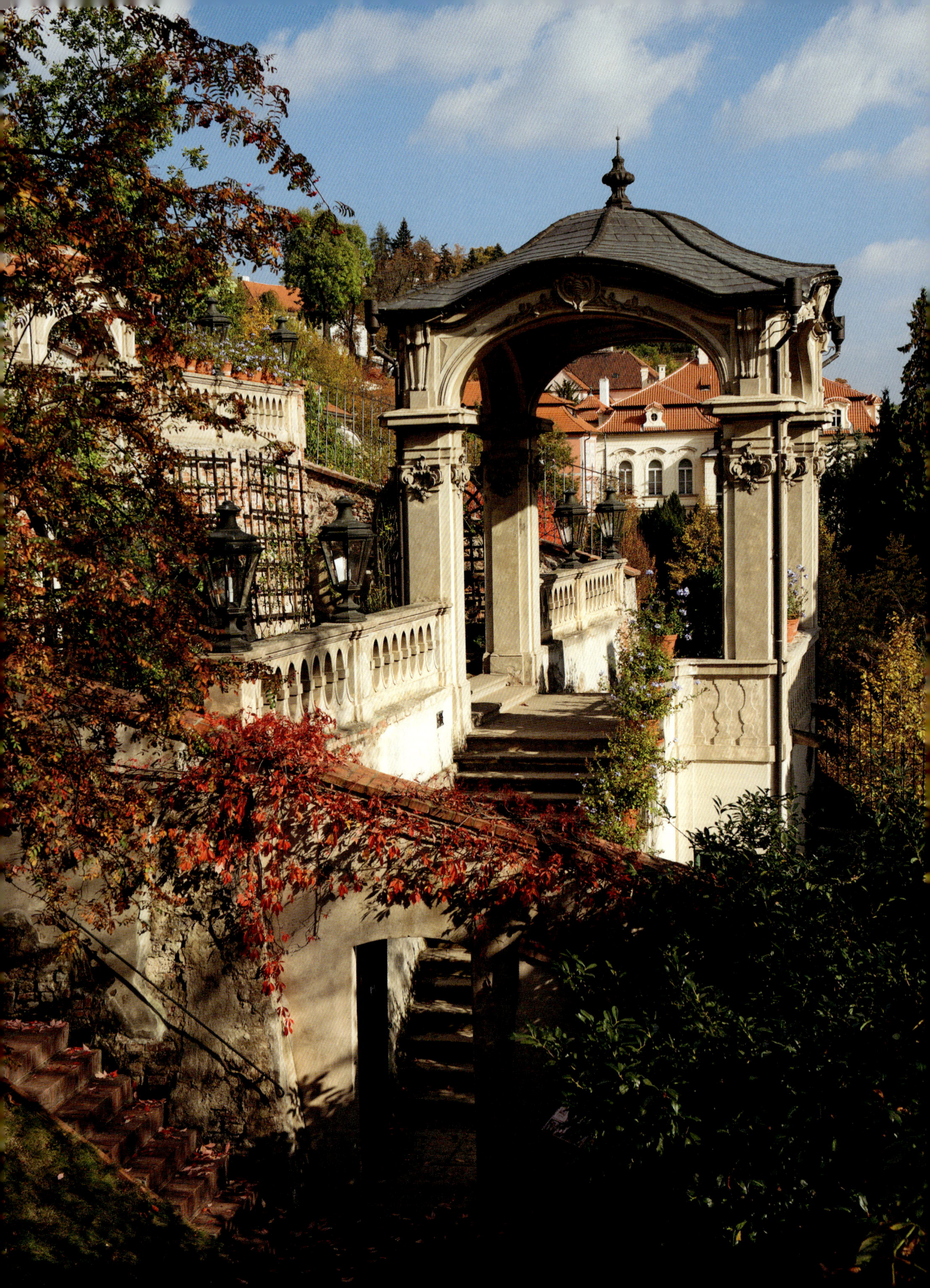

27/ LESSER FÜRSTENBERG GARDEN
(MALÁ FÜRSTENBERSKÁ ZAHRADA)

The terraced garden of Lesser Fürstenberg House (Malý Fürstenberský palác) is quite narrow; its axis is the path linking the lower pavilion with the sala terrena on the upper terrace. Its symmetrical layout dates from the second half of the eighteenth century. The garden also makes use of the earlier circular pavilion on its highest point, affording a panoramic view of the city.

28/ VIEW OF THE LESSER TOWN
FROM THE LESSER FÜRSTENBERG GARDEN
(MALÁ FÜRSTENBERSKÁ ZAHRADA) →

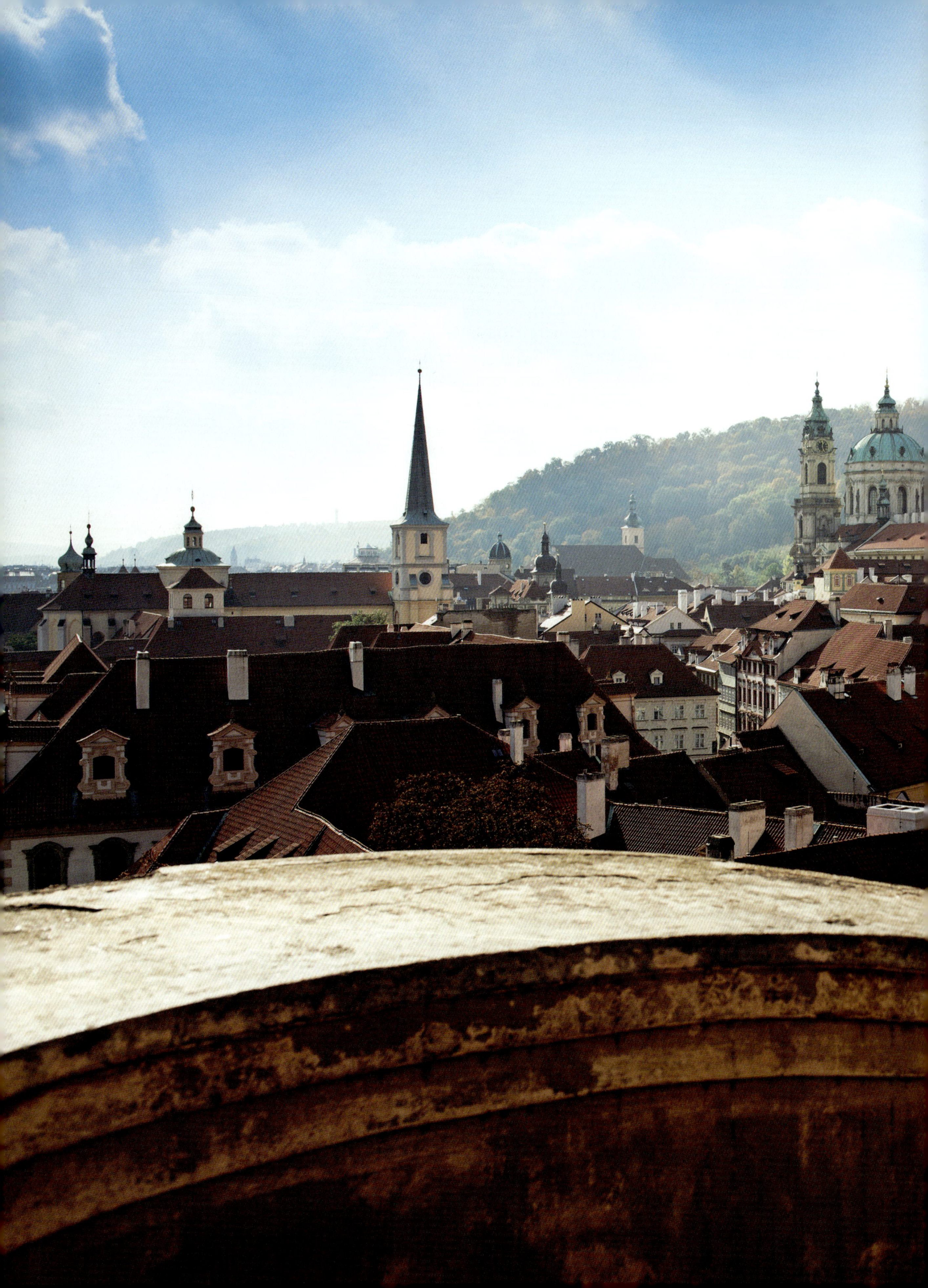

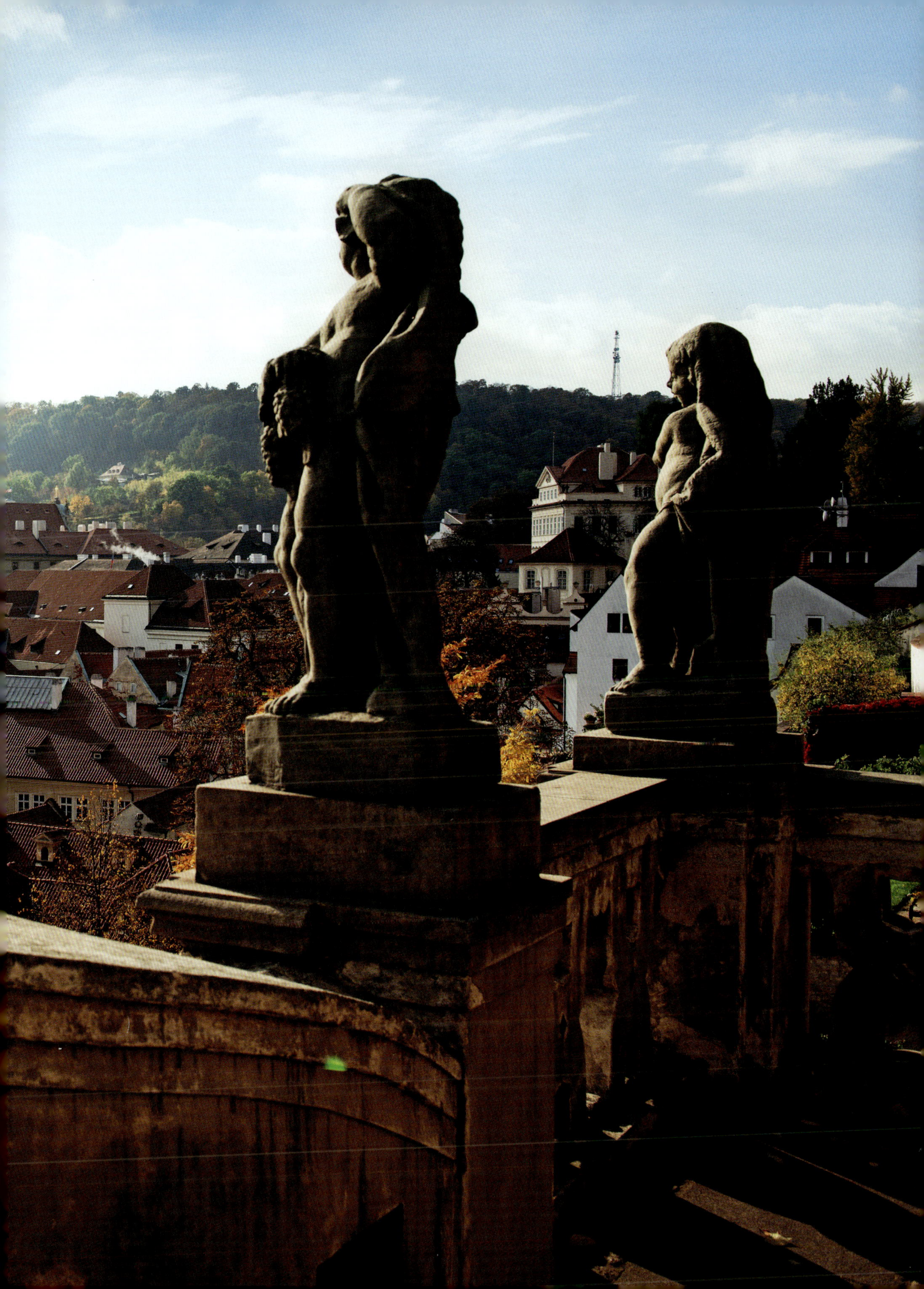

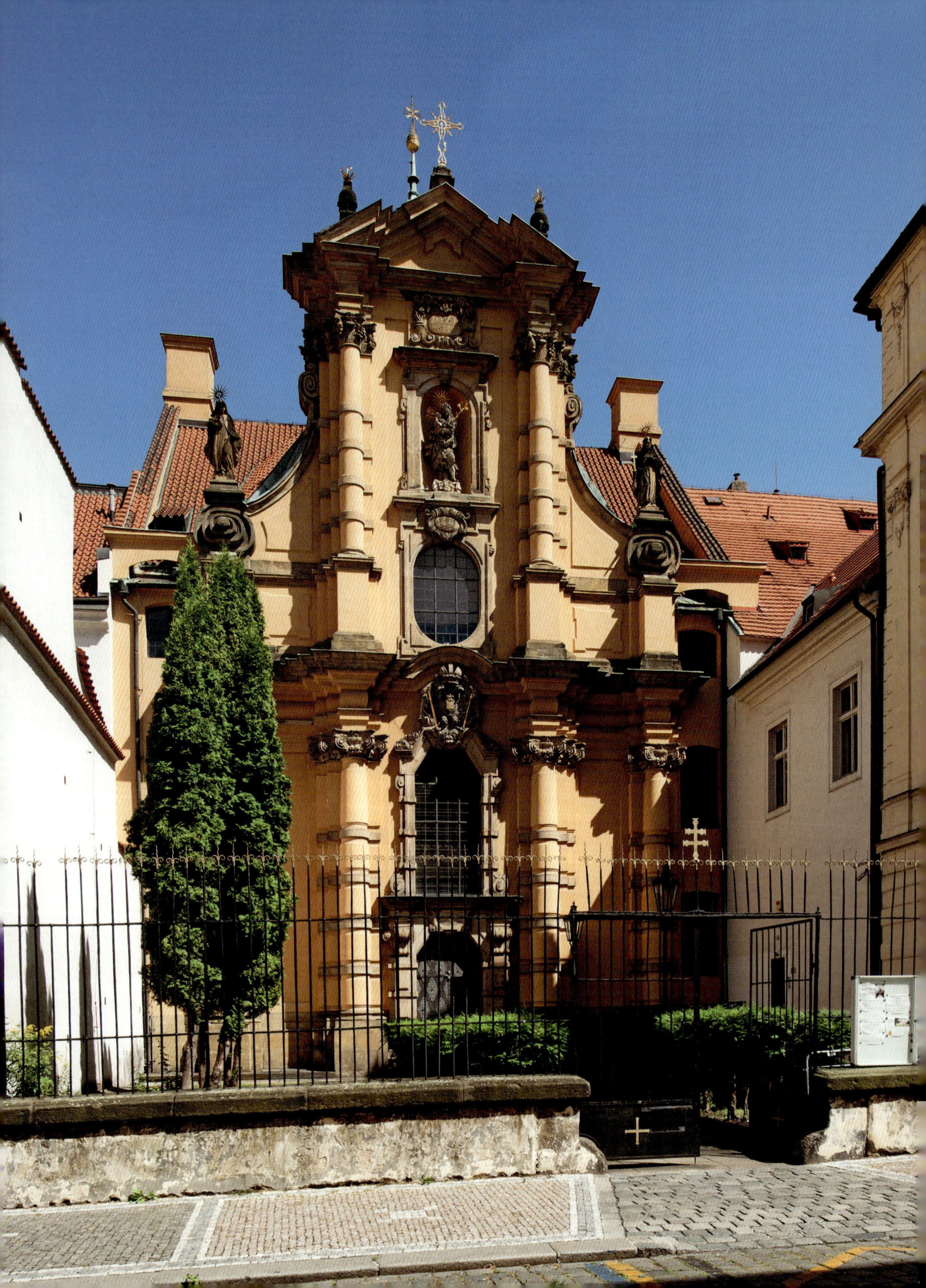

29A/ CHURCH OF ST JOSEPH
(KOSTEL SV. JOSEFA), after 1687

The façade of St Joseph's Church, part of the former convent of the Carmelite nuns, is a unique echo in Prague of seventeenth-century Dutch architecture. It is like a stage backdrop, more or less independent of the space behind it, distinguished by bold rusticated banded pilasters. The archive documents make no mention of the architect of the remarkable plans, but he is generally believed to be Johann Rass of the Carmelite order. Despite its small dimensions, the interestingly designed interior makes a great impression, thanks in part to the central cupola and the double columns of the rhythmically designed wall. An important role here is given to light, which falls primarily on the high altar. This is a remarkable response to Roman church architecture of the period.

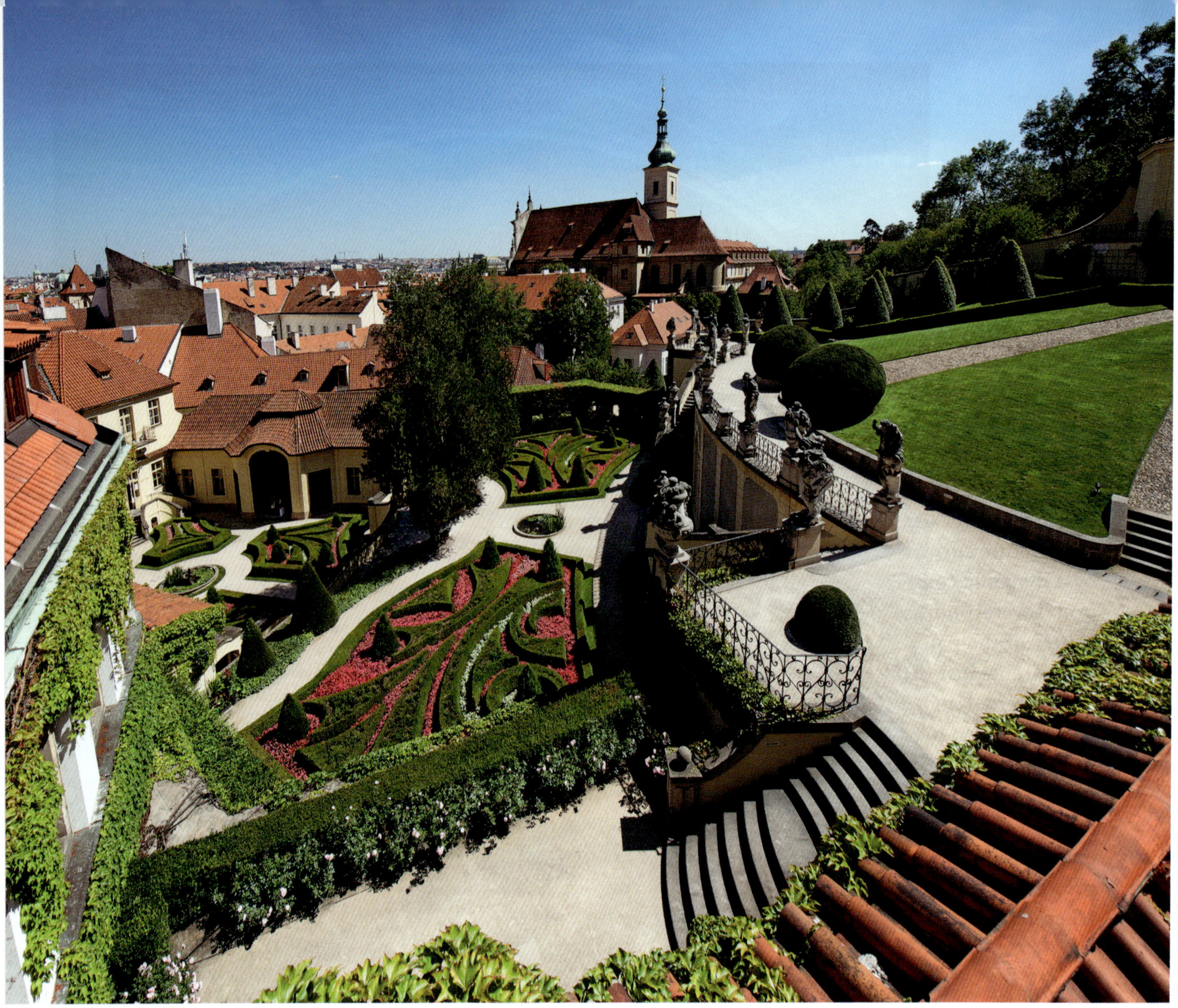

30A–C/ VRTBA GARDEN (VRTBOVSKÁ ZAHRADA)

From the outside, Vrtba House (Vrtbovský palác) in Karmelitská ulice is inconspicuous. At one time the fortified area in front of the Újezd Gate spread out here. By the Renaissance period, houses of burghers were being built on this land. Among their owners was Kryštof Želenský, an influential deputy head of the Bohemian Chancellery in the reign of Rudolph II, and the imperial architect Ulrico Aostalli, but also Kryštof Harant z Polžic a Bezdružic, a highborn Renaissance man. In 1631, Count Sezima z Vrtby united all the properties that he owned here. His grandson Jan Josef the Elder Count z Vrtby began, at the latest in 1718, to build a Baroque terraced garden in the area behind the house on the site of former vineyards. The slope of Petřín Hill in these parts rises up steeply and, moreover, turns at a right angle towards the west. The inventive architect (probably František Maxmilián Kaňka) was able to achieve the maximum effect on this cramped site.

He divided the steep terrain into three tiers coming to a peak with the effective backdrop of a pavilion. Looking along the main axis the garden seems to be much larger than it actually is. The architecture is completed by decorative urns and statues of gods of classical mythology from the workshop of Matthias Bernhard Braun. The intimate sala terrena in the lower part of this Baroque town house garden, the most beautiful in Prague, is adorned with stucco work by Tommaso Soldati and paintings by Wenzel Lorenz Reiner. Unique views of the Lesser Town and Hradčany open up from the terraces. Vrtba Garden is superb evidence of the ability of Baroque art harmonically to link the work of the human spirit and human hands with works of nature. Prague Baroque art and architecture enriched the natural terrain and added value to it, both in the overall landscaping and in the many charming details.

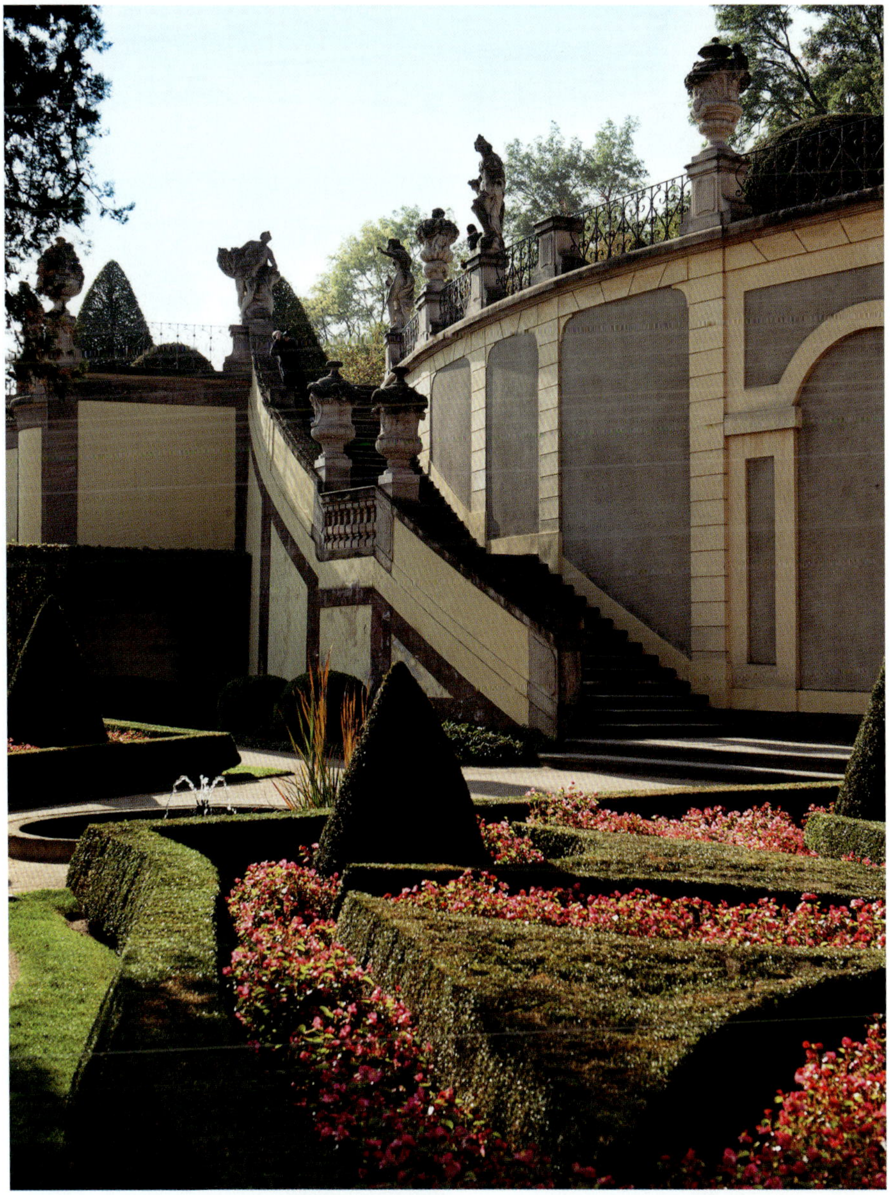

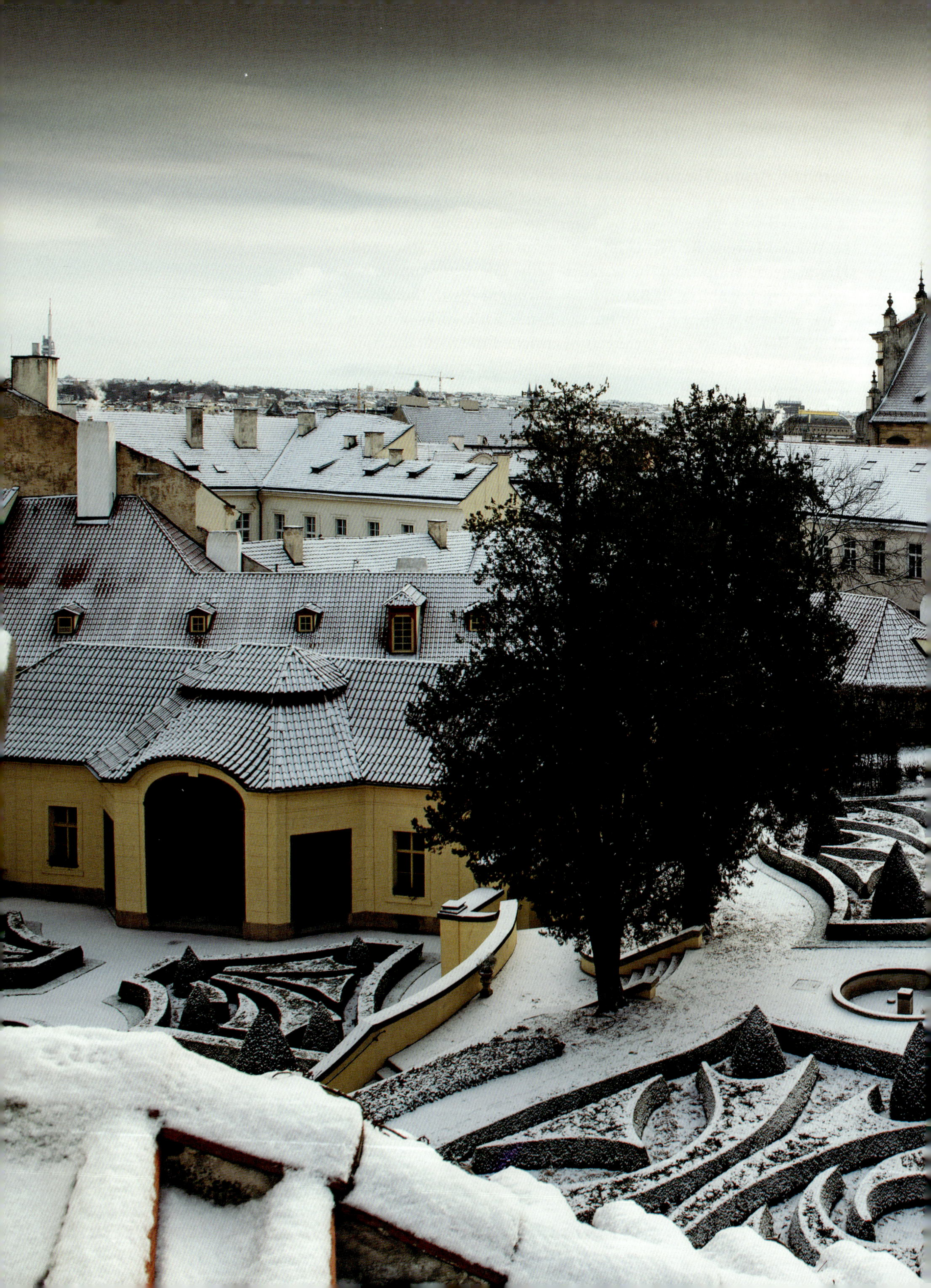

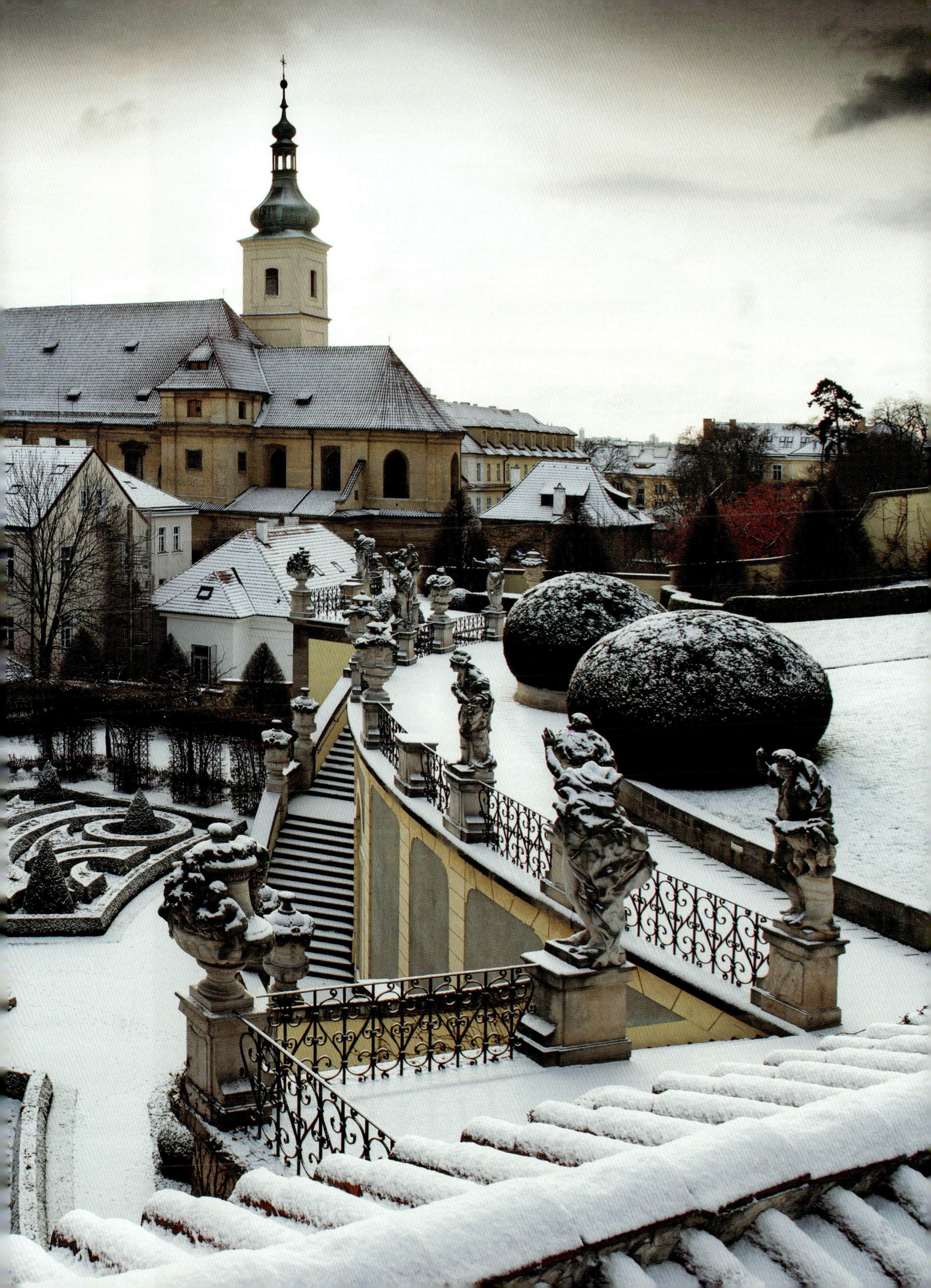

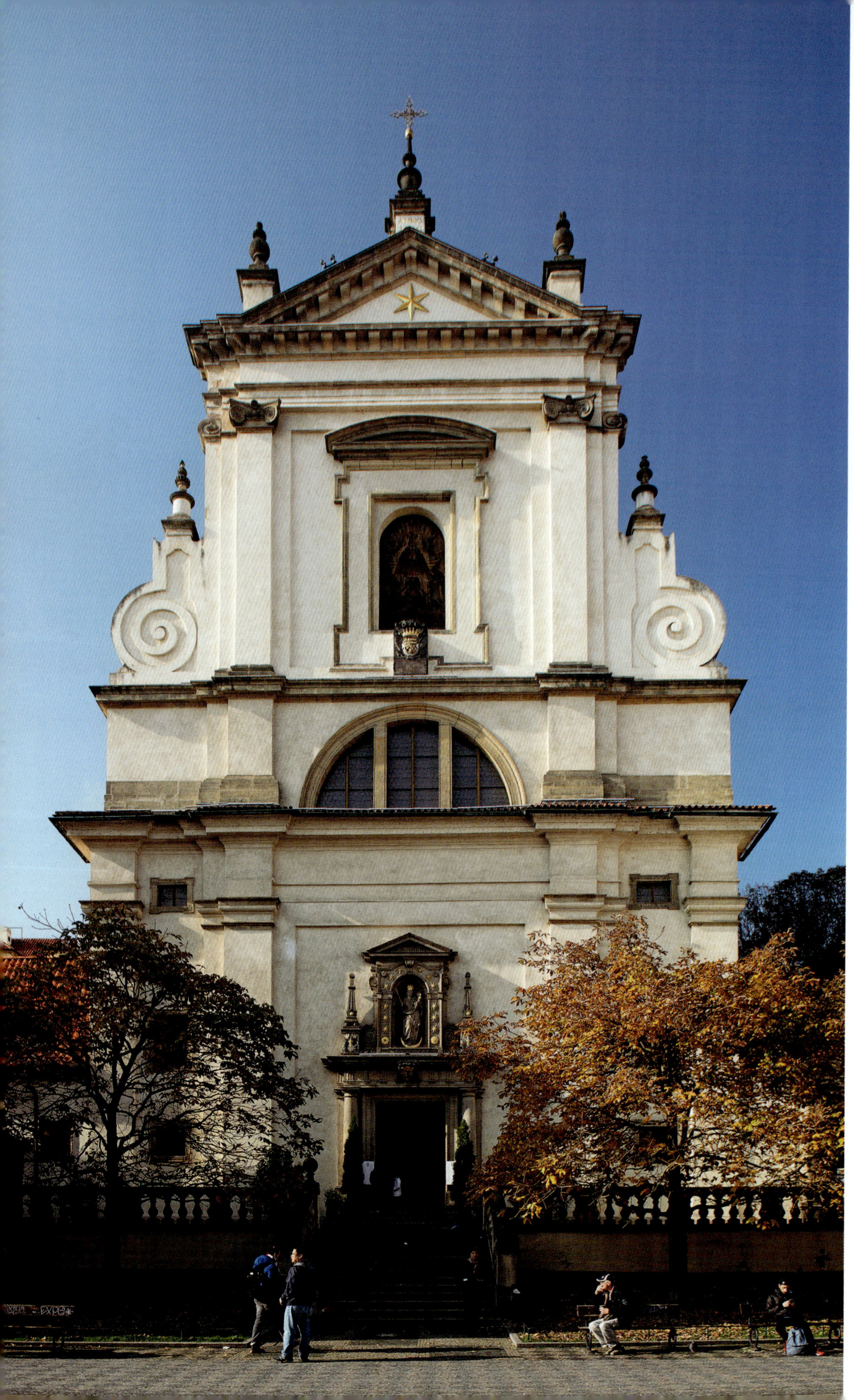

31/ ST MARY OF VICTORY (KOSTEL PANNY MARIE VÍTĚZNÉ)

31A/ FAÇADE

The originally Protestant church of the Holy Trinity (Nejsvětější Trojice) was given by Emperor Ferdinand II to the Discalced Carmelites in 1624. The church was rededicated as Saint Mary of Victory (Panny Marii Vítězné) to commemorate the victory of the Catholics at the Battle of the White Mountain (1620). Built from 1611 to 1613, it is an example of 'proto-Baroque' architecture in Prague. Its architect, Giovanni Maria Filippi, drew inspiration for its main façade from the Church of Santissima Trinità dei Monti in Rome.

31B/ ALTAR OF THE INFANT JESUS OF PRAGUE (PRAŽSKÉHO JEZULÁTKA)

The greatest treasure of the Carmelite church in the Lesser Town is the world-famous sacred little statue of the Infant Jesus. It stands on an altar of red and grey marble, made in 1776 by Franz Martin Lauermann. The statues of St Joseph and the Blessed Virgin Mary, together with the figure of God the Father in the reredos above them, were carved by Peter Prachner. The glazed cabinet of the Infant Jesus was made in the goldsmith's workshop of the Packeny family, together with the richly decorated pedestal, twenty figures of angels and other decoration.

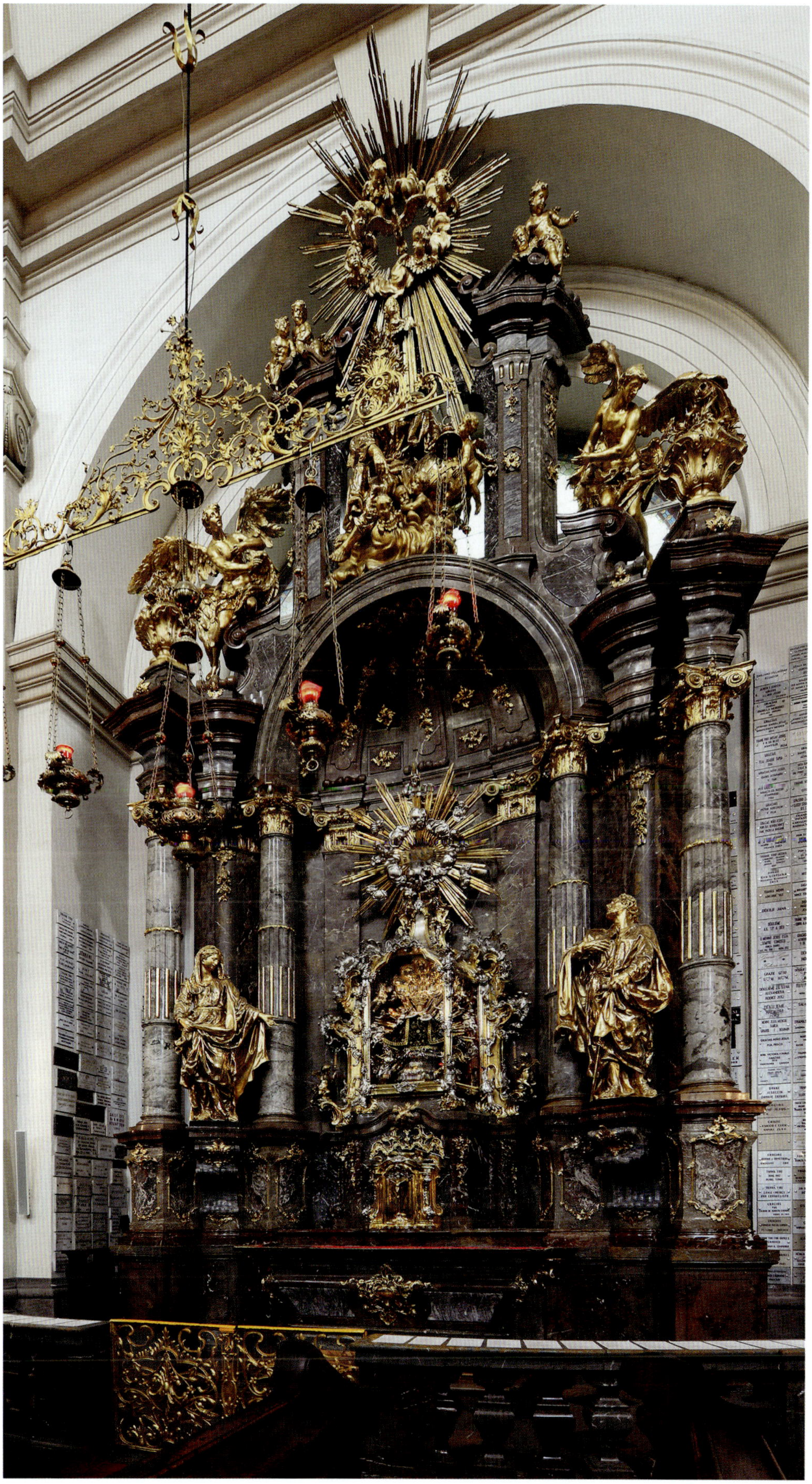

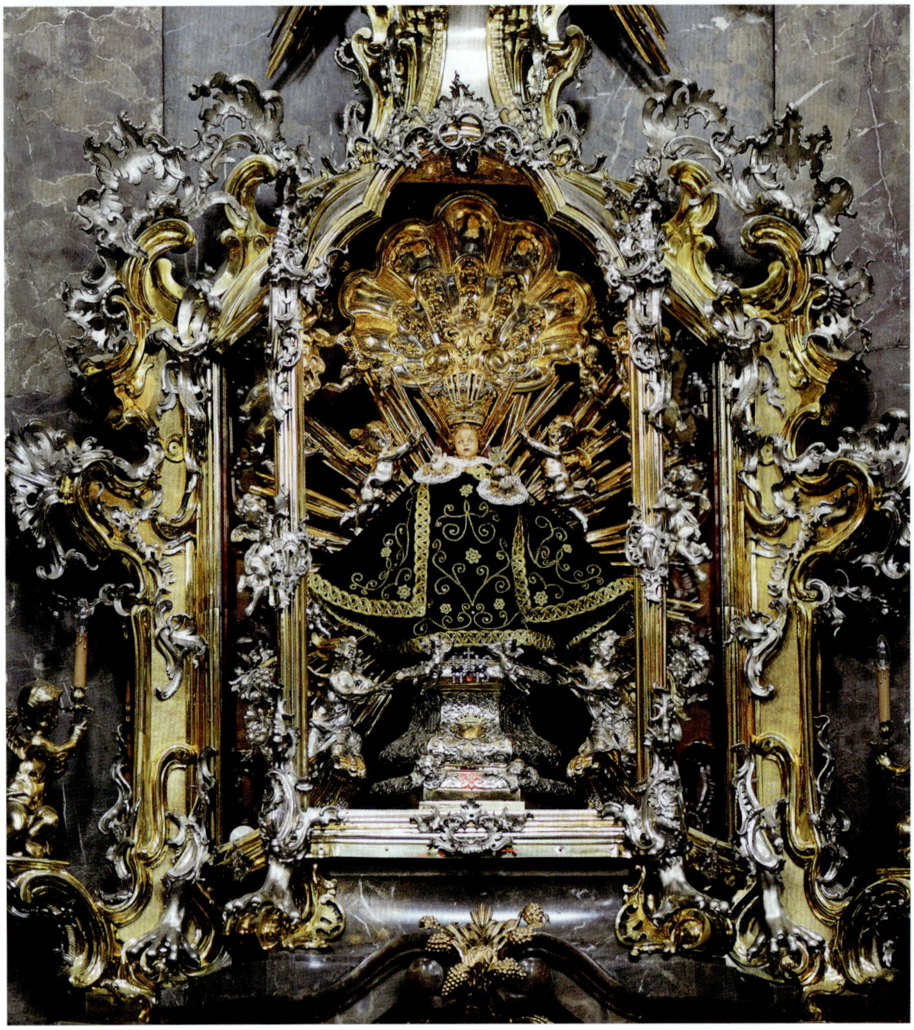

31c/ INFANT JESUS OF PRAGUE (PRAŽSKÉHO JEZULÁTKA)
The wax statue of Spanish origin came to Bohemia in the second half of the sixteenth century thanks to the noble family of Manrique de Lara y Mendoza. After the death of her second husband, in 1628, Polyxena von Lobkowicz (z Lobkovic), the daughter of Marie Manrique de Lara y Mendoza and Vratislav von Pernstein (z Pernštejna), gave the statue to the Carmelites of the Lesser Town. Its cult developed from the mid-seventeenth century onwards and did not fade even with the end of the Baroque period. The Infant Jesus of the Lesser Town has an abundant wardrobe comprising sixty little outfits. The earliest surviving clothes are of green velvet, dating from 1700. The others are gifts from pious venerators not only from all over Europe, but also from Asia and particularly South America. One of the outfits is said to have been donated to the statue by Empress Maria Theresa. The Infant Jesus statue also has lace ruffs, orbs, and gilded crowns. Count Bernhard Ignaz von Martinitz even conferred on the Infant Jesus the Order of the Golden Fleece, which, however, was stolen from the statue by an unidentified thief in 1733.

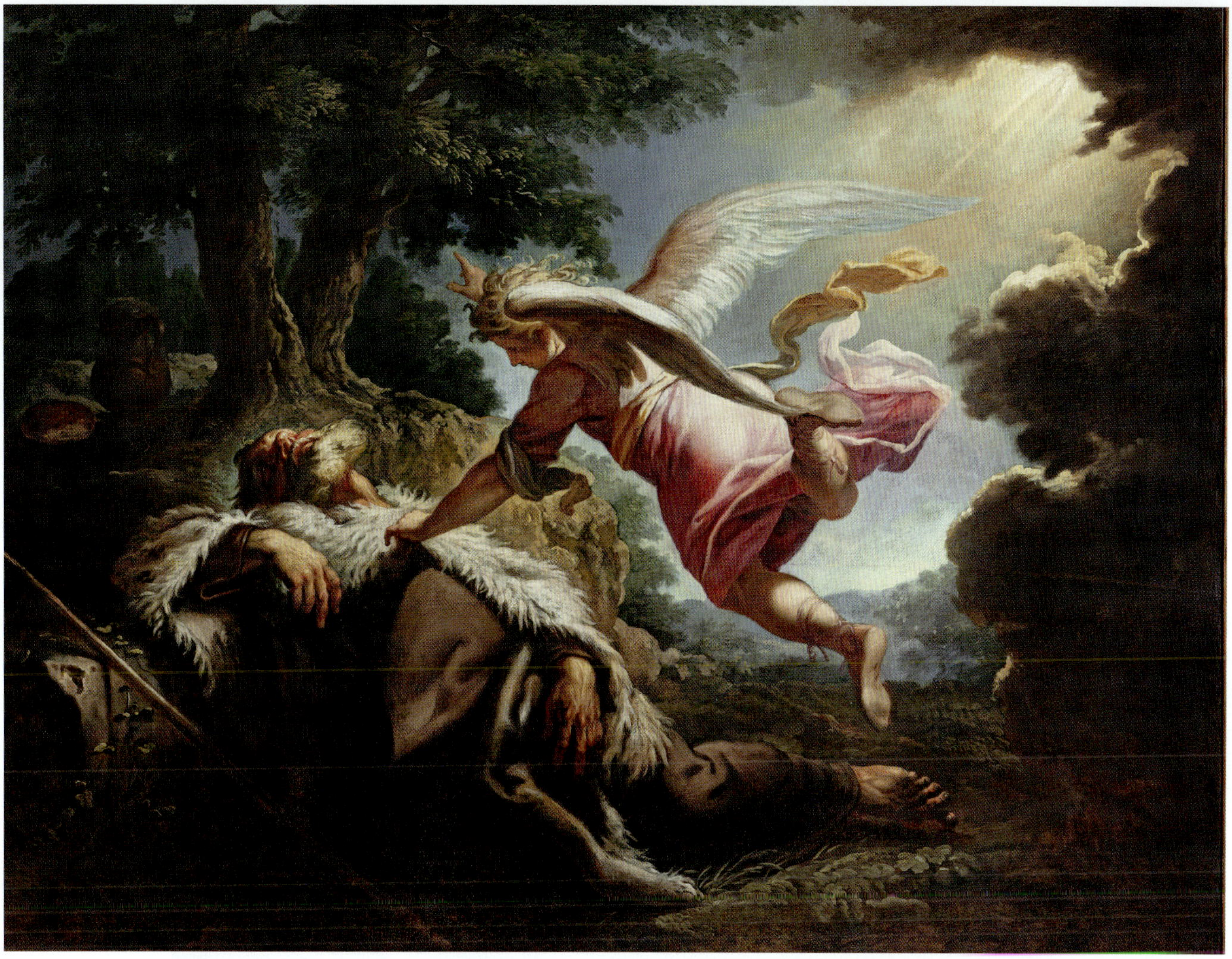

31D/ PETER BRANDL:
THE PROPHET ELIJAH'S DREAM, 1724
This painting is of the miraculous sating of the thirst and hunger of the Old Testament prophet Elijah, considered to be the 'founder' of the Carmelite Order. Peter Brandl has set in motion here the dramatic play of shadow and light, the most powerful source of which is the sun, penetrating the heavy clouds and symbolizing hope and salvation.

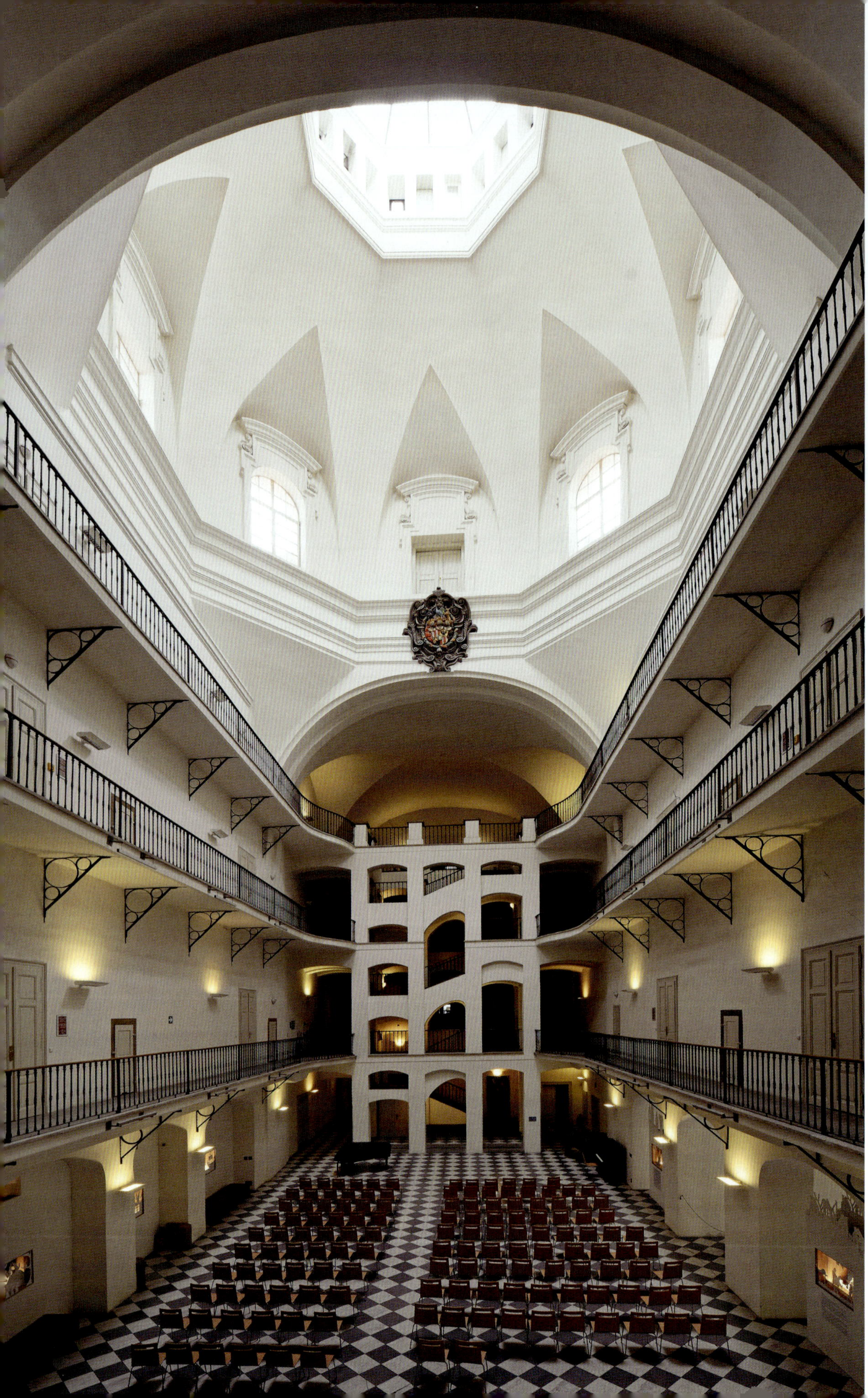

32A–B/ CZECH MUSEUM OF MUSIC

The vast block between what are today Harantova and Hellichova streets is filled with buildings of the former Dominican monastery at the Church of St Mary Magdalene. The first little church dedicated to her here was already built by the early fourteenth century and beside it was a convent of the Order of St Mary Magdalene. The convent ceased to exist during the Hussite Wars (1419–34) and the land was acquired by the Dominicans in 1613. Since the religious order was in financial difficulties, the foundation stone of the new, Baroque church was not laid until 1656. With a temporary roof, the church was used for services only from 1677 onwards, but was not dedicated until 1709. The plans were by Francesco Caratti, who conceived the church on the plan of a Greek-cross with a cupola at the centre and two steeples, one at each side. After the monastery was suppressed in 1783, the deconsecrated church was used for various purposes. Through the years, the building has been a warehouse, an office building, a post office, barracks of the gendarmerie, and a state archive. Currently, it houses the Czech Museum of Music. The utilitarian aspect of the building is reflected in its sober Neoclassical façade from 1853–54, which bears no resemblance to the former 'Roman' Baroque church façade with five vertical divisions. Of Caratti's building, the impressive stucco vaulting that comes to a peak in the cupola has been preserved. The cornice is adorned with the large sculptural coat of arms of the Michna z Vacínova, who generously financed the construction of the monastery.

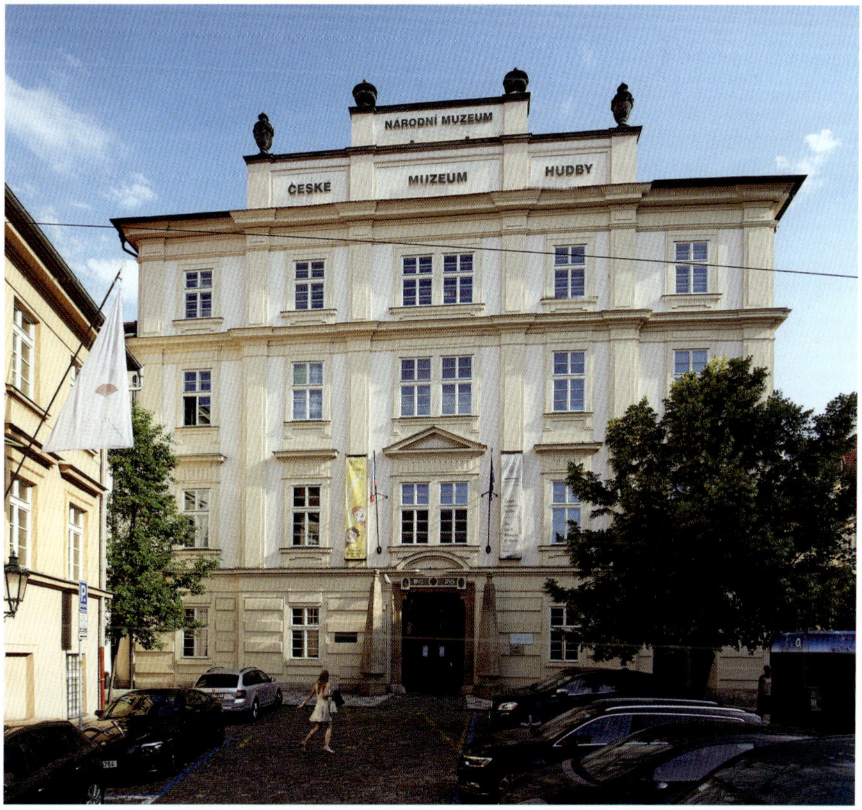

33/ MICHNA HOUSE (MICHNOVSKÝ PALÁC)

Apart from Wallenstein House, Michna House (Michnovský palác), whose garden façade probably dates from between 1631 and 1644, is the most important stately home in Prague from the period of the Thirty Years War. The architecture is stylistically mature and unique in Bohemia. Unfortunately, we do not know who its architect was. The avant-corps (the central pavilion-like projection), as well as the division of the façade, brings to mind Roman architecture of that period, for example, the Villa Doria Pamphili. Some art historians believe it was designed by Italians working for Wallenstein.

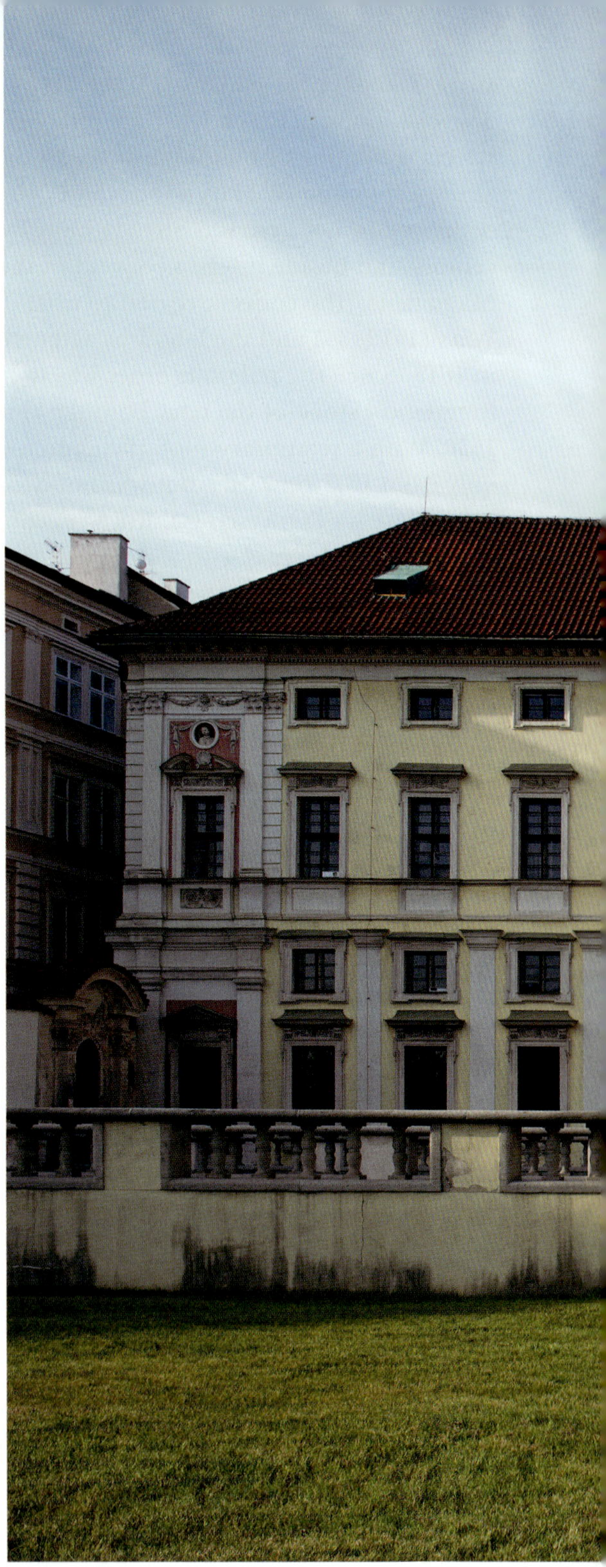

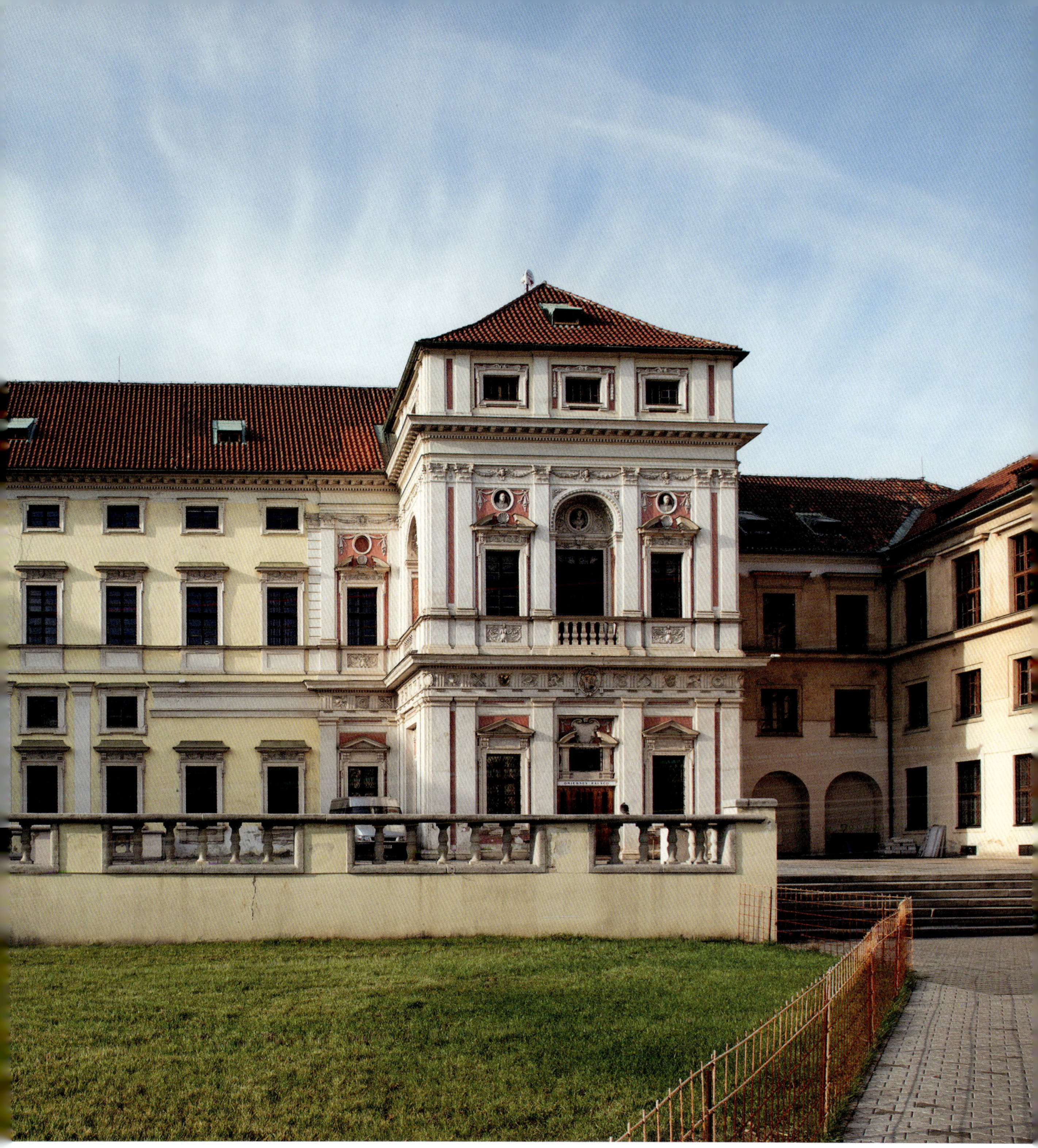

34/ KNIGHTS OF MALTA SQUARE (MALTÉZSKÉ NÁMĚSTÍ)

In 1714, the Knights of Malta (the Order of Knights of the Hospital of Saint John of Jerusalem) commissioned the sculptor Johann Brokoff to make for their Lesser Town monastery a 'lovely work of sculpture' in honour of their patron saint. The figures of St John the Baptist and three angels together with relief sculptures on the pedestal were carved of sandstone from Toužim, a town in Bohemia, by Johann's son, Ferdinand Maximilian. The work was finished in November 1715. Here, Saint John is not holding the usual light cross of reed, but the standard of the Knights of Malta. One of the reliefs on the pedestal commemorates how he appeared to the Christian forces during the famous naval battle against the Turks at Lepanto in 1571.

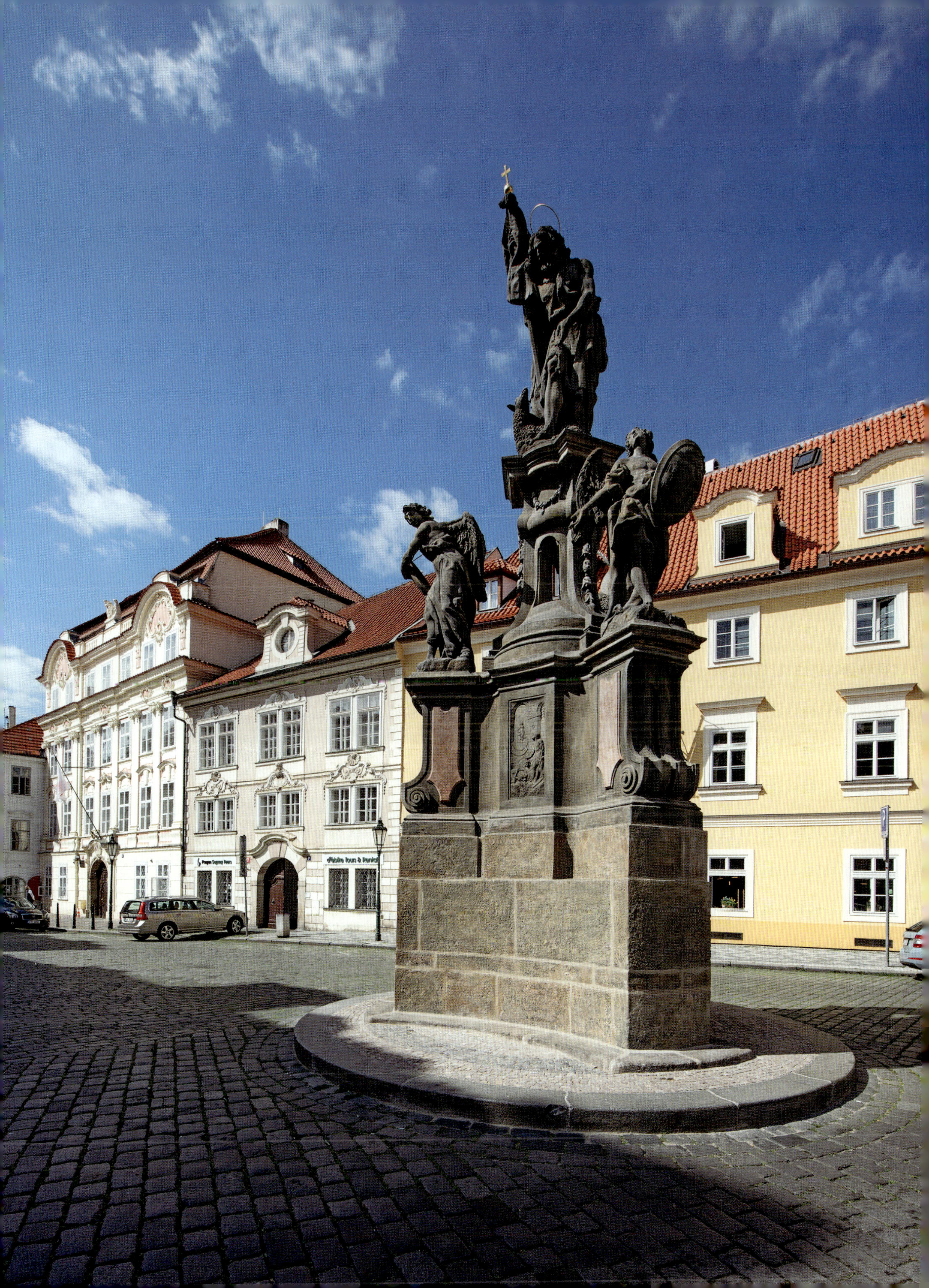

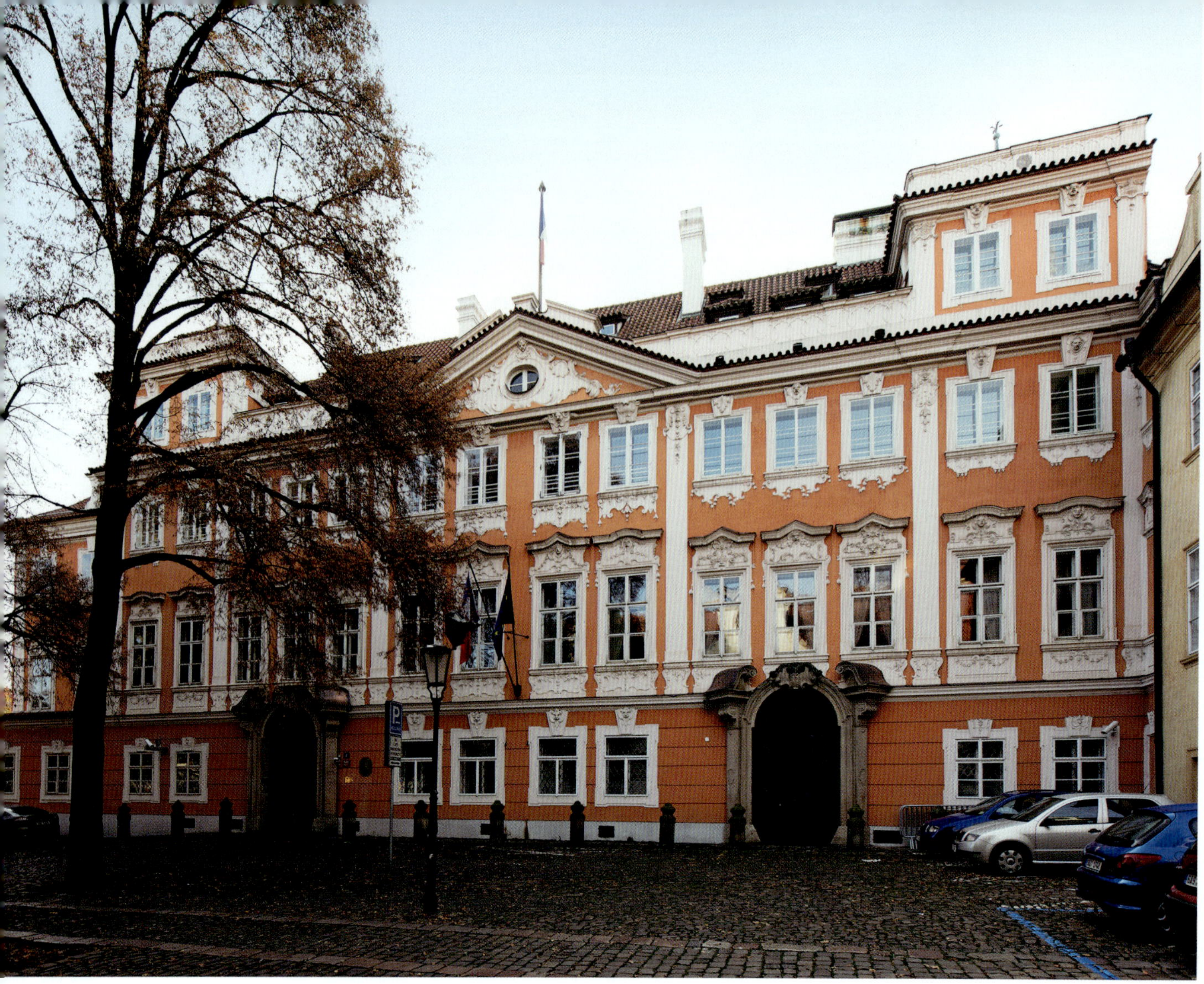

35/ BUCQUOY HOUSE (BUQUOYSKÝ PALÁC)
The house and grounds, which since 1919 have been the site of the French Embassy, spread out between Maltézské náměstí (Knights of Malta Square) and Velkopřevorské naměstí (Grand-Prior Square). The house was gradually built on land where three smaller houses had once stood and it acquired its High Baroque appearance between 1736 and 1748. The work was led by Johann Georg Aichbauer, a master builder who often collaborated with Kilian Ignaz Dientzenhofer. The house became the property of the Counts of Bucquoy in 1748. Its main façade is on Velkopřevorské náměstí, providing a monumental backdrop; the mass of the actual house is only half as large as what the façade suggests. As in several other palatial Prague houses, here too the stone 'bowling-pin' hitching posts have been preserved.

35/ NOSTITZ HOUSE (NOSTICKÝ PALÁC)
The imposing house, enclosing the southern side of Maltézské náměstí (Knights of Malta Square), was built after 1660 by Count Johann Hartwig von Nostitz-Rieneck, the Lord High Chancellor of the Bohemian Kingdom, on the site of two early houses. The façade is divided up by pilasters of the giant order and the similarity between this design and that of the later Czernin House has led art historians to attribute the plans to Francesco Caratti. Nostitz House was remodelled in about 1760 and then again in the Neoclassical period. In the second half of the eighteenth century, it became a meeting place of important figures of Enlightenment Prague, led by Josef Dobrovský and František Martin Pelcel. Their energetic scholarly work developed around the excellent Nostitz Library, which is still housed here to this day. The interior of what was once the gallery contains a hint of the then newly installed former picture gallery of the Counts of Nostitz, whose most important works are now held by the National Gallery in Prague.

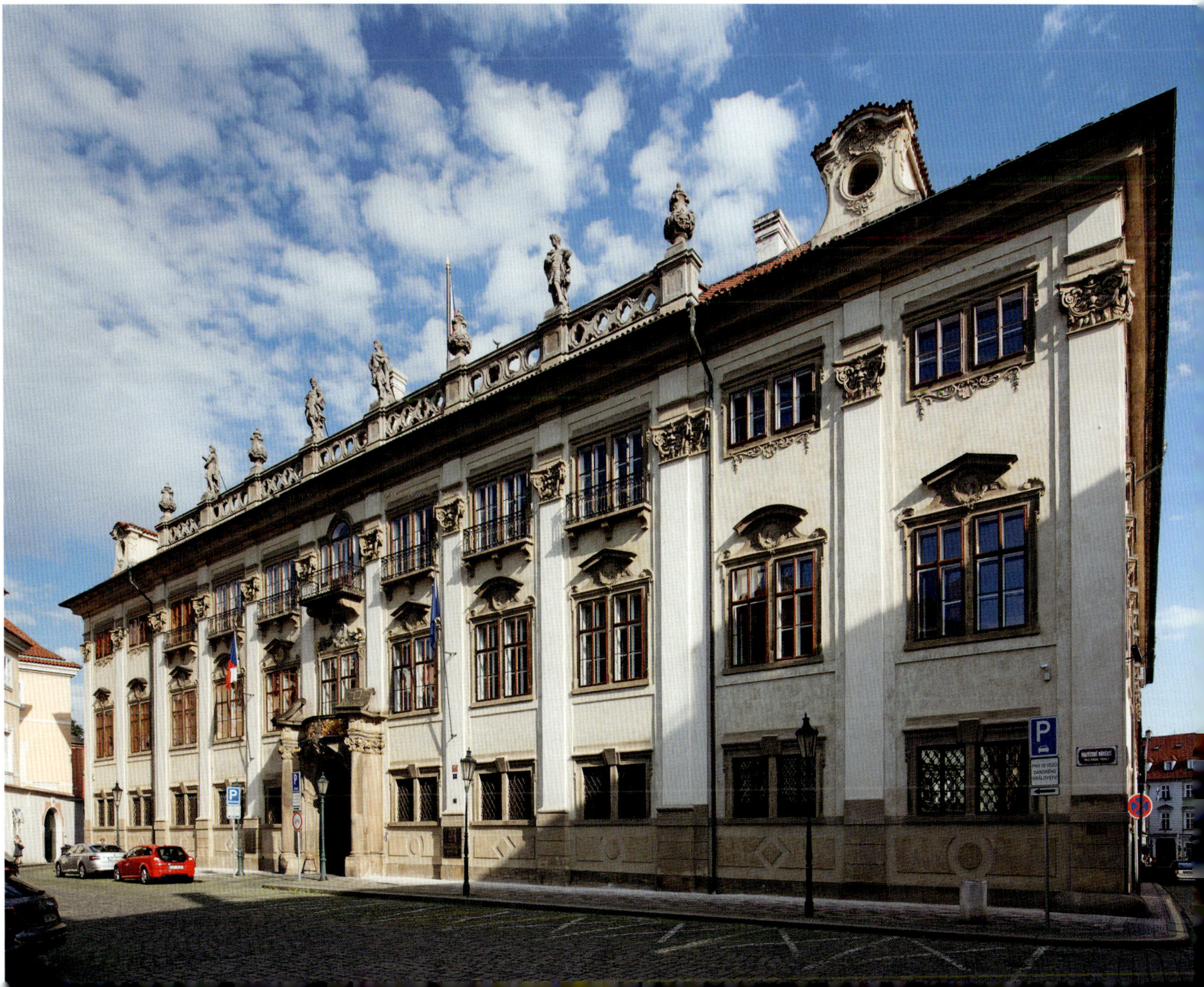

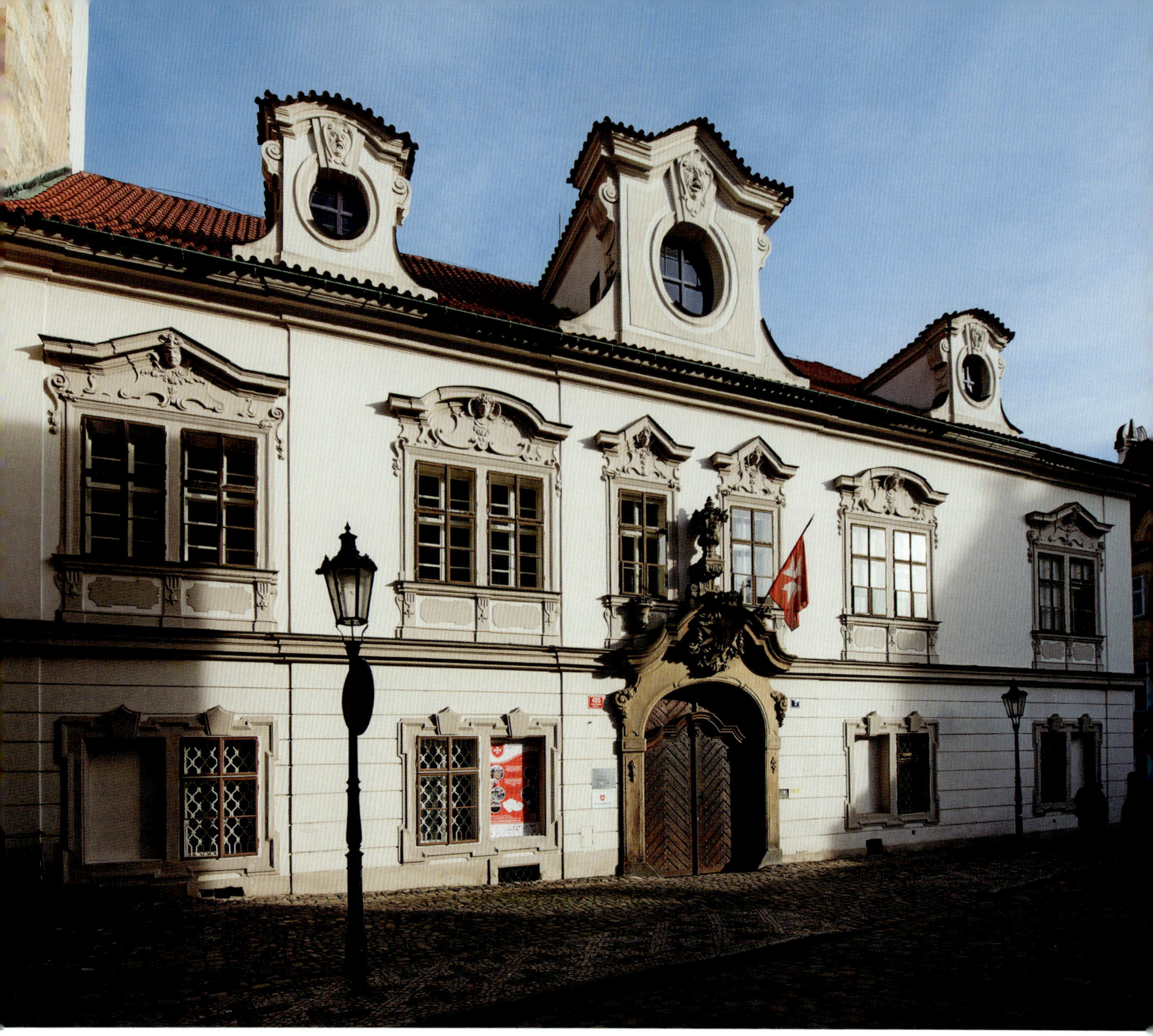

37/ THE GRAND-PRIOR'S HOUSE (VELKOPŘEVORSKÝ PALÁC)
From the second half of the twelfth century onwards, the area round Maltézské náměstí (Knights of Malta Square) belonged to the Knights Hospitaller. They actually constituted a small town covering the area roughly between what is today Karmelitská ulice and the Vltava embankment, protected by its own fortifications. Its centre was the commandery with the adjacent monastery, hospital, and Church of St Mary under the Chain (sv. Panny Marie pod řetězem). The Romanesque masonry of the original building has largely been preserved under today's façades, which are the result of Baroque remodelling from 1638 to 1647 and especially after 1725, when the architect in charge was Bartolomeo Scotti.

38/ THE BLUE FOX, HOUSE SIGN

The originally Renaissance house in Kampa is decorated with a pair of Rococo stucco cartouches. The upper one contains a picture of the Infant Jesus of Prague and the lower one has the somewhat odd depiction of a blue fox with a rose in its muzzle. The house first appears in the records under this name in 1630.

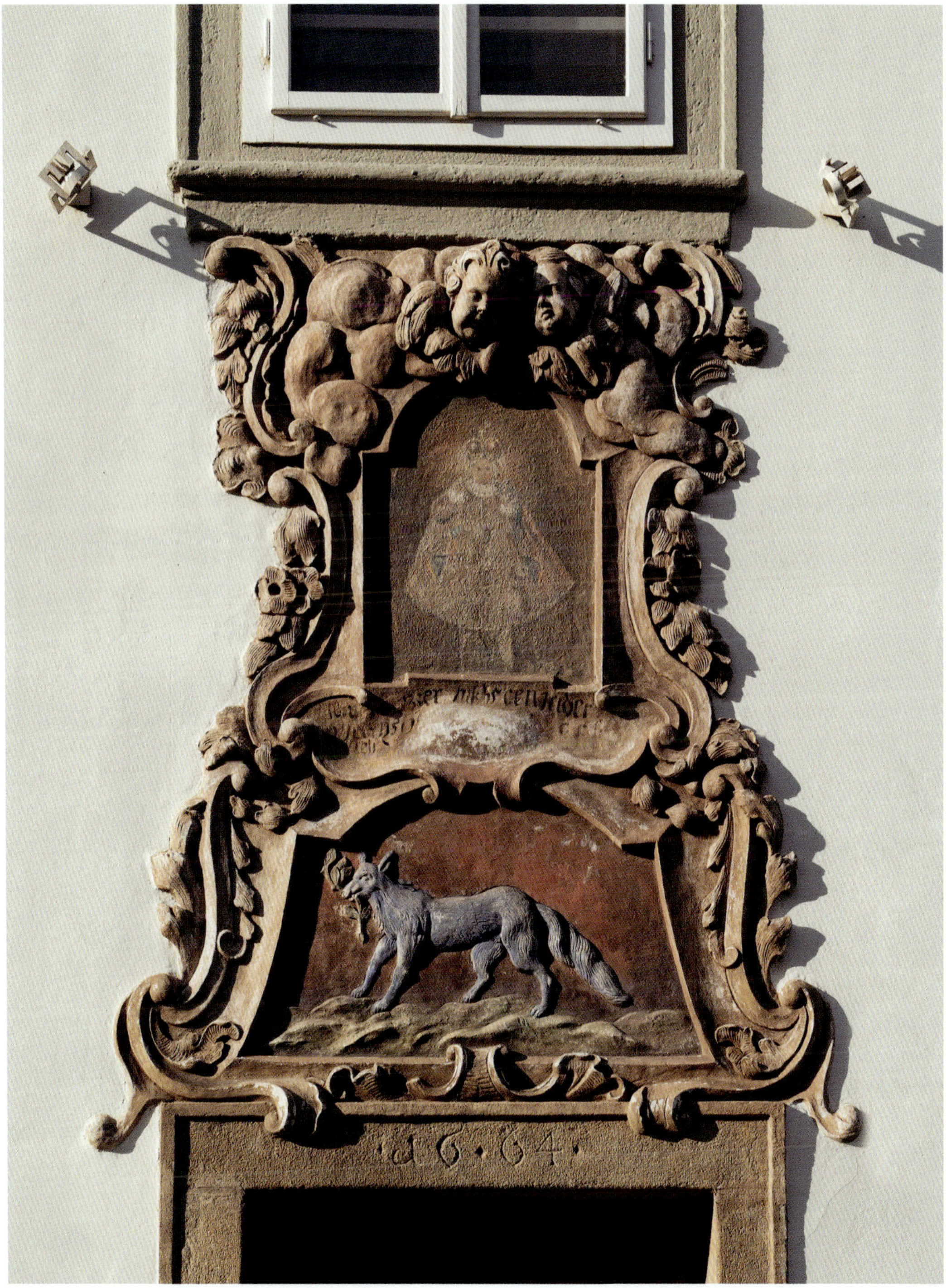

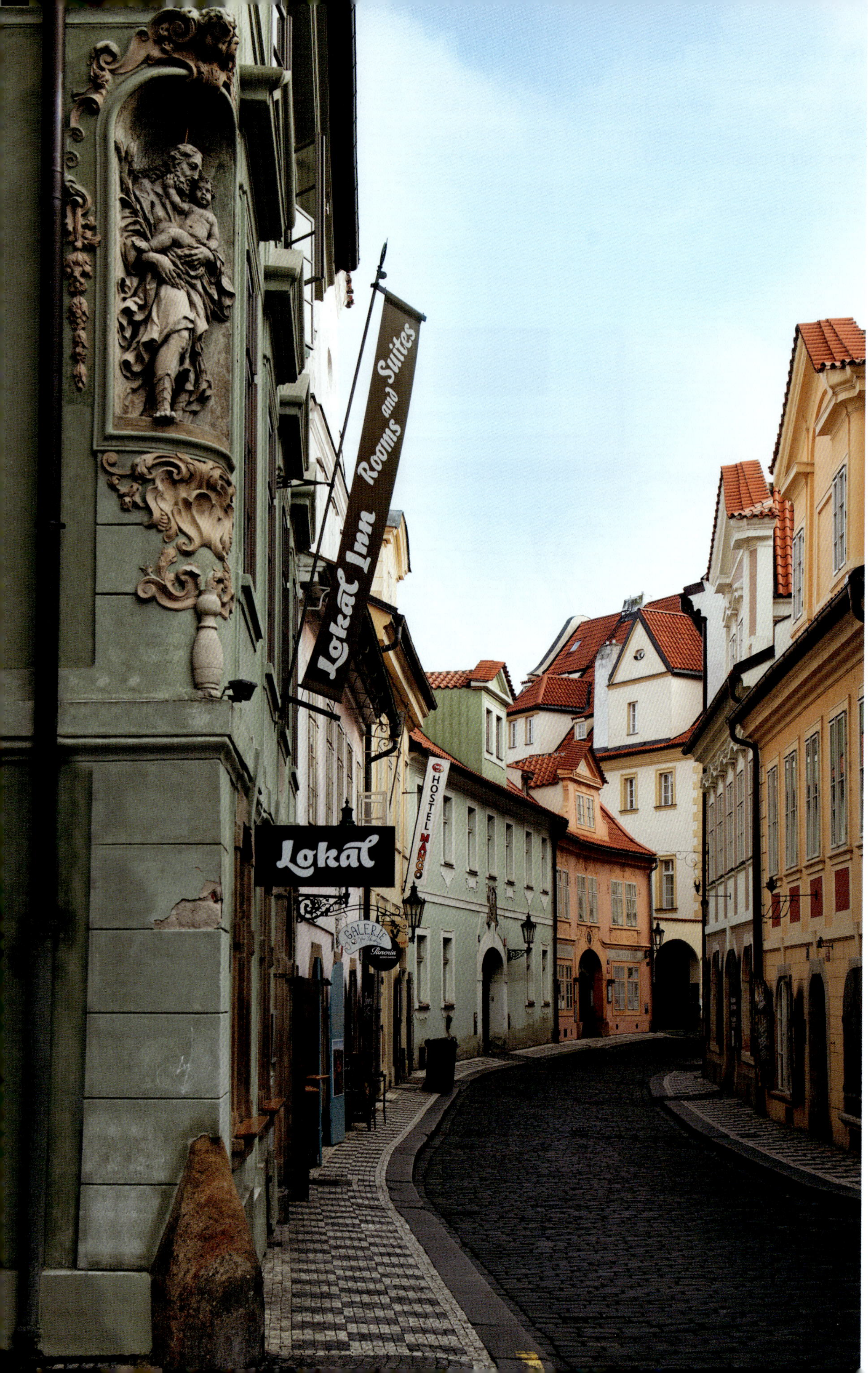
Lokal Inn
Rooms and Suites
Lokal
HOSTEL MANGO
GALERIE

39/ MÍŠEŇSKÁ ULICE (MEISSEN STREET)
The area between Charles Bridge (Karlův most) and the square-like area of Klárov long remained part of the 'outskirts' of the Lesser Town, and its architecture corresponded to that notion. The crescent-shaped Míšeňská ulice (Meissen Street) was not laid out until the early eighteenth century when Thun Garden was subdivided. It was laid out in 1707 by the architect Thomas Haffenecker, following the wall around the former Carmelite convent gardens, today Vojanovy sady (Vojan Gardens). With their gables and stucco decoration, these Baroque houses imitate, in a more modest way, the spectacular Baroque houses that were built at that time on the main streets and squares of the Lesser Town. The south side of Míšeňská ulice was reserved for traffic and business which needed to be near the river. The butcher's guild of the Lesser Town had its abattoir here and the soap factory of the Demartini family was also nearby

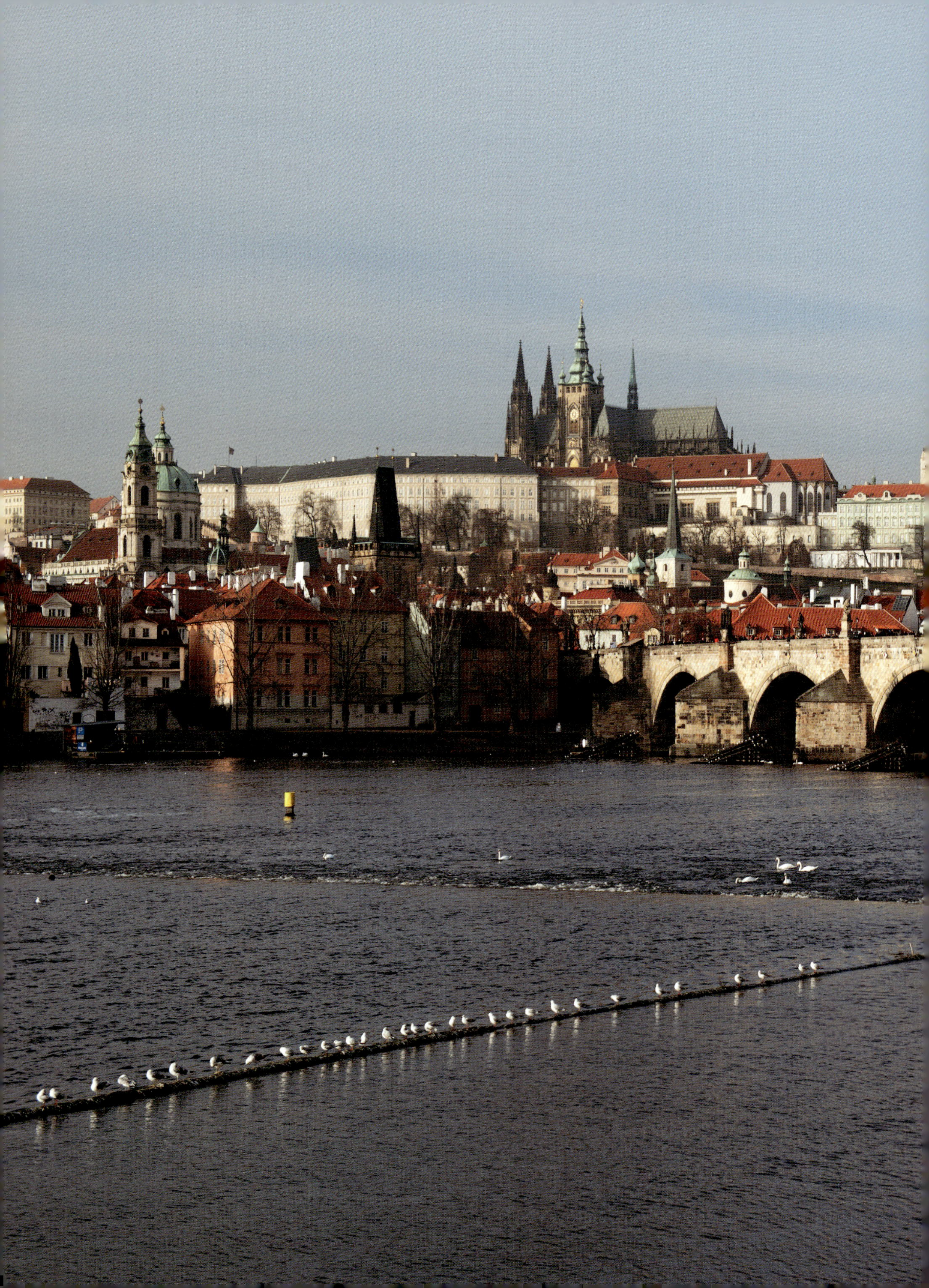

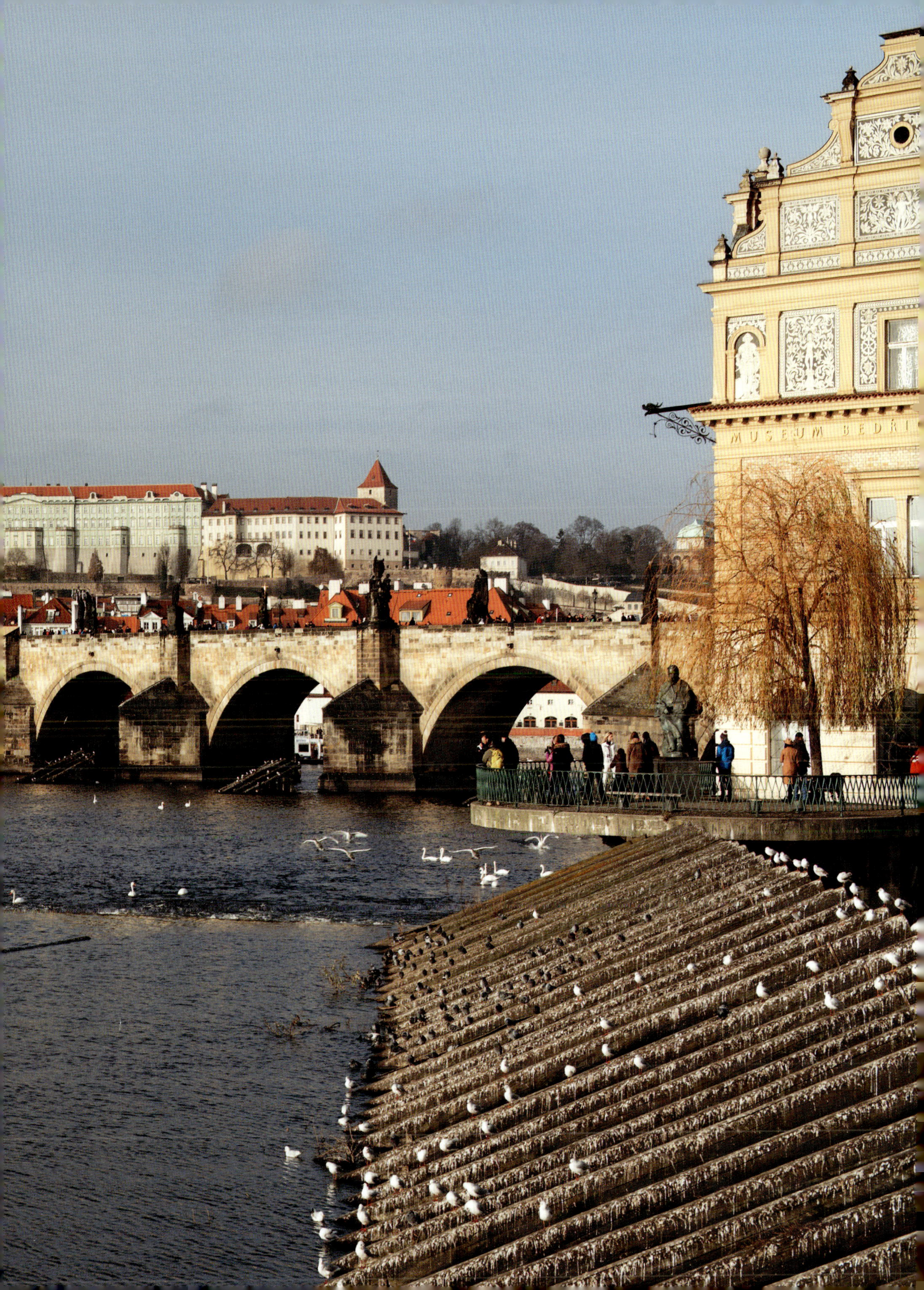

40A/ PANORAMA FROM THE SOUTH

Until the nineteenth century, the Gothic bridge, whose construction was started by Charles IV in 1357, was the only bridge over the River Vltava in Prague. The unique decoration of its piers with Baroque statues dates from 1683 to 1714. Not all of them have been preserved, since some individual figures and even whole sculptural groups were taken down and replaced in the nineteenth and twentieth centuries with new ones. Gradually, the Baroque originals are being replaced with copies. Despite all the changes, however, the bridge remains compelling evidence of the intrinsic link and mutual harmony between the Gothic and the Baroque, two periods of art which have greatly influenced the appearance of Prague.

'The bridge over the Muldaw [Moldau/Vltava] exceeds that of Ratisbon and Dresden in length, being seven hundred and forty-two common paces. The breadth of it is fourteen common paces; so that it affords room for three carriages to go a-breast. It consists of sixteen arches, and is adorned on each side with twenty-eight statues of so many saints. The crucifix and the statue of St. John Nepomuc [sic] are of brass, and the rest of stone. Several votaries are always to be seen here on their knees, paying their devotion to these statues, especially at noon and in the evening.'

Johann Georg Keyßler, 1732

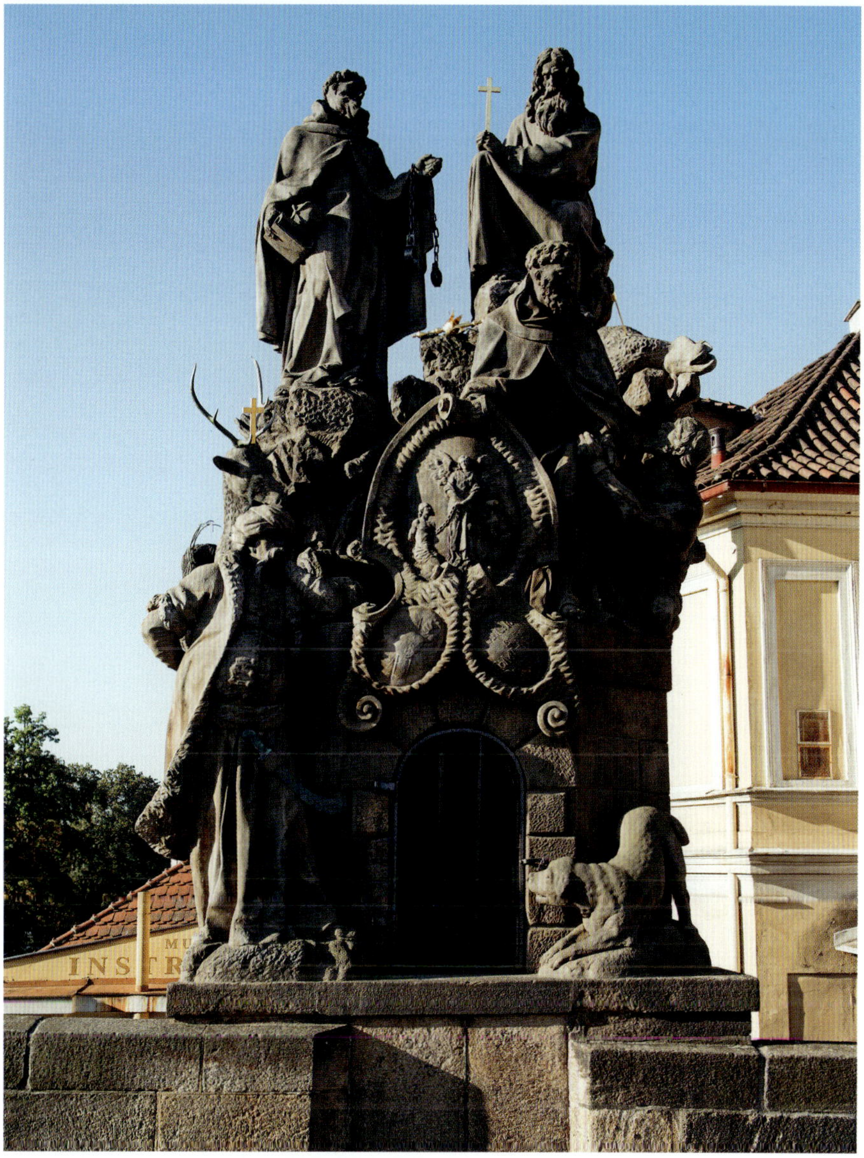

40B/ FERDINAND MAXIMILIAN BROKOFF: ST IVAN WITH ST JOHN OF MATHA AND ST FELIX OF VALOIS, LIBERATING CHRISTIAN SLAVES, 1714

One of the most elaborate sculptural groups on Charles Bridge, this work was paid for by Franz Joseph Count Thun to mark the five-hundredth anniversary of the founding of the Trinitarian Order, which paid the ransom for Christian captives in Muslim occupied lands. In Baroque Bohemia, the almost unknown saints John of Matha and Felix of Valois, the founders of the Trinitarian Order, are linked here with the hermit Ivan, who represents the patron saints of Bohemia. Brokoff has given this conceptually inconsistent group a well-balanced composition and realistic detail; the effect is monumental and sober at the same time. The Turk guarding the imprisoned Christians is a popular figure of old Prague. In his art collection, Franz Joseph Thun had smaller versions of this sculptural group and of another twenty-six statues on the bridge.

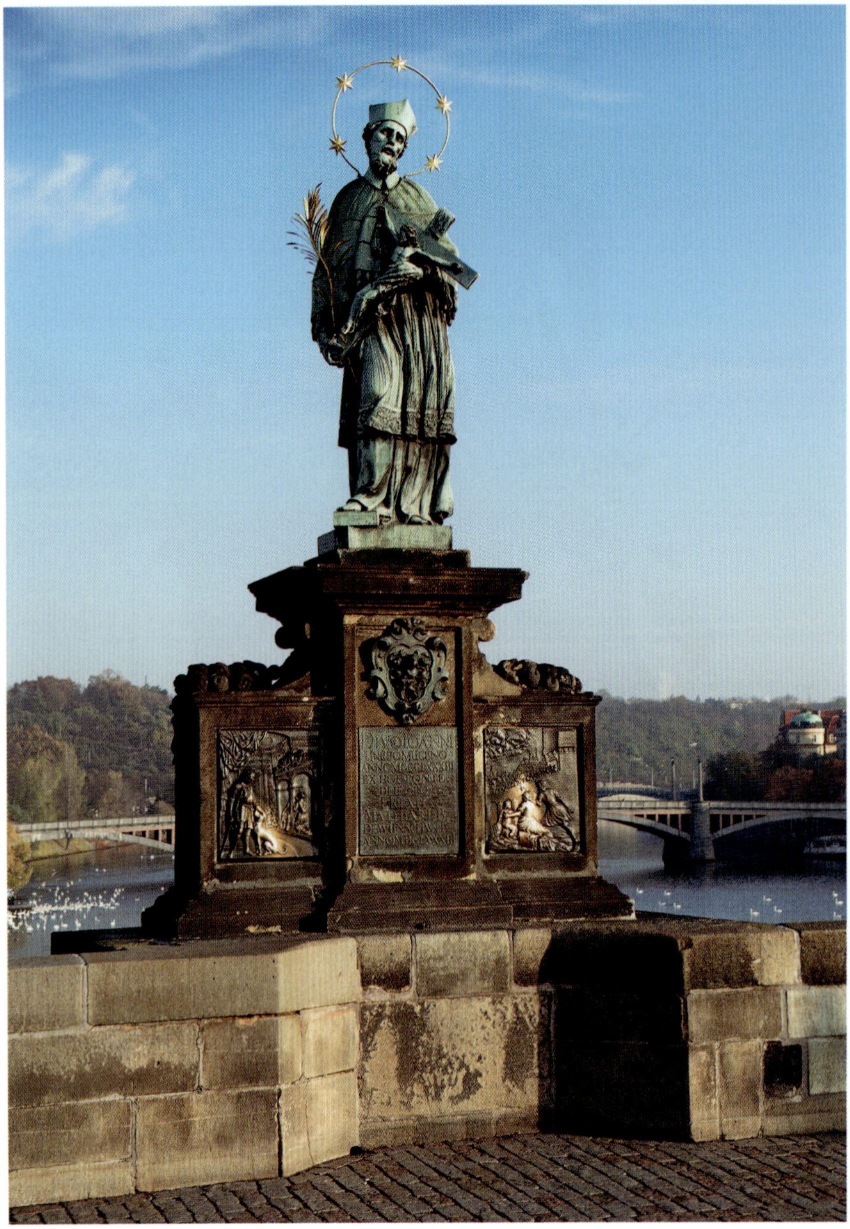

40C/ JOHANN BROKOFF (JAN BROKOF):
ST JOHN NEPOMUCENE, 1683

This bronze of John Nepomucene, placed near where he was martyred, is the oldest statue of a saint on Charles Bridge. It was erected by Baron Matthias Gottfried von Wunschwitz, who revered the saint. It was cast after Brokoff's wooden model (today in the Church of St John Nepomucene on the Rock (sv. Jana Nepomuckého na Skalce), together with the reliefs for the pedestal, by Wolf Hieronymus Herold in Nuremberg. The work provided a firm basis for an iconographic type and became a model for countless subsequent statues of John Nepomucene throughout the world.

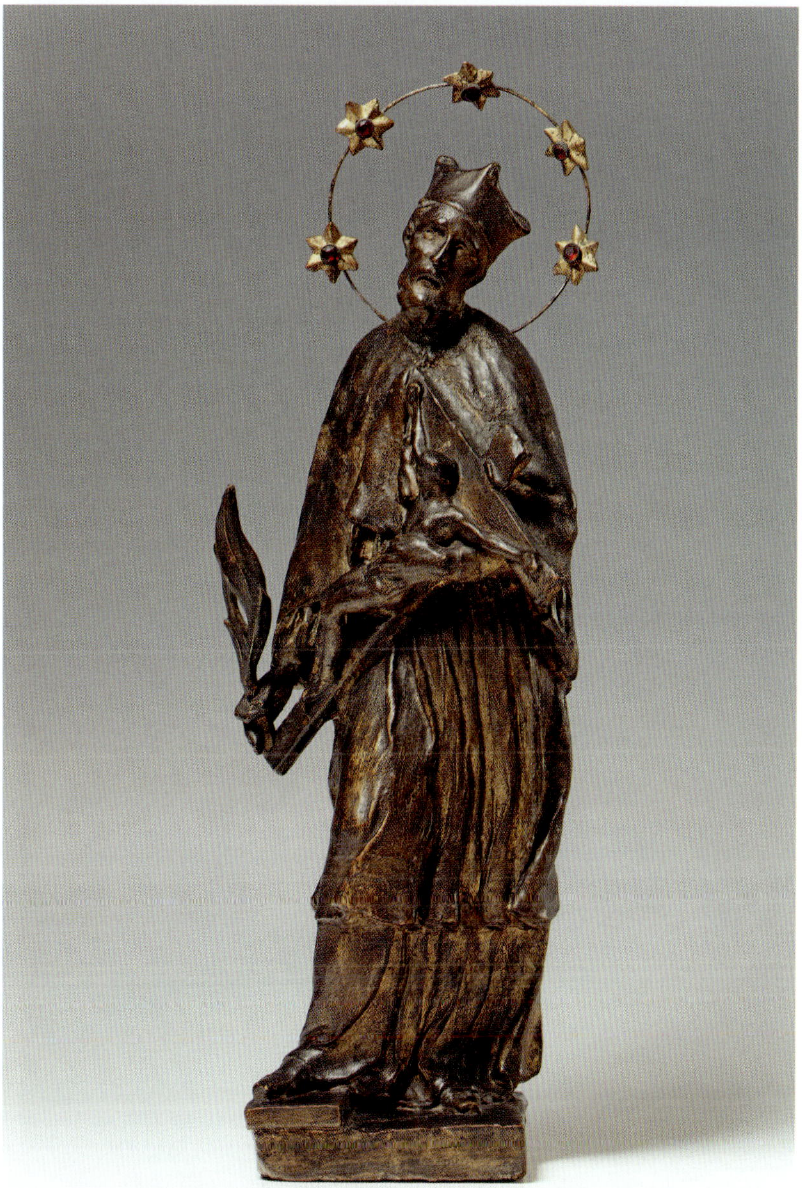

40D/ MATTHIAS RAUCHMILLER:
ST JOHN NEPOMUCENE, bozzetto, 1681

In creating his statue of John Nepomucene, the sculptor Johann Brokoff worked from this small clay model (bozzetto) made for the patron Wunschwitz by the versatile Vienna-based artist Matthias Rauchmiller. He conceived this soon-to-be saint (beatified 1721, canonized 1729), whose appearance had not yet been firmly established, as a bearded canon with a biretta on his head, dressed in a cassock and rochet, with a fur mantle over his shoulders. He is holding a crucifix and the martyr's palm branch.

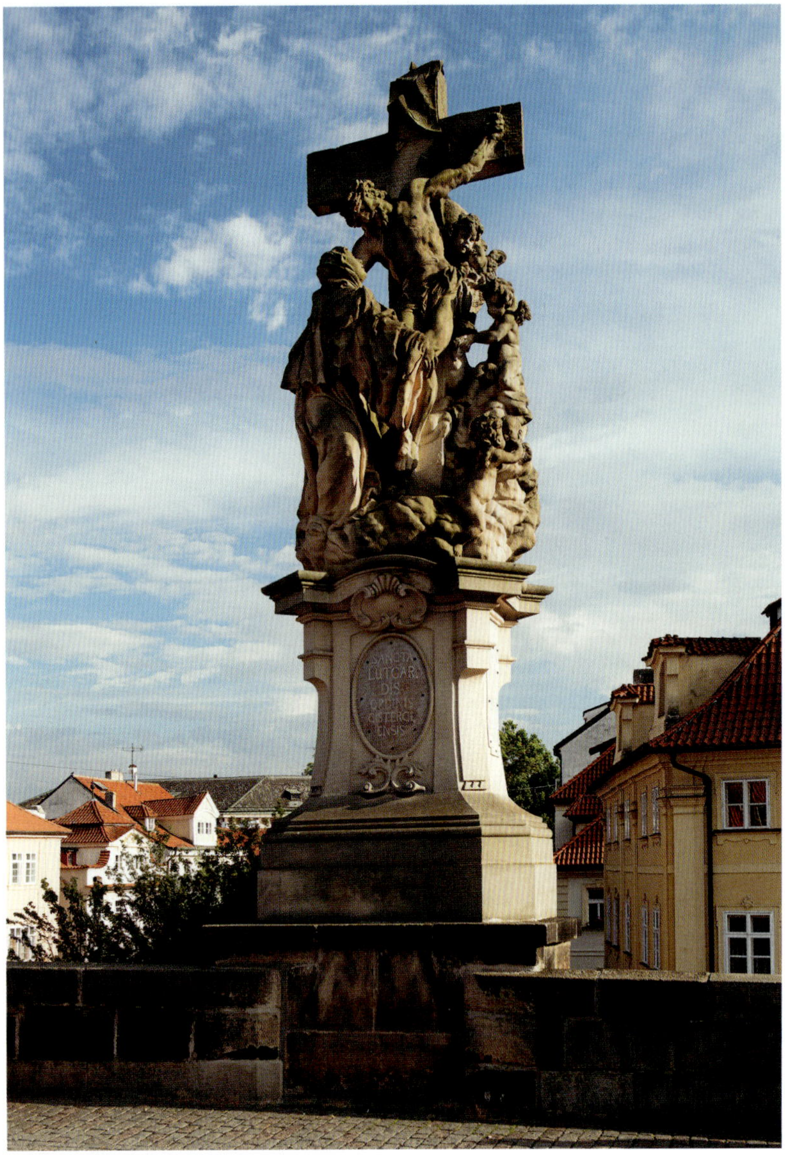

40E/ MATTHIAS BERNHARD BRAUN: THE VISION OF SAINT LUTGARDE OF AYWIÈRES, 1710

This sculptural group was commissioned by the Cistercians in Plasy (about 100 km west of Prague). For its subject matter they chose a medieval legend of the religious order, making it relevant to the Baroque period by means of mystic speculation, which was practised particularly in religious houses of Southern Germany and Silesia. *St Lutgarde* was the first big prestigious commission of the young Matthias Bernhard Braun. Though he drew on Bernini's *Ecstasy of St Teresa*, he conceived the scene more solemnly and more suitable to its spiritual message. Nevertheless, he did not suppress the emotional component, with which the scene of the blind Flemish nun's mystical 'amorous' union with the crucified Christ is deeply imbued. The sculptural group now on Charles Bridge is a modern copy; the original is in the Lapidarium of the National Museum.

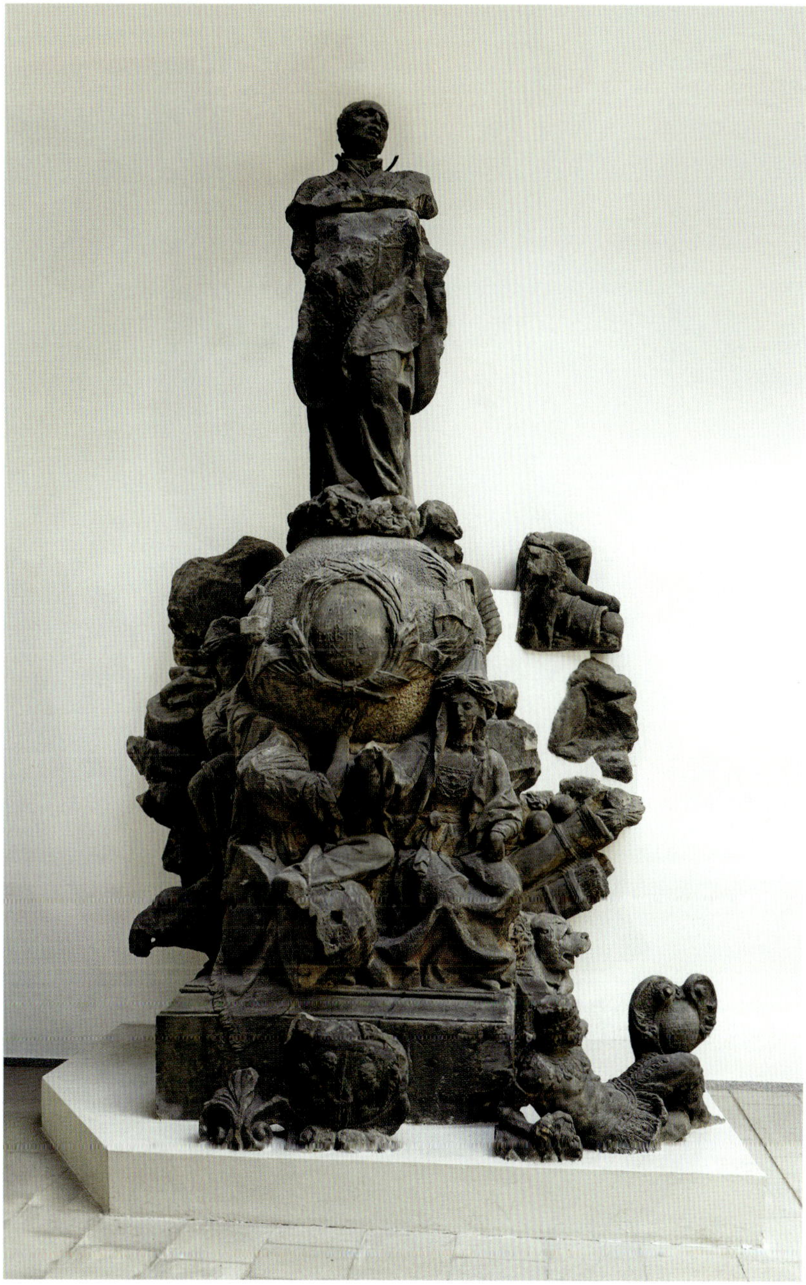

40F/ FERDINAND MAXIMILIAN BROKOFF:
THE GLORIFICATION OF ST IGNATIUS, 1710–11
The New Town Jesuit College made its presence known on Charles Bridge with a sculptural group representing the triumph of the founder of the order, St Ignatius of Loyola, as the propagator of the true faith over all the continents known at the time. In the flood of 1890, the group fell into the River Vltava. About sixty of its fragments were eventually salvaged and, in 1913, the sculptor Čeněk Vosmík assembled a torso of the former whole.

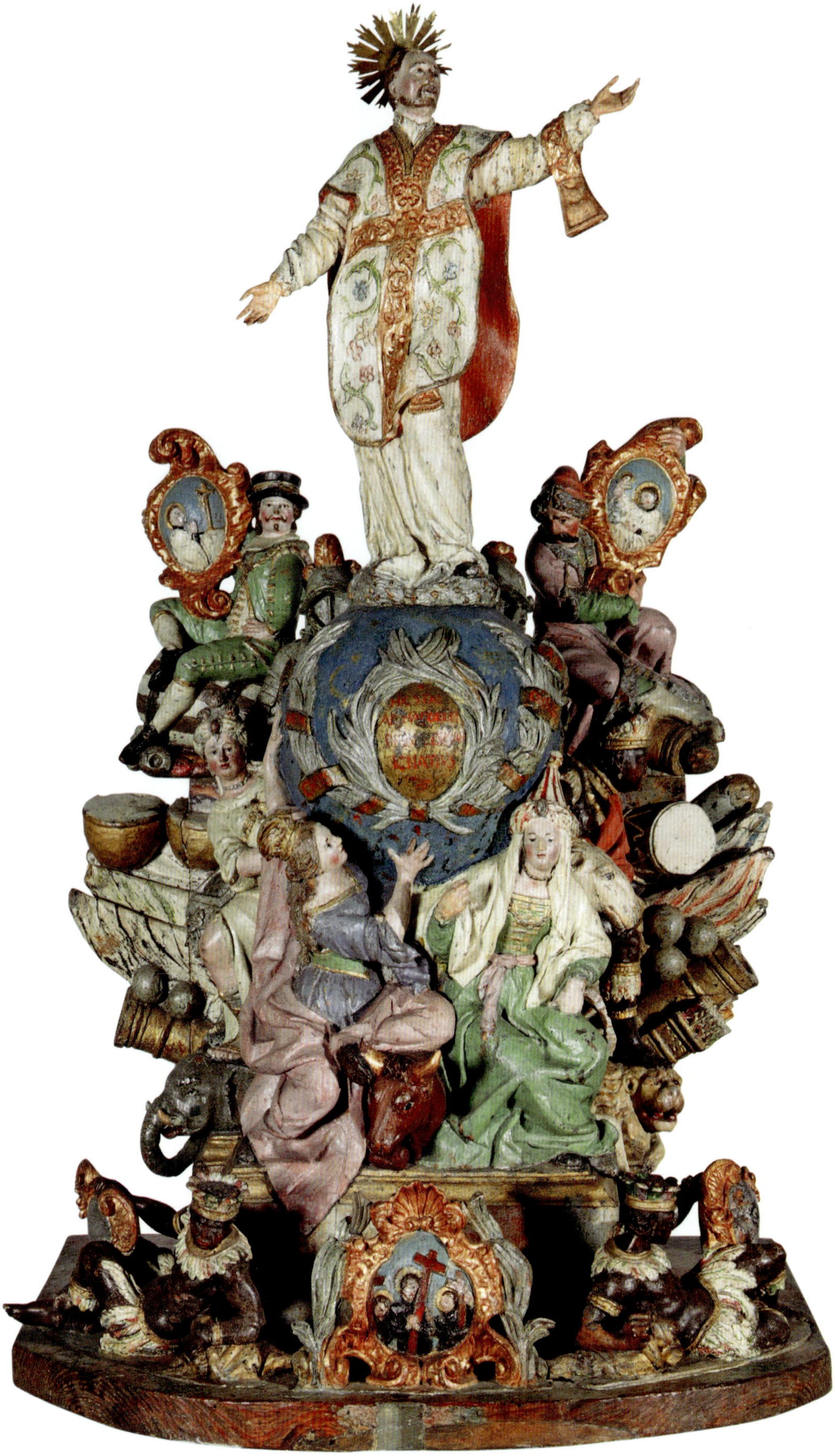

40G/ FERDINAND MAXIMILIAN BROKOFF:
THE GLORIFICATION OF SAINT IGNATIUS,
maquette, 1709–11

Before this sculptural group was made, the Jesuits commissioned a model of it. St Ignatius stands on a globe adorned with a laurel wreath, a symbol of triumph. The globe is borne by allegorical figures of the four continents, from the left: America, Europe, Asia, and Africa. The other four reclining figures symbolize the various nations that provided the Society of Jesus with saints and martyrs. Despite the complicated ideas behind the work, Brokoff has succeeded in maintaining the logical structure of the composition and has made the individual figures convincingly lifelike. For this work he drew on a number of previous compositions using Jesuit iconography.

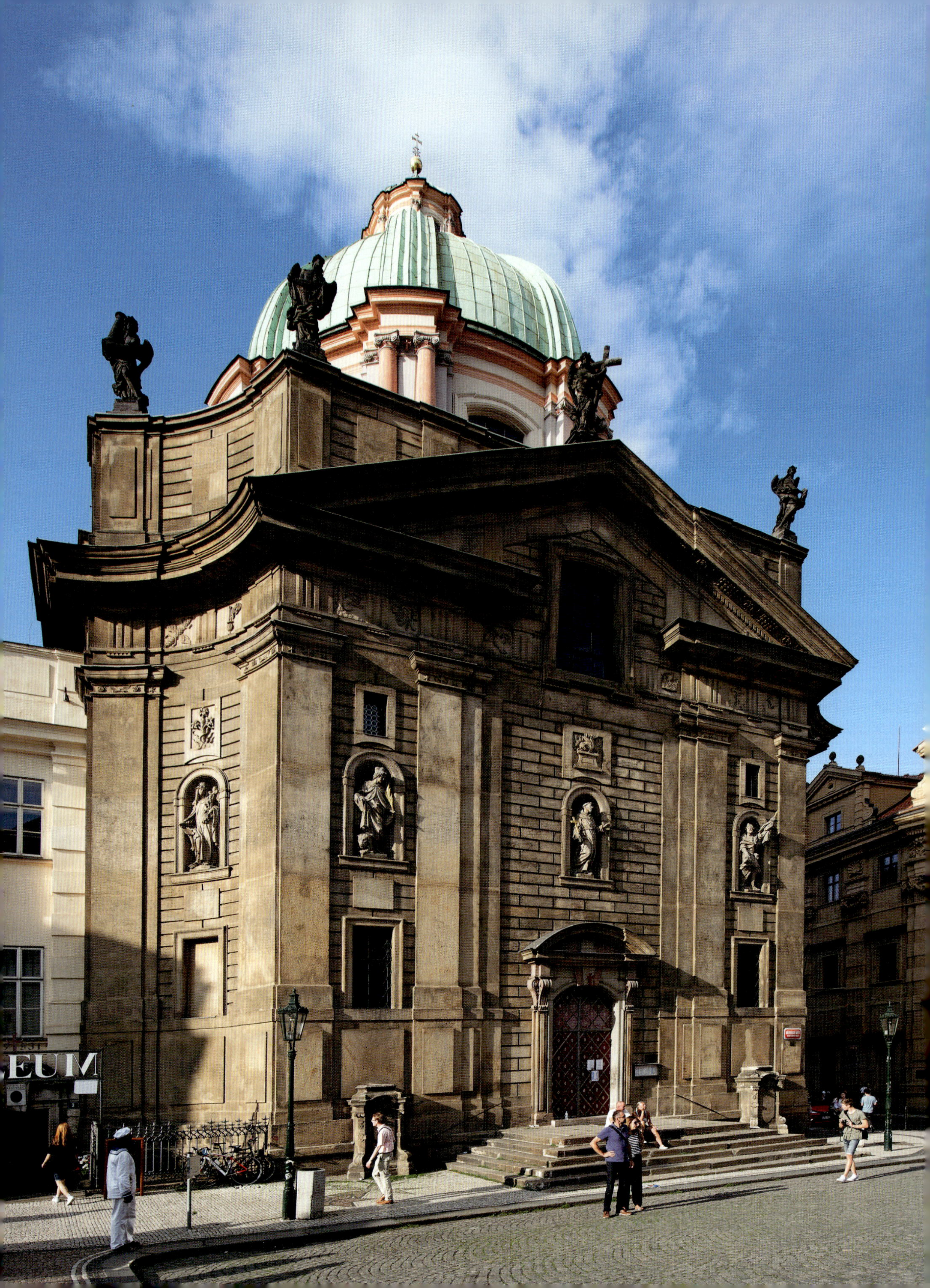
EUM

41/ ST FRANCIS'S CHURCH (KOSTEL SV. FRANTIŠKA SERAFÍNSKÉHO)

41A/ FAÇADE

Křižovnické náměstí (Knights of the Cross Square) is the only square in the Old Town of Prague which was does not date from the Middle Ages. Nevertheless, from the start, the Gothic bridge tower, which affords a view of the Lesser Town and Hradčany, determined the scale for the whole space. The surprisingly intimate area is lined on two sides with the monumental backdrops of the church façades. The Baroque architects ingeniously took advantage of the complicated urban sites and in the course of the seventeenth century created a square that would rightly come to be known as the 'town's drawing-room'. In its Baroque form, built from 1679 to 1688, the church of the Knights of the Cross with the Red Star, dedicated to Saint Francis of Assisi, is a masterpiece of architecture by Jean-Baptiste Mathey. The grand yet delicately shaped block of the main façade leaves a harmonious impression, which is intensified by the perfectly designed layering of lesenes and pilasters. The dynamics of Mathey's architectural language, evident particularly in the shaping of the central avant-corps and in the contrast between the concave corners and the oval drum, in many respects anticipated future developments of Baroque architecture in Prague.

41B/ INTERIOR

The exterior of the church is perfectly matched by its interior, in which architecture, composition, sculpture, and painting come together as a whole. The plan is based on ingeniously linking together the motifs of the Greek cross and the oval. The sophisticated colour scheme combines red and brown tones with white and gold. This unique space is adorned with superb works of art, especially the paintings by Wenzel Lorenz Reiner, Michael Willmann, and Johann Christoph Lischka.

The high altar was remodelled by the sculptor Mathias Wenzel Jäckel into the opened heavens enlivened by a dramatic scene of divine revelation. It was here that this scenographic conception, in which the whole church interior becomes a stage and an auditorium at the same time, was first used in Baroque Prague. The canvas by Lischka, with a scene of St Francis receiving the stigmata, captures the dramatic, expressively conceived scene, whose composition is based on two intersecting diagonals. With an agitated concept and muted colours, Lischka here continues in the style of his step-father and teacher, Willmann, whose lessons he was able to link with experience he had gained during his training in Italy.

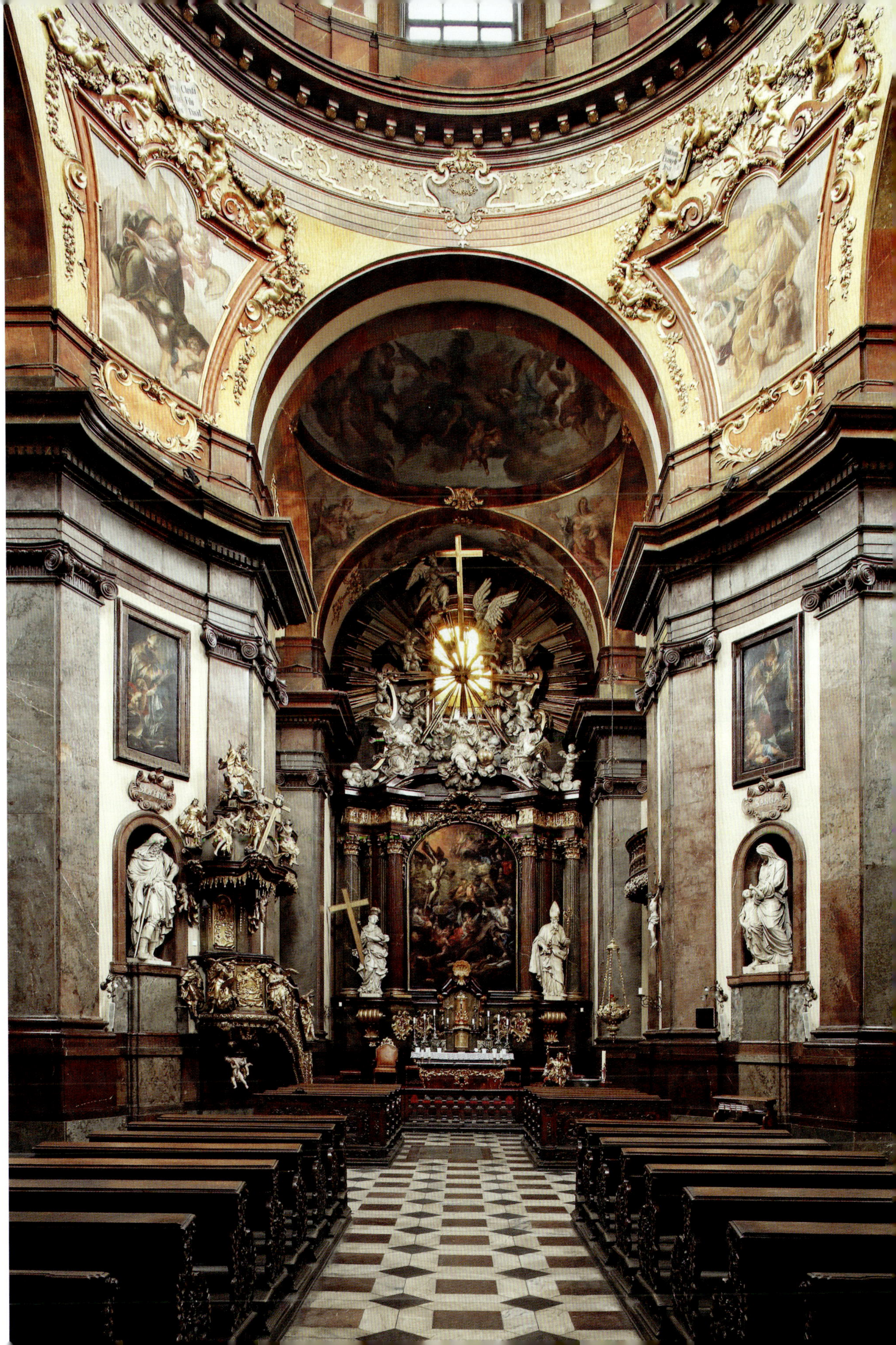

41C/ JOHANN CHRISTOPH LISCHKA: SAINT FRANCIS RECEIVING THE STIGMATA, sketch, before 1700/01
This outstanding sketch, with the artist's energetic, relaxed brushstroke, was made for the altarpiece mentioned in 41B, and was preserved in the former Bucquoy collection. Here, the artist has limited himself to the main participants in the scene, and has suppressed the draughtsmanship aspects in favour of blurs of colour, from which he has constructed the whole composition.

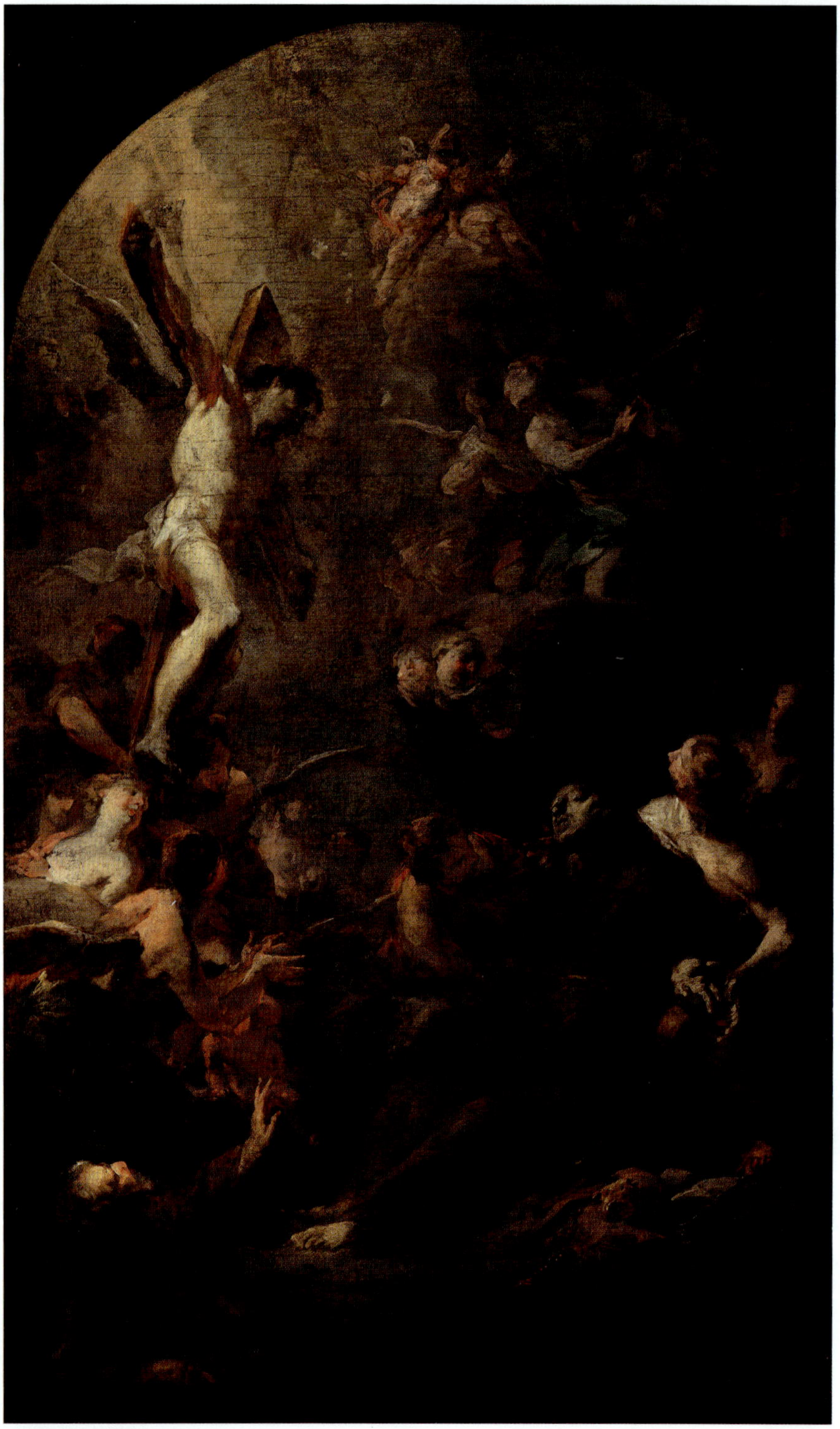

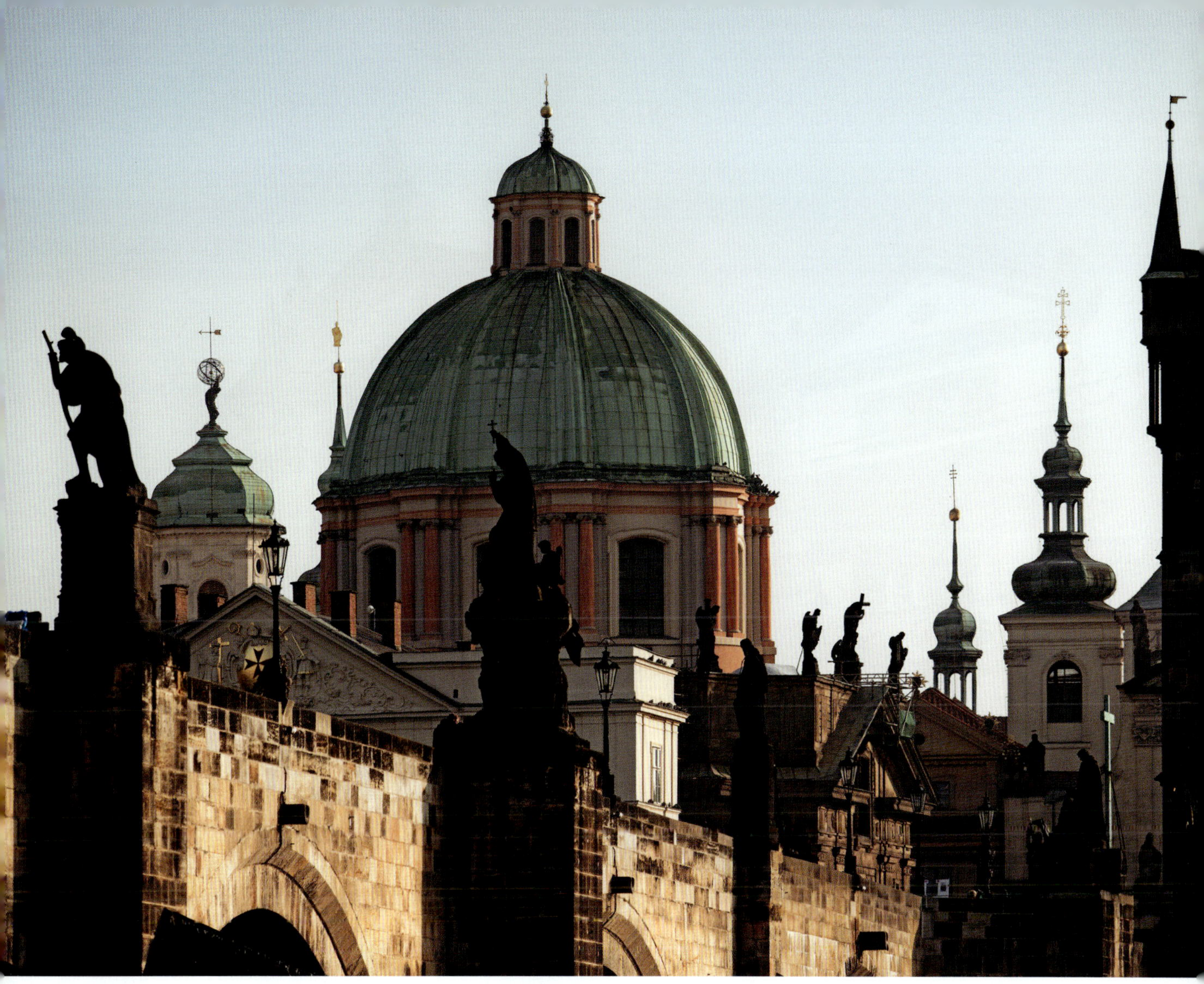

41D/ VIEW OF ST FRANCIS'S CHURCH (KOSTEL SV. FRANTIŠKA SERAFÍNSKÉHO) FROM ACROSS CHARLES BRIDGE

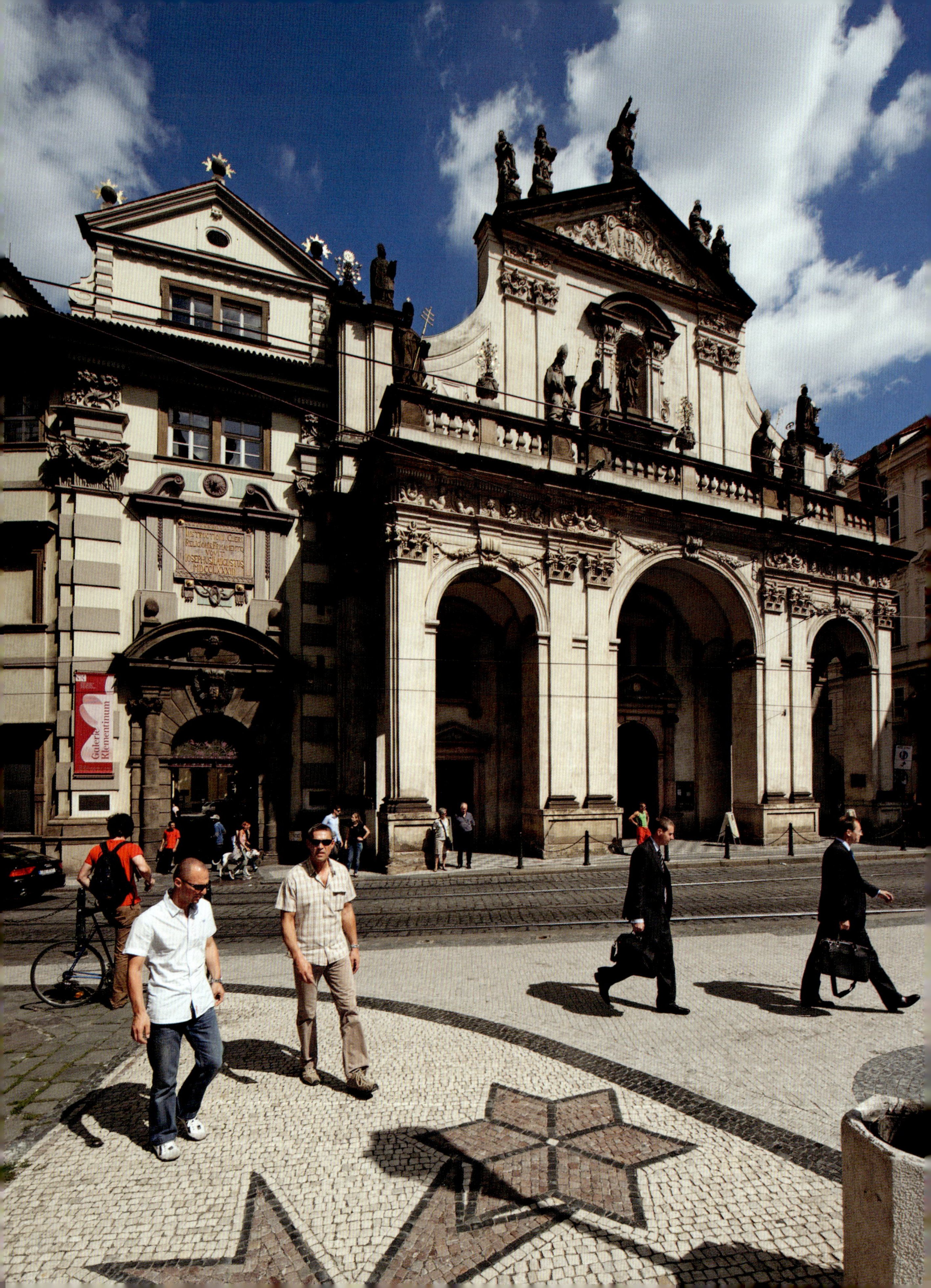
Galerie Klementinum

42/ ST SAVIOUR'S CHURCH (KOSTEL NEJSVĚTĚJŠÍHO SALVÁTORA) IN THE CLEMENTINUM

42A/ FAÇADE

Invited by Emperor Ferdinand I, Jesuits settled in Prague after the middle of the sixteenth century on the site of a medieval Dominican monastery. They built a Renaissance basilica by their college there in two stages, from 1578 to 1582 and in 1600/01. After 1640, it was thoroughly remodelled on Early Baroque plans by Carlo Lurago. These changes culminated in the construction, from 1654 to 1659, of a highly articulated portico, corresponding to the large volume of the Gothic architecture opposite it, the Old Town Bridge Tower. The extraordinarily ambitious artistic design of the main façade of the Jesuit church was unparalleled in Bohemian architecture at that time, and attests to the importance that the Jesuits attributed to their presence on one of the busiest Prague intersections of those days. The statues, made from 1655 to 1660 in the workshop of Johann George Bendl, are in keeping with the ideas behind the decoration. The figures of the Church Fathers on the attic balustrade of the portico are joined by figures of a Bohemian patron saint, Adalbert (Vojtěch), and the guardian of the Clementinum, St Clement. In the niche behind them is Mary the Immaculate, whose guard of honour is formed by the Jesuit saints Ignatius of Loyola and St Francis Xavier, each standing on one side of the gable. The highest statue is of Christ the Saviour (Salvator) among the Four Evangelists.

'Though Prague does not have large squares built in the Baroque and Neoclassical periods, like those that Rome, Paris, and other cities can boast, at least Křižovnické náměstí (Knights of the Cross Square) may rightly be considered a masterpiece of the Baroque sense of space.'
Vojtěch Volavka, 1967

42B/ JOHANN GEORG BENDL: ST ANDREW, 1673–75
The confessionals in the Church of St Saviour (Nejsvětějšího Salvátora) are decorated with Bendl's carvings of the twelve Apostles. This masterpiece was inspired by contemporary Roman sculpture. The realistically conceived figure of St Andrew, turning towards the heavens with a gesture of devotion and readiness for a martyr's death, is based on a statue with the same subject matter by François Duquesnoy in St Peter's Basilica in the Vatican. The classically styled head attests to Bendl's knowledge of the famous sculptural group of classical antiquity, *Laocoön*.

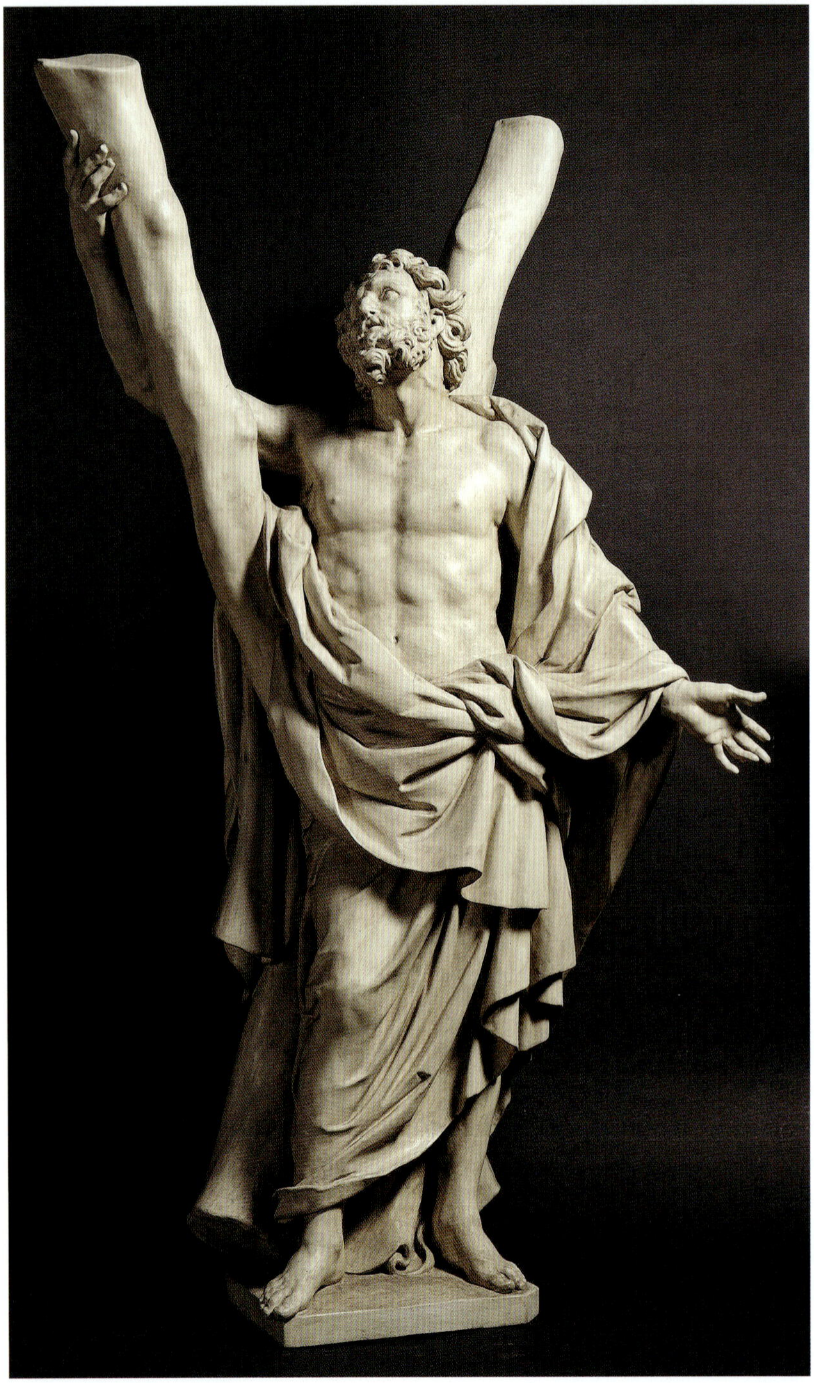

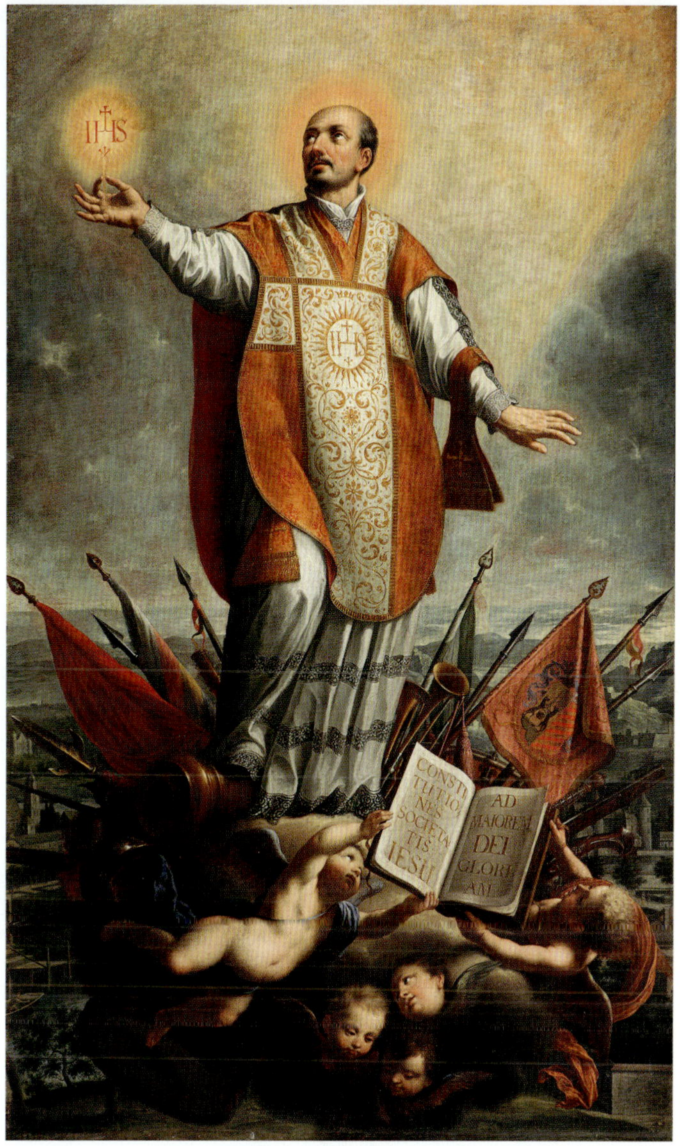

42C/ JOHANN GEORG HEINSCH: ST IGNATIUS OF LOYOLA, 1708

In its conception, this painting of the founder of the Society of Jesus is similar to Brokoff's sculptural group of St Ignatius on Charles Bridge. Both works were made after the same models, in particular the statue by Pierre Le Gros on the altar from 1696 to 1700, designed by Andrea Pozzo, in the Church of the Gesù, Rome. Possibly, Heinsch worked directly with the sculptor on this work, as we know he had when making statues of two Jesuit saints, Francis Xavier and Francis Borgia.

Heinsch tried to achieve a grandly conceived composition, but its monumentality is somewhat diminished by the painter's liking for meticulous detail. Ignatius's main attribute here is the sun in splendour with the Christogram. The angels at the saint's feet bear an open book with writing recalling the Jesuit motto 'Ad maiorem Dei gloriam' (For the greater glory of God) and Ignatius's having laid down the regulations of the Society of Jesus. The military trophies here have several meanings: they recall Ignatius's secular past, but are also symbols of the Jesuit Order as the Soldiers of Christ, whereas the drums and trumpets proclaim the glory of the Society of Jesus on all the continents. The precise depiction of Ignatius's family coat of arms on the banner on the right is particularly noteworthy.

43/ ST CLEMENT'S CHURCH
IN THE CLEMENTINUM

43A/ THE CLEMENTINUM COMPLEX
WITH ST CLEMENT'S CHURCH

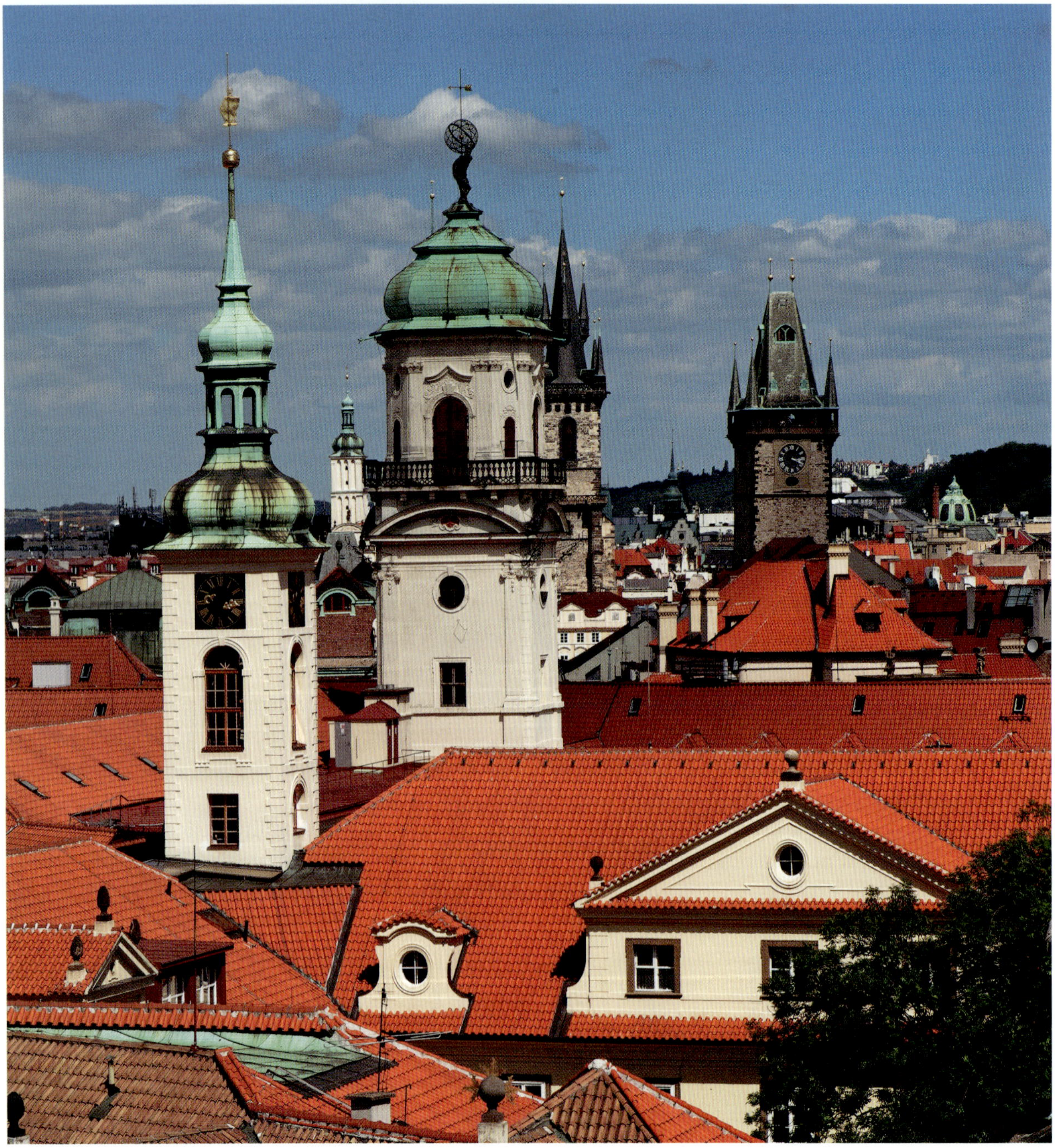

43B–C/ INTERIOR OF THE CHURCH →

Today, St Clement's Church shares only its dedication with its medieval ancestor, which served the Dominican monastery. It was built from 1711 to 1715 on the site of a chapter house, probably on plans by František Maxmilián Kaňka. At present it serves the Greek Catholic Church. The inventive use of space is remarkable: the chancel and entrance area with the choir loft are visually set off from the nave by means of free-standing columns. The ceiling fresco is by Johann Hiebel, and includes, above the choir loft, a painted veduta of the Baroque Clementinum.

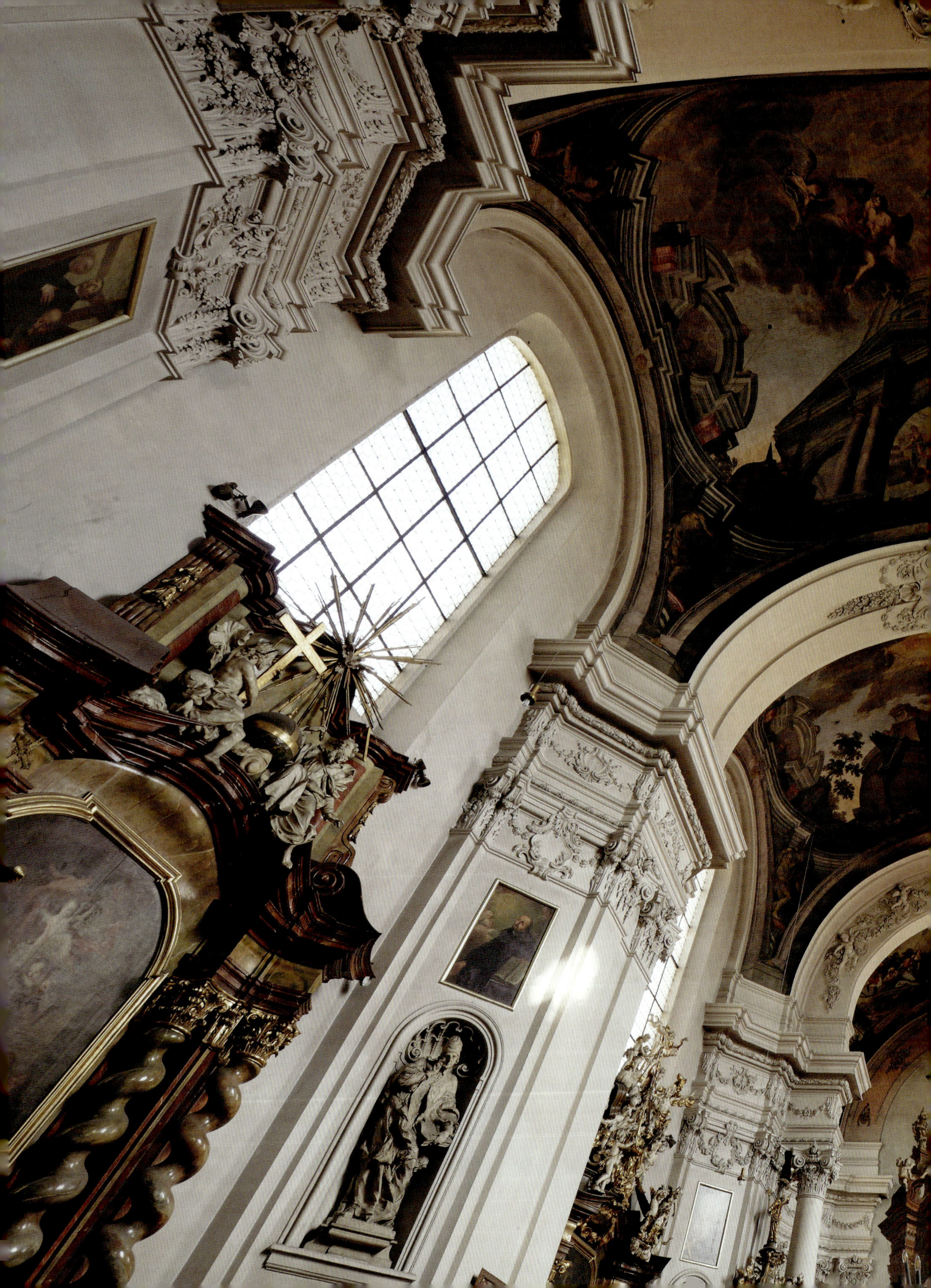

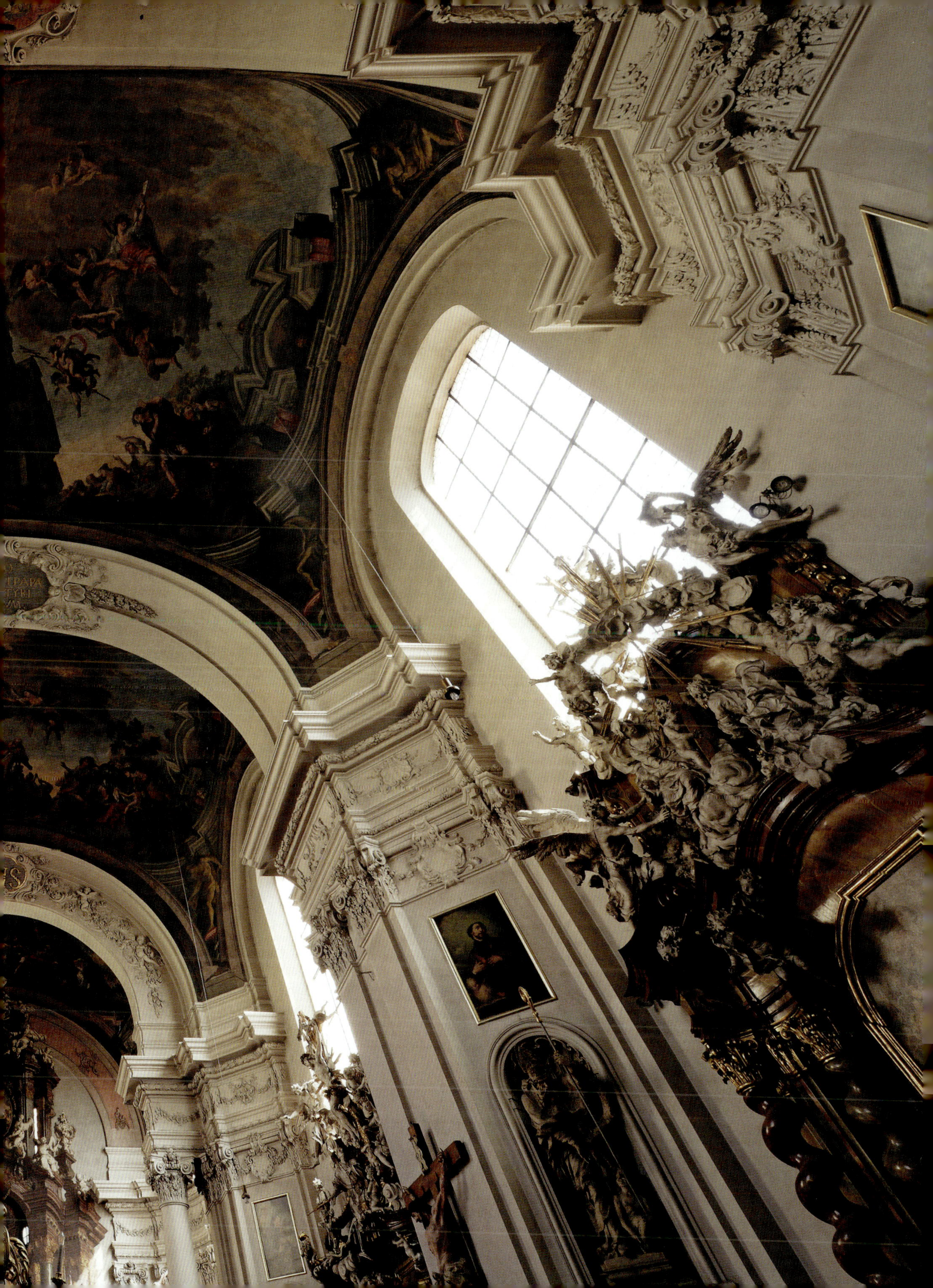

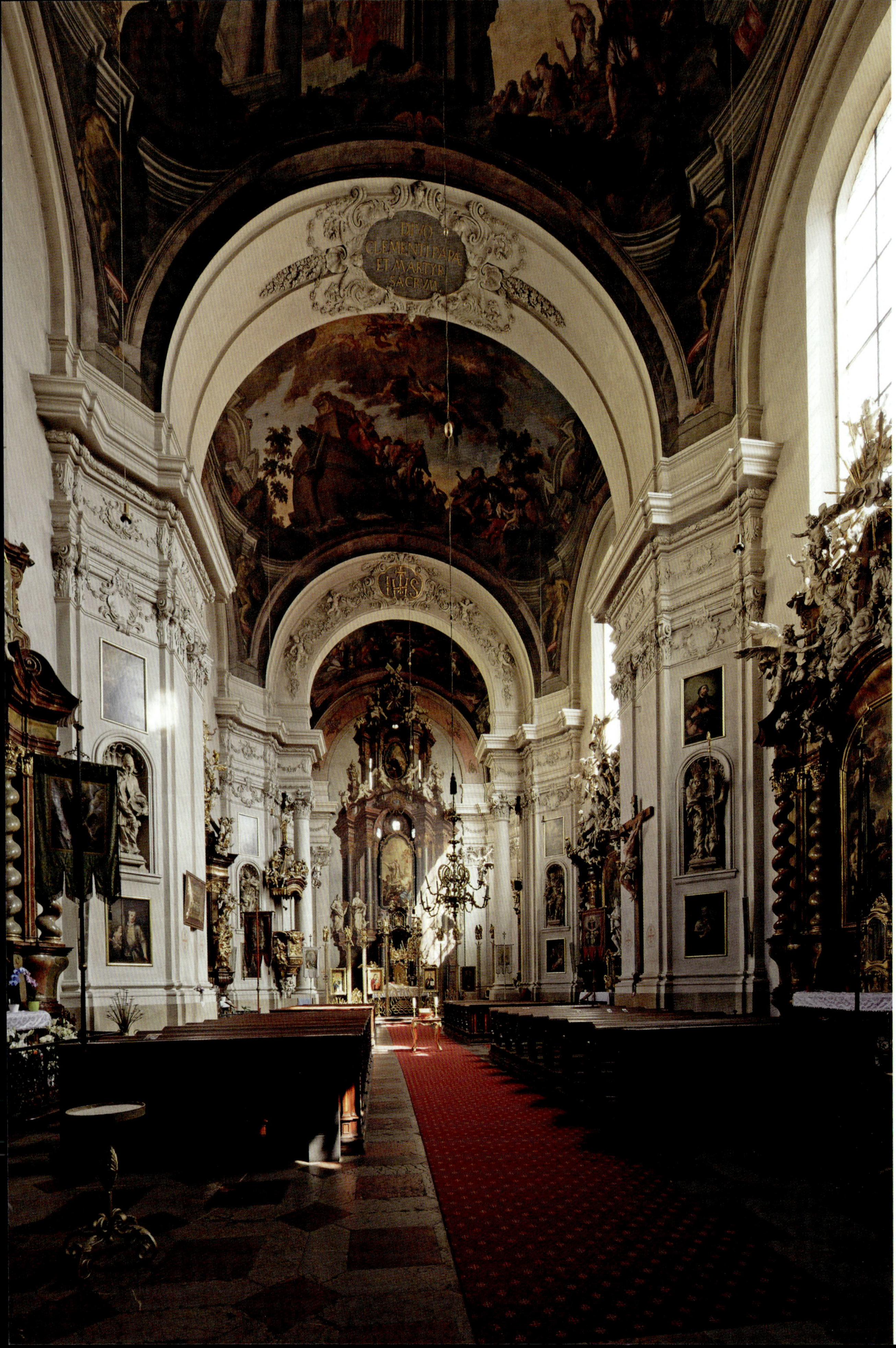
CLEMENTI PAPA
ET MARTYRI
SACRVM

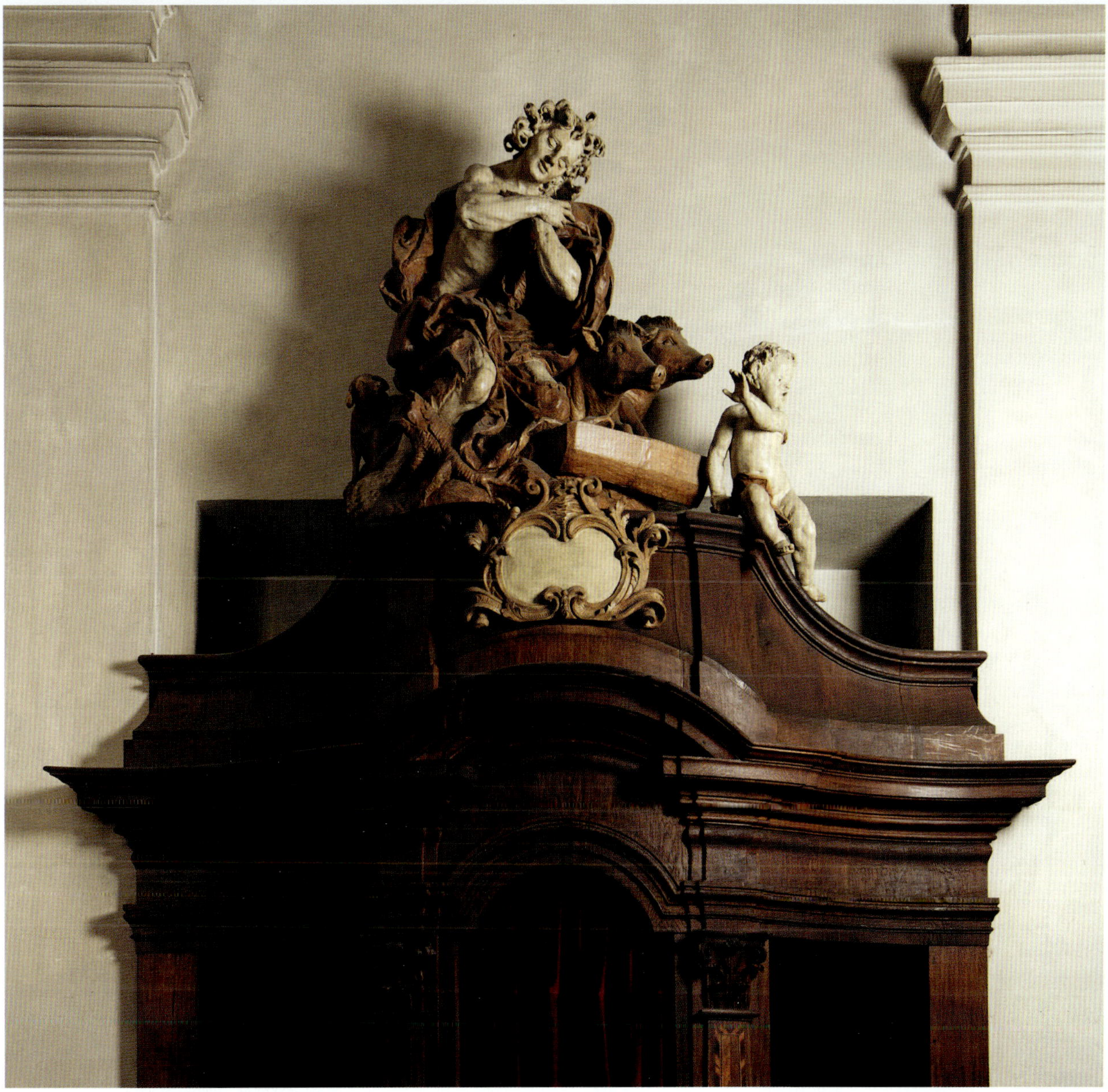

43D/ MATTHIAS BERNHARD BRAUN:
THE PRODIGAL SON, *c.*1720

The real treasure of St Clement's Church is a unique set of statues by Matthias Bernhard Braun and his workshop from 1715 to 1721. Among them are six carvings on the subject of repentance, one on the roof of each confessional. The Prodigal Son is depicted here at the moment of his deepest humiliation, when he is overcome by the desire to return to his father's house and beg forgiveness. The statue is evidence of the artist's supreme mastery in the depiction of emotion connected with an impassioned yet credible external gesture.

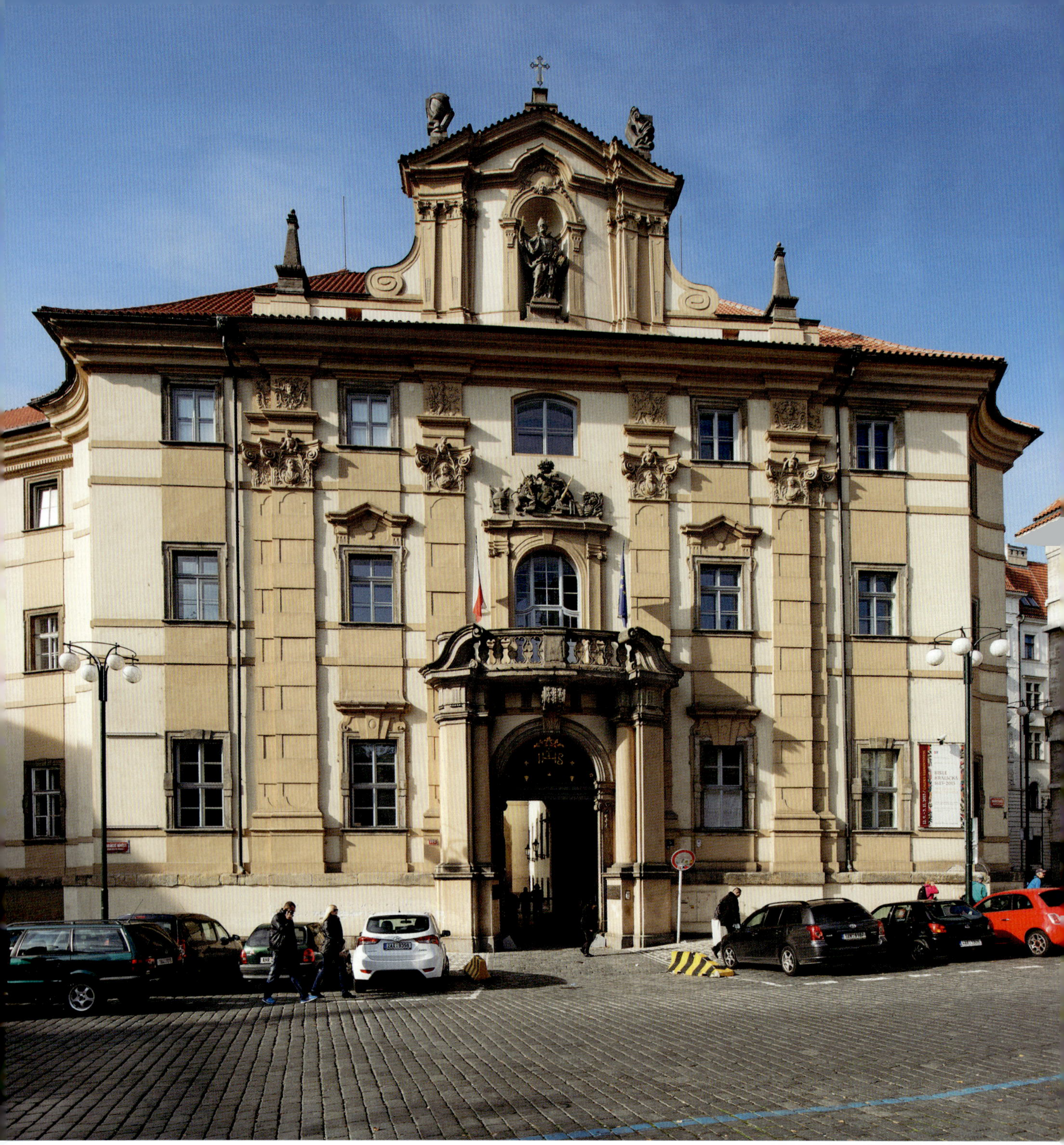

44A/ MAIN ENTRANCE FROM MARIÁNSKÉ NÁMĚSTÍ

The appearance of the vast Old Town college of the Society of Jesus developed gradually from 1653 to the 1720s. The largest and oldest Jesuit house in Bohemia was built on the site of a Dominican friary, of which the ground plan and division into four rectangular blocks have been more or less preserved. In addition to rooms to live and work in, the complex included a schoolhouse, a library, a printing office, the Church of St Clement, the Church of St Saviour, and three chapels.

44B/ BAROQUE MAIN LIBRARY →

The Baroque Main Library, from before 1727, is furnished with the original inlaid cabinets. The *trompe-l'oeil* fresco on the vaulted ceiling is by Johann Hiebel, and depicts allegories of natural and revealed knowledge with regard to the saints and distinguished men of learning from the Jesuit Order. The terrestrial and celestial globes are from the original Clementinum collection and were all made by members of the order.

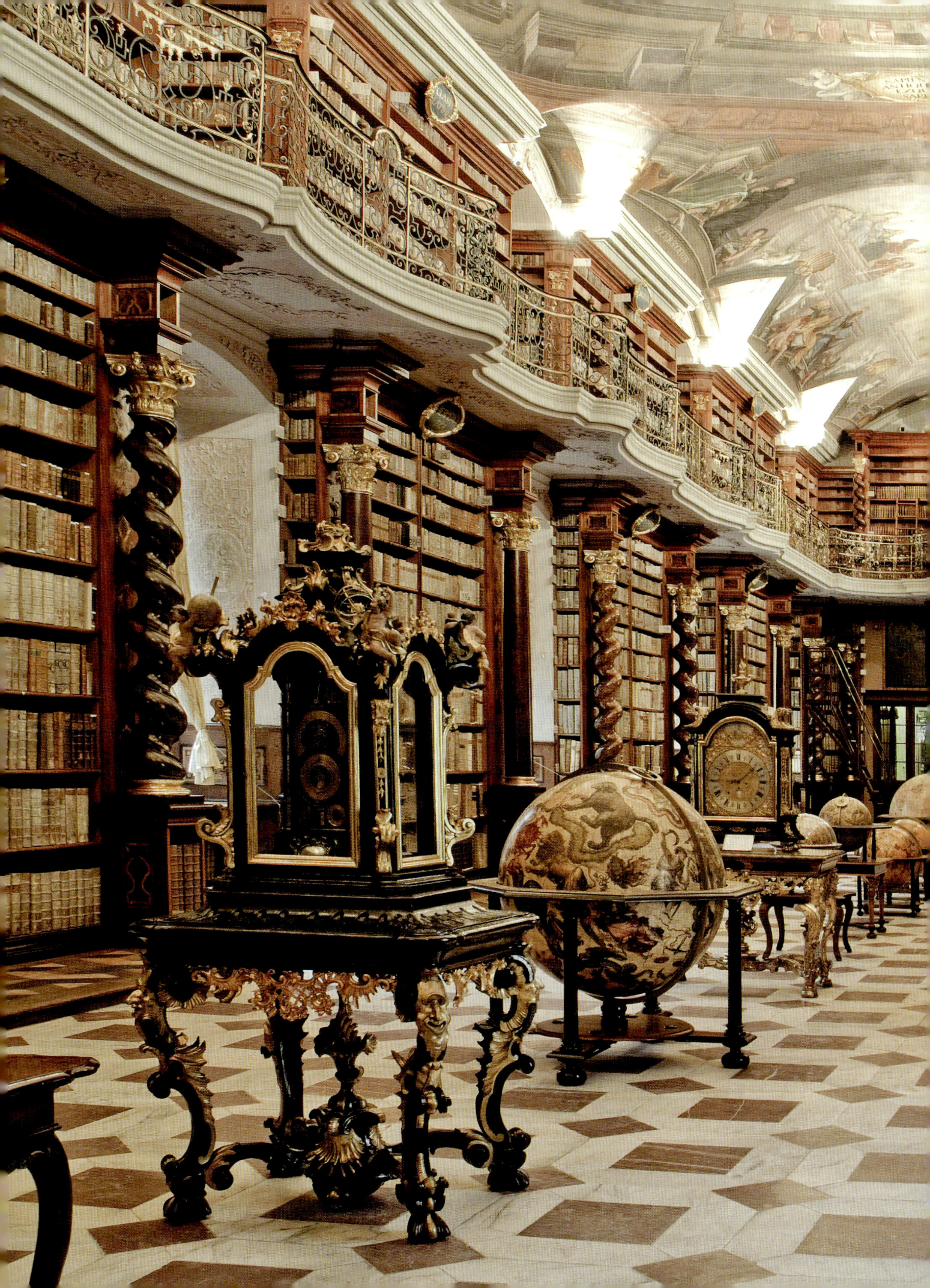

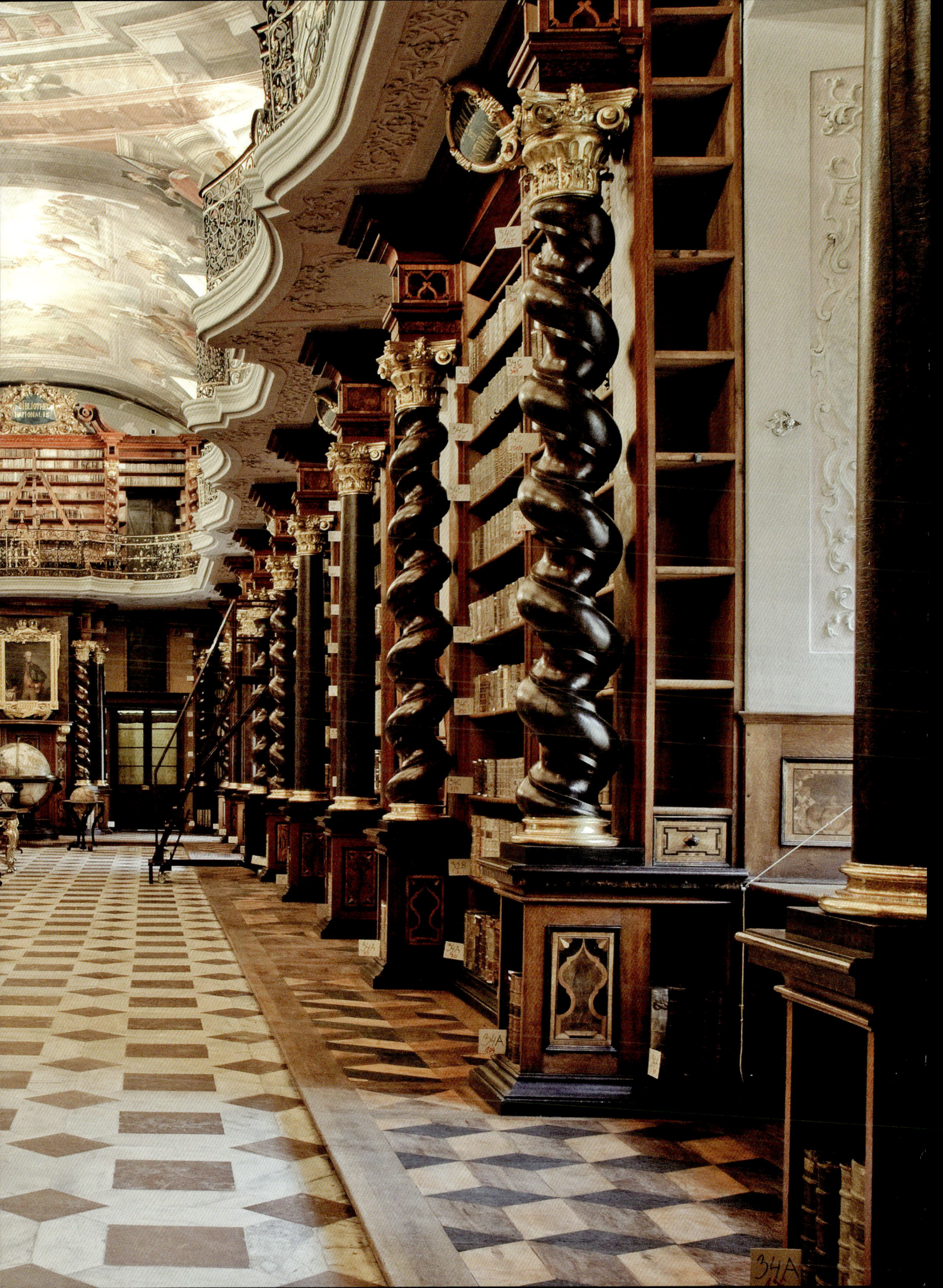
34A

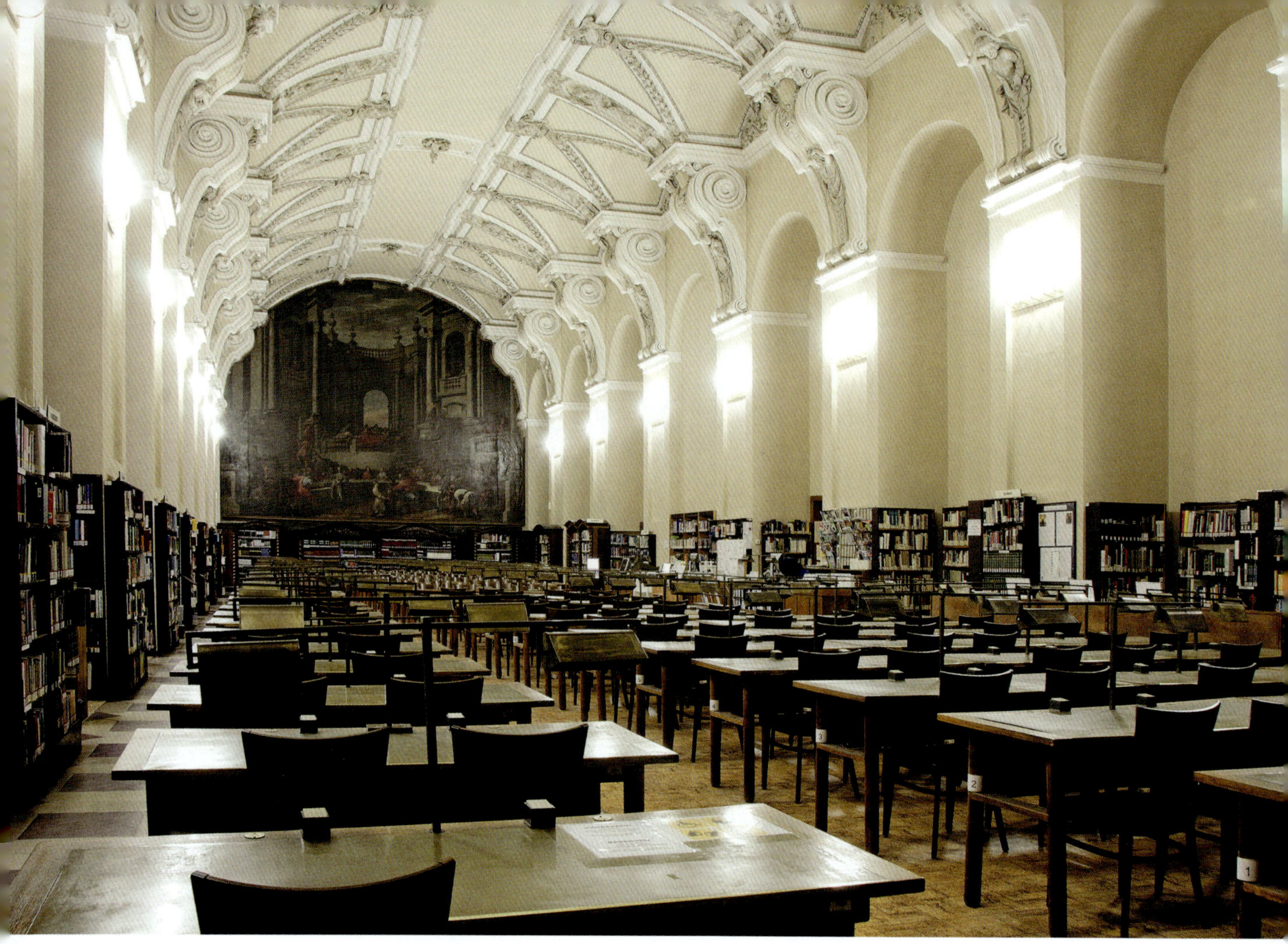

44C/ SUMMER REFECTORY

The former summer refectory today serves as the Reading Room of the National Library of the Czech Republic. It has a barrel-vaulted ceiling with rich stucco decoration from before 1680. Its allegorical figures of the Christian virtues are probably by Johann Georg Bendl. The east wall has a large fresco by Christoph Tausch after *The Marriage at Cana* (1710) by Andrea Pozzo.

44D/ ASTRONOMICAL TOWER

The astronomical tower dates from after 1722 and is connected with the Jesuits interest in astronomy. The upper storey was adapted as an observatory, between 1748 and 1751, on a design by the outstanding Jesuit astronomer and mathematician Joseph Stepling, perhaps on plans by Anselmo Lurago. The top of the tower is decorated with a statue of Atlas bearing a celestial sphere; it is attributed to the workshop of Matthias Bernhard Braun.

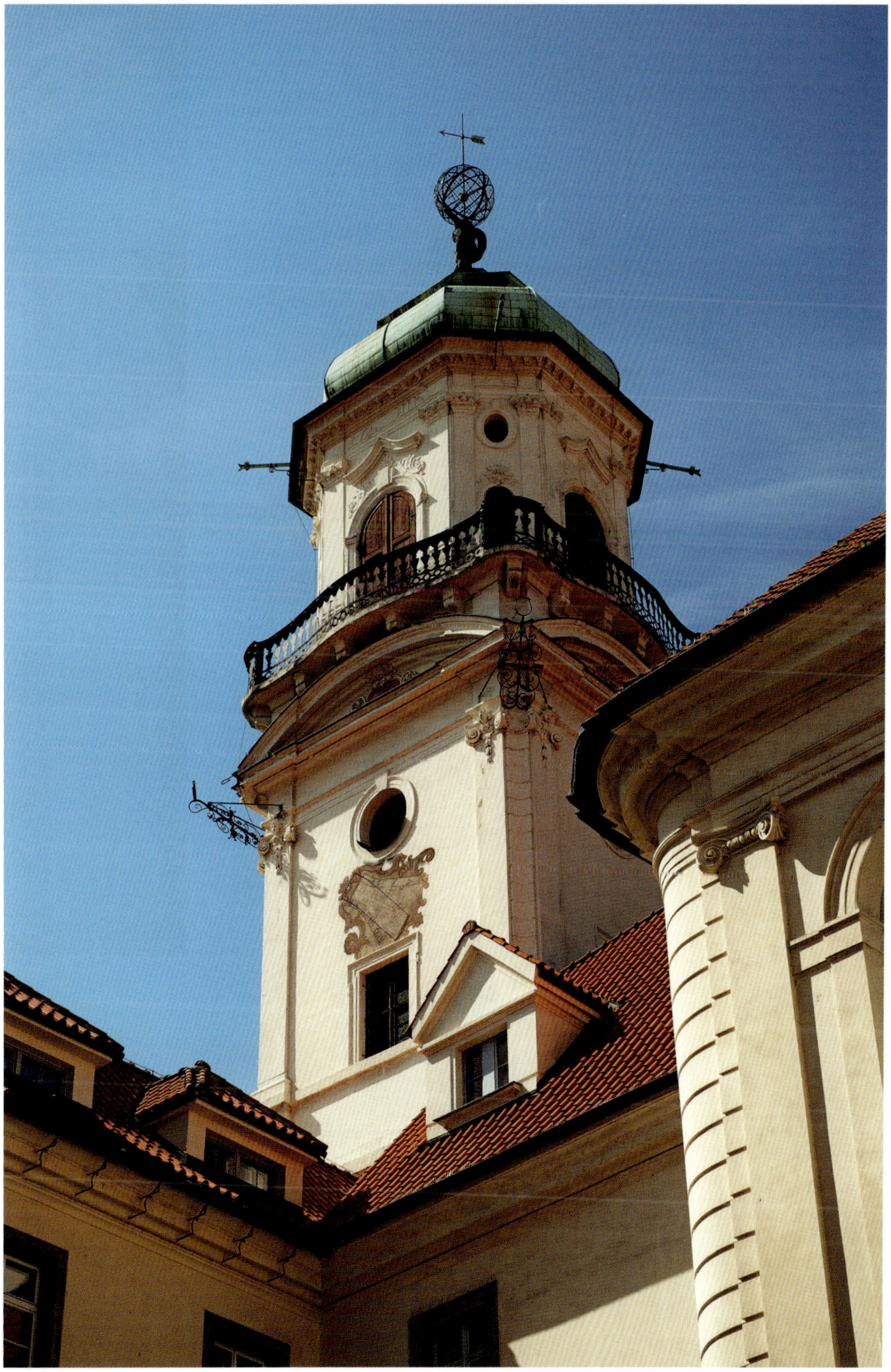

44E/ CHAPEL OF MIRRORS (ZRCADLOVÁ KAPLE)
The Chapel of the Annunciation dates from the later phase of the building of the Jesuit college, that is, from 1722 to 1726. The plans for this oratory, better known as the Chapel of Mirrors of the Congretgatio Latina major, are attributed either to František Maxmilián Kaňka or, less probably, to Kilian Ignaz Dientzenhofer. The interior employs natural and artificial marble in a wide range of colours in harmony with striking stucco decoration by Bernardo Spinetti and frescos by Johann Hiebel, which illustrate the text of the angelic greeting, the prayer Ave Maria (Hail Mary). Four hanging paintings by Wenzel Lorenz Reiner are also intimate depictions of Marian themes.

'Just as thirteen-hundred pharmacists in London are clear evidence of the excellence of the town, so too do a couple of thousand Jesuits in Prague attest to something.'
Charles Patin, 1695

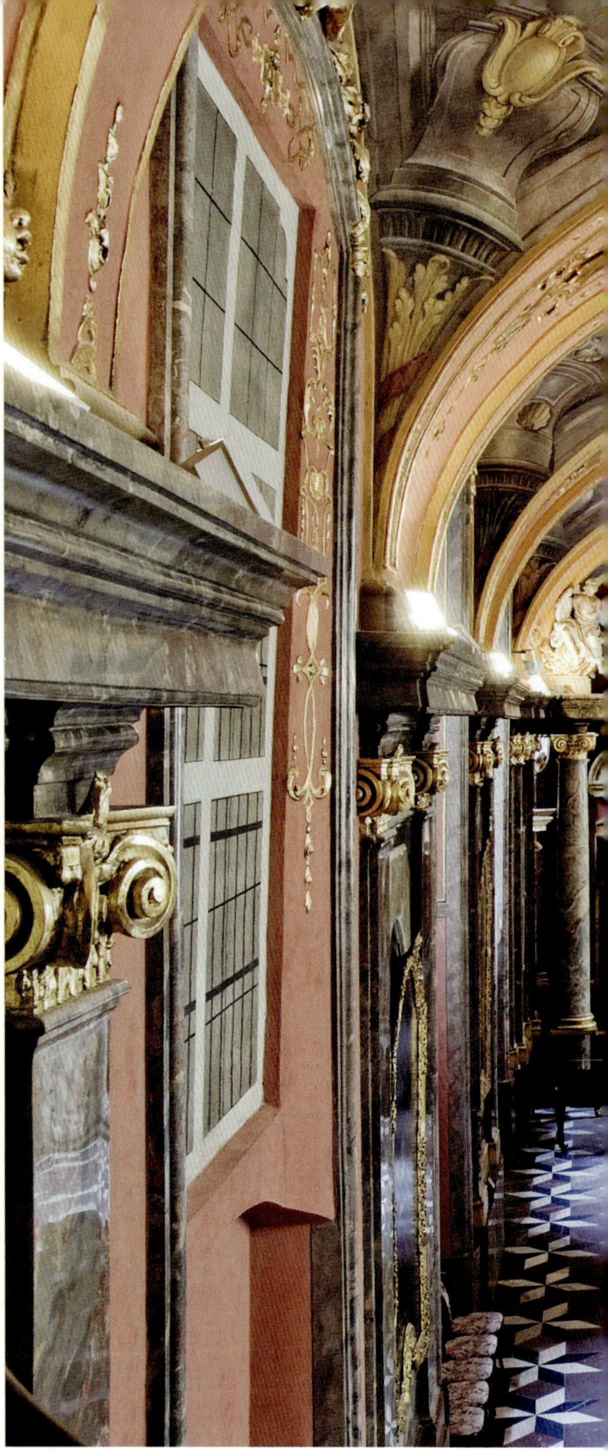

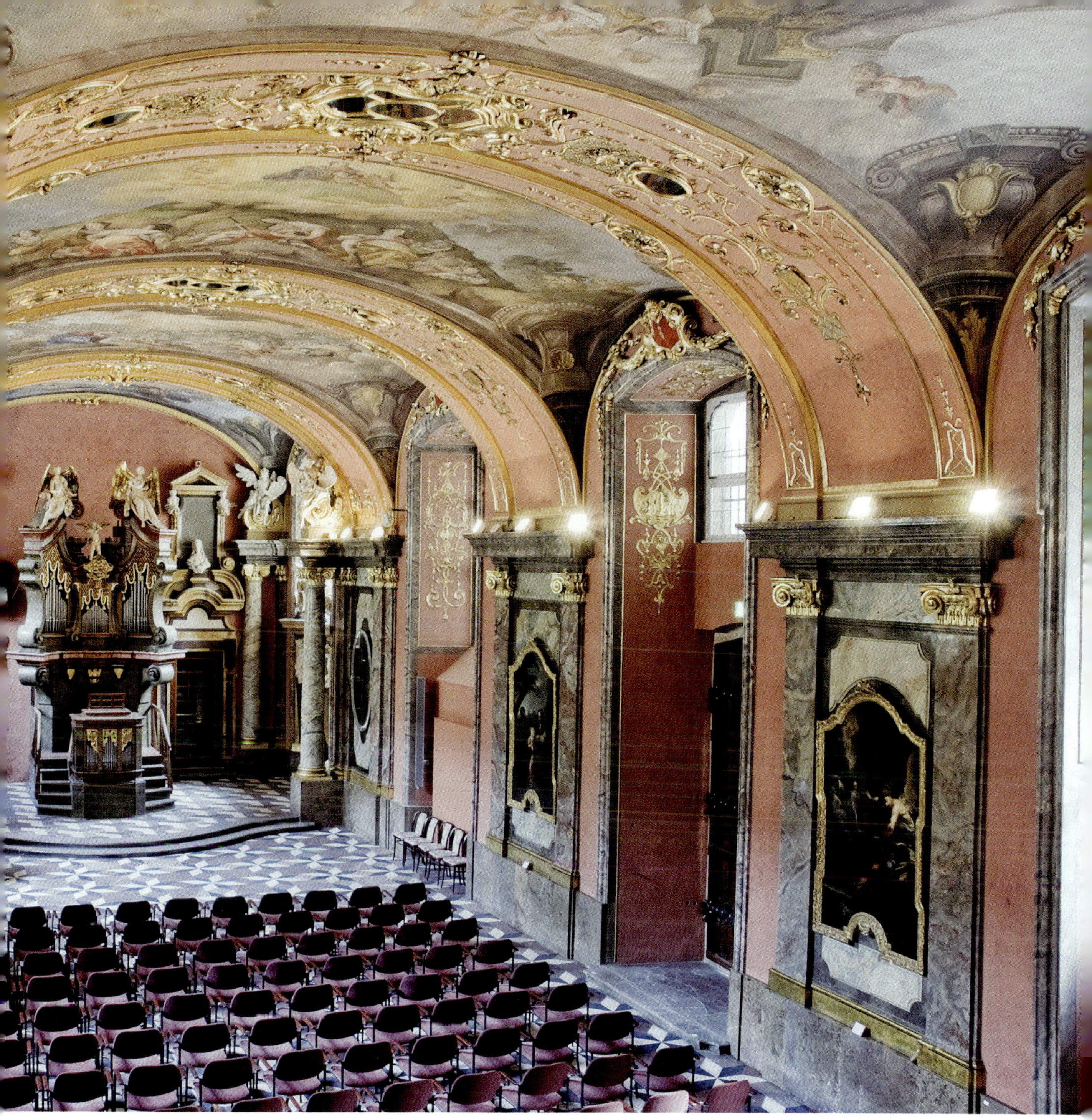

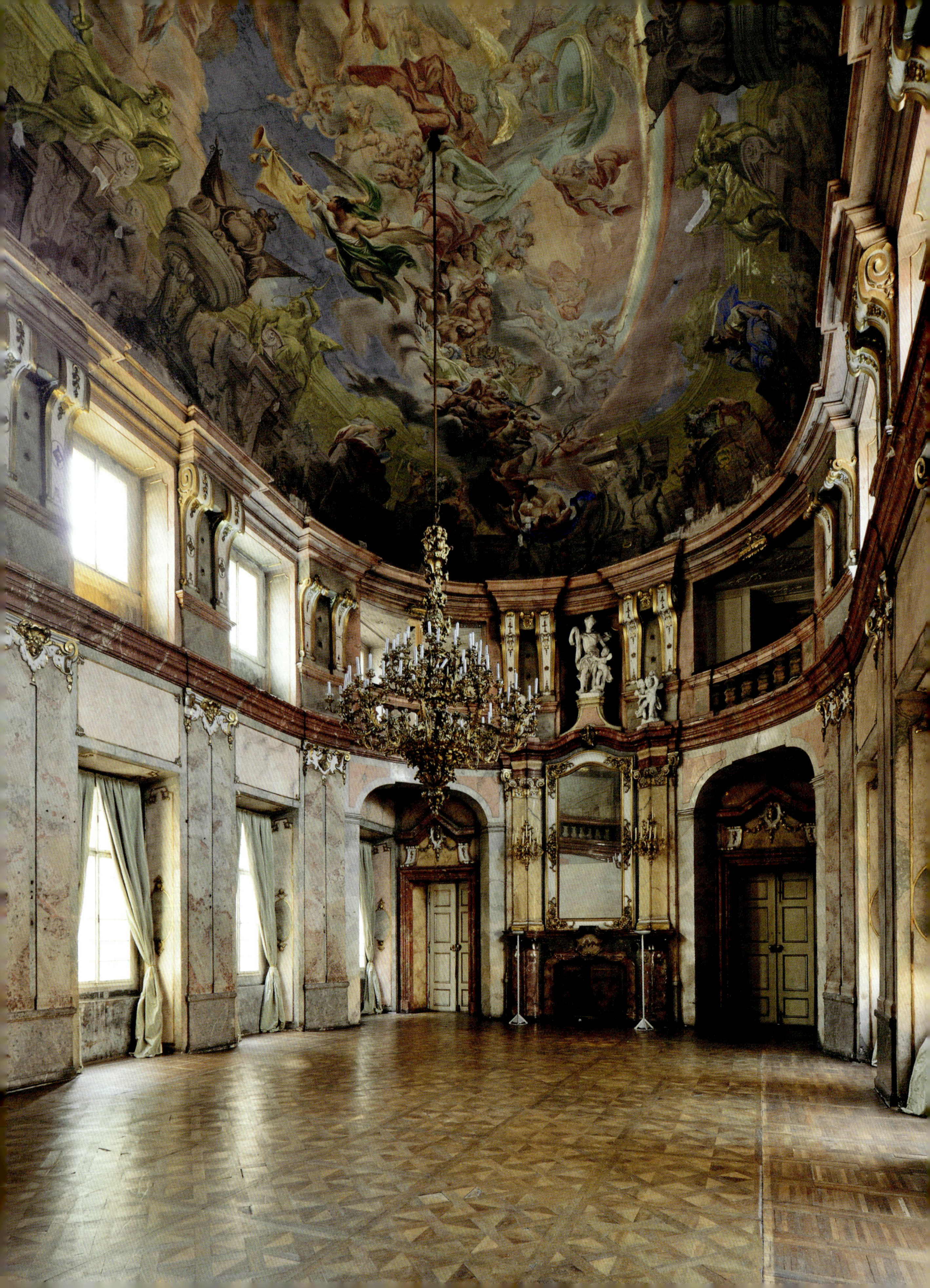

45/ COLLOREDO-MANSFELD HOUSE (COLLOREDO-MANSFELDSKÝ PALÁC) – GREAT HALL

This house on the busy crossroads of what are today Karlova ulice and Křižovnická ulice was remodelled between 1730 and 1735 by the architect František Ignác Prée for Heinrich Paul Franz II Graf von Mansfeld, Fürst von Fondi. It probably preserved a number of features of earlier remodelling carried out after 1700, when the residence belonged to the Counts of Breda. The architect of this High Baroque adaptation is generally considered to be Giovanni Battista Alliprandi. The Great Hall is two storeys high. Its present appearance dates from 1736. The hall manifests influences of earlier Viennese palatial architecture and of the work of František Maxmilián Kaňka. The high voluted brackets below the main cornice further suggest that Alliprandi was involved in the design. The ceiling painting, *The Council of the Gods,* is by Giovanni Battista Zaist (the *trompe-l'oeil* architecture) and Giovanni Pietro Scotti (the figures).

46A–B/ THE GOLDEN WELL (DŮM U ZLATÉ STUDNĚ)
The house on the corner of Karlova and Seminářská streets has a respectable architectural history going back to the Romanesque period. The core of the present building is Renaissance and its appearance is Late Baroque. The House of the Golden Well became famous for the stucco relief on its façade (from before 1701), which is generally attributed to the sculptor Johann Ulrich Mayer. The central motif is the palladium of the Bohemian Lands – a bas relief of the Madonna of Stará Boleslav at the centre of an eight-pointed Marian star being crowned by two putti and guarded by a pair of lions. At its sides stand two Bohemian patron saints – Wenceslas and John Nepomucene. Below them, on the first storey, are St Sebastian and St Roch and, on the top level, St Ignatius and St Charles Borromeo, above whom is a recumbent St Rosalia. With the honourable exception of St Ignatius of Loyola, whose presence may reasonably be explained by the nearness of the Jesuit college, this is a group of protectors against the plague.

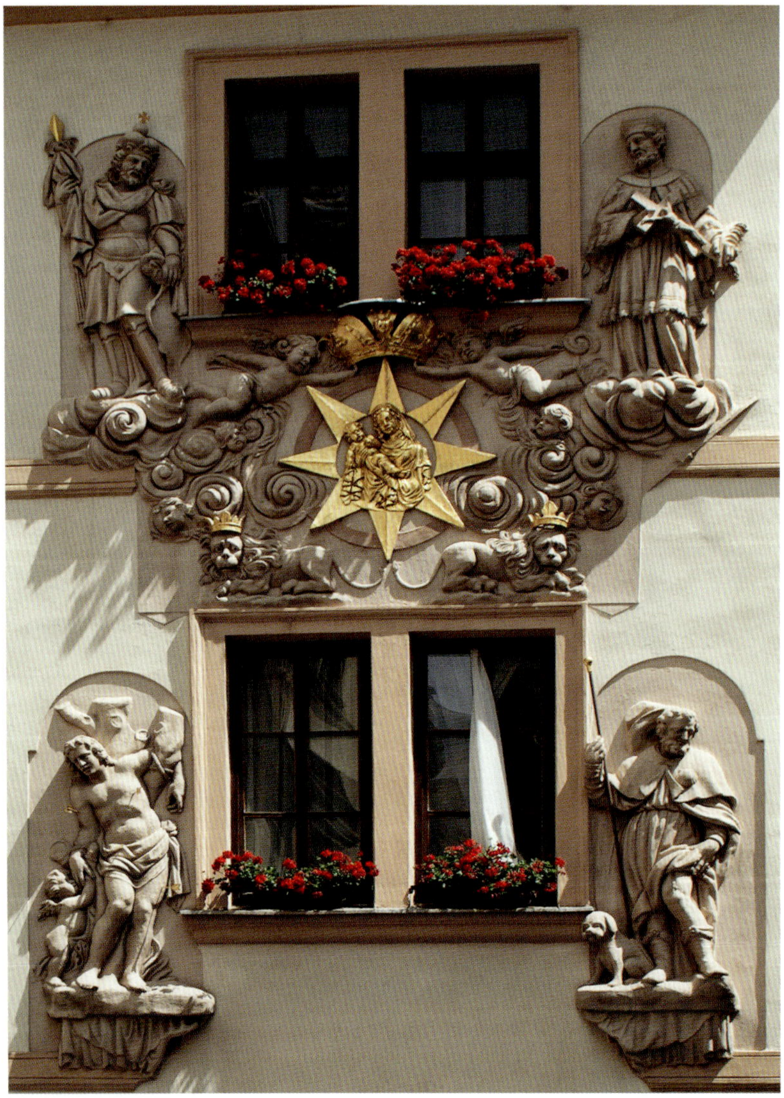

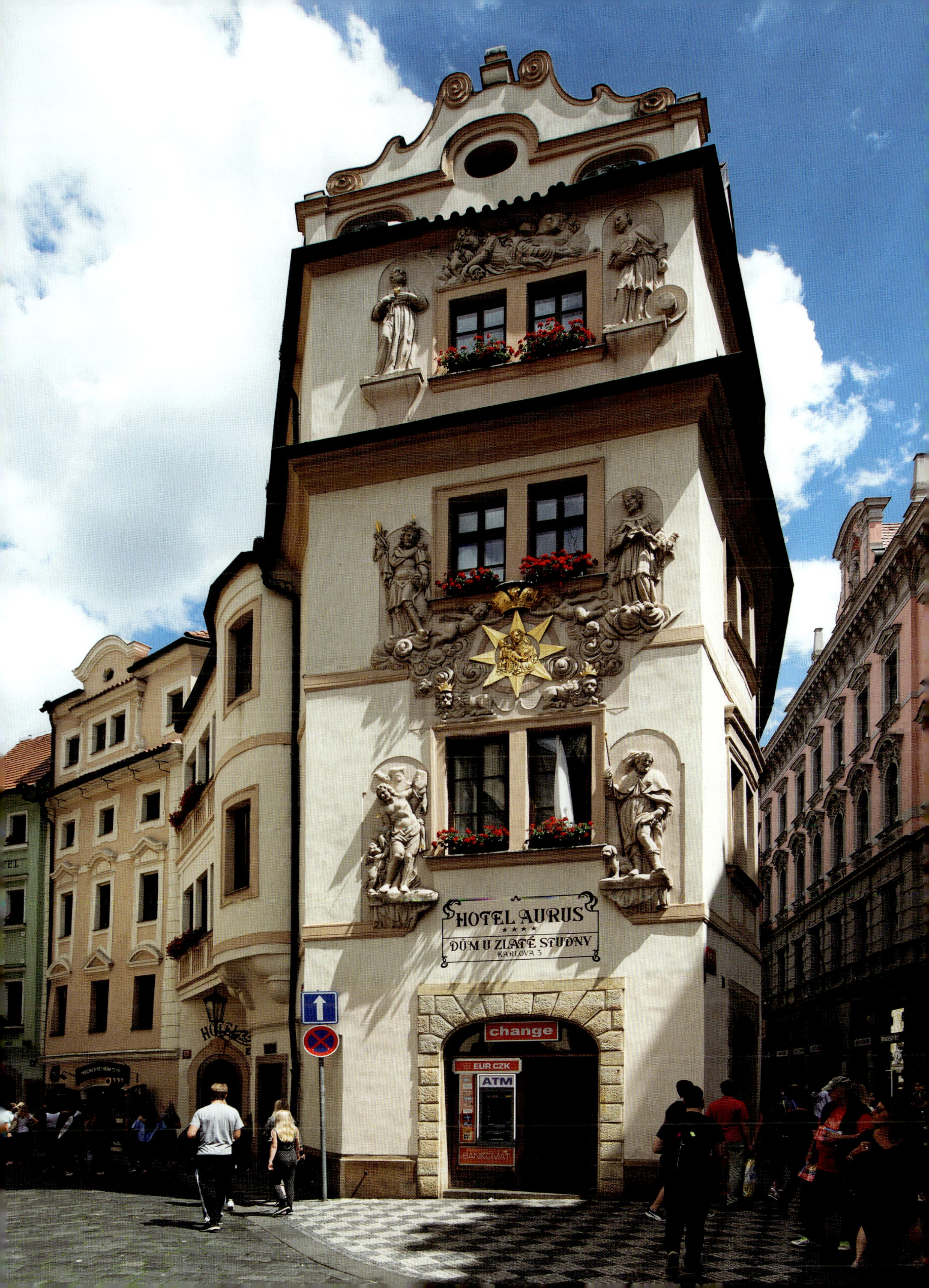

HOTEL AURUS
DŮM U ZLATÉ STUDNY
KARLOVA 3
change
EUR CZK
ATM
BANKOMAT

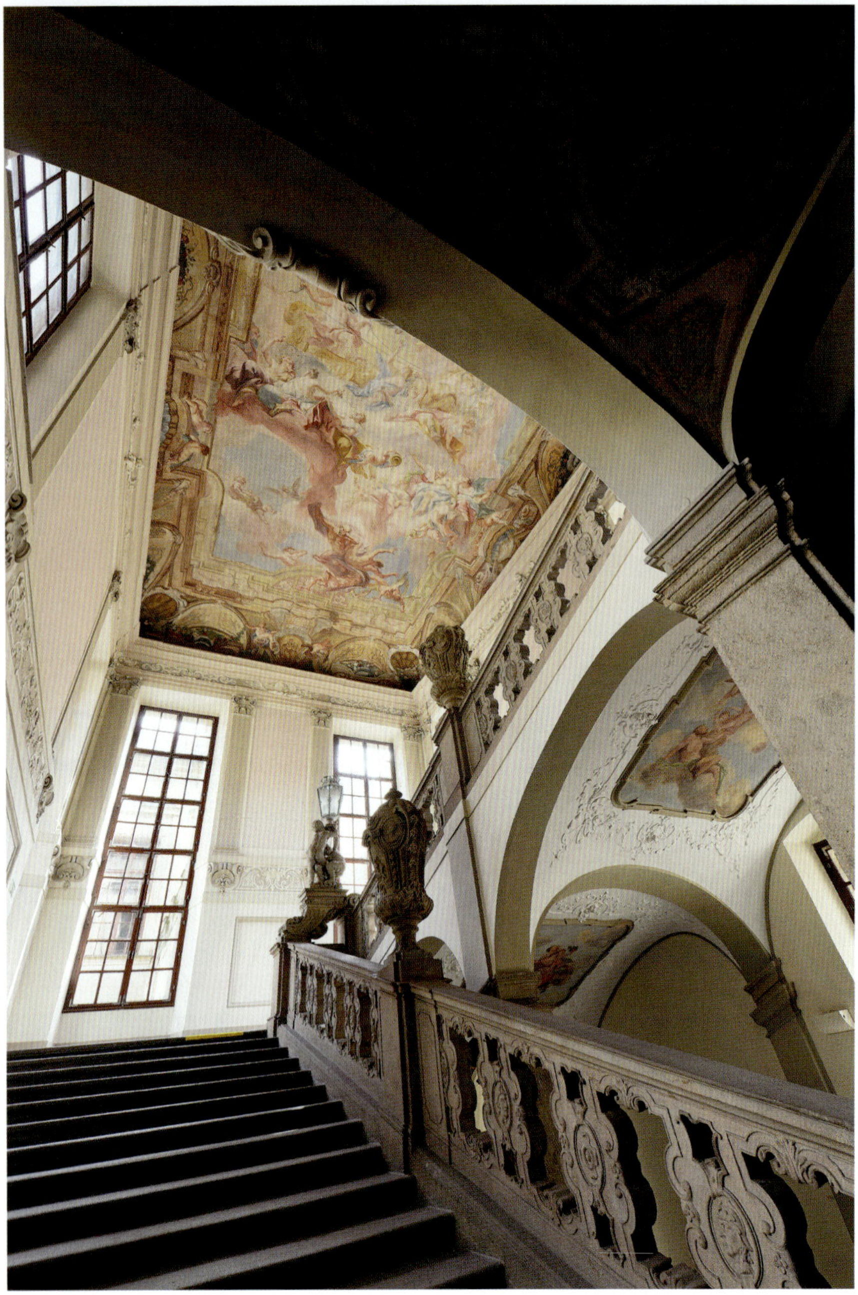

47A–B/ CLAM-GALLAS HOUSE (CLAM-GALLASOVSKÝ PALÁC)

The diplomat and politician Count Johann Wenzel Gallas began building his stately Prague seat in late 1699 or early 1700. After buying up other houses in the area between what are today Husova ulice (Hus Street) and Malé náměstí (Little Square), he began in 1714 to carry out grand new plans provided by Johann Bernhard Fischer von Erlach, an architect at the court in Vienna. When the count died in Naples in July 1719, where he was Viceroy, this extremely costly building was far from finished.

Though Gallas's heirs completed the building, they abandoned some of the original ideas for the decoration and furnishing of the interiors when faced with a shortage of funds. The grand Neoclassical façade of the house is enlivened by the huge portal in the avant-corps on each of the two sides, surmounted with balconies and urns. The balconies are supported by four pairs of atlantes made by Matthias Bernhard Braun, whose workshops provided all the sculptural decoration for the building.
The main staircase is generally considered to be the loveliest in Baroque Prague. It is bordered with a perforated parapet with urns and groups of putti from Braun's workshop. The rich stucco decoration of the walls culminates in the monumental ceiling fresco, *Apollo's Defeat of the Demons of Darkness*, by Carlo Innocenzo Carlone (or Carloni).

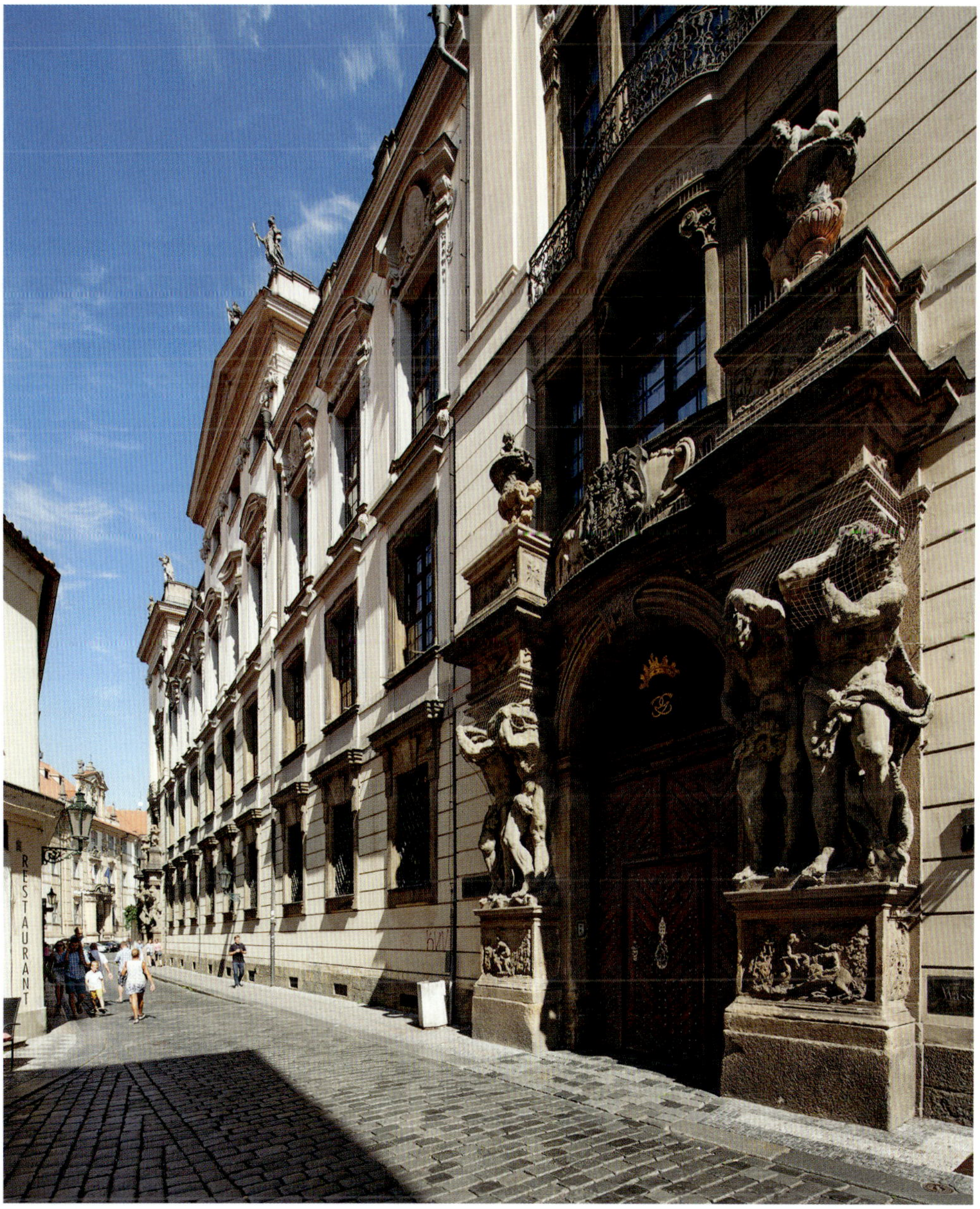

48/ ST NICHOLAS' CHURCH (SV. MIKULÁŠE) ON OLD TOWN SQUARE, 1732–37

This monumental church was designed by Kilian Ignaz Dientzenhofer. It took the place of a medieval church on a cramped plot, next to a now no longer extant Benedictine abbey, in the middle of the densest built-up area in the town. The architect moved the main façade to the front of the south lateral wall, and orientated it to the axis of the little square with its central fountain. The slum clearance in the nineteenth century dramatically changed this situation and made St Nicholas' Church a landmark of Old Town Square where the newly made Mikulášská street, today's Pařížská (Paris), leads into Old Town Square. The sensitively shaped, well-balanced façade is adorned with statues by Anton Braun, who also made some of the decoration inside the church. The furnishings are not original, but the rich stucco decoration by Bernardo Spinetti, framing Cosmas Damian Asam's fresco on the legend of St Benedict, has been preserved.

'Saint Nicholas in the Old Town of Prague did not become one of the loveliest churches in Prague, indeed, in the northern lands, until the hoe and the shovel had removed the house of the abbot and the house of Křenovský, which used to stand in front of the church at the corner of Old Town Square.'
Augustin Vojtěch, 1940

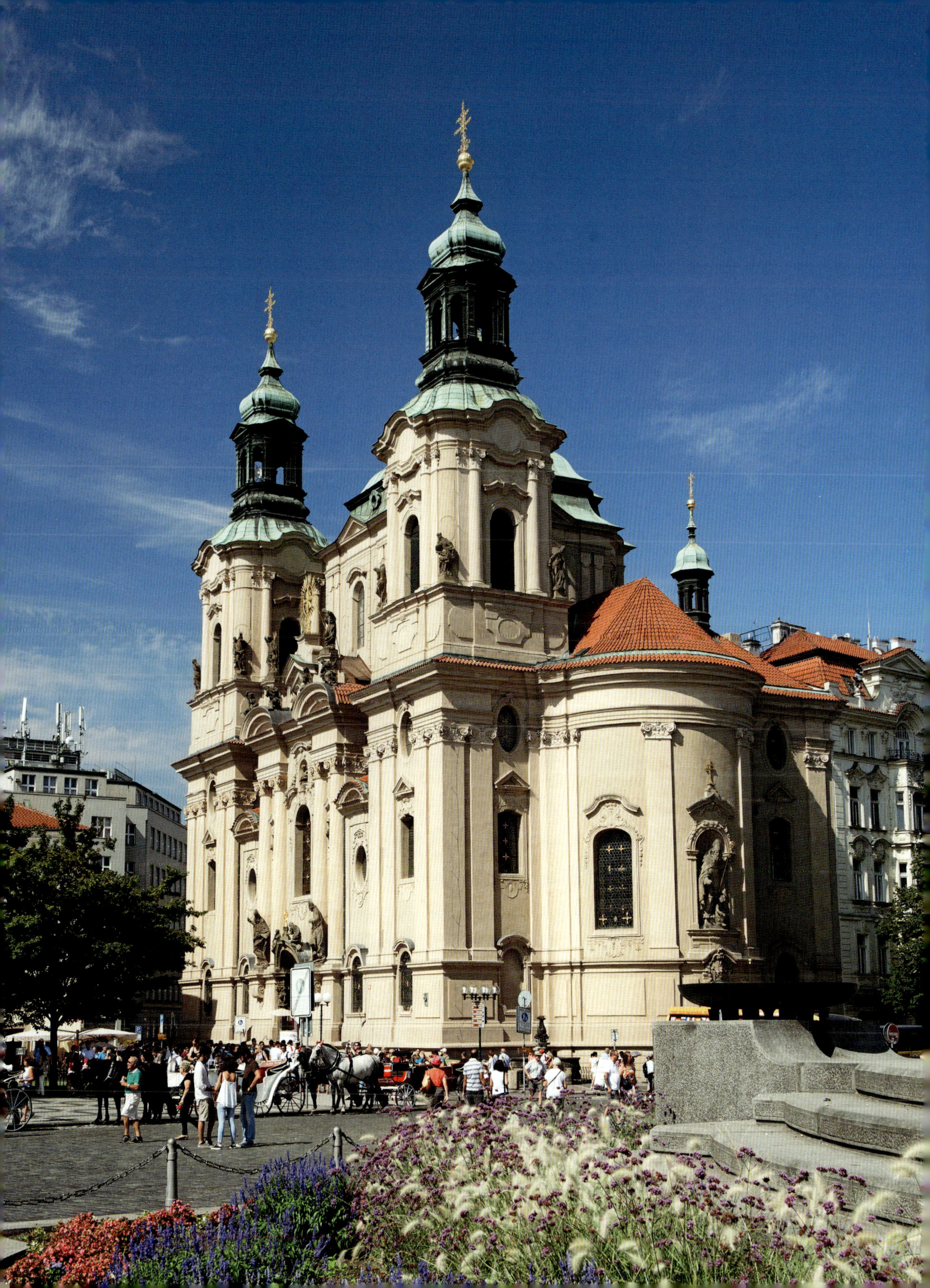

49/ GOLTZ-KINSKÝ HOUSE (PALÁC GOLTZ-KINSKÝCH) (1750–65)

The monumental Rococo house in front of the Thein Church (Týnský chrám) was built by Count Johann Ernst von Goltz, probably on plans by Anselmo Lurago, on the land of three earlier houses. In 1768 the builder sold his new residence to Count Franz Ulrich Kinsky. The rich stuccowork on the façade is by Carlo Giuseppe Bossi; on the first floor, above the middle window of the avant-corps on the left, is the palladium of the Madonna of Stará Boleslav and above the middle window on the right is St John Nepomucene. Ignaz Franz Platzer is the sculptor of the reliefs in the two triangular tympanums surmounting the two avant-corps. They depict scenes from Ovid's *Metamorphoses*, the abductions of Deianeira and of Europa. The statues of gods of classical mythology on the attic (today, copies) are also by Platzer.

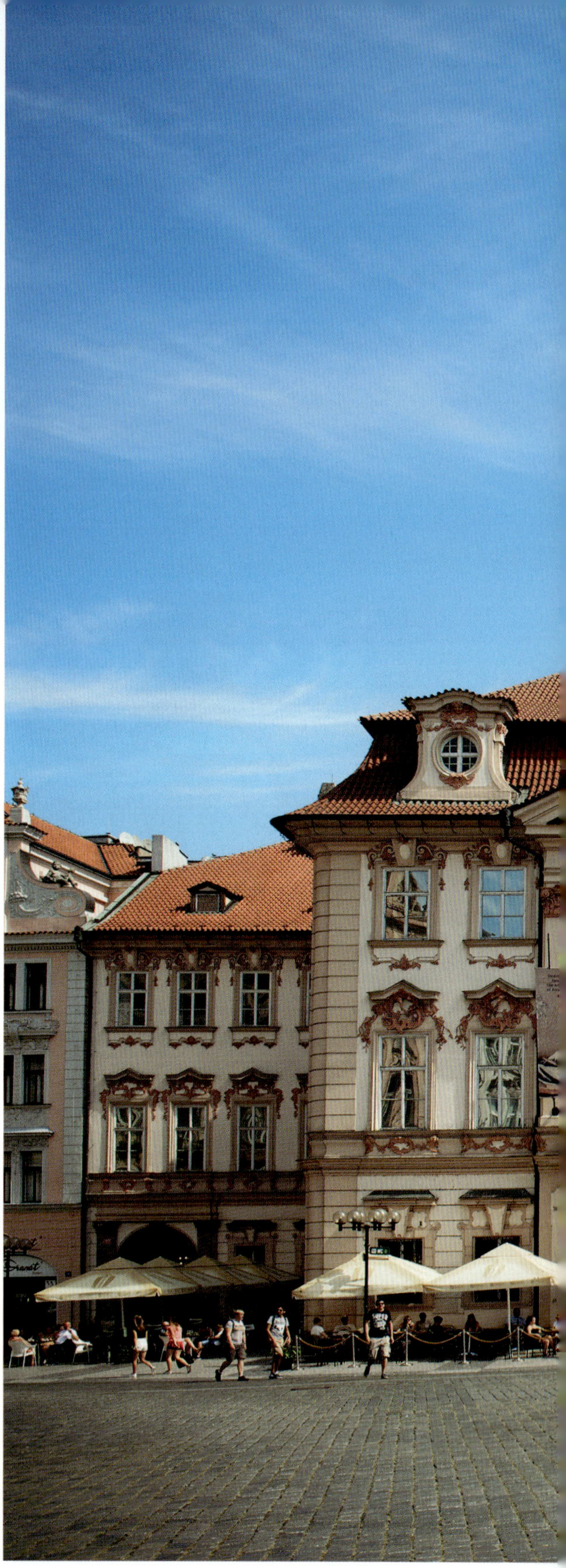

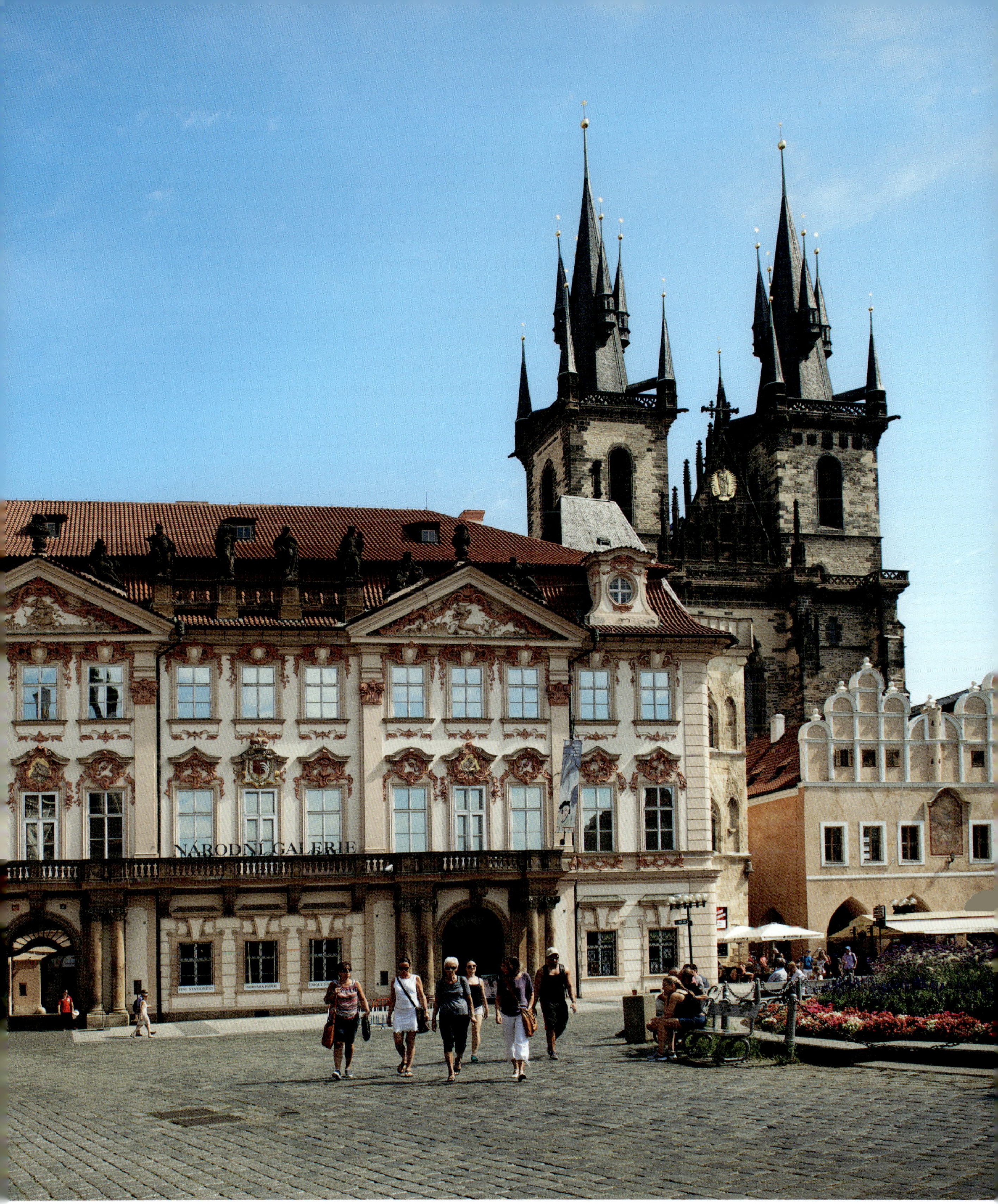
NÁRODNÍ GALERIE

50A/ FROM THE THEIN CHURCH – HIGH ALTAR

After the Battle of the White Mountain, in 1620, the erstwhile spiritual bastion of Utraquist Prague became a model Catholic Marian church and, at the same time, a religious monument to the heroic defence against the Swedish invaders in 1648. Though the prodigious portal-like high altar had already been built in 1645, it was not dedicated until four years later and the paintings were not placed on it until perhaps 1654. The magnificent canvas by Karel Škréta, *The Assumption*, was painted after models with which this famous artist had become acquainted during his Italian sojourn. With the same mastery and grandness, Škréta also painted *The Trinity* in the reredos above the altar.

The side altars of the Thein Church are also decorated with remarkable Baroque works, including other paintings by Karel Škréta, Anton Stevens, and Johann Georg Heinsch, together with statues by Ernst Johann Heidelberger and Johann Georg Bendl.

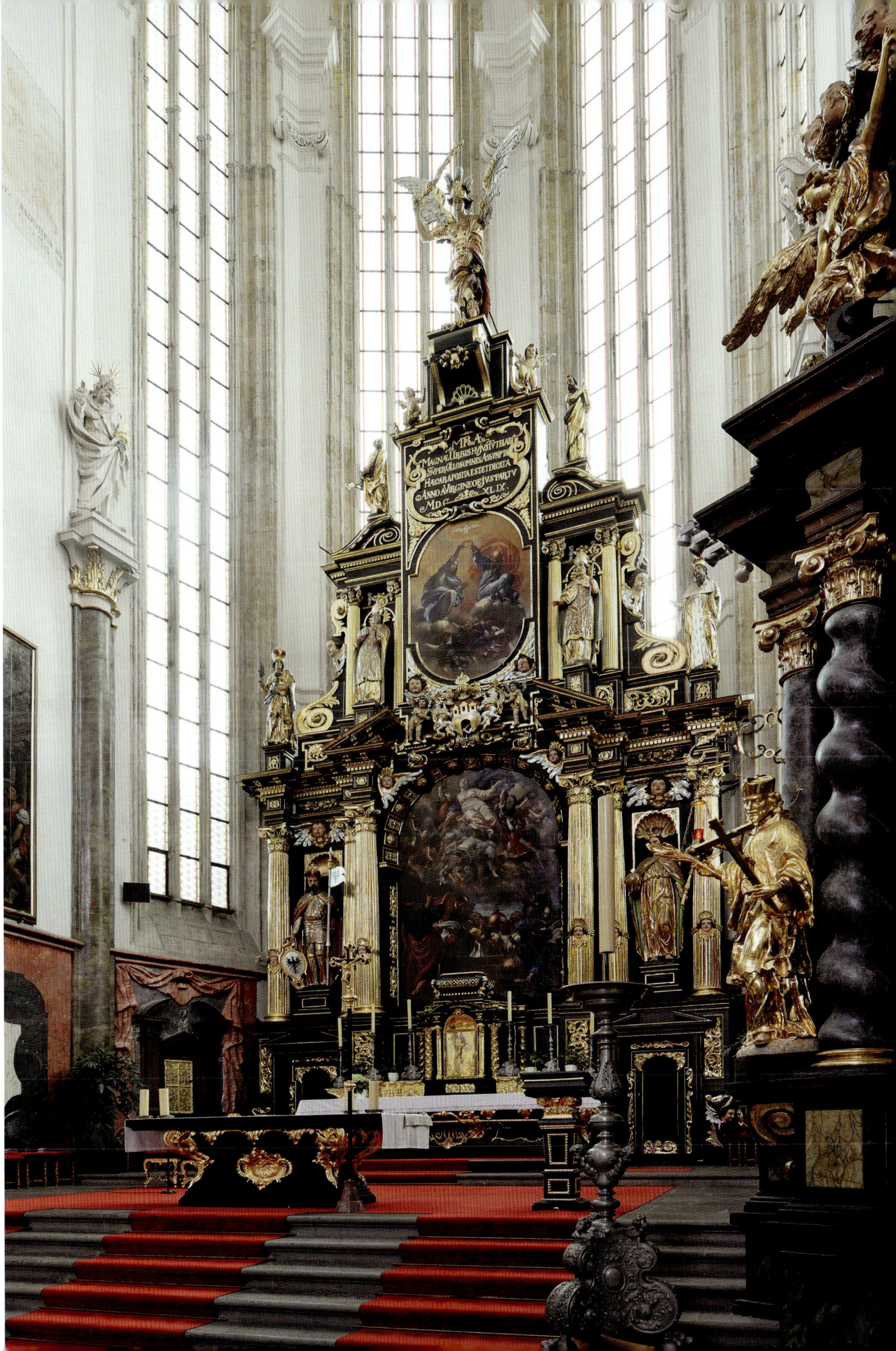
MRÆ
MAGNÆ URBIS HUJUS TUTELARI
SUPER CÆLOS OMNES ASSUMPTÆ
HÆC ARA POSITA EST ET DICATA
ANNO A VIRGINEO EJUS PARTU
MDC XLIX.

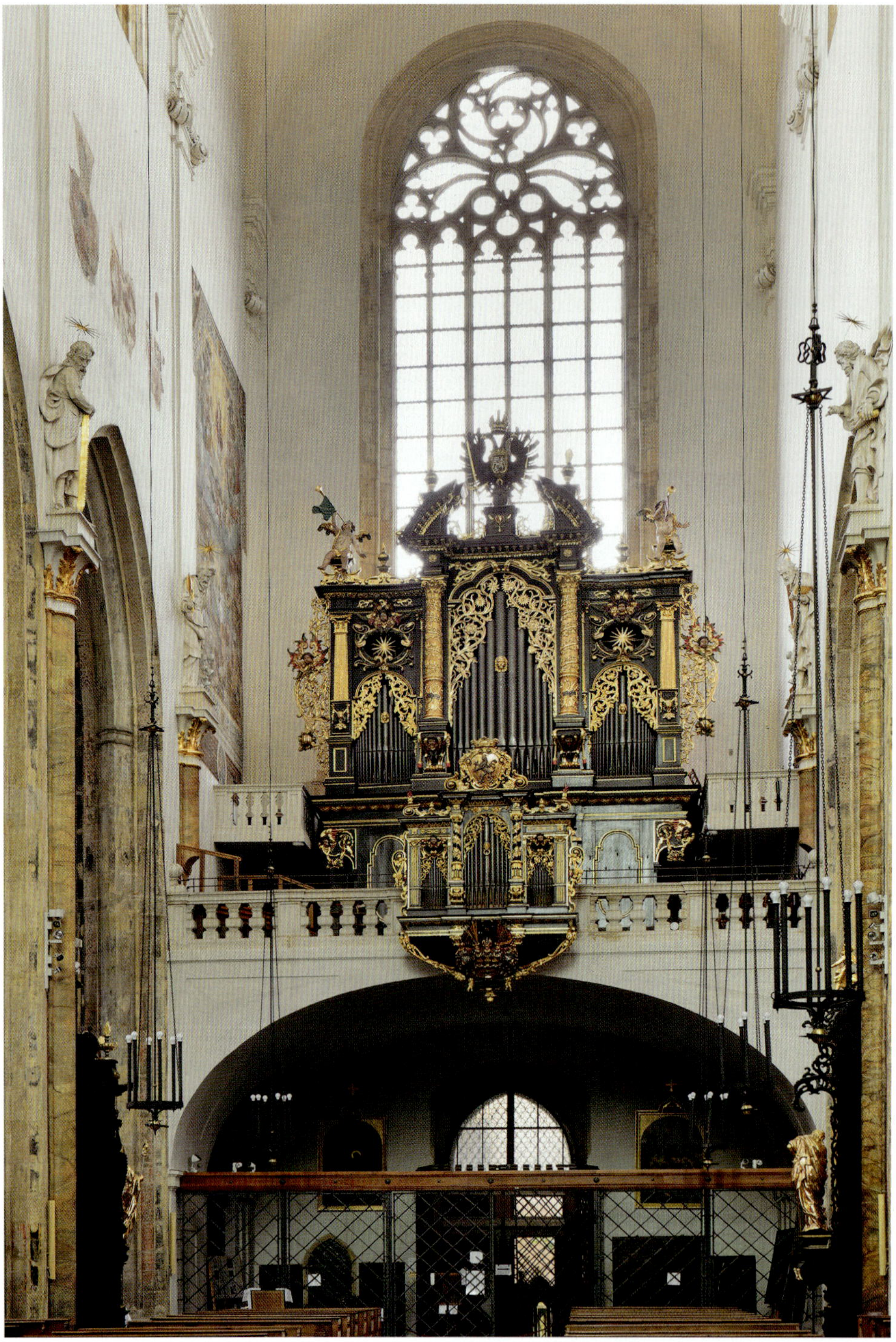

50B/ THE PIPE ORGAN

Among the Early Baroque furnishings of the Thein Church is the richly decorated organ with thirty-two stops and 1,665 pipes. Probably the oldest functioning church organ in Prague today, it was made from 1670 to 1673 by the renowned organ-builder Johann Heinrich Mundt of Cologne.

51A–B/ FROM THE CHURCH OF ST CASTULUS (SV. HAŠTALA) – FERDINAND MAXIMILIAN BROKOFF AND HIS WORKSHOP, *THE PASSION*, 1716
The carvings of the suffering of Christ, from His agony on the Mount of Olives to His crucifixion, were commissioned from Brokoff by the Old Town councillor Johann Paul Petsch. The Passion scenes were part of the original decoration of the altar, but their current location and arrangement are modern.

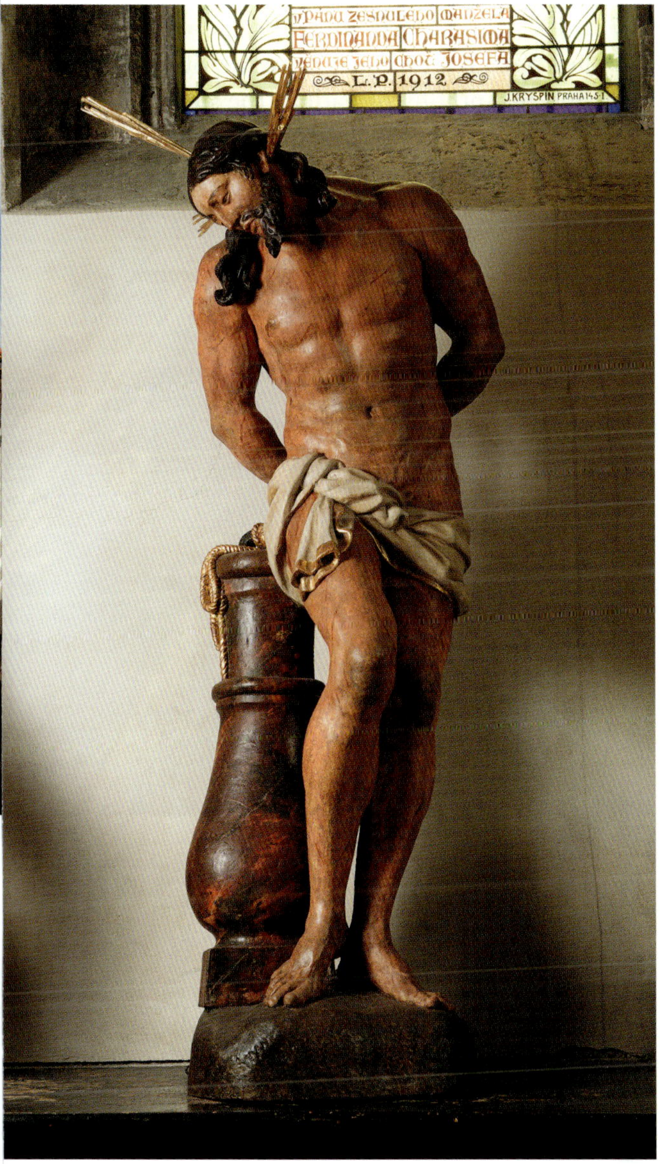

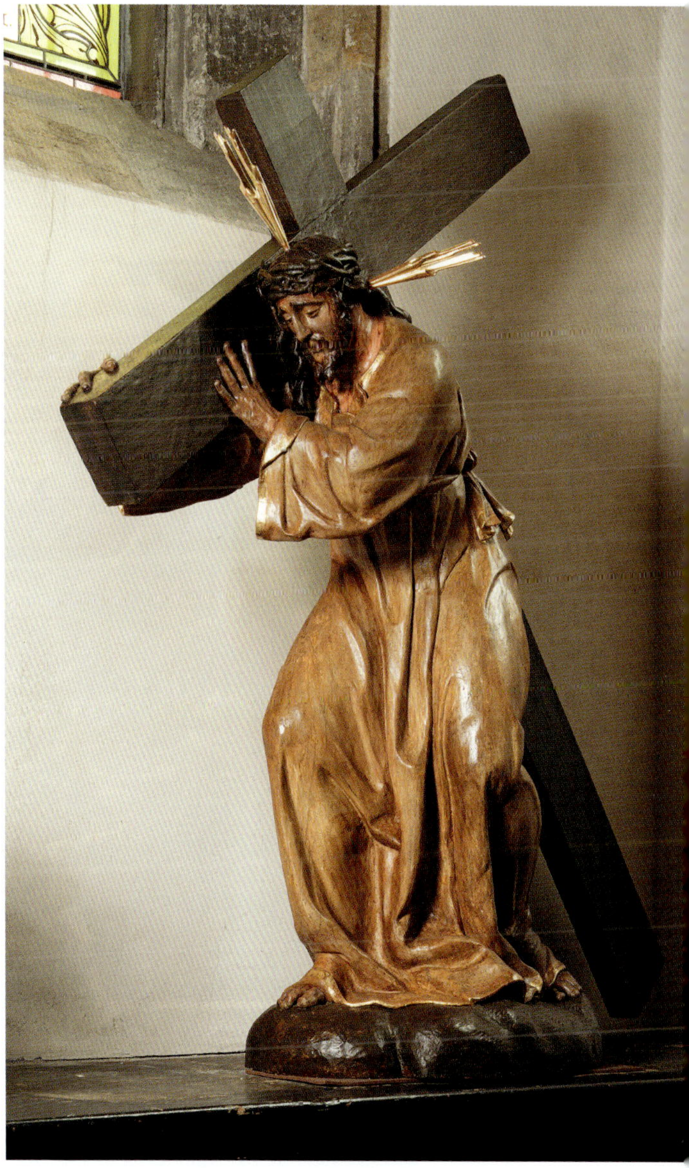

52C/ TOMB MONUMENT TO JOHANN WENZEL WRATISLAW VON MITROWITZ, 1714–16

Count Wratislaw was a distinguished diplomat and politician who contributed greatly to the Habsburg success in the War of the Spanish Succession (1701–14). In Wratislaw's honour, his brother-in-law, Count Leopold Joseph Schlik, commissioned the most spectacular tomb monument of Baroque Prague. The concept behind it was proposed by the polymath poet Carl Gustav Heraeus; the architectural design is by Johann Bernhard Fischer von Erlach. The voluminous subtly shaped statues are by Ferdinand Maximilian Brokoff. Though they seem to be carved out of marble they are in fact sandstone covered with a layer of painted gesso. In the middle, the asymmetrical yet perfectly balanced composition carries the figure of the deceased Wratislaw, who is being raised up and decorated with a wreath by a kneeling Glory. An airborne Fama is inscribing Wratislaw's titles into the pyramidal obelisk, whereas merciless old Saturn (Chronos) is already numbering Wratislaw's days on earth. The lowest figure, seated, grieving, and engrossed in her thoughts, is Contemplation, sometimes also interpreted as History.

'The melancholy exuded by this play of forms affects the historian acquainted with the events in the life of Johann Wenzel Wratislaw von Mitrowitz more deeply than any other contemporaneous monument of its kind [...] the body of our last "Baroque cavalier", in the full sense of the word, which was prematurely broken.'
Zdeněk Kalista, 1939

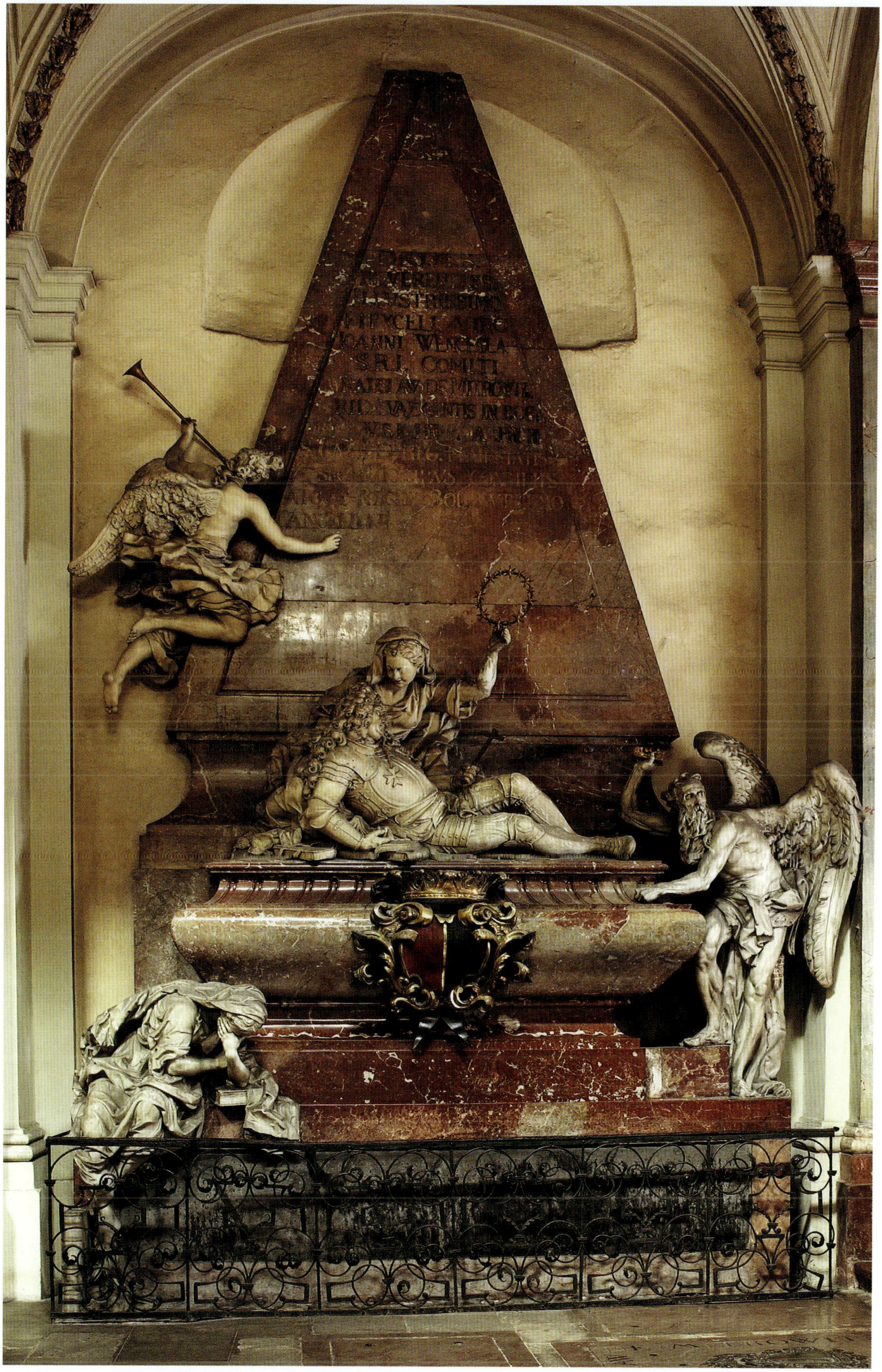

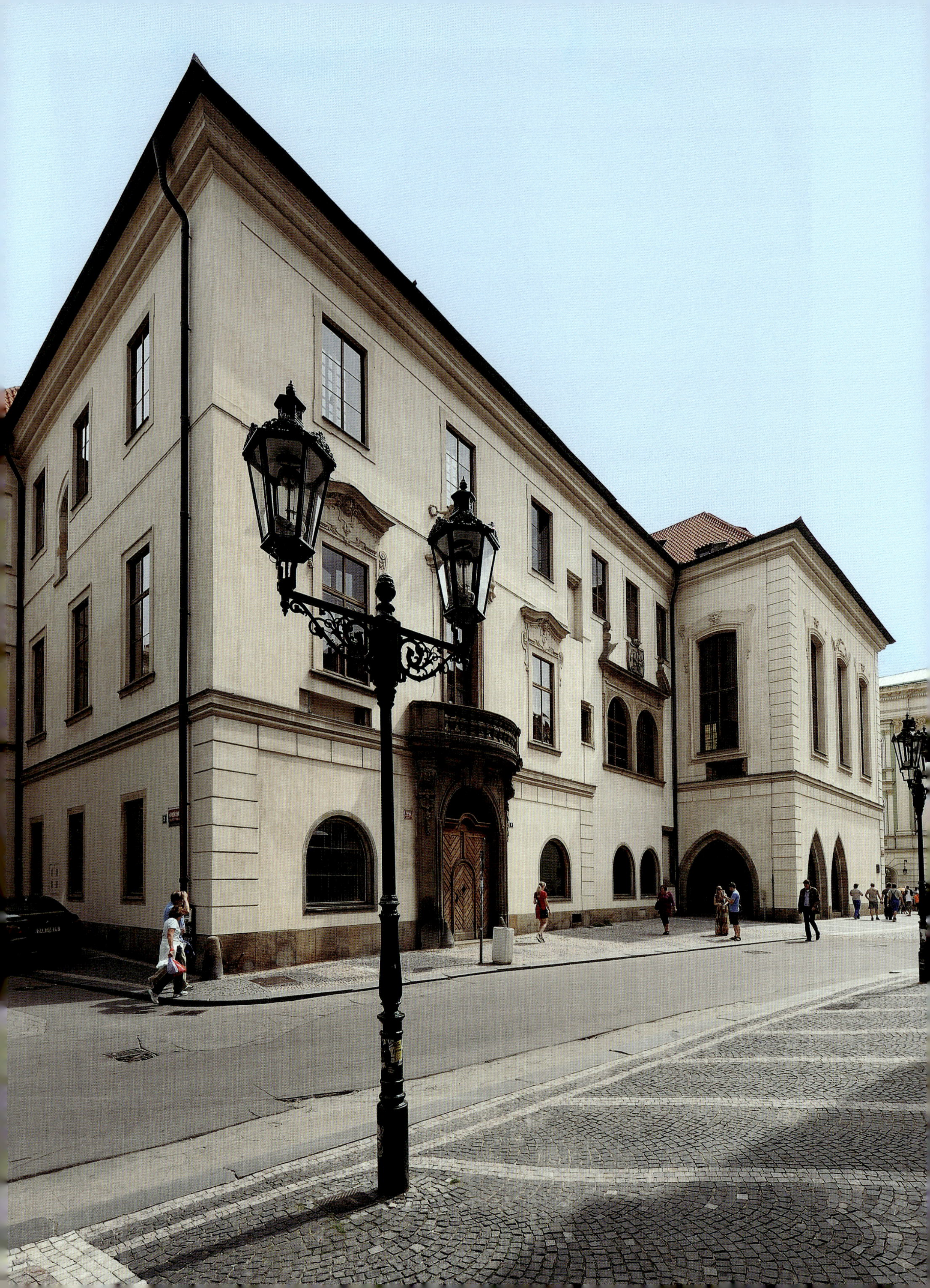

53A/ THE CAROLINUM – FAÇADE
FROM ŽELEZNÁ ULICE

From 1715 to 1718, the historic seat of what is today known as Charles University, once called the Collegium Carolinum, underwent fundamental rebuilding on plans by František Maxmilián Kaňka. At that time, the façade on Železná ulice (Iron Street) was visually unified, acquiring a palazzo-like character with a central portal and balcony. The earlier house in the middle, with twin windows, from 1687, remains preserved in the façade.

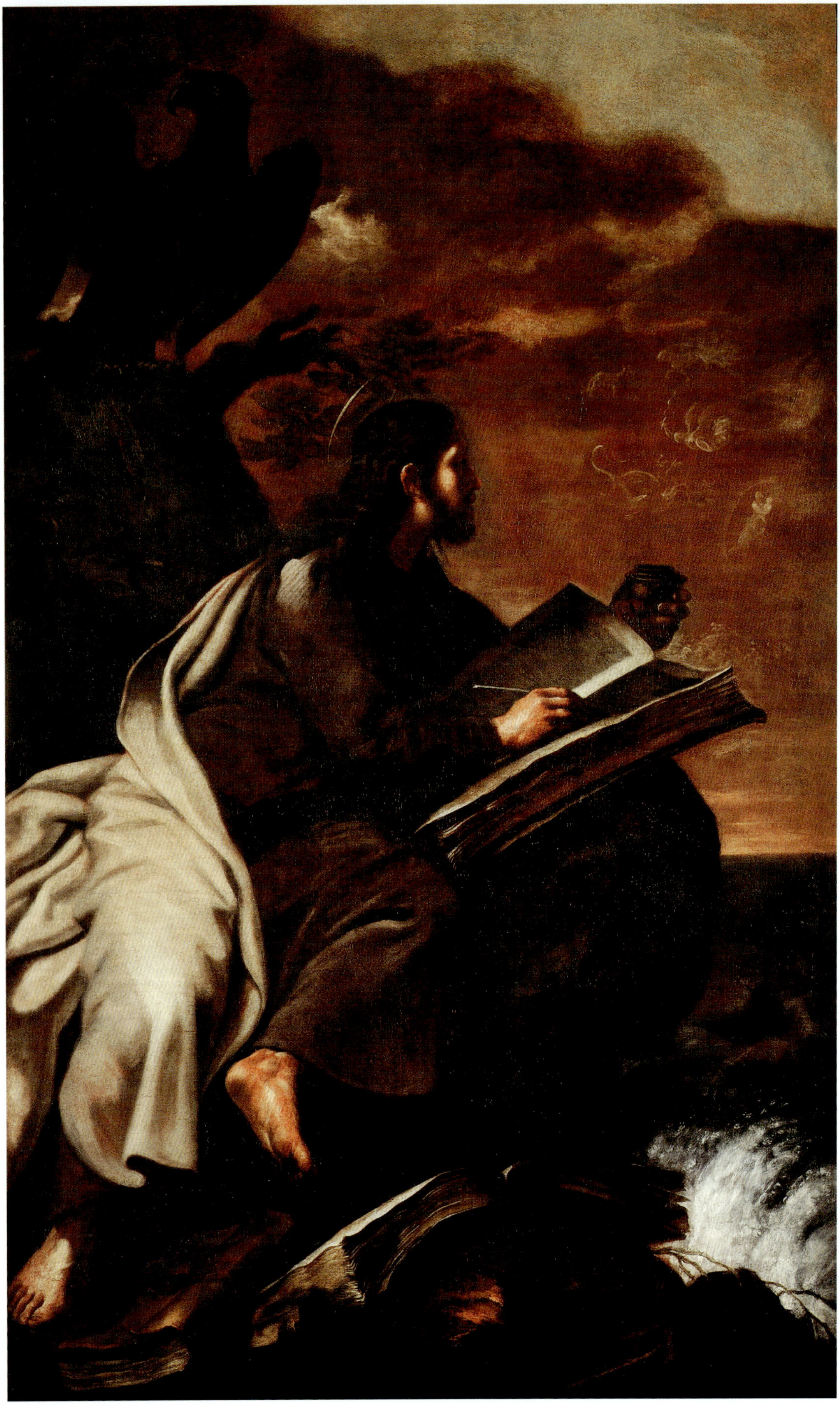

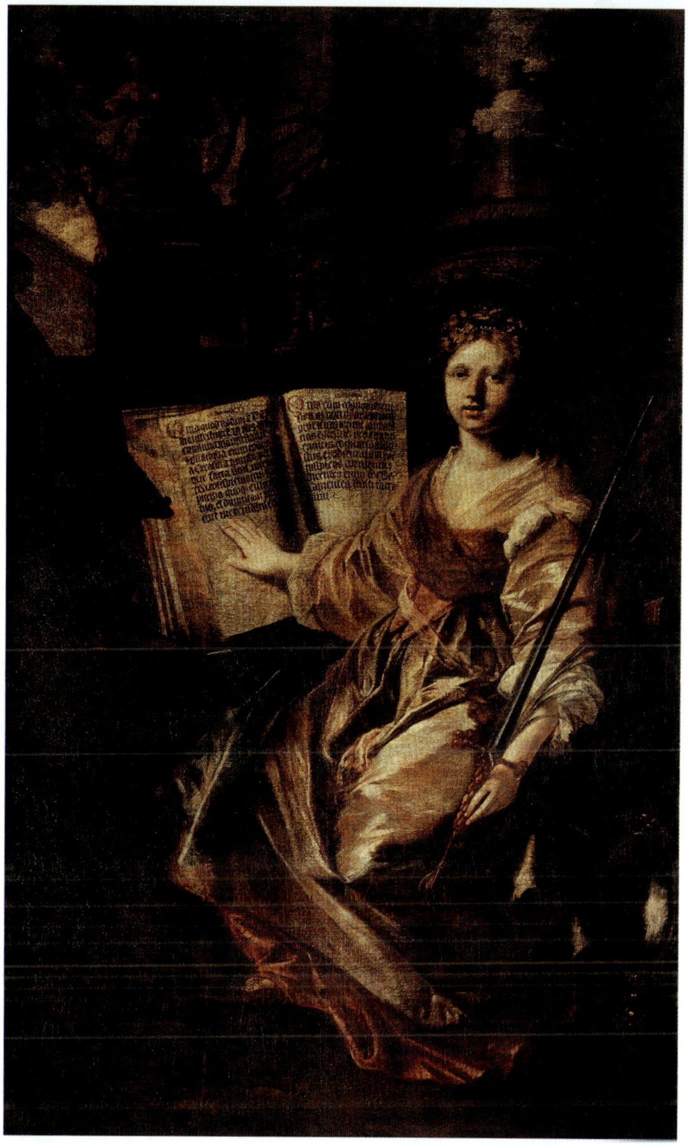

53B/ KAREL ŠKRÉTA: ST JOHN THE EVANGELIST ON PATMOS, 1650S

53C/ KAREL ŠKRÉTA: ST CATHERINE, 1658

In the Baroque period, this painting of St John the Evangelist (the patron of the Faculty of Theology) and its counterpart, St Catherine (the protectress of the Faculty of Arts), adorned the Great Hall (Aula magna) of the Carolinum, where graduations and other academic ceremonies were traditionally held. Here, Škréta has portrayed St John on a barren rocky coast at work upon the Book of Revelation. In the sky, before his eyes, appears a vision of the Woman Clothed with the Sun and the Archangel Michael slaying the dragon (Satan).
The painting of St Catherine was donated to the university by one of its students, Michał Korybut Wiśniowiecki, the future King of Poland. Here, Catherine is surrounded by her attributes of learning, which refer to this young princess's legendary disputation with fifty pagan philosophers. Her right hand rests on the Bible, which is open at the Epistles of St Paul to the Romans, referring to the role that only God can play in the process of true learning.

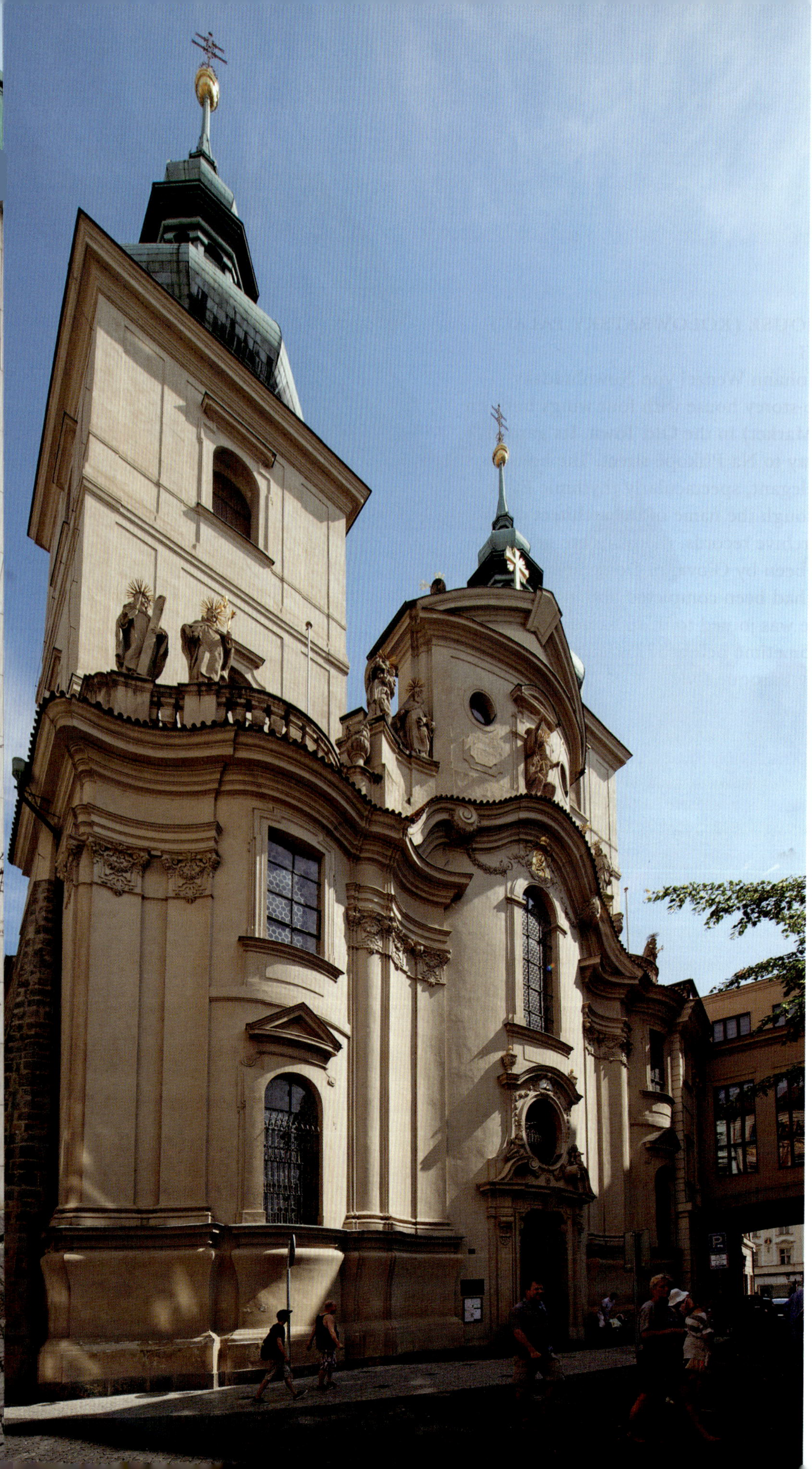

55A/ CHURCH OF ST GALL (KOSTEL SV. HAVLA) – FAÇADE

The Church of St Gall used to be the parish centre of the autonomous Town of Gall (Havelské Město in Czech, Gallusstadt in German), a rich quarter with a mostly German patrician class. During the Hussite Wars (from *c.*1419 to 1434), it became the property of the Utraquists. Consequently, in 1627, Ferdinand II donated it to the Carmelites. The medieval building was remodelled in the Baroque style and from 1722 to 1724 a striking two-towered façade, resembling a piece of stage scenery, was added to it. Stylistically, it combines Early and High Baroque elements, including a curved ground plan. According to period records, the remodelling was designed by Paul Ignaz Bayer.

55B/ FERDINAND MAXIMILIAN BROKOFF:
THE CRUCIFIXION, 1719–20

The carved decoration of the Holy Cross Chapel in the Church of St Gall was commissioned from Brokoff by the local Carmelite friary. In this small space, a truly Baroque 'spiritual theatre' is played out, its participants expressing a wide range of emotions, from the serious compassion of the Evangelists to the grief of the angels to the pain and sadness of the figures below the Cross. The ideas and composition of this group culminate in the nobly tragic expression of the crucified Christ, whose sacrifice is crowned by His death.

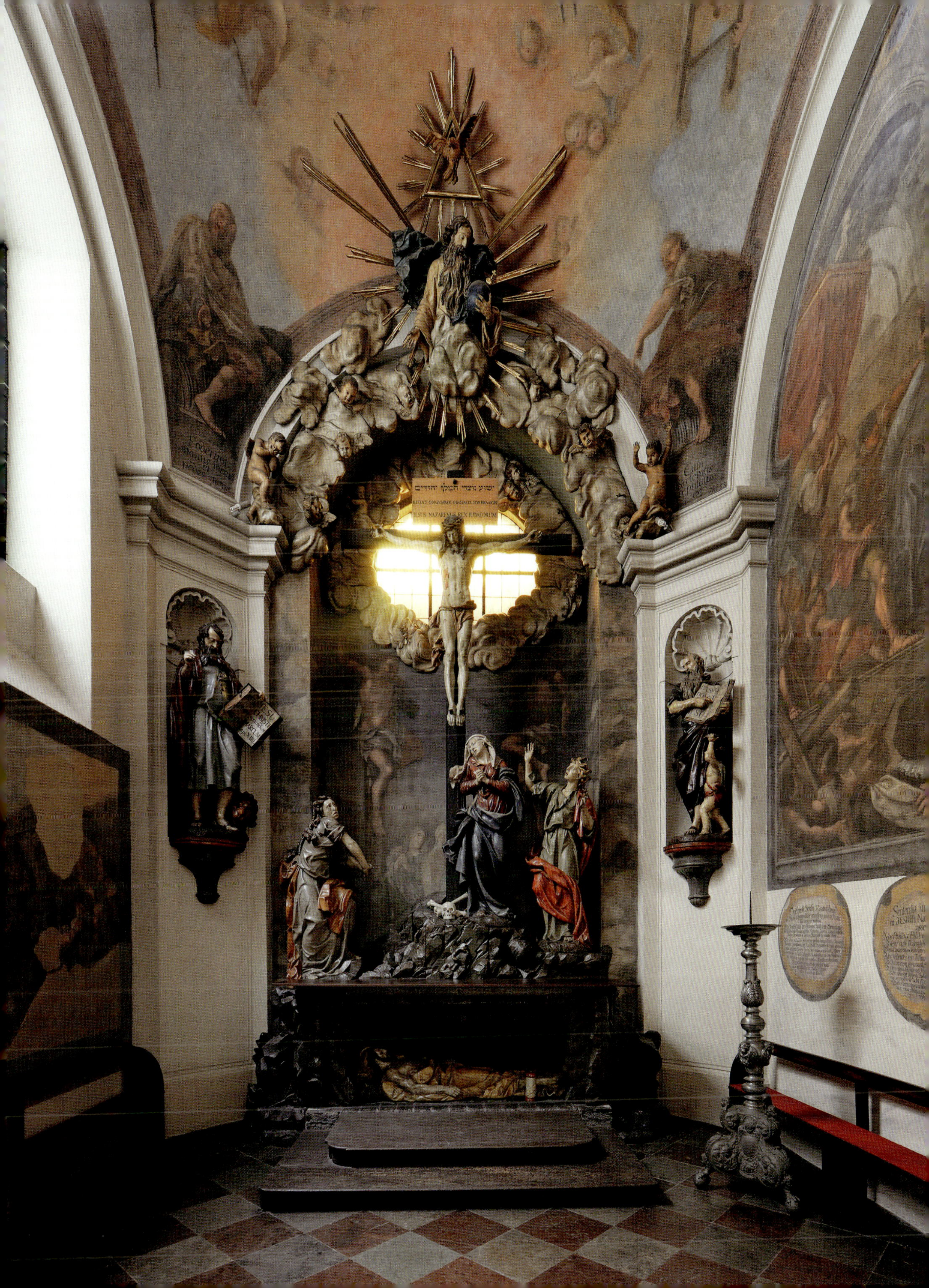

IESUS NAZARENUS REX IUDAEORUM

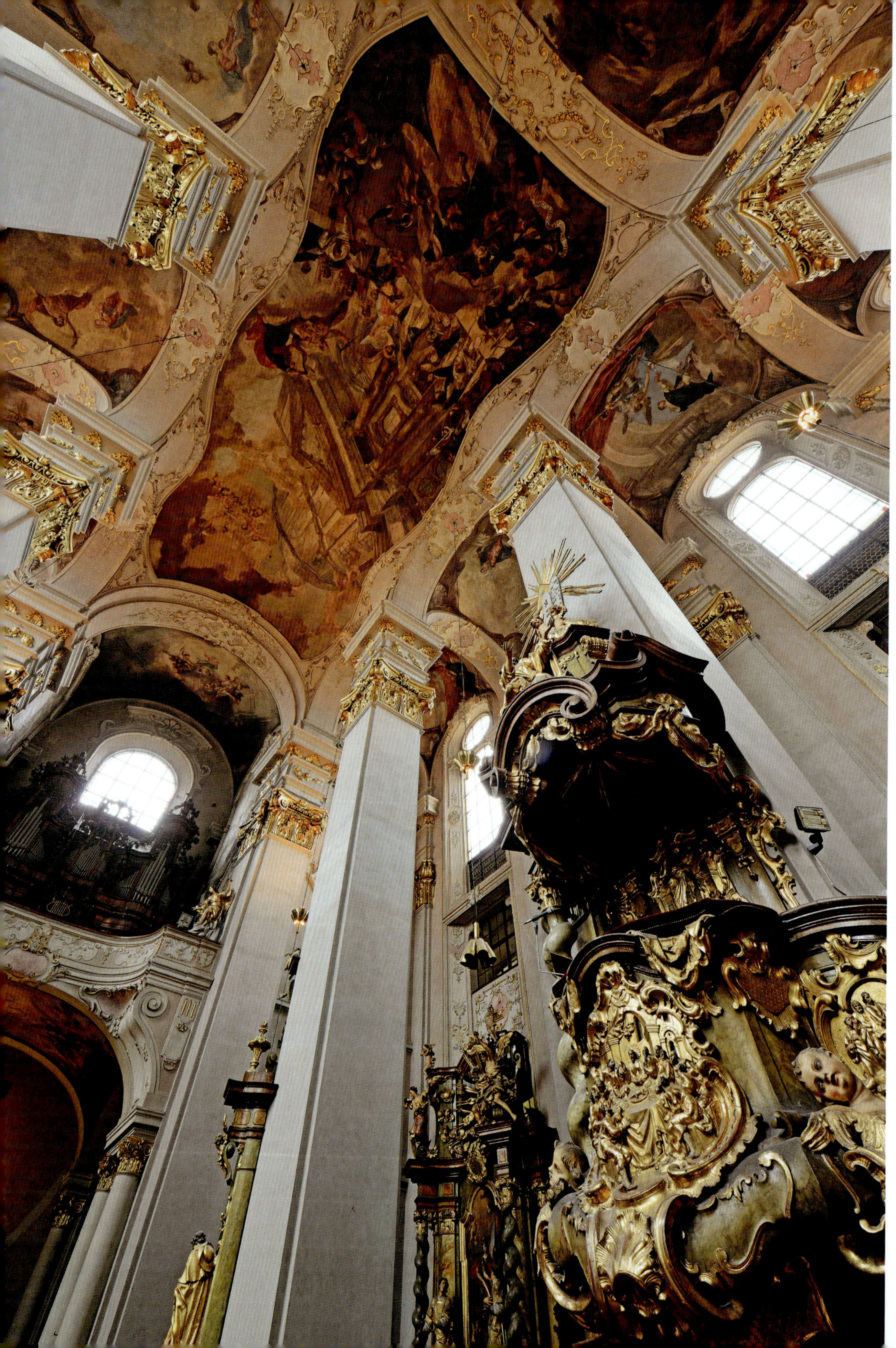

56/ FROM THE CHURCH OF ST GILES – FRESCO WITH SCENES FROM THE HISTORY OF THE DOMINICAN ORDER AND ITS GLORIFICATION, TOGETHER WITH SCENES FROM THE LIVES OF SAINTS GILES, DOMINIC, AND THOMAS AQUINAS BY WENZEL LORENZ REINER, 1734/35

Having been forced to leave the Clementinum, their historic seat at Charles Bridge, to make room for the Jesuits, the Dominicans of Prague acquired the erstwhile collegiate church of St Giles in 1625. The vast Gothic hall underwent Baroque remodelling from 1731 to 1734 on plans by Václav Špaček. Since it was eventually to be decorated with paintings, the ceiling of the nave was first changed into an undulating unified surface. This was a highly original solution, carried out three decades before similar changes to the vaulted ceiling of St Nicholas' Church in the Lesser Town. Reiner's magnificent frescos depict, among other things, the ceaseless aversion that the Dominicans and the Jesuits felt towards each other. The subject matter is mainly the glorification of the Dominican Order, both in its principles and in the figures of its greatest saints, Dominic and Thomas Aquinas. The decoration culminates in an allegorical scene in which the Dominicans protect the Church from heretics, depicted here as a rupturing Lateran Basilica in Rome. What particularly annoyed the Jesuits here of course was the reminder of the mutual philosophical disputations on the fresco depicting the Council of Trent (which took place from 1545 to 1563). The archiepiscopal consistory vindicated the Jesuits and the offensive subject matter was eventually removed from the painting. Reiner was on friendly terms with the Dominicans. He lived on Na Perštýně street, not far from this church, and in his last will and testament he ensured that he would be buried in St Giles' and that Mass would regularly be held here for him.

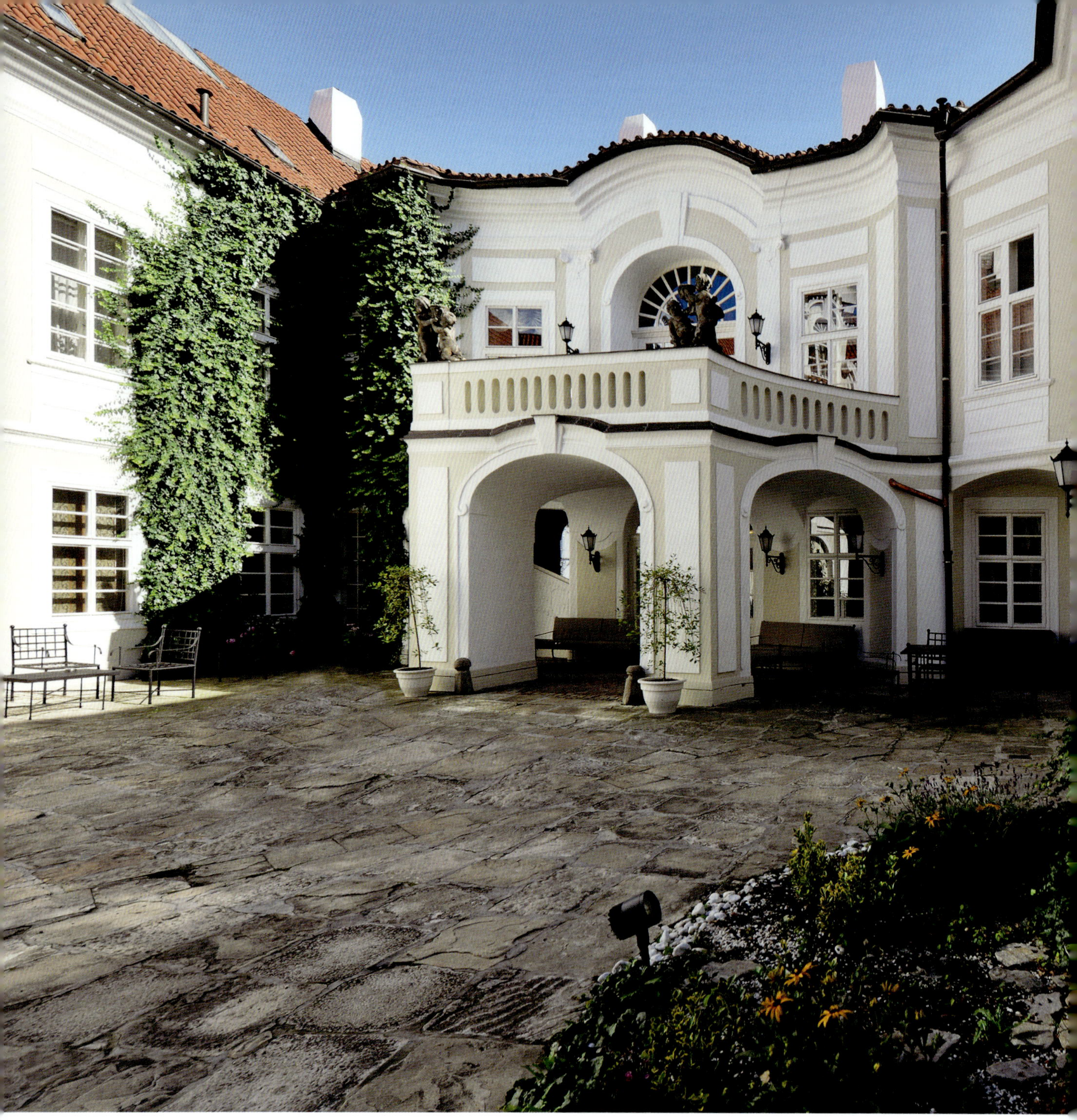

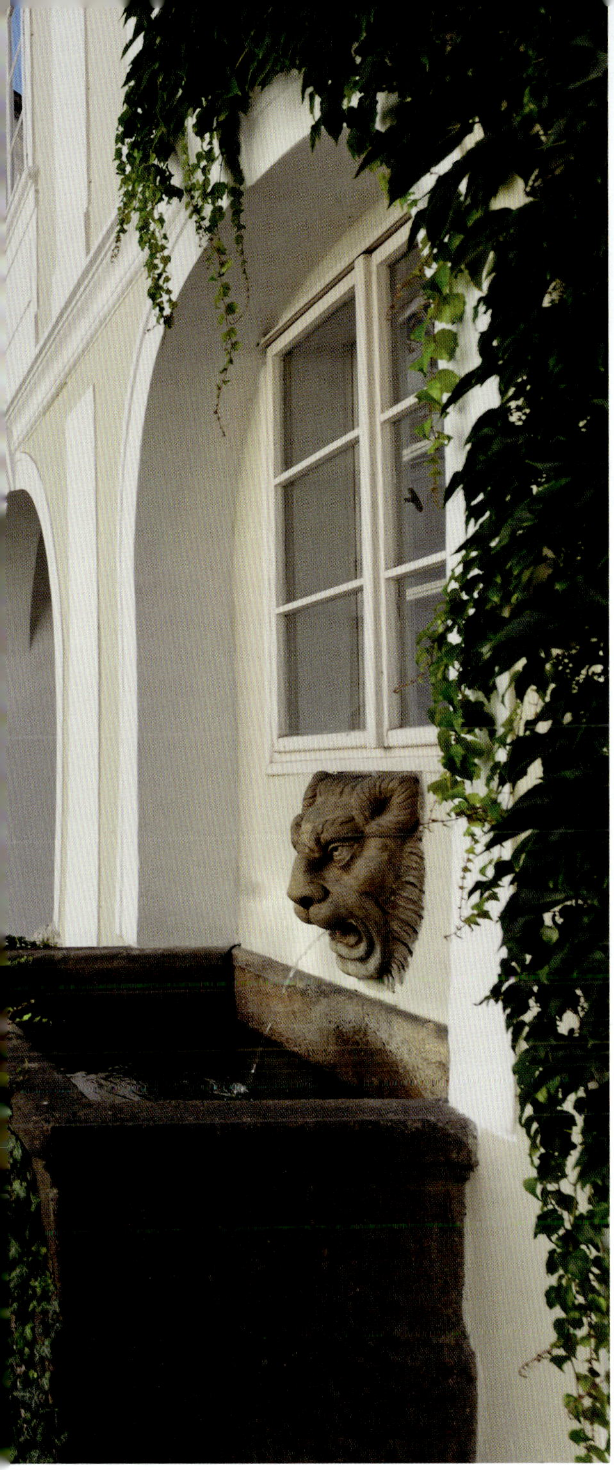

57/ PACHTA VON RAYHOFEN HOUSE

This block of houses, not particularly attractive from the outside, is on St Anne's Square (Anenské náměstí), near the busy Smetana Embankment (Smetanova nábřeží). Concealed inside the block is an architectural gem of the Late Baroque – the original garden façade of the Pachta House from after 1770. The architect was most likely Johann Joseph Wirch, who, in a monumental variant, had used the similar motif of a high central niche with an inserted balcony for the façade of the Archbishop's Palace. On the ground floor, a dynamically composed trapezoid portico, originally for coaches to drop off or pick up passengers, projects from the building. This is how the house looked when, in 1787, Wolfgang Amadeus Mozart visited Count Johann Joseph Pachta von Rayhofen, a renowned music-lover. It was at that time that Mozart wrote the Six German Dances for his host. According to legend, he composed them during his visit and Pachta's musicians learnt them with such alacrity that the assembled company could listen to the latest compositions even before lunch.

58A/ FAÇADE

The magnificent Baroque façade on the street called Národní is actually the north lateral façade of the convent church that the Ursuline nuns built from 1699 to 1704 in honour of their patron saint. It is here that the architect, Marcantonio Canevalle, first used the elements of church architecture in Prague which would later be developed in the buildings of what is known as the 'radically dynamic group'. The sensitively modelled façade is designed to create the impression of unstoppable upward movement. That has also been achieved by emphasizing the avant-corps with three vertical divisions, employing a wide range of architectural elements and decorative detail. The sculptural decoration was made in the workshop of Mathias Wenzel Jäckel.

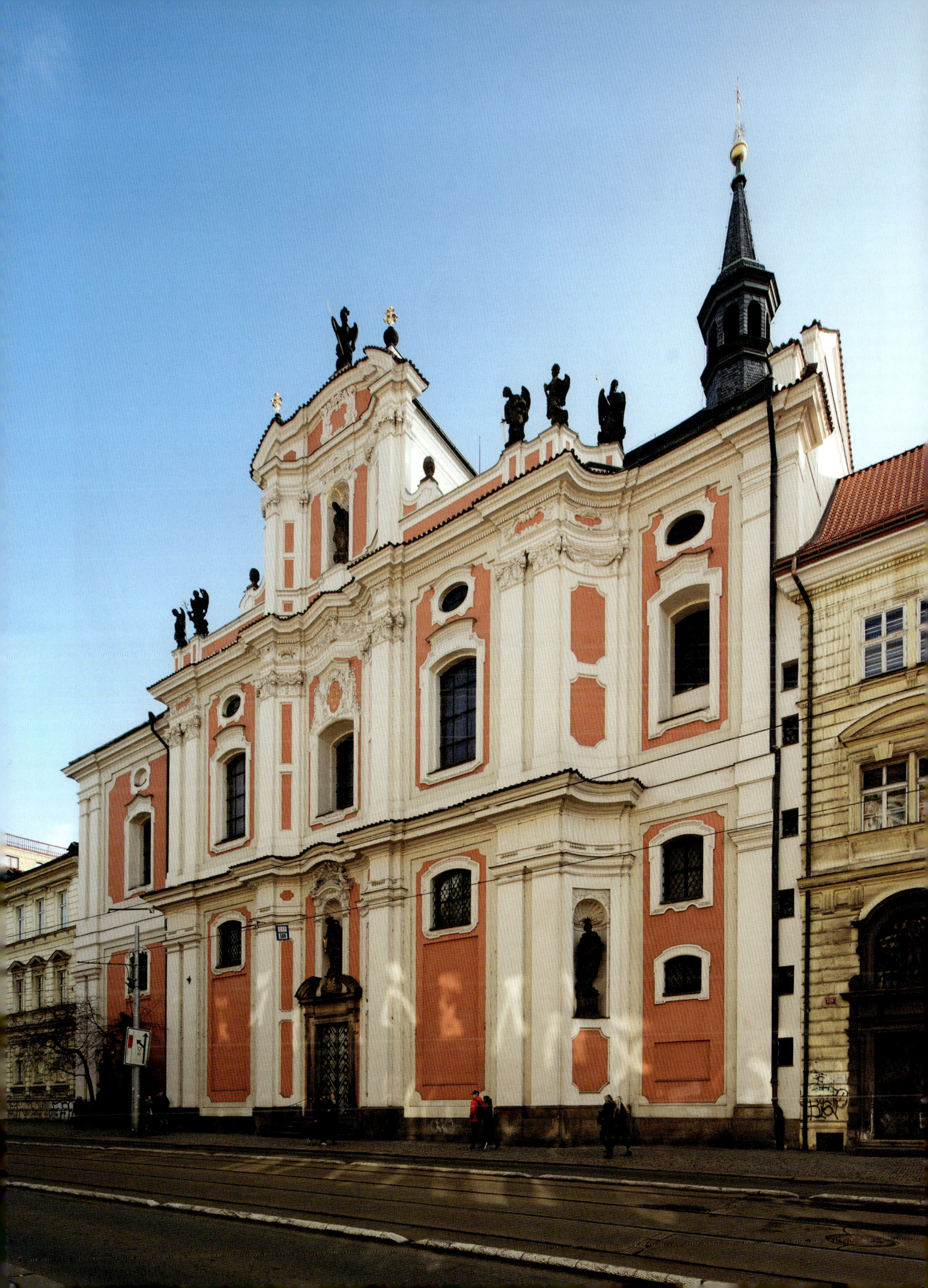

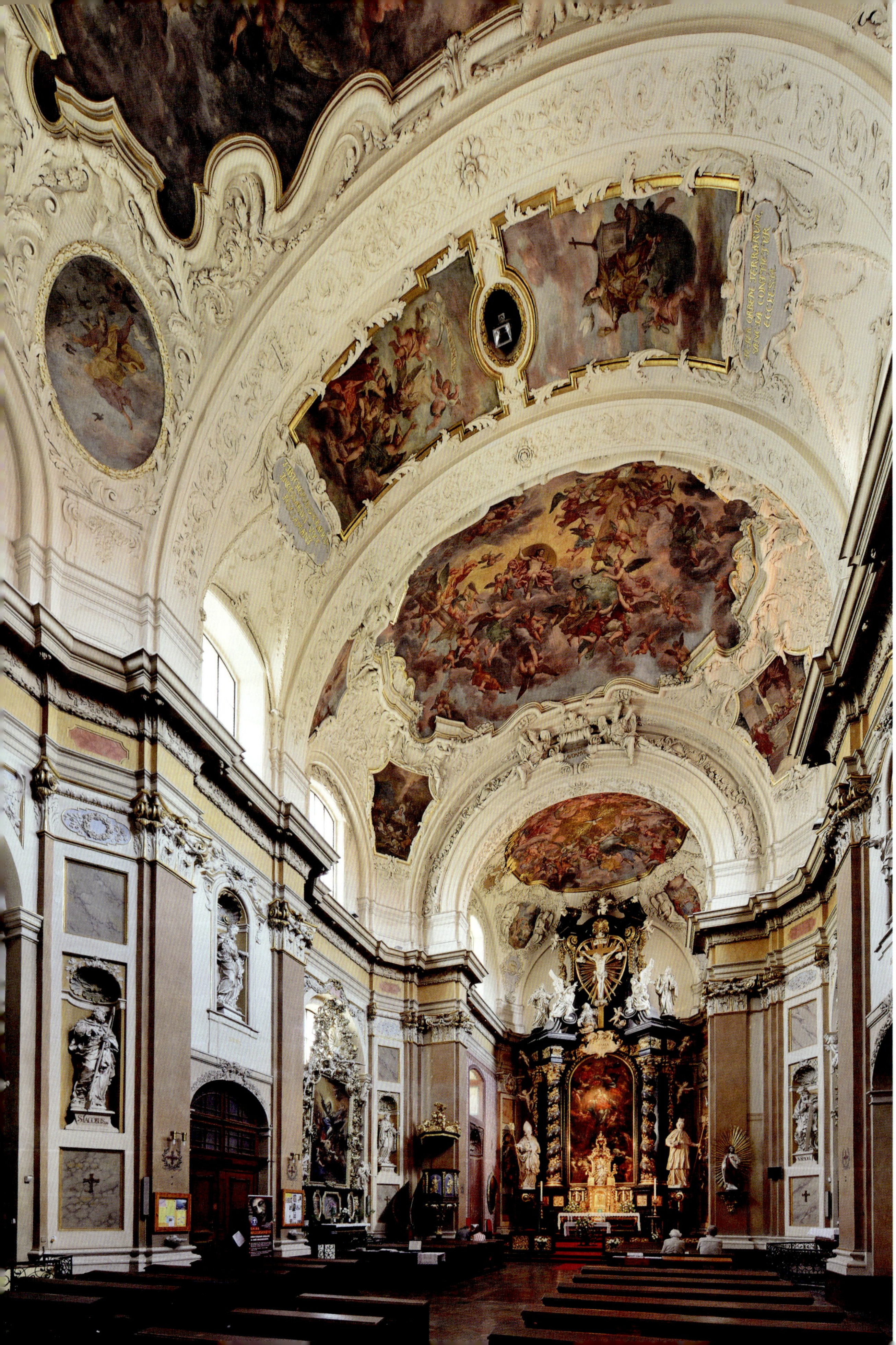

58B/ INTERIOR

The interior of the church is also remarkably designed: a single nave based on a pair of rectangles with chamfered corners, to which an almost square chancel is connected. The complicated spatial composition is dominated by striking sail vaults with rich stucco and painted decoration (frescos by Johann Jacob Stevens von Steinfels, 1707). The superb Baroque furnishings, from the first quarter of the eighteenth century, have been preserved. The altarpieces are by Johann Christoph Lischka and Peter Brandl; the evocative statues by Franz Preiss from 1709–10 are among the most important works of early High Baroque sculpture in Prague before the arrival of Matthias Bernhard Braun.

58C/ IGNAZ FRANZ PLATZER: ST JOHN NEPOMUCENE, 1746–47

This sculptural group at the Church of St Ursula is an early work of the last great sculptor of the Baroque in Prague. It was commissioned by the Ursuline nuns, for whom Platzer made a carefully elaborated wooden model of the central figure. The composition is based on a traditional iconographic type and symmetrical arrangement, but, especially in the figures of putti with cartouches, one already sees the smooth modelling and proportional conception characteristic of early Neoclassicism. The architectural part is the work of Kilian Ignaz Dientzenhofer.

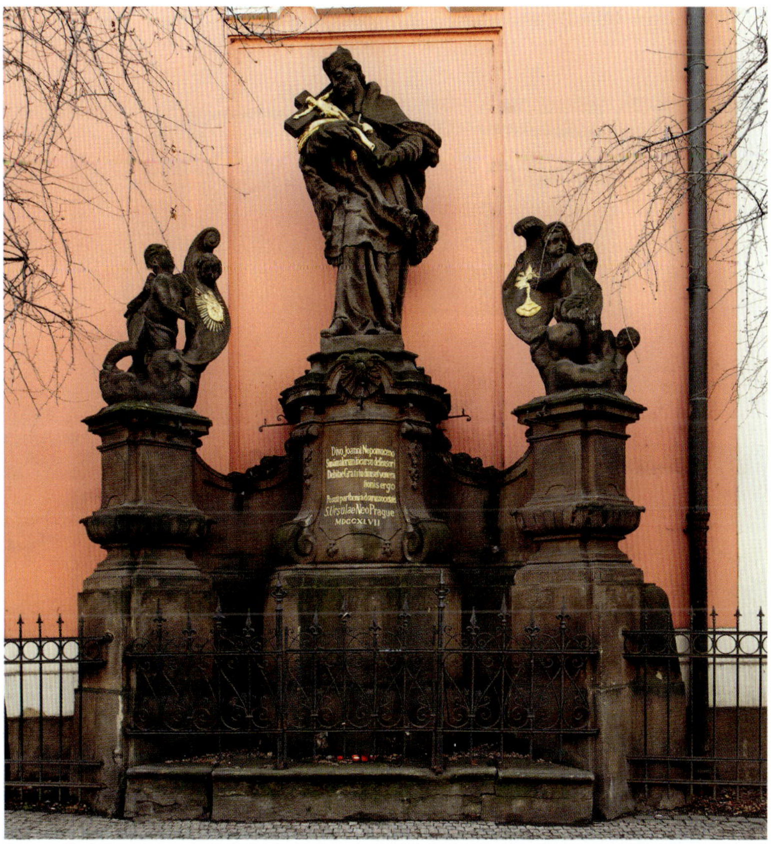

59A/ FROM THE CHURCH OF OUR LADY OF THE SNOW (PANNY MARIE SNĚŽNÉ) – HIGH ALTAR

Though it had been planned in the mid-fourteenth century as the largest Gothic church in the New Town of Prague, by the beginning of the Hussite Wars in about 1419 only the chancel and the side chapels were built. Work on the imposing unfinished church was taken over by the Franciscans in 1603 and in the course of the next two centuries they structurally secured the church and furnished it in the Baroque style. The high altar, from 1649–51, is the tallest in Prague. It stands out for its austere architectural composition and characteristic black-and-gold colour scheme. Its rich sculptural decoration comes from the workshop of the court sculptor Ernst Johann Heidelberger. The altarpiece depicts a legendary event from AD 352: in the middle of a hot Roman summer, so the legend goes, snow fell on the Esquiline Hill, marking the place on which to build the first Marian church, the Basilica of Santa Maria Maggiore. The remarkable composition is attributed to the painter Anton Stevens.

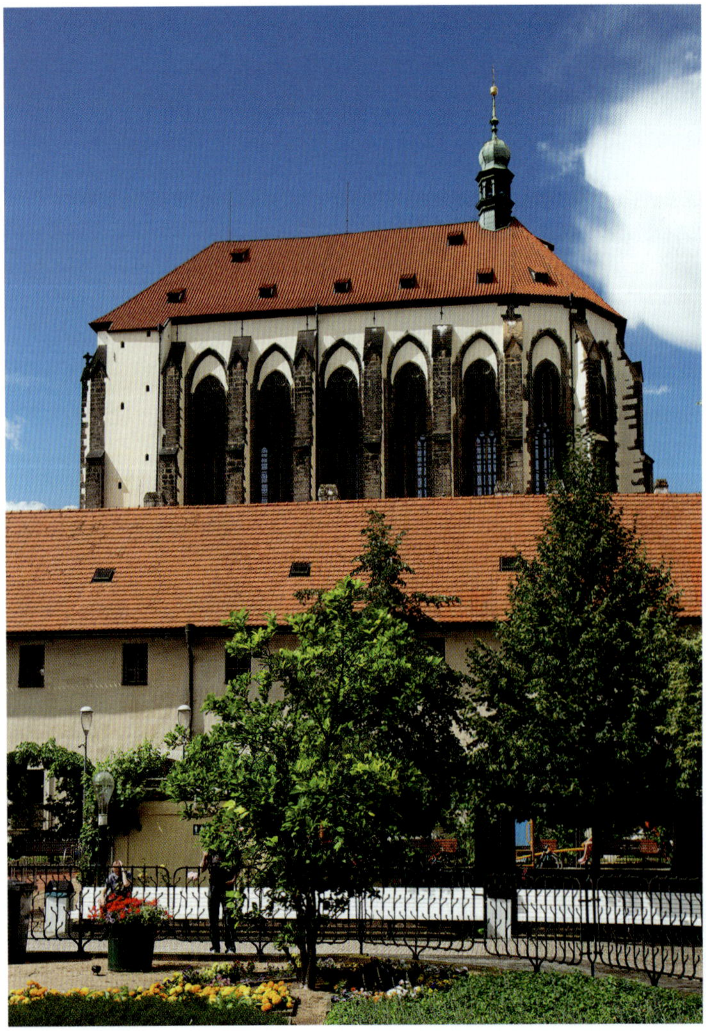

59B/ CHURCH OF OUR LADY OF THE SNOW

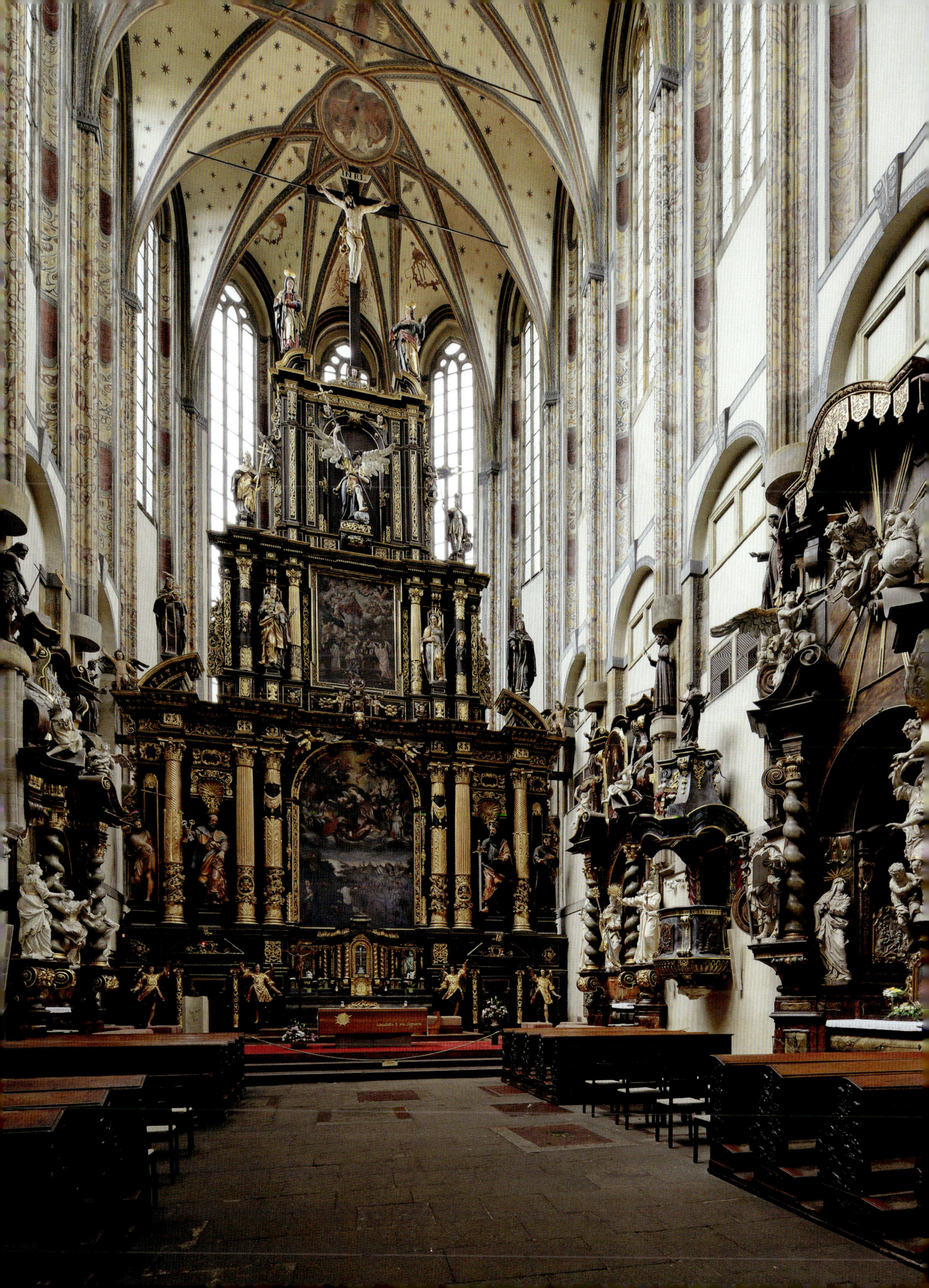

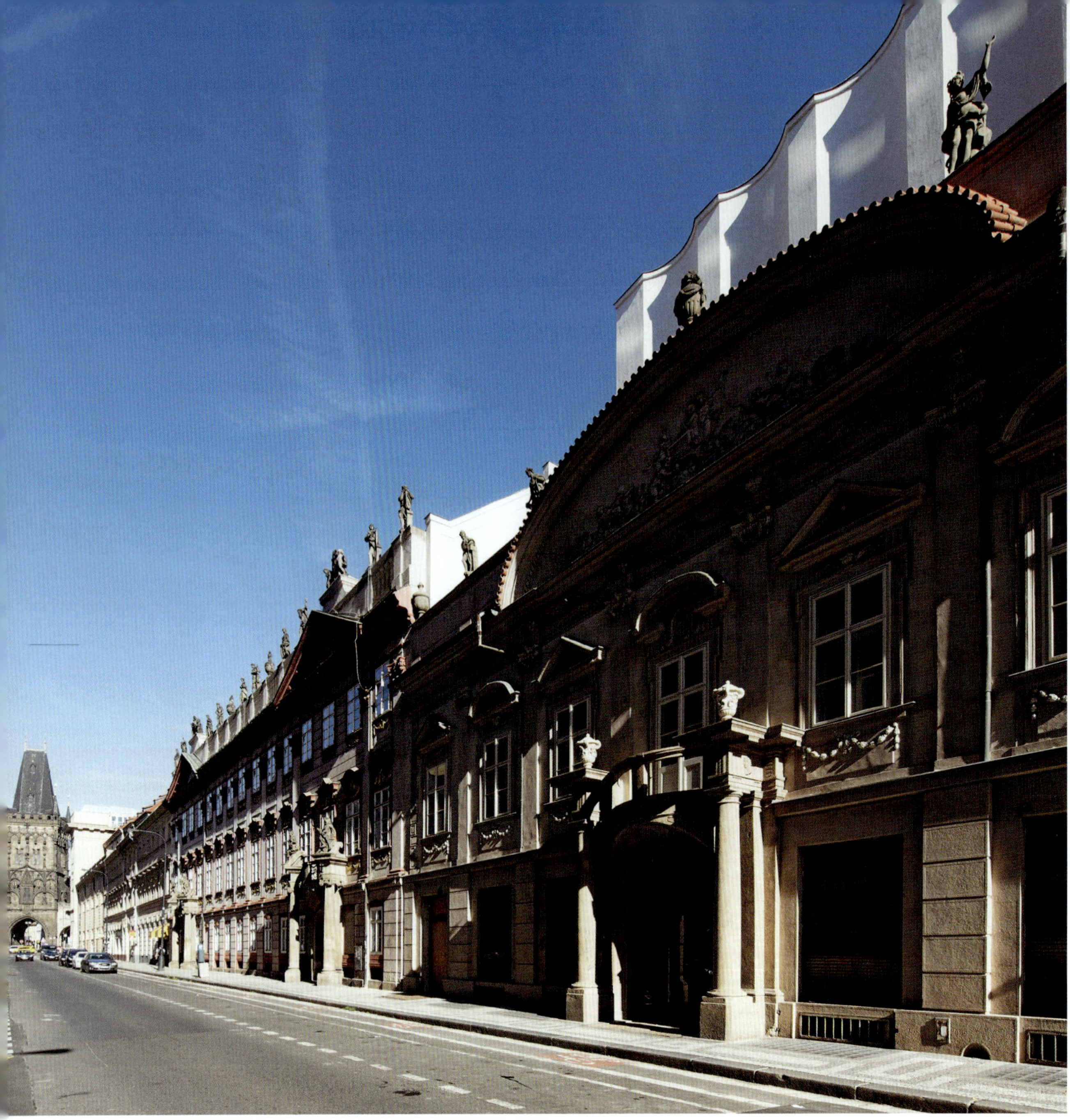

60A–B/ HYBERNSKÁ ULICE

Leading from the boundary of the Old and the New Town, the formerly main Prague street forks near the medieval Powder Tower (Prašná brána). One branch leads along the former Old Town fortifications to the River Vltava, the other leads to the former gate through which the main road to Moravia once ran, and then on to Austria, Hungary, and Poland. Along this important artery, constituting the first section of the Royal Road, an important residential area was built up in the seventeenth century. Today, it is reflected in the palatial houses, whose imposing façades line the busy Hybernská ulice. The first of them, Losy (or Kinský) House, better known today as Lidový dům (the People's House, currently the headquarters of the Social Democrats), was built from 1651 to 1657 by Count Johann Anton the Elder Losy von Losinthal on plans by Carlo Lurago. The count's son, Johann Anton the Younger, expanded the building and made it an important centre of music in Baroque Prague. The Early Baroque appearance of the house is most evident in the courtyard. The main façade was considerably remodelled in the Neoclassical style after 1787.

In the late eighteenth century the two neighbouring houses were owned by Johann Franz Christian Count Swéerts-Reist und von Sporck. Until that time, they had developed separately. Of the former one-storey house on the west (left) side of the Losy House, only the Neoclassical main façade from 1791–92 remained. It comes to a peak in the segmental pediment filled with a delicately shaped relief from the Platzer workshop. The monumental house next door, from the late seventeenth century, belonged to, among others, Count Franz Anton Sporck. In the adjacent garden in 1701, he built the renowned Comoedien-Haus, which in its day was the most important public theatre in Prague. The current appearance of the façade (after 1783) is the work of Anton Haffenecker. Together with the obliquely placed columns flanking the portals, the regular rhythm of the continuous pilasters makes this the last truly Baroque noble house in Prague. The rich sculptural decoration comes from the workshop of Ignaz Michael Platzer.

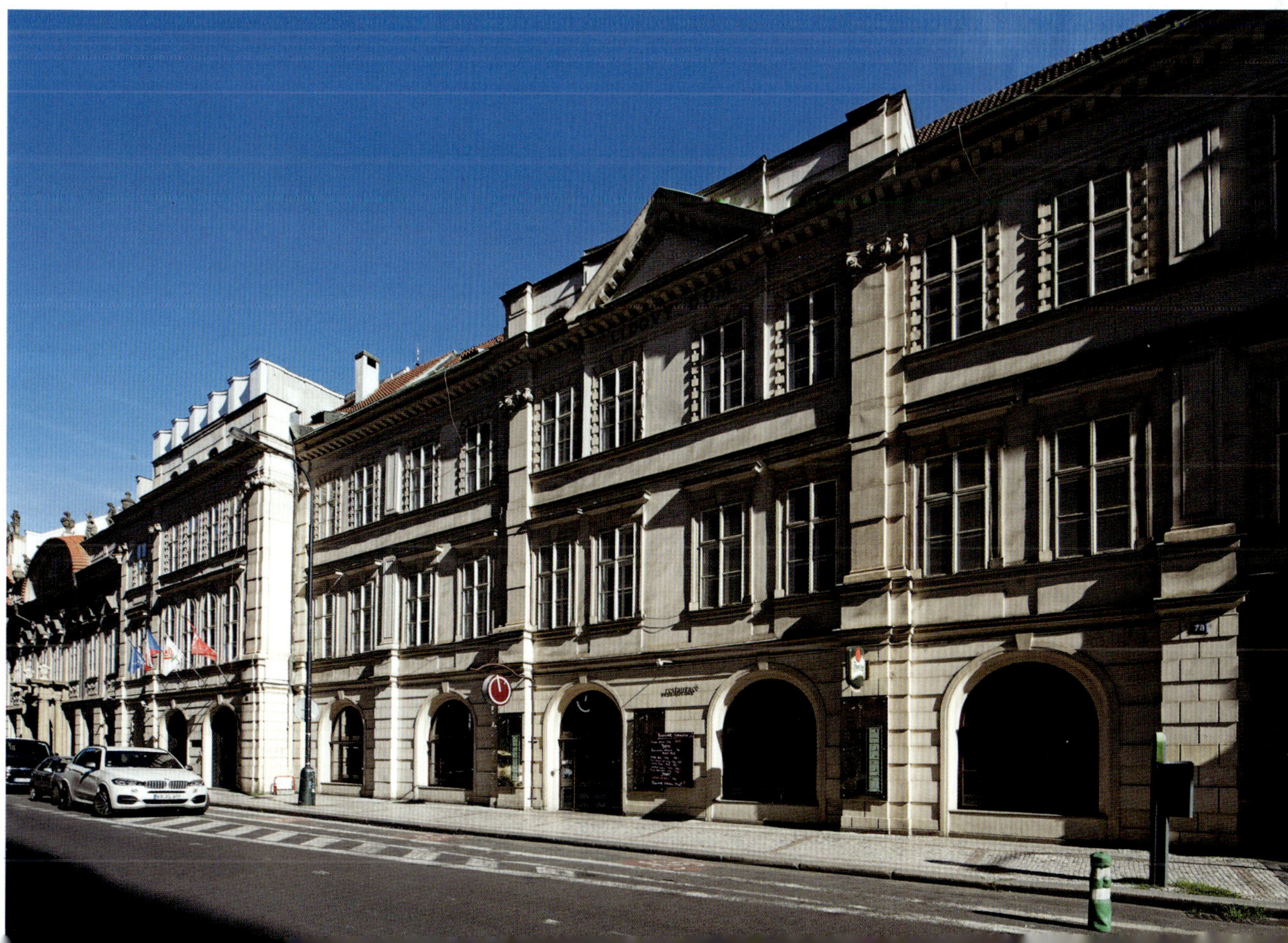

63B/ INTERIOR

The church interior consists of a vast aisleless nave with chapels facing each other below the galleries. The overall impression is achieved in large part by the stucco decoration, made from 1697 to 1699, by artists of the 'Lurago school', among whom Tommaso Soldati in particular left his mark. The colour scheme, based on the contrast of white and pink with gold accents, is also highly effective.

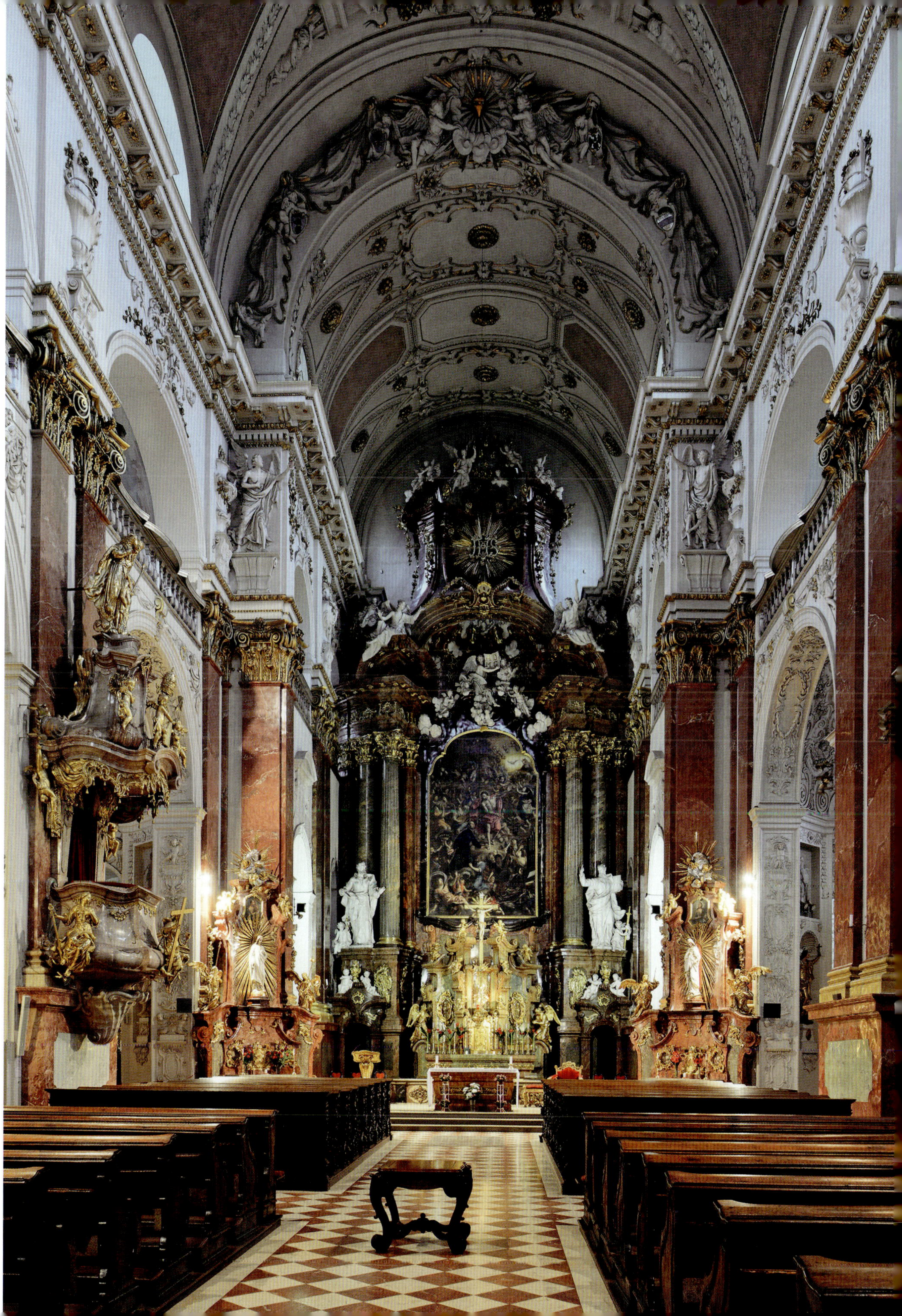

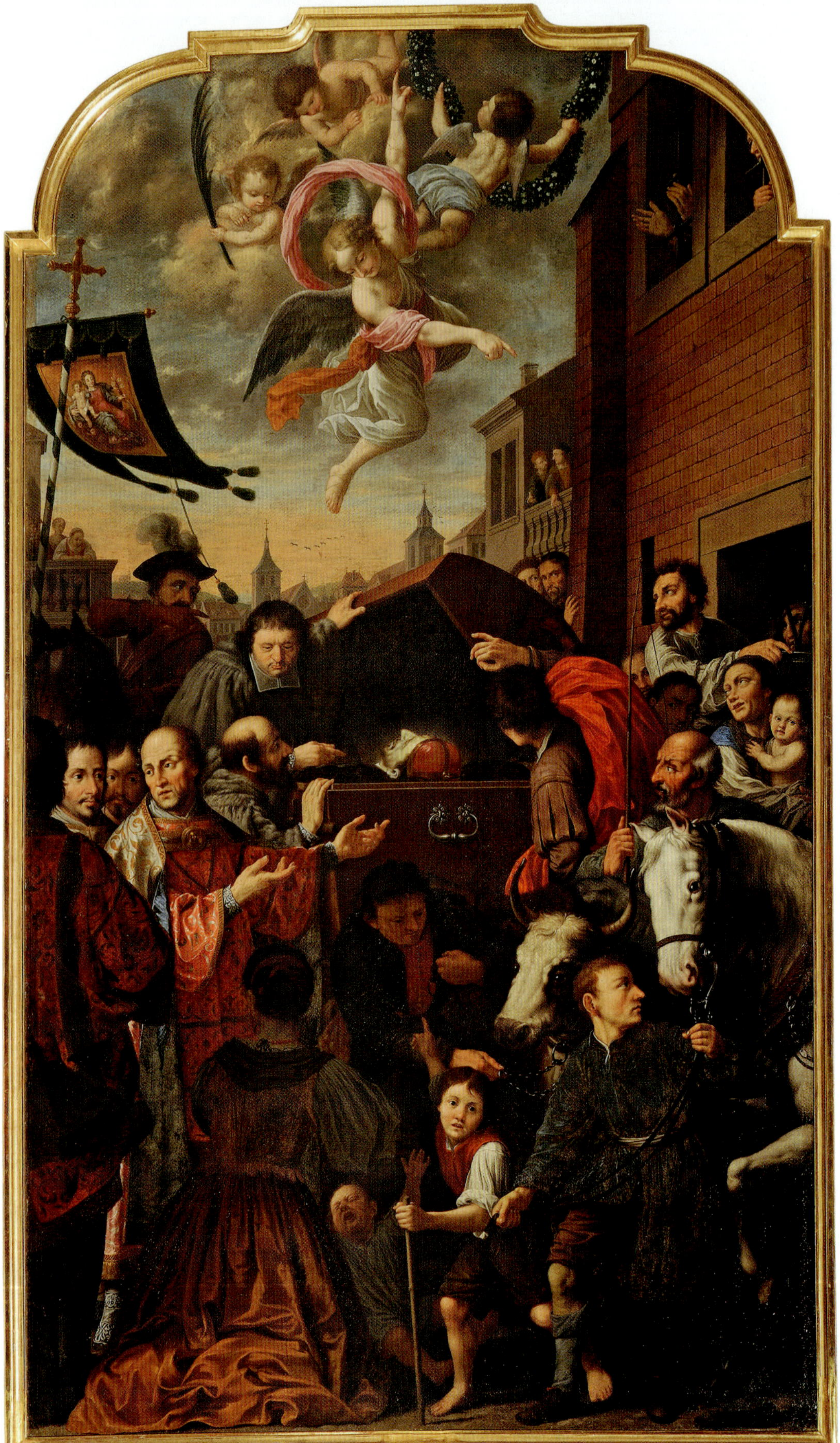

(274)

63C/ JOHANN GEORG HEINSCH: MOVING THE BODILY REMAINS OF ST WENCESLAS FROM BOLESLAV TO PRAGUE, 1692

According to legend, when the body of the murdered Duke Wenceslas was taken to Prague for burial, the waggon with the coffin forded the River Vltava and soon afterwards stopped prematurely at what is today Malostranské náměstí (Lesser Town Square). In vain, the drivers brought additional horses: the waggon would still not budge. The reason was revealed only after a priest was summoned, who then explained that Wenceslas himself had intentionally stopped the waggon in front of the prison, and he pointed out that the saint, in his lifetime, performed various good deeds, among which was releasing prisoners. When the local jail was opened and the convicts' shackles were removed, the waggon could move on again unhindered up the hill to Prague Castle. On the place where this miracle is said to have occurred, the parish church of the Lesser Town, St Wenceslas', was built. In this painting for the high altar Johann Georg Heinsch has effectively depicted the whole event, paying particular attention to characteristic details and the faces of the individual figures, which he has conceived as portraits of some of his contemporaries. After St Wenceslas' Church was dissolved as part of Joseph II's reforms in the late eighteenth century, the painting was moved to the Thein Church and, later, to St Ignatius', the New Town Jesuit church, where it can be seen today.

64/ CHURCH OF SAINTS CYRIL AND METHODIUS (KOSTEL SV. CYRILA A METODĚJE) (FORMERLY, ST CHARLES BORROMEO) IN ZDERAZE

From 1730 to 1740, a house for elderly priests, together with the Church of St Charles Borromeo, was built in Zderaz, an area on the long slope of the New Town above the River Vltava. The building work was first led by Paul Ignaz Beyer, then by Johann Christoph Spannbrucker, and eventually Kilian Ignaz Dientzenhofer. Though the plans were formerly attributed to Dientzenhofer, the main architect was probably Bayer, who has left his best work here. The architecture of the church, dedicated in 1735, is classically well balanced and serene, yet noble and impressive.

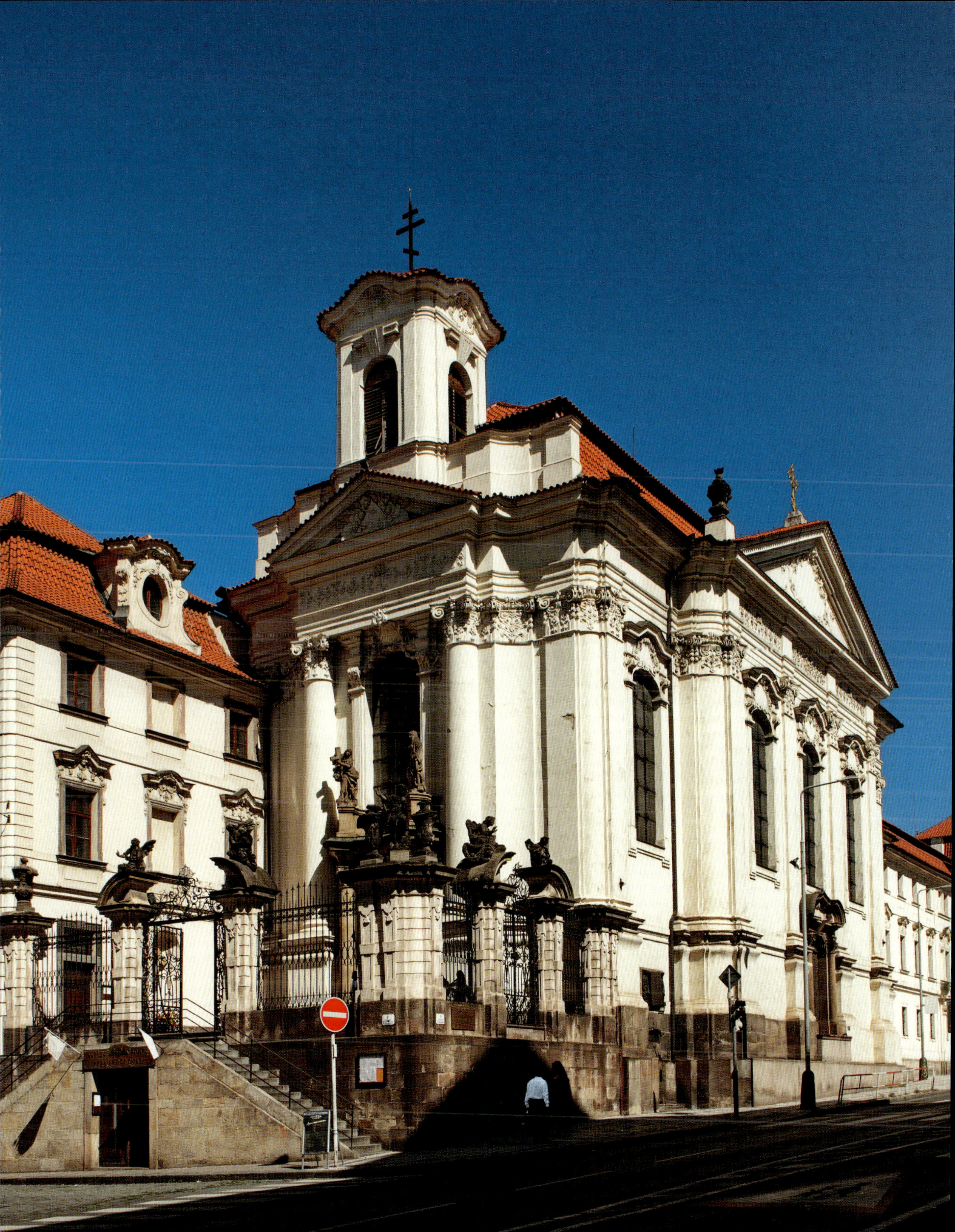

65A–C/ CHURCH OF ST JOHN NEPOMUCENE ON THE ROCK (KOSTEL SV. JANA NEPOMUCKÉHO NA SKALCE), 1730–38

Already in 1697, in the vineyards above the Emmaus monastery a chapel was erected in honour of John Nepomucene (Jan Nepomucký, *c.*1345–1393), though he would not be beatified till 1721, let alone canonized. Ten years later, it became a place for the gatherings of the lay brothers who, after John's canonization in 1729, had the lofty Baroque church built on plans by Kilian Ignaz Dientzenhofer. By means of a spectacular double staircase, the architect has joined the main façade of the church, situated at the height of Karlovo náměstí (Charles Square), with the original sunken lane below the square. The dynamically modelled façade with an aedicula in the middle is dominated by a pair of obliquely turned steeples. On the obelisk between them is a huge gilded representation of Nepomucene's best-known attribute – the relic of his incorrupt tongue.

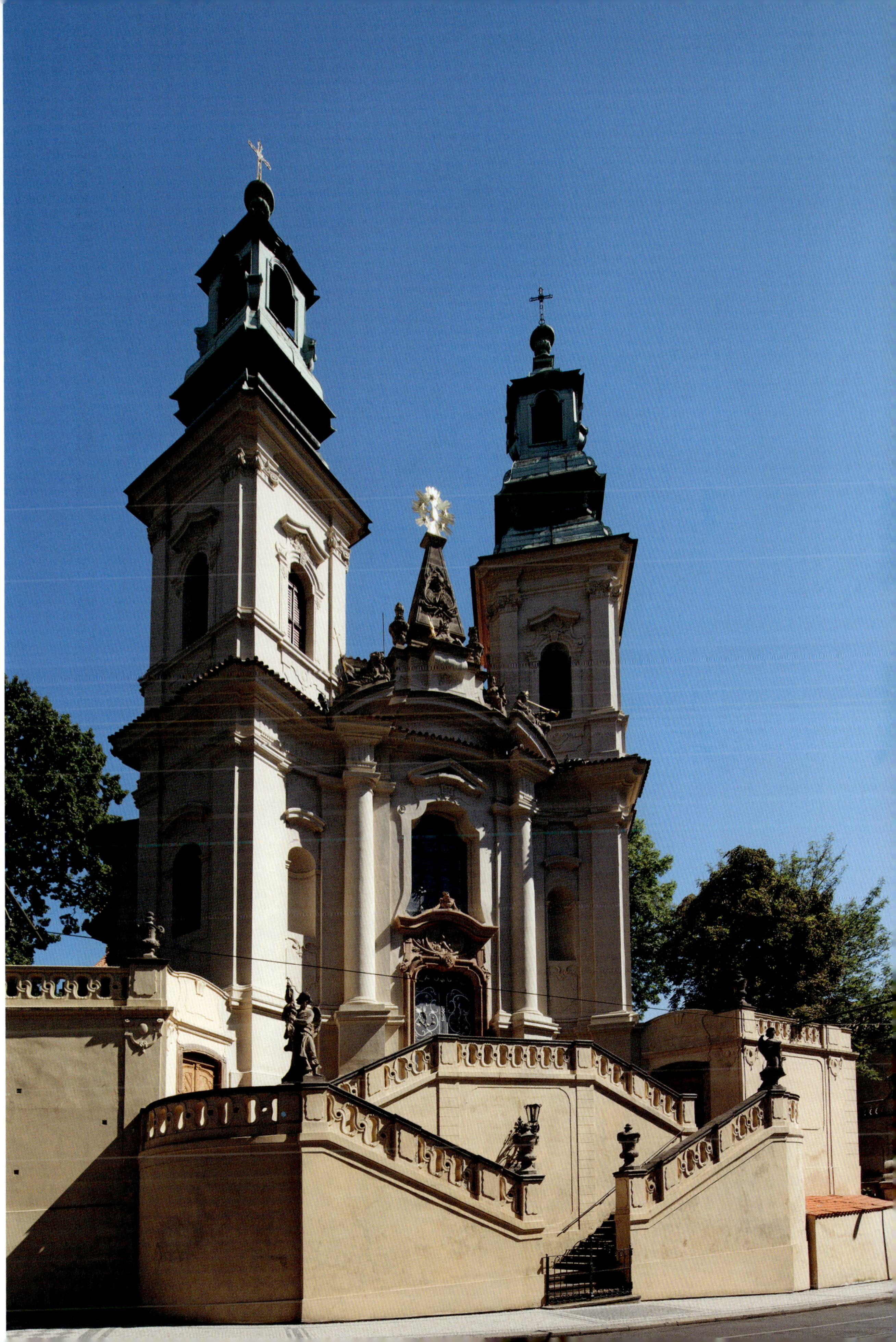

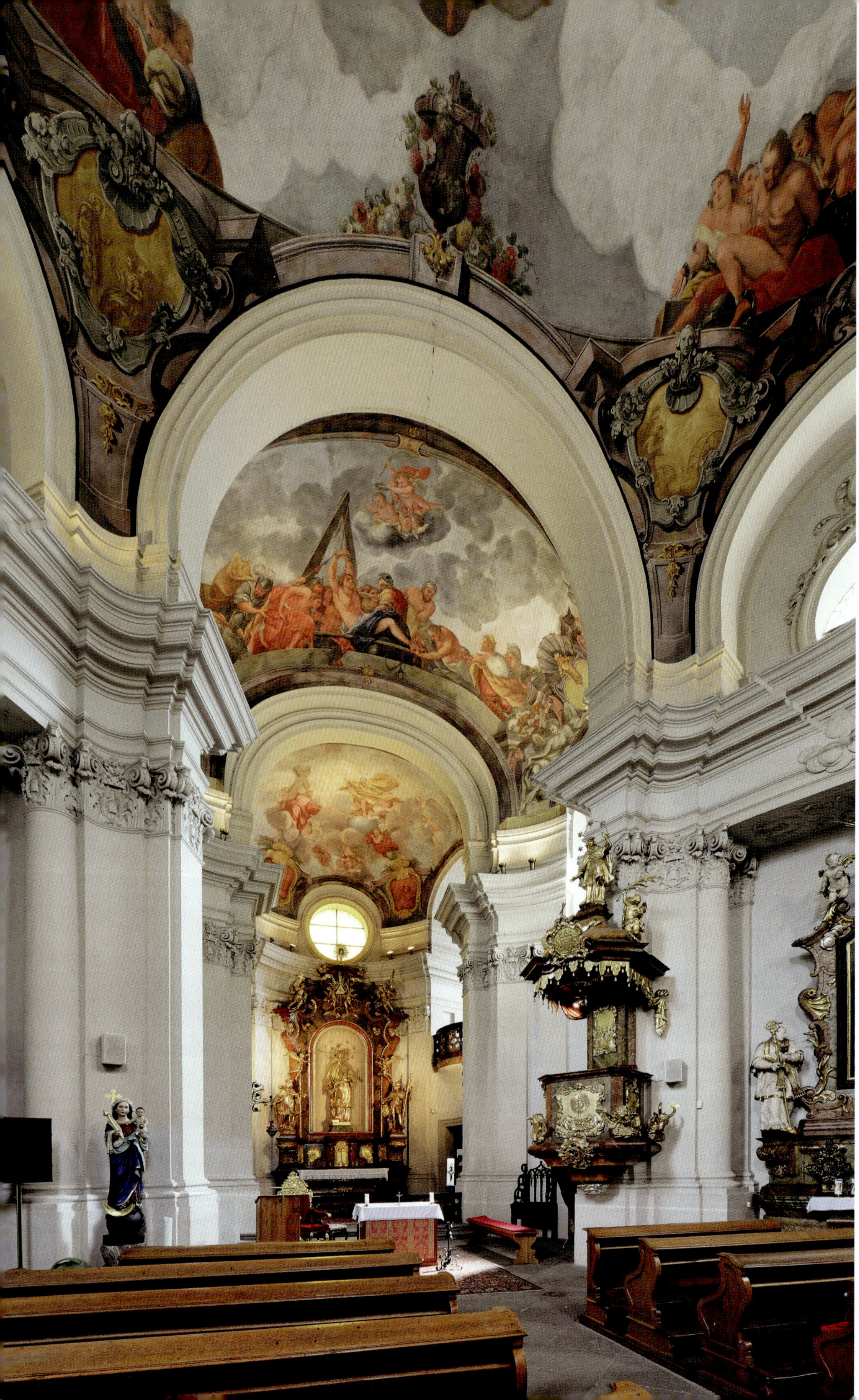

The interior of the church comprises a dynamically composed octagonal central space with large sail vaults. The ceiling fresco (1738), by Franz Anton Müller, illustrates the Nepomucene legend, reminding us of the Baroque saint's miracles, and culminating in his monumental glorification on the ceiling of the central nave.

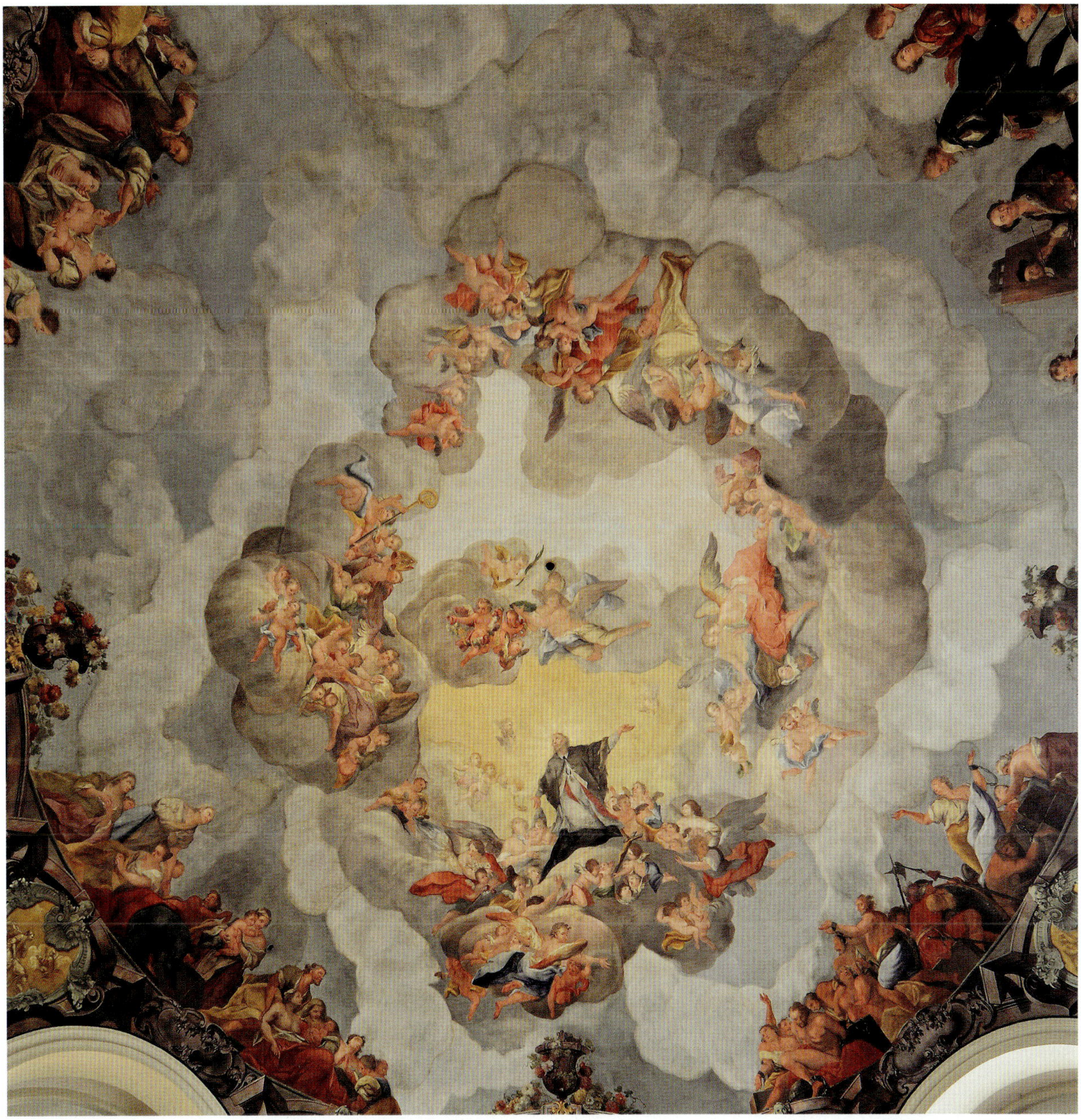

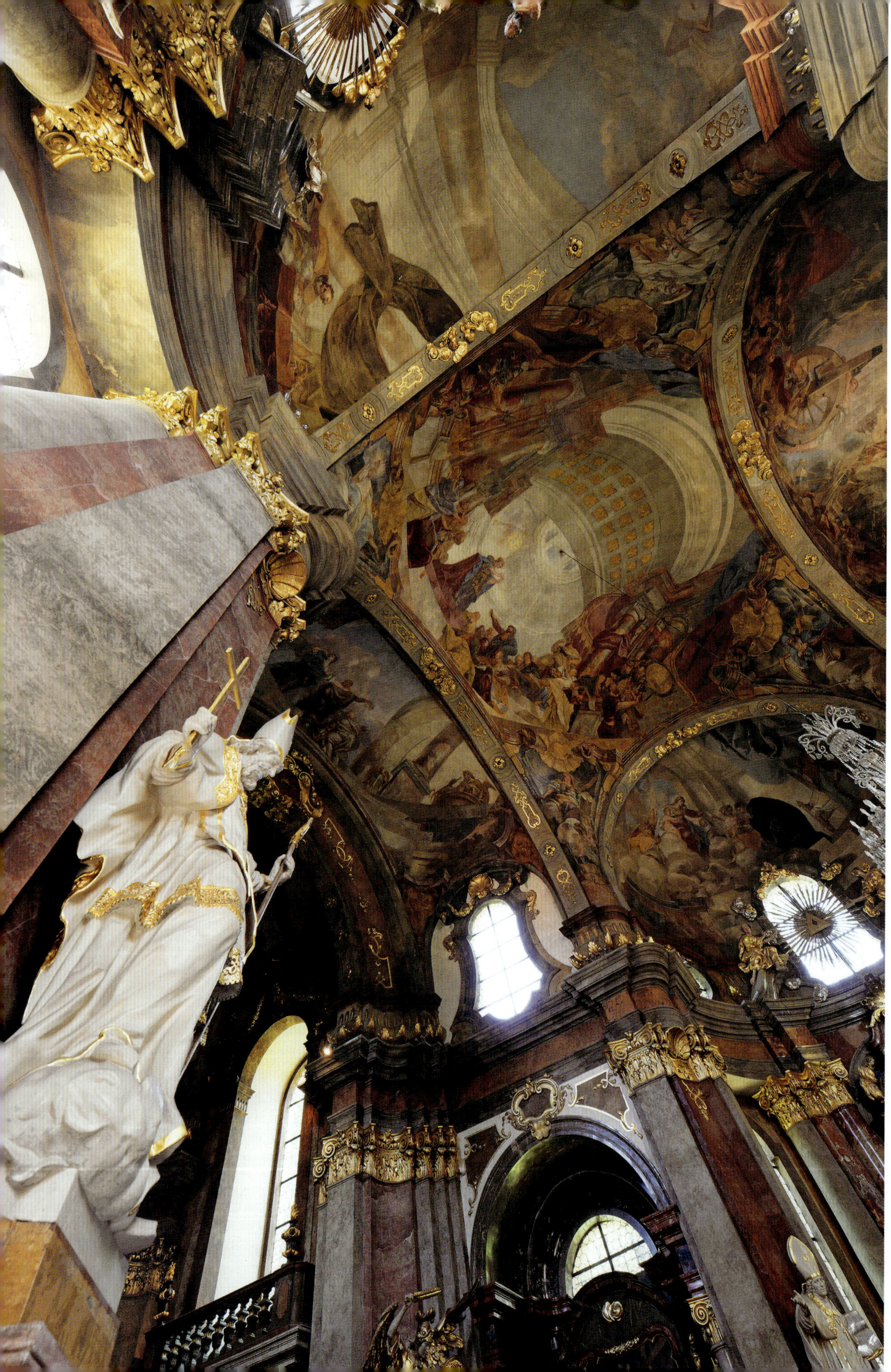

66A–B/ FROM ST CATHERINE'S CHURCH

In 1355, Charles IV founded the convent of Augustinian nuns, whose church was dedicated to St Catherine of Alexandria, his favourite female saint. The new Baroque church, built from 1737 to 1741, retained only the slender tower of its Gothic predecessor, which is today a landmark in this part of the city. Kilian Ignaz Dientzenhofer designed a strikingly long aisleless nave with the transept in the middle. The sophisticatedly structured columns bear sail vaults decorated with frescos by Wenzel Lorenz Reiner in 1741. The overall impression made by the interior of this masterful Baroque building is largely due to the use of light, which enters through the windows and openings in the vaults. Dientzenhofer was doubtless also behind the uniformly designed furnishings of the church, which have been preserved practically intact. The sculptural decoration was provided by the workshop of Franz Ignaz Weiss, the leading master of Early Rococo sculpture in Prague. The high altar is adorned with a canvas of St Catherine and the Fourteen Holy Helpers (1739) by the Rome-born Gregorio Guglielmi.

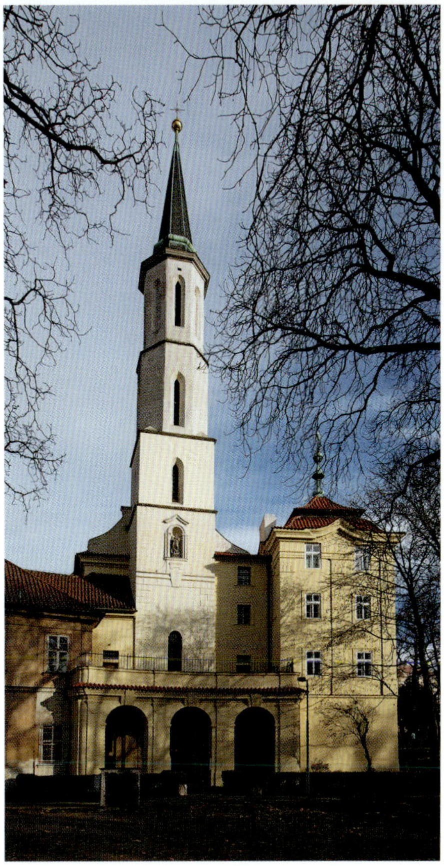

66C/ CHURCH OF ST CATHERINE

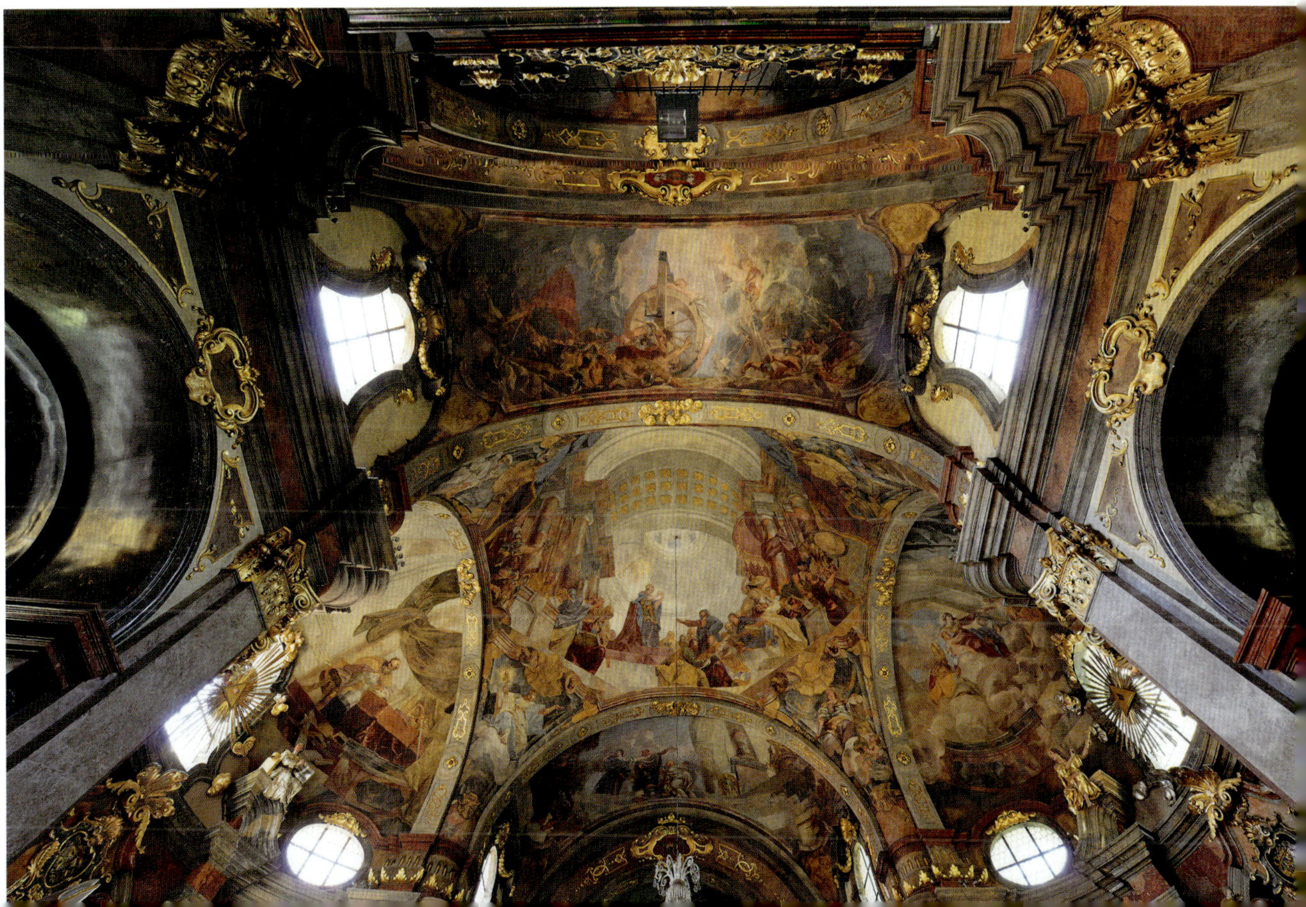

67/ THE MICHNA SUMMER HOUSE, CALLED AMERIKA, 1717

This delightful Baroque house, today surrounded by tall modern buildings, was erected by Count Jan Václav Michna z Vacínova. It is a reminder of a time when the upper part of the New Town was a recreational area for the rich of Prague, who built their summer homes here among gardens and vineyards. The summer house is widely considered to be the first independent work of the young Kilian Ignaz Dientzenhofer, who here probably applied experience he had gained from studying the contemporary architecture not only of Vienna but also of France. The main two-storeyed building, designed as a pavilion with a mansard roof, is flanked by matching free-standing single-storey structures. The garden sculpture was made by the Braun workshop under Anton Braun.

'This architectural plaything is the first independent work of the young Kilian Ignaz Dientzenhofer, inspired by his training in Vienna, and probably carried out as part of his father's business, which he most likely also had a hand in running.'

Milada Vilímková, 1986

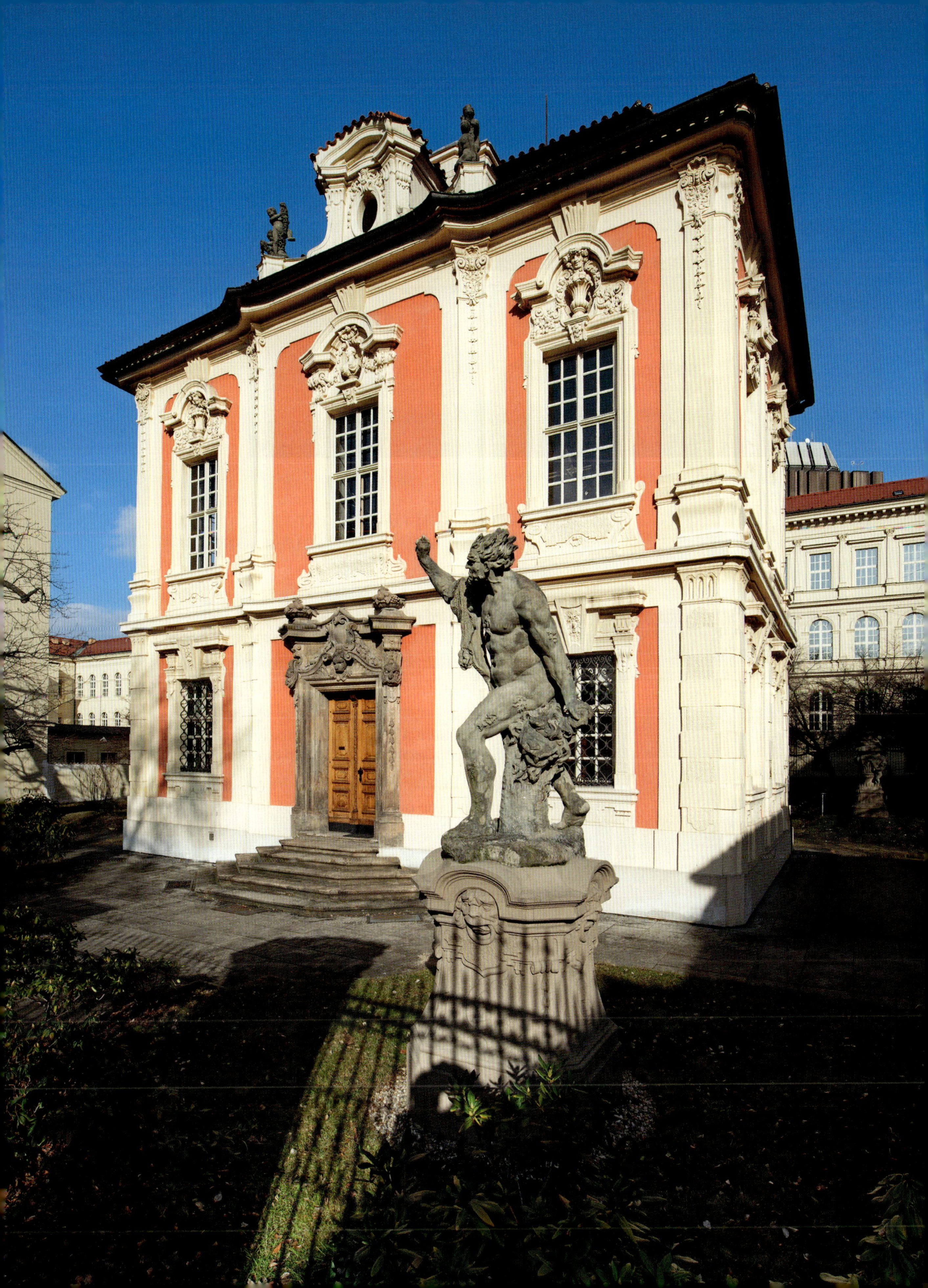

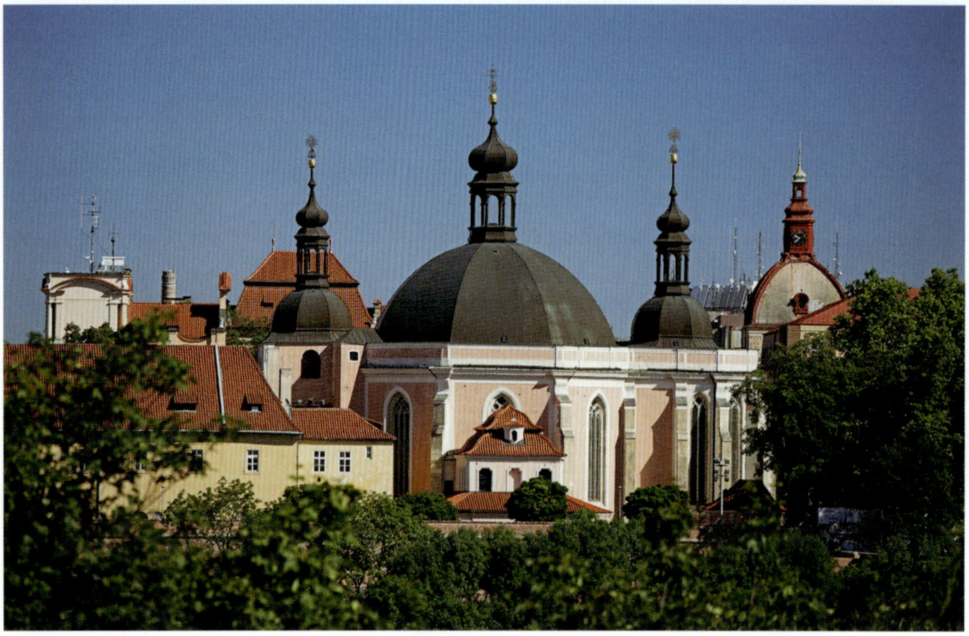

68A/ CHURCH OF ST MARY AND THE BLESSED CHARLAMAGNE

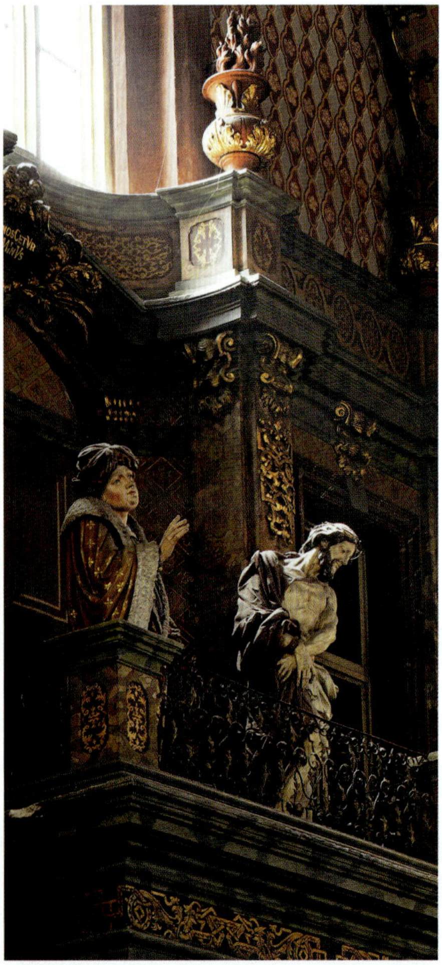

68B–C/ FROM THE CHURCH OF SAINT MARY AND THE BLESSED CHARLEMAGNE AT KARLOV

This church at the former New Town abbey of Augustinian canons is truly a compendium of ideas and styles of architectural revivalism. Charles IV, the king of Bohemia and future emperor, founded it in 1350, recalling Charlemagne's Palatine Chapel in Aix-la-Chapelle (Aachen), which it indeed evokes with its central layout and the octagonal plan of the nave. Though not built until 1575, the vaulting is intended to evoke Gothic architecture. The Baroque remodelling carried out from 1733 to 1740 on plans by František Maxmilian Kaňka, includes gothicizing features. In the same period, the interior of the church was enlivened with theatrically conceived scenes from the Bible. The pilgrims who used to come here to see the cult painting of the Blessed Virgin Mary were meant to be provided with the most convincing illusion and encouraged to feel like direct participants in the New Testament stories. The balcony of 'Pilate's house' is brought to life by the realistic *Ecce Homo* scene with the lushly painted wooden statues, which are making impassioned rhetorical gestures. They are the work of the Austrian-born Jan Jiří Šlanzovský (Johann Georg Schlansowsky). The physical link between visitors and events from the Gospels was meant to continue even after leaving the church. Jesus' birth is commemorated by the Grotto of the Nativity (1708) built on to the south side of the church. Nearby are the Holy Stairs, imitating the Scala Santa in Rome, which were believed to be the stairs of Pontius Pilate's praetorium, preserved near the Archbasilica of Saint John Lateran. The Prague staircase was made before 1711 on plans by Johann Blasius Santini-Aichel.

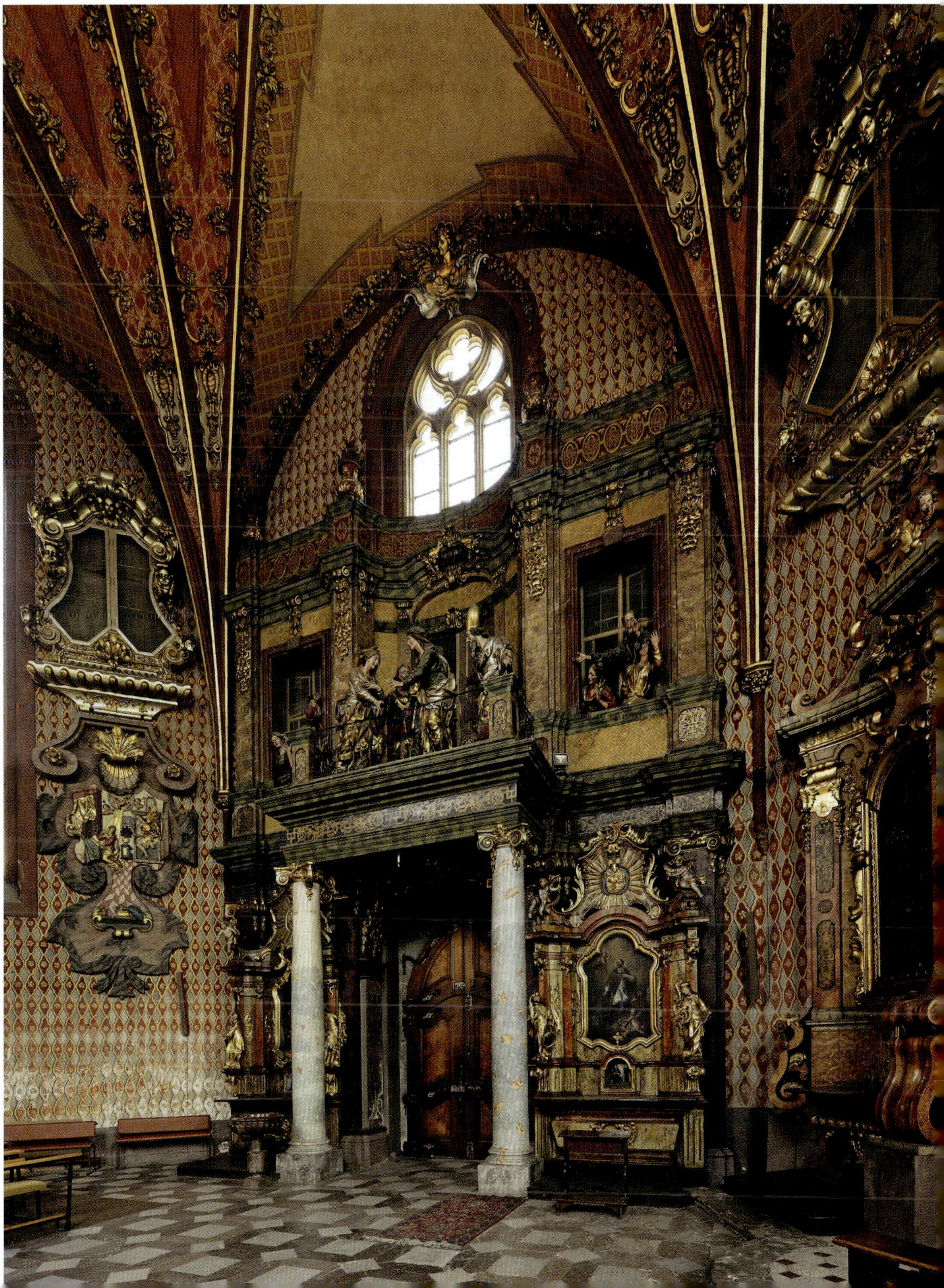

69A/ THE LEOPOLD GATE

After the Thirty Years War (1618–48), it was finally decided to build a citadel for Prague at Vyšehrad. Thus, in 1650, Baroque bastion fortifications began to be erected around the top of the hill. Work on the fortifications did not resume until during the battles for Prague after Maria Theresa came to the throne. The Vyšehrad fortress was not truly finished, however, until the nineteenth century. Shortly after its completion, Prague lost its status as a fortified town and began to demolish its city walls. But Vyšehrad retained the character of a Baroque citadel. One enters the fortress through an Early Baroque gate, named in honour of Emperor Leopold I (r. 1658–1705). The gate was built after 1653, probably on plans by Carlo Lurago, who most likely drew upon the sixteenth-century treatise of Sebastiano Serlio. The impressive front of the gate is decorated not only with a mascaron and the imperial coat of arms but also with statues of two recumbent Bohemian lions and an imperial eagle. The two empty cartouches probably once bore painted coats of arms.

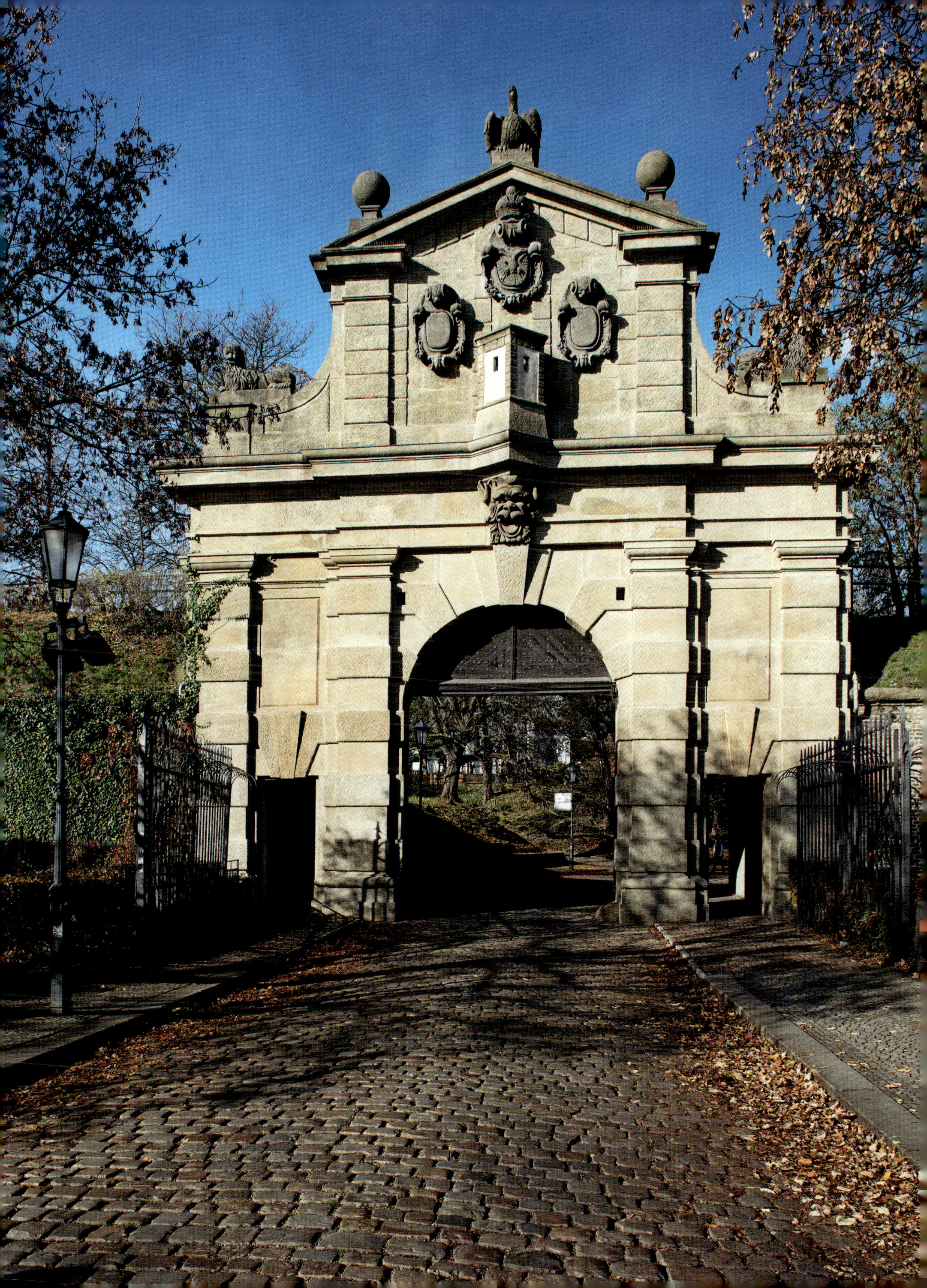

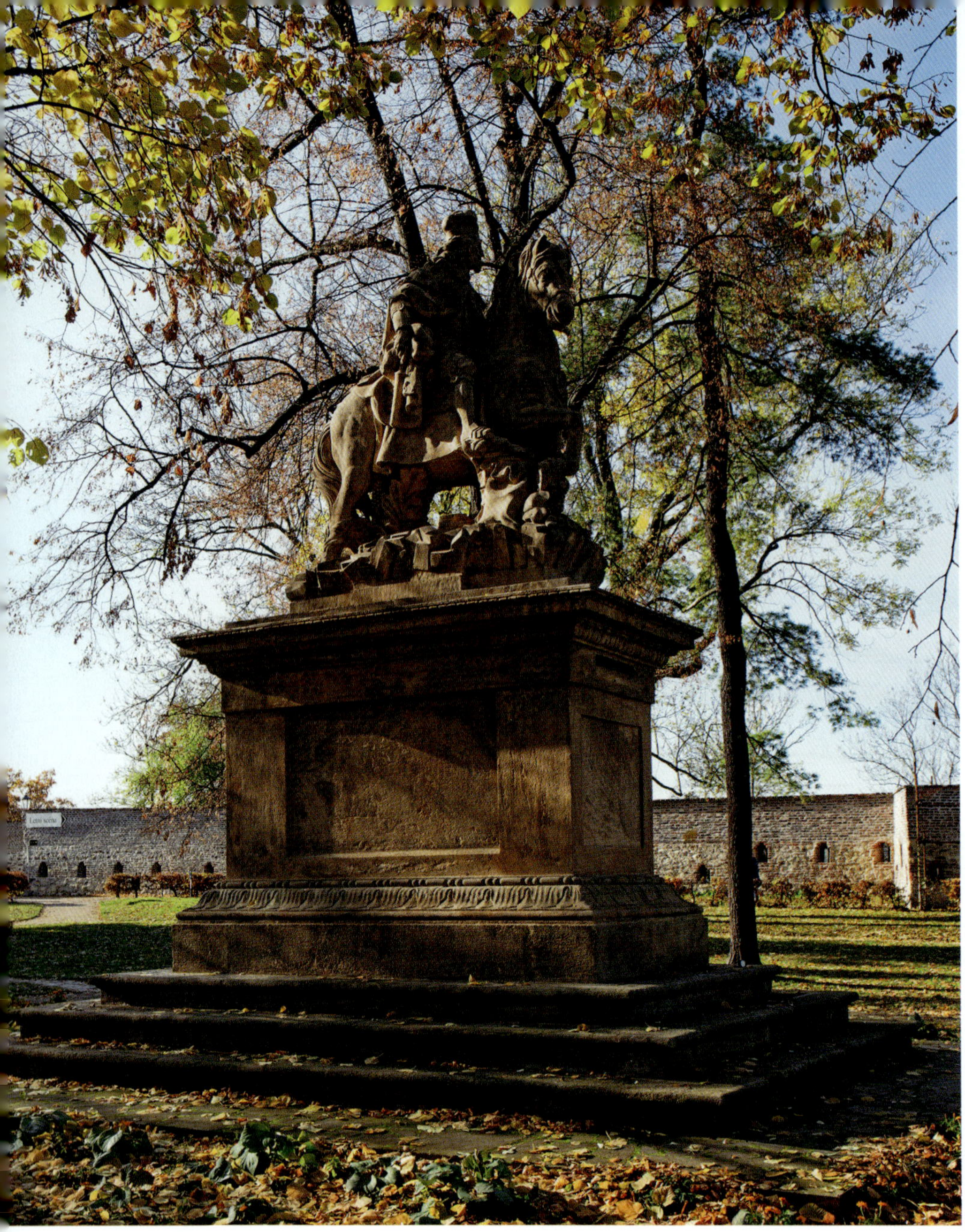

69B/ JOHANN GEORG BENDL: EQUESTRIAN STATUE OF ST WENCESLAS, 1680

According to a contract of 16 November 1678, the sculptor Johann Georg Bendl carved a 'life-size image of St Wenceslas on horseback, in royal garb and holding a banner' for the town hall of the New Town of Prague. This, the first equestrian statue in modern Prague, was eventually erected on the fountain at the Horse Market, today's Wenceslas Square. In 1879, it was moved to Vyšehrad. A copy currently stands in its place; the original is in the Lapidarium of the National Museum.

Bendl's somewhat ponderous statue originates in the iconographic type that, respecting earlier artistic tradition, was made by Karel Škréta before the mid-seventeenth century. In the spirit of Baroque patriotism, the saint's face has the features of a typical portrait of the late Emperor Ferdinand III, who greatly venerated St Wenceslas.

69C/ THE VYŠEHRAD CASEMATES – GORLICE HALL

The builders of the Vyšehrad citadel paid particular attention to securing its north-east face, that is, the side facing the valley of the Botič stream. From the beginning of the construction work, passageways were made inside the Baroque fortifications, which enabled both the transfer of troops and their sorties into the glacis on the one hand and reconnoitring the activities of besiegers and the possible laying of countermines on the other. The gallery inside the St Bernard Bastion (Bastion No. 33) was perfected by the French troops who occupied Prague in 1741–42. After further expansion of the bastion, now by imperial troops, casements with embrasures were built, whose one branch leads into the vast underground hall called Gorlice. It served as an assembly point for the defenders and as a store for provisions and munitions. Today, the original Baroque statues from Charles Bridge are deposited here and copies have been installed in their place.

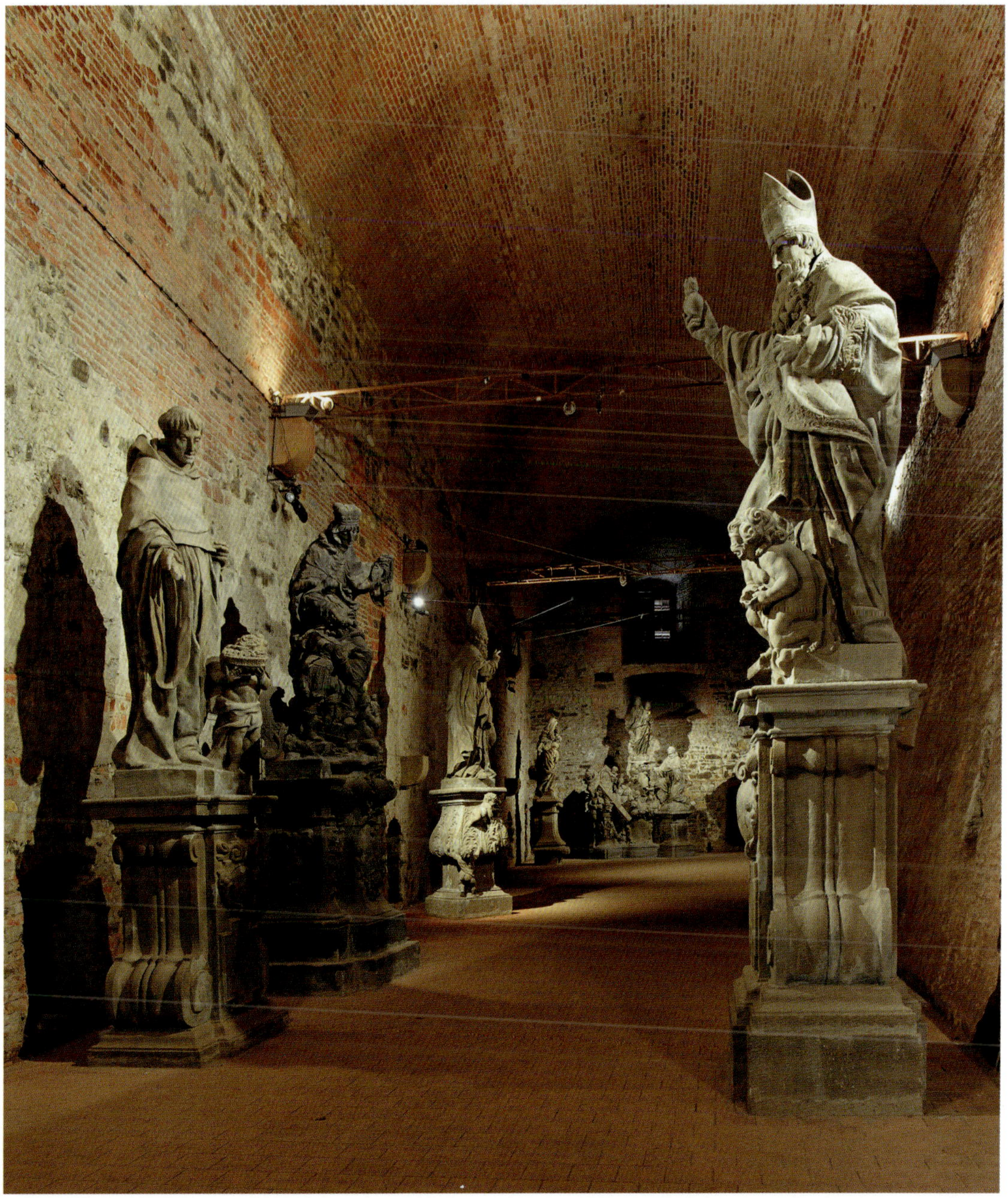

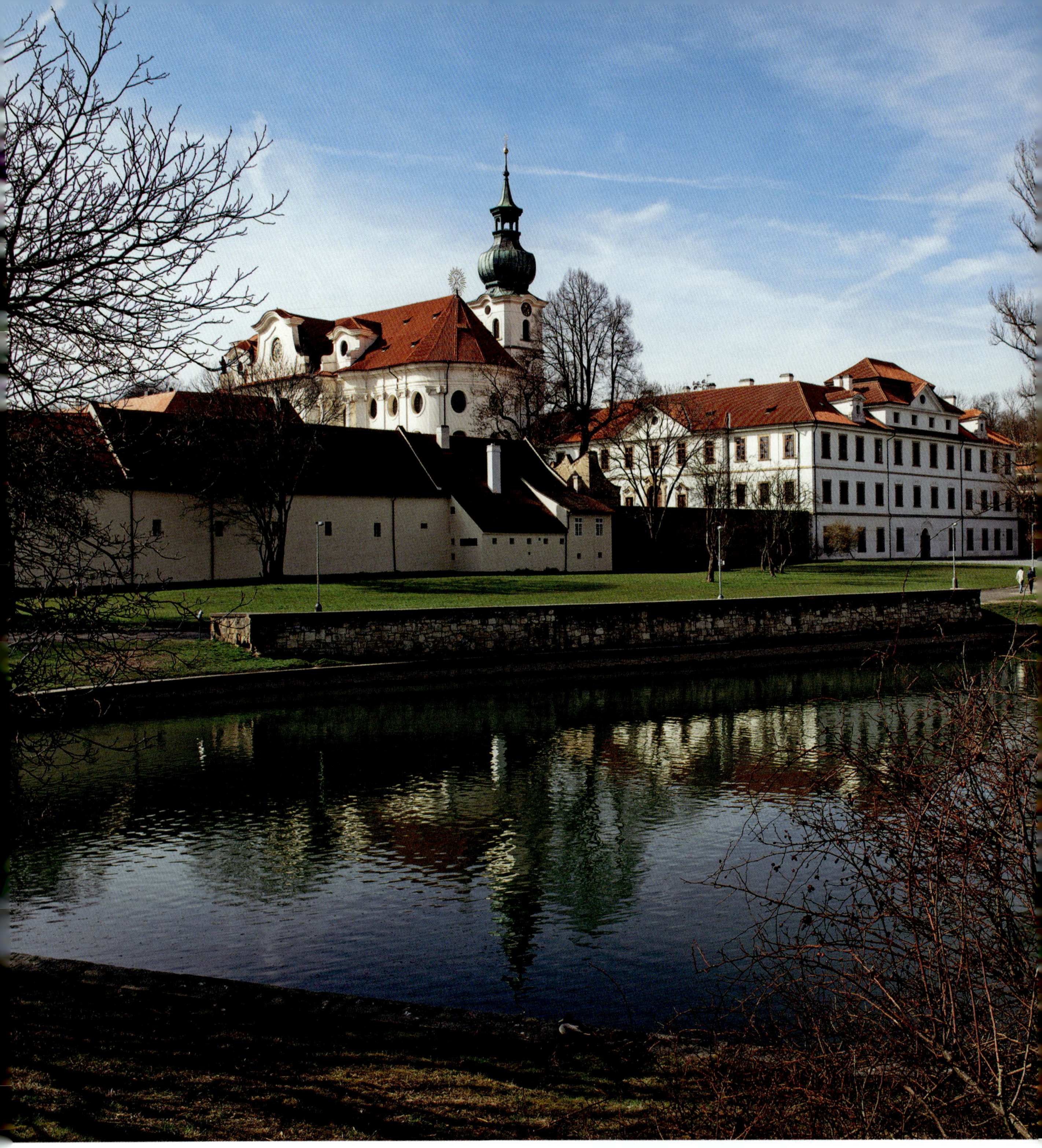

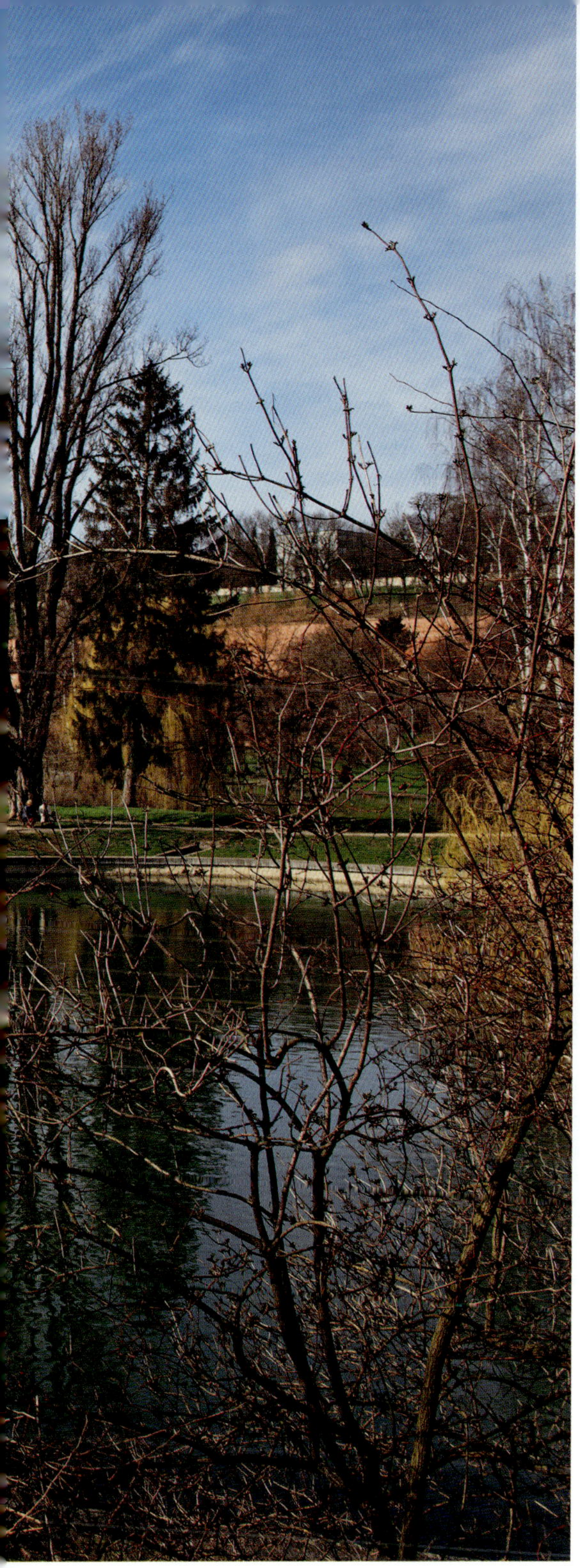

70/ BŘEVNOV – BENEDICTINE ARCHABBEY OF ST ADALBERT AND ST MARGRET (SV. VOJTĚCHA A SV. MARKÉTY)

70A/ BŘEVNOV ABBEY (BŘEVNOVSKÝ KLÁŠTER)

The Benedictine abbey in Břevnov (now a district of Prague), it is generally believed, was founded with the participation of St Adalbert in the late tenth century. It is thus the oldest monastic house in the Bohemian Lands. From 1700 to 1738, under the abbot Othmar Daniel Zinke, it acquired its High Baroque appearance, to which the most renowned artists of their day contributed. The original plans were elaborated by Paul Ignaz Bayer, who, beginning in 1708 was also in charge of carrying them out. As early as 1709, however, the abbot entrusted Christoph Dientzenhofer with heading the construction work, and later made him the abbey architect. From 1716 onwards, the work was overseen by the young Kilian Ignaz Dientzenhofer. He, however, was more involved as an architect in the next phase, after 1735, working on the abbey and its grounds.

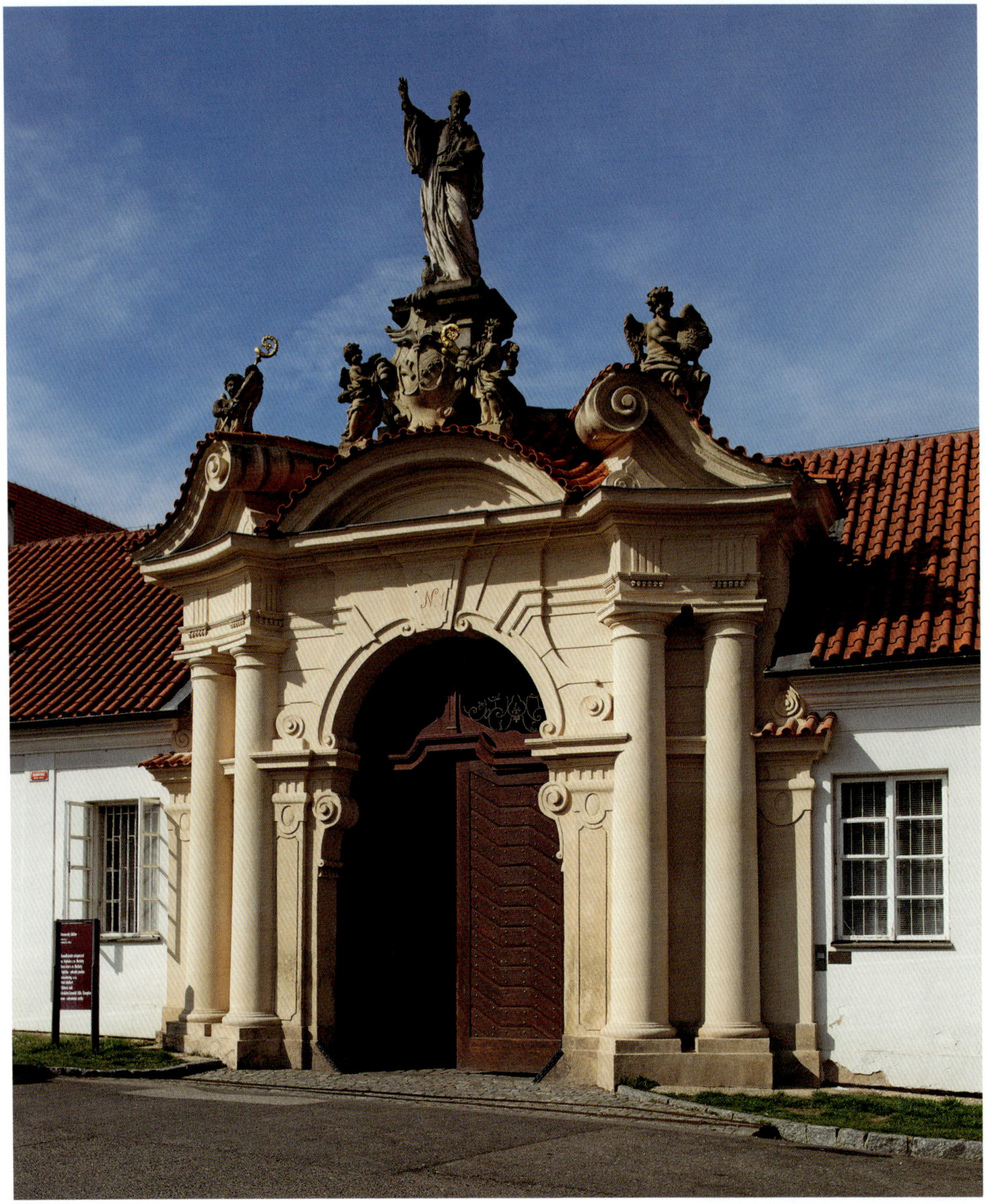

70B/ ABBEY GATE

One enters the abbey through this monumental gate built on plans by Kilian Ignaz Dientzenhofer in 1739/40, while Benno Löbl was abbot (1738–51). It is decorated with the figure of the founder of the order, St Benedict of Nursia, carved by Carl Joseph Hiernle, a tried and tested supplier of sculpture for the Benedictines not only at Břevnov but also at Broumov (Braunau), in north-east Bohemia. Hiernle also made the four angel statues and the sculptural coat of arms of the abbey.

70C/ CHURCH OF ST MARGARET (CHRÁM SV. MARKÉTY)
The abbey church of St Margaret was built in two stages: the nave was made from 1709 to 1712 and the chancel in 1714–15. In this last phase, the architect was Christoph Dientzenhofer, who made changes to the plans even during construction, doubtless at the instigation of Abbot Zinke. The application of radically Baroque principle of intersecting elliptical vaults makes the Břevnov abbey church one of the most important High Baroque works in Bohemia. According to one interpretation, the building was meant to evoke the idea of a ship, that is, the Church, despite the storms, heading to the certainty of salvation under the sign of the Cross (alluded to by the rough-hewn log [*břevno*] from which the abbey derives its name).

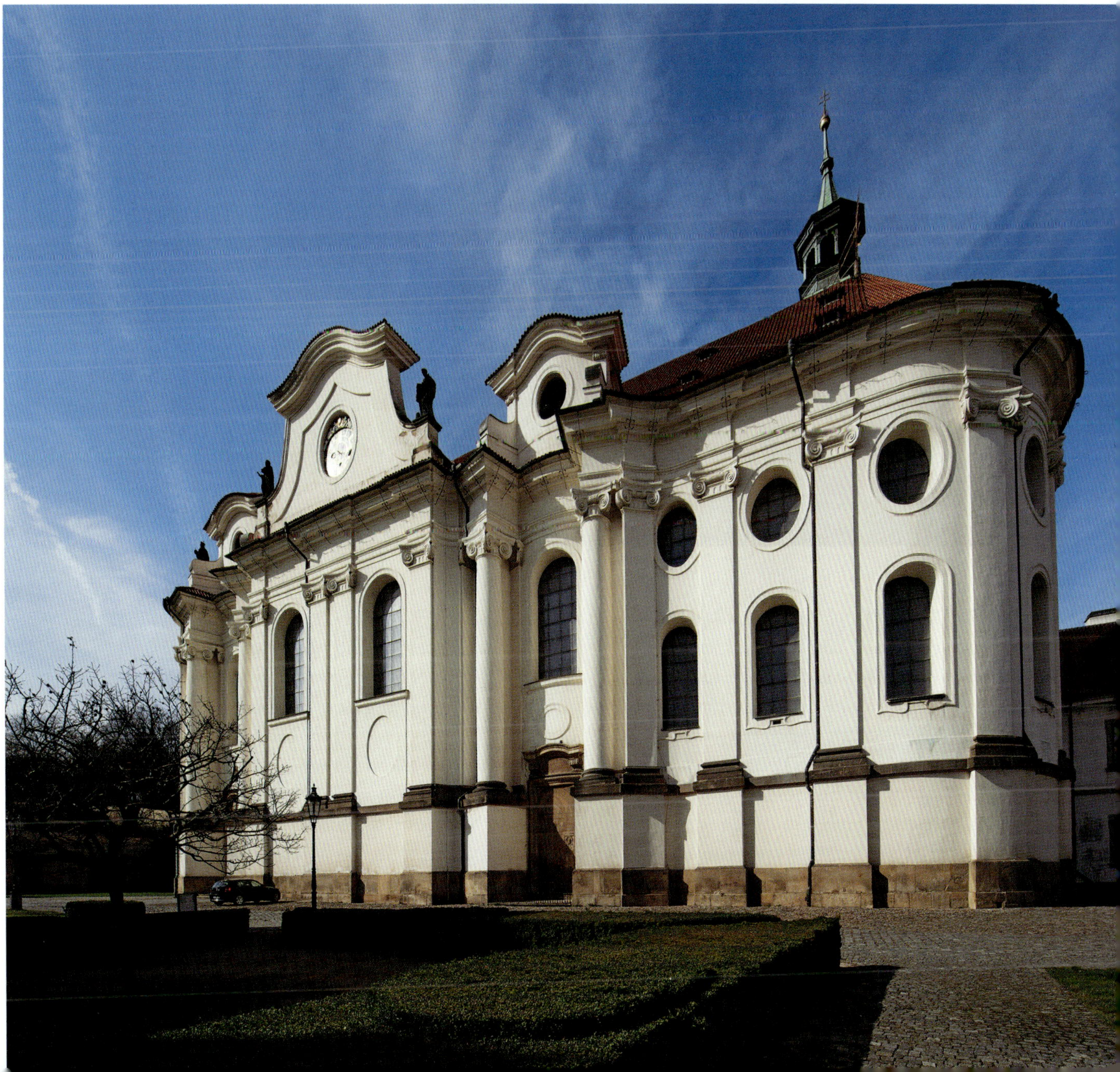

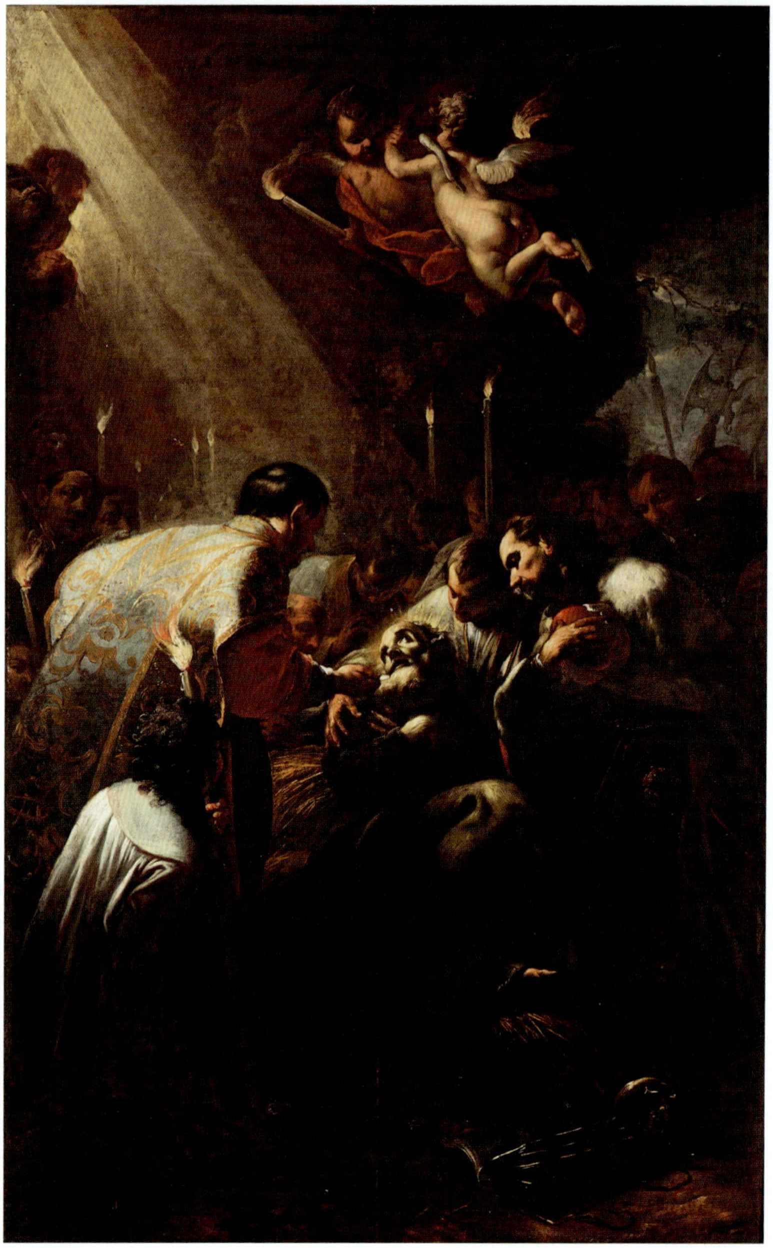

70D/ PETER BRANDL: *THE LAST COMMUNION OF THE HERMIT GUNTHER*, 1718/19
Abbot Zinke entrusted Peter Brandl with making all seven altarpieces for the new church. Despite the low fee he was paid, the famed artist carried out the prestigious commission because so far only one painter in Bohemia during the Baroque period had been given an opportunity to decorate a whole church with his own paintings: that was Karel Škréta in the Cathedral of St Stephan in Litoměřice (Leitmeritz), north Bohemia.
In this painting, one of his best, Brandl has captured the Last Communion of Gunter in his Bohemian Forest hermitage in the presence of Duke Břetislav and Severus (Šebíř), the bishop of Prague. The scene demonstrates the artist's mastery in combining light from various sources. Everything is dominated by the beam of heavenly light falling on the face of the dying old man and the figures around him, who are deeply moved at this moment of the approach of blissful death. Gunther, who came from a noble family in Thüringen, founded several monasteries and worked as a missionary in Bohemia and Hungary. He had been venerated by the Bohemian Benedictines since the Middle Ages, and is buried in Břevnov, in keeping with his wishes.

70E/ THERESA HALL – COSMAS DAMIAN ASAM: THE MIRACLE OF THE HERMIT GUNTHER, 1728

In this fresco on the ceiling of the Theresa Hall of Břevnov Abbey, Cosmas Damian Asam, the great master of the Rococo in Bavaria, depicted another scene from the life of the Blessed Gunther (*Vita s. Guntheri*). According to legend, the hermit was offered a roast peacock at a banquet given by King Stephen I of Hungary. The guest did not want to offend his host, yet he did not want to break the rule of his order, which forbade him to eat meat. He therefore retired to pray, after which the bird miraculously came back to life and flew out an open window. The epic painting is part of the decoration of the stately section of the abbey.

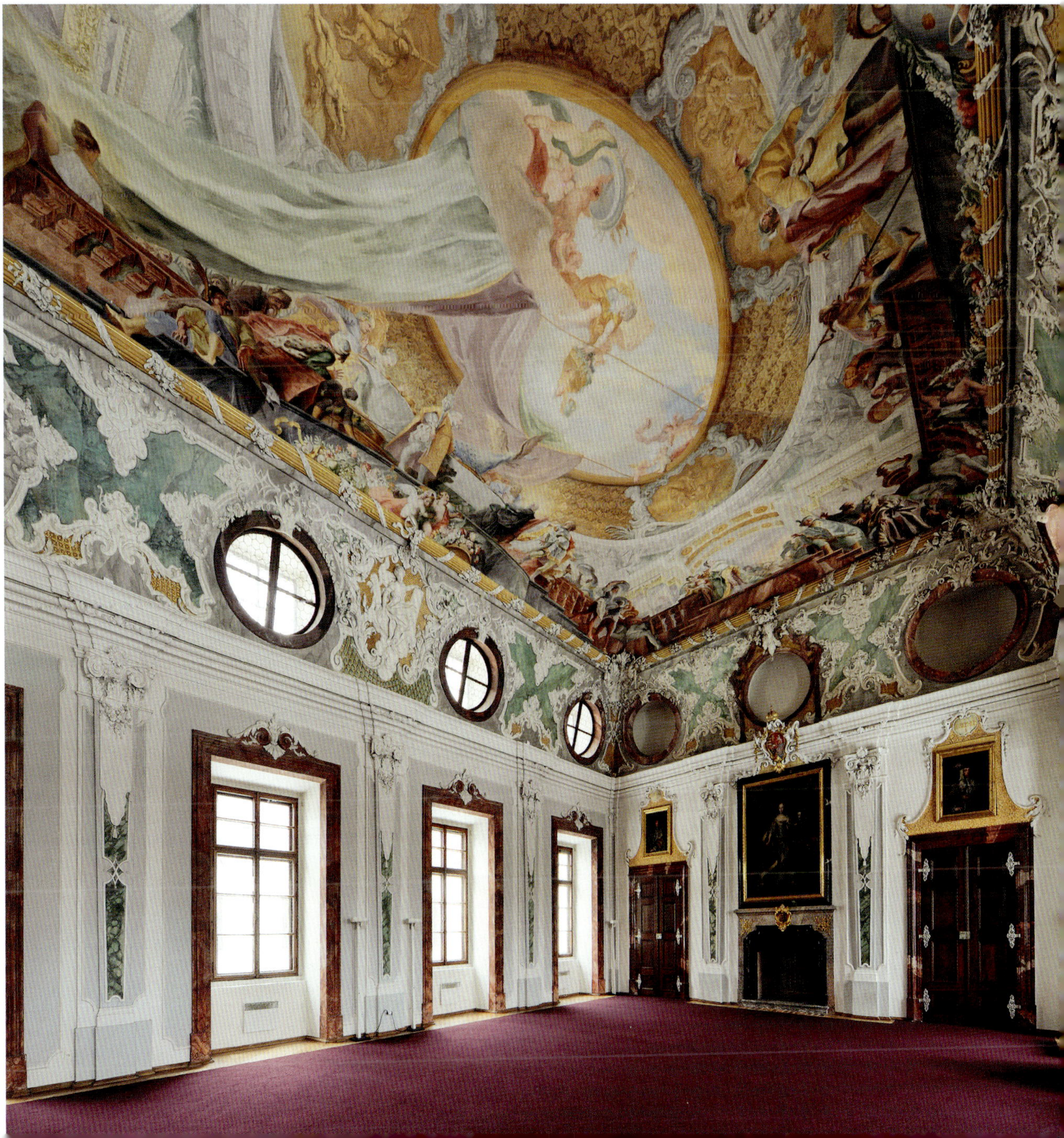

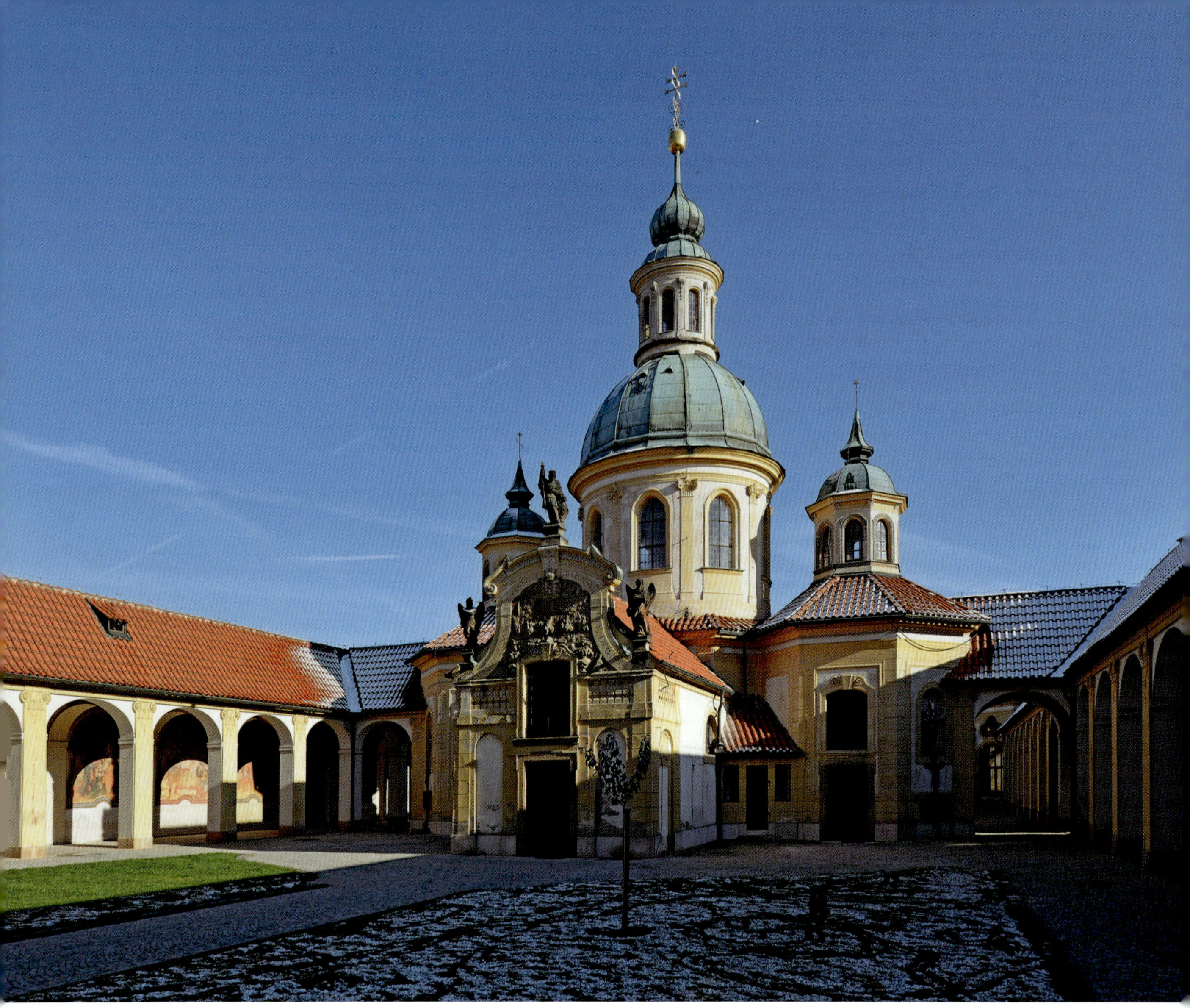

'The Baroque replaces the troops scattered on the tiny hillock of the White Mountain with a splendid cohort of saints, bedraggled statues, which in the spectacular churches and on Charles Bridge dance ecstatically and rise up to the heavens. As the grief of the White Mountain merges with the dramatic character of the Baroque, the distinctive atmosphere of Prague literature emerged, febrile and grotesque, a refuge of rowdies and eccentrics, misfits, and crackpots, who occasionally bring to mind figures on Tarot cards.'

Angelo Maria Ripellino, 1973

71A–B/ THE WHITE MOUNTAIN – PLACE OF PILGRIMAGE WITH THE CHURCH OF ST MARY OF VICTORY

Most of the inhabitants of Baroque Catholic Prague understood the Battle of the White Mountain (1620) as the 'victory' that ended the unfortunate rebellion against the emperor and restored the government of both the legitimate monarch and the Roman Catholic Church. At the level of religion, this conviction was projected into pilgrimages to the Chapel of St Mary of Victory, built on the site of the fateful military clash. From 1704 onwards, the originally small structure was gradually remodelled and enlarged. A fundamental change to this place of pilgrimage was initiated by the Prague painter Christian Luna, the rector of a Marian lay confraternity. According to the plans, attributed to Johann Blasius Santini-Aichel, the chapel was rebuilt from 1710 to 1714 and cloisters were added. In 1728, the central cupola of the newly erected little church was adorned with a fresco by a Bavarian painter and architect, Cosmas Damian Asam. Its subject matter is the triumph of the Roman Catholic Church, depicted on a chariot, whose wheels bear the coats of arms of Bavaria and the Empire. The horses drawing the chariot are led by the patron saint of Bavaria, Archangel Michael, with his sword drawn. The patron saints of Bohemia are in the meantime engaged in the struggle with nonconformists. The composition is completed with the allegorical figures of Faith, Hope, and Charity (a nursing woman, painted in the cupola of the lantern). Asam's work is linked both with the participation of Maximilian I, Elector of Bavaria, in the Battle of the White Mountain, and with the relations between Vienna and Munich at the beginning of the disputes over the Austrian succession. For the fresco, the pious Asam asked for the symbolic payment of a cast of the iron ring from the door of the Wenceslas Chapel at St Vitus' Cathedral, commonly believed to be the ring on the door of the church in Stará Boleslav, which St Wenceslas clutched as he was murdered.

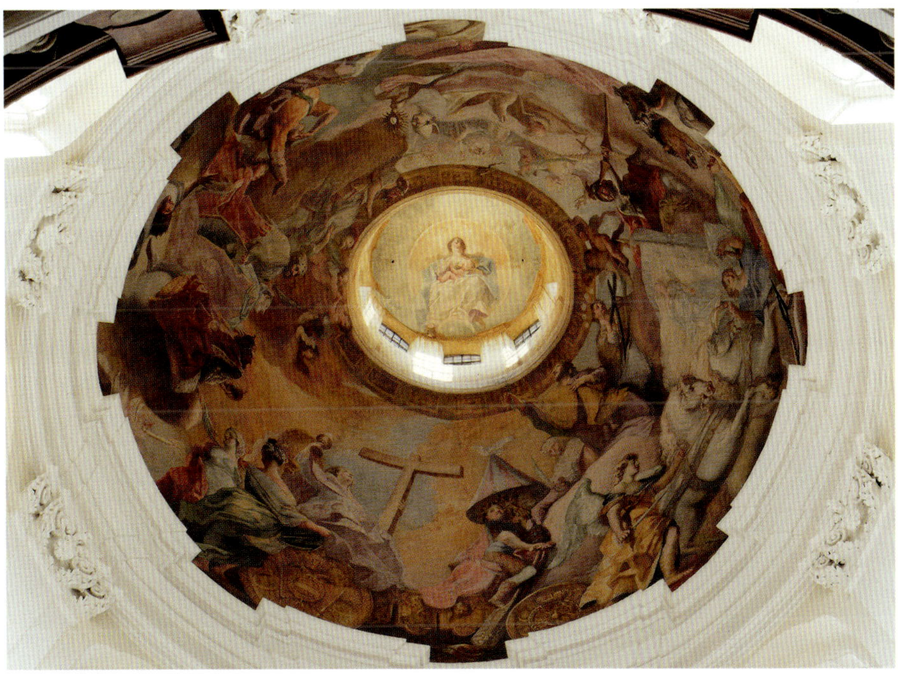

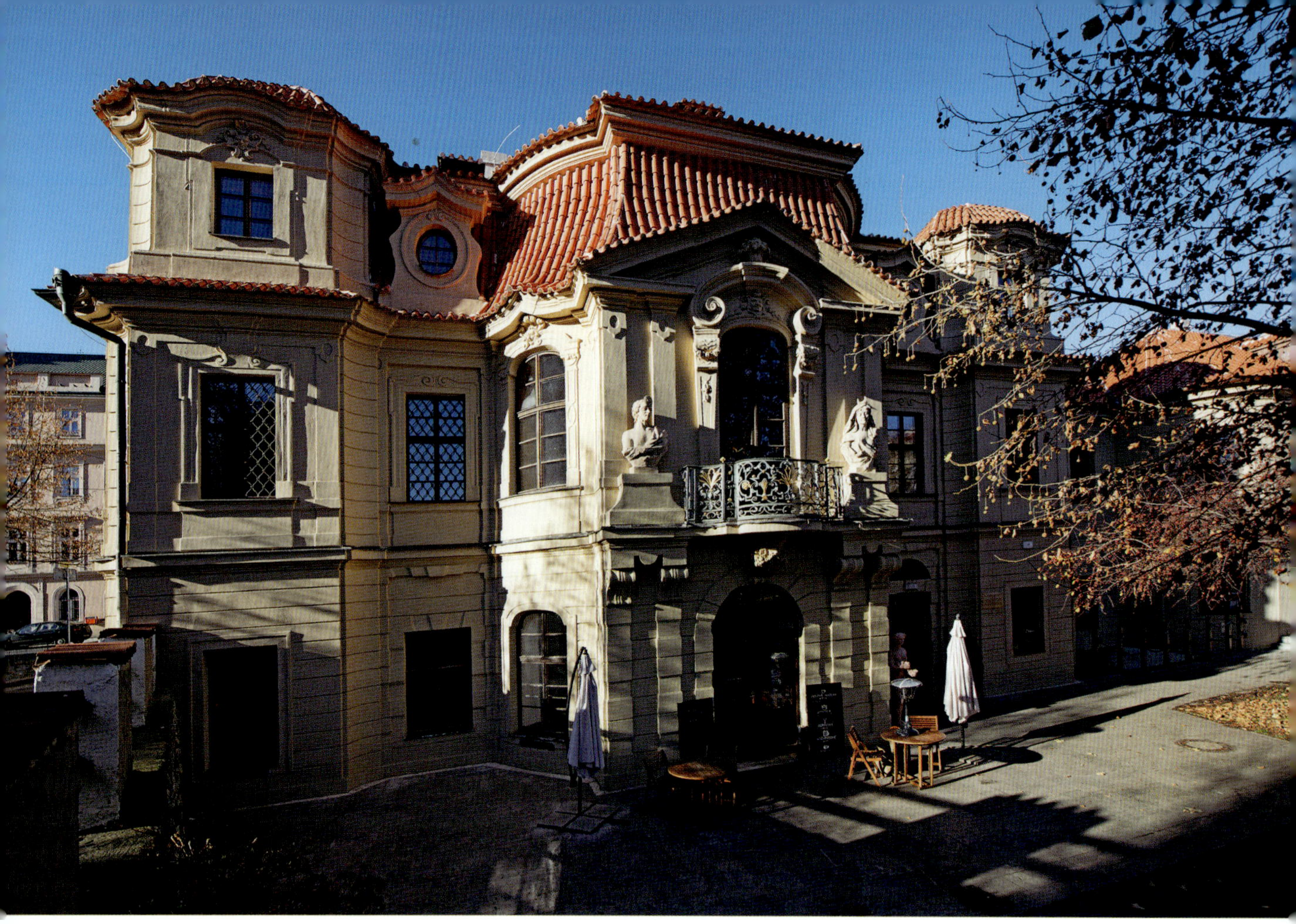

72A–B/ PORTHEIMKA, THE SUMMER HOUSE OF KILIAN IGNAZ DIENTZENHOFER, 1725–28
On the model of other rich inhabitants of Prague, the successful architect and builder Kilian Ignaz Dientzenhofer, an esteemed resident of the Lesser Town, built a summer house for himself beyond the city walls, in front of the Újezd Gate on the left bank of the Vltava, at the centre of what is today the Prague district of Smíchov. The intricately composed, three-dimensionally articulated main façade is surmounted by a mansard roof, reflecting the social standing of the architect, whose 'maison de plaisance' was the equal of the houses of noblemen. Dientzenhofer was undoubtedly not concerned merely to have a comfortable summer residence for his family; rather, he wanted a stately house suitable for meetings with distinguished clients.

The artistic decoration of the house corresponds to his high demands. The main façade is decorated with the allegory *Day and Night* from Braun's workshop. The opulent main hall on the first storey has a vaulted ceiling on which, in 1729, Dientzenhofer's friend, Wenzel Lorenz Reiner, painted the *Bacchanal* fresco. The energetically executed scene, full of *joie de vivre*, was made at the time of the architect's second wedding.

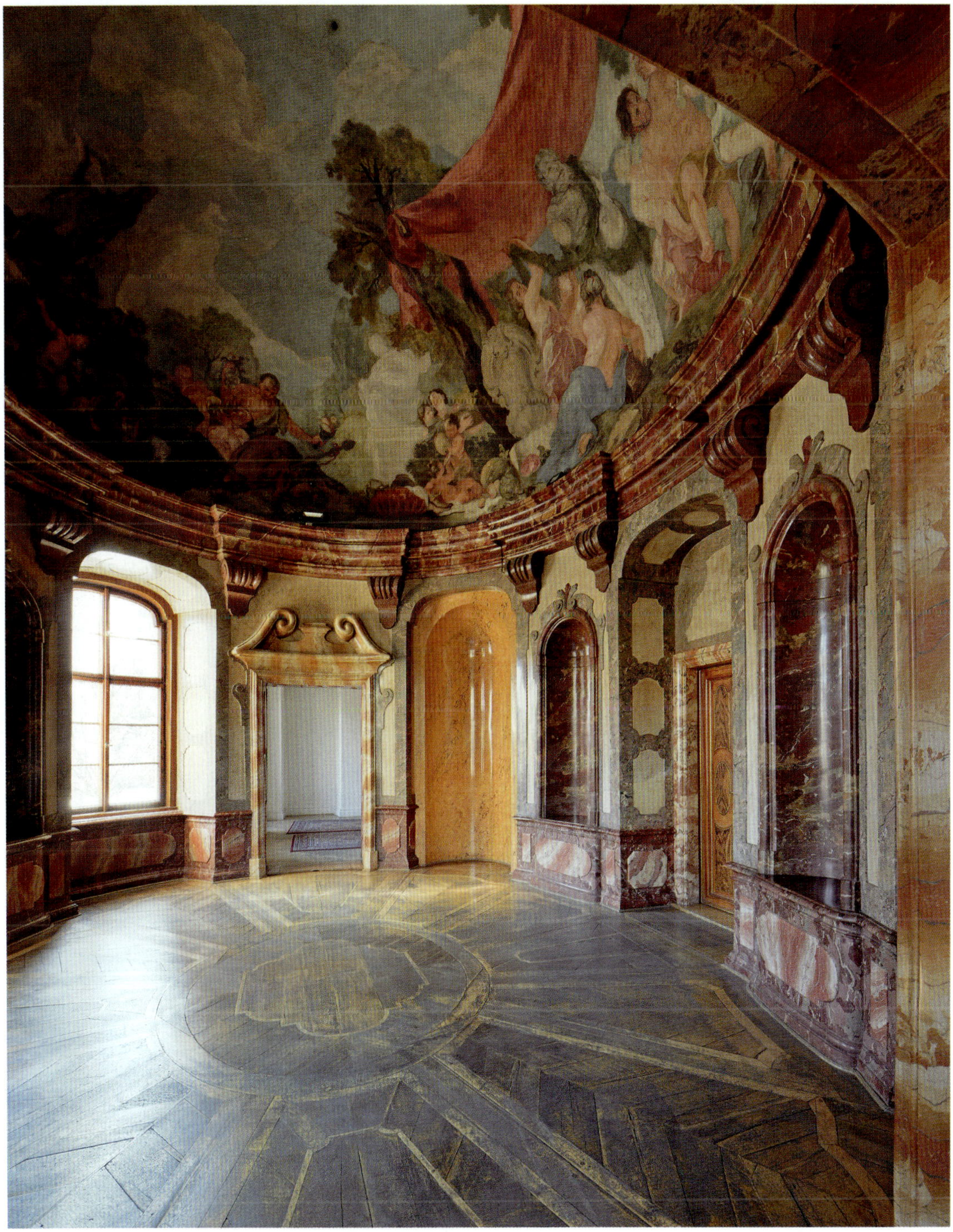

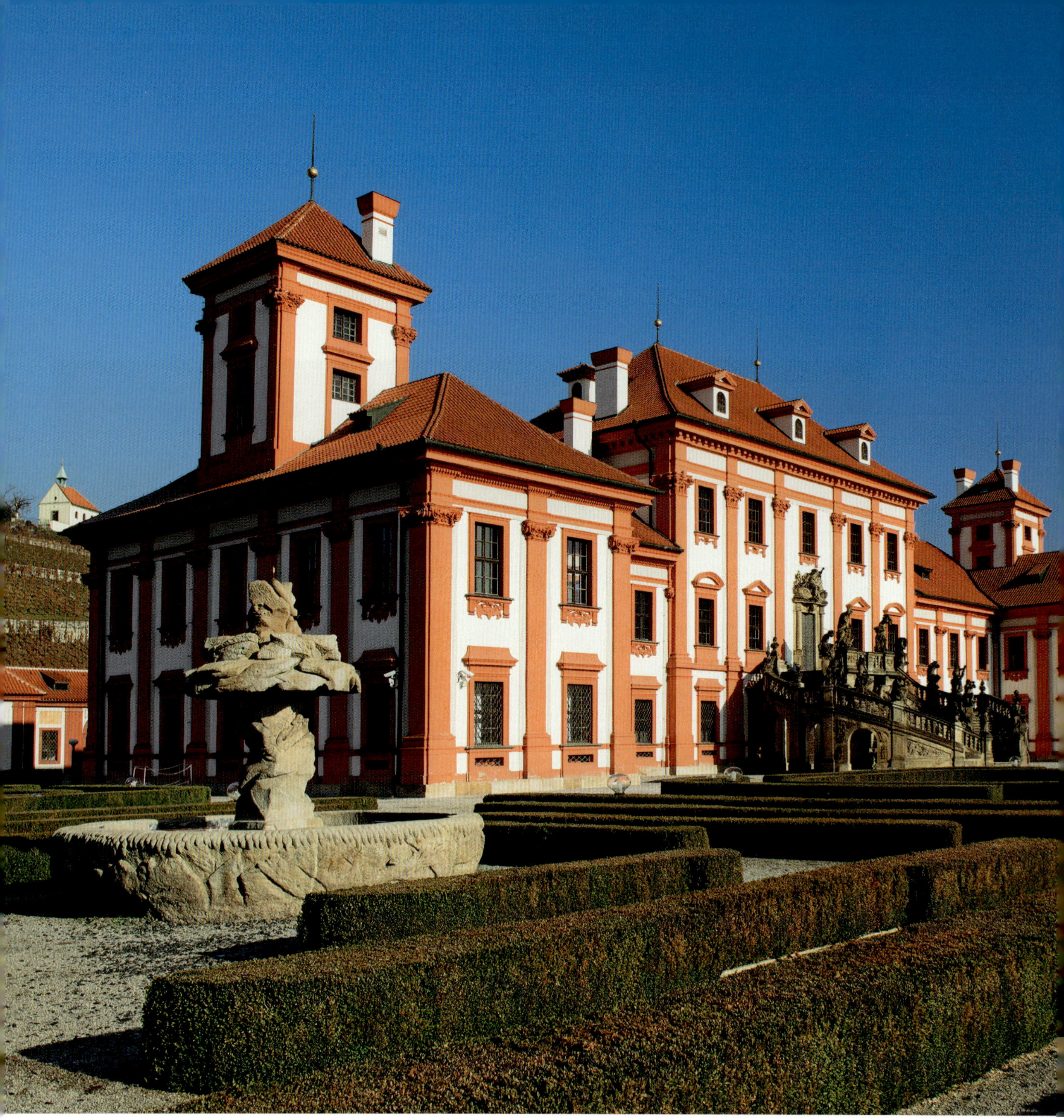

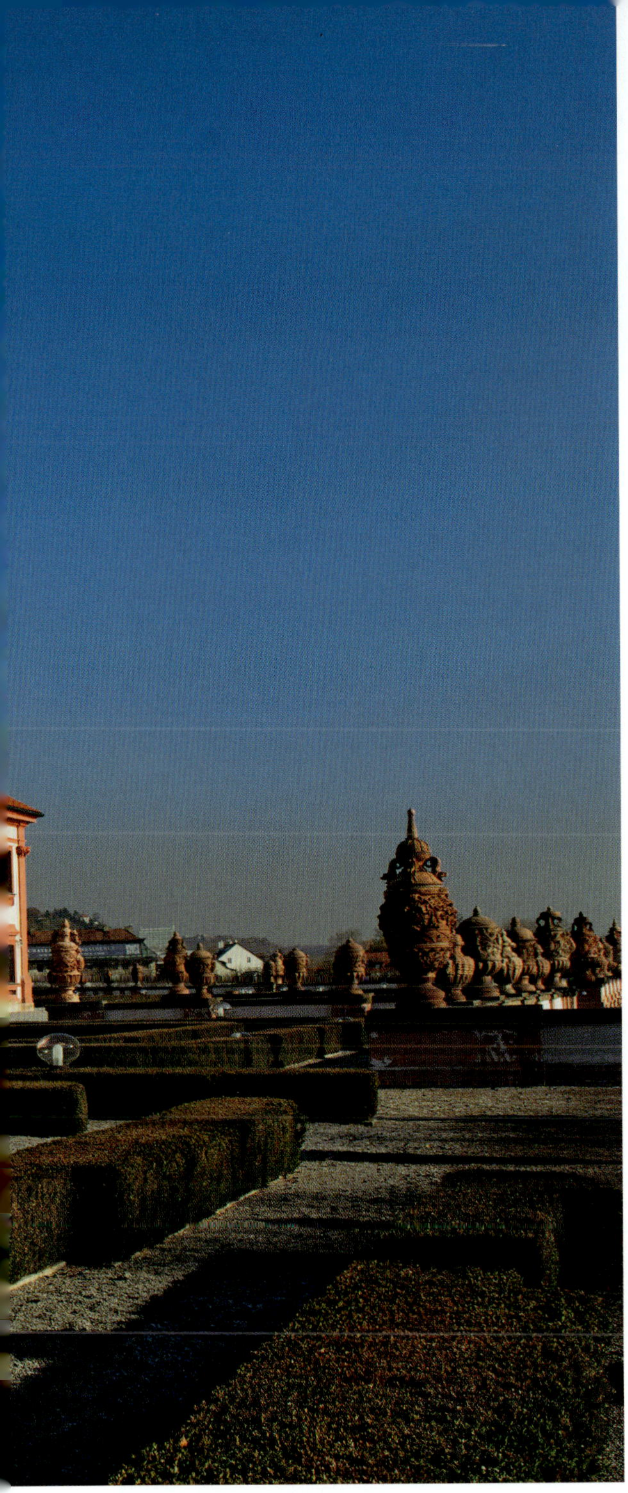

73/ SCHLOSS TROJA (TROJA PALACE) – COUNTRY HOUSE OF WENZEL ADALBERT VON STERNBERG

73A/ SCHLOSS TROJA (TROJSKÝ ZÁMEK)
Count Sternberg (Šternberk) began building his sumptuous suburban summer seat on the bank of the Vltava in 1678. The architect, Jean-Baptiste Mathey, handled the project superbly. The buildings and gardens of Troja, masterly set into the landscape, distinctively follow on from contemporary Italian architecture of the third quarter of the seventeenth century. Just as the terraces of the villas in Frascati afford a view of the Eternal City, so does Troja link the main sightline with Prague Castle. This little schloss served as, among other things, the site of spectacular hunts by members of the court in the nearby Royal Hunting Preserve (today, Stromovka).

'If these Italian palazzi could at least be placed into a glasshouse with the palms during the Bohemian winter. I was continuously haunted by the thought of how cold they must be at night.'
François René de Chateaubriand, 1833

73B/ STAIRCASE WITH A GIGANTOMACHY AND GROTTO

The architecture of this nobleman's seat blends harmoniously with the other arts, particularly the sculpture and monumental painting. On the outer staircase, which projects markedly forward, the Saxon-born sculptor Johann Georg Heermann and his nephew Paul Heermann developed their dramatic *Gigantomachy* (1685–1703), the battle between the Olympian gods and the Giants, an allegorical tribute to the emperor. The artists here have applied their knowledge of the works of Gian Lorenzo Bernini and have created an artistic whole, which, in its expression, is already part of the High Baroque.

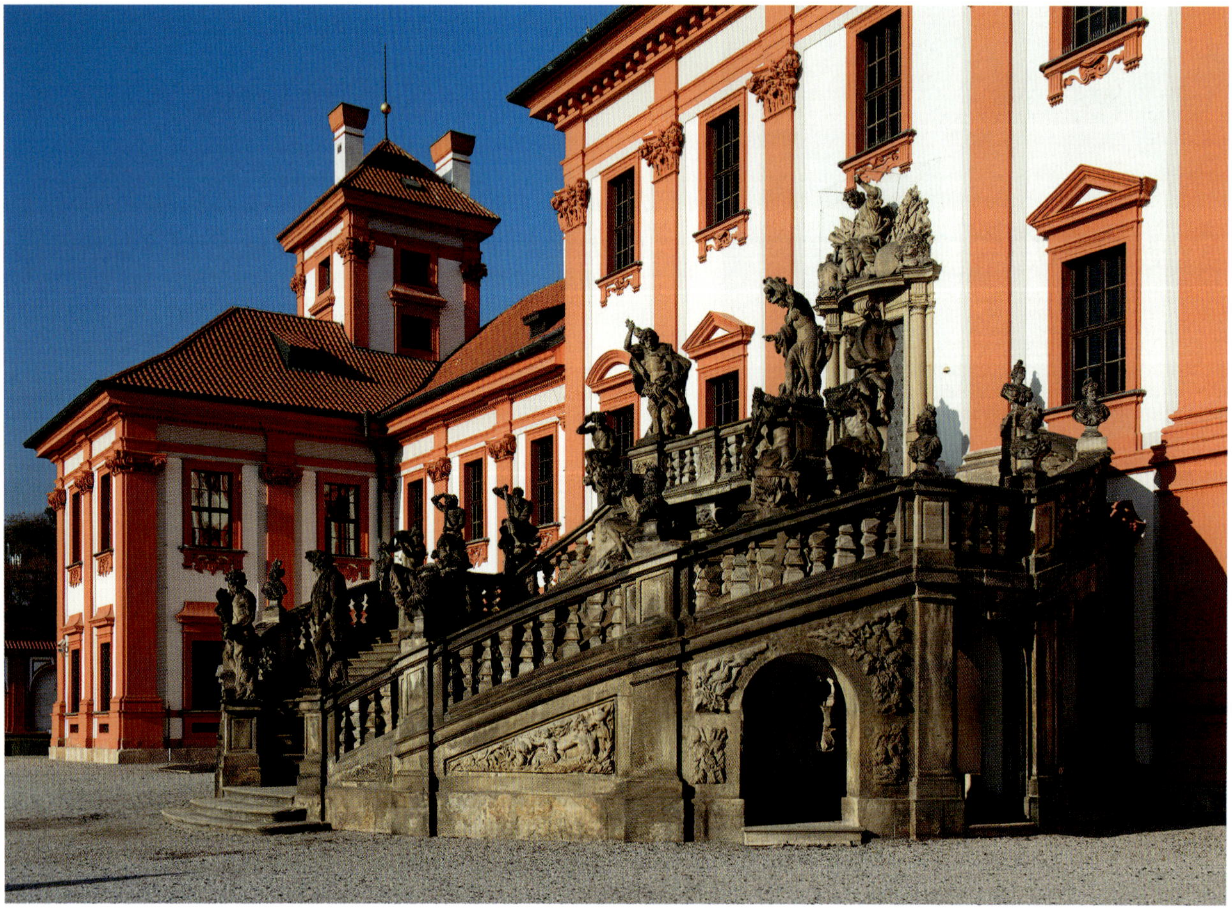

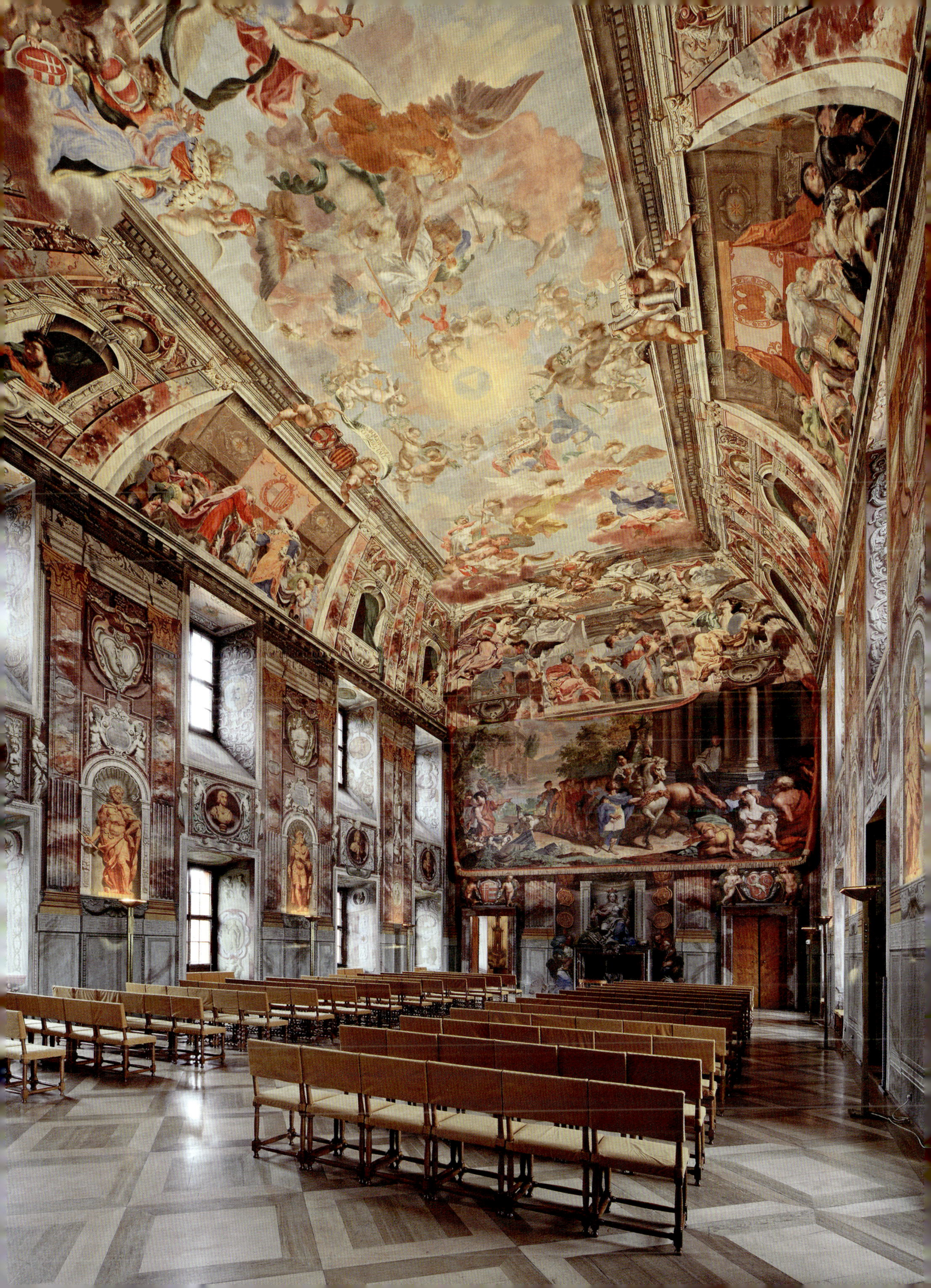

73C–D/ THE GREAT HALL

The painted decoration of the Troja interiors, according to contemporary testimony, is the work of 'various brushes of Bolognese, Milanese, Swiss, Flemish, Polish, and German' artists. The magnificent paintings in the Great Hall were executed from 1691 to 1697 by Abraham Godyn of Antwerp. This is an intricately composed yet conceptually unified and artistically convincing celebration of the Habsburg dynasty, emphasizing events of the war then being fought against the Ottoman Empire.

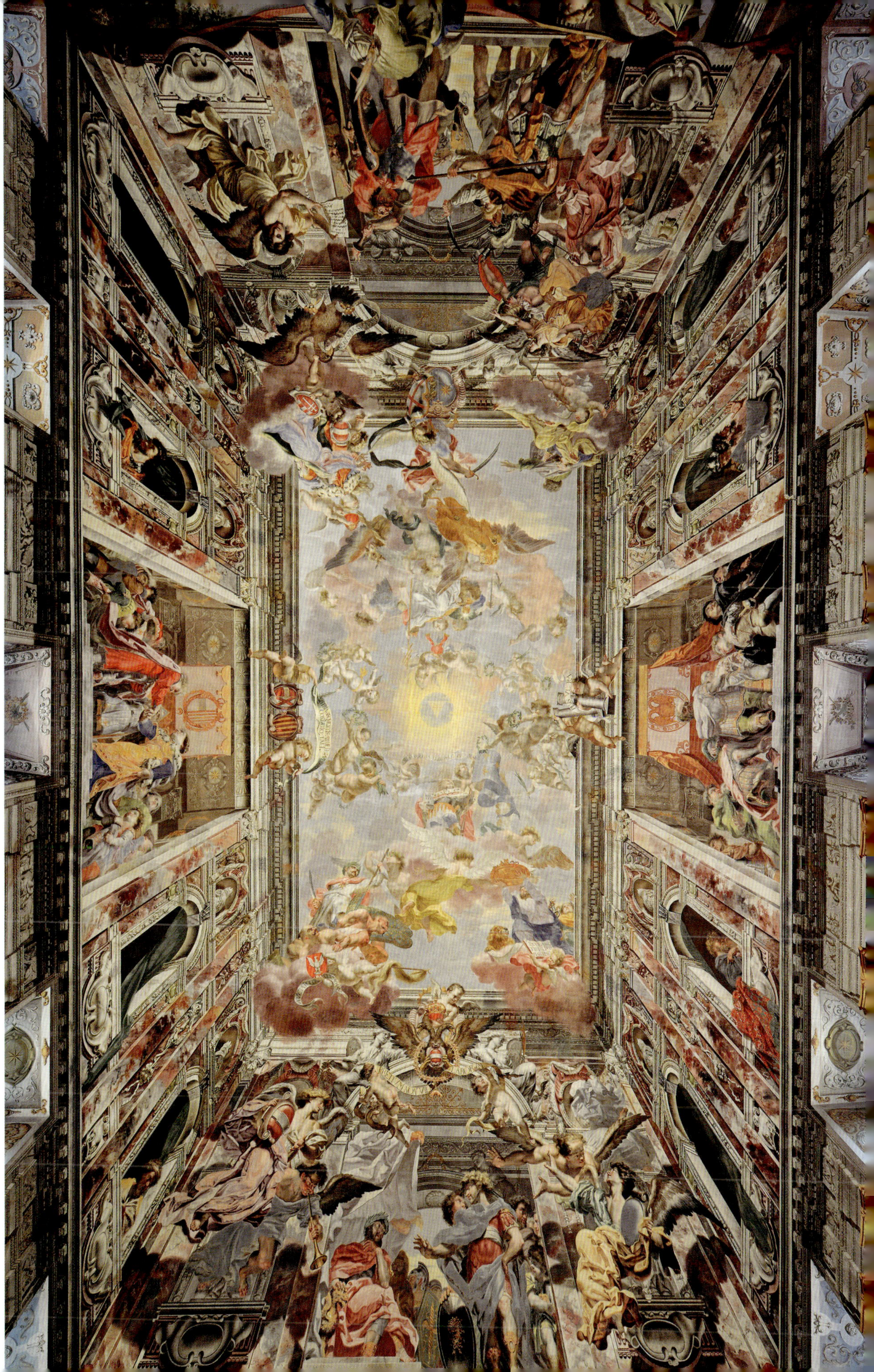

EMINENT PERSONAGES

Abeles, Shimon (1681–1694), Jewish boy who was preparing himself for baptism by the Jesuits in the Clementinum. His death, after a brutal beating by members of his family, led to a trial on trumped-up charges and to a wave of anti-Jewish feeling.

Adlerthurn, von, *see* Putz von Adlerthurn

Aichbauer the Younger, Johann Georg Michael (1680–1737), master mason and builder in Prague, son of the master mason Johann Georg Aichbauer the Elder, step-brother of Kilian Ignaz Dientzenhofer.

Albrecht, Conrad Adolph von (1681–1751), scholar, poet, numismatist and antiquarian, worked as an emblematist and designer of iconographic programmes, particularly for Joseph Emanuel Fischer von Erlach. Was imperial envoy to Portugal from 1734 to 1737.

Alliprandi, Giovanni Battista (after 1685–1720), architect, probably from Laino in the Val d'Intelvi, Northern Italy; trained in Vienna; active in Bohemia from 1690 onwards. An important representative of the classicizing Vienna-style architecture of the High Baroque.

Althann, Gundacker Ludwig (1665–1747), officer and diplomat in the Emperor's service; from 1716 onwards, Imperial Director of Works.

Altman von Eidenberg, David Norbert (after 1617–1656), Prague painter, employed particularly by the Premonstratensians at Strahov.

Anhalt-Bernburg, Christian I, von (1568–1630), diplomat and military commander in the service of the Protestant Union and the Elector Palatine. Supreme commander of the forces of Frederick IV, Elector Palatine, and the Bohemian Estates at the Battle of the White Mountain (1620).

Arnim-Boitzenburg, Hans Georg, von (1583–1641), diplomat and general, active during the Thirty Years War in Poland and then in the service of the Emperor and, later, Saxony. In 1631–32, commander of the Saxon forces occupying Bohemia.

Asam, Cosmas Damian (1686–1739), painter and architect, member of a large family of Bavarian artists. Active in Prague in the 1720s and 1730s, worked mainly for the Benedictines.

Baccio del Bianco, Luigi (1604–1657), Florence-born painter, stucco artist, architect, and mathematician. In Florence, worked with Giovanni Battista Pieroni, whom he went to Vienna with from 1620 to 1622 and then to Prague, where he worked for Wallenstein (*see*). In 1625/26, returned to Italy. From 1650 to the end of his life, worked at the royal and imperial court in Madrid.

Backoffen (Bloch-Backoffen), Elias (after 1667–1719), leading member of the Landesjudenschaft (Jewish autonomous administration); after being denounced by Abraham Aaron Lichtenstadt, was sentenced for allegedly having blasphemed against the Christian faith, but was granted a pardon in 1705. Paid for money from the fine that he had to pay, the Hebrew inscription praising Christ was added to the Crucifixion sculpture on Charles Bridge.

Bassevi von Treuenburg, Jacob (1570–1634), Jewish merchant and financier, supporter and defender of the Jews of Prague. In 1622 the Emperor made him a member of the consortium to improve the state budget. Towards the end of his life, worked for Albrecht von Wallenstein (*see*).

Bayer, Paul Ignaz (*c.*1665–1733), Prague builder and architect.

Bechteler, Caspar (*c.*1580–after 1638), woodworker from Allgäu, Bavaria. Beginning in 1605, worked for Prague Castle. In 1616, was granted the right of domicile in Hradčany. In 1621, was made a court cabinetmaker.

Beckovský, Jan František (1658–1725), member of the Order of the Knights of the Cross with the Red Star; historian and writer.

Belle-Isle, Charles-Louis-Auguste Fouquet, Duc de (1684–1761), French officer and diplomat; in 1741, was awarded the distinction Marshal of France. Initiated the Bohemian campaign of 1741, and was military commander of Prague during the French-Bavarian occupation.

Bendl, Johann Georg (*c.*1620–1680), member of a family of woodcarvers from Southern Germany, a leading sculptor of the Early Baroque in Bohemia.

Birckhardt, Anton (1677–1748), engraver and publisher from Augsburg, operated the most productive printing office in Prague of the High Baroque.

Bossi, Carlo Giuseppe (*c.*1737–1798), of Italian origin, active in Bohemia as a leading artist of stucco architectural decoration in the Rococo style. In 1786 was made a court stucco artist.

Brandl, Peter (1668–1735), painter and one of the most important artists of the Baroque in Bohemia.

Braun, Anton (1709–1742), sculptor of Tyrolean origin, active in Prague beginning in *c.*1730. The most important colleague of Matthias Bernhard Braun (*see*), who was his uncle and whose workshop he took over.

Braun, Matthias Bernhard (1684–1738), artist of Tyrolean origin, of the Italian school. The most important and most prolific sculptor of the High Baroque in Bohemia.

Brixi, František Xaver (1732–1771), composer, beginning in 1759 was choirmaster of St Vitus' Cathedral, Prague.

Broggio, Octavian (1668–1742), builder and architect in the town of Litoměřice (Leitmeritz), north Bohemia. Son of the architect Giulio Broggio.

Brokoff, Ferdinand Maximilian (1688–1731), sculptor, son of Johann Brokoff; with Matthias Bernhard Braun, the leading sculptor of the High Baroque in Bohemia; worked in neighbouring countries as well.

Brokoff, Johann (1652–1718), sculptor from Zips in Upper Hungary (today, Spiš, Slovakia). In 1692, established a family workshop in Prague.

Browne (Brown), Edward (1644–1708), English physician, President of the Royal College of Physicians, traveller, and writer.

Bucquoy, Charles Bonaventure de Longueval, Count (1571–1621), commander of the Imperial Army during the Bohemian Rebellion and at the beginning of the Thirty Years War; fought in the Battle of the White Mountain (1620).

Byss, Johan Rudolf (1660 or 1662–1738), Swiss painter, active in Prague from 1689 to 1712. Was a versatile artist whose work covers many genres, from landscape to mythological scenes to large allegorical compositions on walls and ceilings.

Canevalle, family of builders, architects, and members of other building trades; from the area around Lanzo d'Intelvi, Northern Italy, they began settling in Prague from the first half of the seventeenth century onwards; among its outstanding members are the stucco artist **Domenico** (*fl.* from 1631 onwards), the builder **Giacomo Antonio** (1660–1731), and, especially, the architect **Marcantonio** (1652–1711).

Caratti, Francesco (d.1677), Italian architect from Bissone, Switzerland, settled in Prague at the latest in 1652. Was employed in the service of Bohemian nobles, Dominicans, and Jesuits.

Carlone, Carlo Innocenzo (1686–1775), painter, native of Scaria d'Intelvi, trained in Venice but was also a pupil of Francesco Trevisani in Rome. Beginning in 1724, carried out commissions for Bohemia, and from 1727 to 1730 was active in Prague. Was a master of Venetian colour schemes with touches of Neoclassicism.

Charles X Gustav of Sweden (1622–1660), Count Palatine, and, from 1654 onwards, King of Sweden. In autumn 1648, was the commander of the Swedish forces besieging Prague. On his mother's side, was related to the house of the Electors Palatine and thus to the 'Winter King' of Bohemia, Frederick V of the Palatinate.

Chlumu a Košumberka, z, *see* Slavata z Chlumu a Košumberka

Chřepický z Modlíškovic, Zdeněk Jiří, Count (1677–1755), a Roman Catholic clergyman, canon of the chapters in Litoměřice (Leitmeritz) and Stará Boleslav (Alt-Bunzlau) and the metropolitan chapter of St Vitus' Cathedral in Prague. In 1733, became chapter dean of St Vitus' and in 1734 provost; in 1743, became suffragan bishop of Prague. In 1720 his sister, Antonie Ignácie, married the architect Johann Blasius Santini-Aichl (*see*).

Cometa, Giovanni Bartolomeo (1620–1687), stucco artist from Devoggio near Lugano, worked in Saxony, Lusatia, Bohemia, and perhaps Austria. Probably settled in Prague in the early 1650s; excelled in figurative stucco work.

Corradini, Antonio (1668–1752), sculptor active on the Italian peninsula and central Europe; virtuoso of Early Rococo decorative art.

Czernin von und zu Chudenitz, Franz Joseph, Count (1697–1733), grandson of Humprecht Johann Czernin, was a chamberlain and privy counsellor to Emperor Leopold I; was made a supreme court justice in 1721. An important builder and Baroque nobleman whose debts were the beginning of the Czernins' financial decline.

Czernin von und zu Chudenitz, Humprecht Johann, Count (1628–1682), nobleman with wide ranging interests, including art and architecture; envoy to Venice from 1660 to 1663.

Decker, Coenraet (1650–*c*.1685), Dutch engraver, pupil of Romeyn de Hooghe.

Delsenbach, Johann Adam (1687–1765), Nuremberg painter and engraver.

Dientzenhofer, Christoph (1655–1722), descendent of a large family of Bavarian architects; active in Bohemia at the latest by 1685; principal architect of what is known as the 'radical group' of buildings of the High Baroque in Bohemia.

Dientzenhofer, Kilian Ignaz (1689–1751), Prague architect, son of Christoph Dientzenhofer (*see*); was the chief military engineer and chief architect to the imperial court and one of the most important architects of the High and the Late Baroque in Bohemia.

Dietzler, Johann Joseph (1694–1744), draughtsman at the Office of the Land Rolls (land registry) in Prague, made cityscapes (*vedute*) and plans.

Dittmann von Lavenstein, Christian Sebastian (*c*.1639–1701), painter from Krupka (Graupen) in north Bohemia, settled in Prague *c*.1660.

Dominic a Jesu Maria (1559–1630), Spanish Carmelite, later general of the order. Participated in the Bohemian campaign of the Catholic League and the Battle of the White Mountain (1620).

Erlach, *see* **Fischer von Erlach**

Filippi, Giovanni Maria (*c*.1565–after 1630), architect of South Tyrolean origin, active at the imperial court in Prague from 1602 to 1616; important proponent of Late Mannerist and 'Proto-Baroque' architecture of a Roman orientation.

Fischer von Erlach, Johann Bernhard (1656–1723), architect to the imperial court, also employed by noblemen in Bohemia and Moravia; proponent of monumental Austrian Baroque Neoclassicism.

Fischer von Erlach, Joseph Emanuel (1693–1742), architect, son and pupil of Johann Bernhard Fischer von Erlach (*see*); from 1722 worked for the imperial court.

Frisoni, Giuseppe Donato (1683–1735), stucco artist and architect from Laino in the Val d'Intelvi, Northern Italy. Came to Prague shortly after 1700 and from there, in 1709, went with the stucco artist Tommaso Soldati to Ludwigsburg, in Württemberg. From 1714 onwards, architect at the court of Eberhard Ludwig, Duke of Württemberg.

Fux, Johann Joseph (*c*.1660–1741), Austrian composer, beginning in 1715 kapellmeister at the imperial court.

Gallas, Johann Wenzel von, Count (1669–1719), diplomat in the Emperor's service, Oberstlandmarschall of Bohemia, and, in 1719, Viceroy of Naples.

Galli, Santino (after 1629–after 1670), stucco artist, perhaps from Rovio, near Lugano. Active in the service of Wallenstein (*see*) in Prague and Jičín (Jitschin), north-east Bohemia, later also in Buda (Hungary) and various places in Germany.

Galli da Bibiena, Giuseppe (1696–1757), stage designer and painter, member of a large family of artists from Parma; in 1727, was appointed chief theatrical designer to the imperial court.

Godyn, Abraham (*c.*1665–after 1724), painter from Antwerp, active in Prague from 1687 to 1697/98.
Goltz, Johann Ernst, Count (d.1765), from the Bohemian branch of an originally Brandenburg noble family, in 1724 was elevated to a Bohemian barony, in 1731 he was elevated to the rank of a Bohemian count.
Guglielmi, Gregorio (1714–1773), Rome-born painter, probably a pupil of Francesco Trevisani and Sebastiano Conca. Active mainly as a painter of frescos in various metropolises of central and eastern Europe, including Dresden, Vienna, and Saint Petersburg.
Haffenecker, Anton (1720–1789), Prague-born builder and architect, son of Thomas Haffenecker (*see*), was the Imperial Director of Works. Designed in the style of the transition from the Baroque to early Neoclassicism.
Haffenecker, Thomas (1669–1730), Tyrol-born builder and architect; in 1701, was granted the right of domicile in the Lesser Town of Prague; in 1727, was made Imperial Director of Works.
Halbax, Michael Wenzel (1661–1711), painter from Lower Austria, pupil of Johann Carl Loth in Venice. In Prague, influenced other artists, particularly Peter Brandl (*see*).
Harrach, Ernst Adalbert von, Baron (1598–1667), Roman Catholic priest, became Archbishop of Prague in 1623 and a cardinal in 1626.
Heermann, Johann Georg (1645/6–after 1701), Dresden-based sculptor and architect, active also in Görlitz and Linz among other places. While in Prague, worked intermittently from *c.*1685 to 1703 on the decoration of the Sternberg schloss in Troja. His style reflects the transition from Early to High Baroque.
Heermann, Paul (*c.*1673–1732), Saxon sculptor, nephew of Johann Georg Heermann (*see*), whom he trained with in Prague and worked with on the decoration of the Sternberg schloss in Troja.
Heidelberger, Ernst Johann (d. before 1668), sculptor and woodcarver in the transition from Mannerism to Early Baroque; active, for instance, at Prague Castle and for Wallenstein (*see*).
Heimbach, Wolfgang (*c.*1615–*c.*1678), deaf painter from Lower Saxony, active at the Danish court; in the mid-seventeenth century, worked briefly in Bohemia. A popular portraitist.
Heinsch, Johann Georg (1647–1712), painter from Kladsko (today, Kłodzko, Poland), active in Prague at the latest from 1679 onwards; a prolific painter of works for churches and also made drawings for prints.
Hennevogel, Johann Wilhelm (1700–1754), artist in stucco and marble, sculptor; his son and pupil was Johann Caspar Hennevogel. Active in Prague from the beginning of the 1720s, later moved to Litoměřice (Leitmeritz), north Bohemia, where, in 1745, was granted the right of domicile. Beginning in 1740, court sculptor in marble for Frederick II of Prussia.
Heraeus, Carl Gustav (1671–1725), Stockholm-born antiquarian to the imperial court in Vienna, numismatist, and poet. Designed emblems and iconographic programmes for buildings, medals, and allegorical prints.
Herold, Wolf Hieronymus von (1627–1693), bell founder and metal founder in Nuremberg, cast the bronze statue of John Nepomucene for Charles Bridge.
Hiebel, Johann (1681–1755), born in Ottobeuren, Bavaria; active in Prague, from 1710 onwards, as a painter of frescos, altarpieces, and portraits, and made drawings for prints.
Hiernle, Carl Joseph (*c.*1693–1748), sculptor, descendent of a South German family of sculptors, pupil of Mathias Wenzel Jäckel in Prague, and important member of the first generation of artists of Prague Rococo sculpture.
Hohenlohe, Georg Friedrich, Count (1569–1645), soldier and poet, author of Lutheran devotional verse. In 1620, led the Estates cavalry in the Battle of the White Mountain.

Hollar, Wenceslaus (Václav) (1607–1677), Prague-born graphic artist of European importance, active in Germany, the Netherlands, and England; in 1636, briefly visited his native Prague.
Jäckel, Mathias Wenzel (1655–1738), sculptor from Lusatia; in the late seventeenth century, became master of an important Prague workshop.
Jäger, Josef (*c.*1721–1793), architect and builder from Haldensee in the Tyrol; came to Prague in *c.*1740.
Känischbauer von Hohenried, Johann Baptist (1668–1739), goldsmith from Vienna. Became a master in 1696 and head of the Vienna goldsmiths' guild in 1703. In 1712, was appointed goldsmith to the imperial court and was made an official of the Imperial Treasury. In 1722, was granted the title von Hohenried. A leading goldsmith of the High Baroque in Austria.
Kaňka, František Maxmilián (1674–1766), builder and architect, frequent collaborator of leading artists of the High Baroque, a long-standing architect of buildings for the Czernin von Chudenitz family.
Kaulfersch the Elder, Christian (dates unknown), painter active in the first half of the seventeenth century, specialized in portraiture.
Kern, Anton (1710–1747), painter at the Saxon court, influenced by the Venetian Rococo; also active in Bohemia in the 1730s.
Keyßler, Johann Georg (1693–1743), born in Thurnau, Germany, was a fellow of the Royal Society of Physicians in London, and an author of travel writing (published in English under the name John George Keysler); generally considered the father of protohistory.
Kinsky, Franz Ulrich, Fürst (1634–1699), high-ranking military officer, imperial diplomat, active in the politics of Bohemia; in 1667, chief justice of the court of appeal, and in 1683 was made Lord High Chancellor.
Kogler the Younger, Johann Georg (*c.*1670–1720), native of Gumpoldskirchen, Lower Austria; important goldsmith of the High Baroque, active in Prague after 1704.
Kohl, Hieronymus (1632/35–1709), sculptor born in Horní Slavkov (Schlaggenwald), west Bohemia, settled in Prague at the latest by 1650, and was granted right of domicile in the Lesser Town in 1675. Pupil of Ernst Johann Heidelberger, becoming court sculptor after him.
Kolowrat-Nowohradsky, Johann Wenzel, Count (d.1690), a member of the Bohemian government.
Komenský, Jan Amos (Comenius) (1592–1670), last bishop of the Bohemian Brethren (Unitas Fratrum), spiritual leader of the Czech exiles after the Battle of the White Mountain (1620), theologian and educationalist of European importance.
Königsmarck, Hans Christoph von (1600–1663), German soldier in the service of the Swedes in the Thirty Years War. In July 1648, led the attack against Prague and the subsequent plundering of the imperial art collections at Prague Castle.
Koželuh, Jan Antonín (1738–1814), composer, was appointed kapellmeister of St Vitus' Cathedral in Prague in 1787.
Kracker, Johann Lucas (1717–1779), painter, attended the Academy of Fine Arts in Vienna; also worked in Moravia, Prague, and, particularly, Hungary.
Krakowská z Kolowrat, Ludmila Eva Františka, Countess (1616–1695), née Hiserle von Chodau, married first to Ferdinand de Couriers, then to Sigismund, Count Wolkenstein, and lastly to Vilém Albrecht Count Krakowský z Kolowrat. She was the founder and patron of the Confraternity of Jesus, Mary, and Joseph of the Holy Family at the Loreto, Prague.
Kratochvíl, Jan Václav (1667–1721), specialist in lacquer painting, worked in Bohemia and at Schloss Rastatt in Baden.
Kvasejovic, z, ***see*** **Přehořovský z Kvasejovic**
Lauermann, Franz Martin (1714–1778), mason and marble worker, born in Ploskovice (Ploschkowitz), north Bohemia; from at least 1748 onwards, in Prague.

Lauermann, Josef (1714–1772), twin brother of Franz Martin Lauermann (*see*), mason and marble worker, born in Ploskovice (Ploschkowitz), north Bohemia; his work in Prague is documented from 1743 to 1772.
Leopold Wilhelm, Archduke of Austria (1614–1662), second son of Emperor Ferdinand II. Titular bishop, eventually in five dioceses, including Olomouc and Breslau (Wrocław); from 1639 to 1642, commander of the Imperial Army; from 1646 to 1656, governor of the Spanish Netherlands. A passionate collector, founded, for example, the outstanding new imperial collection at Prague Castle in 1655.

Libsteinsky Kolowrat, **Franz Karl I**, Count (1620–1700), chief justice of the court of appeals and, in 1667, became chief administrator of Moravia.
Lichtenstadt, **Abraham Aaron** (d.1702), son of Naftali Hirz Oettingen; was a Court Jew of the dukes of Lower Saxony; in 1674, was made head of the Landesjudenschaft (Jewish self-administration) in Bohemia. Initiated court proceedings against Elias Backoffen and his friend Berl Tabor for allegedly having blasphemed against the Cross.
Liechtenstein, Karl I. von, Fürst (1569–1627), Moravian politician in the service of the Habsburg emperors; gained the Duchy of Troppau (Opava) in 1613 and the Duchy of Jägerndorf (Krnov) in 1623. Was made the governor of Bohemia in 1621, and was thus responsible for punishing the participants of the Estates Rebellion.
Linek, Jiří Ignác (1725–1791), composer, beginning in 1747, taught music in the town of Bakov nad Jizerou, central Bohemia.
Lischka, Johann Christoph (*c.*1650–1720), painter, stepson and pupil of Michael Leopold Willmann (*see*), in whose workshop he was employed and from whom he adopted a powerfully expressive style, which he developed and enriched with Italian elements. Worked in Prague and elsewhere in Bohemia, particularly for the Cistercians and the Knights of the Cross with the Red Star.
Lobkowicz, Benigna Catherina, von (1594–1653), noblewoman from the Duchcov (Dux) branch of the House of Lobkowicz (z Lobkovic); in 1608, married Vilém the Younger Popel von Lobkowicz, of the branch from Bílina, north Bohemia.
Lobkowicz, Polyxena, von (1566–1642), née von Pernstein (z Pernštejna); in 1587, married Wihelm von Rosenberg (Vilém z Rožmberka) and, then, in 1603, Zdeněk Vojtěch Popel von Lobkowicz, the High Chancellor. She consistently supported Roman Catholic Habsburg policy.
Löbl, Benno the Younger (1688–1751), Benedictine monk; in 1738, was made Abbot of Břevnov abbey and its filial abbey in Broumov, north-east Bohemia. Was important in commissioning buildings and works of art.
Losy von Losinthal, Johann Anton the Elder, Count (*c.*1600–1682), inspector of wine, beer, and salt taxes in Bohemia, privy counsellor, head of the Court Chancellery. Fought in the defence of Prague against the Swedes in 1648, was made a knight in 1647 and a count in 1655.
Losy von Losinthal, Johann Anton the Younger, Count (*c.*1650–1721); in his day, known throughout Europe as a composer as well as a virtuoso of the violin and especially the lute.
Luna, Christian (*c.*1671–1729), Prague painter, woodcarver, specialized in the portrait miniature.
Lurago, Anselmo Martino (*c.*1701–1765), Italian builder and architect, nephew of Bartolomeo Scotti (*see*) and pupil of František Maxmilián Kaňka (*see*).
Lurago, Carlo (1615–1684), Italian architect and builder, worked in Bohemia from 1638 onwards, chiefly for the Jesuits.
Lurago, Francesco Anselmo (1634–1693), Italian architect and builder, cousin of Carlo Lurago (*see*); worked in Prague from at least 1665 onwards.
Mansfeld und Fondi, Heinrich Franz von (1712–1780), nobleman from a large central European family; third of his line to bear the title Fürst.

Maria Anna, Archduchess of Austria (1738–1789), daughter of Emperor Francis I and Maria Theresa; in 1766, was made Abbess of the Institute for Distressed Noblewomen (Das adelige Damenstift/Ústav šlechtičen) at Prague Castle.
Martinelli, Domenico (1650–1718), Italian architect, pupil of Domenico Fontana in Rome. From 1690 to 1705, active in Vienna, where he also made plans for a number of buildings in Bohemia and Moravia.
Martinitz, Bernhard Ignaz von, Count (1615–1685), politician, beginning in 1651, Lord Burgrave of Prague.
Mathey, Jean-Baptiste (*c.*1630–1696), French painter and architect, trained in Rome, active in Bohemia from 1675 to 1695.
Maulbertsch, Franz Anton (1724–1796), Swabian painter, worked in Vienna from 1739 onwards, while also receiving numerous commissions from Hungary, Moravia, and Bohemia. The leading central European painter of the second half of the eighteenth century.
Maximilian I (1573–1651), made Duke of Bavaria in 1597 and Elector in 1623. Led the Catholic League, initiated the Bohemian campaign of the League Army in 1620.
Mayer, Johann Ulrich (1652–1721), sculptor from Lower Austria; granted right of domicile in the Lesser Town of Prague in 1712.
Medici, Gian (Giovanni Battista) Gastone de' (1671–1737), was made Grand Duke of Tuscany in 1723. As the husband of Anna Maria Franziska, Duchess of Saxe-Lauenburg, lived in Prague and north Bohemia from 1697 to 1708.
Michl, Martin (dates unknown), painter, assisted Franz Anton Maulbertsch (*see*) with the ceiling fresco at Strahov monastery, Prague, in 1794.
Michna z Vacínova, Jan Václav, Count (1669–1721), Bohemian nobleman, a knowledgeable and demanding builder.
Michna z Vacínova, Pavel, Count (1589–1632), during the Thirty Years War, was imperial quartermaster general. Established the Michna family's wealth and power.
Mitrovic, z, ***see*** Wratislaw von Mitrowitz
Modlíškovic, z, ***see*** **Chřepický z Modlíškovic**
Montagu, Mary Wortley, Lady (1689–1762), English aristocrat, married the diplomat Edward Wortley Montagu in 1712; together they lived in Constantinople from 1716 to 1718. Known for her letters describing her experiences in the Ottoman Empire and in towns of central Europe, including Prague and Vienna.
Morzin, Wenzel von, Count (1676–1737), important builder and patron of composers, including Joseph Haydn and Antonio Vivaldi.
Mosto, Ottavio (*c.*1659–1701), Padua-born sculptor, active in central Europe (especially Salzburg); arrived in Prague before 1694, where he became the first important artist of Baroque sculptural *trompe-l'oeil.*
Müller, Franz Anton (1693–1753), painter, born in Žatec (Saaz), west Bohemia; pupil of Wenzel Lorenz Reiner. Active in Prague beginning in 1725; appointed painter to the court in 1735.
Mundt, Johann Heinrich (1632–1691), organ builder from Cologne, settled in Prague before 1668.
Neunhertz, Georg Wilhelm (1689–1749), painter from Breslau, pupil of his father-in-law, Michael Leopold Willmann (*see*), and of Johann Christoph Lischka (*see*); in 1724, moved the family workshop from Lubiąż Abbey (Kloster Leubus), Lower Silesia, to Prague.
Neureuter, Augustin Peter (*c.*1673–1749), engraver and publisher, working in Prague from at least 1697 onwards.
Nosecký, Siard (Siardus) (1693–1753), Prague painter and frescoist; in 1714, became a member of the Premonstratensian canonry and its librarian at Strahov, in Prague. Worked mainly for the houses of the Premonstratensians.

Nostitz-Rieneck, Johann Hartwig von, Count (1610–1683), was, from 1644 to 1650, chief justice of the court of appeal, and, from 1652 to 1683, High Chancellor of the Kingdom of Bohemia.

Novák, Ignác (1723–1803), Prague goldsmith.

Orsi, Giovanni Battista (d. before 1641), builder, born in San Fedele in the Val d'Intelvi; active in Vienna and, beginning in 1626, in Prague.

Orsi (sometimes Orsi de Orsini), Giovanni Domenico (1633/34–1679), an architect and builder, son of Giovanni Battista Orsi; worked in Prague from at least 1650 onwards; in 1666, was appointed chief military engineer for fortifications in Bohemia.

Ouden Allen (sometimes Alten-Allen), Folpert van (1635–1715), a Dutch painter, draughtsman, and engraver, specialized in cityscapes. In 1673, was appointed court painter to Emperor Leopold I.

Pacassi, Nicolò (Nikolaus) (1716–1790), in 1748 was appointed architect to the court in Vienna; was the chief architect at the imperial court of Maria Theresa.

Packeny (Pakeni), family of important Prague goldsmiths of the High Baroque and Rococo periods; the founder of the family workshop was **Johann** (1694–1760), originally from Jülich, in the lower Rhineland; in 1724 became a citizen of the Lesser Town of Prague; worked with his sons **Johann Dominik** (1725–1786) and **Franz Emanuel** (1737–1809), both of whom later took over from him.

Palko, Franz Xaver Karl (1724–1767), a painter, trained at the Academy of Fine Arts in Vienna, was particularly influenced by Venetian painting. Active in Bohemia from the end of the 1740s onwards; in 1752 was a painter to the royal court in Dresden.

Pariati, Pietro (1665–1733), Italian poet and librettist (including for works by Handel and Vivaldi), active from 1714 onwards at the court of Emperor Charles VI in Vienna.

Pánek, Jan Šimon (*c.*1654–1734), master mason and builder in Prague, where he was granted right of domicile in the New Town in 1684.

Patin, Charles (1633–1693), French physician and numismatist, wrote about his travels in western and central Europe.

Pernstein, Polyxena, z, *see* **Lobkowicz, z, Polyxena**

Pieroni da Galliano, Giovanni Battista (1586–*c.*1654), architect, military engineer, mathematician, and lawyer. Native of Florence, active as a designer of fortifications in Vienna in 1620/21, and beginning in 1624 worked for Wallenstein (*see*). Returned to Vienna at the latest in 1639.

Plachý, Jiří (Georg) (*c.*1606–1664), Jesuit, taught theology, Hebrew, and ethics at the universities of Olomouc (Olmütz) and Prague; was a popular Czech preacher and spiritual leader of the Academic Legion during the defence of Prague against the Swedes in 1648

Platzer, Ignaz Franz (1717–1787), the leading sculptor of the Late Baroque in Bohemia in the transition from Rococo to Neoclassicism; in 1743, founded the important Platzer family workshop in Prague.

Platzer, Ignaz Michael (1757–1826), sculptor, son and pupil of Ignaz Franz Platzer; took over his father's workshop.

Prachner, Peter (1747–1807), Prague sculptor, son and pupil of Richard Prachner. Attended the Academy of Fine Arts in Vienna; as an architect worked in the early Neoclassical style.

Preiss, Franz (*c.*1660–1712), important Prague sculptor from the beginning of the High Baroque before the arrival of Matthias Bernhard Braun (*see*).

Prée, František Ignác (*c.*1702–1755), architect and builder, pupil of František Maxmilián Kaňka (*see*). Active in Prague as an independent master beginning in 1726.

Přehořovský z Kvasejovic, František Karel, Count (1645–1723), financier and politician active in the Bohemian administration; from 1705 to 1717, Lord Chief Justice.

Příchovský z Příchovic, Antonín Petr, Count (1707–1793), Roman Catholic clergyman; from 1753 to 1763, Bishop of Hradec Králové (Königgrätz); in 1764, made Archbishop of Prague.

Putz von Adlerthurn, Johann Ignaz Dominik, Baron (1647–1718), on the Aulic Council and Imperial Chamber Court.

Quitainer, Andreas Philipp (1679–1729), sculptor from Friedland (Frýdlant), north Bohemia, working in Prague from at least 1694 onwards.

Quitainer, Johann Anton (1709–1765), Prague sculptor of the early Rococo, son and pupil of Andreas Philipp Quitainer (*see*).

Rappa, Domenico Antonio (*fl.* in Bohemia in the 1710s and 1720s), mason, in Prague from at least 1711, when he was granted right of domicile in the Old Town, and at least until his son's baptism in 1727. A frequent collaborator of František Maxmilián Kaňka (*see*).

Rass, Johann Martin, called fra Ignatius a Jesu (1640–1694), builder, born in the Tyrol; from 1667, member of the Order of Carmelites in Belgium. Active in Prague from at least 1686 to 1693 in connection with buildings for the Carmelites and for Johann Georg Joachim Slavata (*see*).

Rauchmiller, Matthias (1645–1686), sculptor, painter, and architect, active in Mainz, Liegnitz (Silesia; today, Legnica, Poland), Passau, and Vienna.

Redel, Carl Adolph (1659–after 1710), Saxon lawyer, author of *Das Sehens-würdige Prag* (The Sights of Prague, 1710).

Reiner, Martin (*c.*1627–1680), builder, in Prague since at least the mid-1650s, where he initially worked with Carlo Lurago (*see*).

Reiner, Wenzel Lorenz (1689–1743), Prague painter, most important fresco artist of the High Baroque in Bohemia. Grandson of Martin Reiner (*see*).

Ringle, Johann Georg (*fl.* first half of the eighteenth century), a copper engraver active in Augsburg.

Rosenberg, Polyxena von, *see* Lobkowicz

Santini-Aichl, Johann Blasius (1677–1723), Prague painter, one of the most original architects of the High Baroque in Bohemia.

Saxe-Lauenburg, Anna Maria Franziska von, Duchess (1672–1741), wife of Prince Philipp Wilhelm August, Count Palatine of Neuburg, from 1690 to 1693, and then of Gian Gastone de' Medici, from 1697 to 1737.

Schlik zu Bassano und Weißkirchen, Leopold Anton Joseph, Count (1663–1723), politician and general; in 1705, was made General War Commissioner, and, in 1707, Field Marshal; in 1713, was made Lord High Chancellor of the Bohemian Kingdom.

Schönherr, Matthias (*c.*1701–1743), sculptor from the Tyrol, was granted right of domicile in the Old Town of Prague in 1734.

Schöpf, Johann Adam (1702–1772), painter from Regensburg, active in Prague from 1724 to 1742.

Scotti, Bartolomeo (1685–1737), builder and architect from Laino, Val d'Intelvi; active in Prague from at least 1715 onwards. In 1718, was made chief military engineer for fortifications.

Scotti, Giovanni Pietro (1695–1747), painter from Laino, Val d'Intelvi, active in the 1730s as an artist of decorative ceiling paintings in Württemberg and Prague.

Škréta Šotnovský ze Závořic, Karel the Elder (1608/12–1674), painter, descendent of an Old Town patrician family. After a study trip to Germany and Italy, returned to Prague where he found employment mainly as a portraitist, a painter of works for churches, and as a draughtsman for prints. The most important artist of the Early Baroque in Bohemia.

Šlanzovský (Schlansowsky), Jan Jiří (Johann Georg) (*c.*1682–1752), Austrian-born sculptor; after arriving in Prague, was probably employed in the workshop of Mathias Wenzel Jäckel (*see*).

Slavata z Chlumu a Košumberka, Johann Georg Joachim, Count (1634/7–1689), imperial privy counsellor; from 1685 to 1688, Lord Chief Justice.
Soldati, Tommaso (*c.*1665–1743), stucco artist from Ponna in the Val d'Intelvi, Northern Italy, active in Prague from at least 1685 onwards. Granted right of domicile in the Old Town of Prague in 1700.
Sonntag, Johann Tobias (1716–1774), painter from Darmstadt, specialized in scenes of hunting and battle.
Šotnovský ze Závořic, *see* Škréta Šotnovský ze Závořic
Špaček, Václav (1689–1751), builder and architect, active mainly in the service of Anna Maria Franziska, Duchess of Saxe-Lauenburg (*see*) at Schloss Ploskovice (Ploschkowitz), north Bohemia.
Spanberger, Jacob (1637–1680), Jesuit, beginning in 1679 was a preacher and confessor in the Bethlehem Chapel in the Old Town of Prague. Was the brother of Simon Spanberger (*see*).
Spanberger, Simon (1631–1680), Jesuit, in 1677 was made a professor of moral theology at Prague University.
Spannbrucker, Johann Christoph (1704–1741/43), builder, son and pupil of Philipp Spannbrucker (*see*). Granted right of domicile in the Old Town of Prague in 1733.
Spannbrucker, Philipp (*c.*1672–1729), builder in Prague, where he was granted right of domicile in the Lesser Town in 1695. His colleagues included Jean-Baptiste Mathey (*see*) and Johann Blasius Santini-Aichel (*see*).
Spezza, Andrea (1580–1628), builder and architect from Arogno, in the Lugano District, in what is today the Swiss canton of Ticino; active, for instance, in Oldenburg, Bielany (a village near Cracow), and, beginning in 1616, on and off in Bohemia, where he worked beginning in 1623 for Wallenstein (*see*).
Spinetti, Bernardo (*c.*1699–1748), stucco artist, in Prague from at least 1728 onwards. From a large Italian family of builders, masons, and stucco artists, some of whom began to settle in Bohemia before the mid-seventeenth century.
Sporck, Franz Anton von, Count (1662–1738), self-centred nobleman, famous as a builder and investor in painting, sculpture, verse, drama, and music. Was a publisher of unconventional devotional literature, a tireless critic, and a somewhat tedious moralizer.
Stegner, Matthias (dates unknown), court goldsmith and jeweller, pupil and collaborator of Johann Baptist Känischbauer (*see*).
Stepling, Joseph (1716–1778), Jesuit, was made a professor at Prague University in 1748. An important mathematician, physicist, and astronomer, organized academic work and the teaching of the natural sciences. Director of the Clementinum observatory (beginning in 1751) and of a mathematics centre.
Sternberg, Wenzel Adalbert von, Count (1643–1708), diplomat; from 1696 to 1704, Lord Chief Justice; in 1704, was made Lord High Chamberlain.
Stevens von Steinfels, Johann Jakob (1651–1730), a Flemish landscape painter at the court of Rudolph II. Employed mainly as a fresco painter, for instance, in the conventual church in Waldsassen, Bavaria (just over the border from Bohemia).
Strachovský ze Strachovic, František Xaver Kazimír, knight (d.1786), Roman Catholic clergyman, was made provost of the metropolitan chapter of St Vitus' Cathedral in 1769.
Swedenborg, Emanuel (1688–1772), Swedish polymath, inventor, philosopher, and theologian of a mystical orientation. Visited Prague in 1733.
Swéerts-Reist und von Sporck, Johann Franz Christian, Count (1729–1802), an imperial privy counsellor and chamberlain, an enlightened Bohemian nobleman. His father, Franz Karl Rudolf Graf von Swéerts-Reist und von Sporck, was the adopted son and heir of Franz Anton von Sporck (*see*).

Tausch, Christoph (1673–1731), Innsbruck-born painter and architect, lay brother of the Jesuit Order, pupil and colleague of Andrea Pozzo, whose designs he carried out in Vienna and Prague. Also active in the Kingdom of Hungary and especially in Silesia.
Tessin the Younger, Nicodemus (1654–1728), Swedish architect and town planner; visited Prague in 1688 and recorded his impressions.
Thun und Hohenstein, Michael Oswald von, Count (1631–1694), imperial privy counsellor, Statthalter in Bohemia, magistrate on the Bohemian Court.
Tyroff, Martin (1704–after 1759), engraver and publisher, from a large Nuremberg family of graphic artists.
Waldstein, Johann Friedrich von, Count (1642–1694), Roman Catholic clergyman; from 1668 to 1675, Bishop of Hradec Králové (Königgratz); in 1675, was made Archbishop of Prague.
Wallenstein (Waldstein), Albrecht Wenzel Eusebius von (1583–1634), imperial general and politician. From 1625 to 1630 and again in 1631, was generalissimo of the Imperial Army. At the height of his power, was the most important man in Europe, but eventually lost the emperor's confidence, was removed by a conspiracy of his own generals, and assassinated by imperial order.
Vogt, Mauritius (1669–1730), Cistercian monk of the monastery in Plasy (Plass), southwest Bohemia. A Baroque polymath, his interests included history, theology, geography, and, especially, music. Was the author of an historical topographical work about Bohemia (1712).
Vrtby, Jan Josef the Elder z, Count (1669–1734), was made Lord High Burgrave of Prague in 1712; an important builder, employed the most renowned artists of the High Baroque.
Weiss, Franz Ignaz (*c.*1695–1756), sculptor, active first in the workshop of Mathias Wenzel Jäckel (*see*), which he took charge of in 1723, and then as a master of his own workshop. An important Prague sculptor of the early Rococo period.
Werner, Friedrich Bernhard (1690–1778), Silesian draughtsman and engraver, much sought after for his cityscapes. Worked in a number of central European cities, including Prague, where he was in charge of stage machinery at the theatre of Count Sporck (*see*).
Willmann, Michael Leopold (1630–1706), painter from Königsberg (today's Kaliningrad), active mostly in Prussia and Silesia but also in Bohemia and Moravia. An important practitioner of Early Baroque painting of a dramatic expressive nature. Was the stepfather of Johann Christoph Lischka (*see*).
Wirch, Johann Joseph (1732–1787), born in the village of Košetice (Koschetitz), south Bohemia, the leading architect of the Rococo style in Prague.
Wiśniowiecki, Michał Tomasz Korybut (1640–1673), Michael I, King of Poland and Grand Duke of Lithuania from 1669 till his death. Attended Jesuit schools in the towns of Brok (in the Masovia Province of Poland) and Nysa (Silesia), and, from 1656 to 1660, attended Prague University.
Wodniansky, Johann Ezechiel (*c.*1673–1758), painter, active in Prague.
Wratislaw von Mitrowitz, Johann Wenzel, Count (1672–1712), distinguished imperial diplomat during the War of the Spanish Succession, was Grand-Prior of the Bohemian Province of the Order of St John, and at various times held several offices in the administration of the Bohemian Lands, including Lord High Chancellor from 1711 until his death.
Wunschwitz, Matthias Gottfried von (1632–1695), lawyer, governor (*procurator regis*) in Moravia, and eventually chief administrator of the Pilsen Region. Was dubbed a knight in 1661, and raised to a barony in 1675. Venerated John Nepomucene and promoted his cult.
Würth, Johann Joseph (1706–1767), silversmith, active in Vienna from 1733 to 1757.

Zaist, Giovanni Battista (1700–1757), Cremona-born painter, specialist in *trompe-l'oeil* architectural painting.
Zatoczil von Löwenbrucken, Johann Norbert (*c.*1625–1691), Prague burgher, scrivener, and, later, chief councillor the Old Town of Prague. A chronicler of the defence of the right bank of Prague against the Swedes in 1648.
Zinke, Othmar Daniel (1664–1738), Benedictine monk; in 1700 was appointed Abbot of Břevnov (today a Prague district), and its filial abbey in Broumov, north-east Bohemia. Generous builder of both abbeys in the Baroque style.

KINGS OF BOHEMIA FROM 1576 TO 1790

HABSBURG DYNASTY (Austrian branch)

Rudolph II, r. 1576–1611
(18 July 1552 Vienna – 20 January 1612 Prague, son of Maximilian II); crowned King of Bohemia in Prague on 22 September 1575, from 1576 to 1608, King of Hungary; in 1576 was elected Holy Roman Emperor.

Matthias, r. 1611–19
(24 February 1557 Vienna – 20 March 1619 Vienna); brother of Rudolph II; in 1608, was crowned King of Hungary; in 1612, was crowned Holy Roman Emperor. In Prague on 23 May 1611, was crowned King of Bohemia; married Anna of Tyrol (1585–1618) on 4 December 1611.

Ferdinand II, r. 1619–37
(9 July 1578 Graz–15 February 1637 Vienna); of the Styrian line of the Habsburgs; was crowned Holy Roman Emperor and King of Hungary in 1619. In Prague, was crowned King of Bohemia on 29 June 1617. In 1600, married Maria Anna of Bavaria (1574–1616) and in 1622 Eleonora Gonzaga (1598–1655).

WITTELSBACH DYNASTY (Palatine branch)

Frederick V of the Palatinate, r. 1619–20
(26 August 1596 Deinschwang near Amberg – 29 November 1632 Mainz). From 1610 to 1623, Elector Palatine. In Prague, was crowned King of Bohemia on 4 November 1619. In 1613, married Elizabeth Stuart (1596–1662).

HABSBURG DYNASTY (Austrian branch)

Ferdinand III, r. 1637–57
(13 July 1608 Graz – 2 April 1657 Vienna); son of Ferdinand II; in 1637, was crowned Holy Roman Emperor and King of Hungary. In Prague, was crowned King of Bohemia on 24 November 1627. In 1631, married Maria Anna of Spain (1606–1646); in 1648, married Maria Leopoldine of Austria-Tyrol (1632–1649); in 1651, married Eleonora Magdalena Gonzaga (1630–1686).

Ferdinand IV, r. 1646–54 (never independently)
(8 September 1633 Vienna – 9 July 1654 Vienna). Son of Ferdinand III. In 1647, was crowned King of Hungary; in 1653, crowned King of the Romans (but never ruled independently). In Prague, crowned King of Bohemia on 5 August 1646.

Leopold I, r. 1657–1705
(9 June 1640 Vienna – 5 May 1705 Vienna). Brother of Ferdinand IV. In 1657, was crowned King of Hungary; in 1658, was crowned

King of the Romans. In Prague, was crowned King of Bohemia on 14 September 1656. In 1666, married Margaret Theresa of Spain (1651–1673); in 1673, married Claudia Felicitas of Austria (1653–1676); in 1676, married Eleonora Magdalene of Neuburg (1655–1720).

Joseph I, r. 1705–11
(26 July 1678 Graz – 17 April 1711 Vienna). Son of Leopold I. In 1705, was crowned King of the Romans and King of Hungary. Was never crowned King of Bohemia. In 1699, married Wilhelmine Amalia of Brunswick-Lüneburg (1673–1742).

Charles VI, r. 1711–40
(1 October 1685 Vienna – 20 October 1740 Vienna). Brother of Joseph I. From 1703 to 1714, King of Spain; in 1711, was crowned King of the Romans and King of Hungary. In Prague, was crowned King of Bohemia on 5 September 1723. In 1708, married Elizabeth Christina of Brunswick-Wolfenbüttel (1691–1750).

Maria Theresa, r. 1740–80
(13 May 1717 Vienna – 29 November 1780 Vienna). Daughter of Charles VI. In 1740, was crowned Queen of Hungary. In Prague, was crowned Queen of Bohemia on 12 May 1743. In 1736, married Francis Stephen, Duke of Lorraine (1708–1765), who, in 1745, was crowned Holy Roman Emperor.

WITTELSBACH DYNASTY (Bavarian branch)

Charles Albert (Charles VII), r. 1741–43
(6 August 1697 Brussels – 20 January 1745 Munich). Son-in-law of Joseph I. In 1726, was made Prince-Elector of Bavaria, and in 1742 was crowned Holy Roman Emperor. Was never crowned King of Bohemia. In 1722, married Maria Amalia of Austria (1701–1756).

HABSBURG-LORRAINE DYNASTY

Joseph II, r. 1780–90
(13 March 1741 Vienna – 20 February 1790 Vienna). Son of Maria Theresa. In 1765, was crowned Holy Roman Emperor, ruled with his mother until 1780; in 1780, was crowned King of Hungary. Was never crowned King of Bohemia. In 1760, married Isabella of Bourbon-Parma (1741–1763); in 1765, married Maria Josepha of Bavaria (1739–1767).

MAPS

Hradčany and the Lesser Town

Hradčany (Castle district)

1. St Vitus' Cathedral (Katedrála sv. Víta)
2. Institute for Distressed Noblewomen (Ústav šlechtičen aka Rožmberský palác), Prague Castle
3. St George's Basilica (Bazilika sv. Jiří), Prague Castle
4. Royal Garden (Královská zahrada), Prague Castle
5. Riding School of Prague Castle (Jízdárna Pražského hradu), U Prašného mostu 3
6. Archbishop's Palace (Arcibiskupský palác), Hradčanské náměstí 16
7. Sternberg House (Šternberský palác), Hradčanské náměstí 15
8. Grand Duke of Tuscany's House (Toskánský palác), Hradčanské náměstí 5
9. The Loreto (Loreta), Loretánské náměstí 8
10. Czernin House (Černínský palác), Loretánské náměstí 5
11. Church of St John Nepomucene (Kostel sv. Jana Nepomuckého na Hradčanech), on the corner of Kanovnická and U Kasáren
12. Stone Column House (Dům u Kamenného sloupu), Úvoz 24

The Lesser Town (Malá Strana)

13. Strahov Monastery (Strahovský klášter), Strahovské nádvoří 1
14. Morzin House (Morzinský palác, also called U Mouřenínů) Nerudova 5
15. Kolowrat House (Thun House) (Kolowratský palác, also called Thunovský palác), Nerudova 20
16. Our Lady of Perpetual Help and St Cajetan (Kostel Panny Marie Matky ustavičné pomoci a svatého Kajetána, earlier Panny Marie pod ochranou Božské prozřetelnosti), Nerudova 22
17. Lobkowicz House (Lobkovický palác, aka palác Přehořovských z Kvasejovic), Vlašská 19
18. Italian Hospice with Chapel of St Mary and St Charles Borromeo (Panny Marie a sv. Karla Boromejského), Vlašská 34/Šporkova 14
19. St Nicholas' Church in the Lesser Town (Chrám sv. Mikuláše na Malé Straně), Malostranské náměstí
20. St Thomas' Church (Kostel sv. Tomáše), Josefská 8
21. Ledebur Garden (Ledeburská zahrada), Valdštejnské náměstí 3/Valdštejnská 14
22. Lesser Fürstenberg Garden (Malá Fürstenberská zahrada), Valdštejnské náměstí 3/ Valdštejnská 14
23. Wallenstein House (Valdštejnský palác), Valdštejnské náměstí 4
24. St Joseph's Church (Kostel sv. Josefa), Josefská 4
25. Vrtba Garden (Vrtbovská zahrada), Karmelitská 5
26. Church of St Mary of Victory (Kostel P. Marie Vítězné) and the Monastery of the Infant Jesus of Prague, Karmelitská 9
27. Michna House (Michnovský palác, palác Michnů z Vacínova, Tyršův dům), Újezd 40
28. Statue of St John the Baptist (sv. Jana Křtitele), Maltézské náměstí
29. Nostitz House (Nostický palác), Maltézské náměstí 1 and Nosticova 9
30. Bucquoy House (Buquoyský palác), Velkopřevorské náměstí 2
31. Grand-Prior's House (Velkopřevorský palác), Velkopřevorské náměstí 4
32. The Blue Fox (Dům U Modré lišky), Na Kampě 1

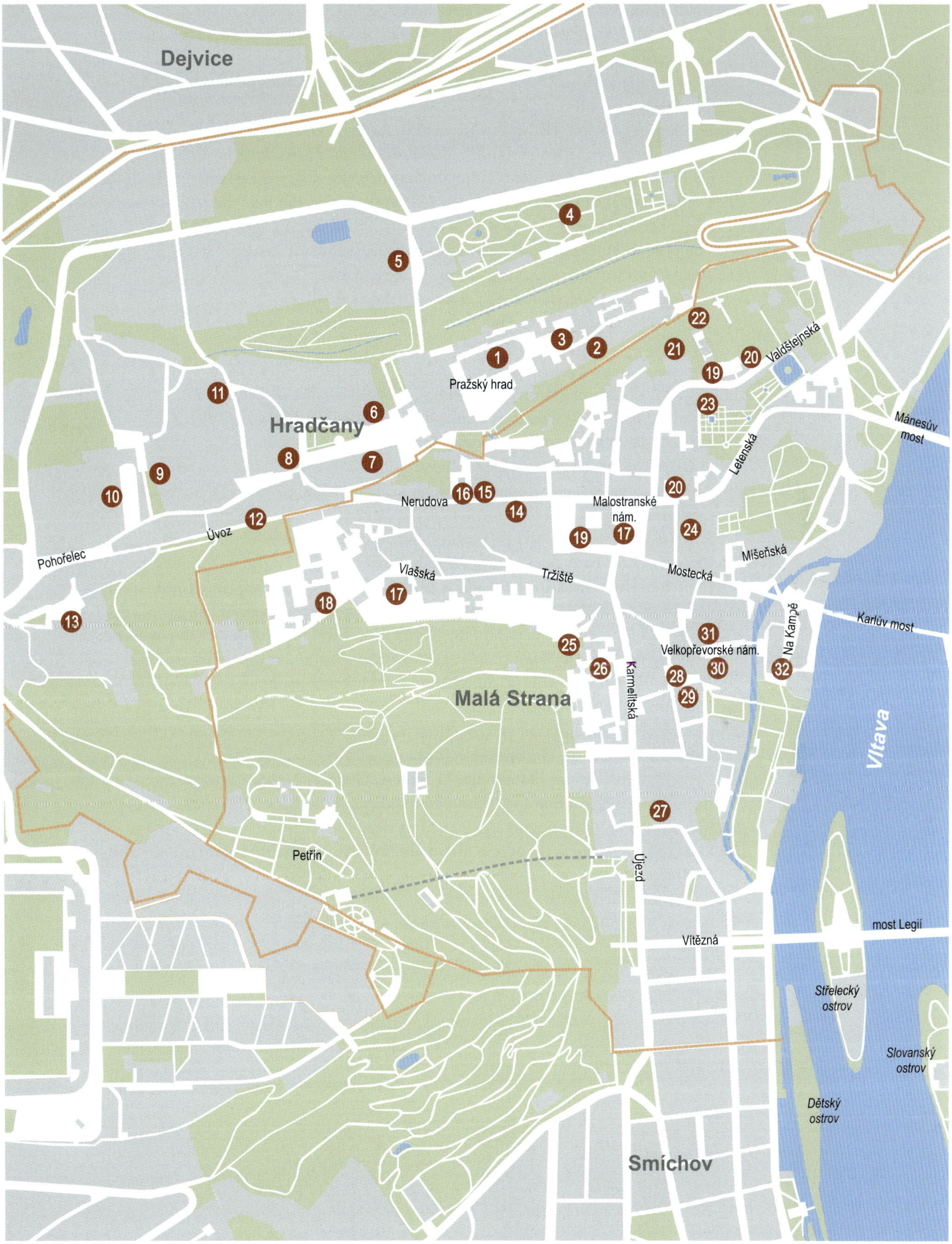

Dejvice
Hradčany
Pražský hrad
Malá Strana
Smíchov
Petřín
Nerudova
Úvoz
Pohořelec
Vlašská
Tržiště
Malostranské nám.
Mostecká
Míšeňská
Letenská
Valdštejnská
Mánesův most
Karlův most
Na Kampě
Velkopřevorské nám.
Karmelitská
Újezd
Vítězná
most Legií
Vltava
Střelecký ostrov
Slovanský ostrov
Dětský ostrov

The Old Town, the New Town, and elsewhere

1. Church of St Francis of Assisi (Kostel sv. Františka z Assisi), Křižovnické náměstí 3, Old Town
2. Church of St Saviour (Kostel Nejsvětějšího Salvátora), Křižovnické náměstí 4 , Old Town
3. St Clement's Church (Kostel sv. Klimenta), Karlova, Old Town
4. The Clementinum (Klementinum), Mariánské náměstí 5/Karlova 1
5. Colloredo-Mansfeld House (Colloredo-Mansfeldský palác), Karlova 2
6. Golden Well (Dům U Zlaté studně or U Červené sesle [The Red Chair]), Karlova ulice 3 / Seminářská 2
7. Clam-Gallas House (Clam-Gallasovský palác), Husova 20
8. Thein Church (Týnský chrám), Staroměstské náměstí
9. Kinsky House (Palác Kinských), Staroměstské náměstí 1/3
10. St Nicholas' Church in the Old Town (Kostel sv. Mikuláše na Starém Městě), Staroměstské náměstí, Old Town
11. St James' Church (Kostel sv. Jakuba), Malá Štupartská 6, Old Town
12. St Castalus' Church (Kostel sv. Haštala), Haštalské náměstí, Old Town
13. Kolowrat House (Kolowratský palác), Ovocný trh 6, Old Town
14. St Gall's Church (Kostel sv. Havla), Havelské náměstí, Old Town
15. St Giles' Church (Kostel sv. Jiljí), Husova ulice, Old Town
16. Pachta House (Palác Pachtů z Rájova, also called Pachtovský palác), Anenské naměstí 4, Old Town
17. St Ursula's Church (Kostel sv. Voršily), Národní třída 8, New Town
18. Church of Our Lady of the Snow (Chrám P. Marie Sněžné), Jungmannovo náměstí 18
19. Church of the Holy Trinity (Kostel Nejsvětější Trojice), Spálená, New Town
20. Church of St Ignatius (Kostel sv. Ignáce), Karlovo náměstí, New Town
21. Church of John Nepomucene on the Rock (Kostel sv. Jana Nepomuckého na Skalce), Vyšehradská 26, New Town
22. The Michna Summer House, called Amerika (Michnův letohrádek or Amerika), Ke Karlovu 20, New Town
23. Church of the Assumption and the Blessed Charlemagne (Kostel Nanebevzetí P. Marie a sv. Karla Velikého), Horská, New Town
24. Church of Sts Cyril and Methodius (Kostel sv. Cyrila a Metoděje) (formerly St Charles Borromeo, sv. Karla Boromejského), on the corner of Resslova and Na Zderaze
25. Břevnov Abbey (Břevnovský klášter), Markétská 1, Břevnov
26. Place of pilgrimage at the White Mountain (Poutní areál na Bílé hoře), Zbečenská, Bílá hora
27. Portheimka, Štefánikova 12, Smíchov
28. Schloss Troja (Trojský zámek), U Trojského zámku 1, Troja

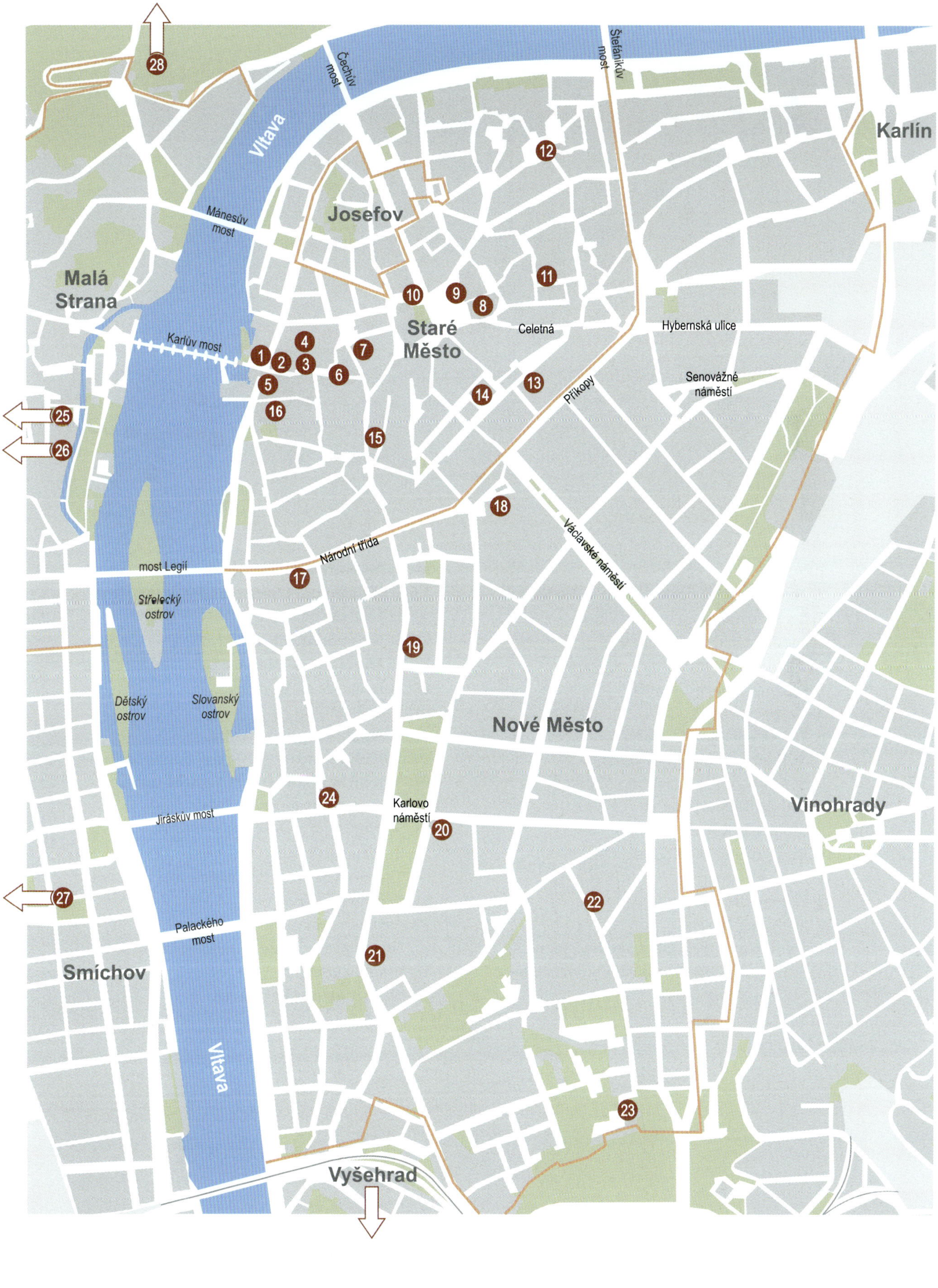

Čechův most
Štefánikův most
Karlín
Vltava
Josefov
Mánesův most
Malá Strana
Staré Město
Celetná
Hybernská ulice
Karlův most
Senovážné náměstí
Příkopy
Václavské náměstí
Národní třída
most Legií
Střelecký ostrov
Dětský ostrov
Slovanský ostrov
Nové Město
Karlovo náměstí
Jiráskův most
Vinohrady
Palackého most
Smíchov
Vltava
Vyšehrad
1
2
3
4
5
6
7
8
9
10
11
12
13
14
15
16
17
18
19
20
21
22
23
24
25
26
27
28

THE STATUES ON CHARLES BRIDGE

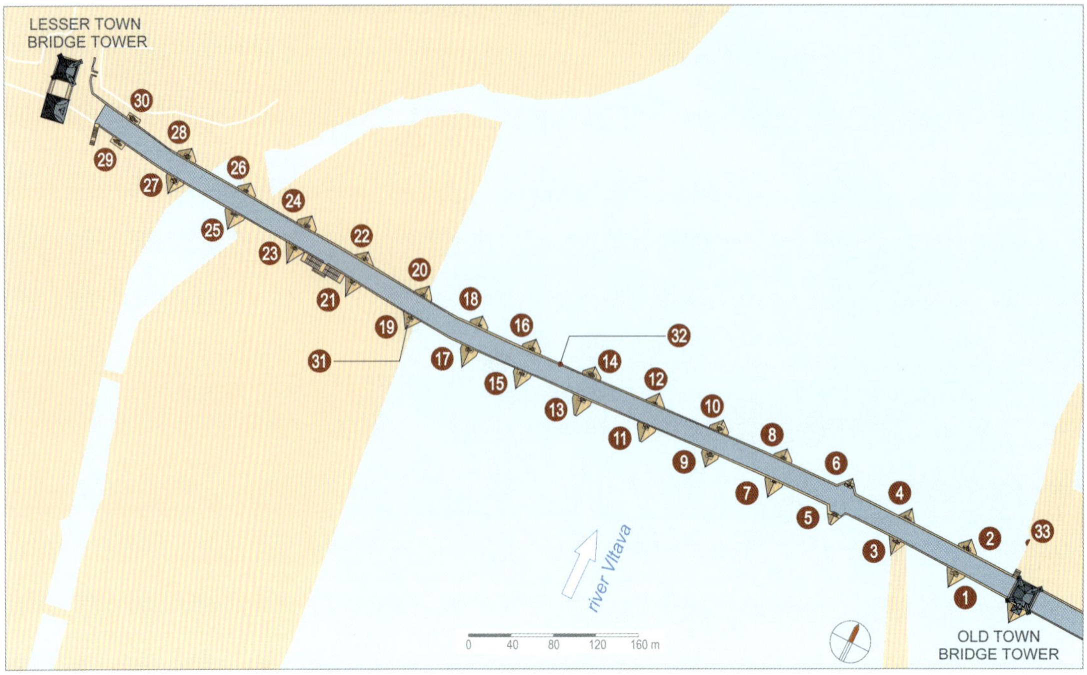

1. St Ivo
2. The Blessed Virgin Mary and St Bernard
3. Sts Barbara, Margaret the Virgin, and Elizabeth of Hungary
4. The Blessed Virgin Mary, St Thomas Aquinas, and St Dominic
5. *Pietà*
6. The Crucifixion (Calvary)
7. St Joseph with the Boy Jesus
8. St Anne with her daughter Mary and the Infant Jesus
9. St Francis Xavier
10. Sts Cyril and Methodius
11. St Christopher
12. St John the Baptist
13. St Francis Borgia
14. Sts Norbert, Wenceslas, and Sigismund
15. St Ludmila of Bohemia with St Wenceslas
16. St John Nepomucene
17. St Francis of Assisi
18. St Anthony of Padua
19. Sts Procopius of Sázava and Vincent Ferrer
20. St Jude the Apostle
21. St Nicholas of Tolentino
22. St Augustine of Hippo
23. St Lutgarde of Aywières
24. St Cajetan
25. St Adalbert
26. St Philip Benizi
27. St John of Matha and St Felix of Valois, the Blessed Ivan, and a Turk
28. St Vitus
29. St Wenceslas
30. The Holy Saviour, St Cosmas, and St Damian
31. Roland (Bruncvík)
32. A cross marking the spot where John Nepomucene is said to have been thrown from the bridge.
33. The Bearded Man (Bradáč)

LIST OF ILLUSTRATIONS

Dust jacket: (front) St Nicholas' Church in the Lesser Town of Prague, looking up into the cupola; (back) a view of the Lesser Town from the Lesser Fürstenberg Garden.
Front flap: St Nicholas' Church in the Lesser Town of Prague, seen from the east.
Introductory pages (unnumbered): (pp. 2–3) Church of St Francis as seen from across Charles Bridge; Baroque hall of the National Library of the Czech Republic, in the Clementinum; (p. 8) Church of St Mary of Victory at Bílá hora; (pp. 10-11) Vrtba Garden; (p. 12), mascaron from the façade of Wallenstein House.

Documentary illustrations

17. Johann Georg Ringle, after Friedrich Bernhard Werner, *Old Town Square with the Krocín Fountain and Marian Column*, *c.*1740, copper engraving, 205 × 302 mm, Muzeum hlavního města Prahy, inv. no. 7275.
18. Anonymous, Mathematics Museum in the Clementinum, cabinet with mineral exhibits (*Theatrum mineralium*), copper engraving, in Joseph Passetzky (presided over by Johann Kisling), *Compendium physicae experimentalis*, Prague, 1747, plate between pp. 68 and 69, Ústav dějin Univerzity Karlovy, sbírka starých tisků, sign. A72-31/4, p. 37.
19. Anonymous, *The French Fire of Prague in 1689*, etching with copper engraving, 89 × 300 mm, Archiv hlavního města Prahy, sbírka grafiky, sign. G 28b, p. 38.
20. Johann Adam Delsenbach, after Johann Bernhard Fischer von Erlach, *House of Johann Wenzel Gallas in the Old Town* (Clam-Gallas), 1721, copper engraving, 300 × 430 mm, Muzeum hlavního města Prahy, inv. no. 8257, p. 39.
21. Christian Dittmann, *St Procopius Commands the Dreaming Burgher Soběslav to Change His House into a Church*, 1668/69, oil on canvas, 98 × 128 cm, Church of All Saints, Prague Castle, Správa Pražského hradu, photo Jan Gloc, p. 40.
22. Karel Škréta, *St Luke Painting the Virgin*, 1661, oil on canvas, 236 × 138 cm, Muzeum hlavního města Prahy, inv. no. D-15, p. 42.
23. David Norbert Altman, *The Holy Family with St Elizabeth and St John the Baptist*, masterpiece of the Prague painters' guild, 1644, oil on wood, 71 × 55.5 cm, private collection, p. 43.
24. Jindřich (Heinrich) Eckert, Garden gate of the former Slavata Summer House in Smíchov, 1880, photo (negative), Archiv hlavního města Prahy, Sbírka fotografií, sign. XII 1005, p. 44.
25. Wenceslaus Hollar, *A Woman of Prague* (*Mulier pragensis*), etching, [P 1810], 93 × 60 mm, Archiv hlavního města Prahy, Sbírka grafiky, sign. G 207, p. 45 (left).
26. Wenceslaus Hollar, *A Prague Merchant's Wife* (*Mercatoris pragensis uxor*), 1642, etching [P 1808], 95 × 62 mm, private collection, p. 45 (right).
27. Johann Joseph Dietzler, Map of Prague, 1741, coloured pen and ink drawing, 429 × 637 mm, Národní galerie v Praze, inv. no. DK 1212, p. 46.
28. Plan of the water mains in the Old Town of Prague, 1684, pen and ink drawing and watercolour, 712 × 1040 mm, Jindřichův Hradec, pracoviště Státního oblastního archivu Třeboň, fond Rodinný archiv Černínů, Historica, p. 47.
29. Johann Georg Heinsch, *The Jesuit Brothers Spanberger during the Plague in Prague in 1680*, sketch for an illustration to Mathias Tanner, *Societas Jesu Apostolorum imitatrix*, Prague, 1694, pen and ink drawing, ink wash, 159 × 110 mm, Národní galerie v Praze, inv. no. K 40354, p. 48.
30. Johann Georg Kogler the Younger, Torah shield, 1708, hammered and chased silver, 28 × 27.8 cm, Prague, Židovské muzeum, inv. no. 4418, p. 49.
31. Anonymous, *Shimon Abeles*, *c.*1694, oil on canvas, 118 × 66 cm, Prague, kostel Matky Boží před Týnem, photo Oto Palán, p. 50.
32. Matthias Trodl, Triumphal Arch built by the New Town of Prague for the Entry of Charles of Austria (Charles III of Spain, later Emperor Charles VI) in 1703, copper engraving, 476 × 286 mm, Muzeum hlavního města Prahy, inv. no. 21347, p. 51.
33. Anton Birckhardt after Johann Ezechiel Wodniansky, *The Festive Decoration of the Area in Front of the West Façade of St Vitus' Cathedral for the Celebrations of the Canonization of St John Nepomucene in October 1729*, copper engraving, 449 × 560 mm, Muzeum hlavního města Prahy, inv. no. 31463, p. 53.
34. Anonymous, *The Decoration of Old Town Square and a Fireworks Display during Celebrations on 9 October 1667 to Mark the Birth of the Son of Emperor Leopold I*, pen and ink, tempera and watercolour, 490 × 840 mm, Národní archiv, Sbírka map a plánů, sign. A XVI 15a, photo Oto Palán, p. 54 (top).

35. Anonymous, *Regatta on the Vltava at Old Town Bridge Tower during the Celebrations on 9 October 1667 to Mark the Birth of the Son of Emperor Leopold I*, pen and ink, coloured with tempera, 370 × 540 mm, Národní archiv, Sbírka map a plánů, sign. A XVI 15b, photo Oto Palán, p. 54 (bottom).
36. Anonymous, *Coronation of Charles VI as King of Bohemia*, [1723], copper engraving, 164 × 264 mm, Muzeum hlavního města Prahy, inv. no. 11 717, p. 55.
37. Benedikt Richter and Daniel Warou, Medal to commemorate the coronation of Charles VI as King of Bohemia and the thousandth anniversary of the founding of Prague, 1723, silver, diam: 4.95 cm, Národní muzeum, inv. no. H5-69ARVIIIa17/H5-50.257, p. 56.
38. Anton Birckhardt, after Giuseppe Galli da Bibiena: *Summer Theatre at Prague Castle: The Opera* Costanza e Fortezza, *produced to mark the coronation of Charles VI in 1723*, 1723, copper engraving, 528 × 665 mm, Muzeum hlavního města Prahy, inv. no. 8622, p. 57.
39. Johann Tobias Sonntag, *Maria Theresa at the Head of the Hungarian Troops as the Saviour of Prague*, 1745, oil on canvas, 54 × 71.5 cm, Muzeum hlavního města Prahy, inv. no. 10531, p. 59.
40. Martin Tyroff, after Johann Joseph Dietzler, *Maria Theresa's Triumphant Entry into Prague on 29 April 1743 (A Procession on Křižovnické náměstí)*, etching with copper engraving, 340 × 710 mm, Prague, Památník národního písemnictví, inv. no. IG 2761, p. 60.
41. Coenraet Decker, after Folpert van Ouden Allen, *View of Prague*, 1685, etching with copper engraving, 800 × 2057 mm, Archiv hlavního města Prahy, Sbírka grafiky, sign. G 37, pp. 62–63.

A Guide to Baroque Prague
All photos, unless otherwise stated, Oto Palán
Opposite title page: Clementinum complex with St Clement's Church
1/ Prague Castle (Pražský hrad) – entrance façade with the cour d'honneur
2/ Institute for Distressed Noblewomen (Das adelige Damenstift/Ústav šlechtičen) – façade
3/ St George's Church (Kostel sv. Jiří) – façade
4/ Riding School of Prague Castle (Jízdárna Pražského hradu)
5/ Royal Garden, Anton Braun, *Night*, 1733
6/ *St Vitus' Cathedral (Katedrála sv. Víta)*
6A–B/ The carved west door, Správa Pražského hradu, photo Jan Gloc
6C/ Tomb of St John Nepomucene, Správa Pražského hradu, photo Jan Gloc
6D/ Augustin Peter Neureuter, Tomb monument to St John Nepomucene, copper engraving, 1717, 335 × 232 mm, private collection
6E/ Tomb monument to Count Joseph Leopold Schlik, photo Správa pražského hradu – Jan Gloc
6F/ Ignaz Franz Platzer, Cenotaph of St John Nepomucene, 1763, photo Správa pražského hradu – Jan Gloc
7/ *Prague Castle Gallery (Obrazárna Pražského hradu)*
7A/ Guido Reni, *The Centaur Nessus Abducting Deianeira*, after 1603, oil on canvas, 257 × 195 cm, Sbírky Pražského hradu, inv. no. O 104, photo Správa Pražského hradu – Jan Gloc
7B/ Peter Paul Rubens, *The Council of the Gods*, 1602, oil on canvas, 204 × 379 cm, Sbírky pražského hradu, inv. no. O 102, photo Správa Pražského hradu – Jan Gloc
8/ Archbishop's Palace
9A/ Sternberg House (Šternberský palác) – garden façade
9B/ Sternberg House – Chinese Room
10/ Marian Column on Hradčanské náměstí
11A/ Grand Duke of Tuscany's House (Toskánský palác) – façade
11B/ Ottavio Mosto, Archangel Michael on the corner of the house

12/ *Prague Loreto*
12A/ Main façade
12B/ Santa Casa
12C–E/ Church of the Nativity (Kostel Narození Páně)
12F/ Diamond monstrance called 'The Prague Sun', photo Capuchin Province of the Czech Republic
13/ *Czernin House (*Černínský *palác)*
13A/ Czernin House seen from the street called Nový svět
13B/ Main façade
13C/ Garden façade, photo Věroslav Škrabánek
13D/ Francesco Caratti, design for vaulted ceiling of the chapel in Czernin House, 1675, technical drawing in India ink, washed and coloured, 434 × 558 mm, Jindřichův Hradec, pracoviště Státní oblastní archiv Třeboň, fond Černínská ústřední správa, Sbírka map a plánů, sign. V/58, photo Státní oblastní archiv Třeboň
14A/ Church of St John Nepomucene at Hradčany (Kostel sv. Jana Nepomuckého na Hradčanech) – façade
14B–C/ Wenzel Lorenz Reiner, frescos with scenes from the life, works, and glorification of St John Nepomucene
15/ *Royal Canonry of the Premonstratensians at Strahov*
15A–B/ Basilica of the Assumption (Kostel Nanebevzetí P. Marie)
15C/ Altar of St Augustine – Franz Xaver Karl Palko, *Saint Augustine*, before 1760, oil on canvas, 180 ×106 cm
15D/ Strahov Library (Strahovská knihovna) – Theology Room
(322)
15E/ Strahov Library – Philosophy Room
15F/ Franz Anton Maulbertsch, *Man's Spiritual Evolution: The Triumph of Divine Wisdom*, modello for the ceiling fresco in the Philosophy Room, 1793, oil on canvas 167 × 93 cm, Strahovská obrazárna, inv. no. O 697
16/ The Stone Column (U Kamenného sloupu), house sign
17/ Church of Our Lady of Perpetual Help and St Cajetan (Kostel P. Marie Ustavičné pomoci a sv. Kajetána) (aka Panny Marie pod ochranou božské prozřetelnosti)
18/ Kolowrat House, also called Thun House (Kolowratský aka Thunovský palác)
19/ Morzin House (Morzinský palác)
20/ Lobkowicz House, aka Přehořovský House (Lobkovický aka Přehořovských palác)
21A–B/ Chapel of St Mary and St Charles Borromeo in the Italian Hospice (sv. P. Marie a Karla Boromejského ve Vlašském špitále)
21C/ Karel Škréta, *St Charles Borromeo Visiting Plague Sufferers in Milan*, 1647, oil on canvas, 210 × 247 cm, Národní galerie v Praze, inv. no. O 2579, photo Národní galerie v Praze
22/ *St Nicholas' Church in the Lesser Town (Kostel sv. Mikuláše)*
22A/ Main façade
22 B–C/ Interior
22D/ Karel Škréta, *The Crucifixion with Our Lady of Sorrows and Souls in Purgatory*, 1644, oil on canvas 350 × 183 cm
22E/ Karel Škréta, *Christ before Caiaphas*, 1673, oil on canvas 234 × 170 cm
22F/ The church seen from the east
23/ *St Thomas' Church (Kostel sv. Tomáše)*
23A–B/ St Thomas' Church – west façade and interior
23C/ Peter Paul Rubens, *St Augustine*, *c.*1636–37, oil on canvas, 232 × 153 cm, Česká provincie řádu sv. Augustina, on loan to the Národní galerie v Praze, photo Národní galerie v Praze
23D/ Peter Paul Rubens, *The Martyrdom of St Thomas*, *c.*1636–37, oil on canvas, 380 × 253 cm, Česká provincie řádu sv. Augustina, on loan to the Národní galerie v Praze, photo Národní galerie v Praze

24/ The Golden Stag (U Zlatého jelena), house sign
25/ *Wallenstein House (Valdštejnský palác)*
25A/ Main façade
25B/ Sala terrena
25C/ Leathern Drawing Room
25D/ Wenceslas Chapel
25E/ Great Hall
25F/ Wallenstein Garden
26A–C/ Ledebur Garden (Ledeburská zahrada): full view, statue of Hercules, sala terrena
27 / Lesser Fürstenberg Garden (Malá Fürstenberská zahrada)
28/ View of the Lesser Town from the Lesser Fürstenberg Garden
29A/ St Joseph's Church (Kostel sv. Josefa) – façade
29B/ Peter Brandl, *The Holy Family*, *c.*1702, oil on canvas, 373 × 232 cm
30A–C/ Vrtba Garden (Vrtbovská zahrada)
31/ *Church of St Mary of Victory (Kostel P. Marie Vítězné)*
31A/ Façade
31B/ Altar of the Infant Jesus of Prague (Pražského Jezulátka)
31C/ Infant Jesus of Prague
31D/ Peter Brandl, *The Prophet Elijah's Dream*, 1724, oil on canvas, 248 × 187 cm, Klášter Pražského Jezulátka, on loan to the Národní galerie v Praze, photo Národní galerie v Praze
32A–B/ Czech Museum of Music (former Church of St Mary Magdalene)
33/ Michna House (Michnovský palác also called Tyršův dům)
34/ Maltézské náměstí (Knights of Malta Square) – statue of St John the Baptist
35/ Bucquoy House (Buquoyský palác)
36/ Nostitz House (Nostický palác)
37/ Grand-Prior's House (Velkopřevorský palác)
38/ The Blue Fox (U Modré lišky), house sign
39/ Míšeňská ulice (Meissen Street)
40/ *Charles Bridge (Karlův most)*
40A/ Panorama from the south
40B/ Ferdinand Maximilian Brokoff, *St Ivan with St John of Matha and St Felix of Valois, Liberating Christian Slaves*, 1714
40C/ Johann Brokoff, *St John Nepomucene*, 1683
40D/ Matthias Rauchmiller, *St John Nepomucene*, 1681, bozzetto, terracotta with plaster of Paris and wooden additions, H: 41 cm, Národní galerie v Praze, inv. no. P 613, photo Národní galerie v Praze
40E/ Matthias Bernhard Braun, *Vision of St Lutgarde of Aywières*, 1710, copy
40F/ Ferdinand Maximilian Brokoff, *Glorification of St Ignatius of Loyola*, torso of the original,1710–11, Lapidárium Národního muzea, inv. no. 38132, photo Národní muzeum
40G/ Ferdinand Maximilian Brokoff, *Glorification of St Ignatius of Loyola*, bozzetto, 1709–11, polychromy 1724, polychromed lime, H: 83.8 cm, Muzeum hlavního města Prahy, inv. no. 10796, photo Muzeum hlavního města Prahy
41/ *Church of St Francis of Assisi (Kostel sv. Františka Serafínského)*
41A/ Façade
41B/ Interior, photo Helena Kodíková
41C Johann Christoph Lischka, *Saint Francis Receiving the Stigmata*, before 1700/01, oil on canvas, 137.5 × 81 cm, Národní památkový ústav, Státní hrad Rožmberk, on loan to the Národní galerie v Praze, photo Národní galerie v Praze
41D/ Church of St Francis of Assisi seen from across Charles Bridge
42/ *Church of St Saviour (Kostel Nejsvětějšího Salvátora) in the Clementinum*
42A/ Façade

The Prague Series *Edited by Milada Motlová*

PUBLISHED

Eliška Fučíková: *Praha rudolfínská* (2014); *Prague in the Reign of Rudolph II* (2015)
Kateřina Bečková: *Praha – město a řeka* (2015); *Prague: The City and Its River* (2016)
Jan Royt: *Praha Karla IV.* (2016); *The Prague of Charles IV* (2016)
Božena Pacáková-Hošťálková: *Praha – zahrady a parky* (2016); *Prague: Its Gardens and Parks* (2017)
Eliška Fučíková: *Praha renesanční* (2017); *Renaissance Prague* (2018)
Vít Vlnas: *Praha barokní* (2017); *Baroque Prague* (2024)
Petr Wittlich: *Praha secesní* (2017); *Art Nouveau Prague* (2020)
Josef and Lydia Petráňovi: *Praha univerzitní* (2018); *Prague: University Town* (2018)
Jan Royt: *Praha středověká* (2019)

SOON TO BE PUBLISHED

Jan Royt: *Medieval Prague*
Vít Vlnas: *Praha – město a válka [Prague: The City and War]*

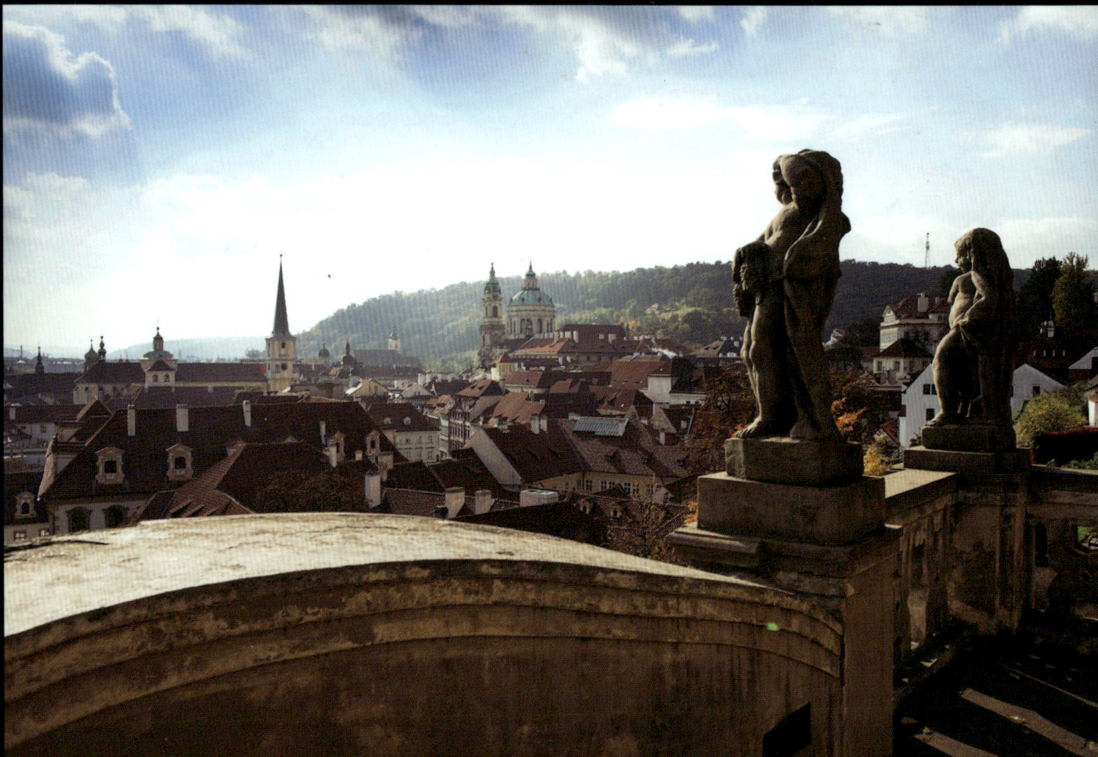

www.karolinum.cz
ISBN 978-80-246-4376-2
9 788024 643762